THE FAMILY
Its Structures
& Functions
SECOND EDITION

THE FAMILY
ITS STRUCTURES
& FUNCTIONS

Second Edition

Rose Laub Coser, editor

STATE UNIVERSITY OF NEW YORK AT STONY BROOK

ST. MARTIN'S PRESS

NEW YORK

Since this page cannot accommodate all of the copyright notices, the two pages that follow constitute an extension of the copyright page.

Acknowledgments

p. 3 "Reciprocity, the Essence of Social Life" by Claude Lévi-Strauss is reprinted by permission of the publisher from *Sociological Theory*, ed. Coser and Rosenberg, New York: The Macmillan Co., 1957, pp. 84-94.

p. 13 "The Incest Taboo in Relation to Social Structure" by Talcott Parsons is reprinted by permission of the author from *The British Journal of Sociology*, Vol. 5 (1954), pp. 101-117.

p. 31 "A Deviant Case: Brother-Sister and Father-Daughter Marriage in Ancient Egypt" by Russell Middleton is reprinted from the *American Sociological Review*, Vol. 27, No. 5 (October 1962), pp. 603-611. Copyright © 1962 by the American Sociological Association.

p. 44 "Structural Differences in Reciprocity" by Bernard Farber is reprinted from pp. 8-14 and 63-66 of *Kinship and Class: A Midwestern Study*, © 1971 by Basic Books, Inc., Publishers, New York.

p. 51 "Parenthood, the Basis of Social Structure" by Bronislaw Malinowski is reprinted by permission from *The New Generation*, ed. V. F. Calverton and S. D. Schmalhausen, New York: Macauley Co., 1930, pp. 113-168.

p. 64 "A Deviant Case: Illegitimacy in the Caribbean" by William J. Goode is reprinted from the *American Sociological Review*, Vol. 25, No. 1 (February 1960), pp. 21-30, by permission of the author and the *Review*. Copyright © 1960 by the American Sociological Association.

p. 78 "Structured Imbalances of Gratification: The Case of the Caribbean Mating System" by Morris Freilich and Lewis A. Coser is reprinted by permission of the publisher from *The British Journal of Sociology*, Vol. 23, No. 1 (March 1972), pp. 1-19.

p. 94 "The Principle of Legitimacy and Its Patterned Infringement in Social Revolutions" by Rose Laub Coser and Lewis A. Coser is reprinted by permission of the publisher from *Cross-National Family Research*, ed. Marvin B. Sussman and Betty E. Cogswell, Leiden, The Netherlands: E. J. Brill, 1973, pp. 119-130.

p. 111 "Social Limitations on Libidinal Withdrawal" by Philip Slater is reprinted from the *American Sociological Review*, Vol. 28 (June 1963), pp. 339-364, by permission of the author and the *Review*. Copyright 1963 by the American Sociological Association.

p. 134 "Love or Marriage" by Ernes van den Haag is reprinted by permission of the author from *Harper's Magazine*, Vol. 224 (May 1962), pp. 43-47.

p. 143 "The Theoretical Importance of Love" by William J. Goode is reprinted from the *American Sociological Review*, Vol. 24, No. 1 (February 1959) pp. 38-47, by permission of the author and the *Review*. Copyright © 1959 by the American Sociological Association.

p. 157 "Marriage and the Construction of Reality" by Peter L. Berger and Hansfried Kellner is reprinted by permission of the publisher from *Diogenes*, No. 46 (Summer 1964), pp. 1-23.

p. 175 "Marriage Among the English Nobility" by Lawrence Stone is reprinted by permission of the author and publisher from *Comparative Studies in Society and History*, Vol. 3 (November-January, 1960-61), pp. 182-206. Copyright 1962 by Mouton & Co., The Hague, Netherlands.

p. 200 "Money, the Job, and Little Women" by Ellen Moers is reprinted by permission of the publisher and Curtis Brown Ltd. from *Commentary*, Vol. 55 (January 1973), pp. 57-65. Copyright © 1973 by the American Jewish Committee.

For my family

Preface

In this second edition, as in the first, I deal with the family not as it appears in the experience of its members but as it relates to society as a whole. My aim is to look at the family as a social institution, not as a source of specific social problems. Hence, problems that are often thought of as originating within the family—such as delinquency, mental illness, or divorce—notwithstanding their saliency for society, have been deliberately omitted. Many books deal with the social dynamics of family life, but few systematically place the family in its broader social context. This anthology is meant to redress the balance.

One reason for this new edition is that new material has appeared in the last decade that could be ignored only at one's peril. Another reason is the change that has occurred in our social thought. For several decades there was a strong emphasis on childhood socialization; it has given way to a more fundamental concern with the social matrix in which this socialization takes place: the social structure of the American family and the changing social roles within it, especially the role of women, have come to the foreground of our attention. This edition reflects these new concerns.

There has been little change in my general conceptual framework, which I owe mainly to my former teachers at Columbia University. My students have continued to challenge me, and one of them, Gerald Rokoff, has engaged me in an intensive dialogue which culminated in a joint paper that is reprinted in these pages. I am also proudly publishing here two papers by my students Peter Dobkin Hall and Jeffrey P. Rosenfeld. I am deeply indebted to all, including my colleagues at Stony Brook, who have made my intellectual life exciting and productive.

As in the past, my work owes a great deal to an intensive exchange of thoughts with Lewis Coser. Whatever little I have been able to achieve derives from his untiring encouragement, stimulation, and creative thought. My children, although they have become young adults since the first edition of this book, have remained true to their parents' interests: Ellen as a young professional and mother, Steven as a college junior, ready to put to work his intellectual alertness and curiosity. Both continue to be sources of inspiration.

Contents

Introduction

The material in this book has been selected and organized according to the basic assumption that the family constitutes an integral part of the structural arrangements of society. The selections focus, in order, on four central questions: What are the universal functions of the family for society? How are some of these universal functions served in concrete instances? How are interpersonal relations within the family adapted to the wider social context? How does the family mediate between its members and their roles and positions in society? The last part of the book deals with changes in the relationships between men and women and with some alternatives to family living. None of the papers in this book deals with concrete social problems, such as divorce or health and disease, that occur in and through family life.[1]

A study of the family as an institution must relate it to the context of the particular society in which it functions, because relationships within the family and its pattern of life must to some extent be congruent with the demands that the community makes upon its members. For example, if there is strong emphasis on individual achievement as the basis of social

1. For a similar approach to the institution of the family, see Kingsley Davis, *Human Society*, New York: The Macmillan Co., 1949, Chapter 15. Davis's conceptual framework informs in large measure the organization of this book.

status—as in our own society, especially in the middle class—the values of individualism and achievement will guide the family's concerns in relation to its young members. For it is in the family that the next generation is prepared for the roles to be occupied in the society at large.

The basic assumption that patterns of family life must be explained in terms of the larger social order is contrary to the view that the political and economic life of the society must be explained by reference to the character and personality of individuals, as they are shaped in the family through its training practices. While it may be true that from the point of view of individuals the family is the first institution to which they are exposed, it is important to remember that from the point of view of society the family is a mediator of social values. As Erich Fromm has aptly stated: "In spite of individual differences that exist in different families [of the same society], the family represents primarily the content of society; the most important social function of the family is to transmit this content, not only through formation of opinions and points of view but through the creation of a socially desirable attitudinal structure." [2]

Following the French anthropologist Claude Lévi-Strauss,[3] the family may be defined as a group manifesting the following organizational attributes: it finds its origin in marriage; it consists of husband, wife, and children born in their wedlock, though other relatives may find their place close to this nuclear group; and the group is united by moral, legal, economic, religious, and social rights and obligations (including sexual rights and prohibitions as well as such socially patterned feelings as love, attraction, piety, and awe).

That the family is a universal institution cannot be explained simply by its manifest functions—such as reproduction, economic activities, socialization of the young—all of which could conceivably be fulfilled outside the institutionalized family. Moreover, the family does not serve exactly the same functions in every society or at every time: it may be an economic enterprise or have no economic function other than consumption; religious worship may center around the family or may be regulated by other social institutions. Nevertheless, though the manifold characteristics of families are as diverse in structure as the cultures in which they are embedded, one feature stands out universally: the family helps place individuals into a patterned network of interweaving social relationships. It does this in two ways: by regulating social alliances between families and by acting as an agent of social placement for the new members of society. The first of these

2. Erich Fromm, "Sozialpsychologischer Teil" in *Autoritaet and Familie,* Max Horkheimer, ed., Paris: Librairie Alcan, 1936, p. 87.
3. "The Family," in *Man, Culture and Society,* Harry L. Shapiro, ed., New York: Oxford University Press, 1960.

is known as the *Principle of Reciprocity,* the second as the *Principle of Legitimacy.*

Though some earlier social theorists—of the evolutionist school, for example—assumed that "in the beginning" (whatever this may mean) there was no family, that men and women lived in a "free" or "promiscuous" state and that their children belonged to the "collectivity," contemporary anthropologists, sociologists, and historians agree that no known society, present or past, exists without groups of two or more adults who are responsible for the reproduction and maintenance of new members as well as for their socialization. The first discoveries of previously unknown territories peopled by "savages" (like early contacts with Eastern civilization) led Westerners to the realization that their social arrangements were not universal or divinely ordained. Early travelers and missionaries regarded patterns of sexual life that they were unfamiliar with as lacking sexual mores and rules. Societies where men had sexual relations with more than one woman, where promiscuity seemed to be the common pattern, or where sexual relations between boys and girls before marriage appeared to be unrestricted seemed to lack any order at all. Yet we now know that in every society that has been discovered so far the relations between men and women, the processes of reproduction and of socialization, and the social exchange of women have been subject to some social control.

It is well established, for example, that polygamous societies institutionalized either polyandry, when a woman has more than one husband, or polygyny, when a man has more than one wife (the latter being much more frequent), but never random mating. Whether the culture practices polyandry or polygyny, there is usually role differentiation and division of labor among the various partners of the same sex, and assignment of offspring to the proper lineage. Furthermore, polygamy is limited primarily, if not exclusively, to those individuals who occupy a high place in the social structure—chiefs or nobles, for example—so that marital selection tends to be related to the status order of the larger society.

The family makes society possible by defining social relationships through a patterned exchange of sexual partners. This reciprocity, which is the essence of social life, is assured by the incest taboo. Whatever the type of social control of sexual activities—whether premarital sexual intercourse is permitted, preferred, prescribed, or proscribed [4]—all societies control pregnancy and birth; and no matter how much license there is for some kind of uncontrolled sexual behavior, generally a rule of exogamy requires that sexual partners be obtained from outside one's immediate family. Since emotional ties between members of the family must necessarily be strong, sexual partners from within the same family group would

4. About these variations in the social control of mores, see Robert K. Merton, *Social Theory and Social Structure,* Glencoe, Ill.: The Free Press, 1957, p. 133.

naturally be the preferred choice; if incest were permitted, ties between individuals would become ever more limited to fewer and fewer persons, and social atomization would replace social process.[5] Despite the fact that "one's immediate family" may be defined differently in various cultures— it may or may not include cousins, for example—the incest taboo makes possible a patterned form of exchange *between* instead of *within* families; it thereby assures the occurrence of social exchange and provides the basis for the operation of the *Principle of Reciprocity.*

If individuals are to be exchanged between families through marital selection, one important aspect of the interrelation between the family and the society is the "placement" function the family has for its members. The family—more specifically, the father—gives the children a social identity; that is, it places them in a specific pattern of social relationships. Indeed, the distinctly social nature of the family is characterized by the universal insistence on fatherhood. If the function of the family were simply reproduction, the link between man and woman could be severed after conception, because no necessary ties arise from the fact of biological descent. The Latin distinction between *genitor* (father as procreator) and *pater* (social father) indicates well the dual nature of fatherhood. The institution of adoption demonstrates that it is the *social father* who assigns status to the children that are said to belong to the family, whether the father or both parents are the physiological agents or not. It is in this way that every society, no matter what its sexual mores, establishes the legitimacy of its new members.

The dyad mother-child, self-sufficient as it might conceivably be economically and emotionally, is always considered incomplete sociologically. This is true of every society, whether patrilineal or matrilineal (that is, whether the father or the maternal uncle has the main control over the children). Even in matrilineal societies, where both mother and offspring belong to the mother's clan, the dyad of mother and child is not considered a complete social unit and has no well-defined social identity. The *Principle of Legitimacy* holds that every child shall have a father, and one father only. The theories of *reciprocity* and *legitimacy* are presented in the first part of this book.

The rule of exogamy implies, of course, that feelings of mutual attraction as a motivation for marital selection are not to be left to chance alone. Cravings for sexual intimacy and mutual attraction through love are not

---

5. The importance of social prescriptions is tested by the reaction to their violation. The exceptional case of Egyptian society during a certain historical period is a case in point (cf. Russell Middleton, "A Deviant Case . . . ," this volume, pp. 31–43). Brother-sister marriage in this instance produced heated controversy and required special legal action to be tolerated.

permitted to reign supreme, since they might threaten patterned social alliances. Furthermore, there is a reluctance in every social milieu to let pairs of lovers withdraw completely from the social scene; if this were possible, society could no longer exist. Indeed, marriage itself, with all its social obligations, is a means of control of love relationships. In marriage, feelings and emotions get redefined in the course of dyadic interaction and in the course of the interaction of the partners with people outside the family. What takes place is an integration of private life with responses to expectations emanating from the various subgroups of society with which the members of the family must interact as well.

If exogamy serves to bring into relation with one another otherwise separated groups—that is, if marriage is to be seen as a form of social alliance—there must exist different preferences for different types of alliances. Alliance with strangers entails the risk of disparity of values, of differences in financial or social status, or other discrepancies between potential allies that are socially defined as undesirable. The families and friends of the future partners are concerned about the alliance that comes from marriage, and the nuclear families and other social groups may express socially prescribed interest in the marital choices of children and peers. Such controls may be exercised by subtle encouragement, as is often the case in our society, or by enforcement of prescribed behavior, as among the traditional Chinese gentry; but in no society is marriage determined by spontaneous sentiments alone. If sentiments are allowed, or expected, to give the immediate impetus to marital choice, they are to be "appropriate" —that is, they are to be so channeled as not to clash with the value system. In modern Western society, where marital choices are made by the young persons themselves, and where there is strong emphasis on love as a basis of that choice, many subtle and informal pressures may be exercised by parents, as well as, in smaller measure, by peers, to prevent choices that are socially considered "wrong." The freedom in marital selection upon which so much emphasis is placed in our culture does not imply lack of restriction or an unlimited range of choice but simply freedom of choice within a socially prescribed framework. Problems dealing with the social control of emotions as well as problems of marital selection are discussed in the second part of this book.

The degree of individual choice permitted in marital selection depends on the distribution of duties and obligations within the family system. When the father has absolute power and authority over the members, as among the traditional Chinese gentry, love between the young couple would weaken the son's allegiance and interfere with expected filial piety. Hence, in a society that rests on rigid and continuous paternal authority, love will have little importance as a basis of marital partnership. In contrast, in a society in which a young man is expected to relinquish his dependency on his parents, it is permissible, even desirable, for the young couple to be bound by strong feelings, since they will have to depend primarily on each other and move to a new abode of their own. The way in which marital choice takes place is related to the internal family organization.

Similarly, the subsequent division of roles within the family is related to the broader social context. Role differentiation would seem to be more sharply marked in societies where the family performs many functions than in those where it is limited mainly to reproduction and socialization. For example, if the family is also a productive unit, division of labor may be expected; if the family is also the center of religious activities, different rituals are assigned to various members. Consequently, the need for role differentiation in the family would seem to be strongly reduced in industrial society, since most of the functions that have traditionally been served by the family are now being performed by outside institutions. Even a large part of the socialization of the young has been taken over by the educational system, and the family as a unit of production has almost disappeared. (Farm families, which by definition do not actively participate in modern industrial societies, are one notable exception.)

Another reason for less rigid role differentiation in the modern family is the fact that in industrial societies, where status tends to be based on achievement rather than on ascribed characteristics, sexual differences are correspondingly less emphasized as a basis for role distribution. It is not simply the woman's participation in the economic process that determines her equality in the family, however, for there would be no contradiction between the need for a woman's hard work and her subordination to her husband if "hard work" were seen only as an obligation. But when high *moral* value is given to personal achievement through hard work, the importance of that achievement as a criterion for evaluating individuals tends to eliminate from consideration other possible sources of inequality. It is the equalitarian value system of which this moral emphasis on individual achievement is a part, rather than a woman's *de facto* participation in economic life, that frees her—in the dominant value system if not quite in reality—from her husband's authority and defines her as a companion.

Under this same value system the children are supposed to be treated equally, irrespective of sex—their age a basis for discrimination only insofar as it makes for differences in maturity and ability. Indeed, since the family prepares its young members for their future roles in society at large, it must emphasize those human qualities that are highly valued in the culture. This is why achievement is so highly valued within the middle-class family. The "equalitarian" family, especially cherished in the

American middle class, is part of a value system that serves the economic process of an industrial society.[6]

However, role differentiation in the family may vary in different sub-groups. For example, the modern middle-class family tends to reveal greater equality between husband and wife, and between siblings in all respects other than age, than the working-class family. Similarly, the emphasis on achievement and mobility is not similar in all socio-economic strata. The upper and middle classes tend to be the representatives of the dominant values; in addition, these values are less pervasive as moral guides in strata where there is little opportunity for their attainment. In periods of social revolution in which a formerly underprivileged class is promised a share of rewards hitherto unattainable, that class may well adopt these values. During the Russian and the Chinese revolutions, for example, the idea of social equality for the working class gave it the necessary impetus for achievement and hard work, and the idea of equality for women freed them from traditional family ties; thus the equalitarian ideology of a social movement became an important force in the rapid industrialization of both these countries.

Even in modern society, sex remains to a very large extent a basis for status assignment. In the American occupational sphere women are usually paid a lower salary than men doing the same work, and many types of positions are given to women rarely and reluctantly. Similarly, in the middle-class family full equality between husband and wife is seldom achieved, and there is often a contradiction between the avowed equality of siblings and the actual differential treatment of boys and girls.[7] One reason for the inequality between men and women is the fact that women are mainly assigned to their *ascribed* roles, while for men it is the *achieved* role that is salient. Women have the cultural mandate to give priority to the care of their families, and this fact gives them less than full status in the occupational sphere. The emphasis on having children and on meeting their need for motherly care helps deny women equal rights in the occupational sphere.

The emphasis on personal achievement also affects relationships within the extended family. Where individuals gain their status through their own achievement rather than through ascription, the family into which

6. It should be understood that changes in family structure similar to those that have taken place in modern Western society do not always "automatically" follow upon industrialization. Some of these changes may sometimes precede and hence facilitate industrialization as a result of the spreading of the ideology of individualism and equality which is often popular with the young, with women, and with an elite of educated. Cf. William J. Goode, *World Revolution and Family Patterns,* New York: The Free Press of Glencoe, 1963.

7. See, for example, Mirra Komarovsky, "Functional Analysis of Sex Roles," in *The Family: Its Structure and Functions,* 1st ed., pp. 290–306.

they are born—*the family of orientation*—loses importance for the young married couple. Many parents give aid to married children, but such aid is considered temporary and is thought of as "influencing the children's status position," [8] until *they can be on their own* and *prove themselves.* In spite of the fact that emotional ties between members of an extended family continue to exist,[9] the modern family is removed, morally and physically, from relatives; it is to the family formed by marriage—*the family of procreation*—that family members owe their primary allegiance. The United States furnishes an excellent example of the modern family in an industrial society. The nuclear family is independent of other consanguine relationships, with husband, wife, and children constituting an independent family unit.

The need of modern industry, business, and the professions to be guided by considerations of competence and achievement has its counterpart in the individual emphasis on personal "improvement" and career, especially among men. To serve this end, individuals must be free to accept changes in location and status, and hence to sever close relations with neighborhood friends. Strong emotional ties to neighbors would impede the geographical movement and status mobility that provide the flexibility needed in modern industry and bureaucratic organization. Studies of army life have shown that privates often refuse promotion because they do not want to leave their "buddies." If such nonrational attachments to friends or relatives were typical of the general way of life, it would be difficult for persons to be placed in a rationally organized enterprise on the basis of their abilities.

A binding allegiance to "buddies," whether or not they are family members, may impede individual achievement. The British discovered in India, for example, that as long as people felt bound to their families and were not permitted to enjoy the fruits of their own achievement because they had to support their families, they had no incentive to "better themselves." In 1930 the Indian government passed the Gains of Learning Act, which stipulated that "all gains of learning are a man's exclusive and separate property." A consequence of the "administration of the Hindu law by British courts was the disintegration of the joint-family organization (although it was retained in name)." [10] Severing family relations made it possible to fill positions in the civil service and in industry.

The strength of the ties between the individual and his family of

8. Marvin B. Sussman, "The Help Pattern in the Middle-Class Family," *American Sociological Review,* 18 (Feb. 1953), pp. 22–28.

9. Cf. Eugene Litwak, "Occupational Mobility and Extended Family Cohesion" and "Geographic Mobility and Extended Family Cohesion," *American Sociological Review,* 25 (Feb. and June 1960 respectively), pp. 9–21 and 385–394.

10. K. M. Kapadia, *Marriage and Family in India,* Bombay: John Brown, Oxford University Press, 1955, pp. 249–251.

orientation is clearly related to the authority relations within the family. Because of the reduction of the number of the family's social functions and the emphasis on individual achievement, authority in the modern family has been restricted. In an increasingly differentiated social order, controls over individuals emanate from a variety of institutions; authority is segmented just as activities are segmented, not only in social life generally but to some extent in the family as well. For example, the child, though he is under his parents' authority in general life style, is controlled by teachers in the educational sphere. And the young man who sets out to work is not, as in some rural societies, subjected to his father's management (and often exploitation) but is away from home, under the control of managers or supervisors expressly hired for the job. If achievement is the measure, and if it takes place mainly outside the family, parental figures can judge the performance of their children in only a limited way—especially in a rapidly changing society where knowledge acquired in the past soon becomes obsolete or supplemented. When children bring new knowledge home from school, for example, parents have to admit that "they don't know everything." [11] Thus authority in the modern family is neither based on the ability of the parent to exploit his children economically nor on his unequivocal superior knowledge in all spheres.

But the modern family need not be regarded as "breaking down," as some writers on the subject have assumed (except where the limitation of authority within the family is not integrated with the value system, as is sometimes the case, for example, with immigrant families [12]). The loosening of control over the children does not necessarily mean that the family is "weak." Where relaxation of authority by the parents is not accompanied by relinquishment of responsibilities, it is used as a deliberate means to teach the children "to be on their own." In families that value the acquisition of knowledge and individual independence, the child who brings home knowledge responds to the parents' ideal of the "independent achiever"; the father does not so much feel his authority threatened as he delights in his child's conformity to his own values. He may be less secure than the traditional parental figure whose control was unequivocally based on his power position, but he derives prestige and self-esteem if he acts as an effective representative of the values of the larger social order.

The emphasis on the value of knowledge as well as on the value of individual independence is not equally shared in all subgroups of modern society. Not all the subgroups are equally privileged in having access to these values, for they are a concomitant of social position. That is, middle

11. The *Scholastic News Time*—a newspaper distributed through elementary schools —reprints the following letter from a reader: "I like *News Time* because . . . now I know things even before my mother does" (Sept. 1963).
12. William I. Thomas and Florian Znaniecki, *The Polish Peasant in Europe and America,* New York: Dover Publications, 1958.

and upper classes in modern society are more geared toward valuing internal dispositions, toward developing the "proper" attitude that will guide behavior, while the working and lower classes tend to value behavior as such and its immediate consequences, without much reference to underlying attitudes. In social classes where individual achievement is stressed, and where individualistic effort seems to be rewarded with some degree of success, the emphasis is on flexibility of behavior because behavior must be adapted to the exigencies of particular situations and to the expectations of a diverse and changing number of people in an individual's various activity systems. In contrast, under social and economic conditions that are harsh and in which rewards, if any, are slow in coming, the emphasis is on staying out of trouble and behaving according to rules and regulations to avoid unpredictable consequences. Role expectations in American society generally, as well as in different social classes, are dealt with in the third part of this book.

It should be clear by now that variations in family structure occur, not because of random cultural relativity, but in terms of the differing functional interrelations between family and the ongoing social order. The family is the main institution for helping individuals, and especially the young, adapt to the requirements of the society by passing on its values, thus assuring at the same time continuity between the generations and hence the continuity of culture. This continuity takes place not only through the transmission of moral and social values but through the transmission of valued goods and property as well. The differential effects of various types of land inheritance illustrate the consequences that family arrangements may have on society. In pre-Communist China, for example, the division of property among all the sons caused landholdings to become smaller with each generation and thus exacerbated the poverty of the Chinese peasant. Where, in contrast, primogeniture is practiced in the passing on of land, younger sons are more likely to leave the land to find their fortunes elsewhere, thus providing the labor power for other occupations and leaving the landholdings intact.

Some investigators believe that in the nineteenth century primogeniture fostered the development of industry in urban centers, while division of property among the sons favored development of local industries in homes or small workshops. In regions where landed property was passed on to a single heir, younger brothers either had to stay with the main household as celibates, migrate to places—often overseas—where land was available, or move to emerging industrial centers. In contrast, where land was divided among all the sons, it was more likely that each would set up his own household on his separate piece of land, which frequently proved insufficient for subsistence. Thus, the way in which goods that are valuable economically, as well as attitudes and behaviors that are valuable morally and socially, are passed on to future generations has an important impact on role distribution in the social, political, and economic life of the society.

It is precisely because of the importance of the family as an agency of transmission that its features cannot be a matter of indifference to political power-holders. In some societies, a limited authority over the young within the family may serve to facilitate direct control by representatives of the political order. In Nazi Germany, for example, young people were required to leave the parental home at prescribed times, to participate in the activities of the Hitler Youth, to go on hikes, or to spend long periods in camps. This system put the young for an important part of their lives under the direct control and influence of representatives of the political regime. Though not always coercive, mechanisms of control over the family operate more or less indirectly everywhere. In the United States, for example, adolescents, especially in the middle class, are weaned away from the influence of the home not through rules and regulations and policy-making but by the fact that a four-year absence from home while acquiring a college education is considered to be good for character building. For the purpose of formal education alone there would be no reason why the college youth should not live at home while attending classes; but attending colleges that are geographically removed from home, or living in college dormitories even if the parents' abode is nearby, is believed to be "good for them," since it "encourages independence" and helps them develop the self-reliance demanded by a highly competitive society.

Even in a democratic society, official policy often influences family life. President Nixon's veto in 1971 of a bill aimed at providing funds for child-care centers is a case in point. The degree to which the social controls over family patterns are enforced explicitly or operate implicitly may differ, but the range of choice open to an individual family is always limited by two factors. First, definite concepts of public welfare, which are the concern of state or government, are enforced deliberately either through coercion, as in the case of compulsory education even in democratic societies, or through incentives, as in the case of financial support for *familles nombreuses* in contemporary France. Second, every family must adapt its choices to the economic and political order in which it exists; the choices available may be many or few, but the possible alternatives for such adaptation are always somewhat limited. Since social arrangements within the family may affect development, they must be subject to some control. Flexibility and informality of controls is associated with flexibility in other social institutions and the degree to which innovation is tolerated in these other spheres.

During periods of social change, the family structure is likely to change as well. The change may be deliberately fostered or even regulated, as during social revolutions; or it may come about gradually, often being noticed only after it has taken place. In any case, it creates tension, and accounts in large part for what has come to be known as the "generation gap." Yet not only the relation between the generations but the role distribution within the family is likely to be affected by a change in the society. The structural and functional significance of inheritance and some of the effects of social change on roles within the family are discussed in the fourth part of this book.

In our own society, recent changes in the economic and social realm, as well as in our value system, will have a lasting effect on our family structure. Changes in the labor force ever since World War II, and changes in the opportunity structure as a result, in large part, of the civil rights movement—these developments of the last thirty years or so are bringing about a reevaluation of the traditional family structure, which already has begun to be modified in an unobtrusive manner.

A new definition of woman's role in the family is about to emerge as a consequence, at least in part, of women's participation in the labor force. The development from World War II, when 6 million women took jobs, and when 75 percent of the new women workers were married,[13] to our day, when women constitute almost 40 percent of the labor force and when one third of all married women age 20–24 with preschool children and husband present are at work, indicates an irreversible trend in women's participation in the world of work as well as a change in the role of the mother-wife and, as a consequence, a change in the role of the husband-father.

Women continued to participate in the labor force all through the fifties and sixties, despite postwar propaganda against such participation. During the war they were hailed for their courage and their ability, for being an "everflowing source of moral and physical energy, working for victory . . . [because] ships and planes and guns [can't be built] without them," but with the return of peace an attempt was made to put them in their place again. The mass media, educators, and academicians joined hands. The *Ladies Home Journal* wrote that "The ideal of every woman is to find the right husband, bear and rear his children and make for them a cozy, gay, happy home," yet had to report that more women workers wanted to continue on the job than return home. Margaret Pickel, dean of Barnard College, declared in the *New York Times Magazine* that women had "less physical strength, a lower fatigue point, and a less stable nervous

13. For an incisive account of the change in the status of women during World War II and later, see William H. Chafe, *The American Woman, Her Changing Social, Economic and Political Roles, 1920–1970,* New York: Oxford University Press, 1972.

system" than men. And the sociologist Willard Waller charged that during the war women had gotten "out of hand" and "women must bear and rear children; husbands must support them." [14]

In fact, women, including those married and with children, not only remained in the labor force but continued to participate in increasing numbers between 1950 and 1970. The reason was that there was increased demand for female labor at a time when the traditional pool of women available for work—the young unmarried ones—decreased in number.[15] The demand was increased by advancing industrialization, in which the office grows faster than the factory, creating a growing need for clerical and service workers. And since the demand could not be met by young and unmarried women, especially since their proportion decreased because of the lower birthrate in the thirties, the earlier age of marriage, and the increased length of schooling, married women had to be recruited.

Although women's wages continued to be lower than men's, women found it both advantageous and possible to respond to the demand. It was *advantageous* because taking jobs permitted them to supplement the family income either out of dire need or to increase the family's living comforts in an economy that was flooding the market with goods to enhance family living. And it was *possible* because the advanced technology of labor-saving devices and the advanced food industry not only reduced significantly the time needed to care for households and families but also reduced the need for a division of labor. That is, at a time when women can operate cranes as readily as men because the technology minimizes differences in physical strength, men can open cans and frozen food packages as readily as women, because the technology minimizes differences in household skills. Nor is the change merely a matter of technical or mechanical operation, for on a more encompassing level the development of industry has eliminated the productive tasks within the family by producing outside the home all the goods needed—not only clothing and food, but prepared food as well—to the point where earlier essential household activities, such as sewing and cooking, tend to become hobbies of the artsy-craftsy and gourmet variety, for those who have the leisure to indulge in them.

As the family is hardly a productive unit any longer, the age-old division of labor within the family has become obsolete. As the home becomes more and more mechanized, the American husband would feel slightly ridiculous claiming that he cannot run the machines, even though he may still claim ineptitude when it comes to sewing on a button. Conversely, the wife would feel silly claiming that she has to wait for her

14. The quotes in this paragraph are taken from Chafe, *op. cit.*
15. For a superb analysis of the demographic trends of supply and demand of female labor, see Valerie Kincade Oppenheimer, "Demographic Influence on Female Employment and the Status of Women," in *Changing Women in a Changing Society,* Joan Huber, ed., Chicago: University of Chicago Press, 1973, pp. 184–199.

husband to fix an electric plug. To be sure, some symbolic division of labor hangs on longer than what is defined as instrumental: the husband takes the wheel at the family outing on Sunday, when all through the week his wife has been the family's chauffeur. Yet these symbolic gestures are quick to disappear. The new generation is busy working out new ways that are more harmonious with the new technology and with the new concepts of division of labor as well.

Technology by itself is not sufficient to change the patterns of living; it must be accompanied by opportunities as well as by the legitimacy of change. After all, washing machines and dishwashers have been around for a long time and have been used whether or not the wife-mother went out to work. Even if housework is facilitated and goods no longer need to be produced in the home, housework tends to multiply to fill the time that is available, or at least enough of the time to maintain the claim on a full-time person to look after it. Yet when opportunities open up, such as the increased demand for female labor mentioned earlier, modern technology can easily be made use of to respond to this demand.

To these opportunities has been added an important argument for the legitimacy of their acceptance: the recent advocacy of zero population growth. The need for motherhood as a career has been seriously questioned in the name of the well-being of future generations, and this questioning has gone hand in hand with the technological improvement of contraceptives, followed by a moral reversal in the American ethos in regard to abortion. All these recent developments cannot help but call the attention of the present young generation to the fact that they have choices never before available, and that not only do they have choices but the moral obligation to choose deliberately rather than let biology be their destiny.

The civil rights movement has had no small share in bringing about a demand for sexual as well as racial equality. This movement has highlighted the contradiction between our society's emphasis on achievement, between the theory that allocation of status takes place according to merit, and the fact that opportunities for achievement have been withheld from people on the basis of ascribed characteristics. Patterns of behavior that have been based on biological differences suddenly seem to many not only irrelevant but illegitimate; they seem to violate the American principle of equality. Coinciding as this movement did with the actual participation of women in the world of work and with an industrial development that made the traditional tasks assigned to them obsolete, it resulted in drastic changes in the status of women, which in turn will bring about a drastic change in the structure of the family. How deep-going a revolution this will be remains to be seen.

The contradictions and changes in the status of the American woman, as well as structural alternatives to present-day family living in America, are dealt with in the fifth part of this book.

THE BASIC FUNCTIONS OF THE FAMILY

Nuclear families are recognized in all societies, whether or not the household consists of conjugal or extended kin. The social process of exchange—i.e., of reciprocity—which is the essence of social life, as Lévi-Strauss points out, accounts for the existence of nuclear families and therefore for the universality of the incest taboo. Talcott Parsons demonstrates that the taboo, by frustrating early sexual desires, helps develop in the young the psychological attributes for becoming active members of society and the parental guides of the next generation.

Russell Middleton describes the case of Ancient Egypt where —unusual as it seems to be—father-daughter and brother-sister unions were considered legitimate. Future theoretical or empirical research in this area will undoubtedly make it possible to refine the theory of the incest taboo. Philip Slater's paper later in this book (Chapter 3) provides some clues in this direction. Slater shows that incest is tabooed because it would lead to ever-increased withdrawal from the community. This raises the question of whether in ancient Egypt there were social mechanisms at work that prevented the father-daughter and sister-brother unions from withdrawing from society.

Exchange of people through marriage takes place between nuclear families, and it is this process that assigns to the families the function of social placement. According to the theories of *reciprocity* and *legitimacy,* the existence of nuclear families makes possible social control of childbirth and social placement of the young, and is a precondition for the social exchange of men and women as well as of goods and services.

Bronislaw Malinowski demonstrates the social importance of fatherhood in giving status to the child. The following three selections deal with the modification of this universal principle. For if social placement is deemed to be important, there is more at stake in it for some families than for others. The importance of placement is directly related to status position. The lower the social class, the less difference it makes how and where the child is placed. This issue is dealt with by Goode. Freilich and Lewis Coser describe a mating system where legitimacy is not controlled, and show the cost for women of the practice of illegitimacy. Finally, Coser & Coser deal with the paradox of the principle: if it is true that the *Principle of Legitimacy* is universal because of society's insistence that children be placed in the social structure, it follows that at certain historical periods a society that wants to transform its status system through a revolution will be helped in its endeavors if the family suspends this function. This further demonstrates the fact that legitimacy—that is, placement in society by a social father—is seen as contributing to the stability of society.

2

1 THE PRINCIPLE OF RECIPROCITY

Claude Lévi-Strauss

Reciprocity, the Essence of Social Life

The conclusions of the famous *Essay on the Gift* are well known. In this study which is considered a classic today, Mauss intended to show first of all that in primitive societies exchange consists less frequently of economic transactions than of reciprocal gifts; secondly, that these reciprocal gifts have a much more important function in these societies than in ours; finally, that this primitive form of exchange is not wholly nor essentially of an economic character but is what he calls "a total social fact," i.e., an event which has at the same time social and religious, magic and economic, utilitarian and sentimental, legal and moral significance. It is known that in numerous primitive societies, and particularly in those of the Pacific Islands and those of the Northwest Pacific coast of Canada and of Alaska, all the ceremonies observed on important occasions are accompanied by a distribution of valued objects. Thus in New Zealand the ceremonial offering of clothes, jewels, arms, food and various furnishings was a common characteristic of the social life of the Maori. These gifts were presented in the event of births, marriages, deaths, exhumations, peace treaties and misdemeanors, and incidents too numerous to be recorded. Similarly, Firth lists the occasions of ceremonial exchange in Polynesia: "birth, initiation, marriage, sickness, death and other social events. . . ."[1] Another observer cites the following occasions for ceremonial exchange in a section of the same region: betrothal, marriage, pregnancy, birth and death; and he describes the presents offered by the father of the young man at the celebration of the betrothal: ten baskets of dry fish, ten thousand ripe and six thousand green coco-nuts, the boy himself receiving in exchange two large cakes.[2]

Such gifts are either exchanged immediately for equivalent gifts, or received by the beneficiaries on the condition that on a subsequent occasion they will return the gesture with other gifts whose value often exceeds that of the first, but which bring about in their turn a right to receive later new gifts which themselves surpass the magnificence of those previously given. The most characteristic of these institutions is the potlatch of the Indians in Alaska and in the region of Vancouver. These ceremonies have a triple function: to give back with proper "interest" gifts formerly received; to establish publicly the claim of a family or social group to a title or privilege, or to announce a change of status; finally, to surpass a rival in generosity, to crush him if possible under future obligations which it is hoped he cannot meet, thus taking from him privileges, titles, rank, authority and prestige.

Doubtless the system of reciprocal gifts only reaches such vast proportions with the Indians of the Northwest Pacific, a people who show a genius and exceptional temperament in their treatment of the fundamental themes of a primitive culture. But Mauss has been able to establish the existence of similar institutions in Melanesia and Polynesia. The main function of the food celebrations of many tribes in New Guinea is to obtain recognition of the new "pangua" through a gathering of witnesses, that is to say, the function which in Alaska, according to Barnett, is served by potlatch. . . . Gift exchange and potlatch is a universal mode of culture, although not equally developed everywhere.

But we must insist that this primitive conception of the exchange of goods is not only expressed in well-defined and localized institutions. It permeates all transactions, ritual or secular, in the course of which objects or produce are given or received. Everywhere we find again and again this double assumption, implicit or explicit, that reciprocal gifts constitute a means of transmission of goods; and that these goods are not offered principally or essentially, in order to gain a profit or advantage of an economic nature: "After celebrations of birth," writes Turner of the Samoan culture, "after having received and given the *oloa* and the *tonga* (that is the masculine gifts and the feminine gifts) the husband and the wife are not any richer than they were before."

. . .

1. Raymond Firth, *Primitive Polynesian Economy*, London, 1939, p. 321.
2. H. Ian Hogbin, "Sexual life of the natives of Ongton Java." *Journal of the Polynesian Society*, Vol. 40, p. 28.

Exchange does not bring a tangible result as is the case in the commercial transactions in our society. Profit is neither direct, nor is it inherent in the objects exchanged as in the case of monetary profit or consumption values. Or rather, profit does not have the meaning which we assign
to it because in primitive culture, there is something else in what we call a
"commodity" than that which renders it commodious to its owner or to
its merchant. Goods are not only economic commodities but vehicles and
instruments for realities of another order: influence, power, sympathy,
status, emotion; and the skillful game of exchange consists of a complex
totality of maneuvers, conscious or unconscious, in order to gain security
and to fortify one's self against risks incurred through alliances and
rivalry.

. . .

Writing about the Andaman Islanders, Radcliffe-Brown states: "The
purpose of the exchange is primarily a moral one; to bring about a friendly
feeling between the two persons who participate." The best proof of the
supra-economic character of these exchanges is that, in the potlatch, one
does not hesitate sometime to destroy considerable wealth by breaking a
"copper," or throwing it in the sea and that greater prestige results from
the destruction of riches than from its distribution; for distribution, although it may be generous, demands a similar act in return. The economic
character exists, however, although it is always limited and qualified by
the other aspects of the institution of exchange. "It is not simply the
possession of riches which brings prestige, it is rather their distribution.
One does not gather riches except in order to rise in the social
hierarchy. . . . However, even when pigs are exchanged for pigs, and
food for food, the transactions do not lose all economic significance for
they encourage work and stimulate a need for cooperation." [3]
The idea that a mysterious advantage is attached to the obtainment of
commodities or at least certain commodities by means of reciprocal gifts,
rather than by production or by individual acquisition is not limited to
primitive societies.

In modern society, there are certain kinds of objects which are especially well suited for presents, precisely because of their non-utilitarian
qualities. In some Iberian countries these objects can only be found, in all
their luxury and diversity, in stores especially set up for this purpose and
which are similar to the Anglo-Saxon "gift shops." It is hardly necessary
to note that these gifts, like invitations (which, though not exclusively, are
also free distributions of food and drink) are "returned"; this is an instance in our society of the principle of reciprocity. It is commonly understood in our society that certain goods of a non-essential consumption
value, but to which we attach a great psychological aesthetic or sensual

3. A. B. Deacon, *Malekula . . . A Vanishing People in the New Hebrides*, London, 1934,
p. 637.

value, such as flowers, candies and luxury articles, are obtainable in the form of reciprocal gifts rather than in the form of purchases or individual consumption.

Certain ceremonies and festivals in our society also regulate the periodic return and traditional style of vast operations of exchange. The exchange of presents at Christmas, during one month each year, to which all the social classes apply themselves with a sort of sacred ardor, is nothing else than a gigantic potlatch, which implicates millions of individuals, and at the end of which many family budgets are confronted by lasting disequilibrium. Christmas cards, richly decorated, certainly do not attain the value of the "coppers"; but the refinement of selection, their outstanding designs, their price, the quantity sent or received, give evidence (ritually exhibited on the mantelpiece during the week of celebration), of the recipient's social bonds and the degree of his prestige. We may also mention the subtle techniques which govern the wrapping of the presents and which express in their own way the personal bond between the giver and the receiver: special stickers, paper, ribbon, etc. Through the vanity of gifts, their frequent duplication resulting from the limited range of selection, these exchanges also take the form of a vast and collective destruction of wealth. There are many little facts in this example to remind one that even in our society the destruction of wealth is a way to gain prestige. Isn't it true that the capable merchant knows that a way to attract customers is by advertising that certain high-priced goods must be "sacrificed"? The move is economic but the terminology retains a sense of the sacred tradition.

. . .

In the significant sphere of the offering of food, for which banquets, teas, and evening parties are the modern customs, the language itself, e.g., "to give a reception," shows that for us as in Alaska or Oceania, "to receive is to give." One offers dinner to a person whom one wishes to honor, or in order to return a "kindness." The more the social aspect takes precedence over the strictly alimentary, the more emphasis is given to style both of food and of the way in which it is presented: the fine porcelain, the silverware, the embroidered table cloths which ordinarily are carefully put away in the family cabinets and buffets, are a striking counterpart of the ceremonial bowls and spoons of Alaska brought out on similar occasions from painted and decorated chests. Above all, the attitudes towards food are revealing: what the natives of the Northwest coast call "rich food" connotes also among ourselves something else than the mere satisfaction of physiological needs. One does not serve the daily menu when one gives a dinner party. Moreover, if the occasion calls for certain types of food defined by tradition, their apparition alone, through a significant recurrence, calls for shared consumption. A bottle of old wine, a rare liqueur, bothers the conscience of the owner; these are delicacies which one would not buy and consume alone without a vague feeling of guilt. Indeed, the group judges with singular harshness the person who does this. This is reminiscent of the Polynesian ceremonial exchanges, in which goods must as much as possible not be exchanged within the group of paternal relations, but must go to other groups and into other villages. To fail at this duty is called "sori tana"—"to eat from one's own basket." And at the village dances, convention demands that neither of the two local groups consume the food which they have brought but that they exchange their provisions and that each eat the food of the other. The action of the person who, as the woman in the Maori proverb *Kai Kino ana Te Arahe,* would secretly eat the ceremonial food, without offering a part of it, would provoke from his or her relations sentiments which would range, according to circumstances, from irony, mocking and disgust to sentiments of dislike and even rage. It seems that the group confusedly sees in the individual accomplishment of an act which normally requires collective participation a sort of social incest.

But the ritual of exchange does not only take place in the ceremonial meal. Politeness requires that one offer the salt, the butter, the bread, and that one present one's neighbor with a plate before serving oneself. We have often noticed the ceremonial aspect of the meal in the lower-priced restaurants in the south of France; above all in those regions where wine is the main industry, it is surrounded by a sort of mystical respect which makes it "rich food." In those little restaurants where wine is included in the price of the meal each guest finds in front of his plate a modest bottle of a wine more than often very bad. This bottle is similar to that of the person's neighbor, as are the portions of meat and vegetables, which a waiter passes around. However, a peculiar difference of attitude immediately manifests itself in regard to the liquid nourishment and the solid nourishment: the latter serves the needs of the body and the former its luxury, the one serves first of all to feed, the other to honor. Each guest eats, so to speak, for himself. But when it comes to the wine, a new situation arises; if a bottle should be insufficiently filled, its owner would call good-naturedly for the neighbor to testify. And the proprietor would face, not the anger of an individual victim, but a community complaint. Indeed, the wine is a social commodity whereas the *plat du jour* is a personal commodity. The small bottle can hold just one glass, its contents will be poured not in the glass of the owner, but in that of his neighbor. And the latter will make a corresponding gesture of reciprocity.

What has happened? The two bottles are identical in size, their contents similar in quality. Each participant in this revealing scene, when the final count is made, has not received more than if he had consumed his own wine. From an economic point of view, no one has gained and no one has lost. But there is much more in the exchange itself than in the things exchanged.

The situation of two strangers who face each other, less than a yard apart, from two sides of a table in an inexpensive restaurant (to obtain an individual table is a privilege which one must pay for, and which cannot be awarded below a certain price) is commonplace and episodical. However, it is very revealing, because it offers an example, rare in our society (but prevalent in primitive societies) of the formation of a group for which, doubtless because of its temporary character, no ready formula of integration exists. The custom in French society is to ignore persons whose name, occupation and social rank are unknown. But in the little restaurant, such people find themselves placed for two or three half-hours in a fairly intimate relationship, and momentarily united by a similarity of preoccupations. There is conflict, doubtless not very sharp, but real, which is sufficient to create a state of tension between the norm of "privacy" and the fact of community. They feel at the same time alone and together, compelled to the habitual reserve between strangers, while their respective positions in physical space and their relationships to the objects and utensils of the meal, suggest and to a certain degree call for intimacy. These two strangers are exposed for a short period of time to living together. Without doubt not for as long a time nor as intimately as when one shares a sleeping car, or a cabin on a transatlantic crossing, but for this reason also no clear cultural procedure has been established. An almost imperceptible anxiety is likely to arise in the minds of the two guests with the prospect of small disagreements that the meeting could bring forth. When social distance is maintained, even if it is not accompanied by any manifestation of disdain, insolence or aggression, it is in itself a cause of suffering; for such social distance is at variance with the fact that all social contact carries with it an appeal and that this appeal is at the same time a hope for response. Opportunity for escape from this trying yet ephemeral situation is provided by an exchange of wine. It is an affirmation of good grace which dispels the reciprocal uncertainty; it substitutes a social bond for mere physical juxtaposition. But it is also more than that; the partner who had the right to maintain reserve is called upon to give it up; wine offered calls for wine returned, cordiality demands cordiality. The relationship of indifference which has lasted until one of the guests has decided to give it up can never be brought back. From now on it must become a relationship either of cordiality or hostility. There is no possibility of refusing the neighbor's offer of his glass of wine without appearing insulting. Moreover, the acceptance of the offer authorizes another offer, that of conversation. Thus a number of minute social bonds are established by a series of alternating oscillations, in which a right is established in the offering and an obligation in the receiving.

And there is still more. The person who begins the cycle has taken the initiative, and the greater social ease which he has proved becomes an advantage for him. However, the opening always carried with it a risk,

namely that the partner will answer the offered libation with a less generous drink, or, on the contrary, that he will prove to be a higher bidder thus
forcing the person who offered the wine first to sacrifice a second bottle
for the sake of his prestige. We are, therefore, on a microscopic scale, it is
true, in the presence of a "total social fact" whose implications are at the
same time social, psychological and economic.

   This drama, which on the surface seems futile and to which, perhaps,
the reader will find that we have awarded a disproportionate importance,
seems to us on the contrary to offer material for inexhaustible sociological
reflection. We have already pointed out the interest with which we view
the non-crystallized forms of social life: the spontaneous aggregations
arising from crises, or (as in the example just discussed) simple sub-
products of collective life, provide us with vestiges that are still fresh,
of very primitive social psychological experiences. In this sense the attitudes of the strangers in the restaurant appear to be an infinitely distant
projection, scarcely perceptible but nonetheless recognizable, of a fundamental situation; that in which individuals of primitive tribes find themselves for the first time entering into contact with each other or with
strangers. The primitives know only two ways of classifying strangers;
strangers are either "good" or "bad." But one must not be misled by a
naive translation of the native terms. A "good" group is that to which,
without hesitating, one grants hospitality, the one for which one deprives
oneself of most precious goods; while the "bad" group is that from which
one expects and to which one inflicts, at the first opportunity, suffering or
death. With the latter one fights, with the former one exchanges goods.

   The general phenomenon of exchange is first of all a total exchange,
including food, manufactured objects, as well as those most precious
items: women. Doubtlessly we are a long way from the strangers in the
restaurant and perhaps it seems startling to suggest that the reluctance of
the French peasant to drink his own bottle of wine gives a clue for the
explanation of the incest taboo. Indeed, we believe that both phenomena
have the same sociological and cultural meaning.

                         .   .   .

   The prohibition of incest is a rule of reciprocity. It means: I will only
give up my daughter or my sister if my neighbor will give up his also. The
violent reaction of the community towards incest is the reaction of a
community wronged. The fact that I can obtain a wife is, in the last
analysis, the consequence of the fact that a brother or a father has given
up a woman.

   In Polynesia Firth distinguishes three spheres of exchange according
to the relative mobility of the articles concerned. The first sphere concerns food in its diverse forms; the second, rope and fabrics made of bark;
the third, hooks, cables, turmeric cakes and canoes. He adds: "Apart
from the three spheres of exchange mentioned a fourth may be recognized

in cases where goods of unique quality are handed over. Such for instance was the transfer of women by the man who could not otherwise pay for his canoe. Transfers of land might be put into the same category. Women and land are given in satisfaction of unique obligations. . . ." [4]

It is necessary to anticipate the objection that we are relating two phenomena which are not of the same type; it might be argued that indeed gifts may be regarded even in our own culture as a primitive form of exchange but that this kind of reciprocal interaction has been replaced in our society by exchange for profit except for a few remaining instances such as invitations, celebrations and gifts: that in our society the number of goods that are being transferred according to these archaic patterns represents only a small proportion of the objects of commerce and merchandising, and that reciprocal gifts are merely amusing vestiges which can retain the curiosity of the antiquary; and that it is not possible to say that the prohibition of incest, which is as important in our own society as in any other, has been derived from a type of phenomenon which is abnormal today and of purely anecdotical interest. In other words, we will be accused, as we ourselves have accused M'Lennan, Spencer, Avebury and Durkheim, of deriving the function from the survival and the general case from the existence of an exceptional one.

This objection can be answered by distinguishing between two interpretations of the term "archaic." The survival of a custom or of a belief can be accounted for in different ways: the custom or belief may be a vestige, without any other significance than that of an historical residue which has been spared by chance; but it may also continue throughout the centuries to have a specific function which does not differ essentially from the original one. An institution can be archaic because it has lost its reason for existing or on the contrary because this reason for existing is so fundamental that its transformation has been neither possible nor necessary.

Such is the case of exchange. Its function in primitive society is essential because it encompasses at the same time material objects, social values and women, while in our culture the original function of exchange of goods has gradually been reduced in importance as other means of acquisition have developed; reciprocity as the basis of getting a spouse, however, has maintained its fundamental function; for one thing because women are the most precious property, and above all because women are not in the first place a sign of social value, but a natural stimulant; and the stimulant of the only instinct whose satisfaction can be postponed, the only one consequently, for which, in the act of exchange and through the awareness of reciprocity, the transformation can occur from the stimulant

4. Firth, *op. cit.*, p. 344.

to the sign and, thereby, give way to an institution; this is the fundamental process of transformation from the conditions of nature to cultural life.

The inclusion of women in the number of reciprocal transactions from group to group and from tribe to tribe is such a general custom that a volume would not suffice to enumerate the instances in which it occurs. Let us note first of all that marriage is everywhere considered as a particularly favorable occasion for opening a cycle of exchanges. The "wedding presents" in our society evidently enter again into the group of phenomena which we have studied above.

In Alaska and in British Columbia, the marriage of a girl is necessarily accompanied by a potlatch; to such a point that the Comox aristocrats organize mock-marriage ceremonies, where there is no bride, for the sole purpose of acquiring privileges in the course of the exchange ritual. But the relation which exists between marriage and gifts is not arbitrary; marriage is itself an inherent part of as well as a central motive for the accompanying reciprocal gifts. Not so long ago it was the custom in our society to "ask for" a young girl in marriage; the father of the betrothed woman "gave" his daughter in marriage; in English the phrase is still used, "to give up the bride." And in regard to the woman who takes a lover, it is also said that she "gives herself." The Arabic word, *sadaqa,* signifies the alm, the bride's price, law and tax. In this last case, the meaning of the word can be explained by the custom of wife buying. But marriage through purchase is an institution which is special in form only; in reality it is only a modality of the fundamental system as analyzed by Mauss, according to which, in primitive society and still somewhat in ours, rights, goods, and persons circulate within a group according to a continual mechanism of services and counter-services. Malinowski has shown that in the Trobriand Islands, even after marriage, the payment of mapula represents, on the part of the man, a counter-service destined to compensate for the services furnished by the wife in the form of sexual gratifications.

. . .

Even marriage through capture does not contradict the law of reciprocity; it is rather one of the possible institutionalized ways of putting it into practice. In Tikopia the abduction of the betrothed woman expresses in a dramatic fashion the obligation of the detaining group to give up the girls. The fact that they are "available" is thus made evident.

It would then be false to say that one exchanges or gives gifts at the same time that one exchanges or gives women. Because the woman herself is nothing else than one of these gifts, she is the supreme gift amongst those that can only be obtained in the form of reciprocal gifts. The first stage of our analysis has been directed towards bringing to light this fundamental characteristic of the gift, represented by the woman in primitive society, and to explain the reasons for it. It should not be surprising then to see that women are included among a number of other reciprocal prestations.

. . .

The small nomadic bands of the Nambikwara Indians of western Brazil are in constant fear of each other and avoid each other; but at the same time they desire contact because it is the only way in which they are able to exchange, and thereby obtain articles which they are lacking. There is a bond, a continuity between the hostile relations and the provision of reciprocal prestations: exchanges are peacefully resolved wars, wars are the outcome of unsuccessful transactions. This characteristic is evidenced by the fact that the passing of war into peace or at least of hostility into cordiality operates through the intermediary of ritual gestures: the adversaries feel each other out, and with gestures which still retain something of the attitudes of combat, inspect the necklaces, earrings, bracelets, and feathered ornaments of one another with admiring comments.

And from battle they pass immediately to the gifts; gifts are received, gifts are given, but silently, without bargaining, without complaint, and apparently without linking that which is given to that which is obtained. These are, indeed, reciprocal gifts, not commercial operations. But the relationship may be given yet an additional meaning: two tribes who have thus come to establish lasting cordial relations, can decide in a deliberate manner to join by setting up an artificial kinship relation between the male members of the two tribes: the relationship of brothers-in-law. According to the matrimonial system of the Nambikwara, the immediate consequence of this innovation is that all the children of one group become the potential spouses of the children of the other group and vice-versa; thus a continuous transition exists from war to exchange and from exchange to intermarriage; and the exchange of betrothed women is merely the termination of an uninterrupted process of reciprocal gifts, which brings about the transition from hostility to alliance, from anxiety to confidence and from fear to friendship.

Talcott Parsons

The Incest Taboo in Relation to Social Structure

After something like a generation in which the attention of anthropologists and sociologists has been focused on the phenomena which differentiate one society from another and the different structures within the same society from each other, in recent years there has been a revival of interest in the problem of what features are common to human societies everywhere and what are the forces operating to maintain these common features. One reason for my present interest in the incest taboo is that it is one of the most notable of these common features. With all the variability of its incidence outside of the nuclear family, there is the common core of the prohibition of marriage and in general of sexual relationships between members of a nuclear family except of course the conjugal couple whose marriage establishes it.

In the older discussions the prevailing tendency was to attempt to find a specific "cause" of the taboo, thus instinctive aversion or Westermarck's contention that aversion was acquired through being brought up in the same household. As our empirical information and theoretical resources have accumulated, however, it seems less and less likely that this is the most fruitful approach. On the contrary anything so general as the incest taboo seems likely to be a resultant of a constellation of different factors which are deeply involved in the foundation of human societies. Analysis in terms of the balance of forces in the social system rather than of one or two specific "factors" seems much more promising. Furthermore, it seems highly probable that a combination of sociological and psychological considerations is involved; that a theory which attempts to by-pass either of these fields will find itself in difficulties.

The element of constancy clearly focuses in the nuclear family. Perhaps the most recent authoritative survey is that of Murdock, [1] and we have his authority that no society is known where incest between mother-son, father-daughter or full brother-sister is permitted except the few cases of brother-sister marriage in royal families, but never for the

---

1. George P. Murdock, *Social Structure*, New York: Macmillan, 1949, chap. 10.

bulk of the people. There are a few cases of marriage permitted between half-brother and half-sister, and similar cases of closeness, but only a few. I shall therefore take the nuclear family as my point of departure and attempt to review a few highlights of it as a subsystem of the society. But the nuclear family is, in my opinion, only the focus of the structural problem, not the whole of it. I shall therefore next attempt to link with the relevant considerations about the family, a series of problems about its place in and articulation with the rest of the society. Then, given this wider setting of social structure, I will attempt to analyze some of the relevant problems of psychological mechanisms in terms of the characteristics and significance of eroticism in personal relationships and in the personality itself.

The Structure and Functions of the Nuclear Family

The universality of some order of incest taboo is of course directly connected with the fact that the nuclear family is also universal to all known human societies. The minimal criteria of the nuclear family are, I suggest, first that there should be a solidary relationship between mother and child lasting over a period of years and transcending physical care in its significance. Secondly, in her motherhood of this child the woman should have a special relationship to a man *outside her own descent group* who is sociologically the "father" of the child, and that this relationship is the focus of the "legitimacy" of the child, of his referential status in the larger kinship system.[2]

The common sense of social science has tended to see in the universality and constancy of structure of the nuclear family a simple reflection of its biological function and composition; sexual reproduction, the generation difference and the differentiation by sex in the biological sense. While I in no way question the importance of this biological aspect and am in agreement with the view that the human family is an "extension" of a subhuman precultural entity, on the human-cultural levels there is, I am sure, another aspect of the problem of constancy. The two biological bases of differentiation, sex and generation, may be regarded, that is, as "points of reference" of a type of social organization the sociological significance of which is general in the structure of small groups.

Evidence from the experimental laboratory study of small groups[3] has shown first that small groups with no prior institutionalized diffentiation of status, differentiate spontaneously on a hierarchical dimension, which I may call "power" in the sense of relative influence on the out-

2. It will be noted that I deliberately assume the incest taboo as part of the constitution of the family itself.

3. See R. F. Bales, "The Equilibrium Problem in Small Groups," in Parsons, Bales and Shils, *Working Papers in the Theory of Action,* New York: The Free Press, 1953.

come of processes in the system. This is the case when this differentiation is measured by any one of a variety of possible measures, both from the point of view of the observer and that of participants in group process. We may say there is a differentiation between "leaders" and "followers."

Secondly, there appears a differentiation which cuts across this one, with reference to qualitative *type of function* in the group. The first broad qualitative type of differentiation which appears in this sense is what Bales and I have called that between primarily "instrumental" function in the group and primarily "expressive" function. An instrumental function is one primarily concerned with the relations of the group to the situation external to it, including adaptation to the conditions of that situation and establishment of satisfactory goal-relations for the system vis-à-vis the situation. Expressive function on the other hand is concerned primarily with the harmony or solidarity of the group, the relations internally of the members to each other and their "emotional" states of tension or lack of it in their roles in the group.

Level of differentiation is of course a function of size of the group. By the time we reach a membership of four there can be a typical four-role pattern, differentiated hierarchically into leadership and followership roles, and qualitatively into more instrumental and more expressive roles. I would like to suggest that it is fruitful to treat the nuclear family as a special case of this basically four-role pattern, with generation as the main axis of superior-inferior or leader-follower differentiation, sex the axis of instrumental-expressive differentiation. Obviously the helplessness of the child, particularly in the first years, is the main basis of the former. The universal fact that women are more intimately concerned with early child care than are men (with lactation playing a very fundamental part) is the primary reason why the feminine role, in the family as well as outside, tends to be *more* expressive in this sense than the masculine.[4]

4. The best documentation of this generalization available so far is I think a paper by M. Zelditch, Jr., "Role Differentiation in the Nuclear Family," in Parsons, Bales, Zelditch and Olds, *Family, Socialization and Interaction Process,* New York: The Free Press, 1955, chap. VI. Zelditch [this book, 256–58] studied a sample of fifty-five societies and found first an overwhelming preponderance of relative instrumentalism in the father role, second no cases where the available evidence was unequivocal that the mother role in the nuclear family is *more* instrumental than that of the father. The greatest difficulties for this thesis occur in the cases of matrilineal kinship systems where the mother's brother takes over some of the functions of the father in other systems. The weight of Zelditch's evidence, however, suggests that even in these cases the *relative* differentiation on this axis holds, though the span of it is greatly narrowed.

The importance of these four roles for family structure is, I think, emphasized by kinship terminology. I believe it is true that, with all the variation of kinship terminology, there is no known system where these four roles, namely mother, father, brother, sister and, conversely, self, spouse, son, daughter, are not discriminated from each other. Of course frequently incumbents of these roles are classified together with other kin, as father with his brothers. But there is no known system which fails to discriminate the four cardinal roles in the nuclear family from each other. This is to say that generation and sex within the family are universally made bases of discrimination. There is no other set of roles in kinship systems of which this is true.

My first point is thus that the nuclear family has certain characteristics common to small groups in general. The effectiveness of its performance of function as a family is, I think, dependent on its having these characteristics. The primary functions I have in mind are a certain significance for maintaining the emotional balances of all members of the family including the adults, and its paramount role as an agency for the socialization of children. The general characteristics I have in mind are three. The first is that it should be a *small* group, especially in its higher status-echelon. Given age-specific death rates as well as birth rates presumably in no society does the effective nuclear family average more than about seven members, and generally fewer. The second characteristic is that the main structural differentiation of the family as a group should be along these two axes, namely that of power or hierarchy and the instrumental-expressive distinction. The third is that *both* the latter should be represented in the "leadership" structure and that there should be a strong "coalition" between them.[5] The fact that the two parents are of opposite sex and that marriage, though with variations, always constitutes an important structural bond of solidarity transcending the parental functions, in a broad way insures this. It should be clear from the above that sex role differentiation in its more generalized sense which impinges on many contexts other than the structure of the nuclear family itself is importantly involved in this structural complex.

But this does not mean that just any kind of small group which met these specifications could perform the functions of the family. It clearly has to be a group which has relatively long duration—a considerable span of years. But it is not indefinite duration. One of its most important characteristics is that the family is a self-liquidating group. On attainment of maturity and marriage the child ceases in the full sense to be a member of his family of orientation; instead he helps in the establishment of a new one. The implications of this basic fact will be briefly discussed in the next section.

Secondly, it must be a group which permits and requires a high level of diffuse affective involvement for its members; though this of course varies with the different roles, being highest for the young child. Clearly no evanescent experimental group could perform the functions of a family. The fact that with few exceptions the nuclear family is the main unit of residence is of critical importance in this connection.

Finally, third, I suggest that it is essential to the family that more than in any other grouping in societies, overt erotic attraction and gratification should be given an institutionalized place in its structure. But when we say this is institutionalized we mean that eroticism is not only permitted but carefully regulated; and the incest taboo is merely a very promi-

5. The connection between the leadership coalition of the small group and the erotically bound marriage partners was first stated by Bales, "The Equilibrium Problem in Small Groups," in Parsons, Bales and Shils, *op. cit.*, chap. IV.

nent negative aspect of this more general regulation.

This aspect will be more fully discussed in the third section of the paper. But at this point it does seem worthwhile to summarize the familiar features of the erotic organization of the family. First genital eroticism is both permitted to and expected of the marital pair. Only in certain special religious groups is its justification even in theory confined to the direct procreative function; it is itself a bond and a very important symbol of the solidarity of the marriage pair as responsible for a family. But at the same time—and this fact accentuates this meaning—the marital couple have a monopoly of the right to genital eroticism within the nuclear family, though of course not necessarily outside.

Secondly, pre-genital eroticism is positively institutionalized, always in the early mother-child relation, and probably usually to some extent in that of father and child. But clearly it is generally far more important in the case of mother and child.

Third, with probably few exceptions, overt erotic expression except possibly autoeroticism in some cases, is tabooed as between post-oedipal children and both parents, and in the relations of the children to each other, except where an older sibling plays a partly parental role to a small child. Finally, no homosexuality is permitted at all within the nuclear family unless we wish to call the attraction between mother and pre-oedipal daughter homosexual. In view of what we know on psychological levels of the erotic potentials of human beings this structure is clearly not one of unrestricted permissiveness, but of a systematic combination of controlled expression and regulatory prohibition. Moreover, in view of the wide variety of human customs in so many respects, its relative uniformity is impressive and deserves to be counted as one of the most important universals of human society.

It would be rash to suggest that the socialization of children could not be carried out except in a group of the specific biological composition of the family, or even without this specific set of erotic relationships. I think, however, that it is fairly safe to contend that the primary socializing agency must be a small group with broadly the sociological characteristics I have suggested, and that even the erotic factor could not vary extremely widely. For example, it could not be completely suppressed, by having all fertilization occur by artificial insemination, and by a careful policy of avoiding arousing any erotic interest on the part of children, or at the other extreme by removing all restrictions on fulfilment of any and all erotic impulses as and when they might be aroused.

The Family and the Wider Social Structure

One of the cardinal uniformities of social structure which is most intimately connected with the incest taboo is the fact that nuclear families are *never* found as independent total "societies" on a human cultural level. There is never simply extra-social biological mating outside the family, but the nuclear family is always a unit within a society which contains a plurality of other families, and other types of units; "solidarity" extends over these areas and the other groupings, and even where they are kinship groupings, sociologically they have characteristics very different from those of the nuclear family.

Undoubtedly one of the main characteristics of the more "primitive" societies lies in the fact that a far larger proportion of the total social structure is organized about kinship than is the case with the more "advanced" societies. Indeed there are some where it is difficult to speak of any "statuses" or groups which are not in some important respect kinship statuses and groups. But two main things need to be said. First, though always including nuclear families, the kinship system always also includes groups which differ fundamentally from nuclear families. Secondly, it can, following Leach,[6] probably be said that a kinship system cannot be a completely "closed" system in that features of it always have to be analyzed with reference to economic, political and other considerations which are not peculiar to kinship relations, which do not disappear in social structures which have entirely cast loose from a kinship base.

Whether the groupings which transcend the nuclear family are organized about kinship or not, relative to the family they have in general—with a few exceptions like friendships—certain characteristics in common. They are groups in which the personal emotional interests of the individual are not so closely bound up as in the family; where the accent is more on impersonal functions of the group. A good kinship case of this type is the lineage as a corporate entity with reference to its political functions. The case of organizations composed primarily of occupational roles in modern society is one where kinship is not prominent. Broadly one may say that in such cases the role or the organization is characterized by primacy of functional responsibility on a social system level, and by relatively severe control of affective spontaneity—by what I have elsewhere[7] called "affective neutrality." These are the structures in which the main functions of direct maintenance and goal-attainment in the society are performed; *viz.* economic provision, political stabilization and defence, religious expression, etc.

Where the main basis of composition of such groupings rests in kinship, marriage has direct functional significance as a mechanism which establishes important direct ties of interpenetration of memberships between the different elements in the structural network. Under such circumstances marriage cannot be merely a "personal affair" of the parties

6. E. R. Leach, *The Structural Implications of Matrilineal Cross-Cousin Marriage,* London: Royal Anthropological Society, 1951.

7. Cf. Parsons, *The Social System,* New York: The Free Press, 1951, chap. II.

to it. Where it is difficult to have solidary relationships which do not involve kinship the intermarriage between groups can establish a pattern of such solidarities cross-cutting those based directly or primarily on relationships by descent.

As Fortune was one of the first to emphasize, and Lévi-Strauss has developed farther,[8] in this kind of situation it is not so much the prohibition of incest in its negative aspect which is important as the positive obligation to perform functions for the subunit and the larger society by marrying out. Incest is a withdrawal from this obligation to contribute to the formation and maintenance of supra-familial bonds on which major economic, political and religious functions of the society are dependent.

Where extended kinship groupings have a critical importance in the social structure, it is considerations of this kind which underlie the patterns of extension of the incest taboo beyond the nuclear family. Broadly, the principles seem to be that intermarriage is forbidden within units which, first, are organized primarily as kinship units, second, have functions in the social system which transcend the personal interests of the members of small family groups, which therefore involve a more impersonal set of disciplines, and, third, groups within which, as kinship groups, daily interaction with reference to these interests is relatively close. The lineage and its segments and the male local succession group which Leach discusses, are prototypes of such groups. Illustrating the last criterion it is typical that exogamy often breaks down within the most extensive lineage groups but is maintained within their lower-order segments.[9]

Recent work on kinship seems to indicate that in a very rough way it is possible to construct a series of types in this respect. At one end is the so-called Kariera type which is characterized by symmetrical cross-cousin marriage. This forms a very "tight" form of organization, but is very limited in the range of different kinds of social ties which can be established through it. It makes for a rigid social structure though probably under certain conditions a relatively stable one.

Lévi-Strauss is probably right that the asymmetrical type of cross-cousin marriage which rests primarily on marriage with the mother's brother's daughter constitutes an important step towards a wider ranging and more flexible set of arrangements as compared both with the Kariera type and with marriage to the father's sister's daughter. It is interesting to note that this is connected with the asymmetry of the structure of the nuclear family itself as that was discussed above. If the masculine role is more instrumental than the feminine in the senses I have discussed, then

---

8. R. F. Fortune, "Incest," in *Encyclopedia of the Social Sciences*, edited by Seligman and Johnson, and Claude Lévi-Strauss, *Les structures élémentaires de la parenté*, Paris: Presses Universitaires de France, 1949 [this book, pp. 3–12].

9. For a recent survey, cf. Murdock, *op. cit.*, chap. X.

the men should have more direct and important anchorages in the extended kinship groupings than the women. Then for a woman who has married out of her descent group, the strongest source of support would not be her sister but her brother. This is first because the sister may well have married either into ego's own post-marital group or into another controlled largely by her husband's agnatic kin and second because in the descent group the men have more control in extrafamilial affairs than the women.

The father's brother, on the other hand, is in a status directly similar to that of the father and not complementary to him, while the father's sister belongs to this same agnatic group. Put a little differently an alliance with the mother's brother is the stablest kind of alliance with a distinctly different group and at the same time bolsters the structure of the nuclear family in such a way as to redress the balance resulting from its internal asymmetry by giving the mother external support through a channel independent of her husband.

Lévi-Strauss therefore seems to be right in saying that asymmetrical cross-cousin marriage through the mother's brother's daughter relationship opens up a wider circle which is both stabler and more extensive than any alternative where the kin involved are so close. Leach,[10] however, has made an important additional contribution by showing that on such a basis the kinship system cannot be closed through marriage-exchange relations alone, but that there are several alternative ways in which such a system can work out. Which of them will develop will depend on the economic and political relations of the exchanging kinship units, and hence on the nature and values of the "considerations" which enter into the marriage arrangements other than the exchange of spouses as such.

But all this is compatible in a broad way with Lévi-Strauss's view that this makes women, though in somewhat different ways also men, a kind of symbolic "counters" in a process of exchange. Perhaps I may state it in somewhat different terms by saying that the woman or man, in marrying outside his own descent group, is performing a role-obligation in a social group or collectivity which transcends his own family of orientation, and one to which to some degree his family is subordinated; it is a superordinate unit in the social structure. He is no more free to marry whom he chooses in such a situation than is an industrial worker free within the organization to perform any job-task he chooses regardless of how it fits into the plan for how the total process is to be organized.

It is in this sense that incest would be socially regressive in the sense in which Lévi-Strauss analyzes the problem. It would, in an area of the higher integrative structures of the society, constitute giving membership in the lower-level structure priority over that in the higher. It is only on the impossible assumption that families should constitute independent

10. *Op. cit.*

societies and not be segmental units of higher-level organizations, that incest as a regular practice would be socially possible.

These considerations give us the basis for a further generalization concerning the difference between extended exogamous systems and those found in modern societies. So far as the higher level functions of the society are performed by collectivities the composition of which is determined in kinship terms, there will be a tendency to extend the incest taboo to such collectivities. So far, however, as a social function, economic, political and religious, comes to be organized in groups not put together out of kin, the whole issue of exogamy with reference to them will cease to be significant.

There is, however, complete continuity between these two types of cases so far as certain aspects of the social functions of the incest taboo are concerned. We may say that there are two primary interconnected but independent aspects of this function. In the first place, it is socially important that the nuclear family should not be self-perpetuating and hence that adults should have a personality structure which motivates them to found new and independent nuclear families. Erotic attraction to persons of opposite sex but outside the nuclear family is clearly a mechanism which aids in this. But, secondly, it is essential that persons should be capable of assuming roles which contribute to functions which no nuclear family is able to perform, which involve the assumption of non-familial roles. Only if such non-familial roles can be adequately staffed can a society function. I suggest that the critical roles in this class are roles in which erotic interests must be altogether subordinated to other interests.

I thus see the "problem" of the incest taboo in the following setting so far as social structure is concerned. It seems to be clear that human personalities are universally socialized in nuclear families, which are small groups of the special type sketched above. Included in their special characteristics is the role of erotic attraction between their members. The incest taboo operates to "propel" the individual out of the nuclear family, not in one but in two senses. He is propelled into a new nuclear family formed by his marriage. Here the erotic component of his personality is positively made use of. But also he is propelled into non-familial roles, which of course are differentiated by sex and other status characteristics, but in some sense such roles must be assumed by all adults. This corresponds to the fact that every known society consists in a plurality of nuclear families the duration of which is limited to one generation and also the fact that these families are always relatively low-level units in a social structure, the higher level units of which have different functions in the society, functions which cannot be performed by family groups.[11] It is in

11. There are good reasons for believing that there is an intimate connection between the overcoming of the excessive autonomy of the nuclear family and the possibility of a cultural level of social development. In the first place such a group is apparently too small to support an independent language with its minimum of extensity of generalization and communicative

this setting that I wish to discuss some of the problems of the psychological characteristics of eroticism and its place in the development of personality.

The Psychological Characteristics and Functions of Eroticism

After all, the most distinctive feature of the incest taboo is the regulation of erotic relationships, within the family and in relation to the establishment of new families. The considerations about social structure which I have advanced therefore need to be supplemented by a discussion of the nature of eroticism and its functions in the development of personality and in the personality of the adult. I shall here put forward a view which has three main emphases. First, eroticism will be held to play a very important part, probably an indispensable one, in the socialization of the child, in taking a raw organism and making a "person" out of it. Second, however, the awakening of erotic interests not only performs functions, it creates problems. There are important psychological reasons why erotic needs seem to be particularly difficult to control. Making use of this instrument of socialization therefore constitutes a kind of "pact with the devil." Once present the question of what is to be done with this force is a serious problem. Finally, third, the view of eroticism I take here will dissociate it considerably from what is ordinarily meant by the "sex instinct" or the instinct of reproduction. Though the interest in genital eroticism of the post-adolescent is undoubtedly genuinely part of the erotic complex, and a very important part, it is only part, and the complex is far broader than such an instinct in two senses. On the one hand its childhood or pregenital aspects are of fundamental importance for our problem and presumably have nothing to do with the reproductive function. Secondly, though there undoubtedly must be a basis on constitutional predisposition, the aspects of eroticism which are important for our purposes involve a very large component which is learned rather than "instinctive" in the usual sense.

I shall rely heavily on Freud for my views of the erotic complex, though I think Freud can be supplemented by some considerations derived from the sociological study of the process of socialization. But after all one of the greatest of Freud's discoveries was the fundamental *importance* of the eroticism of childhood—the fact of its existence was

---

range. It is also probable that it is too "ingrown," culturally rather than biologically. One of the important consequences of the incest taboo is to enforce the mixing of family cultures (on the distinctiveness of the cultures of particular households, see J. M. Roberts, *Three Navaho Households*, Peabody Museum Monographs, Cambridge, Mass., 1951). There is an analogy here to the biological functions of sexual reproduction. If, therefore, I may hazard an extremely tentative hypothesis about socio-cultural origins it would be that the earliest *society* had to be a multifamily unit which enforced an incest taboo.

not discovered by Freud, but as so often in the history of science well-known facts excited little interest because nobody knew how to assess their importance. Furthermore, Freud clearly saw the importance of the processes of learning in the development of erotic interests. I may recall his famous statement that "the infant is polymorph perverse." This I interpret to mean that any normal child has the potentiality of developing *any* of the well-known types of erotic orientation, homosexuality, autoeroticism and the perversions as well as what we think of as normal heterosexuality. This can only mean that the latter is in considerable measure the product of the process of socialization, not simply the expression of an instinct.[12]

What, then, are the most important characteristics of eroticism? Erotic interest is, I think, the interest in securing a particular type of organic pleasure, which is in *one* aspect organically specific in a way comparable to the pleasure of hunger-gratification or warmth. But this is only one aspect of it. What is most important about eroticism is, I think, its dual character, the combination of this organic specificity, the possibility of intense pleasure through the stimulation of specific parts of the body, with a *diffuse* spreading into a general sensation of well-being. From stimulation of an erogenous zone then, it is not a very big step to learning that almost any type of bodily contact with the agent can come to be felt as a source of pleasure. I may take a specific example from early childhood. Being fed by the mother is a source not only of hunger-gratification but very early, according to psychoanalytic views, of oral-erotic gratification as well. But from stimulation of this oral-erotic interest there is generalization to pleasurable sensation from any physical contact with the source of the original oral gratification; hence being held and fondled by the mother is a source of pleasure and a focus of an incipient system of expectations.

Put in psychological terms, erotic gratification is a peculiarly sensitive source of conditioning in the "classical" Pavlovian sense. From desiring the specific stimulation, the child comes to desire diffuse non-specific contact with the object which has served as agent of the original gratification. Eroticism is thus a major, in the earlier stages probably *the* major mechanism for the "generalization of cathexis" by which a diffuse attachment to an object comes to be built up.[13]

The great importance of diffuse attachment in this sense to the process of learning has come to be well-recognized. So long as a socializing agent is only a source of specific segmental gratifications, the omission of such gratification will cause the child very rapidly to lose interest in the

12. The best general reference for this aspect of Freud's work is his *Three Contributions to Sexual Theory*.

13. Freud's views on this problem are most fully developed in the late paper, *Hemmung, Symptom und Angst*. English title: *The Problem of Anxiety*, New York: Norton, 1936.

object. But the process by which the deeper kind of learning[14] is possible involves the building up of need-systems and then their frustration as a preliminary to the learning of new goals and needs.[15] The essential point is that the socializing agent should be in a position to frustrate the child —really seriously—without losing control of him.

Another aspect of the point is that it is by this order of generalization of cathexis that the child is made sensitive to the *attitudes* of the socializing agent, say the mother. This sensitivity to attitude is possible only through transcending the specificity of interest in organic gratifications as such. What matters to the child is whether and how much he feels that his mother "cares." The very fact that erotic gratification is *not* essential to any of the basic physiological needs of the individual organism makes it a suitable vehicle for this generalization.

A further characteristic of eroticism seems to be important in the general situation; it is what underlies my reference above to its arousal constituting in a sense a "pact with the devil." Erotic need, that is, seems to have some of the characteristics of addiction. The erotic interests of childhood cannot be allowed to be dominant in later phases of development, and in normal development are not. But the evidence is that by and large they are not, as the psychologists put it, successfully "extinguished," but rather have to be repressed. From this it comes that the psychoanalysis of any "normal" adult will bring to light "infantile" erotic patterns which are still there, though they have not been allowed overt gratification for many years. The evidence is very clear that normal and pathological differ in this respect only in degree, not in terms of presence or absence.[16] If this general view is correct then the mechanism for handling such permanently repressed material must be of great importance in the normal adult personality.

Let us look at the matter in more of a sociological perspective. A socializing agent at any given major stage of the process plays a dual role, in *two* systems of social interaction. On the one hand he—or she —participates with the child at the level which is appropriate to the beginning of the phase in question, as in the case of the mother-child love attachment of the immediately pre-oedipal period. On the other hand she—the mother in this case—also participates in the full four-role family system. In disturbing the equilibrium of the former interaction system she

14. Meaning the internalization of cultural values—cf. Parsons, *The Social System, op. cit.*, chap. VI.

15. This involves what Olds calls the "law of motive growth." See James Olds, *The Growth and Structure of Motives, Psychological Studies in the Theory of Action*, New York: The Free Press, 1954, chaps. I and II.

16. Eroticism in this respect seems to be a member of a large class of strong affective interests. Thus the work of Solomon and Wynne ("Traumatic Avoidance Learning: The Principles of Anxiety Conservation and Partial Irreversibility," *Psychological Review*, 61, Nov. 1954) on conditioned anxiety in dogs has shown that a sufficiently acute anxiety is almost impossible to extinguish.

acts as an agent of the latter. This act of disturbance constitutes frustration to the child and produces among other things anxiety and aggression. If, on the other hand, there were no positive motivation in his involvement in the relationship other than what he is now denied expression, the attachment would simply break up and no progress could be made, since he is not yet motivated to assume his *new* role in the new and higher level interaction system.

But the specific part of the erotic attachment is a focus of precisely the element of "dependency"—at the relevant level—which has to be overcome if the new level is to be attained. Under the conditions postulated, however, the *diffuse* aspect of the erotic attachment can survive the frustration of the focal specific desire, and it can thus become a main lever by which the child is positively motivated to learn a new role which, it must be remembered, involves learning new goals, not merely new instrumental means for the attainment of given goals.

Thus the child's erotic attachment to the mother is the "rope" by which she pulls him up from a lower to a higher level in the hard climb of "growing up." But because the points of attachment of this "rope" remain sensitive, interest in them is not extinguished, there is a permanent channel back into the still operative infantile motivational system. Serious disturbances of the equilibrium of the personality can always re-open these channels. This is what is ordinarily meant by "regression," and early erotic patterns always play a prominent part in regressive tendencies.[17]

There seem to be three stages at which the mother is the primary object of erotic attraction of the child; these are what Freud identified as the oral, the anal, and the phallic phases. They correspond to three relatively discontinuous "steps" in the process of learning new levels of personality organization; new goals and capacities for independent and responsible performance. Each one leaves a residuum of the erotic structures which have been essential in order to make the step, but which if allowed to remain active would interfere with the subsequent steps. Thus there is in all personalities, granting my hypothesis of addiction, a channel through erotic associations, right down into the lowest and most primitive strata of the Id—the most regressive parts of the personality system. These can be re-activated at any time. The connection of this situation with the problem of the probable psychological significance of incest seems to be clear.

From this point of view the problem of incest fits into the larger context of the structuring of erotic motivation in the personality, over time and with reference to choice of objects. The context includes the

17. This sociological aspect of the socialization process is much more fully analyzed in Parsons, Bales, *et al.*, *Family Socialization and Interaction Process, op. cit.*, especially chaps. IV and VI.

problem of homosexuality and of the status of the perversions. The goal of socialization—with many variations but in its broad pattern universal—is to establish at least the primacy, if not the complete monopoly over other possibilities, of normal genital erotic attraction which includes choice of object outside the family, and stability of orientation to objects.

Only mother-son incest is as such directly involved in the constellation I have sketched. Here the regressive implications seem very clear. This agrees with psychoanalytic opinion that such incest, where it does appear in our society, is always deeply pathological, on both sides but particularly that of the son.

The case of the daughter vis-à-vis her father is somewhat different. But when she is forced to abandon her primary attachment to her mother, it should be clear that the next available alternative is the father. This is further made "plausible" by the fact that she is taught that it is normal for a female to have a primary attachment to a masculine object, but in this case erotic development of the attachment is blocked. This clearly has to do on one level with the internal equilibrium of the nuclear family as a system. The erotic attachment of the parents to each other is a primary focus and symbol of their coalition as the leadership element of the family as a system. To allow the child who has just been forced out of an erotic attachment to the mother to substitute one with the father would immediately weaken this coalition as a source of generalized pressure to grow up for children of both sexes.

But there is a broader "functional" aspect of the problem. If it is exceedingly important that the boy should find a feminine object outside the family, this is obviously only possible in a generalized way if girls also typically do so. Furthermore, in order to perform her functions as a socializing agent, as mother, it is extremely important that a woman's regressive need systems should not be uncontrolled. Indeed it is probably more important than in the case of the man, because as a mother the woman is going to have to enter into much stronger erotic reciprocities with her young children than is her husband, and at the same time she is in due course going to have to act as the agent of their frustration in these respects. If she is not able to control her own regressive needs, then the mother-child system is likely to get "stuck" on one of the early levels and be unable to take the next step. Indeed such phenomena are prominent in the pathology of family relations in relation to the genesis of mental disorders. Thus the "over-protective" mother, instead of, at the proper time, refusing to reciprocate her child's dependency needs, positively encourages them and thereby makes it more difficult for him to grow up.

Finally, there is the case of the prohibition of brother-sister incest. It seems to me, that in the first instance this relates to the symmetry of the nuclear family. Once the oedipal crisis has been passed, the most symmetrical arrangement is that which reserves a monopoly of erotic relations within the family to the married couple. But in a broader context functionally the more important thing is at the relevant time to achieve complete—though temporary—repression of erotic needs for both sexes. Fulfillment of this requirement would be blocked by permissiveness for brother-sister erotic relations.

For childhood eroticism regardless of the sex of the child the original object is the mother. Once this attachment to the mother has ceased to be useful to the development of the personality it tends, I have noted, to be repressed altogether. This means that not only is the original object denied, but those "next in line," that is all other members of the original nuclear family, are tabooed. This in turn, it seems, is an aspect of what I referred to above as the process of self-liquidation of each particular nuclear family.

What Freud called the period of "latency," i.e. from the point of view of overt eroticism, thus seems to be the period in which the individual is above all learning to perform extrafamilial roles. Childhood erotic attachment has played a part in laying the necessary foundations for these processes, but beyond a certain point it becomes a hindrance. Just a word may be said about the first of these steps which seems to have a bearing on the problem of brother-sister attachment.

One of the primary features of the oedipal transition in the course of which the last phase of childhood eroticism is normally repressed is the assumption of sex role, or the first major step in that process. Though the points of reference for the differentiation are unmistakably biologically given, there is strong reason to believe that the role—including the psychological categorization of the self—must be learned to a much greater extent than has ordinarily been appreciated. It seems to be significant that just at this period children begin to be much more independent of their families and to associate particularly with other children. There will be many variations as a function of the structure of extended kinship groups and the nature of residential communities, but it seems to be broadly true that there is a general tendency to segregation of the sexes at this period. The phenomenon so familiar in Western society of the one-sex peer group seems to have a nearly universal counterpart to some extent elsewhere. The turning of primary interests into the channel of relations to friends of the same sex and nearly the same age, seems to have a dual significance. On the one hand, it reinforces the individual's self-categorization by sex by creating a solidarity transcending the family between persons of the same sex. On the other hand, for the first time the individual becomes a member of a group which both transcends the family and in which he is not in the strongly institutionalized position of being a member of the *inferior* generation class. It is the first major step toward defining himself as clearly *independent* of the authority and help of the parental generation.

Adolescence comes only after a considerable period of this latency-level peer group activity. Along with the fact that the emerging genital erotic interest of adolescence and after involves symmetrical attraction to persons of opposite sex, it is of the first importance that now for the first time erotic attraction is experienced with an object which is broadly an equal, instead of a generation-superior. On both counts there must be a considerable reorganization of the erotic complex in the personality and its relation to the other components before mature erotic attachments become possible. It is a psychiatric commonplace that much of the pathology of marriage relationships and of the erotic interests of adults otherwise, has to do with inadequate solution of these two problems, namely how to form a stable attachment to a single person of opposite sex and how to treat the partner as fundamentally an equal, neither to be dependent on him or her in a childish sense nor, by a mechanism which includes reaction-formation to dependency, to take the parental role and have a compulsive need to dominate.

When all this has taken place the circle is closed by the individual's marriage and parenthood. He has had his erotic ties within the nuclear family of orientation broken. But he has also built up the nonerotic components of his personality structure with the double consequences of building a relatively secure dam against his still-present regressive needs and building a positive set of motivational capacities for the performance of the non-familial roles without which no society could operate. Only when this process has reached a certain stage are the gates to erotic gratification reopened, but this time in a greatly restructured way and carefully controlled.

Finally, it must not be overlooked that the erotic motivational component of the adult personality is used not only to motivate the marital attachment, but also constructively as itself an instrument of the socialization of the next generation. For it is clear that eroticism is fundamentally a phenomenon of social relationships. Strong erotic motivation is built up in the child only because the mother, and to a lesser degree the father, *enjoys* reciprocal erotic relations with the child. But as in the case of the genital eroticism of marriage, this must be controlled by strong ego and super-ego structures in the personality, lest the parent be unable to renounce his own need when the time comes.

I expressed agreement above with the view of Fortune and Lévi-Strauss that on the social level incest must be regarded as a regressive phenomenon, a withdrawal from the functions and responsibilities on the performance and fulfilment of which the transfamilial structures of a society rest. The review of the role of eroticism in the development of the personality, which I have just presented, shows a striking parallel. Incestuous wishes constitute the very prototype of regression for the mature person, the path to the re-activation of the primitive layers of his personality structure. But surely this is more than merely a parallel. There is the most intimate causal interdependence. Societies operate only in and through the behavior of persons, and personalities on the human socio-cultural level are only possible as participants in systems of socially in-teractive behavior, as these are related to the needs of human organisms.

I have argued that erotic gratification is an indispensable instrument of the socialization of the human child, of making a personality and a member of society of him. But equally, unrestricted erotic gratification stands directly in the way, both of the maturation of the personality, and of the operation of the society. Indispensable to certain processes of learning, it becomes probably the most serious impediment to further essential stages of maturity. The incest taboo is a universal of human societies. I suggest that this is because it constitutes a main focus of the *regulation* of the erotic factor. The institutionalization of the family pro-vides the organized setting for the positive utilization of the erotic factor, both in socialization and in strengthening the motivation to the assump-tion of familial responsibility. But the taboo in its negative aspect is a mechanism which prevents this positive use from getting "out of hand," which ensures the self-liquidation of the particular family and the produc-tion of personalities by it which are capable of fulfilling the functions of trans-familial roles.

Admittedly, as far as origins are concerned, this is very largely a functional argument and does not solve the problem of how incest taboos came into being. It does, I think, serve to illuminate the manifold ways in which the incest taboo is involved in the functioning of any going society and gives a basis for prediction of the probable consequences of various forms of interference with it or modification of it. It places the problem in the context of analysis of the social system in such a way as also to show the interdependence of social systems with the processes of the personal-ity. Once this level of analysis has been worked out the problem of origins assumes a lesser significance, but also can be approached with better hope of success.

There is one final important point. At the beginning of this paper, I referred to the earlier tendency to attempt to find a specific explanation of the incest taboo, and expressed my own belief that an analysis of the interdependence of a number of factors in a system was much more promising. A common counterpart of this specific factor view, is the demand that an explanation in some one simple formula adequately ex-plain all the variations of incidence of the taboo. It seems to me clear that, on the basis of the analysis I have presented, this is an illegitimate and unnecessary requirement. I have emphasized that there is a solid common core of incidence, namely centering on the nuclear family. But we know that even this is broken through under *very* exceptional circumstances, namely the brother-sister marriage of a few royal families. This case is not an embarrassment for the kind of theory I have presented. For if the taboo is held to be the resultant of a balance of forces, then it is always possible that the balance should be altered so as to relax it under certain circumstances. As Fortune[18] correctly points out a better test case would be the full legitimation of morganatic marriages in royal families—i.e. as taking the place of politically significant alliances. Essentially the same holds where it is a question of variations of incidence outside the nuclear family. Only a sufficiently full analysis of the conditions of stability of the *particular* social system in question can furnish an adequate answer to the question of why this rather than a different pattern is found in a particular case. But such variations, and the elements of contingency involved in them, do not alter the importance of the massive fundamental facts that no human society is known without an incest taboo, and in no case does the taboo fail, for a society as a whole, to include all the relationships within the nuclear family. It is to the understanding of these massive facts that this analysis has been primarily directed.

18. *Op. cit.*

Russell Middleton

A Deviant Case: Brother-Sister and Father-Daughter Marriage in Ancient Egypt*

Almost every sociologist and anthropologist in the last thirty years who has written on the general subject of incest prohibitions has proclaimed the universality of the taboo upon the marriage of brothers and sisters and of parents and children. Most of them hasten to add that there are a few exceptions to this "universal" principle—the cases of brother-sister marriage among the Incas, the Hawaiians, and the ancient Egyptians being most frequently cited. They usually maintain, however, that these exceptions were sanctioned only for the royalty and never for commoners. The marriage of brothers and sisters, they argue, functioned "to preserve the purity of the royal blood line," "to keep privilege and rank rigidly within the group," and to set the divine rulers apart from their mundane subjects, who were required to observe the taboos. Ordinarily the authors do not recognize any cases of parent-child marriage, though a few do cite the case of father-daughter marriage among the Azande kings and the case of orgiastic father-daughter incest among the Thonga.

That the kings of ancient Egypt sometimes married their sisters or half sisters is widely recognized by sociologists and social anthropologists today. Yet they remain almost totally unaware of the evidence painstakingly uncovered by Egyptologists regarding father-daughter marriage among the kings and brother-sister marriage among the commoners. This paper attempts to summarize the present state of knowledge concerning the marriage of near kin among both royalty and commoners in three periods in ancient Egypt: Pharaonic period (prior to 332 B.C.), Ptolemaic period (323–30 B.C.), and Roman period (30 B.C.–324 A.D.).

* I am deeply indebted to the following Egyptologists who have given me the benefit of their advice and encouragement: William F. Edgerton, Rudolf Anthes, Jaroslav Černý, Claire Préaux, William C. Hayes, William Kelly Simpson, Elizabeth Riefstahl, and Alan Samuel. I am further indebted to the Research Council of Florida State University which provided financial help for this study.

Pharaonic Period

Although instances of Pharaohs who married their own sisters or half sisters have been reported from several of the dynasties, the greatest concentration of cases appears to be in the 18th and 19th Dynasties. Indeed, probably a majority of 18th-Dynasty kings (1570–1397 B.C.) married their sisters or half sisters: Tao II, Ahmose, Amenhotep I, Thutmose I, Thutmose II, Thutmose III, Amenhotep II, and Thutmose IV.[1] In the 19th Dynasty, Rameses II (1290–1223 B.C.) and Merneptah (1223–1211 B.C.) probably married sisters or half sisters.[2] Some authorities maintain that there are no well-established cases among the Pharaohs of the marriage of full brothers and sisters; no more than a half-sibling relationship can be proved.

Documented cases of father-daughter marriage among the Egyptian kings are less numerous and more controversial. De Rougé first called attention to evidence that Rameses II married not only two of his sisters, but also at least two of his daughters.[3] Erman, in a footnote in *Aegypten und Aegyptisches Leben im Altertum* published in 1885, denied this, arguing that the title of "Royal Wife," ascribed to the daughters was of mere ceremonial significance and was bestowed upon royal princesses even in infancy. More recent scholarship, however, has demonstrated that Erman was mistaken, and Ranke rightly omitted the footnote in his revision of the work.[4] Many authorities believe that Rameses II was married to three of his daughters: Banutanta, Merytamen, and Nebttaui.[5] There is some doubt about Nebttaui, for she apparently had a daughter, Astemakh, who was not a child of the king. Petrie suggests that she may have been married to a subject after the death of the king—though this is not likely, since she would have been over forty at the time—or As-

1. Marc Armand Ruffer, "On the Physical Effects of Consanguineous Marriages in the Royal Families of Ancient Egypt," in *Studies in the Palaeopathology of Egypt*, Chicago: University of Chicago Press, 1921, pp. 325–337; Adolf Erman, *Life in Ancient Egypt*, London: Macmillan and Co., 1894, p. 154; W. M. Flinders Petrie, *A History of Egypt*, Sixth edition, London: Methuen and Co., 1917, vol. 2, pp. 1, 40; W. C. Hayes, *The Scepter of Egypt*, Cambridge: Harvard University Press, 1959, vol. 2, p. 44; and Alan Gardiner, *Egypt of the Pharaohs*, Oxford: Clarendon Press, 1961, pp. 172–173. There is, however, some dispute among the authorities with regard to some of the kings.

2. Alfred Wiedemann, *Aegyptische Geschichte*, Gotha: F. A. Perthes, 1884, vol. 2, p. 466; Ernest A. Wallis Budge, *Egypt Under Rameses the Great*, London: K. Paul, Trench, Trübner and Co., 1902, p. 69; Ruffer *op. cit.*, pp. 337–340.

3. Emmanuel de Rougé, *Recherches sur les Monuments qu'on Peut Attribuer aux Six Premières Dynasties de Manéthon*, Paris: Imprimerie Impériale, 1866.

4. Adolf Erman, *Aegypten und Aegyptisches Leben im Altertum*, revised by Hermann Ranke, Tübingen: J. C. B. Mohr, 1923, pp. 180–181.

5. Gaston Maspéro, *The Struggle of the Nations*, New York: D. Appleton and Co., 1897, vol. 2, p. 424; Wiedemann, *op. cit.*, vol. 2, p. 466; Budge, *op. cit.*, pp. 69–70. Gardiner also concurs with regard to one of the daughters, Banutanta, and Kees says that it is certain that Rameses II married two of his daughters, if not more. See Gardiner, *op. cit.*, p. 267, and Hermann Kees, "Aegypten," in A. Alt and others, *Kulturgeschichte des Alten Orients*, München: C. H. Beck, 1933, p. 77.

temakh may have been the daughter not of Nebttaui but of princess
Nebta, daughter of Amenhotep.[6]

A second example of father-daughter marriage that is generally accepted by most Egyptologists involves Amenhotep III (1397–1360 B.C.),
who was probably married to his daughter Satamon[7] and possibly to
another daughter as well.[8]

Three alleged cases of father-daughter marriage which were accepted
earlier, however, have now generally been discarded. Brunner concluded
from a fragmentary inscription that Amenhotep IV or Akhenaton
(1370–1353 B.C.) was married to his daughter Ankes-en-pa-Aton and had a
daughter by her who bore the same name as her mother.[9] Most scholars
regard his interpretation as highly subjective, for the inscription nowhere
says that Ankes-en-pa-Aton was married to her father.[10] Wiedemann had
stated that Psamtik I of the 26th Dynasty (663–609 B.C.) married his
daughter Nitocris,[11] but Breasted has published texts which show that
this was not the case.[12] Sethe argued on the basis of an inscription found
above the false door of a tomb that Snefru of the 4th Dynasty (2614–2591
B.C.) was married to his eldest daughter, Nefertkauw, and that they had a
son named Neferma'at.[13] The Harvard-Boston Expedition in 1926, however, found another inscription which Reisner maintains clears up ambiguities in the earlier text and shows that Neferma'at was the grandson
rather than the son of Snefru.[14] This interpretation is now accepted by
most Egyptologists, though some remain unconvinced.

Evidence of brother-sister marriage among commoners in Pharaonic
times is meager. Černý has examined records of 490 marriages among
commoners, but the names of both sets of parents are given for only four
of the couples.[15] In each case they are different. The names of the
mothers are given for 97, however, and the names are the same in two

6. Petrie, *op. cit.*, vol. 3, p. 88.
7. Alexandre Varille, "Toutankhamon Est-il Fils d'Aménophis III et de Satamon?" *Annales du Service des Antiquités de l'Égypte*, 40 (1941), pp. 655–656; S. R. K. Glanville, "Amenophis III and His Successors in the XVIIIth Dynasty," in *Great Ones of Ancient Egypt*, New York: Charles Scribner's Sons, 1930, pp. 122–123; Gardiner, *op. cit.*, p. 212.
8. Percy E. Newberry, "King Ay, the Successor of Tutankhamun," *Journal of Egyptian Archaeology*, 18 (1932), p. 51.
9. Hellmut Brunner, "Eine neue Amarna-Prinzessin," *Zeitschrift für Ägyptische Sprache und Altertumskunde*, 74 (1938), pp. 104–108.
10. Gardiner, *op. cit.*, p. 236.
11. Wiedemann, *op. cit.*, vol. 2, p. 622.
12. James Henry Breasted, *Ancient Records of Egypt*, Chicago: University of Chicago Press, 1906, vol. 4, pp. 477–491.
13. Kurt Heinrich Sethe, "Das Fehlen des Begriffes der Blutschande bei den Alten Ägyptern," *Zeitschrift für Ägyptische Sprache und Altertumskunde*, 50 (1912), p. 57; Kurt Heinrich Sethe, "Zum Inzest des Sneferu," *Zeitschrift für Ägyptische Sprache und Altertumskunde*, 54 (1916), p. 54.
14. George Reisner, "Nefertkauw, the Eldest Daughter of Sneferuw," *Zeitschrift für Ägyptische Sprache und Altertumskunde*, 64 (1929), pp. 97–99.
15. Jaroslav Černý, "Consanguineous Marriages in Pharaonic Egypt," *Journal of Egyptian Archeology*, 40 (December, 1954), p. 27.

instances. These two cases, which have a Middle Kingdom date (c. 2052–1786 B.C.) suggest the possibility of the marriage of at least half brothers and sisters, but the names were common during that period and different individuals of the same name may have been involved. In the 20th Dynasty (1181–1075 B.C.) we also have a census list for a village of workmen, and there is no evidence of consanguineous marriages in the village.[16]

One must be cautious of literal interpretations of Egyptian terms of relationship, for in love songs and other inscriptions a lover or spouse is often referred to as "my brother" or "my sister."[17] Černý argues, however, that the custom of calling one's wife "sister" had its origin in the reign of Thutmose III and thus did not develop prior to the 18th Dynasty.[18] If this conclusion is accepted, there are, then, two probable cases of brother-sister marriage in the Middle Kingdom (c. 12th–13th Dynasties).[19] In the first, the reporter of the Vizier Senwosret was married to a woman called both sister and wife. In the second, the priest Efnaierson was married to a woman named Bob, who was either his sister by the same mother or his niece.

Fischer has recently called attention to another possible case of brother-sister marriage among commoners in the Middle Kingdom.[20] Two stelae deal with the family of a keeper of the chamber of the daily watch. On one, Mr is called "his sister" and Dng.t is named with her in such a manner as to suggest that she is a sister too. On the second Dng.t is called "his wife," but Mr's relationship is not mentioned. Although the wife Dng.t is not explicitly identified as a sister, there is circumstantial evidence that she is. The one fairly certain case of the marriage of a commoner to his sister in the Pharaonic period, however, occurs in the 22nd Dynasty during the reign of Sheshonk III (823–772 B.C.).[21] The genealogy of the Libyan commander Pediese is given on a votive stela, which indicates that he is married to his sister Tere and has two sons by her. He and his wife have the same father, but the stela does not contain evidence regarding their mothers.

Murray has published eleven genealogies of small officials in the Middle Kingdom which she maintains contain several cases of mother-son marriage, several of father-daughter marriage, and one of brother-

16. *Ibid.*, pp. 28–29.
17. Erman, *Life in Ancient Egypt*, p. 154; Gaston Maspéro, *The Dawn of Civilization; Egypt and Chaldaea*, Second edition, London: Society for Promoting Christian Knowledge, 1896, p. 50. Gardiner points out that kinship terms were sometimes used loosely in other circumstances too. Gardiner, *op. cit.*, p. 178.
18. Černý, *op. cit.*, p. 25.
19. *Ibid.*, pp. 25–26.
20. Henry George Fischer, "A God and a General of the Oasis on a Stela of the Late Middle Kingdom," *Journal of Near Eastern Studies*, 16 (October, 1957), p. 231.
21. Breasted, *op. cit.*, vol. 4, p. 386.

sister marriage.[22] Murray assumes, however, that different examples of the same name on the same stela, and even on different stelae, necessarily refer to one and the same individual, even though the names were very common at the time. If one discards unwarranted assumptions and establishes the genealogies properly, there is no substantial evidence in the genealogies of marriages occurring within the nuclear family, and Egyptologists today do not take these cases seriously.

Ptolemaic Period

Upon the death of Alexander the Great in 323 B.C., Ptolemy, one of Alexander's generals, established a new dynasty of Macedonian kings in Egypt. The Ptolemaic kings apparently found it prudent to adopt many of the customs of their royal predecessors, including brother-sister marriage. Greek law probably permitted the marriage of paternal half brothers and half sisters, but it certainly prohibited the union of full brothers and sisters.[23] Ptolemy II, nevertheless, married his full sister Arsinoe. If we may judge by a story told by Athenaeus, who lived in Egypt at the end of the second century A.D., this act probably was regarded as scandalous by the Hellenistic elements of the population. According to Athenaeus, Sotades, a popular Greek writer of obscene verses, described the marriage in a coarse line as incestuous. He was forced to flee Alexandria immediately, but he was caught by the king's general, Patroclus, and thrown into the sea in a leaden jar.[24]

The descendants of Ptolemy II tended to follow his example, marrying half sisters or full sisters. Of the thirteen Ptolemies who came to the throne, seven contracted such marriages. Ptolemy VIII was married to two of his sisters, and both Ptolemy XII and Ptolemy XIII were married to their sister, the famous Cleopatra VI.[25]

Brother-sister marriage during the Greek period in Egypt seems to have been restricted to the royalty, for there is no evidence of its practice among commoners, either Egyptian or Hellenistic.

22. Margaret A. Murray, "Notes on Some Genealogies of the Middle Kingdom," *Ancient Egypt* (June, 1927), pp. 45–51.

23. See Philo Judaeus, "On the Special Laws," in *Philo,* vol. 7, translated by F. H. Colson, Cambridge: Harvard University Press, 1937, book 3, paragraph 4; Plutarch, *Plutarch's Lives,* translated by Bernadotte Perrin, London: William Heinemann, 1948, pp. 87–89.

24. Athenaeus, *The Deipnosophists,* translated by C. B. Gulick, Cambridge: Harvard University Press, 1951, book 14, paragraph 621.

25. Edwyn Bevan, *A History of Egypt under the Ptolemaic Dynasty,* London: Methuen and Co., 1927, p. 60; J. P. Mahaffy, "Cleopatra VI," *Journal of Egyptian Archeology,* 2 (1915), pp. 1–4; Arthur Weigall, *The Life and Times of Cleopatra: Queen of Egypt,* rev. ed., New York: Putnam, 1924, pp. 44, 65; Franz V. M. Cumont, *L'Égypte des Astrologues,* Brussels: La Fondation Égyptologique, 1937, pp. 177–179; Ruffer, *op. cit.,* pp. 341–356.

Roman Period

During the period of Roman rule in Egypt there is, for the first time, an abundance of papyrus documents and records which give evidence that commoners often practiced brother-sister marriage. These documents are of several kinds: personal letters, marriage contracts, other types of contracts, petitions and documents addressed to the administrative authorities, and census documents carrying genealogical information. Unlike some of the earlier types of evidence which may be subject to differing interpretations, these documents of a technical character have an "indisputable precision."[26]

Egyptologists have been aware of this evidence at least since 1883, when Wilcken concluded from his study of some papyri that marriage between brothers and sisters occurred often during the Roman period.[27] Among the marriages recorded in the fragments which he examined, marriages between brother and sister were in an absolute majority. Moreover, most of the marriages were with full sisters, not half sisters. One of the papyri, for example, speaks of "his wife, being his sister by the same father and the same mother."[28]

Grenfell and Hunt published in 1901 the text of an application from a woman named Demetria asking that her son Artemon might be admitted to a group with special tax privileges, on the grounds that he was a descendant of members of the group.[29] The papyrus gives the genealogy for five generations. Although there are no consanguineous marriages on the father's side, during a period extending from about 50 to 120 A.D., Demetria's father, grandfather, and great-grandfather were all married to their full sisters. About the same time Wessely published genealogies of four well-to-do Egyptian families in which marriages between brothers and sisters were in a majority.[30] Only a little later Mitteis and Wilcken published a text dating from the third century A.D. of a card of invitation issued by a mother for the marriage together of her son and daughter.[31]

Approximately 150 papyri have been found dealing with a man named Apollonius, who was the civil administrator of the nome of Apol-

---

26. Marcel Hombert and Claire Préaux, "Les Mariages Consanguins dans l'Égypte Romaine," in *Collection Latomus: Hommages à Joseph Bidez et à Franz Cumont,* Bruxelles: Latomus, 1949, vol. 2, p. 138.

27. U. Wilcken, "Arsinoitische Steuerprofessionen aus dem Jahre 189 n. Chr. und verwandte Urkunden," *Sitzungsberichte der Königlich Preussischen Akademie der Wissenschaft zu Berlin* (1883), p. 903.

28. *Ibid.*

29. Bernard P. Grenfell and Arthur S. Hunt, *The Amherst Papyri,* London: H. Frowde, 1901, part 2, pp. 90–91.

30. Carl Wessely, *Karanis und Soknopaiu Nesos,* Vienna: Carl Gerold's Sohn, 1902, pp. 23–24.

31. Ludwig Mitteis and U. Wilcken, *Grundzüge und Chrestomathie der Papyruskunde,* Leipzig: B. G. Teubner, 1912, vol. 1, p. 568.

lonopolis Heptakomia (c. 117 A.D.).[32] The papyri show clearly that he was married to his sister Aline and that they were deeply attached to each other. "During the Jewish war Aline writes to him begging him to put the burden of the work on to his subordinates as other strategi did and not to run into unnecessary danger; when he went away, she says, she could taste neither food nor drink, nor could she sleep."[33] Romans were not permitted to contract marriages with their sisters, but there was apparently little or no social stigma attached to the custom, for Apollonius had many Roman friends.

Calderini in 1923 examined 122 fragments of papyri from the fourteen-yearly census conducted by the Roman administrators between 6 and 310 A.D.[34] In eleven of the papyri he found evidence of thirteen cases of consanguineous marriages, including eight in which husband and wife had both parents in common. Three of the cases are found in the census year 173–4 A.D. and six in 187–8 A.D. The concentration of cases at these dates, however, is due in large part to the greater number of fragments available for these censuses.

All available evidence of the marriage of brothers and sisters among commoners in Roman Egypt has recently been summarized by Hombert and Préaux as follows:[35]

Place	Consanguine Marriages	Other Marriages
Arsinoe	20	32
Villages of Fayoum	9	39
Oxyrhynchus	0	7
Hermoupolis	5	14
Others	4	32
Total	38	124

Some of these cases involve merely half brothers and sisters, but the majority are full brothers and sisters. Though it is hazardous to generalize from the small and unrepresentative number of cases, it appears that consanguineous marriages were more common in the cities than in the rural villages. There are no examples of brother-sister marriage occurring

32. Johannes Nietzold, *Die Ehe in Ägypten zur Ptolemäisch-Römischen Zeit*, Leipzig: Verlag von Veit und Co., 1903, p. 13; C. H. Roberts, "The Greek Papyri," in S. R. K. Glanville, ed., *The Legacy of Egypt*, Oxford: Clarendon Press, 1942, pp. 276–279.

33. *Ibid.*, pp. 278–279.

34. Aristide Calderini, *La Composizione della Famiglia Secondo le Schede di Censimento dell' Egitto Romano*, Milan: Sociatà Editrice "Vita e Pensiero," 1923.

35. Marcel Hombert and Claire Préaux, *Recherches sur le Recensement dans l'Égypte Romaine, Papyrologica Lugduno-Batava*, Leiden: E. J. Brill, 1952, vol. 5, p. 151.

after 212 A.D., but Diocletian's issuance of an edict in 295 condemning such marriages suggests that they were still occasionally practiced.[36]

A further source of evidence concerning marriage customs in Egypt is in the writings of Greek and Roman observers. The Greeks were notoriously ethnocentric and their accounts of the customs of "barbarians" are often suspect, but when these accounts are taken in conjunction with other evidence, they provide additional corroboration. Diodorus of Sicily, a Greek historian of the first century B.C., who drew heavily on the historical romance of Hecataeus of Abdera, wrote, "The Egyptians also made a law, they say, contrary to the general custom of mankind, permitting men to marry their sisters, this being due to the success attained by Isis in this respect; for she had married her brother Osiris. . . ."[37] The Hellenistic Jewish philosopher Philo Judaeus, who lived in Alexandria (20 B.C.–c. 50 A.D.), made the following statement: "But the lawgiver of the Egyptians poured scorn upon the cautiousness of both [Athenians and Lacedaemonians], and, holding that the course which they enjoined stopped halfway, produced a fine crop of lewdness. With a lavish hand he bestowed on bodies and souls the poisonous bane of incontinence and gave full liberty to marry sisters of every degree whether they belonged to one of their brother's parents or to both, and not only if they were younger than their brothers but also if they were older or of the same age."[38] The Roman philosopher Seneca (c. 4 B.C.–65 A.D.) commented similarly with regard to the marriage of brothers and sisters: *Athenis dimidium licet, Alexandriae totum.*[39] Claudius Ptolemy, a Greek mathematician, astronomer, and geographer living in Alexandria (c. 127–151 A.D.) commented that Egypt, because of the conjunction of certain planets, was "governed by a man and wife who are own brother and sister."[40] Finally, Pausanias, a Greek traveler and topographer (c. 175 A.D.) wrote, "This Ptolemy fell in love with Arsinoe, his full sister, and married her, violating herein Macedonian custom, but following that of his Egyptian subjects."[41]

Conclusion and Discussion

For the Pharaonic period there is reasonably firm evidence that the Egyptian kings, especially those in the 18th and 19th Dynasties, sometimes

36. *Ibid.*, p. 153.
37. *Diodorus of Sicily*, translated by C. H. Oldfather, London: William Heinemann, 1946, book 1, section 27, p. 85.
38. Philo Judaeus, *op. cit.*
39. See William Adam, "Consanguinity in Marriage," *Fortnightly Review*, 2 (1865), vol. 2, p. 714.
40. Ptolemy, *Tetrabiblos*, translated by F. E. Robbins, Cambridge: Harvard University Press, 1940, book 2, chapter 3, p. 151.
41. Pausanias, *Description of Greece*, translated by W. H. S. Jones, London: William Heinemann, 1918, book 1, section 7, paragraph 1, p. 35.

married their sisters or half sisters and perhaps on rare occasions their daughters. For the commoners, on the other hand, there is only one fairly certain case of the marriage of brother and sister, though there are several other possible or even probable cases. In no instance, however, is there proof that the individuals were more than half brother and half sister. Bell[42] and Wilcken[43] believed that the relative lack of evidence of brother-sister marriage among the commoners before Roman times was due to the paucity of documents pertaining to commoners rather than to the absence of the custom among them. Nevertheless, on the basis of evidence now available, we must conclude that, although the marriage of brothers and sisters was probably not forbidden to commoners in the Pharaonic period, it was practiced only very rarely.

In the Ptolemaic period the evidence is conclusive that many of the kings married their sisters or half sisters, but there are no reports of such marriages among commoners. During the Roman period, on the other hand, there is an abundance of evidence that points to a fairly high incidence of marriages between brothers and sisters among commoners.

How can the extensive practice of brother-sister marriage in Egypt be explained? This question has stimulated much speculation, but no final answers are possible on the basis of evidence presently available. Some Egyptologists have argued in favor of a diffusion hypothesis, maintaining that the custom was not indigenous but was adopted as a result of the influence of other cultures. Kornemann, for example, believed that the Ptolemies copied the Persian custom and that the Egyptian commoners later began to follow the practices of the royalty.[44] It is a matter of vigorous controversy whether consanguineous marriages were practiced among the ancient Persians,[45] but the fact that such marriages apparently did exist in the contiguous culture of Egypt lends credence to the Persian case. With scanty information, however, it is difficult to determine the direction of the diffusion process. Moreover, alien cultural elements are not ordinarily adopted by a society unless they have some functional significance in the new setting. Thus the diffusion hypothesis, even if it were possible to establish it firmly, still does not answer the question of why the custom developed in the original host culture or why it was later adopted in a secondary culture.

Several authors, following Diodorus, suggest that the custom of

42. H. I. Bell, "Brother and Sister Marriage in Graeco-Roman Egypt," *Revue Internationale des Droits de l'Antiquité*, 2 (1949), p. 84.

43. Wilcken, *op. cit.*

44. E. Kornemann, "Die Geschwisterehe im Altertum," *Mitteilungen der Schlesischen Gesellschaft für Volkskunde*, 24 (1923), p. 83.

45. See J. S. Slotkin, "On a Possible Lack of Incest Regulations in Old Iran," *American Anthropologist*, 49 (October–December, 1947), pp. 612–617; Ward H. Goodenough, "Comments on the Question of Incestuous Marriages in Old Iran," *American Anthropologist*, 51 (April–June, 1949), pp. 326–328; and J. S. Slotkin, "Reply to Goodenough," *American Anthropologist*, 51 (July–September, 1949), pp. 531–532.

brother-sister marriage in Egypt had its origin in the religious system.[46] The gods Osiris and Set according to legend married their sisters Isis and Nepthys, presumably setting a pattern which was subsequently imitated by their followers. Incestuous origin myths characterize almost every society, however, including those which maintain strict taboos on the marriage of brothers and sisters. Also religious myths tend to be a reflection or popular explanation of more basic cultural elements rather than their source. White, on the other hand, believes that the Ptolemies adopted the practice of marrying their sisters as a means of conciliating the cult of Osiris and of undermining the prestige and authority of the hostile Theban priesthood, who were associated with the rival cult of Amon-Ra.[47]

Another hypothesis that has been advocated by many Egyptologists in the past is that ancient Egypt was in a transitional stage between matrilineal and patrilineal descent systems.[48] The royalty were governed by matrilineal descent with authority handed down through the female line. The king secured his legitimacy only through marriage with the heiress queen. Thus marriages contracted between brothers and sisters were merely an expedient for shifting the succession from the female to the male line. This type of explanation, however, smacks of the now discredited evolutionary schemes of the nineteenth-century anthropologists who maintained that a matrilineal stage preceded the "higher" patrilineal stage in most societies at some distant time in the past. Anomalous customs, for which there was no readily perceived functional explanation, were seized upon as "survivals" and evidences of the earlier period. The bulk of the evidence for Egypt suggests that kingship was not inherited primarily through the female line but through the male line. In the absence of a male heir able to assert his rights effectively, however, it frequently happened that a son-in-law of the king became the new king.

The First Story of Sethon Khamwese, which, as Griffith remarks, is the only account we possess of an early Egyptian betrothal or marriage that is not of the fairy-tale order, suggests that not only was the marriage of brothers and sisters not necessary for the succession, but it tended to endanger it:[49]

46. John Wilkinson, *Manners and Customs of the Ancient Egyptians*, rev. ed., New York: Dodd, Mead, and Co., 1878, vol. 3, p. 113; Ernest A. Wallis Budge, *The Dwellers on the Nile*, London: Religious Tract Society, 1926, p. 23; and Ruffer, *op. cit.*, pp. 323–324.

47. Rachel Evelyn White, "Women in Ptolemaic Egypt," *Journal of Hellenic Studies*, 18 (1898), pp. 238–239.

48. Petrie, *op. cit.*, vol. 2, p. 183; White, *op. cit.*; Kornemann, *op. cit.*; Margaret Murray, "Royal Marriages and Matrilineal Descent," *Journal of the Royal Anthropological Institute*, 45 (1915), pp. 307–325; and Margaret Murray, *The Splendour that Was Egypt*, London: Sidgwick and Jackson, 1949, pp. 100–102, 321–323.

49. F. L. Griffith, "Marriage (Egyptian)," in J. Hastings, ed., *Encyclopaedia of Religion and Ethics*, New York: C. Scribner's Sons, 1955, vol. 8, p. 444.

. . . . The ancient Pharaoh's argument about his son Neferkeptah and his daughter Ahure seems to be that it would be impolitic, when there were only two children in the royal family, to risk the succession by marrying them together. His preference, following a family custom, would be to marry them to a son and a daughter of two of his generals in order to enlarge his family. At a banquet he questioned Ahure, and was won over by her wishes to the other plan; thereupon he commanded his chief steward to take the princess to her brother's house that same night with all necessary things. . . .

It is often stated that the Egyptian kings, like the Incas or the kings of Hawaii, married their sisters or daughters in order to maintain the purity of the royal blood. The frequency with which kings married commoners or even slaves, however, belies this explanation. The offspring of these unions frequently acceded to the throne. Moreover, neither this, nor the preceding explanation that the king had to seek legitimacy by marrying the heiress to the throne, can account for the existence of brother-sister marriage among the commoners. One might argue that the royal custom was established first and that it was gradually adopted by the commoners through a filtering-down process. But again, a custom is not likely to be adopted unless it has some functional significance within the social system or subsystem.

The most plausible explanation that has been advanced for the marriage of brothers and sisters in Egypt is that it served to maintain the property of the family intact and to prevent the splintering of the estate through the operation of the laws of inheritance.[50] Since daughters usually inherited a share of the estate,[51] the device of brother-sister marriage would have served to preserve intact the material resources of the family as a unit. That marriages of brothers and sisters were probably more common in the cities than in the rural communities during Roman times is consistent with this explanation, for there was a greater concentration of wealth among the urban residents. Other societies have, of course, used other means of dealing with the problem of fractionalism—primogeniture, ultimogeniture, or unilineal inheritance through an extended family system. The reason for the Egyptian adoption of the more unusual alternative remains obscure, particularly since the marriage of brothers and sisters could ordinarily be expected to have dysfunctional consequences.[52]

50. See Nietzold, *op. cit.*, p. 13; Budge, *op. cit.*, p. 23.

51. Gaston Maspéro, *Life in Ancient Egypt*, London: Chapman and Hall, 1892, p. 11.

52. See Bronislaw Malinowski, "Culture," *Encylopedia of the Social Sciences*, New York: Macmillan Co., 1930, vol. 4, pp. 629–630; Bronislaw Malinowski, *Sex and Repression in Savage Society*, London: Kegan Paul, Trench, Trubner, and Co., 1927, pp. 244–251; E. B. Tylor, "On a Method of Investigating the Development of Institutions; Applied to Laws of Marriage and Descent," *Journal of the Anthropological Institute*, 18 (1888), pp. 266–267; Leslie A. White, "The Definition and Prohibition of Incest," *American Anthropologist*, 50 (July–Sept., 1948), pp. 422–426; Brenda Z. Seligman, "The Incest Barrier: Its Role in Social Organization," *British Journal of Psychology*, 22 (January, 1932), pp. 274–276; and Talcott Parsons, "Social Structure and the Development of Personality: Freud's Contribution to the Integration of Psychology and Sociology," *Psychiatry*, 21 (November, 1958), pp. 332–336.

There is also a suggestion in the Roman laws that their Egyptian subjects may have employed consanguine marriages as marriages of convenience for the transmission of property that otherwise would have fallen to the state. Roman citizens in Egypt, on the other hand, were specifically enjoined from marrying their sisters, and when a brother married a sister, the state confiscated the property.[53]

In conclusion, the evidence from ancient Egypt, particularly from the Roman period, casts doubt upon the universality of the taboo upon the marriage of brothers and sisters. Apparently brother-sister marriage can be institutionalized for commoners as well as for royalty and it may be practiced on a fairly wide scale. What are the implications of this finding for the theoretical problems which revolve around the incest taboo? First, there is further evidence, if further evidence were needed, of the social nature and origins of incest prohibitions. Second, and more important, it is clear that unicausal explanations of the "universality" of the brother-sister taboo are inadequate. Firth has written perceptively, "I am prepared to see it shown that the incest situation varies according to the social structure of each community, that it has little to do with the prevention of sex relations as such, but that its real correlation is to be found in the maintenance of institutional forms in the society as a whole, and of the specific interest of groups in particular. Where these latter demand it for the preservation of their privileges, the union permitted between kin may be the closest possible."[54] Although the need to maintain clearly differentiated roles within the nuclear family or the need to establish cooperative alliances with other families may serve as the foundation for incest prohibitions in the great majority of societies, these needs may in some cases be offset by other functional requirements of overriding importance. This has long been recognized in connection with small ruling elites, but not with regard to general institutions which may be applicable to the whole society.

Although it is probably the most significant example, the Egyptian case does not stand alone as an exception to the universality of the

53. See Papyrus 206 in A. S. Hunt and C. C. Edgar, *Select Papyri,* Cambridge: Harvard University Press, 1934, vol. 2, p. 47.
54. Raymond W. Firth, *We, the Tikopia,* London: G. Allen and Unwin, 1936, p. 340. Parsons has commented in a similar vein: ". . . Anything so general as the incest taboo seems likely to be a resultant of a constellation of different factors which are deeply involved in the foundations of human societies. Analysis in terms of the balance of forces in the social system rather than of one or two specific 'factors' seems much more promising." Talcott Parsons, "The Incest Taboo in Relation to Social Structure and the Socialization of the Child" [this book, pp. 13–30]. Parsons, however, was misled by Murdock's sweeping statement—based upon the analysis of only 250 societies—that "in no known society is it conventional or even permissible for father and daughter, mother and son, or brother and sister to have sexual intercourse or to marry." George P. Murdock, *Social Structure,* New York: Macmillan Co., 1949, p. 12. Consequently, Parsons fails to recognize that the "balance of forces in the social system" may in some cases be such that marriages between brother and sister or even parent and child are permitted.

brother-sister incest taboo. Wilson has recently reported that forty-two members of a community on a Caribbean island have been carrying on incestuous relations for the past thirty years, including relations between mothers and sons, fathers and daughters, and brothers and sisters.[55] This however, apparently is an aberrant situation which developed because of special circumstances, and the original normative standards are now beginning to be reasserted. At any rate, this does not represent a long-term institutionalized pattern persisting for hundreds of years, as was the case in ancient Egypt.

There is also other evidence, however, that societies which have sanctioned unions between brothers and sisters or between parents and children have not been nearly as rare as has been generally supposed in recent years. In dust-covered volumes, which for the most part have been left unopened and unread on the library shelves by the current generation of social scientists,[56] there are many instances of such cases reported by travelers, government officials, missionaries, ethnographers, and archeologists.[57] Although many of the several dozen reports are of doubtful authenticity, there probably remains a substantial number of societies which are deserving of greater attention. It is important not only that we test the validity of our empirical generalizations, but also that we seek to discover in greater detail the various conditions which may impinge upon the structure of the nuclear family.

55. Peter J. Wilson, "Incest—A Case Study," paper presented at 60th Annual Meeting of the American Anthropological Association, Philadelphia, November, 1961.

56. Earlier social scientists, on the other hand, such as Spencer, Sumner, Frazer, Westermarck, Briffault, Letourneau, and Howard, were aware of many of the reports and called attention to them. Since their works also remain largely unread today, most of the cases have long since been forgotten.

57. I am currently completing a survey of these reports and plan to publish a summary of this material shortly.

Bernard Farber

Structural Differences in Reciprocity

Social Differentiation Emphasis in Kinship.[1] Possibly the most valuable property of a kinship group aside from wealth is its position among other kinship units in terms of honor and status, a position defined by the content of the symbolic estate that the kinship group possesses. This symbolic estate includes the achievements and honors of those individuals, both living and dead, related to the kinship group. More generally, families may become known by a great ancestor (real or fictitious), wealth, or personal achievements. One role of kinship groups in social differentiation is to perpetuate and enhance these symbolic estates, which become an important part of the family culture.

If orderly transmission of this family culture in the next generation is to occur, each family of orientation (that is, the family into which an individual is born) must be organized to produce in its children's families of procreation (the families in which they are parents) patterns of norms and values identical to its own. Restriction of marriage to individuals from families or descent groups with identical norms and values would enhance this continuity of the symbolic estate. In addition, the perpetuation of family norms from one generation to the next is facilitated when the kinship groups of both husband and wife have a stake in controlling the family of procreation.[2]

Marriage systems which either prescribe or encourage marriage between cousins appear ideally suited for maintaining symbolic family estates. Inasmuch as cousins are descended from parents who had been raised together as brothers and sisters, there is a strong probability that the norms and values transmitted to them are similar. If their own children in turn marry the children of their siblings, the continuity would be

---

1. The material on integration and differentiation in this section is based on Bernard Farber, *Comparative Kinship Systems: A Method of Analysis*, New York: Wiley, 1968, pp. 3–21, 24–45. The point of view expressed rests on an analysis of issues raised by such anthropologists as Claude Lévi-Strauss (*Structural Anthropology*, New York: Basic Books, 1963), David M. Schneider ("Some Muddles in the Models: Or, How the System Really Works," in Michael Banton, ed., *The Relevance of Models for Social Anthropology*, New York: Praeger, 1965), and Meyer Fortes, ("The Structure of Unilineal Descent Groups," *American Anthropologist*, 55 (1953), pp. 17–41).

2. See discussion of "orderly replacement" in Bernard Farber, *Family: Organization and Interaction*, San Francisco: Chandler, 1964.

maintained. The systems prescribing marriage between cousins thus appear to be efficient mechanisms of orderly transmission of family culture from one generation to the next in that they require members to marry into groups with similar norms and maximize control over the nuclear family.

Integration Emphasis in Kinship. In contrast to systems emphasizing social differentiation functions of kinship, those systems that stress integration functions are organized in ways which maximize the number of marital liaisons between descent groups. An open system of alliances would maximize the proportion of the adult population who marry, and it would provide little control by kin groups over nuclear family organization. Under an open system each individual would be available for marriage to any person of the opposite sex, regardless of current marital status. This permanent availability for marriage reflects the lack of interest or the inability of kinship groups to sustain the orderly transmission of family culture—including symbolic estates—from one generation to the next or to maintain permanent bonds with other kinship groups. These kinship groups would provide few institutionalized forms of social control over the nuclear family.

Under conditions favoring permanent availability, marriage takes on the form of a voluntary association in which an individual continues membership only as long as his personal commitment to his spouse exceeds his commitments elsewhere. Regardless of his current marital status, the individual is motivated to sustain a high desirability as a mate and tends to develop personal skills and attributes that enhance his position in relation to potential marriage partners. Kinship systems reflect these tendencies in various ways. If courtship-type behavior is permitted between all members who are potential marriage partners, interaction in cross-sex relationships will tend to be informal. There is no necessity to restrict courtship-type behavior to specific individuals or to unmarried persons. To fulfill needs and maintain intimate relationships in an impersonal world individuals are under pressure for both early marriage and later remarriage. Systems tending toward permanent availability would show (1) an increase in expected remarriage during the course of a lifetime, (2) decline in premarital chastity and marital fidelity as a value, (3) lessened effect of children as a deterrent to divorce, and (4) increased emphasis on maintaining personal attractiveness even after marriage.[3]

Differentiation and Integration. The preceding discussion has suggested that kinship systems which facilitate orderly transmission of family norms from one generation to the next differ markedly in organization from those which tend to maximize the number of kin groups connected by marriage. In the first instance marital alliances are confined to those

3. See Farber, *Family: Organization and Interaction,* San Francisco: Chandler, 1964, for a discussion of "permanent availability" and its relationship to courtship, marriage, divorce, family, and kinship norms.

descent groups that are governed by similar norms and values. In this situation cultural similarity as a factor in marital selection would facilitate a highly stratified arrangement of clusters of related descent groups. In the second instance, cultural similarity would have little influence on the formation of marital alliances, and the consequence would be an integration of descent groups through elaborated networks extending throughout the society. Under these latter conditions (facilitating permanent availability) kinsmen would be drawn from diverse cultural backgrounds and would, for lower-class families, facilitate hypergamy.

Kinship and Intimate-Kin Groups

Kinship refers partly to rules by which an individual inherits relatives, accrues them during his lifetime through birth or marriage, and transmits them to the succeeding generation. Continuity of a society over a series of generations demands stability in the kinship system in order to govern the succession of statuses and property rights. Accordingly, sections of legal codes dealing with basic kinship organization tend to persist over long periods of time. In particular, laws pertaining to incestuous marriage are generally stable generation after generation. When they are revised considerably, as they have been in the past fifty years in England, this revision apparently signifies a profound modification in the social structure. With a change in legal codes pertaining to incestuous marriage (and, by implication, the kinship system), other new laws relevant to husband-wife relationships, divorce, and inheritance may be anticipated. These revisions invoke new images of ideal family organization and redefine which relatives an individual can regard as his own.

In contrast to the view that the inheritance, distribution, and transmission of relatives is a primary function of kinship, for Lévi-Strauss social structure obtains its form and endurance through exchange, and marriage is the "archetype" of exchange. He assigns a central role to the prohibition of incestuous marriage in the development of systems of exchange: the proscription of marriage within prohibited degrees of kinship "tends to ensure the total and continuous circulation of the group's most important assets, its wives and daughters."[4] Kinship structures derive their form, according to the Lévi-Strauss position, from the ways they regulate marital exchange.

Yet the universal existence of limitations on marital exchange suggests another line of reasoning. The prohibition of incestuous marriage implies the presence of kin groups within which members cannot be exchanged for one another. The aggregation of these kin groups indicates

4. Claude Lévi-Strauss, *The Elementary Sources of Kinship,* Boston: Beacon Press, 1969, p. 479.

that social structure can be defined in terms of nonreciprocities (as opposed to exchange). Generally, property may be regarded as something which may be withheld or prohibited from exchange (for example, entailed estates cannot be sold). In fact, Lévi-Strauss quotes Proudon: "Property is non-reciprocity."[5] Kin groups can vary in the amount and value of property they possess. Position in the social structure is determined not so much by the expenditure of kin-group assets in exchange, but by the ability of the kin group to withhold exchanges for its members and other goods until the right price is paid. In the final analysis, social position of a kin group depends upon the extent of surplus value of assets over what is required for exchange in dealing with other kin groups. Seen in this light, social structure is molded by regulations which govern the accumulation, distribution, and transmission of kin-group property by inhibiting exchange and dissipation of this property. In particular, persons within the range of prohibited marital relationships are the collective property of the same group, whose interests are to be maximized.

The emphasis on *reluctance* to enter into reciprocities as a basis for social structure appears justified in view of Lévi-Strauss's discussions of the enmity of kin groups entering into marital alliances as well as the prevalence of haggling over dowries and brideprices where these exist. From the viewpoint of perpetuation of kin-group property, marital exchange is a necessary evil unless it can be applied in such a way as (1) to perpetuate this property by requiring persons with preexisting consanguineous ties to marry one another (as in direct exchange of siblings) or to arrange marriages of relatives in a round-robin fashion (as in indirect exchange), or (2) to enhance assets of *both* kin groups involved in the marriage simultaneously. In the former case, to which Lévi-Strauss applies the term "elementary structures," perpetuation of kin-group property is relatively unproblematic.[6]

In the case of "complex structures," however, where greater latitude exists in marital selection, there is necessarily an ambivalence between pressures for exchange and those for accumulation and perpetuation of kin-group property. The resolution of the conflict between forces for exchange and for perpetuation of property would depend upon the value of kinship property. In highly industrial societies, kin groups with valuable property become highly selective in establishing close ties with other kin groups through marriage. Viewed in this manner, some forms of bilateral kinship may represent mechanisms for enhancing the property value of both husband's and wife's kin groups simultaneously at high socioeconomic levels. At low socioeconomic levels, however, marriage would serve a different function, one which emphasizes reciprocity. By

5. *Ibid.*, p. 490.
6. See E. R. Leach, "The Structural Implications of Matrilateral Cross-Cousin Marriage," *Journal of the Royal Anthropological Institute*, 81 (1951), pp. 23–55.

maximizing the number of ties with other kin groups, a family would provide its members with a plethora of sources for mutual assistance pacts. At both extremes in socioeconomic status, marriage could thus be used to enhance the value of property at the disposal of both husband's and wife's families—at one extreme by rigorous selectivity and at the other extreme by the creation of numerous networks of reciprocity.

There are two situations in which marital ties are not desirable. The first is one in which a kin group does not want to establish a cooperative relationship with another group. In American society, religious and racial intermarriage is often discouraged on this basis. The second situation for proscribing marriage is one in which individuals are already regarded as part of the same kin group. Marriage would then be superfluous in the creation of further alliances; the individuals are already closely related. In fact, marriage between members of the same closely related kin group may foster internal conflicts. Individuals in the range of relatives with whom marriage would be considered incestuous may be regarded as members of EGO's *intimate-kin group*.[7]

The composition of intimate-kin groups seems to reflect the manner in which the kinship system handles problems of social stratification and integration of family groups in the society. For example, an analysis of intimate-kin groups of ten societies has suggested that the exclusion of first cousins from the intimate-kin group is associated with estate ownership by the "family" (rather than by the individual) and with severe limitations on testacy. The composition of the intimate-kin group, as implied in laws pertaining to incestuous marriage, thus appears to be related to other aspects of the social structure.[8] The putative existence of two different functions of marriage at high and low socioeconomic strata suggests that the kinds of *persons* who are considered as the property of the intimate-kin group (that is, within degrees of relationship in which marriage is forbidden) will vary by position in the social structure.

. . .

Conclusions

1. One purpose of the investigation of kinship in Champaign-Urbana was to determine whether characteristics of Biblical and Western American kinship systems were associated with socioeconomic status. In general, the tendencies anticipated were found, with Biblical kinship attributes appearing at higher socioeconomic levels and Western American at

7. The term EGO is used to refer to any person whose perspective is taken as a point of reference, such as the respondent in an interview, or the person whose relatives are reckoned genealogically.

8. Farber, *Comparative Kinship Systems*, pp. 14–21 and 127–132.

lower levels. The results, however, were somewhat equivocal and suggest that at all socioeconomic levels, some proclivity exists to mix the systems.

Higher socioeconomic persons tended to use *mother* and *father* as terms of address for in-laws (with these terms being associated with feelings of closeness) and, in this way, acknowledged at least a symbolic incorporation into the spouse's family of orientation. In contrast, for low socioeconomic persons, feelings of closeness to in-laws were related to use of first names to address them.

Possibly, the use of *mother* and *father* as terms for addressing in-laws can be interpreted as a "courtesy" to the spouse.[9] As "courtesy kin," in-laws would not "gain a son" nor would any new rights or obligations to the spouse's parents be accrued with marriage. However, that interpretation would not explain the difference in usage by socioeconomic status, that is, the use of *mother* and *father* at higher socioeconomic levels and use of first names at lower levels when EGO felt close to in-laws. It seems as reasonable to interpret the findings as representing different tendencies in kinship organization—with *kinship status* emphasized in feelings of closeness at higher socioeconomic levels (consistent with the Biblical system) and *personal relationships* emphasized in feelings of closeness at lower levels since, consistent with the Western American system, the spouse's parents are not really part of EGO's intimate-kin group.

2. As in other societies, in American society the paternal descent group seems to serve primarily to provide the child with legitimacy and community status. Its major role is therefore to create and sustain marriages. Data were examined concerning differences in feelings of closeness to paternal and maternal relatives when EGO's parents were divorced. As compared with feelings of closeness to kin when the parents were still married, respondents with divorced parents felt more distant to their fathers and paternal grandparents. In the analysis pertaining to paternal versus maternal aunts and uncles, the data revealed little difference when EGO's parents were married but considerably greater feelings of closeness to maternal aunts and uncles when EGO's parents had been divorced. The effect of divorce on feelings of closeness toward paternal and maternal consanguineous kin can be traced to the influence of divorce on in-law relationships. Only occasionally does a woman report feeling close to her siblings- or parents-in-law after divorce. Since almost all children live with their mothers or maternal kin following divorce, their feelings of closeness toward paternal kin are affected by the general decline in their mothers' closeness to former affines.

9. David M. Schneider, "American Kin Terms for Kinsmen: A Critique of Goodenough's Componential Analysis of Yankee Kinship Terminology," *American Anthropologist,* 67 (1965), No. 5, Part 2, pp. 288–308.

This state of affairs suggests that, consistent with the Western American kinship system, at lower socioeconomic levels ties with affines are maintained in deference to the married consanguineous relative; when the marriage ends, the ties tend to be broken.[10] The affinal quality of the paternal line in the Western American kinship system is also reflected in these findings.

3. The matrifocal family represents the most fleeting connection between affines. This situation makes the matrifocal family particularly appropriate for studying long-run consequences of the absence of a paternal line. The absence of paternal grandparents creates relationships across generations which deviate from generally accepted norms. An analysis of data supplied by Negro women indicates that when both grandmothers have been known to EGO, she tends to call her FaMo "grandmother" and her MoMo "mother." However, when she has known only MoMo, she uses "grandmother" as a term of address. The maternal grandmother then seems to substitute for the paternal grandmother in a position of respect. Since one of the kinship functions of a paternal line of descent is to provide for a respectable community status, this finding suggests that in matrifocal families paternal functions are not eliminated but are taken over by the maternal side. Insofar as maternal kin accumulate functions normally performed by paternal kin, the importance of affinal relationships is minimized; consanguineous relatives can perform these functions equally well—after all, among the *lumpenproletariat,* affines can offer little in the way of a respectful community status anyway. This accrual of paternal functions by maternal kin precludes symbolic incorporation of husband and wife into their spouse's family of orientation and separates their respective kindred as distinct entities. In this respect, as well as in others, the matrifocal family can be contrasted with high socioeconomic families, in which there tends to be at least the symbolic overlapping of kindreds characteristic of the Biblical kinship system.

10. It would be of interest to compare effects of divorce and widowhood on feelings of closeness for families at different socioeconomic levels. Presumably, families at higher socioeconomic levels would to a greater extent maintain ties with (or feel close to) "divorced affines" than would families of lower SES. It must also be of value to determine how terms of address toward in-laws change after divorce or widowhood when contact is maintained.

2 THE PRINCIPLE OF LEGITIMACY

Bronislaw Malinowski

Parenthood, the Basis of Social Structure

The Child in Power Again

"Daddy, what an ass you are!" This was the final sentence in an argument which I had with my youngest daughter, aged five. I had not been able to convince her or to sway her opinion. . . . I ceased arguing and reflected. I tried to imagine what would have happened had I thus addressed my father some forty years ago. I shuddered and sighed. Fate was unkind in making me appear forty years too soon.

Four hundred years earlier for such a reply a child would have been beaten, put into a dark room, tortured or disciplined into death or moral annihilation. Four thousand years ago, perhaps, in the Bronze Age, a bloodthirsty patriarch would have killed it outright. But forty thousand years back or thereabouts (I am not very strong on dates or hypotheses) the weak, matrilineal father might have smiled on his offspring even more indulgently than I was able to do, and without that wry twist on his face which comes, I suppose, from undigested patriarchal traditions. In any case, among my present-day Stone Age savages of the South Seas, I have heard children address a father as frankly and unceremoniously, with the perfect equivalent in native of the English "you dam' fool!" while he argued back without any show of patriarchal dignity.

. . . The relations between parents and children, as well as our views on them, are undoubtedly undergoing a profound change. As our knowledge increases the very facts themselves shift and modify under our eyes. Psychoanalysis has no sooner delved its complexes out of the Unconscious, than we see them enacted in real tragedies, individual and collective. The so-called freeing of children in the Soviet Republic has assumed catastrophic dimensions. The same new liberty takes less acute, but not less puzzling, forms, in the United States, in England and in Germany. The facts revealed by Judge Ben Lindsey, and in the works of W. I. Thomas, G. V. Hamilton and other students of juvenile delinquency, seem to disclose an entirely new world of precocious vice. The champions of the old order try, above all, to silence the denouncers, to put a taboo on any discussion. When that seems an insufficient remedy they suggest crude, repressive measures. The Fascist State and its imitative fellow-dictatorships of Southern Europe are Prussianizing education, and they thus hope to stem the evil and to produce, under stern state control, the ideal citizen and moral being at high speed and under high pressure.

The relations between the two generations are in the melting pot. New forces are at work, the old principles are in solution, and we really cannot foretell what the results will be. The sober scientific outlook, the weight of facts on which it must be based, the breadth of vision which it can give, seem more urgently needed than ever.

. . . At first sight, the typical savage family, as it is found among the vast majority of native tribes—of the few apparent exceptions I shall speak presently—seems hardly to differ at all from its civilized counterpart. Mother, father and children share the camp, the home, the food and the life. The intimacy of the family existence, the daily round of meals, the domestic occupations and outdoor work, the rest at night and the awakening to a new day, seem to run on strictly parallel lines in civilized and in savage societies, allowance being made for the difference in the level of culture. The members of the family are evidently as closely bound together in a native tribe as they are in an European society. Attached to each other, sharing life and most of its interests, exchanging counsel and help, company and cheer, and reciprocating in economic cooperation, the same bonds unite them as those of our family; similar distances and barriers separate them from other families. In Australia and among most North American Indians, in Melanesia and in Siberia, among the majority of African tribes and in South America, the individual undivided family stands out conspicuous, a definite social unit marked off from the rest of society by a clear line of division.[1] An observer would have to close his eyes or read himself blind in the works of Morgan, Kohler, Cunow or Rivers not to see this.

1. The generalizations of this essay will be fully substantiated in a forthcoming volume on *Primitive Kinship*. Compare also the article s.v. *Kinship* in the 14th Ed. *Encyclopaedia Britannica* and the writer's *The Family among the Australian Aborigines* (1913).

Had our ethnographic Robinson Crusoe an abundance of time for the study of native customs and sufficient intelligence and method to reflect upon them, he could substantiate his first impression by weighty arguments. Thus he would find that what could be called the instinctive foundation of maternal love is clearly traceable in his native society. The expectant mother is interested in her future offspring, she is absorbed in it from the moment of its birth, and in the carrying out of her social duties of suckling, nursing and tending it, she is supported by strong biological inclinations. In a tribe where there are such practices as infanticide or frequent adoption, the natural innate tendencies of maternal love may become rebelliously subservient to custom and tribal law, but they are never completely stifled or obliterated. In any case, once a child is spared, kept and nursed by the mother, maternal love grows into a passion. And this passion develops as the mother has to guide, watch over and educate her child, and lasts through life. To this the child responds with an exclusive personal attachment to the mother, and the mutual bond remains one of the strongest sentiments in any human society.

What might strike an observer with even greater force would be the position of the father. Expecting, perhaps, from a savage man a certain degree of ferocity towards wife and children, he might be astonished to find instead a kind and considerate husband and a tender father. At his worst—I mean in tribes where, through custom and tradition, he plays the not always amiable role of a stern patriarch—he is still the provider of the family, the helpmate at home, and the guardian of the children up to a certain age. At his best and mildest, in a typical matrilineal community, he is a drudge within the household, the assistant nurse of his children, the weaker and fonder of the two parents, and later on the most faithful and often the most intimate friend of his sons and daughters.

If our observer wanted to lay yet deeper foundations for his initial view of the permanence and importance of the individual family, he might point out a number of traditional usages, customary and legal norms referring to common habitation, household occupations and mutual economic duties—all of them making the undivided individual family a definite legal unit. The relation of mother to child, clearly dictated by natural inclinations, is yet not entirely left to them. The mother, besides feeling inclined to do all she does for her child, is none the less obliged to do it. An unnatural mother would be not only blamed but punished, and the bad or careless father would equally have to suffer under the lash of public opinion or be punished by some definite legal measure.

Thus, as likely as not, the final conclusion of our authority would be that in matters of kinship, family life and children, matters among primitive people are much as they are with us. That is to say, the personal bonds of kinship are the same in primitive tribes and in civilized societies; and the affection within the family, the habits, uses and laws of the savage household are entirely reminiscent of a peasant's or poor man's home in

Europe. The mother, tied by psysiological bonds to her children, fulfills the same part as every mother has to fulfill; the father in a savage community seems to be there for exactly the same purpose as the patriarchal head of the family in modern European society; to watch over the safety of his children, to provide for them and to guide them through life.

The picture here attributed to a supposed ethnographic Robinson Crusoe is not imaginary. It is just this sort of information about parental love, the kindly treatment of children, their obedience and affection in return, the enduring of family bonds throughout life, which some of our earliest and best authorities present in their ethnographic accounts. Nor is this picture at all unreal, though it is certainly one-sided. Our early ethnographic information, which shows us the individual family as a universal unit in mankind, which emphasizes motherhood, dwells on the impressive facts of family intimacy and common habitation, and tells us what the native feels and how he behaves; this information gives us not only a true picture, but it brings into relief some of the most essential and valuable features of kinship. . . .

Puzzles of Kinship

Longer residence among the savages, better acquaintance with their language and culture, and above all patient and mature reflection upon what he saw, would have suggested to our observer certain questions and revealed certain anomalies in the typical family life. Thus, for instance, had he been stranded in a matrilineal society he would, in due course, have been impressed by the constant appearance of the mother's brother, by the assumption of authority on his part over his sister's household, and by the number of obligations which he had to fulfill towards it; and this, despite the fact that the husband was still on the spot, endowed with a great deal of marital and paternal influence.

Following up this line of inquiry our observer would have been found to strike the rich vein of native theories of procreation and descent. Perhaps he would have found that in the tribe where he lived the natives had no idea of physiological paternity, that instead they alleged that certain spiritual agencies were responsible for the birth of the child. If, fired by this discovery, our observer had traveled to other countries to follow up his research, he would have been extremely puzzled to find a surprising variety in theories of procreation, in the conclusions drawn from them, and in the institutions which embody these theories.

In certain tribes the mother is regarded as the only parent related by the bond of body and blood to the child. Maternal kinship is exclusive, the mother's brother is head of the family, the father is not united by any kinship tie to the child, there are no legal rights, no inheritance, no solidarity in the agnatic line. Yet, and this might have puzzled our observer considerably, the father, even in such tribes, is in many respects very much like the ordinary patriarchal father, and his position is defined by certain rival customs and laws, apparently in disharmony with the general matrilineal constitution.

Again, in another community, the observer would have found that, in spite of the ignorance of fatherhood, kinship is traced in the paternal line; the mother has very little influence over the legal affairs of the household and no influence in the determining of descent. In some cultures, on the contrary, the father would be considered as the only real procreative agent, while the mother is there regarded but as the soil that receives the seed.

In yet another community descent—that is, the system of determining the child's social status—is reckoned neither through father nor through mother, but is determined by the circumstances of the child's birth, or by some social act performed during the woman's pregnancy or after her confinement, as is the case among the Todas, in Central Australia, and in certain parts of Oceania.

Thus in the study of the problems of descent the inquirer would be led into a complicated network of social rules, beliefs and ideas, astonishingly complex, abstruse and involved, if compared with his initial conclusion that "in the matter of kinship things are much the same with the savages as they are with us."

. . .

The concept of the Initial Situation of Kinship, which I first introduced in my article on *Kinship* in the 14th Edition of the *Encyclopaedia Britannica,* places the emphasis on the study of the first stages of kinship sentiments. And, indeed, if the study of any and all human sentiments must be done along the life history of the individual, in a biographical treatment so to speak, this must be done in the case of kinship above all things. Because in kinship the most typical and the fundamental process is that in which biological facts are transformed into social forces, and unless this be understood well, the whole question is placed on a false foundation and we get the chaos of controversy with which we are faced at present.

It is hardly necessary, perhaps, to add that in laying down the problem of the Initial Situation we are doing more than merely introducing a concept and a terminological entity. In doing this we are really opening a number of definitely empirical questions referring to the cultural transformation of the biological elements, sex, maternity and fatherhood; we are focusing our argument on the linking-up of courtship, marriage and kinship; last, but not least, we are demanding a clear answer to the question as to the relation between procreation, domesticity, and the legal or political aspects of kinship.

Let us then proceed to the analysis of the Initial Situation of kinship and try, through a comparative survey along the widest range of variations, to see whether some general principles can be established with reference to it.

Individual Maternity as a Cultural and Social Fact

Maternity is the most dramatic and spectacular as well as the most obvious fact in the propagation of species. A woman, whether in Mayfair or on a coral island of the Pacific, has to undergo a period of hardship and discomfort; she has to pass through a crisis of pain and danger, she has, in fact, to risk her own life in order to give life to another human being. Her connection with the child, who remains for a long time part of her own body, is intimate and integral. It is associated with physiological effects and strong emotions, it culminates in the crisis of birth, and it extends naturally into lactation.

Now what is it that the advocates of "group-motherhood" want us to believe? Neither more nor less than that, with birth, the individual link is severed and becomes merged in an imaginary bond of "collective motherhood." They affirm that such powerful sociological forces are at work, such strong cultural influences, that they can override and destroy the individual attitude of mother-to-child. Is this true? Do we really find any sociological mechanisms which succeed in severing the mother-child relationship, dumping each into the group of collective mothers and collective children? As a matter of fact all these hypotheses are pure figments and, looking at facts as we did through the eyes of our imaginary observer, we were led to the conclusion that maternity is as individual culturally as it is biologically. The point is of such capital importance, however, that we must look more in detail at the arguments by which individual maternity has been challenged by such writers as Rivers and Briffault.

They have alleged that communal suckling, the frequent and indiscriminate adoption or exchange of infants, joint cares and joint responsibilities, and a sort of joint ownership of children create an identical bond between the one child and several mothers, which would obviously mean that every mother would have also a group of joint children. In these views there is also implied the assumption that conception, pregnancy and childbirth, which obviously are individual and not communal, are completely ignored by society as irrelevant factors, and that they play no part in the development of maternal sentiments.

Let us examine the implication of the group-motherhood hypothesis first, and then decide whether a communal game of share and exchange in children and infants is, or ever could have been, played.

Now, in the first place, it is a universal fact that conception, pregnancy, childbirth and suckling are sociologically determined; that they

are subjects of ritual, or religious and moral conceptions, of legal obligations and privileges. There is not one single instance on record of a
primitive culture in which the process of gestation is left to nature alone.
Conception, as a rule, is believed to be due as much to spiritual as to
physiological causes. Conception, moreover, is not a process which is
allowed to take its natural course as a result of prenuptial intercourse.
Between the freedom of sexual life and the freedom of becoming a mother
a sharp distinction is drawn in all human societies including our own, and
this is one of the most important sociological factors of the problem and to
it we shall presently return.

Most important of all, a legitimate, socially approved of conception
must always be based on an individual legal contract—the contract of
marriage.²

Once conception has taken place the prospective mother has always
to keep taboos and observe ceremonial rules. She has to abstain from
certain foods and carry out lustrations; she has to undergo more or less
complicated pregnancy ceremonies; she has to wear special decorations
and clothes; she is regarded sometimes as holy, sometimes as unclean;
last, not least, she is very often sexually tabooed even to her own husband. All these ceremonial, moral and legal rules are, by the very nature
of the facts, individual. Their motive is invariably the welfare of the future
offspring. Most of them establish individual ties between the prospective
mother and her future offspring. Maternity is thus determined in anticipation by a whole cultural apparatus of rules and prescriptions, it is established by society as a moral fact, and, in all this, the tie of kinship between
mother and child is defined by tradition long before birth, and defined as
an individual bond.

At the crisis itself, that is, at birth, the ceremonies of purification, the
idea of special dangers which unite mother and child and separate them
from the rest of the community, customs and usages connected with
midwifery and early lactation—this whole cultural apparatus continues to
reaffirm and to reshape the bond of maternity, and to individualize it with
force and clearness. These anticipatory moral influences always put the
responsibility upon one woman and mark her out as the sociological or
cultural mother over and above her physiological claims to that title.

All this might appear to refer only to the mother. What about the
child? We can indeed completely discount Freud's assumption that there
is an innate bond of sexual attraction between mother and child; we must
reject further his whole hypothesis of "the return to the womb." With all
this we have to credit psychoanalysis with having proved that the earliest
infantile experiences, provided that they are not completely broken and
obliterated in childhood, form a foundation of the greatest importance for

2. In order to avoid possible misunderstandings I should like to remind the reader that
plural marriages, such as polygyny and polyandry, are always based on an individual legal
contract between one man and one woman, though these contracts may be repeated.

the later individual relationship between the child and its mother.

Now here again, the continuity between prenatal cares, the earliest infantile seclusion of mother and child, and the period of lactation, which in native society is much longer than with us, the continuity of all these experiences and their individual unity is in primitive societies as great as, if not greater than, with us.

And this is the point at which we have to deal with the unprofitable assumption of communal lactation. In the relatively small savage communities where there occur perhaps one or two childbirths in a year within reach of each other the idea of mothers synchronizing conception and pregnancy and clubbing together to carry out lactatory group-motherhood, at the greatest inconvenience to themselves, the babies and the whole community, is so preposterous that even now I cannot think how it could ever have been promulgated by Dr. Rivers and upheld by Mr. Briffault.

As to a "communalizing" adoption, in the first place, even where it is most frequent, as in certain Polynesian and Melanesian communities, it simply substitutes one maternity for another. It proves undoubtedly that cultural parenthood can override the biological basis, but it does not introduce anything even remotely like group-maternity. In fact the severance of one bond before another is established is a further proof of the individuality and exclusiveness of motherhood. In the second place the custom of indiscriminate adoption is prevalent among a few savage societies only.

We can thus say that motherhood is always individual. It is never allowed to remain a mere biological fact. Social and cultural influences always indorse and emphasize the original individuality of the biological fact. These influences are so strong that in the case of adoption they may override the biological tie and substitute a cultural one for it. But statistically speaking, the biological ties are almost invariably merely reinforced, redetermined and remolded by cultural ones. This remolding makes motherhood in each culture a relationship specific to that culture, different from all other motherhoods, and correlated to the whole social structure of the community. This means that the problem of maternity cannot be dismissed as a zoological fact, that it should be studied by every field-worker in his own area, and that the theory of cultural motherhood should have been made the foundation of the general theory of kinship.

The Principle of Legitimacy and the Right to Sexual Freedom

What about the father? As far as his biological role is concerned he might well be treated as a drone. His task is to impregnate the female and then to disappear. And yet in all human societies the father is regarded by tradition as indispensable. The woman has to be married before she is allowed legitimately to conceive. Roughly speaking, an unmarried mother is under a ban, a fatherless child is a bastard. This is by no means only a European or Christian prejudice; it is the attitude found amongst most barbarous and savage peoples as well. Where the unmarried mother is at a premium and her offspring a desirable possession the father is forced upon them by positive instead of negative sanctions.

Let us put it in more precise and abstract terms. Among the conditions which define conception as a sociologically legitimate fact there is one of fundamental importance. The most important moral and legal rule concerning the physiological side of kinship is that no child should be brought into the world without a man—and one man at that—assuming the role of sociological father, that is, guardian and protector, the male link between the child and the rest of the community.

I think that this generalization amounts to a universal sociological law and as such I have called it in some of my previous writings *The Principle of Legitimacy*.[3] The form which the principle of legitimacy assumes varies according to the laxity or stringency which obtains regarding prenuptial intercourse; according to the value set upon virginity or the contempt for it; according to the ideas held by the natives as to the mechanism of procreation; above all, according as to whether the child is a burden or an asset to its parents. Which means according as to whether the unmarried mother is more attractive because of her offspring or else degraded and ostracized on that account.

Yet through all these variations there runs the rule that the father is indispensable for the full sociological status of the child as well as of its mother, that the group consisting of a woman and her offspring is sociologically incomplete and illegitimate. The father, in other words, is necessary for the full legal status of the family.

In order to understand the nature and importance of the principle of legitimacy it is necessary to discuss the two aspects of procreation which are linked together biologically and culturally, yet linked by nature and culture so differently that many difficulties and puzzles have arisen for the anthropologist. Sex and parenthood are obviously linked biologically. Sexual intercourse leads at times to conception. Conception always means pregnancy and pregnancy at times means childbirth. We see that in the chain there are at least two possibilities of a hiatus; sexual intercourse by no means always leads to conception, and pregnancy can be interrupted by abortion and thus not lead to childbirth.

The moral, customary and legal rules of most human communities step in, taking advantage of the two weak links in the chain, and in a most remarkable manner dissociate the two sides of procreation, that is, sex

3. Compare article s.v. *Kinship* in the *Encyclopaedia Britannica*, 14th Edition; also *Sex and Repression* (1927) and Chapter VI of *The Family among the Australian Aborigines* (1913). In this latter the relevant facts are presented though the term is not used.

and parenthood. Broadly speaking, it may be said that freedom of inter-course though not universally is yet generally prevalent in human societies. Freedom of conception outside marriage is, however, never allowed, or at least in extremely few communities and under very excep-tional circumstances.

Briefly to substantiate this statement: it is clear that in those societies, primitive or civilized, where prenuptial intercourse is regarded as immoral and illegitimate, marriage is the *conditio sine qua non* of legitimate children—that is, children having full social status in the com-munity.

In the second place, in most communities which regard prenuptial intercourse as perfectly legitimate, marriage is still regarded as essential to equip the child with a full tribal position. This is very often achieved without any punitive sanctions, by the mere fact that as soon as preg-nancy sets in a girl and her lover have to marry. Often in fact pregnancy is a prerequisite of marriage or the final legal symptom of its conclusion.

There are tribes, again, where an unmarried mother is definitely penalized and so are her children. What is done under such conditions by lovers who want to live together sexually and yet not to produce children is difficult to say. Having had in my own field-work to deal with the case in point, I was yet unable to arrive at a satisfactory solution. Contracep-tives, I am firmly convinced, do not exist in Melanesia, and abortion is not sufficiently frequent to account for the great scarcity of illegitimate children. As a hypothesis, I venture to submit that promiscuous inter-course, while it lasts, reduces the fertility of woman. If this side of the whole question still remains a puzzle it only proves that more research, both physiological and sociological, must be done in order fully to throw light upon the principle of legitimacy.

There is still one type of social mechanism through which the princi-ple of legitimacy operates, and that is under conditions where a child is an asset. There an unmarried mother need not trouble about her sociological status, because the fact of having children only makes her the more desir-able, and she speedily acquires a husband. He will not trouble whether the child is the result of his love-making or not. But whether the male is primed to assume his paternity, or whether the child and mother are penalized, the principle of legitimacy obtains throughout mankind; the group of mother and child is incomplete and the sociological position of the father is regarded universally as indispensable.

The Control of Sexuality by Parenthood

Liberty of parenthood, therefore, is not identical with liberty of sexual intercourse. And the principle of legitimacy leads us to another very important generalization, namely, that the relations of sexuality to parenthood must be studied with reference to the only relevant link: marriage, conceived as a contract legitimizing offspring.

From the foregoing considerations, it is clear that marriage cannot be defined as the licensing of sexual intercourse, but rather as the licensing of parenthood.

Since marriage is the institution through which the inchoate, at times even disruptive, drives of sex are transformed and organized into the principal system of social forces, it is clear that sexuality must be discussed, defined and classified in relation to marriage. From our point of view we have to inquire as to what is its function in relation to marriage.

We have first to inquire, is chartered and limited sexual liberty subversive and destructive of marriage and family; does it ever run counter to these institutions? Or, on the contrary, is regulated and limited intercourse outside matrimony one of those cultural arrangements which allow of a greater stability of marriage and the family, of easier adjustment within it, and of a more suitable choice of partner?

It is obvious that once we erect chastity as a positive ideal, once we accept the Christian principle of monogamous marriage as the only decent way of regarding this institution, we have prejudged all these questions and stultified the whole inquiry. And it is astounding how even those who attack the institutions of Christian morality and marriage and regard themselves as absolutely free of preconceptions, still remain under the influence of the ideal or at least of its pretenses. Thus all sociologists, from Bachofen to Briffault, were inclined to regard communistic orgies, relaxations of the marital tie, forms of prenuptial freedom, as "survivals," as traces of a primeval sexual communism. That, I think, is an entirely wrong view, due to an involuntary tendency to regard sexual intercourse outside marriage as something anomalous, as something which contravenes marriage; a view directly implied in our Christian ideal of monogamy.

Let us look at facts in the correct perspective; see, that is, how sexuality is related to marriage in various primitive communities. Let us first classify the various types of regulation in relation to marriage. Those communities where virginity is a prerequisite of decent and legal marriage, where it is enforced by such surgical operations as infibulation; where wives are jealously guarded and adultery is a rigorously punished offense—those communities present no problem to us. There sex is as absolutely subordinated to marriage as in the Christian monogamous ideal, and far more so than in our Western practice. But such communities are comparatively rare, especially at a primitive level, and generally we find some form of customary license outside marriage.

Here again we must distinguish with direct reference to marriage, which really means to parenthood. Prenuptial license, that is, the liberty of free intercourse given to unmarried youths and girls, is by far the most prevalent form of chartered freedom, as well as the most important. What is its normal course and how is it related to marriage? Does it as a rule develop habits of profligacy; does it lead to a more and more promiscuous attitude?

Even a study of those forms which are nearest to us and should be best known—that is, the prenuptial usages of European peasants—should have furnished the clue to the comparative anthropologist. The German peasant speaks of "trial nights"; he justifies his institution of *Fensterln* (windowing, i.e., entering through the window) by the commonsense axiom that unless he has full sexual experience of his future bride he is unable to make a sound empirical choice. The same view is taken by the savage Melanesian, by the West African, by the Bantu, and by the North American Indian; last, but not least, by some of the new generation —young intellectuals. We have, therefore, in prenuptial license, in the first place, an institutionalized method of arranging marriage by trial and error.

And this is by no means a mere pretense, though often the desire for trial leads to errors. In fact, however, the general course of prenuptial intrigue conforms naturally to the pattern of the principle. The number of intrigues does not increase, the appetite for change and variety does not grow with experience. On the contrary, with age and a ripening insight into the nature of sexual relations, two definite phenomena occur. On the one hand the character of the intrigues changes: they become stronger and deeper. New elements enter into them; the appreciation of personality and the integration of erotic attraction with the spiritual character of the lover. On the other hand, and correlated with the first process, we find that the mere attraction of sexual experiences loses a great deal of its charm.

We see, therefore, that if we look at prenuptial sexuality in a dispassionate sociological spirit, and if we contemplate it in its relation to marriage, we find that it fulfills two functions. It serves as an empirical foundation to a mature, more spiritual choice of a mate, and it serves to drain off the cruder sexual motives from affection and attraction. It is thus, on the one hand, the sowing of wild oats, on the other a trial-and-error method of concluding marriage.

If we look at the relaxations of the matrimonial bond we see that they fulfill a not altogether dissimilar function. There is the temporary exchange of wives. We find it in wife-lending at tribal feasts or during the occurrence of catastrophes; in the institution of *pirraru* in Central Australia; in the prolonged wife-lending among the Eskimos or in Siberia. Such customs simply mean that from time to time a man and a woman already married are allowed to have sexual experiences with other people.

Sexual, let us keep in mind, is not synonymous with conjugal, though the polite parlance of puritanic hypocrisy has made it so. Temporary cohabitation, above all, never implies community of children. Its function consists, in the first place, in that it once more satisfies in an approved, licensed way the desire for change which is inherent in the sexual impulse. In the second place it sometimes leads to the discovery that the new, temporary partnership is more suitable, and so, through divorce, it leads to a marriage on the whole more satisfactory. Here, again, postmarital extra-connubial sexuality is an arrangement both of trial and error, and also a safety vent. The first function is more prominent in the standardized forms of wife-lending for more prolonged periods; the second, in the occasions of orgiastic license at big tribal festivals, where often many of the usual bonds and restrictions are suspended.

. . . We see, therefore, that parenthood and marriage furnish the key to the functional understanding of regulated sexuality. We see that sexual regulations, the liberties and the taboos, constitute the road to marriage and the way of escape from its too rigid bonds and consequent tragic complications. The sexual impulse has to be selective in human as well as in animal communities, but its selectiveness under culture is more complicated in that it has to involve cultural as well as biological values. Trial and error are necessary and with this is definitely connected the interest in variation and impulse towards novelty. To satisfy the fundamental function of sex we have the institution which makes full sex, that is parenthood, exclusive and individual. To satisfy the correlated selective components of sex, we have the dependent institutions of regulated license. To sum up, we have found that parenthood gives us the key to marriage, through the principle of legitimacy, and that marriage is the key to a right understanding of sexual customs. It may be added at once that the dissociation of some sexual experiences from the primitive idea of marriage, coupled with the real interrelation of the two, yields to the sociologist an interesting background for the consideration of modern problems of sexuality, marriage and divorce.

William J. Goode

A Deviant Case:
Illegitimacy in the Caribbean

Over a generation ago Malinowski enunciated a principle which he said amounted to a universal sociological law, that "no child should be brought into the world without a man—and one man at that—assuming the role of sociological father. . . ."[1] This rule is not based on the social disapproval of premarital or extramarital sexual freedom. Malinowski's Trobrianders, for example, indulged in considerable sex play before marriage, but were shocked at illegitimacy. Rather, the rule expresses the interest of the society in fixing responsibility for the child upon a specific individual. Marriage, therefore, is not primarily the legitimation of sex, but the legitimation of parenthood.[2] Whether Malinowski's principle is indeed a universal sociological law has not been analyzed, except to the degree that the recurring debate as to whether the "nuclear family" is universal implicitly includes that principle.[3] It seems safe enough to claim at least that all societies have family systems and that possibly a sociological father is required everywhere.[4]

1. Bronislaw Malinowski, "Parenthood, the Basis of Social Structure," in V. F. Calverton and Samuel D. Schmalhausen, editors, *The New Generation*, New York: Macaulay, 1930, pp. 137–138. [See pp. 51–63 of this volume.]
2. Malinowski was puzzled as to how the Trobrianders could be sexually so free without numerous illegitimates, especially since they denied any connection between sexual intercourse and pregnancy and took no contraceptive precautions. It was not until W. F. Ashley-Montagu's *Coming Into Being Among the Australian Aborigines*, London: Routledge, 1937, that the solution seemed to be clear.
   See also M. F. Ashley-Montagu, *The Reproductive Development of the Female*, New York: Julian, 1957.
3. For a recent discussion of this point, see Melford E. Spiro, "Is the Family Universal?" *American Anthropologist*, 56 (October, 1954), pp. 839–846.
4. The most notable case which raises doubts is the Nayar of Malabar Strait. See K. M. Panikkar, "Some Aspects of Nayar Life," *Journal of the Royal Anthropological Institute*, 48 (July-December, 1918), esp. pp. 260 ff; E. Kathleen Gough, "Changing Kinship Usages in the Setting of Political and Economic Change among the Nayar of Malabar," *Journal of the Royal Anthropological Institute*, 81 (Parts I and II, 1951), pp. 71–88. Gough's latest report ("The Nayars and the Definition of Marriage," *Journal of the Royal Anthropological Institute*, 89 [1959], p. 31) asserts that Nayar marriage does establish paternity legally. Another possible case is the Minang-Kabau; see E. N. Loeb, "Patrilineal and Matrilineal Organization in Sumatra, Part 2," *American Anthropologist*, 36 (January-March, 1934), pp. 26–56.

Illegitimacy in the Caribbean

Malinowski's principle is not refuted by data from the United States or Western Europe, where illegitimacy rates range from perhaps four or five per cent to about eleven percent.[5] However, in the Caribbean area illegitimacy rates are often over fifty percent, as Table 1 shows.

Under such conditions, doubt may be raised as to whether a "sociological father" exists, and indeed various writers have spoken of a

TABLE 1. Illegitimacy Rates in Selected Caribbean Political Units[6]

Political Unit	Year	Percent
British Guiana	1955	35
French Guiana	1956	65
Surinam (excluding Bush Negroes and aborigines)	1953	34
Barbados	1957	70
Bermuda	1957	30
Dominican Republic	1957	61
Guadeloupe	1956	42
Jamaica	1954	72
Antigua	1957	65
Martinique	1956	48
Trinidad and Tobago	1956	47
Grenada	1957	71
Puerto Rico	1955	28
Haiti	—	67–85

5. In Iceland, illegitimate births constituted 27.9 percent of live births in 1950, and the rate in Stockholm and a few other areas in Sweden has remained at about 15 percent in recent years. Cf. Meyer Nimkoff. "Illegitimacy," *Encyclopaedia Britannica*, 1954.

6. All figures except those for Puerto Rico, British Guiana, Surinam, Dominican Republic, Trinidad and Tobago, Grenada, and Haiti were taken from the United Nations Year Book Questionnaire for the years in question. Data were furnished to the U.N. by the statistical offices of the country, and contain all the errors of their own registration procedures. Data for other countries, excluding Haiti and the Dominican Republic, were kindly furnished by the Caribbean Commission. The Dirección General de Estadística of the Dominican Republic graciously sent me the figure for 1957. I have found no recent figure for Cuba; presumably it was 30 percent in 1939. For Surinam, Rudolf van Lier, *Samenleving in een Grensgebied,* 's-Gravenhage: Marthinus Nijhoff, 1949, p. 287, gives 70 percent for 1940. The rate has also dropped in British Guiana from the 41 percent reported in 1946 in *British Guiana Annual Report of the Registrar-General, 1954*, Georgetown, Demerara, British Guiana, 1956, p. 9. I have found no official figure for Haiti. Bastien reports two-thirds for Marbial (Remy Bastien, *La Familia Rural Haitiana*, Mexico: Libra, 1951, p. 85); George E. Simpson reports about 85 percent for one Haitian area in "Sexual and Family Institutions in Northern Haiti," *American Anthropologist*, 44 (October-December, 1942), p. 664.

"matrifocal" family.[7] Certainly so high a rate of deviation would suggest that the norm, if it does exist, might have a very different meaning than in a society in which the rate is less, say, than ten percent. But we must keep in mind that Malinowski was stating a proposition about a *cultural* element: he asserted that the *norm* would always be found, not that the members of the society would obey it under specified conditions.

It is precisely with reference to Malinowski's principle that many students of the Caribbean have taken an opposing position—without developing its implications for family theory. The claim has often been made for various Caribbean lands that when a couple is living together in a consensual union "the family may be said to exist in much the same way as it does in peasant communities throughout the world,"[8] and the child therefore suffers no disadvantage from being illegitimate.[9] Henriques, also writing about Jamaica, comments that there is no moral sanction against "concubinage," by which he means a man and woman keeping house together and raising children, and even claims that respectable black people would rather have their daughter become mistress or concubine to a white or fair colored man than marry a black one.[10] Otherwise put, the consensual union is the marriage form of the lower classes in the Caribbean, and is "sociologically as legitimate" as a legal union. It is, in short, a "cultural alternative," as permissible a way of founding a family as any other.[11] If this interpretation is correct, Malinowski's principle would be erroneous, and one of the apparently major functions of the father would have to be redefined as unessential.

Comments similar to those given above about Jamaica have been made about other Caribbean areas. Herskovits and Herskovits make a similar claim for Trinidad, noting what a "false perspective on the thinking of the people is given by the application of legal terms such as 'legitimate' and 'illegitimate' to the offspring."[12] Similarly, they assert that "there is no social disability imposed by the community because of

7. "One of the regularities of social organization, which has appeared in the literature from Herskovits to Henriques, is the concept of the 'matrifocal' family." Vera Rubin, "Cultural Perspectives in Caribbean Research," in Vera Rubin, editor, *Caribbean Studies: A Symposium,* Jamaica: Institute of Social and Economic Research, 1957, p. 117. 'Such comments are often applicable as well to one period in the development of the Negro family in this country. Cf. E. Franklin Frazier, *The Negro Family in the United States,* New York: Dryden, revised edition, 1948.

8. T. S. Simey, *Welfare and Planning in the West Indies,* Oxford: Clarendon Press, 1956, p. 15.

9. "The fact of illegitimate birth is one completely taken for granted. An illegitimate child does not consider himself disadvantaged. . . ." *Ibid.*, p. 88.

10. Fernando Henriques, *Family and Colour in Jamaica,* London: Eyre and Spottiswoode, 1953, pp. 87, 90.

11. "Thus, the matrifocal family . . . is a subcultural norm. . . ." John V. Murra, "Discussion," in *Caribbean Studies, op. cit.,* p. 76.

12. Melville J. Herskovits and Frances S. Herskovits, *Trinidad Village,* New York: Knopf, 1947, p. 17.

legitimacy or illegitimacy."[13] The common-law marriage is for many the accepted form.[14]

With respect to Haitian children of a placée union which is legalized, of a legal union, or of a union outside of an existing marriage the claim is made that "none of these classes of children are at any special social disadvantage."[15] With reference to the forms of Haitian unions: "In the main, especially in the countryside, socially sanctioned matings which do not enjoy the approval of the Church endure as long and hold as respected a place in the community. . . ."[16] In a parallel vein, Bastien remarks that when a man has "good intentions" with respect to a girl, but does not have enough money with which to marry, he may "establish himself" with the girl, with marriage as a publicly acknowledged, later goal, but does not thereby "incur the scorn of the community."[17]

In Martinique, we are told, in place of the rule of legitimacy, which is absent here, other values have emerged such as ingroup solidarity, status equality, and conviviality, which express family organization.[18] There is "no unequivocally preferred type of bond between parents."[19] The legitimate and illegitimate share the same status.

Although the illegitimacy rate in Puerto Rico is lower than in the areas noted above, here too the claim has been made that the rule of legitimacy fails. It is said of the consensual union that it is "a cultural alternative," that is, marriage is split into two culturally permissible alternatives.[20] Similarly, ". . . the prevalence of consensual unions ought to be considered in terms of local lower-class conceptions of what is considered 'moral.' " It is not that the lower class prefer illegal behavior, but that consensual unions are not seen as immoral.[21] It is asserted, too, that "the consensual union is considered a binding marriage truly cemented at the birth of the first child."[22]

At first glance, then, Malinowski's rule of legitimacy is refuted. A substantial number of societies in the West appear not to accept the norm.

13. *Ibid.*, pp. 82–83; see also p. 107.
14. Lloyd Braithwaite, "Social Stratification in Trinidad," *Social and Economic Studies,* 2 (October, 1953), p. 125.
15. Melville J. Herskovits, *Life in a Haitian Valley,* New York: Knopf, 1937, p. 118.
16. *Ibid.*, p. 106.
17. Bastien, *op. cit.*, pp. 72–73. However, Bastien also presents the prestige rankings of the three forms of matings.
18. Mariam Kreiselman, *The Caribbean Family. A Case Study in Martinique,* Columbia University, Ph.D. thesis, 1958, pp. 271, 292.
19. *Ibid,* p. viii.
20. J. Mayone Stycos, *Family and Fertility in Puerto Rico,* New York: Columbia University Press, 1955, p. 110. I assume here the meaning of "culturally equivalent" or "normatively equal."
21. Sidney W. Mintz, "Cañamelar, The Subculture of a Rural Sugar Plantation Proletariat," in Julian Steward *et al., The People of Puerto Rico,* Urbana: University of Illinois Press, 1956, p. 377.
22. Robert A. Manners, "Tabara: Subcultures of a Tobacco and Mixed Crop Municipality," in *The People of Puerto Rico, op. cit.*, p. 144.

If this is the case, then several fundamental notions in family theory would have to be discarded.

Yet a closer examination of these and other reports prove conclusively that the norm exists, since in fact marriage is the ideal, and those who violate the rule do suffer penalties. The fact that perhaps a majority of certain of these populations do live in unions outside marriage, at some time in their lives, does not change the normative status of the rule. On the other hand, as we shall later indicate, Malinowski's rule must nevertheless be reformulated.

Let us first look more closely at Jamaica. As against the assertion that illegitimacy is not stigmatized, we note the opposing facts. Both upper- and middle-class opinion is set against "concubinage."[23] The priests may shame the couple about the matter. When a young girl is found to be pregnant, her family is angry.[24] Few men (Rocky Roads) allow their women to bring their illegitimate children into the union, if they do marry.[25] In the same community, illegitimate children are subjected to more physical rejection and pressures of sibling rivalry.[26] Moreover, as individuals move through the life cycle, an increasing proportion are actually married, a phenomenon which would be inexplicable if the consensual unions were backed by a set of alternative norms. This process is illustrated by the proportions of persons ever married by selected ages in the major areas of the British West Indies, as shown in Table 2.[27] Thus, though the average British West Indian ages at marriage are among the highest in the world (for example, for Jamaica, 34.1 years for males; for Barbados, 31.7, and for Grenada, 33.0[28]), most individuals do marry. In sum, these various mating forms are "not regarded as alternative forms of conjugal associations between which any individual was free to choose."[29]

Similarly, in Trinidad, a couple may finally marry after living to-

23. Henriques, op. cit., pp. 87, 164.

24. Ibid., p. 88. See also Edith Clarke, My Mother Who Fathered Me, London: Allen & Unwin, 1957, p. 99; and Kreiselman, op. cit., p. 189.

25. Yehudi Cohen, "Structure and Function: Family Organization and Socialization in a Jamaican Community," American Anthropologist, 58 (August, 1956), p. 669.

26. Ibid., p. 672.

27. G. W. Roberts, "Some Aspects of Mating and Fertility in the West Indies," Population Studies, 8 (March, 1955), p. 223. The figures for Jamaica in Table 2 presumably refer to 1943.

28. Ibid., p. 205. More fundamental data are the actual expressions of norms and ideals, to be found in Judith Blake's Family Structure: The Social Context of Reproduction, Ph.D. thesis, Columbia University, 1959, a study of the lower-class Jamaican family. It is the first detailed investigation of the mechanisms through which the norms lose much of their coercive power. For a preliminary report from this study, see Blake, "Family Instability and Reproductive Behavior in Jamaica," Current Research in Human Fertility, New York: Milbank Fund, 1955, pp. 24–41.

29. Clarke, op. cit., pp. 77–78. It is significant that Clarke and Blake, who appear to be the only investigators to take seriously the Jamaican's own normative statements, assert unequivocally the normative underpinnings of a legal marriage.

TABLE 2. British West Indies: Percent of Mates Ever Married by Age, 1946

Age	Jamaica	Barbados	Windwards	Leewards
20–24	10.1	8.5	4.1	4.0
25–34	21.0	37.6	27.6	27.3
35–44	41.9	61.7	54.9	53.4
45–54	55.0	70.8	68.2	63.7
55–64	66.3	75.2	78.4	75.5
65 and over	74.7	85.2	83.1	78.9

gether for some time, "for the position it gives the family." Among other things, "marriage is . . . a prestige phenomenon in terms of social or religious values." Though a couple will usually begin life together as "keepers," "such an episode is outside correct procedure." The unmarried keeper woman wears no ring, and only the married woman is called *Madam*.[30] Many people who rise in class find that their new rank is incompatible with the type of union they once entered. Moreover, when working-class women quarrel, one may point out that the other is not properly married.[31]

Although the case of Haiti seems more complex, the same conclusion seems inescapable. The prestige from the legal, Church union is of sufficient significance to "motivate weddings at which the children and even children of the principals act as attendants."[32] The legal union cannot be broken as easily as the plaçage. When the unmarried girl becomes pregnant, she is beaten.[33] The woman in a placée union cannot demand as much from her man, and her children have no right to the name of the father.[34] Most persons would prefer to marry, and this is especially true of women.[35] Contemporary pressures are increasing the proportion who marry, but some gradations of prestige remain.[36] The plaçage is not stable: "Perhaps three-fourths of the peasant men, and possibly more, have or have had at one time one or more mates in addition to a legal wife or *femme caille*."[37] "The consciousness of their social inferiority so

30. Herskovits and Herskovits, *op. cit.*, pp. 82, 84, 87, 93–94.
31. Lloyd Braithwaite, "Social Stratification in Trinidad," *Social and Economic Studies*, 2 (October, 1953), pp. 125, 126.
32. Herskovits, *op. cit.*, pp. 106, 107.
33. *Ibid.*, p. 110; George Eaton Simpson, "Sexual and Familial Institutions in Northern Haiti," *American Anthropologist*, 44 (October-December, 1942), p. 665.
34. Herskovits, *op. cit.*, pp. 116, 119.
35. Simpson, *op. cit.*, pp. 655, 658.
36. Rhoda Metraux, *Kith and Kin*, Ph.D. thesis, Columbia University, 1951, pp. 197, 205–209.
37. Simpson, *op. cit.*, p. 656. The *femme caille* shares her consort's house. Bastien, *op. cit.*, p. 73, gives three main categories of unions, in order of social rank: (1) marriage; (2) a union established with the idea of later marriage; and (3) the ordinary plaçage, some forms of which involve several women living apart from one another.

troubles . . . [them] . . . that few resist the temptation to explain the cause of their situation. . . ."[38]

In Martinique, too, parents are angry at the pregnancy of the unmarried girl, who may have to leave her home. When talking about the consensual relationships of others, the term "concubine" is used. Many men will promise marriage, but deceive the girl. In a few reported cases of girls having babies, the parents pretended that the children were their own.[39] The consensual union is easily dissolved, and no social obligations are incurred by entering it.[40]

Perhaps more conclusive for Martinique is an important finding, which grew out of an effort to understand the *fête*. In possibly every study of illegitimacy in the Caribbean, people are described as saying—most researchers have accepted this assertion—that they cannot marry because they cannot afford the wedding feast, without which the ceremony is a mockery. The couple will be laughed at later. The "cost of the wedding" is not the church expenses; in every country the Catholic Church (or others, where they are important) has offered nearly free weddings—but with rare acceptance. A few observers have doubted that the expense of the *fête* was the crucial item, even though it is substantial, emphasizing rather that the *fête* is an expression of community solidarity, a *rite de passage*, and a community validation of the union. Kreiselman is unique among observers in offering and, within limits, testing the hypothesis that most persons who can afford to live *en ménage* can also afford a *fête* and therefore a marriage, but that most who do not marry early or later do not have the same rank.[41]

Whether the rank differences among people of a lower stratum are so crucial, and whether a broad sample of stable consensual unions would show that it is mainly those of equal status who marry, remains to be seen. But if this is the case even in Capesterre (Martinique), the relationship shows that the rule of legitimacy holds there. For the rule has as a major function the prevention of unions between wrong lineages, and in nearly every society the rules of marriage serve to confine legal unions mainly to men and women of equal rank.[42]

In Puerto Rico, there is social disapproval of the consensual union,

38. Bastien, *op. cit.*, p. 73.
39. Kreiselman, *op. cit.*, pp. 189, 223, 201, 191, 188.
40. *Ibid.*, p. 231. All unions involve social obligations, of course, but the fact that the investigator makes this observation underlines the lack of community support for this type of union.
41. *Ibid*, pp. 221–231. After a long consensual union, may marriage occur because the man and woman come to have the same rank?
42. Perhaps the Natchez were an exception. See Kingsley Davis, "Intermarriage in Caste Societies," *American Anthropologist*, 43 (July-September, 1941), pp. 382 ff. Of course, a "free courtship system" achieves the same end; and one may date a person whom one may not marry without censure.

even though the sanction does not necessarily lead to conformity. Fathers become angry when their daughters elope, and almost everyone pays "lip service" to the superiority of marriage.[43] People may say that they get married in order to baptize the children.[44] Girls have "idealized feelings" about marriage ceremonies,[45] and often the girls' parents request or insist upon legal unions.[46]

Two-thirds of both men and women in a national sample of Puerto Rico said that a consensual union is a bad life for a man, and over 80 percent of the respondents made the same assertion for women.[47] Perhaps a more penetrating test of the normative status of the consensual union may be found in the attitudes expressed about a *daughter* entering a consensual union: only 7.4 percent of the men and 5.5 percent of the women admitted that this arrangement would either be "all right" or that "it's up to her; doesn't matter."[48]

We are similarly told that in British Guiana the children born outside wedlock "are not sharply differentiated by any stigma of illegitimacy," while the consensual union is a "socially sanctioned one," and "part of the lower-class tradition."[49] Once again, however, we can note that parents are angry at the daughter and beat her when she becomes pregnant while still in the home. An unmarried mother will usually ask another person to take her illegitimate child to church for baptism.[50] And, although the scholar here quoted agrees with a turn-of-the-century French writer on the Congo who asserted that among the Bavili "birth sanctifies the child," a man's "outside" children in British Guiana do not rank equally with his legitimate children, and not all of a woman's children remain with her in a new marital union.[51] Moreover, only the married woman is called "Mistress," while her marital rights are clearer and more secure.[52] Marriage confers a different status on the woman. Women wish to marry, and after they have begun to have illegitimate children they

43. Stycos, *op. cit.,* pp. 108, 110–111.
44. Eric R. Wolf, "San José: Subcultures of a "Traditional' Coffee Municipality," in *The People of Puerto Rico, op. cit.,* p. 220. In Puerto Rico, the girl is usually a virgin when she enters a consensual union. Bastien makes the same claim for the Marbial area in Haiti, but to my knowledge no observer of other Haitian areas has done so; and Bastien is inconsistent. See Bastien, *op. cit.,* pp. 64, 65, 72.
45. Mintz, *op. cit.,* p. 378.
46. Elena Padilla Seda, "Nocora: The Subculture of Workers on Government-Owned Sugar Plantation," in *The People of Puerto Rico, op. cit.,* p. 293.
47. Paul K. Hatt, *Backgrounds of Human Fertility in Puerto Rico,* Princeton: Princeton University Press, 1952, p. 127.
48. *Ibid.,* p. 64. I would suppose, however, that the percentage would be much less on the mainland of the United States.
49. Raymond T. Smith, *The Negro Family in British Guiana,* New York: Grove Press, 1956, pp. 109, 149, 182.
50. *Ibid.,* pp. 126, 145, 132.
51. *Ibid.,* pp. 102, 120, 156, 178.
52. *Ibid.,* pp. 179–180; see also pp. 59, 148–149.

understand that they can achieve this status only by gambling that a quasi-marital union may develop into a marriage.[53] Finally, most people do marry eventually, and the legal, monogamic union is clearly the ideal.[54]

Differential Intensity of Norm Commitment

Several conclusions and problems emerge from such a confrontation of general assertions with specific observations. In order to proceed to further related propositions, these conclusions may be summarized: (1) Unequivocally, Malinowski's Principle of Legitimacy holds even for these societies, for which various observers have asserted that it did not hold. Birth out of wedlock is not a "cultural alternative." There is no special approval of the consensual union, no "counter-norm" in favor of such a union. Of course, the parental anger aroused by a clandestine pregnancy will not be repeated when the girl has entered a consensual union. Nevertheless, in none of these societies does the unmarried mother or her child enjoy the same status as the married mother and her legitimate children. A union based on a marriage enjoys more respect than do other types of unions. (2) Equally clear, however, is the corroboration of another principle: that the degree of norm commitment varies from one segment of the population to another. Not only do some individuals reject particular norms, but the members of some strata are less concerned than those of others about given norms.[55] (3) A more specific inference from the latter principle is also corroborated, namely, that the lower social strata are less committed than the middle or upper strata to a variety of family norms, in this instance that of legitimacy,[56] and also obey them less.

More important, however, is a reformulation of Malinowski's principle. As stated, it gives too little emphasis to the real foundation on which it rests, and ignores the differences in norm commitment among different strata, doubtless because neither problem was important in the societies

53. *Ibid.*, p. 138. The highest illegitimacy rate occurs among births to females 15–19 years of age; British Guiana, *Annual Report . . . , op. cit.*, p. 9.

54. *Ibid.*, Chapter 5.

55. Thus, one can find individuals who specifically reject marriage for one reason or another in all these societies. However, the empirical question is: what percentage of the society or stratum? In our society, too, any public opinion poll will locate a few such individuals.

56. There is substantial literature on this point. See, e.g., William J. Goode, *After Divorce*, Glencoe, Ill.: Free Press, 1956, Chapters 4 and 5; Ruth S. Cavan, *The Family*, New York: Crowell, 1953, Chapters 5, 6, and 7; and William F. Whyte, "A Slum Sex Code," *American Journal of Sociology*, 49 (July, 1943), pp. 24–31. For other data relevant to the subsequent discussion, see Herbert Hyman, "The Value Systems of Different Classes . . . ," in R. Bendix and S. M. Lipset, editors, *Class, Status, and Power*, Glencoe, Ill.: Free Press, 1953, pp. 426–442.

with which Malinowski was concerned. The principle in fact rests primarily upon the function of status placement, not that of locating a father as "protector": the bastard daughter of a count is still illegitimate even if he "protects" her. Violation of the norm creates some status ambiguity with respect to the child, the parents, and the two kin lines. Consequently, (4) commitment to the norm of legitimacy will be greater among the strata *or* kin lines which enjoy a higher prestige, or in which concern with the kin relation is higher. Although in general this concern is more marked in the upper strata, in every stratum there will be *some* family lines which possess "traditions," pride, a sense of kin identity, and so on. Illegitimacy rates can be expected to be higher among the lower strata in all societies. (5) Correlatively, to the extent that a given society possesses a high proportion of lower-strata families who are concerned little or not at all with their lineage, that society will exhibit a higher total rate of illegitimacy than it would have if the proportion were lower.

Given a high rate of illegitimacy, two further inferences may be made. (6) The actual amount of stigma suffered by the average illegitimate child cannot be great, relative to legitimate children in his same stratum and neighborhood. (7) The "matrifocality" of the Caribbean family is merely the result of the mother being left with her children, by either a casual lover, a consensual partner, or husband. The "matriarch" who is in charge has power precisely because no other adult of her generation is there to exercise it. Very likely a different personality configuration as well as a different self-image can and sometimes does develop from this experience.[57] The loyalty of children to the mother is stronger under such a system, since the father is not likely to be around during much of the infancy and youth of the offspring.[58]

On the other hand, early in the union, or continuously when the father remains in the union, the male behaves in a fashion which might be called "patriarchal" in the United States. It is possible that some observers have been misled, in their evaluation of the mother's power, by a false image of male behavior in such patriarchal societies as Japan, China, and India, where in fact the older mother is likely to have great authority in the home even when she pays considerable overt deference to the male head of family.

57. Nor should the matter of *self-selection* be forgotten. Given the social option, individuals will find this role more congenial and choose it against other alternatives.

58. Although almost every writer points to "some" consensual unions which have "lasted as long as" legal ones, the instability of both types seems indubitable, and consensual unions are less stable; see R. T. Smith, "Family Organization in British Guiana," *Social and Economic Studies,* 1 (No. 1, 1953), p. 101; Simpson, *op. cit.,* p. 656; Braithwaite, *op. cit.,* p. 147; Seda, *op. cit.,* p. 293; Mintz, *op. cit.,* p. 375; Stycos, *op. cit.,* p. 119; Simey, *op. cit.,* p. 16. (Kreiselman, by contrast, asserts stability for both types: *op. cit.,* p. 180.) That matrifocality is by default has been noted by others, e.g., Kreiselman, *op. cit.,* p. 282; Simey, *op. cit.,* p. 43; Braithwaite, *op. cit.,* p. 147.

Role Bargaining and Illegitimacy

An "explanation" of these high rates may properly take two directions. One of these would widen our empirical perspective to include other areas of the world, especially the countries south of the Rio Grande where high illegitimacy rates are found, and locate the cultural elements which are common to them. In a related paper, I am making such an analysis, with special reference to the cultural structure of a society and conformity to its norms. This analysis seeks to answer the question: in what types of societies are high rates found?

The second direction is to focus on the more immediate social forces which create a high illegitimacy rate in the Caribbean. It may be granted that the lower norm commitment in the lower strata of this area would, other things being equal, decrease conformity. Intensity of norm commitment, however, is only one element in the decision to risk pregnancy. The social pattern of primary importance is that the young woman in her courtship behavior must make essentially an *individual role bargain*. This apparent contrast with courtship patterns which produce low illegitimacy rates requires only little attention.

By "making an individual role bargain," I refer to the fact that in any role relationship both ego and alter are restricted in what services they may agree to perform for one another, by the expectations of others and thus by the sanctions which others will apply. For example, father and daughter owe, and feel they owe, certain obligations to one another, and in part these obligations are met because of the rewards and sanctions which either can direct toward the other. However, even if both of them are willing to agree to a different set of obligations—say, those appropriate to lovers—there is a "third layer" of persons who have role relationships with either ego and alter, or both of them, and who will act to force both of them to perform properly. These actions include pressures on ego or alter to punish the other for improper performance.

All courtship systems are market systems, in which role bargains are struck. They differ from one another with respect to the commodities which are more or less valuable on that market (beauty, personality, kinship position, family prestige, wealth) and who has the authority to do the marketing. Modern Western societies seem to constitute the only major historical civilization in which youngsters have been given a substantial voice in this bargaining (Imperial Rome might be added by some historians). Even in the U. S., however, where this trend is most fully developed, numerous studies have shown that youngsters make their choices within a highly restricted market, with respect to age, race, religion, social class, and so on. Precisely because courtship systems are bargaining systems, apparently hypergamous marriages (the woman marries upward in class) usually are, in most societies, unions in which a high ranking on one or more variables (wealth, beauty) is traded for a high ranking on other variables (power, prestige, race).[59] As a consequence, most marriages occur between individuals of like rank, or at least like bargaining power,[60] whether youngsters or their elders have the greater authority to conduct the bargaining process. When one party has much less bargaining power, he may be unable to pay as much as the other demands, or will have to pay much more than another family with greater bargaining power.

Although these principles hold with respect to both the choice of marital partner and the decision to marry at all, they are upheld, as is any market system, by a community-wide or stratum-wide set of agreements about *what* is valuable and *how* valuable those characteristics are, and a set of corresponding pressures which prevent the individual from paying too much. In our society, for example, even if a middle-class girl is willing to bear a child outside of marriage, usually her parents will oppose this behavior strongly because she would be giving more than need be under the operating market system.

By contrast, what is striking in the Caribbean community studies are the anonymity and isolation within which the decision is made to enter a union, and the fact that under those social conditions the girl has little chance of being married at all unless she is willing to risk a union outside of marriage. Not only does she become pregnant without her parents' knowing that she is courting, but she is also likely to enter the consensual union without any prior ritual or public announcement.[61]

A synthesis of the factors of importance in the decision to marry or to enter a consensual union can be made from the existing studies (although in many cases needed data are lacking because the appropriate questions were not asked[62]). Especially important are the following five points:

1. The class pattern of marriage has been suggested above. This may be clarified here by noting that not only do middle- and upper-class individuals marry (though of course males from those strata may have mistresses whom they do not marry), but that most members of the lower strata also marry eventually. Some lower-class persons never enter a consensual union, but begin their conjugal career by a wedding. Others begin with a consensual union, but marry sooner or later, usually after the male has somewhat improved his social position. In certain communities which seem to enjoy a higher social standing, a substantial majority of all marital unions are legal.[63]

59. See Davis, *op. cit.*, p. 386.
60. Of course, the principle of least interest operates in courtship as in marital conflict; the individual who is more deeply in love has less bargaining power. Willard Waller and Reuben Hill, *The Family: A Dynamic Interpretation*, New York: Dryden, 1953, pp. 190–192.
61. Smith, *op. cit.*, pp. 101, 137.
62. For Jamaica, as noted in footnote 28, the most complete synthesis has been made by Blake, *op. cit.*
63. E.g., Orange Grove reported in Clarke, *op. cit.*; Better Hope reported in Smith, *op. cit.*; and apparently San José as reported in Wolf, *op. cit.*

2. Kreiselman's finding for Martinique concerning marriages between persons of similar rank can be extended to every Caribbean community. Notwithstanding the frequently voiced assumption to the contrary, many fine distinctions of prestige are made within the lower class, in spite of its apparent homogeneity to the (usually white) outside observer.[64] If there were no other index, we could rely on the fact that certain members of the lower class do marry without entering a consensual union.[65] However, other data are also available, for example, the higher ranking of unskilled laborers with *steady* jobs. Granted, these differences are less sharp or refined than the gross differences between upper and lower strata, but within the narrower class horizon of persons in the bottom stratum they may nevertheless loom large. From this fact, we can suppose that when marriage does occur, the man and woman are more likely to be "rank equals," within the more generalized terms proposed above—which include not merely family prestige but also personal qualities such as beauty.[66]

3. Given a system in which consensual unions are common, it follows that the punishments for entering them cannot be severe, and the rewards for marrying cannot be great. (This proposition is an inference from a well-known principle of social control.) Consequently, the girl's parents or relatives (there is no extended kin group which acts as a unit) are punished or rewarded very little if, in turn, they make or fail to make her behavior conform to "ideal" norms.

4. In the Caribbean, there is no "free" adolescent courtship system such as our own, in which an as yet ineligible male is permitted to approach an immature girl, under the protection of her relatives and peer group. Many or most of the men she first meets are ineligible because of the great cost of a wedding. Most of them have not accumulated enough wealth to finance the formal union and to support its subsequent requirement of a higher level of living than a consensual union.[67] Consequently, the girl's first love and sex contacts occur away from home, and without the knowledge of the family. These first contacts take place essentially in social anonymity, so that she must make the best bargain she can, without the family's support.[68] Parental anger, reported in most studies, is at least in part a reaction to the knowledge that the girl has entered the world of

64. For example, although Smith, *op. cit.*, pp. 218–220 *et passim*, refers to a lack of status differentiation, his detailed descriptions show considerable differentiation.

65. See, for example, Smith's description (*ibid.*, pp. 169–170) of a formal engagement; Seda's comment that parents may insist on a wedding ceremony (*op. cit.*, p. 293); and Clarke, *op. cit.*, pp. 85–88.

66. Here the variable of rank is generalized, of course, and Kreiselman's observation (*op. cit.*, p. 278) from Martinique is extrapolated to the rest of the Caribbean.

67. Cf. Clarke, *op. cit.*, pp. 78, 99; Herskovits and Herskovits, *op. cit.*, p. 84.

68. Kreiselman, *op. cit.*, p. 99; Herskovits and Herskovits, *op. cit.*, p. 88; Smith, *op. cit.*, pp. 109, 137, 145.

adulthood without parental permission and has acted independently while presumably still a child.[69]

5. The Caribbean girl with unusual qualities may be able to demand marriage. However, the average girl has little chance at marriage, early or late, unless she is willing to gamble that a more permanent union will grow from one relationship or another. Without reliable data on the number of unions in the average individual's life, we cannot state what these chances are. Motherhood lowers the girl's value in the market, but if she does not produce a child for the man with whom she is living, or with whom she has a liaison, her chance of a stable union is low.[70] The decision to marry, within the existing social structure, is his rather than hers, and she gains more from marriage than he does. Consequently, as noted previously, it is the women who press toward marriage, while they must take the only road which can—and, apparently, eventually does—lead to marriage. Meanwhile, however, a woman may have children by several men, and may leave some or all of them with her parents or relatives when entering a new union[71]—a practice often resulting in the "grandmother" family. The widespread adoption pattern in the Caribbean is in part a method of taking care of these children. Ideally, a man wants only his own children in his home, especially if he is marrying.

Summary

Although Malinowski's Principle of Legitimacy has been called into question by several students of the Caribbean, the detailed descriptions of family and courtship patterns in that area show that it is generally valid. Derived from societies in which conformity to this norm was high, however, the principle requires revision. This should emphasize status placement rather than "paternal protection," and should specify the lower strata as the part of the society in which deviation from the norm is greatest. In addition, revision of the principle should note the weaker norm commitment in these strata, and the resulting lowering of both punishment for deviation and reward for conformity. . . .

69. Smith, *op. cit.*, p. 145, makes this point clearly, citing a common statement, "If you want to play a big woman go find yourself a man."

70. At the same time a pregnancy may frighten him away, as being too great a burden to assume. Clarke, *op. cit.*, pp. 75, 91, 100–102; Smith, *op. cit.*, p. 138. Blake, *op. cit.*, also reports this fact.

71. Herskovits and Herskovits, *op. cit.*, pp. 104–105, 131; Clarke, *op. cit.*, p. 91; Smith, *op. cit.*, Chapter 4.

Morris Freilich
and Lewis A. Coser

Structured Imbalances of Gratification: The Case of the Caribbean Mating System

A description and analysis of the sex life of Negro peasants in a community of Eastern Trinidad will reveal how a social system that is based on complementarity between sexual partners nevertheless presents such asymmetry that its equilibrium is extremely precarious.

The notion of equilibrium, if useful at all, must be seen in relation to those disequilibrating forces which seemingly stable systems create in the course of their operation. Just as a figure cannot be perceived except in relation to the ground in which it is imbedded, so the notion of balance gains significance only when it is examined in relation to the imbalances which it may occasion even as it attempts to contain them.

In order to search for sources of disequilibrium, we can turn to the same theoretician who originated the notion of equilibrium in social systems. Strangely enough, when modern sociologists discovered in Pareto the concept of social system, they overlooked Pareto's equally important notions concerning disequilibrium. The idea of disturbance and imbalance is implicit in Pareto's distinction between what he calls "utility *for*" and "utility *of*" a community.

An item that can be said to have maximum utility *for* the community is one through which each individual attains the maximum possible satisfaction. In contrast, utility *of* a community refers to the maximum utility not of individuals but of the group or society as a whole. Economists, Pareto argued, can only treat the problems of utility *for* the community since they can only consider wants of individuals which are heterogeneous and whose satisfactions therefore cannot be added up to yield a measure of the maximum utility for the entire group or society. In sociology, however, matters are different, "[A community] can be considered, if not a person, at least as a unity." [1] The maximum utility to a society can

---

1. Vilfredo Pareto, *The Mind and Society,* New York: Harcourt Brace, 1935, para. 2133.

be analyzed sociologically, and, this being the crux of the matter for our present purposes, it may not necessarily coincide with the maximum satisfaction of the wants of the individual members. What is more, there may well exist divergencies between utilities accruing to a total social system and maximum satisfactions of sub-groups, such as social classes. For example, in regard to an increase in population, the utility *of* the community and the utility *for* the community may well diverge. "If we think of the utility *of* the community as regards prestige and military power, we will find it advisable to increase population to the fairly high limit beyond which the nation would be diminished and its stock decay. But if we think of the maximum utility *for* the community, we find a limit that is much lower. Then we have to see in what proportions the various social classes profit by the increase in prestige and military power, and in what different proportions they pay for their particular sacrifices. . . ."[2]

The distinction between the two types of utilities, according to Pareto, is often deliberately obfuscated for manipulative purposes by ruling groups which make it appear as if component individuals or sub-groups would benefit from certain measures when this is not the case. ". . . The ruling classes oftentimes show a confusion of a problem of maximum utility *of* the community and a problem of maximum utility *for* the community. They [try] to make the 'subject' classes believe that there is an indirect utility which, when properly taken into account, turns the sacrifice required of them into a gain. . . . In reality, in cases such as these, non-logical impulses can serve to induce the subject classes to forget the maximum of individual utility, and work for the maximum *of* the community, or merely *of* the ruling classes. . . ."[3] To give another example, maximum wealth may be considered a prime goal for the society as a whole, but this may not coincide with the satisfactions of some of its members and may create great inequalities and major pockets of poverty in the society.

Pareto departed from classical liberal economics, where it was assumed that total benefits for a community simply involved adding up the benefits derived by each individual member ("the greatest happiness of the greatest number") and advanced a sociological view in which system needs and individual or sub-group needs are distinguished. He stressed that, "Even in cases where the utility of the individual is not in opposition to that of the collectivity, the points of maximum in the two cases . . . generally do not coincide."[4]

Among modern functional analysts, Merton stands almost alone in having developed this Paretian notion by stressing that "social usages or sentiments may be functional for some groups and dysfunctional for

2. *Ibid.*, para. 2134.
3. *Ibid.*
4. *Ibid.*, para. 2138.

others in the same society."[5] Merton goes on to state that, "The theoretic framework of functional analysis . . . must expressly allow for a given item having diverse consequences, functional and dysfunctional, for individuals, for subgroups, and for the more inclusive social structure and culture."[6]

Asymmetry and Exploitation

Marx remains the most powerful analyst of asymmetrical relationships. He shows why, when resources or power positions are unequal, the resultant relationship between actors is likely to be unbalanced, unilateral rather than multilateral. Marx's analytical focus is on institutionalized exploitation, "the right to something for nothing," to use Veblen's telling phrase.[7]

Marx's insights have been further developed in two seminal papers by Alvin Gouldner which have not yet been given the attention they deserve.[8] Gouldner argues in particular that reciprocity is indeed a pervasive feature of social interaction in all social systems but that the norm of symmetrical reciprocity can be infringed upon when power relations between two parties are such that one of them is in a position to coerce the other. Such unequal exchanges based on unequal power may be said to be exploitative in that they are based on asymmetrical dependence. "Power arrangements may serve to compel continuances of services for which there is little functional reciprocity."[9] Peter Blau puts the matter well: "A person upon whom others are dependent for vital benefits has the power to enforce his demands. A person who commands services others need, and who is independent of any at their command, attains power over others by making the satisfaction of their need contingent upon their compliance."[10]

The notion of exploitation is, of course, central to the Marxist critique of capitalist relations of production, but as Gouldner points out, it may also serve us well in other areas. In particular it has upon occasion been used in the sociological analysis of sexual relations as when males of higher status are said to use their position of superiority to take advantage

5. Robert K. Merton, *Social Theory and Social Structure*, rev. ed., New York: The Free Press, 1957, p. 27.

6. *Ibid.*, p. 30.

7. Cf. Lewis A. Coser, *Continuities in the Study of Social Conflict*, New York: The Free Press, 1968, pp. 147ff.

8. Alvin Gouldner, "Reciprocity and Autonomy in Functional Theory" in Llewellyn Gross (ed.), *Symposium on Sociological Theory*, Evanston: Row and Peterson, 1959; and Alvin Gouldner, "The Norm of Reciprocity: A Preliminary Statement," *Amer. Sociol. Rev.*, vol. 25, no. 2 (April 1960), pp. 161–78.

9. Gouldner, "Reciprocity," *op. cit.*, p. 250.

10. Peter Blau, *Exchange and Power in Social Life*, New York: Wiley, 1964, p. 22.

of women of lower status, or, more generally, when one partner in a sexual relationship takes advantage of the attachment and dependence of the other in order to extract favors and advantages without adequate compensatory acts of his own.[11]

A detailed analysis of sexual life in a small peasant community in Trinidad will show that complementarity of expectations between the sexes does not preclude a serious imbalance in the reward system for males and females.

Life in Anamat, Eastern Trinidad

Anamat is a dispersed settlement community, spread over six or so square miles of land at an elevation of approximately 5,000 feet. For the Anamatians the relative isolation of their community—due to poor roads, a lack of direct public transportation to larger towns, and the derogatory label of "the bush country"—helps them to live "cool, cool" away from "uncivilized" town living. For the townsfolk only a savage or someone with a deranged mind would spend a lifetime in "the bush," doing without such basic comforts as electricity, gas, running water, indoor latrines and telephones.

The peasants of Anamat farm holdings ranging from 10 to 30 acres of land, with cocoa as the major cash crop and coffee and citrus fruits as subsidiary cash crops. Most of the peasants have full title to all the land they work. The land not owned is rented to make kitchen gardens which provide a regular supply of food for the table. At the time of the study,[12] Anamat had a population of 651 men, women, and children made up of two major and conflicting groups: East Indians (whose ancestors had been brought to Trinidad from India, as indentured servants) and Negroes (whose ancestors had been brought to Trinidad as slaves).

Since this paper focuses on the sexual life of Negro peasants little more wll be said about the Indians, and the hate which exists between Negro and Indian. In passing it should be noted, however, that sexual relations do occur between Negroes and Indians and the form it most frequently takes is between an Indian male and Negro woman. These

11. This idea can already be found in earlier work, E. A. Ross advanced a "Law of Personal Exploitation" according to which, "In any sentimental relation the one who cares less can exploit the one who cares more." (*Principles of Sociology,* New York: Century, 1921, p. 136.) W. W. Waller and R. Hill propounded the "Principle of Least Interest." "That person is able to dictate the conditions of association whose interest in the continuation of the affair is least." (*The Family,* New York: Dryden Press, 1951, p. 191.)

12. Conducted by Morris Freilich from July 1957 through July 1958. For further details, cf. Morris Freilich, "Serial Polygyny, Negro Peasants, Model Analysis," *Amer. Anthropologist,* vol. 63, no. 5 (Oct. 1961), pp. 958–75. And Morris Freilich, "Mohawk Heroes and Trinidadian Peasants," in M. Freilich (ed.), *Marginal Natives: Anthropologists at Work,* New York: Harper and Row, 1970, pp. 185–250.

kinds of relationships are greatly frowned upon by almost all Anamatians, and almost invariably Negro-Indian love affairs are of short duration, and are kept far more secret than sexual affairs between two Negroes.

The sexual life of the Negro peasant must be understood within the context of his socio-economic standing and within the framework of his mating system. It is necessary therefore to comment briefly on these two areas of social living.

Rank, Mating and Sex

As Trinidadians, the Anamatian peasants consider themselves as the cream of Caribbean society. As Anamatians they discuss the superiority of their community over other places in Trinidad. And as peasants they constantly refer to their personal good fortune in not having to work for anyone, and being independent enough to work when, and if, they please. The concept of "independence" provides a major prestige-giving criteria in Anamat. Those who are economically independent are always socially superior to those whose livelihood is dependent on the whim of another man. Hence, the peasant farmers are seen, and see themselves as the upper-class members of their community: a status they share with the *school teachers* and *government overseers* of local projects. Below them, forming a kind of middle class, were the *semi-peasants* (those who owned some land, but who had to work for others part of the year) and the *shopkeepers*. And, on the bottom of this three-class system were those who always worked for others and were therefore completely non-independent: the *laborers* on nearby estates and those who did *road-work* for the government.

Other things being equal, the more independent the Anamatian the more he could afford many love affairs, and the more he actually had them. His freedom to pursue women, however, is also a function of his marital status. Other things being equal, men currently unmarried had more time and more opportunities for sexual involvement and this fact contributed to the "divorce" rate: in local, operational terms, to the frequency with which a given man left a given spouse. To some extent therefore sex functions as a marriage breaker; but this whole matter must be understood within its cultural context.

The terms used in Anamat to describe the sex act are: "breed" and "brush." The term "breed" seems to designate several phenomena: first, it refers to a situation where the male has some sexual right over a woman; second, it points to his ability to exercise such rights because of frequency of contact under the same roof; and third, it emphasizes the offspring. The term "breed" is most frequently used to refer to the relationship of a given man and his spouse. It is, however, at times extended to refer to an implied right of a man to sexual intercourse with any female living in his house, with whom such intercourse would not constitute incest. [13]

Prestige from a "breeding" situation is obtained, not by the sexual act itself, since the man gets only that which is already his, but at such times when children are born.

A "brush" is a sex act where the male has no right over a given woman, and he must therefore approach her as a suppliant. The term used for this kind of approach is "beg." A man telling another of a recent conquest will frequently use the following sentence: "I begged and begged for a brush . . . and she couldn't refuse me." This kind of "stooping to conquer" carried prestige. A man who has many love affairs becomes known as a "hot boy," [14] a prestigeful status denoting a *real man*.

Entering a "breeding" situation, which usually means taking a wife, is part of the following sequence. First, a lot of "begging" is done while still under the parental roof. On leaving school, whether a job is obtained within the village or outside the village, a man rarely stays very long in his parents' house if the father is still alive. The young adult male leaves home and gets an apartment for himself. At this time he is in a position to take a spouse. He has a place to put the spouse, and he is earning money. The forces that usually spur a man to take a wife are several: (1) he needs someone to cook, clean the house, wash his clothes; (2) his "begging" may have produced a child; (3) entering a "breeding" situation does not put him out of the "begging" market, so why not get the best of both worlds?

In local terminology when a man takes a spouse he "gets married" and local terminology, while not always consistent with the language used by Trinidadian church officials, is congruent with Murdock's views of marriage: "Marriage is a complex of customs centering upon the relationship between a sexually associating pair of adults . . . (it) defines the manner of establishing and terminating such a relationship, the normative behavior and recipient obligations within it and the locally accepted restrictions upon its personnel." [15]

A marriage is established in Anamat by a man bringing a woman into a house and living with her. The woman then has the status of wife. In some cases a religious service precedes the woman's entrance into the status of wife. Irrespective of the presence or the absence of the religious sanction, a woman who goes to live with (say) Mr. Jones, is referred to

13. Only two cases of incest were discovered. One was a single incident between a brother and his full sister and the other was a long-term relationship which led the girl to bear two children sired by her father. In the latter case, the girl and her father, and indeed everyone living in that household, were ostracized by the rest of the community.
14. "Hot-boy" is a term used to define a *real man* in contrast to a "sissie boy" who has no or very few sexual relations with women.
15. George Peter Murdock, *Social Structure,* New York: Macmillan, 1949, p. 1.

directly and indirectly as "Ma Jones," that is, the wife of Jones. A marriage is terminated by one of the parties leaving the household. No third party is brought into such a "divorce," whether or not the marriage was religiously sanctioned. For Anamat (and we suspect for many of the Negro villages in the Caribbean) generally, there is little purpose in differentiating between legal marriage, common law marriage, etc. In terms of most problems which are meaningful to Trinidadian peasants, these terms are all structurally and functionally the same.

In Anamat, according to many informants, marriage is a highly formalized procedure. A man is supposed to write "a demand" for a girl, stating that he wished to frequent the house with intentions to marry at a future specified date. Actually this rarely happens. Young adults usually meet informally and a female decides that she will go and live with a male. Three factors are usually involved here: (1) The male must have a place to put the female, ideally this should be his own house; (2) he must be able to support her; and (3) her consent is necessary. In the final analysis, there is freedom of movement based on individual choice.

Once set up in a household, the couple is recognized as man and wife. "Mr. Brown" has the usual obligations of economic support, while his wife, "Ma Brown," is expected by the community to provide the husband with meals, sexual services, and a clean house.

A given marriage is expected to last only as long as a couple can "cooperate together." Each party to the union is understood to be quite capable of judging when and if cooperation exists. At the break-up of a union the wife usually leaves the house in which she has been living (unless she owned the house) and goes with her children, either to her mother's house or to the house of a new husband. In some rare occasions, she may rent a room somewhere in the village. The male may live alone for a while in his house or may have another woman ready to move in with him.

A given household is thus a temporary dwelling for a woman and her children, paralleled by the fact that a given marriage is a temporary union for a given couple. Although many of the peasants will probably change their spouses again at least once before they die, and one young peasant had not yet taken a wife, the average Anamatian peasant has lived with three spouses; and 45 percent of the group have lived with three or more spouses.

Even when a peasant has lived with a given spouse for many years, he still does not consider this a union for life. Marriage according to the Anamatian Negroes is a "now-for-now affair"; and any given union is therefore considered a temporary one. . . .

[The] pattern [of change] may be charted [as follows]: A given male leaves his house on an evening to have a little fête, either with some of the boys or with a girl friend. His wife, now alone, can be visited by one of her admirers. This second male, by leaving his own house, provides a place for a third man and so forth.

. . . In return for sexual favors received from the paramour, a man is supposed to provide goods and services. A richer peasant can thus afford to have more outside women than a poorer peasant. Many peasants frequently made envious and sarcastic remarks about the many outside affairs of one of the oldest and richest peasants in the community. The economic aspect of outside affairs is further indicated by the the following. One Creole peasant showed little sympathy when a shapely Anamatian woman complained about her economic situation. After staring at her body for several minutes the peasant finally said: "Your have lots of ways to make money, but you don't make enough use of what you have."

That similar "outside affairs" occur in other Creole communities in the Caribbean area is evident from R. T. Smith's writings. For example: "Within the household these [sexual services] are provided only between spouses in non-incestuous unions, but they may be provided across the boundaries of household groups between persons who will be referred to as 'lovers.' "[16]

From a male viewpoint sexual involvements are for fun and fame. Unlike what appears to be the case in "Puritan Ethic" countries, in Trinidad love affairs carry no attachment of guilt, which automatically gets transferred to the "players." Hence sexual involvements are here simple, and purely pleasurable. In addition broadcasts of conquests carry "fame" for the virile and eloquent male. Understandably, the sex game in Trinidad, like the money game in America, keeps the players constantly and passionately interested. Men whose sexual needs are almost insatiable are referred to as "hot boys," "sweet men," and "wild men."

The critical factors which appear to account for who plays in the sex-fame game and why some play more often than others are (1) beliefs of males; (2) beliefs of females; and (3) a set of operational rules—rules which help actors predict the probable outcome of given actions. Men believe that all women—single or married—may be begged for sex, and that all men may play the role of sexual beggar.

Two general exceptions exist to these beliefs: first, a given male believes that his sister—if single—is not approachable for sex, and—if married—is only approachable by her husband. Second, a given male believes that his wife is approachable by none but himself for sexual favours. In sum, men believe that they and the husbands of their sisters have monopolistic sexual privilege with their wives, but other men have only preferential sexual privileges. Other husbands thus only have first call (so to speak) for their wives' sexual services; they themselves have the only call.

16. Raymond T. Smith, *The Negro Family in British Guiana*, London: Routledge and Kegan Paul, 1956, p. 67.

Women's beliefs in the area of sexual relations are strongly associated with a more fundamental female belief; that men and women are social equals and that therefore social rules apply equally to males and females. Since their husbands never give up the sex-fame game after marriage, and since other men continue to approach them for sex, sooner or later most women come to believe that outside sex is permissible, as long as such affairs are kept secret. These beliefs, almost invariably, are of the "general" kind, translatable here as "it's all right if *other* husbands have lovers as long as they keep things secret." However, most wives of Negro peasants are annoyed by the sexual exploits of their husbands. Thus a goal of Anamatian females—rarely attained—is to have a husband who does not "run all about." However, the emotional reaction of women to the sexual exploits of their husbands is not uniform; some women get more upset than others, and some express their annoyance more violently than others. Some of the women, temperamentally, are more jealous than others, and very jealous wives will at times make embarrassing scenes and do their utmost to break up an outside affair. Generally, the wives of the community, even the jealous ones, find such confrontations extremely distasteful. A crisis in family relations is always created when the lover initiates a confrontation with the wife and publicly proclaims that she is "the outside woman." Such a broadcast usually includes verbal attacks on the wife's ability to fulfill her sexual role. The reactions of the wife to the taunts of the lover are always extreme. The wife always becomes very angry and frequently either threatens the lover with bodily harm or attacks her then and there.

Wives who "do not jealous their husbands" pride themselves on the control they maintain over their feelings, and describe their reactions as "cool, cool."

No matter how little a woman "jealouses her husband" and how "cool, cool" she is, the money spent on outside women is frequently a major source of conflict between husbands and wives. What many wives find particularly annoying is the fact that they help their husbands economically by "working in the cocoa," and then income that they helped create is spent on other women. Other things being equal, the amount of concern a woman shows appears to be inversely related to her age: the older the wife the less the emotional reaction to her husband's exploits.

Women translate their beliefs and sexual experiences into a set of operational rules which guides their behavior in the sex-fame game. These operational rules for sexual involvements—information which the women of Anamat share with each other—include data as to (1) how well given men keep their conquests secret; (2) the spending abilities (economic standing) and the spending habits (economic "personality") of various "hot boys"; (3) the marital position of the males (legally married, common-law married, "promised" or engaged, free and loose); and (4) men's reputation as lovers. The richer the male, other things being equal, the more economically rewarding the love affair will be. The man who is legally married must work harder to be believed, when he promises his lover that he intends to marry her. Legally married wives are harder to dispose of than common law wives.[17]

Some men have reputations for great power and artistic ability in bed, and such great lovers have far less trouble getting into sexual involvements than old Mister F. The latter, although rich and "always good to his friends," will on rare occasions be denied. It is well known that Mr. F., a hard worker with honorable intentions, often "just can't get it up."

Irrespective of the reputation given males have for keeping secrets, men regularly—and quite often eloquently—broadcast their sexual escapades. They obviously have to, since their fame depends on (1) their sex activities, (2) their abilities to distribute personal sex information, and (3) their abilities to make such information appear credible.

The men, just like the women, have a set of operational rules which guides their behavior in the sex-fame game. Men know that the probability of successful "begging" is higher (1) with women who are currently husbandless than with women currently living with a man, (2) with lower-class women than with the wives of peasants, (3) with women whose husbands stray frequently than with those whose husbands are relatively faithful, (4) with women who need the goods and services they receive in exchange for sexual favours, than with women for whom such goods and services are but extra luxury items. The men also know that some of the peasants' wives firmly believe that marriage puts an end to past affairs and to any possible future ones. Women with such beliefs will rarely be approached for sexual favours. How much begging a woman receives is also a function of her attractiveness. Younger women, generally, are considered more attractive then older women; and virginity is considered a most attractive feature. As one Negro peasant put it, mimicking British understatement, "Some men have preference for a virgin, but to achieve that is hard."

The men spend considerable time and energy discussing their own sexual exploits and such conversations always include statements concerning "fooling." A "great man" is able to fool any woman into believ-

17. In actual fact legally married wives are not harder to "dispose of." The wife who is *legal,* who is a "mistress" of the house, is left as quickly and as easily as the common law wife. However, the female lover *believes* that husbands are more strongly tied to legal wives. The enigma is solved, we believe, as follows: "divorce," operationally speaking, meant physical leaving, for the Anamatians. Such *physical leaving* never included court proceedings in the past in this village; but it could. The fear of possible legal repercussions seems to lie at the base of female beliefs here.

ing all of his promises. In begging for sex there is nothing which is considered wrong, as long as physical force is not used. A woman is supposed to succumb to a man's attractiveness and eloquence, not his brute force. And the eloquent beggar is given great verbal latitude. One peasant boasting of his own superior abilities as a woman-fooler said:

> Some of the fellows here don't know how to fool a woman. They don't know how to speak to a woman properly; they can't tell her, "I love you." After I get a woman alone for a while and talk to her, I begin to beg for a brush. I beg and beg and she can't refuse me.

The information of a given broadcaster is generally evaluated rather critically. Both his message and the analysis of it then get communicated through informal community channels. Since the the siring of an outside child is proof positive of a conquest, a strategy used by some men to achieve greater fame is to claim paternity over children whose parentage is in doubt. Anamatians generally achieve a consensus as to who sired a given child; and males other than the agreed-on father, who continue to claim paternity, are referred to as "trying to give themselves fame." A more subtle strategy used by a few is to deny paternity in situations where there is general agreement that the child is theirs. The latter situation generates much talk involving the "denying father" who thereby increases his "fame." Thus, and to put it conservatively, for males there is little reason to worry about contraceptive measures. In the words of one informant:

> If I had an outside child I would try to keep it. I would offer it first to my mother and then to my sister. My mother would not be vexed [in this kind of situation]. The son becomes a hero, like a fellow goes to war and returns with medals. The women can't push this boy around; he pushes them around.

An outside child, while a sign of fame for a man, is a source of trouble for the woman. As one woman said: "For a girl to bring an outside child home is to disgrace the family. They will take you in, but you will see much trouble." For the married woman, any extra child is more work and more restrictions on her freedom of movement. As one woman put it: "The children hold the Creole women back so they don't want many; with many they can't go to dances as they like, nor to wakes. Nor can they get about the way they like to."

Attempts to guard against pregnancy are common; and generally they require the woman to do something. The contraceptive devices used most frequently include: gynomin tablets, "withdrawal," Epsom salts placed inside the vagina prior to intercourse, drinking quicksilver and rum, and eating young pineapples. Since most of the adult males have sired some outside children—uncertainty existed on exactly how many a given male had sired—clearly these contraceptive devices are frequently ineffective.

The System

The data presented can be described as a system by (1) isolating the critical elements involved, and (2) showing how these elements have functional interconnections. This can be done as in Table 1.

The system, *qua* system, has tendencies making both for states of equilibrium and states of disequilibrium. The former can be described as follows:

Sexual encounters have a dualistic quality for women; sexual experiences, while intrinsically pleasurable, have a possible unfortunate consequence: pregnancy. For men, sexual encounters are intrinsically enjoyable and are avenues to social applause. Since men and women are equals in a sexual encounter, its rewards are equalized by defining women as giving and men taking sex. The "takers" must beg and reciprocate for favors received. By keeping their sex "expenses" low, men have "funds" for many affairs and they receive extra fame for their fooling power. Such fooling tends to cut short given affairs. Short duration affairs with one woman are congruent with men's desires for variety in sexual experiences and for fame—partly a function of the number of women with whom involvements exist.

The richer the peasant the more he can afford sexual affairs, the more his promises are believed and the more affairs he actually has. The poorer his lover the more often she will accept lovers. The sex-fame game is thus a mechanism for the distribution of surplus goods within the community. Marriage is considered by the peasant as a "now-for-now" affair; and the sex-fame game helps to lead a peasant from wife to wife—that is, facilitates serial polygamy—by providing him with relationships with many women, each of which can be evaluated as a possible future wife. The disruptive element of the sex-fame game on marital relations weakens the nuclear family and (consequently) strengthens the martrifocal family: a membership unit peasants consider of prime importance in their lives. The children produced by outside affairs create pseudo-kin ties between males, females, and their offspring. Community bonds are enhanced by these pseudo-kin links which also act as mechanisms for the distribution of surplus goods.

Viewed as a system in a general state of equilibrium, the sex-fame game has a major flaw; male and female players have diametrically opposite goals. Indeed our label for this game, though well fitting the man's viewpoint, does little justice to that of the woman's. *The Secret-Sex Game* is a more appropriate title for her views of these encounters. Since it is the male's goals which are generally met (see Table 2), the sex-fame game remains an appropriate label for this system. Most community members know the "secret" sex life of most community members: women's attempts to avoid pregnancy are not always successful; prom-

TABLE 1. The Sex-Fame Game

I. Players	Men	Women
II. Beliefs	1. Sex is good	Sex is good
	2. Real men want sex often, with many women	"Hot boys" are exciting
	3. Women give sex	Women give sex
	4. Men give valued objects for sex	Men must pay for sex
	5. Clever men "pay" far less than they promise	Beware of men who are good at fooling
	6. Sexual affairs must be broadcast discreetly	Sexual affairs are secret
	7. The successful beggar is a "famous man"	The "cool cool" wife is a wise woman
III. Goals	8. To be famous as a "hot-boy"	To have their love affairs kept secret
	9. To get prestige as a great fooler	To have promises kept
	10. To avoid confrontation with irate husbands	To avoid confrontation with "outside" women
	11. To have wives who do not have lovers	To have a husband who rarely takes an outside woman
IV. Strategies	12. To broadcast real and fictional involvements eloquently and convincingly	To act as if their home life is perfect
	13. To exaggerate promises, to minimize sexual "payments"	To take lovers with reputations of honesty
	14. To keep watch on the behaviour of the wife	Not to marry "hot boys"
	15. To get women pregnant; to claim fatherhood of children of doubtful parentage and to deny fatherhood in cases where everyone knows the "denier" is really the father	To avoid pregnancy in a love affair; and to deny fatherhood claims of outside men
V. Sentiments associated with sexual affairs	16. Excitement, freedom and pleasure	Excitement, freedom and pleasure

TABLE 2. Contrasting Male and Female Goals

Sex-Fame (Male)	Secret-Sex (Female)
1. Maximal movement of sexual information (loud broadcasts)	1. Minimal movement of sexual information (secrecy)
2. To get lovers pregnant for greater fame	2. To avoid pregnancy to maintain secrecy
3. To keep few promises, for the broadcast of "fooling-power"	3. To have promises kept to maintain "social equality"
4. To have many outside women for greater fame	4. To have a husband who does not spend money on *any* outside women

ises made are rarely kept in their entirety; conjugal relations are rarely lasting and husbands have many, not few, outside women.

Given the system's apparent preference for male goals, what options are available to the women? The women can elect to avoid the sex-fame game; or, they can play cautiously—selecting partners who are comparatively honorable; or, they can play "normally" and create crises when partners do them wrong. Avoidance means giving up the positive consequences of active involvement—companionship, pleasure, goods and services, and presentation-of-self as an equal of the males. Playing cautiously helps little, for in order to achieve their goal of fame men must fool and they must broadcast their conquests. Playing and creating crises is the only realistic option left; it is the option generally taken, and is not totally satisfying.

The angry, tearful, and upset wife loses community prestige and sees her husband rarely. The wife who accosts her husband's lover loses even more prestige and creates considerable problems for herself (see below). The lover who, because of broken promises, acts like an angry wife, quickly loses her lover. Should she accost his wife, the lover gets to be known as "a shameless woman" from whom married men stay away. Men are blamed as much as their "shameless" lovers when a wife is accosted by their "sweethearts." As one wife put it: "Every man has a girl friend and that is all right if kept secret. But many men allow the girl to give the wife words: that is unmoral. These things make the woman at home feel bad."

The socio-cultural system described is not adequately presented as being in a state of equilibrium. From a systems viewpoint, two factions exist with many contradictory goals. From the viewpoint of individuals in interaction, this is a *man against woman situation*: fame versus secrecy, fooling against promise-keeping.

Yet, the system contains mechanisms which allow it to minimize undue threats to its stability. Among these, perhaps the most important, is secrecy concerning the operation of the sex-fame game. Secrecy serves to allow the operation of the game while partially neutralizing its potentially destructive impact.

Secrecy and Its Functions

. . . The system's "efforts" at maintaining a state of equilibrium frequently fall short of desired goals. Actors find it difficult to live in terms of the compromise solution. As the tensions of individuals increase, acts eroding the fiction of secrecy pile up: broadcasts to get fame are made too openly; sexual information is distributed too publicly; wives chastise lovers and lovers confront wives. At those times actors accept the negative sanctions of the system, for the personal rewards they receive. Open broadcasts of sexual conquests—although considered bad form by some of the listeners—have valuable feed-back effects: weakening egos are invigorated. Confrontations with wives or lovers function as problem-airing and problem-sharing devices. Tensions are temporarily reduced by a direct confrontation with an assumed cause of one's problems—a husband's lover, a wife. Sufferings are lessened by distributing them into the realm of men's lives—by quarrels with husbands or with lovers.

Secrecy helps contain the potential conflict between males and females, thus preventing disruptive consequences for the community. Secrecy helps keep expression of hostilities within bounds. It is system-maintaining not only in the sense that social life can run more smoothly than if secrecy would not obtain, but in the sense that it helps maintain the respective power positions of the actors.

Yet, while serving as a lightening rod, so to speak, it cannot prevent a recurrent gathering of the clouds, it cannot prevent repeated accumulation of tensions.[18] The basic structural asymmetries between men and women cannot be hidden, nor can they be compensated for through secrecy.

One could argue that continued secrecy between people who engage in frequent and intensive interaction, such as wives, husbands, and lovers in a small community where everybody knows everyone, is in itself tension-producing. It requires much energy on everybody's part to keep the game going. While each one of the partners knows that he is engaged in a game of "make-believe," they all have to cooperate in spite of the fact that all of them have antagonistic interests in regard to each other.

Hence, it is at the expense of much tension that secrecy keeps the

18. Cf. Lewis A. Coser, *The Functions of Social Conflict*, New York: The Free Press, 1956, pp. 35ff.

system going. Moreover, secrecy does not alter the fact that the system as a whole primarily benefits the men. We have here an almost classical case of exploitation, of asymmetrical types of relations, where benefits received by no means equal benefits conferred. Given the superior power positions of males, they manage to utilize their resources so as to shore up their positions *vis-à-vis* the women. The system does not bestow equal rewards to both sides in the sexual equation; the game is rigged in favor of the males.

The sex-fame game is positively functional for the male members of the community since it allows them the maximum of sexual gratification with a minimum of responsibility. Moreover, it allows them to attain secure bases for invidious status appraisal in a society where other means of attaining such status are unavailable. Matters are fundamentally different for females. From their point of view, dysfunctional elements seem to loom at least as large as functional ones. They gain some advantages, to be sure, especially if the game is played within the bounds of secrecy. Non-cooperation would yield even fewer rewards than the sparse ones they can attain now.

Yet the women are basically but the objects, or counters, in a game in which the males are the sole autonomous players. It would be an exaggeration to say that the males receive something for nothing in this game, but they get much in return for comparatively little. The terms of exchange are unequal, so that what prevails is exploitation rather than reciprocity.

In view of their minimal rewards, woman will gladly turn to alternatives if such should present themselves. They will have much to gain from modernization which would offer them some means for reducing their dependency on their sexual partners. When forces of industrialization or urbanization begin seriously to impinge on the system, the male-female relationship will emerge as one of the weakest links in the structure. Here, as elsewhere, exploitative relationships will be resisted, and strains toward complete reciprocity will emerge in full force once traditional impediments to equalization have begun to crumble.[19]

19. The implied question here, "How will these anticipated changes enter the system?" can be briefly answered with: "Through the institutionalization of new *operational rules*." Cf. Morris Freilich, *The Meaning of Culture*, Lexington, Mass., Xerox College Publishing, 1972, pp. 290ff.

Rose Laub Coser
and Lewis A. Coser

The Principle of Legitimacy
and Its Patterned Infringement
in Social Revolutions*

At the basis of the social regulation of procreation, according to Bronislaw Malinowski, is the universal rule "that no child should be brought
into the world without a man—and one man at that—assuming the role of
sociological father." This rule, which Malinowski calls *The Principle of
Legitimacy,* is said to be universal. It "obtains throughout mankind; . . .
the sociological position of the father is regarded universally as indispensable." This is the case, argues Malinowski, because, despite all cultural
variations, "there runs the rule that the father is indispensable for the full
sociological status of the child," because the social father is "the male
link between the child and the rest of the community."[1]

At first blush this proposition would seem to be refuted by the well-
known fact of very high rates of illegitimacy in, for example, the Caribbean or contemporary African societies in cultural transition where social
controls have been weakened.[2] It should be realized, however, that
Malinowski was not concerned with the factual existence of illegitimacy
but with its normative regulation. Even high rates of deviance from a
norm are no evidence that the deviating individuals are unaware of the
norm or deny its legitimacy. On the contrary, the relation of deviance to
conformity is always that of figures to the ground setting them off. Figures cannot be perceived except in relation to their grounds, and deviance
is definable only against the ground of normalcy.[3]

* Prepared for delivery at the 7th World Congress of Sociology, Varna, Bulgaria,
September 1970.
1. Bronislaw Malinowski, "Parenthood, The Basis of Social Structure," ed. Rose Laub
Coser, *The Family, Its Structure & Functions,* New York: St. Martin's Press, 1964, pp.
3–19 [this edition, pp. 51–63].
2. William J. Goode, "Illegitimacy in the Caribbean Social Structure," *American
Sociological Review* 25 (1960): 21–30 [this book, pp. 64–77], and "Illegitimacy, Anomie, and
Cultural Penetration," *American Sociological Review* 26 (1961): 910–925.
3. Cf. Lewis A. Coser, "Some Functions of Deviant Behavior and Normative Flexibility," in Lewis A. Coser, *Continuities in the Study of Social Conflict,* New York: The Free
Press, 1967, pp. 111–133.

Furthermore, the results of a number of inquiries seem to have established the fact that deviance from the norm.of legitimacy is by no means due to individual happenstance. It is socially patterned. Indeed, from Malinowski's *Principle,* which rests on the proposition that the sociological father gives status to his son, it follows that it is attenuated, disregarded or abolished, as the case may be, whenever or wherever the transmission of ascribed status is considered to be a matter of some indifference or is negatively valued. This may happen under at least four conditions:

(1) If a subgroup or a substratum in a society has no stake in transmitting status from father to son.

(2) If the stability of the stratification system is not threatened by non-conformity in some of its subgroups.

(3) If status placement depends less on ascription and relies heavily on achievement.

(4) When a ruling elite finds it advisable and desirable to break rather than to assure the continuity of the status system: in times of social revolution.

Conditions (1) and (2) account for the fact that the norms of legitimacy are likely to be enforced with much more laxity in the lower strata,[4] but are adhered to strictly in the upper strata of a society where there is much more at stake in the transmission of status from father to son, and where therefore individuals will be highly motivated to adhere to the *Principle.* In contrast, those who have little wealth, reputation or prestige to pass on from father to son will be less concerned about conforming to the norm.[5]

The norms of a stable society tend to be geared to the needs of the upper strata. If the maintenance and stability of a system are not threatened by lower strata adhering less strictly to some normative requirements, their infringement may not bring forth negative sanctions. What is more, the upper strata may even favor departures from the norms on the part of lower strata if this strengthens the stability of the system. In antiquity, or in the antebellum South, slaves were not expected to abide by the principle of legitimacy. Not only did a slave's son become a slave whether or not he had a sociological father, but illegitimacy helped reinforce the basic separation between slaves and free men and symbolized the fact that slaves were *in* but not *of* society.

The third condition, where ascribed status is not the main basis for status placement, obtains in societies with high rates of mobility on the basis of achievement. Where achievement is more highly valued than

4. Cf. Goode *op. cit.,* as well as his *The Family,* Englewood Cliffs, New Jersey: Prentice-Hall, 1964, Chapter 3, and *World Revolution and Family Patterns,* New York: The Free Press, 1963, *passim.*

5. Cf. Kingsley Davis, "Illegitimacy and the Social Structure," *The American Journal of Sociology* 45 (1939): 215–233.

ascription as a criterion for status position, sanctions against illegitimacy are less severe than where status is transmitted through the family. When the emphasis upon inheritance of wealth, prestige and social standing is diminished, the *Principle* is weakened. This accounts for the "progressive" reform of initially stringent laws against bastardy in most modern European and American jurisdictions and for the decreased stigma attached to persons of illegitimate birth.

Where not only changes in individual status positions are welcomed on the basis of such criteria as individual merit but a transformation of the relations between the social classes is programmatically advocated, illegitimacy is condoned on a broad scale and becomes a matter of ideological reevaluation. This is the fourth case, that of social (not political) revolutions, which is the subject matter of this paper.

Four major social revolutions—the French, the Russian, the Chinese, and the Cuban—despite their otherwise often divergent aims and values show a common pattern of dealing with illegitimacy. In each of them there was an attempt to erase the legal disabilities and moral stigmata that had previously been attached to bastards. In all of them there emerged a wish to eradicate the distinctions between persons born in legitimate and those born in nonsanctioned unions. In each of these revolutions it was attempted to do away with the distinction between biological and social fathers; in each of them it was claimed that every child, legitimate or illegitimate, had the right to be treated as a fully equal citizen.

The main target of attack in social revolutions is the old status order. A break with all aspects of the past is advocated through a change of values, through a rejection of the political, legal and social norms that hitherto governed conduct. The fundamental transformation of the social structure and the change in power relations between the strata of society is implemented through a comprehensive transvaluation of previously held values and beliefs. The efforts to break with the heritage of the past, to write on a clean sheet of history, are expressed in symbolic changes such as forms of dress or forms of address. The French in revolutionary France were to call one another *citoyen,* just as the Russians in their revolution were to call one another comrade, and the Russian rejection of bourgeois formal and rigid attire was but a repetition of the more colorful change in dress of the *sans culottes,* with simple long trousers replacing the "unnatural" knee breeches of the aristocracy. In France, the discontinuity with the past was even symbolized by a change in the calendar; the twelve months of the year were no longer to be named after old gods or dead tyrants but after the works of "beneficent nature."[6]

The call for civil rights for bastards serves the double purpose of

6. Cf. Lewis A. Coser, *Men of Ideas,* New York: The Free Press, 1965, pp. 150–153.

denying the need for social placement of the child according to the old status order and of emphasizing the equality of all men. Appeals for social justice and for raising the status of the underdog accompany the attempt to discontinue placement along the old lines of status division.

There Are No More Bastards in France

In France, appeals for equality found their philosophical basis in the idea of *nature* as beneficent and healthy. Nature was counterposed, in Rousseauist fashion, to convention which was seen as artificial, unnatural, confining and oppressive. The old order was condemned as failing to be in accord with the true and natural dispositions of men. The status order was attacked as being "unnatural." The "artificial" distinctions between men according to ascribed social status position was to give way to a new order in which all men were to be treated equally, in tune with their equal natural rights.

The attempt to eradicate the previous status structure with its differential rights and privileges lies at the root of revolutionary legislation attempting to eradicate the stigma of illegitimacy.[7] In a law of the 12 brumaire of the year II (Nov. 2, 1793), the Convention decreed that illegitimate children born after Bastille Day—the symbolic beginning of the new era—shall have equal rights of inheritance with legitimate children. The debates that led to this revolutionary legislation are instructive. Most legislators appealed to *nature*, and they never referred to bastards or even illegitimate children, but invariably to "natural children" or "children born out of wedlock." Cambacérès, the chief proponent of the law, argued that the civil laws on bastardy of the *ancien régime* were in conflict with natural law and made full parenthood dependent on mere ceremony. "Strange alteration, where respect is given the form and outrage done to nature." "Nature, which has imposed upon us the law of dying, has not made it a crime for us to be born." Oudot proposed to restore to those born out of wedlock the tenderness and the care of their parents "by destroying all these barbarous distinctions between illegitimate children, simple bastards, and adulterous and incestuous bastards." He stated that "all children are legitimate" and that those children unfortunate enough not to know who their parents were should be called "orphans" like children who had lost their parents.

The law of the 12 brumaire does not quite eliminate all distinctions between children born in and those born out of wedlock. Children of adulterous unions, for example, are granted only "one-third in property

7. This whole section on the French Revolution is based on Crane Brinton's seminal *French Revolutionary Legislation on Illegitimacy, 1789*–1804, Cambridge: Harvard University Press, 1936.

of the portion to which they would have had a right had they been born in wedlock." But, as a whole, the law came near to realizing the boast of its proponents that "there are no longer any bastards in France."

By passing the law of the 12 brumaire, the revolutionary legislators thought they had managed to strike another major blow to the "unnatural" status system of the past, and to have laid one more foundation stone of a new order in which the worth of a man was to depend exclusively on his own attainments rather than on the legitimate transmission of status from father to son. But soon after passing this law, the legislators began to have severe doubts about it.

As a revolution proceeds to break down the old order, there is a simultaneous attempt to stabilize the new. Hence, there is a basic ambiguity in denying the need for "social placement" in general, as there is an ambiguity in weakening the position of the family as a mediator between the individual and society, which is a requisite for the maintenance of the new status system. Although the old principle of status placement must be abolished, and the old status quo destroyed, the new social order needs props for stabilization. To this end, status placement is necessary and the social functions of the family have to be reaffirmed.

And so we see that in revolutionary France, as soon as the revolutionary enthusiasm began to wane, many legislators began to have second thoughts. They insisted that they did not reject monogamous marriage as the basis of republican society. They disavowed any desire to undermine the family. They soon began to realize, as did members of the judiciary who had to apply and interpret the new law, that this law contradicts their proclaimed devotion to the monogamous family.

Already during the debates on the law of the 12 brumaire, Berlier, one of its vocal proponents, made an extremely revealing speech in which he said: "Citizens, I too respect the salutary institution of marriage. Not that I see in it the necessary origin of legitimate procreation, but as *an act which assigns everyone to his place* (emphasis ours), and maintains, in a great society, the harmony necessary to its existence." This rather illogical juxtaposition of the abolishment of illegitimacy and the recognition of the functions of status placement of the legitimate family was to characterize many pronouncements of French legislators and judicial officials in subsequent years. As Crane Brinton put it: "For most Frenchmen, attachment to the *legal* family conflicted with the desire to emancipate the *natural* family, and the respectable sentiments were in the long run far stronger than the advanced ones."[8]

With the thermidorian reaction to what were now conceived as the revolutionary excesses of the men of the Convention, concern for the maintenance of the bourgeois family began to take primacy over Rous-

8. *Ibid.*, p. 37.

seauistic appeals to the natural order. As French society began to be stabilized, as a new bourgeois status order emerged, the legislators began to elaborate a new family code in which *puissance paternelle,* rigid rules of inheritance and defense of the double standard were major objectives. When the new code was finally adopted under Napoleon, it stated that "the natural child, even though acknowledged by the father, cannot have the rights of a legitimate child," and declared furthermore that "natural children cannot be heirs," and specifically stated that children born of adulterous or incestuous unions are forbidden to inherit and must be content with support and training in a trade. Moreover, by enshrining the rule *la recherche de la paternité est interdite,* it explicitly proclaimed male dominance by making it illegal for the mother of an illegitimate child or for that child himself to search out the natural father and to make him responsible for mother and child.

By 1803 there again were bastards in France! For but one brief moment enthusiastic revolutionary legislators had sought to remake the whole status order by destroying the *principle of legitimacy.* As a new status order crystallized, as the now dominant middle class felt the need to shore up the stability of the family and the secure transmission of status from father and son, the old stigma against legitimacy was reinstated and indeed strengthened.

In the Soviet Union All Children Were Equal–for a While

The revolutionary founders of the Soviet Union were beholden to Karl Marx rather than to Rousseau. Their ideological pronouncements did not reject the previous status order as "unnatural," but as "bourgeois." But, just like their French revolutionary forebears, their aim was to destroy the old hierarchical order and to put in its place a new order based on full social equality of all citizens.

Marx and Engels conceived of monogamous marriage as enshrining "the subjugation of one sex by the other," and the principle of private property. The whole structure of the bourgeois family in particular was in their view geared to property ownership and male dominance. They taught that since the bourgeois is vitally concerned with the transmission of his property to his lawful heirs and does not wish the status of the *pater familias* to be threatened, bourgeois law, as expressed in the Code Napoleon, proclaimed that *la recherche de la paternité est interdite* and stigmatized the child born out of wedlock. Bourgeois law and morality make an outcast of the illegitimate child so as better to insure the orderly transmission of paternal wealth to legitimate heirs. Marx and Engels foresaw that in the socialist society of the future "the two bases of traditional marriage, the dependence, rooted in private property, of woman on the man and of children on the parents" would be removed. Marriage was to be based on equality and love instead of on property. Illegitimacy would carry no stigma and society would care for the legitimate and illegitimate alike.[9]

The makers of the Russian revolution attempted to realize Marxist ideas in the new legal structure of revolutionary Russia. Their first Code of Laws concerning the family, enacted as early as October 1918, not only established full equality between husband and wife, but also stated: "Actual descent is regarded as the basis of the family, without any difference between relationships established by legal or religious marriage or outside marriage. Children descended from parents related by non-registered marriage have equal rights with those descended from parents whose marriage was registered." Whether a civil marriage had been performed or not, men and women were to be registered as father and mother in the Bureau of Births. "The interested parties, including the mother, are entitled to prove the true descent of a child. . . . Children of parents related by non-registered marriage may be known either by the father's or the mother's or by their joint surname."[10] The subsequent Code of Laws on Marriage and Divorce, the Family and Guardianship of 1926, was even more specific in its attempt to erase all distinctions between legitimate and illegitimate children. It states; "Children whose parents are not married possess the same rights as children born in wedlock . . . . In order to protect the interests of the child, the mother is granted the right . . . to file a declaration of paternity. . . . If the putative father . . . does not raise any objection, he is recorded as the father of the child." If he does object, a paternity suit will decide the matter.[11]

The 1918 family code abolished inheritance altogether and proclaimed that "testate and intestate succession are abolished. Property of an owner becomes after his death the domain of the . . . Soviet Republic." The 1926 Code reinstated the principle of inherited property but made it subject to a strongly progressive inheritance tax.[12] In both cases, legitimate and illegitimate children were treated alike. While neither could inherit property according to the early law, both could inherit according to the later legislation.

During the early period of the Russian revolution Russian writers hailed its achievements in having eradicated the "bourgeois" stigma at-

9. Cf. Friedrich Engels, *The Origin of the Family, Private Property and the State,* New York: International Publishers, 1942, and H. Kent Geiger's fine chapter on "The Marxist Theory of the Family" in his *The Family in Soviet Russia,* Cambridge: Harvard University Press, 1968, pp. 11–40.

10. Rudolf Schlesinger, *The Family in the U.S.S.R.,* London: Routledge & Kegan Paul, 1949, pp. 37–38.

11. *Ibid.,* p. 159.

12. Geiger, *op. cit.,* p. 49f.

tached to illegitimacy. "We have no legal and illegal children," writes one of them, "here all children are equal, they are all legal." [13]

In the early years of the revolution, the Soviet lawgivers seem to have had less difficulty in applying their principles concerning the legal equality of the illegitimate child than had their French predecessors. Being committed in principle to a weakening of the family, which they conceived as a potential center of divided loyalty that might prevent citizens from giving their total allegiance and devotion to the state, they did not have to worry about, indeed they applauded, the tendency of laws on illegitimacy to undermine the monogamic family. Being devoted to the idea that a man's status placement should depend on his contribution to party, state and society at large, they welcomed any piece of legislation that undermined status transmission from father to son.

Some revolutionary publicists argued for a theory of revolutionary sublimation according to which excessive sexual activity was "robbing the Revolution." [14] Others, such as the leftwing Communist Alexandra Kollontai, pleaded for maximum sexual freedom but maintained at the same time that "contemporary love . . . isolates, and separates off the loving pair from the collective." [15] They were at one, however, in seeing the family as a bulwark of the old order, as an obstacle to the full and total integration of the Soviet citizen. If individuals can be shielded by a private family sphere, they reasoned, if sons are dependent on fathers for their status placement, they can escape, at least in part, from the all-pervasive social control of state and party.

But the new Soviet order also had to be stabilized in its status structure. And so, to the surprise of many Western supporters of the Russian Revolution, who had proclaimed that the Russian family legislation was the most "advanced in the world," the new Family Law adopted in 1944 reversed drastically all previous legislation.[16] The new law abolished the institution of *de facto* marriage and stated that thereafter only registered marriages would be recognized by law. Unmarried mothers would no longer have the right to appeal to the courts for establishing paternity and obtaining alimony. The child of an unmarried mother was to be registered in the mother's name. Under the new law, fatherhood outside wedlock created no rights or obligations, whether for the father himself or for his children.[17] Support of the children of unmarried mothers was assumed by the state. From now on, a child born out of wedlock had no right to claim the name or estate of his father and could easily be identified since he

13. V. F. Calverton, "The Illegitimate Child," eds. Calverton and Schmalhausen, *The New Generation*, New York: The Macaulay Co., 1930.

14. Geiger, *op. cit.*, p. 84f.

15. *Ibid.*, p. 63.

16. Schlesinger, *op. cit.*, pp. 367–390.

17. *Ibid.*, p. 401.

carried the mother's name. The new law created a special stigmatized status for the illegitimate child.[18] Since the offspring of unregistered marriages as well as truly illegitimate children had a blank after the word "father" in the birth certificate, the Soviet Union bred an unusually high number of bastards. A Soviet legal specialist estimated that there were 11,000,000 illegitimate children in the USSR in 1947.[19] It was apparently a common occurrence from then on that school children addressed certain of their peers as: "Hey you, fatherless."[20] What had previously been considered a bourgeois prejudice was now hailed as a progressive achievement of Soviet society. Between 1918 and 1944 the wheel had come full circle.

The Russian policy makers, who had once seen the family as a possible center of divided loyalty, changed their course once Russian society was being stabilized. The equalitarian ethos of the first few years was at odds with the new status structure. Trotsky's quip, that the stabilization of the Russian family runs parallel with the stabilization of the ruble, is most perceptive. As the hierarchical structure of the society became stabilized, the child had to fit more tightly into the social framework. The state now attempted to strengthen the family and recognized its functions as a transmission belt for social controls. The elite of Russian society, having now assured for its members privileges and immunities denied the underlying population, realized that the family, through transmission of skills, connections and wealth, served to insure the transmission of social status from parents to children.

The rights of illegitimate children waxed as long as the state wished to undermine the status transmission from parents to children, but they waned as soon as the state resolved to make the legitimate family a bulwark of the new social order and to assure status transmission from father to son in the privileged strata.[21]

The Chinese and Cuban Revolutions

Evidence on how the Chinese and Cuban revolutions have dealt with the problem of illegitimacy is much more scanty than on their French and Russian predecessors. It is, however, quite remarkable that in both cases legislation to outlaw illegitimacy was introduced at an early stage.

The Marriage Law of the People's Republic of China promulgated on May 1, 1950, states unequivocally: "Children born out of wedlock shall

18. Geiger, *op. cit.*, p. 93.
19. *Ibid.*, p. 259.
20. *Ibid.*, p. 108. The law providing for a dash instead of the father's name in birth certificates of illegitimate children was repealed in 1965.
21. Lewis A. Coser, "Some Aspects of Soviet Family Policy," *The American Journal of Sociology* 56 (1951): 424–434 [this book, pp. 412–29].

enjoy the same rights as children born in lawful wedlock. No person shall be allowed to harm or to discriminate against children born out of wedlock. Where the paternity of a child born out of wedlock is legally established by the mother of the child, by other witnesses, or by other material evidence, the identified father must bear the whole or part of the cost of maintenance and education of the child until it has attained the age of eighteen."[22]

In traditional China, and at least through the 1930's, illegitimate birth stemming from casual associations or from dating and courtship, which are the common sources of illegitimate birth in the West, were in fact quite rare. However, concubinage was a traditional Chinese institution of long standing and many concubines bore children to their consorts. These children were not considered illegitimate. They lived within the paternal household, could inherit if the wife had no children, and had a claim on the father for maintenance.[23] The legitimate wife exercised some power over her husband's concubines and her offspring. As concubines were not ostracized, their offspring did not suffer the stigma associated with illegitimacy in the West. Although status was normally transmitted from father to legitimate son, his children from concubines were permitted a kind of reflected status. The patterned status difference between the children born from a legitimate wife and those from a concubine helped maintain the status quo in the stratification system.

The revolutionary legislation on the outlawing of illegitimacy was therefore enacted not so much in favor of those persons usually considered illegitimate in the West but rather in order to accord full legal status to the children of concubines who had previously existed in a legal penumbra. Even so, the parallel with the Russian case is salient; the revolutionary Chinese legislators were most concerned with removing one of the main props of the traditional gentry family. Their target was the institution of concubinage, an institution peculiar to the gentry. As the children of concubines were now on an equal footing with legitimate children it would become very difficult to maintain the gentry family and its exclusive status placement mechanisms. The privileges of the gentry would be undermined by permitting equal access to those of lower rank. The revolutionary legislation, in this respect as in many others, aimed at undermining the stratification system upon which the pattern of concubinage among the gentry rested.

We lack evidence about the working of the new legislation. But even in the absence of such evidence, we might surmise, following William Goode,[24] that with the decline of arranged marriages and the emergence

---

22. C. K. Yang, *The Chinese Family in the Communist Revolution,* Cambridge: The Technology Press, 1959, p. 223.
23. Goode, *World Revolution, op. cit.,* p. 295.
24. *Ibid.*

of courtship as the recognized and preferred avenue to marriage,[25] Western forms of illegitimacy are now likely to become more prevalent in China. If that should indeed be the case, and if Chinese society will gradually follow in the steps of the Russian in stabilizing a new system of stratification, we may expect a reversal of the Marriage Law of 1950. It took the Russians twenty-six years to move from outlawing illegitimacy to its legal reestablishment. It may take the Chinese, who have in recent years attempted to return to the purity of revolutionary ardor, a bit longer.

The Cuban Fundamental Law of 1959 resembles in all relevant respects the early Russian and Chinese legislation. It specifies, "Parents are obliged to support, aid, train and educate their children whether or not they were married when the children were conceived. . . . No record of the marital status of the parents can be entered on birth certificates and similar documents."[26] The Law also guarantees equal rights to married women and assures them control over wages and their own property.[27]

As is well known, in pre-revolutionary Cuba as in the rest of the Caribbean, common-law marriages were exceedingly frequent in the lower classes, while the upper classes adhered to stricter marital norms and upheld the sanctity of official marital bonds. The Fundamental Law of 1959 in its paragraphs on legitimacy is directed specifically at the upper class where the transmission of status was assured through strict official adherence to the *Principle of Legitimacy* combined with fairly widespread unofficial affairs with mistresses. Here, as in China, and as in Russia earlier, the acceptance of illegitimacy is an attack on the privileges of the upper class. If all children, and not only those by the legitimate wife, have the right of inheritance of status, the traditional transmission of status advantages will become most difficult, and correlatively, opportunities to lower-class children for accession to higher status positions would become available. This would undermine the previous basis of the stratification system through an "inflationary" process.

Yet, there is some evidence that the revolutionary regime also wishes to reduce the incidence of common-law marriage by transforming irregular unions into registered marriages. The regime, following a Mexican precedent, conducted mass ceremonies through which common-law marriages were given the blessing of official recognition. By late 1960, 20,000 couples were so married, and 400,000 such mass marriages were anticipated by the end of the following year.[28] This was a further step in the process of equalization in the stratification system.

25. Morton Fried, "The Family in China: The People's Republic," in Ruth N. Anshen, ed., *The Family,* New York: Harper and Row, 1959.

26 Wyatt MacGuffey and Clifford R. Barnett, *Cuba,* New Haven: H.R.A.F. Press, 1967, p. 52.

27. *Ibid.*

28. *Ibid.,* p. 53.

The evidence is too scant to allow a clearer picture of the present status of the illegitimate child in revolutionary Cuba. All that can be said with certainty is that in this case, like in the others discussed here, the revolutionary legislators attempted to equalize the rights and privileges of legitimate children and those born out of wedlock and conceived of this measure as an attack on the old order, more particularly the mores and institutions of the previous elite. At the same time they attempted to reduce the high rate of illegitimacy that had resulted from the customary existence of common-law marriages in the lower classes. They hence were apparently striving for the institutionalization of a model conjugal family of the Western type while at the same time approving legislation that tended to undermine this family type. Whether they will in time face obstacles similar to those experienced in the Soviet Union, only time will tell. Theoretical reasoning, in any case, would lend support to this expectation.

Summary and Conclusion

Following William J. Goode's lead, this paper has attempted to demonstrate the ways in which the *Principle of Legitimacy* provides the link between the kinship and the stratification system. The degree of tolerance a society has for illegitimacy can be taken as an indicator of (1) the importance attached to the role of the father as a mediator between the family and the society, (2) the rigidity of the hierarchical status structure, (3) the normative insistence on ascribed status.

Rather than trying to examine the degrees of tolerance of illegitimacy (as expressed by the difference in sanctions, for example) in various societies or at different historical periods, in relation to the social role of the father, the rigidity of the hierarchical structure and the normative insistence on ascribed status, this paper focuses on extreme cases of social revolution, that is, when there is a deliberate attempt to transform the social order. At such times, it is to be expected that the role of father would be weakened because as mediator between the family and the class structure he would be seen as helping maintain rather than transform the social order. Since the hierarchical status structure is to be broken down, the normative insistence on ascribed status has to be opposed so as to facilitate the establishment of a new social order. Therefore, it is to be expected that the *Principle of Legitimacy* is likely to be abandoned at such times.

Four cases of social revolutions have been examined. And in all these cases the revolutionary legislators moved to eradicate the differential treatment of legitimate and illegitimate children. In all these cases such legislation can be interpreted as a move to change the status structure and, more specifically, as a strategy that undermines the previous mode of transmission of status from fathers to sons. It was an attack on the stability of the upper class which had been served by the *Principle of Legitimacy,* a stability which the revolution attempted to break. An ideology of humanitarian concerns for the welfare of unwed mothers and their offspring helped strengthen the attempt to abolish this conservative principle.

As a corollary, it is to be expected that the newly established social order will in turn support its own stability through a return to the *Principle of Legitimacy.* After the revolutionary breakthrough, millions of men will acquire a stake in the new system, having absorbed a sense of continuity and maybe even acquired some property. They will, therefore, just like the new elite, be interested in continuity of status placement.[29]

After stabilization of the new status structure, the social role of the father will again be emphasized and illegitimacy will call forth negative sanctions. This was indeed the case after the French and the Russian Revolutions. As to Cuba and China, it is too early to tell. We hope that future reseachers will test our prediction.

29. This point was suggested to us by William J. Goode, to whom we are obliged for reading an earlier draft of this paper.

CONTROL AND PROCESS

To the point made by Parsons in Part One, that the incest taboo helps young people channel their libidinal energies outward, Slater adds that not only incest but any love relationship that monopolizes all libidinal energies would prevent the partners from participating in the community. By thus combining Freud's concept of libidinal diffusion with Durkheim's concept of social constraint, Slater prepares the way for another important contribution to the theory of the family: the synthesis of the *Principle of Reciprocity* and the *Principle of Legitimacy*. The community relations that parents must maintain for the sake of their children's socialization are one basic reason for the rule that every child must have a social father to facilitate the maintenance and extension of the outside network of relationships of the marital partners. Lévi-Strauss's point that "the incest taboo is the basis of social life" and Malinowski's statement that "parenthood is the basis of social structure" can now be summarized in one proposition. Slater teaches us that social life means that there can be no libidinal withdrawal, whether through incest or any of its functional equivalents. Hence it becomes clear that *social parenthood and the incest taboo serve the same social function: the prevention of the separation of small groups from the community.*

Slater has opened the discussion of a problem that has preoccupied social thought ever since the work of Freud and Durkheim: the tension between the desire for emotional gratification and social constraint. Van den Haag defends the point of view that the latter has been victorious over the former, claiming that love is incompatible with marriage and that the passion that characterizes love relationships dies out within this institutionalized setting. Goode reviews the various means by which potential love relationships are channeled into socially approved patterns and shows the social processes by which individual feelings are so channeled as to make possible the integration of kinship and stratification structures. He thus illustrates Malinowski's thesis that parenthood, i.e., the agency through which the young are placed in society, is the basis of social structure. Berger and Kellner show how the mutual adjustment between the marriage partners takes place so as to create a common understanding and definition of the reality that governs their individual lives, their lives in common, and their lives within the social network and the society which demands their services.

In every society there are socially preferred forms of marital alliance, and marital choice is never left to the partners alone. For if exchanges of marital partners are basic elements of social structure because they create alliances between families, it follows that there are preferences as to who the exchange partners will be. The four papers reprinted here show, in concrete instances, how patterns of intermarriage are associated with family lineages, stratification factors such as chieftainship or social mobility, economic factors such as ownership and allocation of wealth, and occupational factors such as partnership in business or other occupational choices. In general it turns out that choices of marriage partners are patterned even where there is much leeway of individual choice, and that marital selection is integrated with the stratification system.

3 THE PRINCIPLE OF ADULT SOCIALIZATION

Philip Slater

Social Limitations on Libidinal Withdrawal

Without getting too deeply into a rather abstruse issue we . . . might point out the competitive advantage in natural selection enjoyed by those organisms which participate in collectivities, and the still further advantage held by collectivities which are highly organized and integrated. Libidinal diffusion is the social cement which binds living entities together. The more objects an individual can cathect at once, the larger the number of individuals who can co-operate in a joint endeavor. Furthermore, as libido becomes further diffused, and gratification becomes less complete, the individual experiences a constant tension and restless energy which can be harnessed to serve socially useful ends.

This characteristic of libidinal diffusion is implicit in psychoanalytic writings. Thus Flügel, for example, describes normal sexual development as a series of successive displacements of libidinal cathexis, from the mother, to the father, to siblings, to parental surrogates, to peers with resemblances to the original incestuous objects, to peers who neither resemble nor contrast with these objects but are simply independent of them.[1]

Yet it should be abundantly clear from clinical analysis of dreams and

1. J. C. Flügel, *The Psychoanalytic Study of the Family,* London: Hogarth, 1957.

projective materials collected from normal individuals, not to mention the universality of incestuous longings in mythology and folklore, that these earlier libidinal cathexes are never entirely uprooted. Indeed, so long as there is sufficient libido left over for completely free choice of objects, it is not important that they should be. But let us consider the consequences of this fact: "healthy" human growth in all existing societies *requires* that libidinal gratification must always be partial and incomplete. For no matter how perfectly gratifying the individual's mature erotic relationships may be, they cannot discharge those fragments of libidinal tension which have been "left behind," attached to their original incestuous objects.

This is, of course, of little practical psychological significance. Such residual libidinal tensions can be discharged in dreams or humor, or sublimated into filial devotion or artistic creativity. But it is important for social theory, since it means that *so long as an individual cathects more than one object he will be unable to achieve a complete absence of libidinal tension,* and hence remains always available for collectivization.

One of the best examples of the way in which libidinal diffusion provides competitive advantages in natural selection may be found in Parsons' analysis of the functions of the incest taboo. Parsons points out that the actual prevention of incest is less important than the fact that it enforces "marrying out." That is, it bars the nuclear family from becoming a completely autonomous collectivity, and blocks the withdrawal of libidinal cathexis from those larger coordinated aggregates the maintenance of which has long been essential in most parts of the world to tolerable human existence. "It is only on the impossible assumption that families should constitute independent societies and not be segmental units of higher-level organizations, that incest as a regular practice would be socially possible." Involvement in incestuous relationships, in which emotional needs could be more fully and immediately gratified, would weaken the individual's bonds to the larger collectivity. Parsons seems to be referring to this issue when he talks about the necessity of "propelling the child from the family."[2]

Limitations of Libidinal Diffusion

At this point, however, we find ourselves in another dilemma. Whereas at first we were puzzled to discern the basis for the prevalence of an inferior mode of gratification, we now seem to be in the antipodal difficulty of wondering why there should be any limit to libidinal diffusion. For while

2. Talcott Parsons, "The Incest Taboo in Relation to Social Structure and the Socialization of the Child," *British Journal of Sociology,* 5 (June, 1954), pp. 101–117. [See this volume, pp. 13–30.]

one can assume that the superior gratificatory attraction inhering in libidinal contraction would always exert a kind of gravitational drag on this trend, the advantages in terms of natural selection would seem to push inevitably toward endless increases in the diffusional direction.

Even from a societal viewpoint, however, unlimited libidinal diffusion would be a doubtful blessing.[3] The most obvious limitation is the necessity for motivation of procreation. Those few attempts, by totalitarian religious communities of a utopian nature, to sublimate and diffuse all sexual tendencies, illustrate this point rather dramatically. Ultimate diffusion led to ultimate extinction. We must thus qualify our statement that natural selection favors libidinal diffusion, and say rather that it favors individuals and groups in whom diffusion is ascendant but nonetheless strongly opposed by tendencies toward libidinal contraction—in other words, those who are strongly conflicted on this dimension.

Such a modification helps to explain the intensity of the incest taboo, which may be attributed to the fact that it is indeed the conflicted who have survived. Ultimately, it derives from the specificity of the prohibition; libidinal contraction must be permitted to go far enough to ensure sexual union and procreation but not far enough to threaten the existence of suprafamilial collectivities. Since the incest prohibition marks the point at which prescription is suddenly transformed into proscription, and since the forces propelling the individual across the line are very powerful, the barrier required to interrupt this momentum must be correspondingly powerful.

Three Threats to Aggregate Maintenance

Although violation of the incest prohibition constitutes the nearest danger to suprafamilial collectivities, there are other and more extreme forms of libidinal contraction than that against which the taboo most specifically militates. If libidinal cathexis can be withdrawn from larger collectivities and centered in the nuclear family, it can also be withdrawn from the family and centered in any single dyadic relationship, and finally, it can be withdrawn from all object relationships and centered in the ego, as in the classical psychoanalytic discussions of narcissism. All three are simply positions on a continuous dimension of social regression. Incest itself has long been viewed in this manner, with Parsons twice referring to it as a socially regressive withdrawal, from the "obligation to contribute to the formation and maintenance of suprafamilial bonds on which the major economic, political, and religious functions of the society are depen-

---

3. In raising this issue I do not mean to imply a disbelief in the possibility of further vast increases in the collectivization of human life.

dent," and citing Fortune and Lévi-Strauss in support of this position.[4]

The normal response of others to signs of libidinal contraction in an individual with whom these others participate in some collectivity, is what we shall call "social anxiety." They may also display anger, moral indignation, ridicule, or scorn, but the anxiety is clearly the primary response from which the others are derived. Since it is a rather common and familiar sensation to all of us, experienced whenever someone deserts, either physically or psychically, a group in which we are emotionally involved, little need be said about it. The latent danger with which it is concerned is the collapse of the group. It does not spring, however, from any rational consideration of the advantages of societal existence, but is emotional and automatic, and appears concurrently with awareness of group membership, whether in the family of orientation or elsewhere. Presumably its universality is a result of natural selection.

Social anxiety generally elicits, in those who experience it, behavior designed to reform this deviant member who has "regressed," i.e., transferred his libido from a more inclusive to a less inclusive object. But social control is never entirely *post hoc,* and in all surviving societies we find an elaboration of anticipatory institutions which serve to hinder such cathectic withdrawal. It is primarily with these institutions that the remainder of this paper will deal, although post hoc sanctions will also be discussed.

We have said that there exist three principal forms of libidinal contraction or cathectic withdrawal. Each of these forms has a primary anticipatory institution which tends to preclude its emergence:

1. The most immediate form—withdrawal of cathexis from larger aggregates to within the confines of the nuclear family—we will call "familial withdrawal." Its principal anticipatory institution is the incest taboo.

2. Withdrawal of cathexis from larger aggregates to a single intimate dyad we will call "dyadic withdrawal." Its principal anticipatory institution is marriage.

3. The most extreme form—withdrawal of cathexis from all objects to the self—we will call "narcissistic withdrawal." Its principal anticipatory institution is socialization.

These institutions are for the most part so successful in counteracting libidinal contraction that we are usually unaware of the conflict taking place; it is only at certain rough spots in the social fabric that it becomes visible. Since space limitations forbid detailed discussion of all three forms of withdrawal, I shall concentrate . . . on the second or dyadic type,

4. Reo F. Fortune, "Incest," in *Encyclopedia of the Social Sciences,* New York: Macmillan, 1930; and Claude Lévi-Strauss, *Les Structures élémentaires de la parenté,* Paris: Presses Universitaires de France, 1949 [see this book, pp. 3–12].

which yields some of the most dramatic examples.[5] Little can in any case be added to Parsons' discussion of the function of the incest taboo in preventing familial withdrawal, while narcissistic withdrawal receives extensive treatment in the psychoanalytic literature.[6]

Dyadic Withdrawal

An intimate dyadic relationship always threatens to short-circuit the libidinal network of the community and drain off its source of sustenance. The needs binding the individual to collectivities and reinforcing his allegiance thereto are now satisfied in the dyadic relationship, and the libido attached to these collectivities and diffused through their component members is drawn back and invested in the dyad.

5. *Editor's Note*. The author's discussion of the first and the third type of cathectic withdrawal is omitted here. The first type, the single individual's (narcissistic) withdrawal, lies outside the scope of this volume; and the third type, familial withdrawal which is prevented through the incest taboo, has been dealt with in Chapter 1.

However, since some problems were raised in Chapter 1 by the deviant case presented there, it would seem important to indicate Slater's refinement of the idea of "social contraction" that would be served by incest. To the points made by Fortune, Lévi-Strauss and Parsons about the function of the incest taboo in preventing family withdrawal, Slater adds that it is the strong narcissistic component in the incestual relationship that would present to society the danger of dyadic withdrawal. That is, narcissism in such a relationship would be so strong due to the emotional ties that develop in the immediate family between children and parents of the opposite sex, as well as between siblings of the opposite sex, where the love object is first experienced as an extension of the self. Incest does not simply imply partnership within the nuclear family; it implies a union that would permit the partners to indulge in unmitigated narcissism, to "fall back onto themselves," so to speak. "Incestuous relationships are in part tabooed for the reason that they are closer to absolute narcissism than any other relationship can be." The author goes on to show that of the three possible forms of incest, father-daughter, brother-sister and mother-son, it is the latter which is the most threatening to society "simply because the potential for dyadic withdrawal would be so high. . . . The narcissistic component is particularly strong" in this relationship since mother and son have each "at one time viewed the other as a part of or extension of the self. It is in part for this reason that mother-son incest is of all forms the most severely prohibited."

Slater's hypothesis could be examined through an analysis of incestual relationships in Ancient Egypt (which, by the way, do not seem to have included mother-son unions) as to the measure of narcissistic withdrawal these entailed and as to the possible counteracting social mechanisms that were in operation there.

6. The examples which follow are presented, for the sake of clarity and simplicity, in an interpersonal form, pitting individuals experiencing cathectic withdrawal against others who are not. This should not mislead the reader into assuming that there is no inner struggle in all this, or that we are talking of different types of people. There is no one who does not at some time in his life experience and defend cathectic withdrawal, and no one who never fights against it.

In the same way I have ignored the issue of guilt. Guilt is not aroused by libidinal contraction itself, but only by violation of the norms associated with the anticipatory institutions. For to the extent that cathectic withdrawal has occurred the individual is by definition emotionally unavailable to the collectivity in question. He feels no commitment to it and cannot therefore perceive himself as having violated that commitment.

There are several reasons why the dyad lends itself so well to this kind of short-circuiting. One is that, as Simmel pointed out, "the secession of either would destroy the whole. The dyad, therefore, does not attain that superpersonal life which the individual feels to be independent of himself." [7] Another is that all other groups consist of multiple relationships which influence one another, while the dyad consists of only one relationship, influenced by none. In triads and larger groups the libidinal cathexis of the individual is divided and distributed, and there are many points of "leverage" at which he may be influenced or controlled. Furthermore, if part of the attachment of two persons is based upon a common attachment to a third party it may also be based upon attachment to a superindividual concept, to collective ideals. [8]

One may, of course, exaggerate the special qualities of the dyad. In part it is merely the extreme case of a general law which says that intimate involvement of an individual with a group is an inverse function of its size. It is possible, however, to make a sharp separation of the dyad from other forms by virtue of its low combinatorial potential. The intimate dyadic relationship thus forms a nodal point for libidinal contraction. Libidinal cathexis which is withdrawn from larger collectivities can "stick" to the dyad, in a manner analogous to the stopping-places in Freud's parable of fixation. [9]

The Dyad and the Community. If we assume a finite quantity of libido in every individual, then it follows that the greater the emotional involvement in the dyad, the greater will be the cathectic withdrawal from other objects. This accords well with the popular concept of the oblivious lovers, who are "all wrapped up in each other," and somewhat careless of their social obligations. All of the great lovers of history and literature were guilty of striking disloyalties of one kind or another—disregard for the norms governing family and peer group ties, in the story of Romeo and Juliet, becomes, in the affair of Antony and Cleopatra, a disregard for societal responsibilities which embrace most of the civilized world. In Shakespeare's drama, a war of global significance is treated by the lovers as a courtly tournament, and their armies are manipulated as if the outcome were related only to the complexities of the internal dyadic relationship. This is epitomized in a remark by Cleopatra, who expresses her satisfaction with a day of military victory by saying to Antony, "Comest thou smiling from the world's great snare uncaught?"

Given this inverse relationship between dyadic cathexis and societal cathexis, another correlation suggests itself. We may hypothesize that the

7. Kurt H. Wolff (trans.), *The Sociology of Georg Simmel,* Glencoe, Ill.: The Free Press, 1950, pp. 123–124.
8. Theodore M. Mills, "A Sociological Interpretation of Freud's Group Psychology and the Analysis of the Ego" (unpublished).
9. Sigmund Freud, *A General Introduction to Psychoanalysis,* Garden City Books, 1952, pp. 297–299.

more totalitarian the collectivity, in terms of making demands upon the individual to involve every area of his life in collective activity, the stronger will be the prohibition against dyadic intimacy. . . .

Strong opposition to dyadic intimacy is often found in youth groups which are formed on the basis of common interests such as music, camping, travel, or mountain-climbing. Solidarity in such groups often runs high, and avoidance of even momentary pairing is usually a firmly upheld norm. Extreme prohibitions are also characteristic of utopian communistic communities, religious and otherwise, such as the Oneida experiment. In some instances the dyadic intimacy prohibition is enforced at the same time that sexual promiscuity is encouraged, thus clearly revealing that the basis of the proscription is not fear of sexuality but fear of libidinal contraction—fear lest the functions which the state performs for the individual could be performed for each other by the members of the dyad. Soviet Russia[10] and Nazi Germany also made abortive experiments in this direction, before realizing that as a device for providing societal control over dyadic intimacy, the institution of marriage could scarcely be improved upon.[11]

In some nonliterate societies, the prevention of privacy is managed through such devices as barracks-type living arrangements. I stress this fact because of the widespread notion that "romantic love" is simply an idiosyncrasy of Western civilization, and has no relevance for primitive societies. This view has been challenged by Goode, who argues that it is less rare than supposed, and seems to associate its infrequency, as we have done here, with the notion that "love must be controlled." He sees the need for such control, however, as based on the more limited necessity of preventing the disruption of lineage and class strata. Of particular interest to our purpose is the passage from Margaret Mead which he cites as illustrating the presumed irrelevance of romantic love to primitive living. This passage states that the Samoans "laughed with incredulous contempt at Romeo and Juliet."[12] Similar laughter is often evoked by this drama among pre-adolescents and adolescents in our own society, but I wonder if we would infer from this that it had no meaning to them. Primitive peoples often laugh at hypothetical and "unheard-of" violations of major taboos, and it would perhaps be more appropriate to interpret the laughter as an expression of social anxiety rather than of the "irrelevance" of romantic love.

Goode cites many types of control of dyadic intimacy, similar to

10. *Editor's Note:* The reader is referred to Chapter 8 of this volume, "Some Aspects of Soviet Family Policy" by Lewis A. Coser, pp. 412–29.

11. An insightful literary portrayal of this antagonism may be found in Orwell's *1984* (New York: Harcourt, Brace, 1949), in which a highly centralized collectivity evinces overwhelming hostility to dyadic intimacy, as a potential refuge from the all-pervasive state.

12. William J. Goode, "The Theoretical Importance of Love," *American Sociological Review,* 24 (February, 1959), pp. 38–47. [See this book, pp. 143–56.]

those we will discuss in relation to Western society: child marriages, restriction of the pool of eligible spouses, isolation of adolescents from prospective mates, and peer group control. Of isolation he says, "It should be emphasized that (its) primary function . . . is to minimize informal or intimate social interaction." He also notes that relatively free mate choice (in *formal* terms) is always associated with the "strong development of an adolescent peer group system," for reasons "that are not yet clear." From our perspective, the reasons are simply that societal control has shifted to the peer group, and thus does not need to be exercised parentally.[13]

One principal issue, then, in this conflict between dyadic intimacy and collective life, is whether the relationship shall be an end in itself (as in "romantic love") or a means to a socially desired end. In this connection let us consider Alexander's remark that *"the erotic value of an action is inversely related to the degree to which it loses the freedom of choice and becomes coordinated* and subordinated to other functions and becomes a part of an organized system, of a goal structure." On the individual level he points to the fact that the growing child "first practices most of his biological functions playfully for the mere pleasure he derives from them," but that later they are directed toward utilitarian goals, integrated into a larger system of action, and lose their erotic value. Similarly he sees society as "losing its playful hedonistic qualities as it becomes more and more organized and thus restricts the freedom of the activities of its members. . . . Play requires utmost freedom of choice, which is lost when the activities of man become closely knit into a social fabric." He contrasts the individualistic and playful cat to the collectivistic, organized and unplayful ant, and goes on to note that in the insect states "organization progressed so far that the majority of the members became asexual and what erotic expression remains for them consists in an occasional communal ritualistic performance consisting in to and fro rhythmic movements collectively performed."[14]

This discussion pinpoints the source of the antagonism of "totalitarian" collectivities toward dyadic intimacy. The intimate, exclusive dyadic relationship is essentially "playful" and non-utilitarian. Some kind of organized societal intrusion, as in the institution of marriage, is required to convert it into a socially useful relationship, and insofar as this intrusion is successful the playful aspect of the relationship will tend to disappear. As Alexander points out, "the process toward increased

13. *Ibid.* [this book, p. 152]: This perhaps explains the one important departure of the musical "West Side Story" from its Shakespearean original, which is otherwise as timely as when it was written. But "Romeo and Juliet" portrays decathexis of *both* family and peer group, and is thus the best single portrayal of dyadic withdrawal in adolescence. Even "Marty" adds little to the street corner scenes Shakespeare depictied.

14. Franz Alexander, "Unexplored Areas in Psychoanalytic Theory and Treatment," *Behavioral Science,* 3 (October, 1958), pp. 302–303.

organization or less freedom of choice takes place at the cost of erotic gratification of the individual members of a system, be these organic functions of the body or members of a social organization."[15] Parsons is stressing precisely the same point in his paper on the incest taboo, when he says: "marriage has direct functional significance as a mechanism which establishes important direct ties of interpenetration of membership between different elements in the structural network. Under such circumstances marriage cannot be merely a 'personal affair' of the parties to it."[16] We may thus directly equate libidinal diffusion with the de-eroticizing of the sexual life of the individual—the transformation of hedonistic activity into utilitarian activity as Alexander describes it.

Freud and Bion lay similar emphasis on the opposition between hetero-sexual dyadic attachments and group solidarity. Both view the latter as dependent upon sublimation of sexuality, and see the dyadic bond as a subversion of this sublimation. Freud says flatly that "directly sexual tendencies are unfavorable to the formation of groups," remarking that the sexual act is the one condition "in which a third person is at the best superfluous."[17]

> Two people coming together for the purpose of sexual satisfaction, in so far as they seek for solitude, are making a demonstration against . . . the group feeling. The more they are in love, the more completely they suffice for each other. . . .
>   Even in a person who has in other respects become absorbed in a group the *directly sexual tendencies preserve a little of his individual activity.* . . . Love for women breaks through the group ties of race, of national separation, and of the social class system. . . .[18]

The Premarital Dyad. Let us now look at examples of dyadic withdrawal in our own society. Although it first appears much earlier, as we shall see, its most familiar manifestations are those occurring in adolescence, when experiments in enduring heterosexual intimacy are first essayed, and soon encounter various kinds of resistance and control from parents, other authorities, and the peer group. The arena of the struggle is often the issue of "going steady," which is generally opposed by adults whether it involves a cathectic withdrawal or not, but which is handled by the peer group with the ardent inconsistency characteristic of fledgling social enterprises. In some groups zealous opposition is the rule, while in others there is an equally enthusiastic group endorsement of the

15. *Ibid*. The process is thus analogous to the "routinization of charisma" at the level of narcissistic withdrawal. Cf. Weber, *The Theory of Social and Economic Organization*, New York: Oxford University Press, 1947, pp. 363–368. Cf. also footnote 1.

16. Parsons, *op. cit.*

17. Sigmund Freud, *Group Psychology and the Analysis of the Ego*, New York: Liveright, 1951, pp. 92, 120 ff.; W. R. Bion, "Experiences in Groups: III," *Human Relations*, 2 (No. 1, 1949), pp. 13–22.

18. Freud, *op. cit.*, pp. 121–123. Italics mine.

practice, transformed in such a way, however, by group regulation, as no longer to constitute dyadic withdrawal. Criteria of sexual desirability are established with fanatical specificity by group norms, so as virtually to eliminate the importance of personal psychological characteristics. The partners are expected to spend the bulk of their time in group activities and to have a relationship of short duration (often measured in weeks). Such institutionalization of the "going steady" relationship is clearly a far more effective instrument against libidinal contraction than adult opposition.

A special example of this type of peer group control is found in the "rating-and-dating complex" described by Waller.[19] Here the most desirable dyadic partner becomes the one who best lives up to group norms, which tend to replace sexual strivings with status and prestige needs. Under these conditions personal intimacy is rarely achieved. If by some accident compatible partners should come together, the rules regulating behavior in the situation would tend to prevent the existence of this compatibility from becoming known to either person.

Norms in many such groups also emphasize sexual antagonism and exploitation. The male often achieves prestige within the male group by maximizing physical contact and minimizing expenditure of money on a date. The female achieves prestige within her group by maximizing expenditure and minimizing sexual contact. The date becomes, in the ideal case, a contest between adversaries. Each has much to win or lose in the way of prestige, depending upon how effectively control of tender and sexual feelings can be maintained. It is not difficult to see how dyadic intimacy is minimized in this situation. If each partner, even in the midst of sexual caresses, is "keeping score" in terms of the peer group norms, little emotional involvement can take place. The boy, for example, knows that his friends will later ask him if he "made out," and his sexual behavior may be determined more by this than by any qualities inherent in his partner.[20] It is of no little significance that the beginning of dyadic intimacy and withdrawal is always signalled by the boy's sudden reluctance to talk about the relationship, a reluctance which invariably arouses social anxiety and ridicule.

The control mechanisms of the adult community during this early period are less subtle. Like the peer group, adults depend heavily on ridicule, and lay similar stress upon promiscuity and an exploitive attitude toward the opposite sex. In the adult's exhortation to the adolescent, however, to "play the field," or "keep 'em guessing," or "don't get tied down at your age," it is not difficult to detect the expression of

19. Willard Waller, "The Rating and Dating Complex," *American Sociological Review*, 2 (1937), pp. 727–734.
20. David Riesman sees this as a peculiarly "other-directed" phenomenon, but it undoubtedly occurs whenever the peer group is strong. *The Lonely Crowd*, pp. 96–97.

suppressed promiscuous urges—so that the advice serves a psychological function as well as a societal one.[21]

Adult opposition is not limited to these casual admonitions, however, but often takes more organized forms, and were it not for some such concept as social anxiety it would be difficult to explain why a practice which seems admirably suited to prepare the adolescent for a monogamous adult life should be decried by church and school authorities. "Going steady" is in practice a form of serial monogamy, through which the individual learns not only how to select those qualities most important to him in a mate, but also the obligations and interpersonal expectations appropriate to a monogamous system.

Prohibitions by these authorities are an expression of the breakdown, under changing social conditions, of older and more subtle methods of control. Institutions such as marriage or peer group regulation of dyadic relationships block dyadic withdrawal through social intrusion upon the dyad—ritualizing and regulating it, and drawing its members back into their other relationships. For the most part these forms of control are so effective that it is only in large, "loose," pluralistic societies such as our own that dyadic withdrawal occurs with sufficient frequency and intensity to permit easy observation of the forces opposing it. In many primitive societies dyadic relationships are so highly institutionalized and diluted by group bonds that withdrawal has little opportunity to emerge.

In more mutable societies, however, sudden outbreaks of dyadic intimacy in unexpected areas are always occurring, due to the obsolescence of old mechanisms (e.g., chaperonage) or the emergence of new and unregulated areas of contact (e.g., earlier dating). Sporadic accelerations in the process of collectivization (such as occur in utopian religious communities) may also generate a demand for more extreme action. In such circumstances prohibition becomes more common.

The "going steady" controversy in our society is a good example of this phenomenon, in that it revolves around an extension of heterosexual dyadic intimacy into a younger and younger age group in an era in which teen-age marriage is felt to be socially undesirable. In the colonial period, when an unmarried girl of twenty was considered an old maid, the threat of dyadic withdrawal in adolescence was dissipated by marriage, but this is less feasible today, when the educational process is so prolonged and so

21. Cf. Talcott Parsons, "Age and Sex in the Social Structure of the United States," *American Sociological Review*, 7 (1942), pp. 604–616 [this book, pp. 243–55]. The requirement that the adolescent unlearn this injunction upon marrying constitutes a discontinuity of the type discussed by Ruth Benedict, "Continuities and Discontinuities in Cultural Conditioning," *Psychiatry*, 1 (1938), pp. 161–167. But as in so many other instances, the adult's response to his own stress perpetuates the conflict in the next generation.

valued.[22] Furthermore, we have entered an age in which, through geographical mobility and mass communication, libidinal diffusion has achieved new heights of virtuosity.

Our hypothesis would lead us to expect that the strongest opposition to "going steady" would come from the more "totalitarian"[23] collectivities, and this seems to be the case. A few years ago a Roman Catholic organ expressed unqualified disapproval of the practice, and a parochial school "banned" it. Arguments stressed, as usual, the dangers of sexual transgression, but since sexual intercourse may also occur within the context of a promiscuous dating pattern, something more than sexuality is clearly involved. Other remarks concerning the parochial school ban revealed the intense social anxiety over possible dyadic withdrawal and consequent loss of interest in (i.e., decathexis of) church, state, school, community and God. Thus the priests argued that going steady "creates distractions to *make concentrated study impossible,*" and often leads to marriages between couples too immature emotionally to assume the *obligations of the married state,*" while a school superintendent claimed that it "interferes with good school work, and robs the youngster of one of the finer experiences of growing up: the friendship and companionship of *as wide a circle of acquaintances of both sexes as possible.*"[24] It is, of course, not the "youngster" but the community and the peer group which are "robbed" in these ways, and the absolute and unqualified nature of the italicized phrase reveals the chronic anxiety of the social man when he is reminded that the entire societal structure, upon which he is so utterly dependent, rests upon borrowed libidinal cathexis, the creditors for which are never still.[25]

The Marriage Ceremony as an Intrusion Ritual. The real focal point of the conflict between dyadic intimacy and societal allegiances is, of course, the marital relationship. It would be tedious to review here the many functions of marriage, but it may be profitable to examine the mechanisms which serve to maintain its social nature and prevent dyadic withdrawal. For every marriage poses the threat of this type of social regression, inasmuch as it creates the possibility of a self-sufficient and exclusive sub-unit, emotionally unaffiliated with the larger collectivity.

This danger is not a particularly serious one in many primitive societies, where the proverb "blood is thicker than water" is not merely a psychodynamic reality but also a sociological one. Even in monogamous

22. It may again become the solution, however, as in-school marriages are on the increase. It is interesting how seldom, in these two popular controversies, going steady and early marriage are seen as alternatives.

23. Once again it should be stressed that this term refers to the diminutiveness of that sphere which is considered private and personal by the collectivity, rather than to the degree of autocracy which it evinces.

24. *The Boston Globe,* October 19, 1956. Italics mine.

25. Parsons, in his paper on the incest taboo, makes this same point in relation to socialization. *Op. cit.* [This book, pp. 13–30.]

societies such as that of Dobu, the marital bond is often a very weak one due to the divisive effects of exogamy.[26]

In a society such as ours, however, with small nuclear family units, monogamy, neolocal residence, and relatively weak kinship ties, the threat is a very real one. The marriage ritual then becomes a series of mechanisms for pulling the dyad apart somewhat, so that its integration complements rather than replaces the various group ties of its members. The discussion which follows is primarily concerned with the social rituals surrounding the typical Protestant middle-class marriage in our society, but the pattern differs only in detail from those found elsewhere.

As the marriage approaches there is a rapid acceleration of the involvement of the families of the couple in their relationship. Increasing stress is placed upon an awareness of the ritual, legal, and economic significance of the relationship, and the responsibilities which must be assumed. In addition to the traditional evaluations made at this juncture of the bread-winning and home-making capabilities of the two individuals, there may even be, as Whyte has suggested, a concern about the social appropriateness of the wife for the organizational setting in which the husband must move.[27]

But societal invasion of the free and exclusive intimacy of the couple (assuming this to have been the nature of the relationship prior to this time) is not limited to such overt influence. The entire ceremony constitutes a rehearsal for the kind of societal relationship which is expected of them later. First of all, the ceremony is usually a sufficiently involved affair to require a number of practical social decisions from the couple in preparation for the occasion. Much of their interaction during this period will thus concern issues external to their own relationship, and there will be a great deal of preoccupation with loyalties and obligations outside of the dyad itself. Guests must be invited, attendants chosen, and gifts for the attendants selected. The ceremony has the effect of concentrating the attention of both individuals on every *other* affectional tie either one has ever contracted.

Similarly, the ceremony serves to emphasize the *dependence* of the dyadic partners on other collectivities. In addition to the gifts given to the couple, it is made clear to them that much of the responsibility for their wedding rests with their families, who bear a far greater burden in this regard than they themselves. They are, in essence, "given" a wedding.

Their feelings of harassment and anxiety over the coming event,

26. Reo F. Fortune, *The Sorcerers of Dobu*, London: Routledge, 1932. The kinship systems of many primitive societies, particularly those involving complex exagamous clans and unilineal descent, often seem themselves to be, in part, elaborate defenses against dyadic and familial withdrawal—defenses that are reminiscent, in their rigid, hypertrophied quality, of the neurotic mechanisms of individuals.

27. William H. Whyte, Jr., "The Wife Problem," in Robert F. Winch and Robert McGinnis, *Selected Studies in Marriage and the Family*, New York: Holt, 1953, pp. 278–295.

coupled with the realization that their role is at the moment a relatively minor one, and will throughout be a passive one, inculcates a feeling that the dyadic relationship is not their "personal affair." They become more aware that after marriage, too, life will involve instrumental responsibilities, extra-dyadic personal obligations, and societal dependence. It is usually during this period that the impulse toward dyadic withdrawal reasserts itself, and one or the other will half-seriously suggest elopement. By now there is a feeling that they have set in motion a vast machine over which they no longer have any control. But it is usually felt that things have "gone too far"—parents and friends would be disappointed and hurt, eyebrows would be raised—there is no turning back. The impulse is overwhelmed by the feelings of loyalty and obligation which the impending ceremony has aggravated, and the crucial moment passes.

The role of the clergyman who is to unite the pair is of the utmost importance during this period. It is he who usually verbalizes the societal intrusion most explicitly, and he speaks from a position of considerable prestige, regardless of the religiosity of the betrothed couple. In the first place he is the central person in the proceedings, and represents, emotionally, the paternal figure who can fulfill or deny their wishes. It is he who will speak the magic words which will join them, and the accumulated experience of hundreds of movies, novels, serials, and comic strips tells them that until the last word is spoken the marriage is in danger of being thwarted.

Second, he is the only person on the scene with expert knowledge regarding the ceremony itself. As such he is also typically the least anxious person involved, and thereby provides an important source of support. Sometime prior to the wedding he generally has a "talk" with the couple partly to reassure, but more important, to stress their societal and religious obligations.

The form of this statement is of particular relevance to the concept of societal intrusion. In many denominations it is explicitly stated that marriage is a contract involving three parties—husband, wife, and God, and that He is always "present" so long as the marriage lasts. It would be difficult to find a more vivid symbol of the institutionalization of the dyad than this, nor a more clear illustration of the Durkheimian equation of God with society. The dyadic relationship not only is no longer a "personal affair," it is no longer even a dyad. The privacy of the relationship is seen as permanently invaded. It is interesting to note how this supernatural symbol of societal intrusion is given more concrete form in Orwell's *1984,* in which the dyad cannot escape from Big Brother, who is "always watching."[28]

---

28. One wonders what effect this fantasy of an omnipresent parental figure has on the sexual relationship of couples who take it seriously. Ultimately, of course, societal intrusion is incarnated in a child, and the notion of a scoptophilic deity dwindles into the reality of the curious child before the primal scene.

The actual process of intrusion, however, is more mundane. As the time for the wedding draws near, the forces drawing the couple apart become more intense. It is often believed to be "bad luck" for the groom to see the bride in her wedding dress before the ceremony, and, in general, contact between the couple on the day of the wedding is considered bad form. When they enter the church it is from opposite ends, as leaders of separate hosts of followers. Prior to the wedding day there are showers or a bridal supper for the bride and a "bachelor's dinner" for the groom, in which peer group ties are very strongly underlined. This tends to create the impression that in some way the couple *owe* their relationship to these groups, who are preparing them ceremonially for their marriage. Often this is made explicit, with family and friends vying with one another in claiming responsibility for having "brought them together" in the first place. This impression of societal initiative is augmented by the fact that the bride's father "gives the bride away." The retention of this ancient custom in modern times serves explicitly to deny the possibility that the couple might unite quite on their own. In other words, the marriage ritual is designed to make it appear as if somehow the idea of the dyadic union sprang from the community and not from the dyad itself. In this respect, marriage in our society resembles the ritual of the parent who discovers a child eating candy, and says, "I didn't hear you ask for that," whereupon the child says, "May I?" and the parent says, "Yes, you may." The families and friends may actually have had nothing to do with the match, or even have opposed it. The members of the wedding party often come from far away, and some of them may be strangers to one another. The ceremony itself, however, its corollary rituals, and the roles which pertain to it, all tend to create an image of two individuals, propelled toward each other by a united phalanx of partisans.

The Honeymoon. To everything that has been said thus far the honeymoon would seem to be an exception. The wedding ritual seems designed to emphasize the fact that, indeed, marriage is *not* a honeymoon. Yet this wedding is actually followed immediately by a socially sanctioned dyadic withdrawal, involving the very kind of exclusive, private intimacy—undisturbed by any external ties or obligations—which is at all other times in the life of an individual forbidden. The couple is permitted, even expected, to "get away from it all," and remove themselves entirely from collective life. To facilitate this withdrawal they typically absent themselves from the community, travelling to a place where they are unknown. Some secrecy is usually preserved about their destination, with only a few chosen persons "in on" the secret. Seldom in the life of the average individual are the threads binding him to society so few and so slackened.

At the honeymoon resort they are entirely without obligations or responsibilities. No one knows them or expects anything from them. They are more or less taboo, and others leave them to themselves. The emotional privacy so difficult to obtain at all other times, before and after, is for the moment almost universally granted. But the period of license is characteristically brief, save for the very wealthy; the couple return to the community, establish a household, resume old ties, assume new responsibilities, "put away childish things," and "the honeymoon is over."

But how are we to account for this exception? Should we write it off as simply another example of the universal social tendency to permit norms to be violated on certain festive occasions? The most reasonable interpretation would seem to be the same as was applied to the narcissistic leader: the married couple are allowed to hoard their libido between themselves, "as a reserve against their later momentous constructive activity." By this I refer not merely to the begetting and raising of children, but rather to the more general process of creating a home and becoming a family—the basic unit upon which the societal structure is built. For marriage is after all a compromise institution—one which attempts to generate a substructure which will be solidary enough to perform its social functions without becoming so solidary that it ceases to be a substructure and begins to seek autonomy. The wedding ceremony tends to guard against the latter, while the honeymoon helps to ensure the former. Some marriages, after all, do not begin with a withdrawn dyad, but with one which has scarcely experienced any privacy, intimacy or freedom. Either extreme is socially inutile, as we have noted.

At the same time we should not be carried away by this functional interpretation to the point of assuming that some sort of folk wisdom is operating here. It is not the community, nor the individual's allegiance to it which inspired this custom, but rather his hatred and fear of society and its pressures towards rationalization and de-eroticization of his instinctual life. In other words, the honeymoon is a manifestation of dyadic withdrawal which is tolerated because it has never in fact (for the reasons given above) showed the slightest sign of being socially disruptive.

Nor do I mean by this to attribute any undue rationality or reality-sense to individuals in their group identities. It would be perfectly reasonable to expect that, although the practice never called attention to itself as a social danger, the very threat of dyadic withdrawal in so concrete a form would arouse social anxiety, and that despite the experience of centuries the participants would stupidly reiterate this anxious reaction and the types of behavior to which it gives rise.

This is indeed the case, the reaction expressing itself primarily in going-away pranks of various kinds, whereby the most serious honeymoon taboos may be broken in a joking context. A great deal of hostility is expressed directly toward the departing couple in the form of diffuse anal-expulsive gestures such as throwing rice and confetti. Some of the customary jokes unveil the basis of this hostility, in that they have the covert purpose of hindering the couple's departure. These include tampering with the couple's automobile, hiding their luggage, etc. Furthermore, a number of devices, such as signs, streamers, or tin cans fastened to the automobile, stones placed in the hub caps, and again, the confetti, serve to make the couple conspicuous, and thus have the effect of minimizing or negating the sense of privacy which has been granted to them. The importance of this maneuver appears when we recall that lack of self-awareness is commonly seen as an essential attribute of intimate lovers. Finally, attempts are often made to invade the privacy of the couple directly, and to forestall by symbolic means the breaking of peer group bonds. Thus objects may be placed in the couple's suitcases, or the couple's clothes may be tied in knots—a rather pathetic blending of hostile and wistful sentiments. In the more extreme case every effort is made to find out the couple's destination, and to communicate with them in some way.

In these practical jokes the intensity of the social anxiety aroused by this institutionalized dyadic withdrawal is graphically displayed. It should be noted, however, that physical withdrawal is not a prerequisite to this type of reaction. In more totalitarian communities in which the honeymoon does not exist, the mere possibility of an emotional withdrawal on the part of the newly-weds may call forth more extreme anticipatory anti-withdrawal mechanisms such as the shivaree, which serve as a reminder that the couple has not and cannot evade the community in which it is rooted.

Post-Marital Intrusion. The advent of the first child in itself tends to weaken the exclusive intimacy of the dyad, first by providing an important alternative (and narcissistic) object of cathexis for each member, and second, by creating responsibilities and obligations which are partly societal in nature, and through which bonds between the dyad and the community are thereby generated. [29]

In addition, the marital partners are to a considerable extent drawn apart by their participation in same-sex groups in the community, particularly in the occupational sphere. But the phenomenon is also

29. Simmel makes the following comment on the impact of the child on the marital partners: "It is precisely the very passionate and intimate husband and wife who do not wish a child: it would separate them: the metaphysical oneness into which they want to fuse alone with one another would be taken out of their hands and would confront them as a distinct, third element, a physical unit, that mediates between them. But to those who seek immediate unity, mediation must appear as separation." *Op. cit.*, pp. 128–9.

This "immediate unity" is the same desire for fusion that de Rougement discusses at such length in contrasting "passion-love" with "Christian love," and in his analysis of the Catharist heresy, *Love in the Western World*, Garden City, N.Y.: Doubleday, 1957. It involves loss of identity and essential rejection of role relationships—i.e., relationships that are collectively defined. In *Civilization and Its Discontents*, Freud also emphasizes this point. "When a love-relationship is at its height no room is left for any interest in the surrounding world: the pair of lovers are sufficient unto themselves, do not even need the child they have in common to make them happy." London: Hogarth, 1953, pp. 79–80.

striking in recreational activities, which fall largely into two categories: those which separate the sexes, and those which involve a reshuffling of partners. Occasionally we find both, as in the case of the traditional Victorian dinner party, during which husband and wife are always seated apart and after which the sexes retire to separate rooms. In our society separation by sexes is perhaps the more dominant form in the lower class, while the reshuffling of partners prevails in the middle class. It would not, in fact, be too much of an exaggeration to say that all types of mixed-group recreational activities in the middle class are rooted in more or less larval forms of adulterous flirtation. Married couples who stay too much together in such situations are disapproved.

The extent of such flirtation varies a good deal. The more traditional groups limit themselves to mixing bridge and dancing partners, etc., and frown on spontaneous expressions of sexual interest. Today one more frequently finds groups in which open flirtation in a joking context is expected, but must be carried on in the presence of the group. A third type, found in many sophisticated upper middle-class communities, involves less rigid control. Couples may indulge in sexual caresses away from the group, but it is felt that these should not culminate in intercourse nor lead to any expectation of future interpersonal involvement on the part of either individual (a norm which is perhaps more honored in the breach than in the observance). Finally, there are those communities which are organized on a completely adulterous basis, wherein "wife-trading" is widely practiced. Here the group norms merely proscribe permanent attachments.

While this latter form is something of a special case, it may in general be said that adulterous flirtation in social groups is a cohesive force which prevents the marital bond from atomizing the community. We have noted at many points, particularly with regard to the adolescent dyad, how dyadic intimacy may be blocked by converting sexual drives into strivings for status and prestige. In the married community, however, these strivings tend to unite rather than divide the couple, inasmuch as their status position is shared. This is important in neighborhood gatherings, in which there is typically a fair amount of competitive conversation centering around children and material possessions (such as houses, furnishings, cars, lawns and gardens). Extramarital flirtation tends to vitiate the divisive effect of such invidious comparisons (and vice versa).

Societal Intrusion in Extramarital Dyads. If the marital dyad is institutionalized, the extramarital dyad usually is not. In our society extramarital sexualtiy is generally prohibited, although often sanctioned by sub-groups within it. Since it is forbidden, one would expect the extramarital dyad to be the most free from societal intrusion and control. It would thus provide, theoretically, the most favorable context for dyadic withdrawal.

To a certain extent this seems to be the case. It is not accidental that most of the great love affairs of history and fiction are extramarital, nor is it due entirely to the Oedipal cast provided by triangularity. In most societies, past and present, there has been very little free choice in marriage, and dyadic intimacy has often been restricted to the more voluntary extramarital relationship. But it is easy to exaggerate the freedom of such relationships. In general it may be said that the higher the incidence of extramarital affairs in a given collectivity, the greater will be the societal intrusion upon such affairs, especially with regard to sexual choice. In many societies in which extramarital sexuality is universal, choice is restricted to a few relatives.[30] This means, in effect, that the degree of freedom of choice is relatively constant. The stronger the prohibition, the more individual choice will be thereby limited by situational factors; while the weaker the prohibition the more choice will be limited by group norms.

To begin with, there are the general norms which of course apply to all relationships, not only the extramarital. Thus sexual appeal has been based upon painting the face and body, wearing bizarre clothing, putting rings in the nose, in the ears, around the neck, on the wrists, fingers, ankles, or arms; disfiguring (by scarring, stretching or pitting) parts of the body—to mention only the cosmetic conventions. To foreigners these embellishments often seem strikingly ugly and sexless, and in a complex society such as our own, it is not unusual to hear complaints to this effect even from natives.

Left to themselves, human beings would mate entirely in response to instinctual demands and psychological affinity. The establishment of socially defined aesthetic norms brings sexual choice under social control—one can maximize one's sexual attractiveness by conforming to social canons of taste. The fact that such canons may create an effect which is asexual or even repulsive (by some absolute standard) is merely an indicator of the need and ability of collectivities to control eroticism —to socialize sexuality.

An excellent example of this process may be found in our own society. Comments have often been made upon the enormous emphasis placed upon deodorants, perfumes, and colognes in the United States. Body odors are of paramount importance in the sexual life of animals, and have always played a large, but apparently decreasing role in human sexuality. Sexual appeal was once determined primarily by the intensity of odors emanating from sexual secretions. But these have now become taboo. Erotic value is instead attached to *absence* of natural odors, the interest in which has been displaced onto odors which are advertised and packaged and may be purchased in a store. This means that sexual appeal

30. George P. Murdock, *Social Structure*, New York: Macmillan, 1949, pp. 4 ff.

can be restricted to certain people, and made conditional upon certain acts. It also means that the criteria of attractiveness may be integrated with the other values of the society (e.g., if beauty can be bought it becomes a part of the monetary reward system).

But societal conditioning extends beyond visual and olfactory canons of sexual taste. We have seen how in adolescent peer groups the appeal of personality affinities is transformed into a group-defined appeal, wherein the sexually attractive individual is one who behaves appropriately.

What applies to choice also applies to the conduct of the affair. When extramarital relationships are tolerated or encouraged by a community, they are usually governed by a variety of restrictive conventions which tend to forestall the kind of dyadic intimacy which leads to cathectic withdrawal. These conventions may be grouped roughly into three categories:

(1) *Impermanency*. It is usually considered poor form in such groups to retain the same mistress or lover for long periods. The individual who changes partners rapidly gains the most prestige, while the one who is slow in shifting cathexes suffers ridicule from the group. In such a situation the termination of the relationship becomes almost a more important issue than its inauguration. Each partner is constantly on the alert for signs of flagging interest in the other, lest he or she be caught in the embarrassing predicament of not being the first to find a new partner. (This anxiety is a prominent theme, e.g., in Restoration Comedy, which is a fairly accurate reflection of aristocratic life during that era.) The effect of this pattern is to keep the dyadic ties weak and shallow, and prevent the kind of emotional commitment which is a pre-condition for dyadic withdrawal.

(2) *Romantic Stylization*. Collectivities which sanction extramarital sexuality often develop elaborate and detailed customs for initiating, maintaining, and terminating love affairs. This has generally been the rule in aristocratic groups. When it occurs, intimacy (except in the purely physical sense) becomes difficult, due to the formal, gamelike manner in which the affair is conducted.

Romantic stylization is simply one further example of the socialization of sexuality through appeal to vanity. It is the behavioral counterpart of societal influence over sexual choice. Just as there are fashions in sexual desirability, so also are there fashions in sexual etiquette, and these rules, while they last, will be just as indispensable and just as asexual as a ring in the nose or paint on the face. The important issue is that behavior, like perception, be socially conditioned, and not left to the instinctual tendencies of the dyadic partners. In any given collectivity, behavior which is defined as seductive will often seem as bizarre to the outsider as those cosmetic factors which are socially defined as beautiful.

(3) *Temporal-Spatial Constriction*. Whether an extramarital relation-

ship is ephemeral or lasting, stylized or free, it is often the rule that it must be conducted only at specified times and places. Such constriction of the relationship may, of course, arise purely from situational factors, i.e., factors associated with the fact that these relationships are forbidden. But often it is a socially prescribed limitation. The affair is approved so long as it is "kept in its place."

One example of the operation of this factor is the frequent existence of a demand that affairs be conducted on a clandestine basis even when everyone knows of their existence. The explanation usually offered for this phenomenon is the alleged attractiveness of "forbidden fruit," [31] but this does not account for the motivation of the community to collaborate in this pretence. I would suggest that the demand for clandestine behavior is a mechanism for limiting the scope and depth of the relationship. Temporal-spatial constriction ensures that each of the partners is drawn away from the dyad and into the community during the greater part of his or her everyday life. The intimacy of the relationship is decreased by the fact that each partner knows the other only in a very limited and narrow context. Each is unfamiliar with those personality traits in the other which are irrelevant to the secret rendezvous, and would be unlikely to manifest themselves even in an infinite number of them. Should a degree of intimacy nevertheless arise in such a relationship, its first expression is a demand for more freedom and "sunlight," but should the couple come into the open the reaction among other group members is typically one of shock and contempt. Extension of the dyadic relationship into other areas of everyday life is considered "out of place."

Dyadic Withdrawal and Death. In the preceding discussion it might seem as if we had pursued dyadic withdrawal into its last remaining stronghold only to watch this stronghold collapse. Insofar as such intimacy is frequent, it appears to be ephemeral, and insofar as it is lasting, it seems to be rare. Societal intrusion and absorption seems effectively to forestall tendencies toward dyadic withdrawal whenever and wherever they appear.

It is perhaps for this reason that dyadic withdrawal is such a popular theme in the myths, legends, and dramas of Western Civilization. Yet even in fantasy such withdrawals are always short-lived, ending usually in dissolution or death. Apparently a permanent lifelong dyadic withdrawal is unimaginable, for to my knowledge there is no instance of such a phenomenon in the fantasy productions of any culture. [32]

This statement, however, is somewhat misleading. In death a kind of permanent dyadic withdrawal *is* achieved, and this is the appeal that

31. Cf. Freud, "Contributions to the Psychology of Love. The Most Prevalent Form of Degradation in Erotic Life," *Collected Papers,* Vol. IV, pp. 211–212.

32. George du Maurier's *Peter Ibbetson* comes rather close, but the dyad is subject to a rather severe form of temporal-spatial constriction.

stories of tragic lovers hold. In real life, and in comedies, dyadic withdrawal usually ends in societal absorption, unless the couple separates. This does not mean, of course, that the relationship is any less satisfying—the couple may indeed "live happily ever after" as in the fairy tale. It means only that the dyad loses some of its exclusiveness and self-sufficiency and ceases to be a social threat. Some of the cathexis previously withdrawn into the dyad flows back onto larger collectivities, and some of the needs funneled into the dyad for satisfaction there now begin to seek fulfillment in a wider setting.

The great tragic lovers of fiction, however, are always set in opposition to societal forces and are always destroyed by them. But their relationship is not. They always die or are buried together, with the dyadic bond untainted by societal intrusion. The immortality of this bond and of their withdrawal is often symbolized by plants or trees growing out of their graves and entwining. . . . [Thus, dyadic withdrawal] is initially achieved, satisfying the desire of the spectator for libidinal contraction, and subsequently punished, relieving his social anxiety and assuaging his moral outrage. But in spite of the punishment, society is really cheated, since the withdrawal is never reversed, and both the dyad and the withdrawal remain immortally intact. A moral victory is won for the forces of regression—one in which the spectators can privately participate with secret applause, like Irishmen applauding an Irish villain in an English play.

. . . Freud maintained that condensation, rather than brevity, was the soul of wit, and it may also be responsible for the fact that the best examples of social and psychological processes always come from literature. Although inadmissable as evidence, they provide superior illustrations, by forcefully condensing many processes into a compact and dramatic instance.

Thus the best example of libidinal contraction is a story by Thomas Mann entitled "The Blood of the Walsungs," which deals with an incestuous relationship between a twin brothèr and sister, identical in feature, personality and attitude.[33] Familial withdrawal is expressed in the contrast drawn between the family and outsiders; dyadic withdrawal in the twins' gaze "melting together in an understanding from which everybody else was shut out"; narcissistic withdrawal by Mann's comparing them to "self-centered invalids," in the brother's constant contemplation of his own image in the mirror, and in the final outburst of identification which immediately precedes their climatic copulation, an outburst in which the brother mutters (with rather careless oversight), "everything about you is just like me."[34]

The "erotic" (in Alexander's sense), non-utilitarian quality of the

33. *Stories of Three Decades,* New York: Knopf, 1936, pp. 279–319.
34. *Ibid.,* pp. 301, 305, 307, 317–319.

relationship is emphasized repeatedly by Mann. He speaks of their absorbing themselves in "trifles," of days passing "vacantly," of their having "doffed aside the evil-smelling world and loved each other alone, for the priceless sake of their own rare uselessness." The lower senses, particularly the olfactory, are insistently stressed: "they loved each other with all the sweetness of the senses, each for the other's spoilt and costly well-being and delicious-fragrance." [35]

Finally, the absence of other social ties is conveyed both explicitly and symbolically. The most telling expression, however, is their journey to the theatre in a carriage, in which their social isolation is dramatized by the nearness of the city: "round them roared and shrieked and thundered the machinery of urban life. Quite safe and shut away they sat among the wadded brown silk cushions, hand in hand." [36]

This relationship epitomizes libidinal contraction in its introversiveness, its rejection of partial and scattered libidinal cathexes, its conservatism. One can argue about its satisfactoriness at a psychological level, but it is clear that it does not leave a sufficient residue of tension upon which to build a group structure. Only when an individual falls in love with a stranger while some of his libido is still harnessed to an incestuous object will he be inclined to attach himself to a larger agglomeration which embraces them both. In so doing he sacrifices total gratification and gains whatever benefits accrue from societal existence. One might also maintain that he gains life, for it is only in death that utter quiescence is found.

35. *Ibid.*, pp. 305, 307–8, 309, 316, 317, 319.
36. *Ibid.*, pp. 307, 309, 312, 314, 316.

Ernest van den Haag

Love or Marriage

If someone asks, "Why do people marry?" he meets indignation or astonishment. The question seems absurd if not immoral: the desirability of marriage is regarded as unquestionable. Divorce, on the other hand, strikes us as a problem worthy of serious and therapeutic attention. Yet marriage precedes divorce as a rule, and frequently causes it.

What explains marriage? People divorce often but they marry still more often. Lately they also marry—and divorce, of course—younger than they used to, parcticularly in the middle classes (most statistics understate the change by averaging all classes). And the young have a disproportionate share of divorces. However, their hasty exertions to get out of wedlock puzzle me less than their eagerness to rush into it in the first place.

A hundred years ago there was every reason to marry young —though middle-class people seldom did. The unmarried state had heavy disadvantages for both sexes. Custom did not permit girls to be educated, to work, or to have social, let alone sexual, freedom. Men were free but since women were not, they had only prostitutes for partners. (When enforced, the double standard is certainly self-defeating.) And, though less restricted than girls shackled to their families, single men often led a grim and uncomfortable life. A wife was nearly indispensable, if only to darn socks, sew, cook, clean, take care of her man. Altogether, both sexes needed marriage far more than now—no TV, cars, dates, drip-dry shirts, cleaners, canned foods—and not much hospital care, insurance, or social security. The family was all-important.

Marriage is no longer quite so indispensable a convenience; yet we find people marrying more than ever, and earlier. To be sure, prosperity makes marriage more possible. But why are the young exploiting the possibility so sedulously? Has the yearning for love become more urgent and widespread?

What has happened is that the physical conveniences which reduced the material usefulness of marriage have also loosened the bonds of family life. Many other bonds that sustained us psychologically were weakened as they were extended: beliefs became vague; associations impersonal, discontinuous, and casual. Our contacts are many, our relationships few:

134

our lives, externally crowded, often are internally isolated; we remain but tenuously linked to each other and our ties come easily undone. One feels lonely surrounded by crowds and machines in an unbounded, abstract world that has become morally unintelligible; and we have so much time now to feel lonely in. Thus one longs, perhaps more acutely than in the past, for somebody to be tangibly, individually, and definitely one's own, body and soul.

This is the promise of marriage. Movies, songs, TV, romance magazines, all intensify the belief that love alone makes life worthwhile, is perpetual, conquers the world's evils, and is fulfilled and certified by marriage. "Science" hastens to confirm as much. Doesn't popular psychology, brandishing the banner of Freud with more enthusiasm than knowledge, tell us, in effect, that any male who stays single is selfish or homosexual or mother-dominated and generally neurotic? and any unmarried female frustrated (or worse, not frustrated) and neurotic? A "normal" person, we are told, must love and thereupon marry. Thus love and marriage are identified with each other and with normality, three thousand years of experience notwithstanding. The yearning for love, attended by anxiety to prove oneself well-adjusted and normal, turns into eagerness to get married.

The young may justly say that they merely practice what their parents preached. For, indeed, the idea that "love and marriage go together like a horse and carriage" has been drummed into their heads, so much that it finally has come to seem entirely natural. Yet, nothing could be less so. Love has long delighted and distressed mankind, and marriage has comforted us steadily and well. Both, however, are denatured —paradoxically enough, by their staunchest supporters—when they are expected to "go together." For love is a very unruly horse, far more apt to run away and overturn the carriage than to draw it. That is why, in the past, people seldom thought of harnessing marriage to love. They felt that each has its own motive power: one primed for a lifelong journey; the other for an ardent improvisation, a voyage of discovery.

More Than a Frenzy?

Though by no means weaker, the marital bond is quite different from the bond of love. If you like, it is a different bond of love—less taut, perhaps, and more durable. By confusing these two related but in many ways dissimilar bonds, we stand to lose the virtues and gain the vices of both: the spontaneous passion of love and the deliberate permanence of marriage are equally endangered as we try to live up to an ideal which bogs down one and unhinges the other.

Marriage is an immemorial institution which, in some form, exists everywhere. Its main purpose always was to unite and to continue the families of bride and groom and to further their economic and social position. The families, therefore, were the main interested parties. Often marriages were arranged (and sometimes they took place) before the future husbands or wives were old enough to talk. Even when they were grown up, they felt, as did their parents, that the major purpose of marriage was to continue the family, to produce children. Certainly women hoped for kind and vigorous providers and men for faithful mothers and good housekeepers; both undoubtedly hoped for affection, too; but love did not strike either of them as indispensable and certainly not as sufficient for marriage.

Unlike marriage, love has only recently come to be generally accepted as something more than a frenzied state of pleasure and pain. It is a welcome innovation—but easily ruined by marriage; which in turn has a hard time surviving confusion with love. Marriage counselors usually recognize this last point, but people in love seldom consult them. Perhaps their limited clientele colors the views of too many marriage counselors: instead of acknowledging that love and marriage are different but equally genuine relationships, they depict love as a kind of dependable wheel horse that can be harnessed to the carriage of married life. For them, any other kind of love must be an "immature" or "neurotic" fantasy, something to be condemned as Hollywood-inspired, "unrealistic" romanticism. It is as though a man opposed to horse racing—for good reasons perhaps—were to argue that race horses are not real, that all real horses are draft horses. Thus marriage counselors often insist that the only "real" and "true" love is "mature"—it is the comfortable workaday relation Mommy and Daddy have. The children find it hard to believe that there is nothing more to it.

They are quite right. And they have on their side the great literature of the world, and philosophers from Plato to Santayana. What is wrong with Hollywood romance surely is not that it is romantic, but that its romances are shoddy cliches. And since Hollywood shuns the true dimensions of conflict, love in the movies is usually confirmed by marriage and marriage by love, in accordance with wishful fantasy, though not with truth.

Was the love Tristan bore Isolde "mature" or "neurotic"? They loved each other before and after Isolde was married—to King Mark. It never occurred to them to marry each other; they even cut short an extramarital idyll together in the forest. (And Tristan too, while protesting love for Isolde, got married to some other girl.) Dante saw, but never actually met, Beatrice until he reached the nether world, which is the place for permanent romance. Of course, he was a married man.

It is foolish to pretend that the passionate romantic longing doesn't exist or is "neurotic," i.e., shouldn't exist; it is foolish to pretend that romantic love can be made part of a cozy domesticity. The truth is simple enough, though it can make life awfully complicated: there are two things, love and affection (or marital love), not one; they do not usually pull together as a team; they tend to draw us in different directions, if they are present at the same time. God nowhere promised to make this a simple world.

In the West, love came to be socially approved around the twelfth century. It became a fashionable subject of discussion then, and even of disputation, in formal "courts of love" convoked to argue its merits and to elaborate its true characteristics. Poets and singers created the models and images of love. They still do—though mass production has perhaps affected the quality; what else makes the teen-age crooners idols to their followers and what else do they croon about? In medieval times, as now, manuals were written, codifying the behavior recommended to lovers. With a difference though. Today's manuals are produced not by men of letters, but by doctors and therapists, as though love, sex, and marriage were diseases or therapeutic problems—which they promplty become if one reads too many of these guidebooks (any one is one too many). Today's manuals bear titles like "Married Love" (unmarried lovers can manage without help, I guess); but regardless of title, they concentrate on sex. In handbooks on dating they tell how to avoid it; in handbooks on marriage, how to go about it. The authors are sure that happiness depends on the sexual mechanics they blueprint. Yet, one doesn't make love better by reading a book any more than one learns to dance, or ride a bicycle, by reading about it.

The Use of "Technique"

The sexual engineering (or cook-book) approach is profitable only for the writer: in an enduring relationship, physical gratification is an effect and not a cause. If a person does not acquire sexual skill from experience, he is not ready for it. Where basic inhibitions exist, no book can remove them. Where they do not, no book is necessary. I have seen many an unhappy relationship in my psychoanalytic practice, but none ever in which sexual technique or the lack of it was more than a symptom and an effect. The mechanical approach never helps.

The troubadours usually took sex and marriage for granted and dealt with love—the newest and still the most surprising and fascinating of all relationships. And also the most unstable. They conceived love as a longing, a tension between desire and fulfillment. This feeling, of course, had been known before they celebrated it. Plato described love as a desire for something one does not have, implying that it is a longing, not a fulfillment. But in ancient Greece, love was regarded diffidently, as rather undesirable, an intoxication, a bewitchment, a divine punishment —usually for neglecting sex. The troubadours thought differently, although, unlike many moderns, they did not deny that love is a passion, something one suffers.[1] But they thought it a sweet suffering to be cultivated, and they celebrated it in song and story.

The troubadours clearly distinguished love and sex. Love was to them a yearning for a psychic gratification which the lover feels only the beloved can give; sex, an impersonal desire anybody possessing certain fairly common characteristics can gratify by physical actions. Unlike love, sex can thrive without an intense personal relationship and may erode it if it exists. Indeed, the Romans sometimes wondered if love would not blunt and tame their sexual pleasures, whereas the troubadours fretted lest sex abate the fervor of love's longing. They never fully resolved the contest between love and sex; nor has anyone else. (To define it away is, of course, not to solve it.)

We try to cope with this contest by fusing love and sex. (Every high-school student is taught the two go together.) This, as Freud pointed out, does not always succeed and may moderate both, but, as he also implied, it is the best we can hope for. In the words of William Butler Yeats, "Desire dies because every touch consumes the myth and yet, a myth that cannot be consumed becomes a specter. . . ."

Romantics, who want love's desiring to be conclusive, though endless, often linked it to death: if nothing further can happen and rival its significance, if one dies before it does, love indeed is the end. But this is ending the game as much as winning it—certainly an ambiguous move. The religious too perpetuate longing by placing the beloved altogether out of physical reach. The "bride of Christ" who retired to a convent longs for her Redeemer—and she will continue to yearn, as long as she lives, for union with a God at once human and divine, incarnating life and love everlasting. In its highest sense, love is a reaching for divine perfection, an act of creation. And always, it is a longing.

Since love is longing, experts in the Middle Ages held that one could not love someone who could not be longed for—for instance, one's wife. Hence, the Comtesse de Champagne told her court in 1174: "Love cannot extend its rights over two married persons." If one were to marry one's love, one would exchange the sweet torment of desire, the

1. . . . I am in love
  And that is my shame.
  What hurts the soul
  My soul adores,
  No better than a beast
  Upon all fours.

  So says W. B. Yeats. About eight centuries earlier, Chrétien de Troyes expressed the same sentiment.

yearning, for that which fulfills it. Thus the tension of hope would be replaced by the comfort of certainty. He who longs to long, who wants the tension of desire, surely should not marry. In former times, of course, he married—the better to love someone else's wife.

When sexual objects are easily and guiltlessly accessible, in a society that does not object to promiscuity, romantic love seldom prospers. For example, in imperial Rome it was rare and in Tahiti unknown. And love is unlikely to arouse the heart of someone brought up in a harem, where the idea of uniqueness has a hard time. Love flowers best in a monogamous environment morally opposed to unrestrained sex, and interested in cultivating individual experience. In such an environment, longing may be valued for itself. Thus, love as we know it is a Christian legacy, though Christianity in the main repudiates romantic love where the object is wordly, and accepts passion only when transcendent, when God is the object—or when muted into affection: marital love.

Shifting the Object

Let me hazard a Freudian guess about the genesis of the longing we call love. It continues and reproduces the child's first feeling for his parent —the original source of unconditioned and unconditional love. But what is recreated is the child's image, the idealized mother or father, young and uniquely beautiful, and not the empirical parent others see. The unconsummated love for this ideal parent (and it could be someone else important in the child's experience) remains as an intense longing. Yet any fulfillment now must also become a disappointment—a substitute, cheating the longing that wants to long. Nonetheless most of us marry and replace the ideal with an imperfect reality. We repudiate our longing or we keep it but shift its object. If we don't, we may resent our partners for helping us "consume the myth," and leaving us shorn of longing—which is what Don Giovanni found so intolerable, and what saddens many a faithful husband.

Sexual gratification, of course, diminishes sexual desire for the time being. But it does more. It changes love. The longing may become gratitude; the desire tenderness; love may become affectionate companionship—"After such knowledge, what forgiveness?" Depending on character and circumstance, love may also be replaced by indifference or hostility.

One thing is certain though: if the relationship is stabilized, love is replaced by other emotions. (Marriage thus has often been recommended as the cure for love. But it does not always work.) The only way to keep love is to try to keep up—or re-establish—the distance between lovers that was inevitably shortened by intimacy and possession, and thus, possibly, regain desire and longing. Lovers sometimes do so by quarreling. And some personalities are remote enough, or inexhaustible enough, to be longed for even when possessed. But this has disadvantages as well. And the deliberate and artificial devices counseled by romance magazines and marriage manuals ("surprise your husband . . .")—even when they do not originate with the love of pretense—are unlikely to yield more than the pretense of love.

The sexual act itself may serve as a vehicle for numberless feelings: lust, vanity, and self-assertion, doubt and curiosity, possessiveness, anxiety, hostility, anger, or indifferent release from boredom. Yet, though seldom the only motive, and often absent altogether, love nowadays is given as the one natural and moral reason which authorizes and even ordains sexual relations. What we have done is draw a moral conclusion from a rule of popular psychology: that "it is gratifying, and therefore healthy and natural, to make love when you love, and frustrating, and therefore unhealthy and unnatural not to; we must follow nature; but sex without love is unnatural and therefore immoral."

Now, as a psychological rule, this is surely wrong; it can be as healthy to frustrate as it is to gratify one's desires. Sometimes gratification is very unhealthy; sometimes frustration is. Nor can psychological health be accepted as morally decisive. Sanity, sanitation, and morality are all desirable, but they are not identical; our wanting all of them is the problem, not the solution. It may be quite "healthy" to run away with your neighbor's wife, but not, therefore, right. And there is nothing unhealthy about wishing to kill someone who has injured you—but this does not morally justify doing so. Finally, to say "we must follow nature" is always specious: we follow nature in whatever we do—we can't ever do what nature does not let us do. Why then identify nature only with the nonintellectual, the sensual, or the emotional possibilities? On this view, it would be unnatural to read: literacy is a gift of nature only if we include the intellect and training in nature's realm. If we do, it makes no sense to call a rule unnatural merely because it restrains an urge: the urge is no more natural than the restraint.

The combination of love and sex is no more natural than the separation. Thus, what one decides about restraining or indulging an emotion, or a sexual urge, rests on religious, social, or personal values, none of which can claim to be more natural than any other.

Not that some indulgences and some inhibitions may not be healthier than others. But one cannot flatly say which are good or bad for every man. It depends on their origins and effects in the personalities involved. Without knowing these, more cannot be said—except, perhaps, that we should try not to use others, or even ourselves, merely as a means—at least not habitually and in personal relations. Sex, unalloyed, sometimes leads to this original sin which our moral tradition condemns.

Psychologically, too, the continued use of persons merely as instruments ultimately frustrates both the user and the used. This caution, though it justifies no positive action, may help perceive problems; it does not solve them; no general rule can.

How Long Does It Last?

What about marriage? In our society, couples usually invite the families to their weddings, although the decision to marry is made exclusively by bride and groom. However, a license must be obtained and the marriage registered; and it can be dissolved only by a court of law. Religious ceremonies state the meaning of marriage clearly. The couple are asked to promise "foresaking all others, [to] keep thee only unto her [him], so long as ye both shall live." The vow does not say, "as long as ye both shall want to," because marriage is a promise to continue even when one no longer wishes to. If marriage were to end when love does, it would be redundant: why solemnly ask two people to promise to be with each other for as long as they want to be with each other?

Marriage was to cement the family by tying people together "till death do us part" in the face of the fickleness of their emotions. The authority of state and church was to see to it that they kept a promise voluntarily made, but binding, and that could not be unmade. Whether it sprang from love did not matter. Marriage differed from a love affair inasmuch as it continued regardless of love. Cupid shoots his arrows without rhyme or reason. But marriage is a deliberate rational act, a public institution making the family independent of Cupid's whims. Once enlisted, the volunteers couldn't quit, even when they didn't like it any longer. That was the point.

The idea that marriage must be synchronous with love or even affection nullified it althogether. (That affection should coincide with marriage is, of course, desirable, though it does not always happen.) We would have to reword the marriage vow. Instead of saying, "till death do us part," we might say, "till we get bored with each other"; and, instead of "forsaking all others," "till someone better comes along."Clearly, if the couple intend to stay "married" only as long as they want to, they only pretend to be married: they are having an affair with legal trimmings. To marry is to vow fidelity regardless of any future feeling, to vow the most earnest attempt to avoid contrary feelings altogether, but, at any rate, not to give in to them.

Perhaps this sounds grim. But it needn't be if one marries for affection more than for love. For affection, marital love may grow with knowledge and intimacy and shared experience. Thus marriage itself, when accepted as something other than a love affair, may foster affection.

Affection differs from love as fulfillment differs from desire. Further, love longs for what desire and imagination make uniquely and perfectly lovable. Possession erodes it. Affection, however—which is love of a different, of a perhaps more moral and less aesthetic kind—cares deeply also for what is unlovable without transforming it into beauty. It cares for the unvarnished person, not the splendid image. Time can strengthen it. But the husband who wants to remain a splendid image must provide a swan to draw him away, or find a wife who can restrain her curiosity about his real person—something that Lohengrin did not succeed in doing. Whereas love stresses the unique form perfection takes in the lover's mind, affection stresses the uniqueness of the actual person.

One may grow from the other. But not when this other is expected to remain unchanged. And affection probably grows more easily if not preceded by enchantment. For the disenchantment which often follows may turn husband and wife against each other, and send them looking elsewhere for re-enchantment—which distance lends so easily. Indeed, nothing else does.

William J. Goode

The Theoretical
Importance of Love

Because love often determines the intensity of an attraction[1] toward or away from an intimate relationship with another person, it can become one element in a decision or action.[2] Nevertheless, serious sociological attention has only infrequently been given to love. Moreover, analyses of love generally have been confined to mate choice in the Western World, while the structural importance of love has been for the most part ignored. The present paper views love in a broad perspective, focusing on the structural patterns by which societies keep in check the potentially disruptive effect of love relationships on mate choice and stratification systems.

Types of Literature on Love

For obvious reasons, the printed material on love is immense. For our present purposes, it may be classified as follows:

1. Poetic, humanistic, literary, erotic, pornographic: By far the largest body of all literature on love views it as a sweeping experience. The poet arouses our sympathy and empathy. The essayist enjoys, and asks the reader to enjoy, the interplay of people in love. The storyteller—Boccaccio, Chaucer, Dante—pulls back the curtain of human souls and lets the reader watch the intimate lives of others caught in an emotion we all know. Others—Vatsyayana, Ovid, William IX Count of Poitiers and Duke of Aquitaine, Marie de France, Andreas Capellanus—have written how-to-do-it books, that is, how to conduct oneself in love relations, to

---

1. On the psychological level, the motivational power of both love and sex is intensified by this curious fact (which I have not seen remarked on elsewhere): Love is the most projective of emotions, as sex is the most projective of drives; only with great difficulty can the attracted person believe that the object of his love or passion does not and will not reciprocate the feeling at all. Thus, the person may carry his action quite far, before accepting a rejection as genuine.

2. I have treated decision analysis extensively in an unpublished paper by that title.

143

persuade others to succumb to one's love wishes, or to excite and satisfy one's sex partner.[3]

2. Marital counseling: Many modern sociologists have commented on the importance of romantic love in America and its lesser importance in other societies, and have disparaged it as a poor basis for marriage, or as immaturity. Perhaps the best known of these arguments are those of Ernest R. Mowrer, Ernest W. Burgess, Mabel A. Elliott, Andrew G. Truxal, Francis E. Merrill, and Ernest R. Groves.[4] The antithesis of romantic love, in such analyses, is "conjugal" love; the love between a settled, domestic couple.

A few sociologists, remaining within this same evaluative context, have instead claimed that love also has salutary effects in our society. Thus, for example, William L. Kolb[5] has tried to demonstrate that the marital counselors who attack romantic love are really attacking some fundamental values of our larger society, such as individualism, freedom, and personality growth. Beigel[6] has argued that if the female is sexually repressed, only the psychotherapist or love can help her overcome her inhibitions. He claims further that one influence of love in our society is that it extenuates illicit sexual relations; he goes on to assert: "Seen in proper perspective, [love] has not only done no harm as a prerequisite to marriage, but it has mitigated the impact that a too-fast-moving and unorganized conversion to new socio-economic constellations has had upon our whole culture and it has saved monogamous marriage from complete disorganization."

In addition, there is widespread comment among marriage analysts, that in a rootless society, with few common bases for companionship, romantic love holds a couple together long enough to allow them to begin marriage. That is, it functions to attract people powerfully together, and to hold them through the difficult first months of the marriage, when their different backgrounds would otherwise make an adjustment troublesome.

3. Vatsyayana, *The Kama Sutra, Delhi:* Rajkamal, 1948; Ovid, "The Loves," and "Remedies of Love," in *The Art of Love,* Cambridge: Harvard University Press, 1939; Andreas Capellanus, *The Art of Courtly Love,* translated by John J. Parry, New York: Columbia University Press, 1941; Paul Tuffrau, editor, *Marie de France: Les Lais de Marie de France,* Paris: L'edition d'art, 1925; see also Julian Harris, *Marie de France,* New York: Institute of French Studies, 1930, esp. Chapter 3. All authors but the first *also* had the goal of writing literature.
4. Ernest R. Mowrer, *Family Disorganization,* Chicago: The University of Chicago Press, 1927, pp. 158–165; Ernest W. Burgess and Harvey J. Locke, *The Family,* New York: American Book, 1953, pp. 436–437; Mabel A. Elliott and Francis E. Merrill, *Social Disorganization,* New York: Harper, 1950, pp. 366–384; Andrew G. Truxal and Francis E. Merrill, *The Family in American Culture,* New York: Prentice-Hall, 1947, pp. 120–124, 507–509; Ernest R. Groves and Gladys Hoagland Groves, *The Contemporary American Family,* New York: Lippincott, 1947, pp. 321–324.
5. William L. Kolb, "Sociologically Established Norms and Democratic Values," *Social Forces,* 26 (May, 1948), pp. 451–456.
6. Hugo G. Beigel, "Romantic Love," *American Sociological Review,* 16 (June, 1951), pp. 326–334.

3. Although the writers cited above concede the structural importance of love implicity, since they are arguing that it is either harmful or helpful to various values and goals of our society, a third group has given explicit if unsystematic attention to its structural importance. Here, most of the available propositions point to the functions of love, but a few deal with the conditions under which love relationships occur. They include:

(1) An implicit or assumed descriptive proposition is that love as a common prelude to and basis of marriage is rare, perhaps to be found as a pattern only in the United States.

(2) Most explanations of the conditions which create love are psychological, stemming from Freud's notion that love is "aim-inhibited sex."[7] This idea is expressed, for example, by Waller who says that love is an idealized passion which develops from the frustration of sex.[8] This proposition, although rather crudely stated and incorrect as a general explanation, is widely accepted.

(3) Of course, a predisposition to love is created by the socialization experience. Thus some textbooks on the family devote extended discussion to the ways in which our society socializes for love. The child, for example, is told that he or she will grow up to fall in love with some one, and early attempts are made to pair the child with children of the opposite sex. There is much joshing of children about falling in love; myths and stories about love and courtship are heard by children; and so on.

(4) A further proposition (the source of which I have not been able to locate) is that, in a society in which a very close attachment between parent and child prevails, a love complex is necessary in order to motivate the child to free him from his attachment to his parents.

(5) Love is also described as one final or crystallizing element in the decision to marry, which is otherwise structured by factors such as class, ethnic origin, religion, education, and residence.

(6) Parsons has suggested three factors which "underlie the prominence of the romantic context in our culture": (a) the youth culture frees the individual from family attachments, thus permitting him to fall in love; (b) love is a substitute for the interlocking of kinship roles found in other societies, and thus motivates the individual to conform to proper marital role behavior; and (c) the structural isolation of the family so frees the married partners' affective inclinations that they are able to love one another.[9]

(7) Robert F. Winch has developed a theory of "complementary needs" which essentially states that the underlying dynamic in the

7. Sigmund Freud, *Group Psychology and the Analysis of the Ego,* London: Hogarth, 1922, p. 72.
8. Willard Waller, *The Family,* New York: Dryden, 1938, pp. 189–192.
9. Talcott Parsons, *Essays in Sociological Theory,* Glencoe, Ill.: Free Press, 1949, pp. 187–189.

process of falling in love is an interaction between (a) the perceived psychological attributes of one individual and (b) the complementary psychological attributes of the person falling in love, such that the needs of the latter are felt to be met by the perceived attributes of the former and *vice versa*. These needs are derived from Murray's list of personality characteristics. Winch thus does not attempt to solve the problem of why our society has a love complex, but how it is that specific individuals fall in love with each other rather than with someone else.[10]

(8) Winch and others have also analyzed the effect of love upon various institutions or social patterns: Love themes are prominently displayed in the media of entertainment and communication, in consumption patterns, and so on.[11]

4. Finally, there is the cross-cultural work of anthropologists, who in the main have ignored love as a factor of importance in kinship patterns. The implicit understanding seems to be that love as a pattern is found only in the United States, although of course individual cases of love are sometimes recorded. The term "love" is practically never found in indexes of anthropological monographs on specific societies or in general anthropology textbooks. It is perhaps not an exaggeration to say that Lowie's comment of a generation ago would still be accepted by a substantial number of anthropologists:

> But of love among savages? . . . Passion, of course, is taken for granted; affection, which many travelers vouch for, might be conceded; but Love? Well, the romantic sentiment occurs in simpler conditions, as with us—in fiction. . . . So Love exists for the savage as it does for ourselves—in adolescence, in fiction, among the poetically minded.[12]

A still more skeptical opinion is Linton's scathing sneer:

> All societies recognize that there are occasional violent, emotional attachments between persons of opposite sex, but our present American culture is practically the only one which has attempted to capitalize these, and make them the basis for marriage. . . . The hero of the modern American movie is always a romantic lover, just as the hero of the old Arab epic is always an epileptic. A cynic may suspect that in any ordinary population the percentage of individuals with a capacity for romantic love of the Hollywood type was about as large as that of persons able to throw genuine epileptic fits.[13]

In Murdock's book on kinship and marriage, there is almost no mention, if any, of love.[14] Should we therefore conclude that, cross-culturally, love is not important, and thus cannot be of great importance structurally? If

10. Robert F. Winch, *Mate Selection*, New York: Harper, 1958.
11. See, e.g., Robert F. Winch, *The Modern Family*, New York: Holt, 1952, Chapter 14.
12. Robert H. Lowie, "Sex and Marriage," in John F. McDermott, editor, *The Sex Problem in Modern Society*, New York: Modern Library, 1931, p. 146.
13. Ralph Linton, *The Study of Man*, New York: Appleton-Century, 1936, p. 175.
14. George Peter Murdock, *Social Structure*, New York: Macmillan, 1949.

there is only one significant case, perhaps it is safe to view love as generally unimportant in social structure and to concentrate rather on the nature and functions of romantic love within the Western societies in which love is obviously prevalent. As brought out below, however, many anthropologists have in fact described love *patterns*. And one of them, Max Gluckman,[15] has recently subsumed a wide range of observations under the broad principle that love relationships between husband and wife estrange the couple from their kin, who therefore try in various ways to undermine that love. This principle is applicable to many more societies (for example, China and India) than Gluckman himself discusses.

The Problem and Its Conceptual Clarification

The preceding propositions (except those denying that love is distributed widely) can be grouped under two main questions: What are the consequences of romantic love in the United States? How is the emotion of love aroused or created in our society? The present paper deals with the first question. For theoretical purposes both questions must be reformulated, however, since they implicitly refer only to our peculiar system of romantic love. Thus: (1) In what ways do various love patterns fit into the social structure, especially into the systems of mate choice and stratification? (2) What are the structural conditions under which a range of love patterns occurs in various societies? These are overlapping questions, but their starting point and assumptions are different. The first assumes that love relationships are a universal psychosocial possibility, and that different social systems make different adjustments to their potential disruptiveness. The second does not take love for granted, and supposes rather that such relationships will be rare unless certain structural factors are present. Since in both cases the analysis need not depend upon the correctness of the assumption, the problem may be chosen arbitrarily. Let us begin with the first.[16]

We face at once the problem of defining "love." Here, love is defined as a strong emotional attachment, a cathexis, between adolescents or adults of opposite sexes, with at least the components of sex desire and tenderness. Verbal definitions of this emotional relationship are notoriously open to attack; this one is no more likely to satisfy critics than others. Agreement is made difficult by value judgments: one critic would exclude anything but "true" love, another casts out "infatuation," another objects to "puppy love," while others would separate sex desire

15. Max Gluckman, *Custom and Conflict in Africa,* Oxford: Basil Blackwell, 1955, Chapter 3.
16. I hope to deal with the second problem in another paper.

from love because sex presumably is degrading. Nevertheless, most of us have had the experience of love, just as we have been greedy, or melancholy, or moved by hate (defining "true" hate seems not to be a problem). The experience can be referred to without great ambiguity, and a refined measure of various degrees of intensity or purity of love is unnecessary for the aims of the present analysis.

Since love may be related in diverse ways to the social structure, it is necessary to forego the dichotomy of "romantic love—no romantic love" in favor of a continuum or range between polar types. At one pole, a strong love attraction is socially viewed as a laughable or tragic aberration; at the other, it is mildly shameful to marry without being in love with one's intended spouse. This is a gradation from negative sanction to positive approval, ranging at the same time from low or almost nonexistent institutionalization of love to high institutionalization.

The urban middle classes of contemporary Western society, especially in the United States, are found toward the latter pole. Japan and China, in spite of the important movement toward European patterns, fall toward the pole of low institutionalization. Village and urban India is farther toward the center, for there the ideal relationship has been one which at least generated love after marriage, and sometimes after betrothal, in contrast with the mere respect owed between Japanese and Chinese spouses.[17] Greece after Alexander, Rome of the Empire, and perhaps the later period of the Roman Republic as well, are near the center, but somewhat toward the pole of institutionalization, for love matches appear to have increased in frequency—a trend denounced by moralists.[18]

This conceptual continuum helps to clarify our problem and to interpret the propositions reviewed above. Thus it may be noted, first, that individual love relationships may occur even in societies in which love is viewed as irrelevant to mate choice and excluded from the decision to marry. As Linton conceded, some violent love attachments may be found in any society. In our own, the Song of Solomon, Jacob's love of Rachel, and Michal's love for David are classic tales. The Mahabharata, the great Indian epic, includes love themes. Romantic love appears early in Japanese literature, and the use of Mt. Fuji as a locale for the suicide of star-crossed lovers is not a myth invented by editors of tabloids. There is

17. Tribal India, of course, is too heterogeneous to place in any one position on such a continuum. The question would have to be answered for each tribe. Obviously it is of less importance here whether China and Japan, in recent decades, have moved "two points over" toward the opposite pole of high approval of love relationships as a basis for marriage than that both systems as classically described viewed love as generally a tragedy; and love was supposed to be irrelevant to marriage, i.e., noninstitutionalized. The continuum permits us to place a system at some position, once we have the descriptive data.

18. See Ludwig Friedländer, *Roman Life and Manners under the Early Empire* (Seventh Edition), translated by A. Magnus, New York: Dutton, 1908, Vol. 1, Chapter 5, "The Position of Women."

the familiar tragic Chinese story to be found on the traditional "willow-plate," with its lovers transformed into doves. And so it goes—individual love relationships seem to occur everywhere. But this fact does not change the position of a society on the continuum.

Second, reading both Linton's and Lowie's comments in this new conceptual context reduces their theoretical importance, for they are both merely saying that people do not *live by* the romantic complex, here or anywhere else. Some few couples in love will brave social pressure, physical dangers, or the gods themselves, but nowhere is this usual. Violent, self-sufficient love is not common anywhere. In this respect, of course, the U.S. is not set apart from other systems.

Third, we can separate a *love pattern* from the romantic love *complex*. Under the former, love is a permissible, expected prelude to marriage, and a usual element of courtship—thus, at about the center of the continuum, but toward the pole of institutionalization. The romantic love complex (one pole of the continuum) includes, in addition, an ideological prescription that falling in love is a highly desirable basis of courtship and marriage; love is strongly institutionalized.[19] In contemporary United States, many individuals would even claim that entering marriage without being in love requires some such rationalization as asserting that one is too old for such romances or that one must "think of practical matters like money." To be sure, both anthropologists and sociologists often exaggerate the American commitment to romance;[20] nevertheless, a behavioral and value complex of this type is found here.

But this complex is rare. Perhaps only the following cultures possess the romantic love value complex: modern urban United States, North-western Europe, Polynesia, and the European nobility of the eleventh and twelfth centuries.[21] Certainly, it is to be found in no other major civilization. On the other hand, the *love pattern*, which views love as a basis for the final decision to marry, may be relatively common.

19. For a discussion of the relation between behavior patterns and the process of institutionalization, see my *After Divorce*, Glencoe, Ill.: Free Press, 1956, Chapter 15.

20. See Ernest W. Burgess and Paul W. Wallin, *Engagement and Marriage*, New York: Lippincott, 1953, Chapter 7 for the extent to which even the engaged are not blind to the defects of their beloveds. No one has ascertained the degree to which various age and sex groups in our society actually believe in some form of the ideology.

Similarly, Margaret Mead in *Coming of Age in Samoa*, New York: Modern Library, 1953, rates Manu'an love as shallow, and though these Samoans give much attention to love-making, she asserts that they laughed with incredulous contempt at Romeo and Juliet (pp. 155–156). Though the individual sufferer showed jealousy and anger, the Manu'ans believed that a new love would quickly cure a betrayed lover (pp. 105–108). It is possible that Mead failed to understand the shallowness of love in our own society: Romantic love is, "in our civilization, inextricably bound up with ideas of monogamy, exclusiveness, jealousy, and undeviating fidelity" (p. 105). But these are *ideas* and ideology; *behavior* is rather different.

21. I am preparing an analysis of this case. The relation of "courtly love" to social structure is complicated.

Why Love Must Be Controlled

Since strong love attachments apparently can occur in any society and since (as we shall show) love is frequently a basis for and prelude to marriage, it must be controlled or channeled in some way. More specifically, the stratification and lineage patterns would be weakened greatly if love's potentially disruptive effects were not kept in check. The importance of this situation may be seen most clearly by considering one of the major functions of the family, status placement, which in every society links the structures of stratification, kinship lines, and mate choice. (To show how the very similar comments which have been made about sex are not quite correct would take us too far afield; in any event, to the extent that they are correct, the succeeding analysis applies equally to the control of sex.)

Both the child's placement in the social structure and choice of mates are socially important because both placement and choice link two kinship lines together. Courtship or mate choice, therefore, cannot be ignored by either family or society. To permit random mating would mean radical change in the existing social structure. If the family as a unit of society is important, then mate choice is too.

Kinfolk or immediate family can disregard the question of who married whom, only if a marriage is not seen as a link between kin lines, only if no property, power, lineage honor, totemic relationships, and the like are believed to flow from the kin lines through the spouses to their offspring. Universally, however, these are believed to follow kin lines. Mate choice thus has consequences for the social structure. But love may affect mate choice. Both mate choice and love, therefore, are too important to be left to children.

The Control of Love

Since considerable energy and resources may be required to push youngsters who are in love into proper role behavior, love must be controlled *before* it appears. Love relationships must either be kept to a small number or they must be so directed that they do not run counter to the approved kinship linkages. There are only a few institutional patterns by which this control is achieved.

1. Certainly the simplest, and perhaps the most widely used, structural pattern for coping with this problem is child marriage. If the child is betrothed, married, or both before he has had any opportunity to interact intimately as an adolescent with other children, then he has no resources with which to oppose the marriage. He cannot earn a living, he is physically weak, and is socially dominated by his elders. Moreover, strong love attachments occur only rarely before puberty. An example of

this pattern was to be found in India, where the young bride went to live with her husband in a marriage which was not physically consummated until much later, within his father's household.[22]

2. Often, child marriage is linked with a second structural pattern, in which the kinship rules define rather closely a class of eligible future spouses. The marriage is determined by birth within narrow limits. Here, the major decision, which is made by elders, is *when* the marriage is to occur. Thus, among the Murngin, *galle*, the father's sister's child, is scheduled to marry *due*, the mother's brother's child.[23] In the case of the "four-class" double-descent system, each individual is a member of *both* a matri-moiety and a patri-moiety and must marry someone who belongs to neither; the four classes are (1) ego's own class, (2) those whose matri-moiety is the same as ego's but whose patri-moiety is different, (3) those who are in ego's patri-moiety but not in his matri-moiety, and (4) those who are in neither of ego's moieties, that is, who are in the cell diagonally from his own.[24] Problems arise at times under these systems if the appropriate kinship cell—for example, parallel cousin or cross-cousin—is empty.[25] But nowhere, apparently, is the definition so rigid as to exclude some choice and, therefore, some dickering, wrangling, and haggling between the elders of the two families.

3. A society can prevent widespread development of adolescent love relationships by socially isolating young people from potential mates, whether eligible or ineligible as spouses. Under such a pattern, elders can arrange the marriages of either children or adolescents with little likelihood that their plans will be disrupted by love attachments. Obviously, this arrangement cannot operate effectively in most primitive societies, where youngsters see one another rather frequently.[26]

Not only is this pattern more common in civilizations than in primitive societies, but is found more frequently in the upper social strata.

22. Frieda M. Das, *Purdah*, New York: Vanguard, 1932; Kingsley Davis, *The Population of India and Pakistan*, Princeton: Princeton University Press, 1951, p. 112. There was a widespread custom of taking one's bride from a village other than one's own.

23. W. Lloyd Warner, *Black Civilization*, New York: Harper, 1937, pp. 82–84. They may also become "sweethearts" at puberty; see pp. 86–89.

24. See Murdock, *op. cit.*, pp. 53 ff. *et passim* for discussions of double-descent.

25. One adjustment in Australia was for the individuals to leave the tribe for a while, usually eloping, and then to return "reborn" under a different and now appropriate kinship designation. In any event, these marital prescriptions did not prevent love entirely. As Malinowski shows in his early summary of the Australian family systems, although every one of the tribes used the technique of infant betrothal (and close prescription of mate), no tribe was free of elopements, between either the unmarried or the married, and the "motive of sexual love" was always to be found in marriages by elopement. B. Malinowski, *The Family Among the Australian Aborigines*, London: University of London Press, 1913, p. 83.

26. This pattern was apparently achieved in Manus, where on first menstruation the girl was removed from her playmates and kept at "home"—on stilts over a lagoon—under the close supervision of elders. The Manus were prudish, and love occurred rarely or never. Margaret Mead, *Growing Up in New Guinea*, in *From the South Seas*, New York: Morrow, 1939, pp. 163–166, 208.

Social segregation is difficult unless it is supported by physical segregation—the harem of Islam, the zenana of India[27]—or by a large household system with individuals whose duty it is to supervise nubile girls. Social segregation is thus expensive. Perhaps the best known example of simple social segregation was found in China, where youthful marriages took place between young people who had not previously met because they lived in different villages; they could not marry fellow-villagers since ideally almost all inhabitants belonged to the same *tsu*.[28]

It should be emphasized that the primary function of physical or social isolation in these cases is to minimize informal or intimate social interaction. Limited social contacts of a highly ritualized or formal type in the presence of elders, as in Japan, have a similar, if less extreme, result.[29]

4. A fourth type of pattern seems to exist, although it is not clear cut; and specific cases shade off toward types three and five. Here, there is close supervision by duennas or close relatives, but not actual social segregation. A high value is placed on female chastity (which perhaps is the case in every major civilization until its "decadence") viewed either as the product of self-restraint, as among the seventeenth-century Puritans, or as a marketable commodity. Thus love as play is not developed; marriage is supposed to be considered by the young as a duty and a possible family alliance. This pattern falls between types three and five because love is permitted before marriage, but only between eligibles. Ideally, it occurs only between a betrothed couple, and except as marital love, there is no encouragement for it to appear at all. Family elders largely make the specific choice of mate, whether or not intermediaries carry out the arrangements. In the preliminary stages youngsters engage in courtship under supervision, with the understanding that this will permit the development of affection prior to marriage.

I do not believe that the empirical data show where this pattern is prevalent, outside of Western Civilization. The West is a special case, because of its peculiar relationship to Christianity, in which from its

27. See Das, *op. cit.*
28. For the activities of the *tsu*, see Hsien Chin Hu, *The Common Descent Group in China and Its Functions*, New York: Viking Fund Studies in Anthropology, 10 (1948). For the marriage process, see Marion J. Levy, *The Family Revolution in Modern China*, Cambridge: Harvard University Press, 1949, pp. 87–107. See also Olga Lang, *Chinese Family and Society*, New Haven: Yale University Press, 1946, for comparisons between the old and new systems. In one-half of 62 villages in Ting Hsien Experimental District in Hopei, the largest clan included 50 percent of the families; in 25 percent of the villages, the two largest clans held over 90 percent of the families; I am indebted to Robert M. Marsh who has been carrying out a study of Ching mobility partly under my direction for this reference: F. C. H. Lee, *Ting Hsien. She-hui K'ai-K'uang t'iao-ch'a*, Peiping: Chung-hua p'ing-min Chiao-yu ts'u-chin hui, 1932, p. 54. See also Sidney Gamble, *Ting Hsien: A North China Rural Community*, New York: International Secretariat of the Institute of Pacific Relations, 1954.
29. For Japan, see Shidzué Ishimoto, *Facing Two Ways*, New York: Farrar and Rinehart, 1935, Chapters 6, 8; John F. Embree, *Suye Mura*, Chicago: University of Chicago Press, 1950, Chapters 3, 6.

earliest days in Rome there has been a complex tension between asceticism and love. This type of limited love marked French, English, and Italian upper class family life from the eleventh to the fourteenth centuries, as well as seventeenth-century Puritanism in England and New England.[30]

5. The fifth type of pattern permits or actually encourages love relationships, and love is a commonly expected element in mate choice. Choice in this system is *formally* free. In their 'teens youngsters begin their love play, with or without consummating sexual intercourse, within a group of peers. They may at times choose love partners whom they and others do not consider suitable spouses. Gradually, however, their range of choice is narrowed and eventually their affections center on one individual. This person is likely to be more eligible as a mate according to general social norms, and as judged by peers and parents, than the average individual with whom the youngster formerly indulged in love play.

For reasons that are not yet clear, this pattern is nearly always associated with a strong development of an adolescent peer group system, although the latter may occur without the love pattern. One source of social control, then, is the individual's own 'teen age companions, who persistently rate the present and probable future accomplishments of each individual.[31]

Another source of control lies with the parents of both boy and girl. In our society, parents threaten, cajole, wheedle, bribe, and persuade their children to "go with the right people," during both the early love play and later courtship phases.[32] Primarily, they seek to control love relationships by influencing the informal social contacts of their children: moving to appropriate neighborhoods and schools, giving parties and helping to make out invitation lists, by making their children aware that

30. I do not mean, of course, to restrict this pattern to these times and places, but I am more certain of these. For the Puritans, see Edmund S. Morgan, *The Puritan Family*, Boston: Public Library, 1944. For the somewhat different practices in New York, see Charles E. Ironside, *The Family in Colonial New York*, New York: Columbia University Press, 1942. See also: A. Abram, *English Life and Manners in the Later Middle Ages*, New York: Dutton, 1913, Chapters 4, 10; Emily J. Putnam, *The Lady*, New York: Sturgis and Walton, 1910, Chapter 4; James Gairdner, editor, *The Paston Letters, 1422–1509*, 4 vols., London: Arber, 1872–1875; Eileen Power, "The Position of Women," in C. G. Crump and E. F. Jacobs, editors, *The Legacy of the Middle Ages*, Oxford: Clarendon, 1926, pp. 414–416.

31. For those who believe that the young in the United States are totally deluded by love, or believe that love outranks every other consideration, see: Burgess and Wallin, *op. cit.*, pp. 217–238. Note Karl Robert V. Wikman, *Die Einleitung Der Ehe. Acta Academiae Aboensis (Humaniora)*, 11 (1937), pp. 127 ff. Not only are reputations known because of close association among peers, but songs and poetry are sometimes composed about the girl or boy. Cf., for the Tikopia, Raymond Firth, *We, the Tikopia*, New York: American Book, 1936, pp. 468 ff.; for the Siuai, Douglas L. Oliver, *Solomon Island Society*, Cambridge: Harvard University Press, 1955, pp. 146 ff. The Manu'ans made love in groups of three or four couples; cf. Mead, *Coming of Age in Samoa, op. cit.*, p. 92.

32. Marvin B. Sussman, "Parental Participation in Mate Selection and Its Effect upon Family Continuity," *Social Forces*, 32 (October, 1953), pp. 76–81.

certain individuals have ineligibility traits (race, religion, manners, tastes, clothing, and so on). Since youngsters fall in love with those with whom they associate, control over informal relationships also controls substantially the focus of affection. The results of such control are well known and are documented in the more than one hundred studies of homogamy in this country: most marriages take place between couples in the same class, religious, racial, and educational levels.

As Robert Wikman has shown in a generally unfamiliar (in the United States) but superb investigation, this pattern was found among eighteenth-century Swedish farmer adolescents, was widely distributed in other Germanic areas, and extends in time from the nineteenth century back to almost certainly the late Middle Ages.[33] In these cases, sexual intercourse was taken for granted, social contact was closely supervised by the peer group, and final consent to marriage was withheld or granted by the parents who owned the land.

Such cases are not confined to Western society. Polynesia exhibits a similar pattern, with some variation from society to society, the best known examples of which are perhaps Mead's Manu'ans and Firth's Tikopia.[34] Probably the most familiar Melanesian cases are the Trobriands and Dobu,[35] where the systems resemble those of the Kiwai Papuans of the Trans-Fly and the Siuai Papuans of the Solomon Islands.[36] Linton found this pattern among the Tanala.[37] Although Radcliffe-Brown holds that the pattern is not common in Africa, it is clearly found among the Nuer, the Kgatla (Tswana-speaking), and the Bavenda (here, without sanctioned sexual intercourse).[38]

A more complete classification, making use of the distinctions suggested in this paper, would show, I believe, that a large minority of known societies exhibit this pattern. I would suggest, moreover, that such

33. Wikman, *op. cit.*

34. Mead, *Coming of Age in Samoa, op. cit.*, pp. 97–108; and Firth, *op. cit.*, pp. 520 ff.

35. Thus Malinowski notes in his "Introduction" to Reo F. Fortune's *The Sorcerers of Dobu,* London: Routledge, 1932, p. xxiii, that the Dobu have similar patterns, the same type of courtship by trial and error, with a gradually tightening union.

36. Gunnar Landtman, *Kiwai Papuans of the Trans-Fly,* London: Macmillan, 1927, pp. 243 ff.; Oliver, *op. cit.*, pp. 153 ff.

37. The pattern apparently existed among the Marquesans as well, but since Linton never published a complete description of this Polynesian society, I omit it here. His fullest analysis, cluttered with secondary interpretations, is in Abram Kardiner, *Psychological Frontiers of Society,* New York: Columbia University Press, 1945. For the Tanala, see Ralph Linton, *The Tanala,* Chicago: Field Museum, 1933, pp. 300–303.

38. Thus, Radcliffe-Brown: "The African does not think of marriage as a union based on romantic love, although beauty as well as character and health are sought in the choice of a wife," in his "Introduction" to A. R. Radcliffe-Brown and W. C. Daryll Forde, editors, *African Systems of Kinship and Marriage,* London: Oxford University Press, 1950, p. 46. For the Nuer, see E. E. Evans-Pritchard, *Kinship and Marriage Among the Nuer,* Oxford: Clarendon, 1951, pp. 49–58. For the Kgatla, see I. Schapera, *Married Life in an African Tribe,* New York: Sheridan, 1941, pp. 55 ff. For the Bavenda, although the report seems incomplete, see Hugh A. Stayt, *The Bavenda,* London: Oxford University Press, 1931, pp. 111 ff., 145 ff., 154.

a study would reveal that the degree to which love is a usual, expected prelude to marriage is correlated with (1) the degree of free choice of mate permitted in the society and (2) the degree to which husband-wife solidarity is the strategic solidarity of the kinship structure.[39]

Love Control and Class

These sociostructural explanations of how love is controlled lead to a subsidiary but important hypothesis: From one society to another, and from one *class* to another within the same society, the sociostructural importance of maintaining kinship lines according to rule will be rated differently by the families within them. Consequently, the degree to which control over mate choice, and therefore over the prevalence of a love pattern among adolescents, will also vary. Since, within any stratified society, this concern with the maintenance of intact and acceptable kin lines will be greater in the upper strata, it follows that noble or upper strata will maintain stricter control over love and courtship behavior than lower strata. The two correlations suggested in the preceding paragraph also apply: husband-wife solidarity is less strategic relative to clan solidarity in the upper than in the lower strata, and there is less free choice of mate.

Thus it is that, although in Polynesia generally most youngsters indulged in considerable love play, princesses were supervised strictly.[40] Similarly, in China lower class youngsters often met their spouses before marriage.[41] In our own society, the "upper upper" class maintains much greater control than the lower strata over the informal social contacts of their nubile young. Even among the Dobu, where there are few controls and little stratification, differences in control exist at the extremes: a child

39. The second correlation is developed from Levy, *op. cit.*, p. 179. Levy's formulation ties "romantic love" to that solidarity, and is of little use because there is only one case, the Western culture complex. As he states it, it is almost so by definition.

40. E.g., Mead, *Coming of Age in Samoa, op. cit.*, pp. 79, 92, 97–109. Cf. also Firth, *op. cit.*, pp. 520 ff.

41. Although one must be cautious about China, this inference seems to be allowable from such comments as the following: "But the old men of China did not succeed in eliminating love from the life of the young women. . . . Poor and middle-class families could not afford to keep men and women in separate quarters, and Chinese also met their cousins. . . . Girls . . . sometimes even served customers in their parents' shops." Olga Lang, *op. cit.*, p. 33. According to Fried, farm girls would work in the fields, and farm girls of ten years and older were sent to the market to sell produce. They were also sent to towns and cities as servants. The peasant or pauper woman was not confined to the home and its immediate environs. Morton H. Fried, *Fabric of Chinese Society*, New York: Praeger, 1953, pp. 59–60. Also, Levy (*op. cit.*, p. 111): "Among peasant girls and among servant girls in gentry households some premarital experience was not uncommon, though certainly frowned upon. The methods of preventing such contact were isolation and chaperonage, both of which, in the 'traditional' picture, were more likely to break down in the two cases named than elsewhere."

betrothal may be arranged between outstanding gardening families, who try to prevent their youngsters from being entangled with wastrel families.[42] In answer to my query about this pattern among the Nuer, Evans-Pritchard writes:

> You are probably right that a wealthy man has more control over his son's affairs than a poor man. A man with several wives has a more authoritarian position in his home. Also, a man with many cattle is in a position to permit or refuse a son to marry, whereas a lad whose father is poor may have to depend on the support of kinsmen. In general, I would say that a Nuer father is not interested in the personal side of things. His son is free to marry any girl he likes and the father does not consider the selection to be his affair until the point is reached where the cattle have to be discussed.[43]

The upper strata have much more at stake in the maintenance of the social structure and thus are more strongly motivated to control the courtship and marriage decisions of their young. Correspondingly, their young have much more to lose than lower strata youth, so that upper strata elders *can* wield more power.

Conclusion

In this analysis I have attempted to show the integration of love with various types of social structures. As against considerable contemporary opinion among both sociologists and anthropologists, I suggest that love is a universal psychological potential, which is controlled by a range of five structural patterns, all of which are attempts to see to it that youngsters do not make entirely free choices of their future spouses. Only if kin lines are unimportant, and this condition is found in no society as a whole, will entirely free choice be permitted. Some structural arrangements seek to prevent entirely the outbreak of love, while others harness it. Since the kin lines of the upper strata are of greater social importance to them than those of lower strata are to the lower strata members, the former exercise a more effective control over this choice. Even where there is almost a formally free choice of mate—and I have suggested that this pattern is widespread, to be found among a substantial segment of the earth's societies—this choice is guided by peer group and parents toward a mate who will be acceptable to the kin and friend groupings. The theoretical importance of love is thus to be seen in the socio-structural patterns which are developed to keep it from disrupting existing social arrangements.

42. Fortune, *op. cit.*, p. 30.
43. Personal letter, dated January 9, 1958. However, the Nuer father can still refuse if he believes the demands of the girl's people are unreasonable. In turn, the girl can cajole her parents to demand less.

Peter L. Berger
and Hansfried Kellner

Marriage and the Construction
of Reality

Ever since Durkheim it has been a commonplace of family sociology that
marriage serves as a protection against anomie for the individual.
Interesting and pragmatically useful though this insight is, it is but the
negative side of a phenomenon of much broader significance. If one
speaks of *anomic* states, then one ought properly to investigate also the
nomic processes that, by their absence, lead to the aforementioned states.
If, consequently, one finds a negative correlation between marriage and
anomie, then one should be led to inquire into the character of marriage as
a *nomos*-building instrumentality, that is, of marriage as a social arrangement that creates for the individual the sort of order in which he can
experience his life as making sense. It is our intention here to discuss
marriage in these terms. While this could evidently be done in a
macrosociological perspective, dealing with marriage as a major social
institution related to other broad structures of society, our focus will be
microsociological, dealing primarily with the social processes affecting
the individuals in any specific marriage, although, of course, the larger
framework of these processes will have to be understood. In what sense
this discussion can be described as microsociology of knowledge will
hopefully become clearer in the course of it.[1]

Marriage is obviously only *one* social relationship in which this
process of *nomos*-building takes place. It is, therefore, necessary to first
look in more general terms at the character of this process. In doing so,
we are influenced by three theoretical perspectives—the Weberian perspective on society as a network of meanings, the Meadian perspective on
indentity as a social phenomenon, and the phenomenological analysis of
the social structuring of reality especially as given in the work of Schutz

1. The present article has come out of a larger project on which the authors have been
engaged in collaboration with three colleagues in sociology and philosophy. The project is to
produce a systematic treatise that will integrate a number of now separate theoretical
strands in the sociology of knowledge.

and Merleau-Ponty.[2] Not being convinced, however, that theoretical lucidity is necessarily enhanced by terminological ponderosity, we shall avoid as much as possible the use of the sort of jargon for which both sociologists and phenomenologists have acquired dubious notoriety.

The process that interests us here is the one that constructs, maintains and modifies a consistent reality that can be meaningfully experienced by individuals. In its essential forms this process is determined by the society in which it occurs. Every society has its specific way of defining and perceiving reality—its world, its universe, its overarching organization of symbols. This is already given in the language that forms the symbolic base of the society. Erected over this base, and by means of it, is a system of ready-made typifications, through which the innumerable experiences of reality come to be ordered.[3] These typifications and their order are held in common by the members of society, thus acquiring not only the character of objectivity, but being taken for granted as *the* world *tout court*, the only world that normal men can conceive of.[4] The seemingly objective and taken-for-granted character of the social definitions of reality can be seen most clearly in the case of language itself, but it is important to keep in mind that the latter forms the base and instrumentality of a much larger world-erecting process.

The socially constructed world must be continually mediated to and actualized by the individual, so that it can become and remain indeed *his* world as well. The individual is given by his society certain decisive cornerstones for his everyday experience and conduct. Most importantly, the individual is supplied with specific sets of typifications and criteria of relevance, predefined for him by the society and made available to him for the ordering of his everyday life. This ordering or (in line with our opening considerations) nomic apparatus is biographically cumulative. It begins to be formed in the individual from the earliest stages of socialization on, then keeps on being enlarged and modified by himself throughout his biography.[5] While there are individual biographical differences making for differences in the constitution of this apparatus in specific individuals, there exists in the society an overall consensus on the range of differences deemed to be tolerable. Without such consensus, indeed, society would be impossible as a going concern, since it would then lack the ordering

2. Cf. especially Max Weber, *Wirtschaft und Gesellschaft* (Tuebingen: Mohr 1956), and *Gesammelte Aufsaetze zur Wissenschaftslehre* (Tuebingen: Mohr 1951); George H. Mead, *Mind, Self and Society* (University of Chicago Press 1934); Alfred Schutz, *Der sinnhafte Aufbau der sozialen Welt* (Vienna: Springer, 2nd ed. 1960) and *Collected Papers*, I (The Hague: Nijhoff 1962); Maurice Merleau-Ponty, *Phénoménologie de la perception* (Paris: Gallimard 1945) and *La structure du comportement* (Paris: Presses universitaires de France 1953).
3. Cf. Schutz, *Aufbau*, 202–20 and *Collected Papers*, I, 3–27, 283–6.
4. Cf. Schutz, *Collected Papers*, I, 207–28.
5. Cf. especially Jean Piaget, *The Child's Construction of Reality* (Routledge & Kegan Paul 1955).

principles by which alone experience can be shared and conduct can be mutually intelligible. This order, by which the individual comes to perceive and define his world, is thus not chosen by him, except perhaps for very small modifications. Rather, it is discovered by him as an external datum, a ready-made world that simply is *there* for him to go ahead and live in, though he modifies it continually in the process of living in it. Nevertheless, this world is in need of validation, perhaps precisely because of an ever-present glimmer of suspicion as to its social manufacture and relativity. This validation, while it must be undertaken by the individual himself, requires ongoing interaction with others who co-inhabit this same socially constructed world. In a broad sense, *all* the other co-inhabitants of this world serve a validating function. Every morning the newspaper boy validates the widest co-ordinates of my world and the mailman bears tangible validation of my own location within these co-ordinates. However, some validations are more significant than others. Every individual requires the ongoing validation of his world, including crucially the validation of his identity and place in this world, by those few who are his truly significant others.[6] Just as the individual's deprivation of relationship with his significant others will plunge him into anomie, so their continued presence will sustain for him that *nomos* by which he can feel at home in the world at least most of the time. Again in a broad sense, all the actions of the significant others and even their simple presence serve this sustaining function. In everyday life, however, the principal method employed is speech. In this sense, it is proper to view the individual's relationship with his significant others as an ongoing conversation. As the latter occurs, it validates over and over again the fundamental definitions of reality once entered into, not, of course, so much by explicit articulation, but precisely by taking the definitions silently for granted and conversing about all conceivable matters on this taken-for-granted basis. Through the same conversation the individual is also made capable of adjusting to changing and new social contexts in his biography. In a very fundamental sense it can be said that one converses one's way through life.

If one concedes these points, one can now state a general sociological proposition: the plausibility and stability of the world, as socially defined, is dependent upon the strength and continuity of significant relationships in which conversation about this world can be continually carried on. Or, to put it a little differently: the reality of the world is sustained through conversation with significant others. This reality, of course, includes not only the imagery by which fellowmen are viewed, but also includes the way in which one views oneself. The reality-bestowing force of social relationships depends on the degree of their

6. Cf. Mead, *op. cit.*, 135–226.

nearness,[7] that is, on the degree to which social relationships occur in face-to-face situations and to which they are credited with primary significance by the individual. In any empirical situation, there now emerge obvious sociological questions out of these considerations, namely, questions about the patterns of the world-building relationships, the social forms taken by the conversation with significant others. Sociologically, one must ask how these relationships are *objectively* structured and distributed, and one will also want to understand how they are *subjectively* perceived and experienced.

With these preliminary assumptions stated we can now arrive at our main thesis here. Namely, we would contend that marriage occupies a privileged status among the significant validating relationships for adults in our society. Put slightly differently: marriage is a crucial nomic instrumentality in our society. We would further argue that the essential social functionality of this institution cannot be fully understood if this fact is not perceived.

We can now proceed with an ideal-typical analysis of marriage, that is, seek to abstract the essential features involved. Marriage in our society is a *dramatic* act in which two strangers come together and redefine themselves. The drama of the act is internally anticipated and socially legitimated long before it takes place in the individual's biography, and amplified by means of a pervasive ideology, the dominant themes of which (romantic love, sexual fulfilment, self-discovery and self-realization through love and sexuality, the nuclear family as the social site for these processes) can be found distributed through all strata of the society. The actualization of these ideologically pre-defined expectations in the life of the individual occurs to the accompaniment of one of the few traditional rites of passage that are still meaningful to almost all members of the society. It should be added that, in using the term "strangers," we do not mean, of course, that the candidates for the marriage come from widely discrepant social backgrounds—indeed, the data indicate that the contrary is the case. The strangeness rather lies in the fact that, unlike marriage candidates in many previous societies, those in ours typically come from different face-to-face contexts—in the terms used above, they come from different areas of conversation. They do not have a shared past, although their pasts have a similar structure. In other words, quite apart from prevailing patterns of ethnic, religious and class endogamy, our society is typically exogamous in terms of nomic relationships. Put concretely, in our mobile society the significant conversation of the two partners previous to the marriage took place in social circles that did not overlap. With the dramatic redefinition of the situation brought about by the marriage, however, all significant conversation for the two new

7. Cf. Schutz, *Aufbau,* 181–95.

partners is now centered in their relationship with each other—and, in fact, it was precisely with this intention that they entered upon their relationship.

It goes without saying that this character of marriage has its root in much broader structural configurations of our society. The most important of these, for our purposes, is the crystallization of a so-called private sphere of existence, more and more segregated from the immediate controls of the public institutions (especially the economic and political ones), and yet defined and utilized as the main social area for the individual's self-realization.[8] It cannot be our purpose here to inquire into the historical forces that brought forth this phenomenon, beyond making the observation that these are closely connected with the industrial revolution and its institutional consequences. The public institutions now confront the individual as an immensely powerful and alien world, incomprehensible in its inner workings, anonymous in its human character. If only through his work in some nook of the economic machinery, the individual must find a way of living in this alien world, come to terms with its power over him, be satisfied with a few conceptual rules of thumb to guide him through a vast reality that otherwise remains opaque to his understanding, and modify its anonymity by whatever *human relations* he can work out in his involvement with it. It ought to be emphasized, against some critics of "mass society," that this does not inevitably leave the individual with a sense of profound unhappiness and lostness. It would rather seem that large numbers of people in our society are quite content with a situation in which their public involvements have little subjective importance, regarding work as a not too bad necessity and politics as at best a spectator sport. It is usually only intellectuals with ethical and political commitments who assume that such people must be terribly desperate. The point, however, is that the individual in this situation, no matter whether he is happy or not, will turn elsewhere for the experiences of self-realization that do have importance for him. The private sphere, this interstitial area created (we would think) more or less haphazardly as a by-product of the social metamorphosis of industrialism, is mainly where he will turn. It is here that the individual will seek power, intelligibility and, quite literally, a name—the apparent power to fashion a world, however Lilliputian, that will reflect his own being: a world that, seemingly having been shaped by himself and thus unlike those other worlds that insist on shaping him, is translucently intelligible to him (or so he thinks); a world in which, consequently, he is *somebody*—perhaps

8. Cf. Arnold Gehlen, *Die Seele im technischen Zeitalter* (Hamburg: Rowohlt 1957), 57–69 and *Anthropologische Forschung* (Hamburg: Rowohlt 1961), 69–77, 127–40; Helmut Schelsky, *Soziologie der Sexualitaet* (Hamburg: Rowohlt 1955), 102–33. Also cf. Thomas Luckmann, "On religion in modern society," *Journal for the Scientific Study of Religion* (Spring 1963), 147–62.

even, within its charmed circle, a lord and master. What is more, to a considerable extent these expectations are not unrealistic. The public institutions have no need to control the individual's adventures in the private sphere, as long as they really stay within the latter's circumscribed limits. The private sphere is perceived, not without justification, as an area of individual choice and even autonomy. This fact has important consequences for the shaping of identity in modern society that cannot be pursued here. All that ought to be clear here is the peculiar location of the private sphere within and between the other social structures. In sum, it is above all and, as a rule, only in the private sphere that the individual can take a slice of reality and fashion it into his world. If one is aware of the decisive significance of this capacity and even necessity of men to externalize themselves in reality and to produce for themselves a world in which they can feel at home, then one will hardly be surprised at the great importance which the private sphere has come to have in modern society.[9]

The private sphere includes a variety of social relationships. Among these, however, the relationships of the family occupy a central position and, in fact, serve as a focus for most of the other relationships (such as those with friends, neighbors, fellow-members of religious and other voluntary associations). Since, as the ethnologists keep reminding us, the family in our society is of the conjugal type, the central relationship in this whole area is the marital one. It is on the basis of marriage that, for most adults in our society, existence in the private sphere is built up. It will be clear that this is not at all a universal or even cross culturally wide function of marriage. Rather has marriage in our society taken on a very peculiar character and functionality. It has been pointed out that marriage in contemporary society has lost some of its older functions and taken on new ones instead.[10] This is certainly correct, but we would prefer to state the matter a little differently. Marriage and the family used to be firmly embedded in a matrix of wider community relationships, serving as extensions and particularizations of the latter's social controls. There were few separating barriers between the world of the individual family and the wider community, a fact even to be seen in the physical conditions under which the family lived before the industrial revolution.[11] The same social life pulsated through the house, the street and the community. In our terms, the family and within it the marital relationship were part and parcel of a considerably larger area of conversation. In our contemporary society, by contrast, each family constitutes its own

9. In these considerations we have been influenced by certain presuppositions of Marxian anthropology, as well as by the anthropological work of Max Scheler, Helmuth Plessner and Arnold Gehlen. We are indebted to Thomas Luckmann for the clarification of the social-psychological significance of the private sphere.

10. Cf. Talcott Parsons and Robert Bales, *Family: Socialization and Interaction Process* (Routledge & Kegan Paul 1956), 3–34, 353–96.

11. Cf. Philippe Ariès, *Centuries of Childhood* (New York: Knopf 1962), 339–410.

segregated sub-world, with its own controls and its own closed conversation.

This fact requires a much greater effort on the part of the marriage partners. Unlike an earlier situation in which the establishment of the new marriage simply added to the differentiation and complexity of an already existing social world, the marriage partners now are embarked on the often difficult task of constructing for themselves the little world in which they will live. To be sure, the larger society provides them with certain standard instructions as to how they should go about this task, but this does not change the fact that considerable effort of their own is required for its realization. The monogamous character of marriage enforces both the dramatic and the precarious nature of this undertaking. Success or failure hinges on the present idiosyncrasies and the fairly unpredictable future development of these idiosyncrasies of only two individuals (who, moreover, do not have a shared past)—as Simmel has shown, the most unstable of all possible social relationships.[12] Not surprisingly, the decision to embark on this undertaking has a critical, even cataclysmic connotation in the popular imagination, which is underlined as well as psychologically assuaged by the ceremonialism that surrounds the event.

Every social relationship requires objectivation, that is, requires a process by which subjectively experienced meanings become objective to the individual and, in interaction with others, become common property and thereby massively objective.[13] The degree of objectivation will depend on the number and the intensity of the social relationships that are its carriers. A relationship that consists of only two individuals called upon to sustain, by their own efforts, an ongoing social world will have to make up in intensity for the numerical poverty of the arrangement. This, in turn, accentuates the drama and the precariousness. The later addition of children will add to the, as it were, density of objectivation taking place within the nuclear family, thus rendering the latter a good deal less precarious. It remains true that the establishment and maintenance of such a social world make extremely high demands on the principal participants.

The attempt can now be made to outline the ideal-typical process that takes place as marriage functions as an instrumentality for the social construction of reality. The chief protagonists of the drama are two individuals, each with a biographically accumulated and available stock of experience.[14] As members of a highly mobile society, these individuals have already internalized a degree of readiness to re-define themselves and to modify their stock of experience, thus bringing with them considerable psychological capacity for entering new relationships with

12. Cf. Georg Simmel (Kurt Wolff ed.), *The Sociology of Georg Simmel* (Collier-Macmillan 1950), 118–44.
13. Cf. Schutz, *Aufbau*, 29–36, 149–53.
14. Cf. Schutz, *Aufbau*, 186–92, 202–10.

others.[15] Also, coming from broadly similar sectors of the larger society (in terms of region, class, ethnic and religious affiliations), the two individuals will have organized their stock of experience in similar fashion. In other words, the two individuals have internalized the same overall world, including the general definitions and expectations of the marriage relationship itself. Their society has provided them with a taken-for-granted image of marriage and has socialized them into an anticipation of stepping into the taken-for-granted roles of marriage. All the same, these relatively empty projections now have to be actualized, lived through and filled with experiential content by the protagonists. This will require a dramatic change in their definitions of reality and of themselves.

As of the marriage, most of each partner's actions must now be projected in conjunction with those of the other. Each partner's definitions of reality must be continually correlated with the definitions of the other. The other is present in nearly all horizons of everyday conduct. Furthermore, the identity of each now takes on a new character, having to be constantly matched with that of the other, indeed being typically perceived by people at large as being symbiotically conjoined with the identity of the other. In each partner's psychological economy of significant others, the marriage partner becomes the other *par excellence*, the nearest and most decisive co-inhabitant of the world. Indeed, all other significant relationships have to be almost automatically re-perceived and re-grouped in accordance with this drastic shift.

In other words, from the beginning of the marriage each partner has new modes in his meaningful experience of the world in general, of other people and of himself. By definition, then, marriage constitutes a nomic rupture. In terms of each partner's biography, the event of marriage initiates a new nomic process. Now, the full implications of this fact are rarely apprehended by the protagonists with any degree of clarity. There rather is to be found the notion that one's world, one's other-relationships and, above all, oneself have remained what they were before—only, of course, that world, others and self will now be shared with the marriage partner. It should be clear by now that this notion is a grave misapprehension. Just because of this fact, marriage now propels the individual into an unintended and unarticulated development, in the course of which the nomic transformation takes place. What typically *is* apprehended are certain objective and concrete problems arising out of the marriage—such as tensions with in-laws, or with former friends, or religious differences between the partners, as well as immediate tensions between them. These are apprehended as external, situational and practical difficulties. What is *not* apprehended is the subjective side of these difficulties, namely, the

15. David Riesman's well-known concept of ,"other-direction" would also be applicable here.

transformation of *nomos* and identity that has occurred and that continues to go on, so that all problems and relationships are experienced in a quite new way, that is, experienced within a new and ever-changing reality.

Take a simple and frequent illustration—the male partner's relationships with male friends before and after the marriage. It is a common observation that such relationships, especially if the extra-marital partners are single, rarely survive the marriage, or, if they do, are drastically re-defined after it. This is typically the result of neither a deliberate decision by the husband nor deliberate sabotage by the wife. What rather happens, very simply, is a slow process in which the husband's image of his friend is transformed as he keeps talking about this friend with his wife. Even if no actual talking goes on, the mere presence of the wife forces him to see his friend differently. This need not mean that he adopts a negative image held by the wife. Regardless of what image she holds or is believed by him to hold, it will be different from that held by the husband. This difference will enter into the joint image that now must needs be fabricated in the course of the ongoing conversation between the marriage partners—and, in due course, must act powerfully on the image previously held by the husband. Again, typically, this process is rarely apprehended with any degree of lucidity. The old friend is more likely to fade out of the picture by slow degrees, as new kinds of friends take his place. The process, if commented upon at all within the marital conversation, can always be explained by socially available formulas about "people changing," "friends disappearing" or oneself "having become more mature." This process of conversational liquidation is especially powerful because it is onesided—the husband typically talks with his wife about his friend, but *not* with his friend about his wife. Thus the friend is deprived of the defense of, as it were, counter-defining the relationship. This dominance of the marital conversation over all others is one of its most important characteristics. It may be mitigated by a certain amount of protective segregation of some non-marital relationships (say "Tuesday night out with the boys," or "Saturday lunch with mother"), but even then there are powerful emotional barriers against the sort of conversation (conversation *about* the marital relationship, that is) that would serve by way of counter-definition.

Marriage thus posits a new reality. The individual's relationship with this new reality, however, is a dialectical one—he acts upon it, in collusion with the marriage partner, and it acts back upon both him and the partner, welding together their reality. Since, as we have argued before, the objectivation that constitutes this reality is precarious, the groups with which the couple associates are called upon to assist in co-defining the new reality. The couple is pushed towards groups that strengthen their new definition of themselves and the world, avoids those that weaken this definition. This in turn releases the commonly known pressures of group association, again acting upon the marriage partners to change their definitions of the world and of themselves. Thus the new reality is not posited once and for all, but goes on being redefined not only in the marital interaction itself but also in the various maritally based group relationships into which the couple enters.

In the individual's biography marriage, then, brings about a decisive phase of socialization that can be compared with the phases of childhood and adolescence. This phase has a rather different structure from the earlier ones. There the individual was in the main socialized into already existing patterns. Here he actively collaborates rather than passively accommodates himself. Also, in the previous phases of socialization, there was an apprehension of entering into a new world and being changed in the course of this. In marriage there is little apprehension of such a process, but rather the notion that the world has remained the same, with only its emotional and pragmatic connotations having changed. This notion, as we have tried to show, is illusionary.

The re-construction of the world in marriage occurs principally in the course of conversation, as we have suggested. The implicit problem of this conversation is how to match two individual definitions of reality. By the very logic of the relationship, a common overall definition must be arrived at—otherwise the conversation will become impossible and, *ipso facto,* the relationship will be endangered. Now, this conversation may be understood as the working away of an ordering and typifying apparatus—if one prefers, an objectivating apparatus. Each partner ongoingly contributes his conceptions of reality, which are then "talked through," usually not once but many times, and in the process become objectivated by the conversational apparatus. The longer this conversation goes on, the more massively real do the objectivations become to the partners. In the marital conversation a world is not only built, but it is also kept in a state of repair and ongoingly refurnished. The subjective reality of this world for the two partners is sustained by the same conversation. The nomic instrumentality of marriage is concretized over and over again, from bed to breakfast table, as the partners carry on the endless conversation that feeds on nearly all they individually or jointly experience. Indeed, it may happen eventually that no experience is fully real unless and until it has been thus "talked through."

This process has a very important result—namely, a hardening or stabilization of the common objectivated reality. It should be easy to see now how this comes about. The objectivations ongoingly performed and internalized by the marriage partners become ever more massively real, as they are confirmed and reconfirmed in the marital conversation. The world that is made up of these objectivations at the same time gains in stability. For example, the images of other people, which before or in the earlier stages of the marital conversation may have been rather ambiguous and shifting in the minds of the two partners, now become hardened into definite and stable characterizations. A casual acquaintance, say, may sometimes have appeared as lots of fun and sometimes as quite a bore to the wife before her marriage. Under the influence of the marital conversation, in which this other person is frequently "discussed," she will now come down more firmly on one *or* the other of the two characterizations, or on a reasonable compromise between the two. In any of these three options, though, she will have concocted with her husband a much more stable image of the person in question than she is likely to have had before her marriage, when there may have been no conversational pressure to make a definite option at all. The same process of stabilization may be observed with regard to self-definitions as well. In this way, the wife in our example will not only be pressured to assign stable characterizations to others but also to herself. Previously uninterested politically, she now identifies herself as a liberal. Previously alternating between dimly articulated religious positions, she now declares herself an agnostic. Previously confused and uncertain about her sexual emotions, she now understands herself as an unabashed hedonist in this area. And so on and so forth, with the same reality—and identity—stabilizing process at work on the husband. Both world and self thus take on a firmer, more reliable character for both partners.

Furthermore, it is not only the ongoing experience of the two partners that is constantly shared and passed through the conversational apparatus. The same sharing extends into the past. The two distinct biographies, as subjectively apprehended by the two individuals who have lived through them, are overruled and re-interpreted in the course of their conversation. Sooner or later, they will "tell all"—or, more correctly, they will tell it in such a way that it fits into the self-definitions objectivated in the marital relationship. The couple thus construct not only present reality but reconstruct past reality as well, fabricating a common memory that integrates the recollections of the two individual pasts.[16] The comic fulfilment of this process may be seen in those cases when one partner "remembers" more clearly what happened in the other's past than the other does—and corrects him accordingly. Similarly, there occurs a sharing of future horizons, which leads not only to stabilization, but inevitably to a narrowing of the future projections of each partner. Before marriage the individual typically plays with quite discrepant daydreams in which his future self is projected.[17] Having now considerably stabilized his self-image, the married individual will have to

16. Cf. Maurice Halbwachs, *Les Cadres sociaux de la mémoire* (Paris: Presses universitaires de France 1952), especially 146–77; also cf. Peter Berger, *Invitation to Sociology–A Humanistic Perspective* (Garden City, N.Y.: Doubleday-Anchor 1963), 54–65 (available in Penguin).

17. Cf. Schutz, *Collected Papers*, I, 72–3, 79–82.

project the future in accordance with this maritally defined identity. This narrowing of future horizons begins with the obvious external limitations that marriage entails, as, for example, with regard to vocational and career plans. However, it extends also to the more general possibilities of the individual's biography. To return to a previous illustration, the wife, having "found herself" as a liberal, an agnostic and a "sexually healthy" person, *ipso facto* liquidates the possibilities of becoming an anarchist, a Catholic or a Lesbian. At least until further notice she has decided upon who she is—and, by the same token, upon who she will be. The stabilization brought about by marriage thus affects the total reality in which the partners exist. In the most far-reaching sense of the word, the married individual "settles down"—and *must* do so, if the marriage is to be viable, in accordance with its contemporary institutional definition.

It cannot be sufficiently strongly emphasized that this process is typically unapprehended, almost automatic in character. The protagonists of the marriage drama do *not* set out deliberately to re-create their world. Each continues to live in a world that is taken for granted —and keeps its taken-for-granted character even as it is metamorphosed. The new world that the married partners, Prometheus-like, have called into being is perceived by them as the normal world in which they have lived before. Re-constructed present and re-interpreted past are perceived as a continuum, extending forwards into a commonly projected future. The dramatic change that has occurred remains, in bulk, unapprehended and unarticulated. And where it forces itself upon the individual's attention, it is retrojected into the past, explained as having always been there, though perhaps in a hidden way. Typically, the reality that has been "invented" within the marital conversation is subjectively perceived as a "discovery." Thus the partners "discover" themselves and the world, "who they really are," "what they really believe," "how they really feel, and always have felt, about so-and-so." This retrojection of the world being produced all the time by themselves serves to enhance the stability of this world and at the same time to assuage the "existential anxiety" that, probably inevitably, accompanies the perception that nothing but one's own narrow shoulders supports the universe in which one has chosen to live. If one may put it like this, it is psychologically more tolerable to be Columbus than to be Prometheus.

The use of the term "stabilization" should not detract from the insight into the difficulty and precariousness of this world-building enterprise. Often enough, the new universe collapses *in statu nascendi*. Many more times it continues over a period, swaying perilously back and forth as the two partners try to hold it up, finally to be abandoned as an impossible undertaking. If one conceives of the marital conversation as the principal drama and the two partners as the principal protagonists of the drama, then one can look upon the other individuals involved as the supporting chorus for the central dramatic action. Children, friends, relatives and casual acquaintances all have their part in reinforcing the tenuous structure of the new reality. It goes without saying that the children form the most important part of this supporting chorus. Their very existence is predicated on the maritally established world. The marital partners themselves are in charge of their socialization *into* this world, which to them has a pre-existent and self-evident character. They are taught from the beginning to speak precisely those lines that lend themselves to a supporting chorus, from their first invocations of "Daddy" and "Mummy" on to their adoption of the parents' ordering and typifying apparatus that now defines *their* world as well. The marital conversation is now in the process of becoming a family symposium, with the necessary consequence that its objectivations rapidly gain in density, plausibility and durability.

In sum: the process that we have been inquiring into is, ideal-typically, one in which reality is crystallized, narrowed and stabilized. Ambivalences are converted into certainties. Typifications of self and of others become settled. Most generally, possibilities become facticities. What is more, this process of transformation remains, most of the time, unapprehended by those who are both its authors and its objects.[18]

We have analyzed in some detail the process that, we contend, entitles us to describe marriage as a nomic instrumentality. It may now be well to turn back once more to the macrosocial context in which this process takes place—a process that, to repeat, is peculiar to our society as far as the institution of marriage is concerned, although it obviously expresses much more general human facts. The narrowing and stabiliza-tion of identity is functional in a society that, in its major public institutions, must insist on rigid controls over the individual's conduct. At the same time, the narrow enclave of the nuclear family serves as a macrosocially innocuous "play area," in which the individual can safely exercise his world-building proclivities without upsetting any of the important social, economic and political applecarts. Barred from expand-ing himself into the area occupied by these major institutions, he is given plenty of leeway to "discover himself" in his marriage and his family, and, in view of the difficulty of this undertaking, is provided with a number of auxiliary agencies that stand ready to assist him (such as counseling, psychotherapeutic and religious agencies). The marital ad-venture can be relied upon to absorb a large amount of energy that might otherwise be expended more dangerously. The ideological themes of familism, romantic love, sexual expression, maturity and social adjust-ment, with the pervasive psychologistic anthropology that underlies them all, function to legitimate this enterprise. Also, the narrowing and

18. The phenomena here discussed could also be formulated effectively in terms of the Marxian categories of reification and false consciousness. Jean-Paul Sartre's recent work, especially *Critique de la raison dialectique,* seeks to integrate these categories within a phenomenological analysis of human conduct. Also cf. Henri Lefebvre, *Critique de la vie quotidienne* (Paris: l'Arche 1958–61).

stabilization of the individual's principal area of conversation within the nuclear family is functional in a society that requires high degrees of both geographical and social mobility. The segregated little world of the family can be easily detached from one milieu and transposed into another without appreciably interfering with the central processes going on in it. Needless to say, we are not suggesting that these functions are deliberately planned or even apprehended by some mythical ruling directorate of the society. Like most social phenomena, whether they be macro- or microscopic, these functions are typically unintended and unarticulated. What is more, the functionality would be impaired if it were too widely apprehended.

We believe that the above theoretical considerations serve to give a new perspective on various empirical facts studied by family sociologists. As we have emphasized a number of times, our considerations are ideal-typical in intention. We have been interested in marriage at a normal age in urban, middle-class, western societies. We cannot discuss here such special problems as marriages or remarriages at a more advanced age, marriage in the remaining rural subcultures, or in ethnic or lower-class minority groups. We feel quite justified in this limitation of scope, however, by the empirical findings that tend towards the view that a global marriage type is emerging in the central strata of modern industrial societies.[19] This type, commonly referred to as the nuclear family, has been analyzed in terms of a shift from the so-called family of orientation to the so-called family of procreation as the most important reference for the individual.[20] In addition to the well-known, socio-economic reasons for this shift, most of them rooted in the development of industrialism, we would argue that important macrosocial functions pertain to the nomic process within the nuclear family, as we have analyzed it. This functionality of the nuclear family must, furthermore, be seen in conjunction with the familistic ideology that both reflects and reinforces it. A few specific empirical points may suffice to indicate the applicability of our theoretical perspective. To make these we shall use selected American data.

The trend towards marriage at an earlier age has been noted.[21] This has been correctly related to such factors as urban freedom, sexual emancipation and equalitarian values. We would add the important fact

19. Cf. Renate Mayntz, *Die moderne Familie* (Stuttgart: Enke 1955); Helmut Schelsky, *Wandlungen der deutschen Familie in der Gegenwart* (Stuttgart: Enke 1955); Maximilien Sorre (ed.), *Sociologie comparée de la famille contemporaine* (Paris: Centre National de la Recherche Scientifique 1955); Ruth Anshen (ed.), *The Family—Its Function and Destiny* (New York: Harper 1959); Norman Bell and Ezra Vogel, *A Modern Introduction to the Family* (Routledge & Kegan Paul 1961).

20. Cf. Talcott Parsons, *Essays in Sociological Theory* (Collier-Macmillan 1949), 233–50.

21. In these as well as the following references to empirical studies we naturally make no attempt at comprehensiveness. References are given as representative of a much larger body of materials. Cf. Paul Glick, *American Families* (New York: Wiley 1957), 54. Also cf. his "The family cycle," *American Sociological Review* (April 1947), 164–74. Also cf. Bureau of the Census, *Statistical Abstracts of the United States* 1956 and 1958; *Current Population Reports,* Series P-20, no. 96 (Nov. 1959).

that a child raised in the circumscribed world of the nuclear family is stamped by it in terms of his psychological needs and social expectations. Having to live in the larger society from which the nuclear family is segregated, the adolescent soon feels the need for a "little world" of his own, having been socialized in such a way that only by having such a world to withdraw into can he successfully cope with the anonymous "big world" that confronts him as soon as he steps outside his parental home. In other words, to be "at home" in society entails, *per definitionem*, the construction of a maritally based sub-world. The parental home itself facilitates such an early jump into marriage precisely because its controls are very narrow in scope and leave the adolescent to his own nomic devices at an early age. As has been studied in considerable detail, the adolescent peer group functions as a transitional *nomos* between the two family worlds in the individual's biography.[22]

The equalization in the age of the marriage partners has also been noted.[23] This is certainly also to be related to equalitarian values and, concomitantly, to the decline in the "double standard" of sexual morality. Also, however, this fact is very conducive to the common reality-constructing enterprise that we have analyzed. One of the features of the latter, as we have pointed out, is the re-construction of the two biographies in terms of a cohesive and mutually correlated common memory. This task is evidently facilitated if the two partners are of roughly equal age. Another empirical finding to which our considerations are relevant is the choice of marriage partners within similar socio-economic backgrounds.[24] Apart from the obvious practical pressures towards such limitations of choice, the latter also ensure sufficient similarity in the biographically accumulated stocks of experience to facilitate the described reality-constructing process. This would also offer additional explanation to the observed tendency to narrow the limitations of marital choice even further, for example in terms of religious background.[25]

There now exists a considerable body of data on the adoption and mutual adjustment of marital roles.[26] Nothing in our consideration

22. Cf. David Riesman, *The Lonely Crowd* (New Haven: Yale University Press 1953), 29–40; Frederick Elkin, *The Child and Society* (New York: Random House 1960), *passim*.

23. Cf. references given above note 21.

24. Cf. W. Lloyd Warner and Paul Lunt, *The Social Life of a Modern Community* (New Haven: Yale University Press 1941), 436–40; August Hollingshead, "Cultural factors in the selection of marriage mates," *American Sociological Review* (October 1950), 619–27. Also cf. Ernest Burgess and Paul Wallin, "Homogamy in social characteristics," *American Journal of Sociology* (September 1943), 109–24.

25. Cf. Gerhard Lenski, *The Religious Factor* (Garden City, N.Y.: Doubleday 1961), 48–50.

26. Cf. Leonard Cottrell, "Roles in marital adjustment," *Publications of the American Sociological Society* (1933), 27, 107–15; Willard Waller and Reuben Hill, *The Family—A Dynamic Interpretation* (New York: Dryden 1951), 253–71; Morris Zelditch, "Role differentiation in the nuclear family," in Parsons and Bales, *op. cit.*, 307–52. For a general discussion of role interaction in small groups, cf. especially George Homans, *The Human Group* (Routledge & Kegan Paul 1951).

detracts from the analyses made of these data by sociologists interested primarily in the processes of group interaction. We would only argue that something more fundamental is involved in this role-taking—namely, the individual's relationship to reality as such. Each role in the marital situation carries with it a universe of discourse, broadly given by cultural definition, but continually re-actualized in the ongoing conversation between the marriage partners. Put simply: marriage involves not only stepping into new roles, but, beyond this, stepping into a new world. The *mutuality* of adjustment may again be related to the rise of marital equalitarianism, in which comparable effort is demanded of both partners.

Most directly related to our considerations are data that pertain to the greater stability of married as against unmarried individuals.[27] Though frequently presented in misleading psychological terms (such as "greater emotional stability," "greater maturity," and so on), these data are sufficiently validated to be used not only by marriage counselors but in the risk calculations of insurance companies. We would contend that our theoretical perspective places these data into a much more intelligible sociological frame of reference, which also happens to be free of the particular value bias with which the psychological terms are loaded. It is, of course, quite true that married people are more stable emotionally (i.e. operating within a more controlled scope of emotional expression), more mature in their views, (i.e. inhabiting a firmer and narrower world in conformity with the expectations of society), and more sure of themselves (i.e. having objectivated a more stable and fixated self-definition). *Therefore* they are more liable to be psychologically balanced (i.e. having sealed off much of their "anxiety," and reduced ambivalence as well as openness towards new possibilities of self-definition) and socially pre-dictable (i.e. keeping their conduct well within the socially established safety rules). All of these phenomena are concomitants of the overall fact of having "settled down"—cognitively, emotionally, in terms of self-identification. To speak of these phenomena as indicators of "mental health," let alone of "adjustment to reality," overlooks the decisive fact that reality is socially constructed and that psychological conditions of all sorts are grounded in a social matrix.

We would say, very simply, that the married individual comes to live in a more stable world, from which fact certain psychological conse-quences can be readily deduced. To bestow some sort of higher ontological status upon these psychological consequences is *ipso facto* a symptom of the mis- or non-apprehension of the social process that has produced them. Furthermore, the compulsion to legitimate the stabilized marital world, be it in psychologistic or in traditional religious terms, is another expression of the precariousness of its construction.[28] This is not the

27. Cf. Waller and Hill, *op. cit.*, 253–71, for an excellent summation of such data.
28. Cf. Dennison Nash and Peter Berger, "The family, the child and the religious revival in suburbia," *Journal for the Scientific Study of Religion* (Fall 1962), 85–93.

place to pursue any further the ideological processes involved in this. Suffice it to say that contemporary psychology functions to sustain this precarious world by assigning to it the status of "normalcy," a legitimating operation that increasingly links up with the older religious assignment of the status of "sacredness." Both legitimating agencies have established their own rites of passage, validating myths and rituals, and individualized repair services for crisis situations. Whether one legitimates one's maritally constructed reality in terms of "mental health" or of the "sacrament of marriage" is today largely left to free consumer preference, but it is indicative of the crystallization of a new overall universe of discourse that it is increasingly possible to do both at the same time.

Finally, we would point here to the empirical data on divorce.[29] The prevalence and, indeed, increasing prevalence of divorce might at first appear as a counter-argument to our theoretical considerations. We would contend that the very opposite is the case, as the data themselves bear out. Typically, individuals in our society do not divorce because marriage has become unimportant to them, but because it has become so important that they have no tolerance for the less than completely successful marital arrangement they have contracted with the particular individual in question. This is more fully understood when one has grasped the crucial need for the sort of world that only marriage can produce in our society, a world without which the individual is powerfully threatened with anomie in the fullest sense of the word. Also, the frequency of divorce simply reflects the difficulty and demanding character of the whole undertaking. The empirical fact that the great majority of divorced individuals plan to remarry and a good majority of them actually do, at least in America, fully bears out this contention.[30]

The purpose of this article is not polemic, nor do we wish to advocate any particular values concerning marriage. We have sought to debunk the familistic ideology only insofar as it serves to obfuscate a sociological understanding of the phenomenon. Our purpose has rather been twofold. First, we wanted to show that it is possible to develop a sociological theory of marriage that is based on clearly sociological presuppositions, without operating with psychological or psychiatric categories that have dubious value within a sociological frame of reference. We believe that such a sociological theory of marriage is generally useful for a fully conscious awareness of existence in contemporary society, and not only for the sociologist. Secondly, we have used the case of marriage for an exercise in the sociology of knowledge, a discipline that we regard as

29. Cf. Bureau of the Census, *op. cit.*
30. Cf. Talcott Parsons, "Age and Sex in the Social Structure of the United States," *American Sociological Review* (December 1942), 604–16; Paul Glick, "First marriages and remarriages," *American Sociological Review* (December 1949), 726–34; William Goode, *After Divorce* (Chicago: Free Press 1956), 269–85.

most promising. Hitherto this discipline has been almost exclusively concerned with macrosocialogical questions, such as those dealing with the relationship of intellectual history to social processes. We believe that the microsociological focus is equally important for this discipline. The sociology of knowledge must not only be concerned with the great universes of meaning that history offers up for our inspection, but with the many little workshops in which living individuals keep hammering away at the construction and maintenance of these universes. In this way, the sociologist can make an important contribution to the illumination of that everyday world in which we all live and which we help fashion in the course of our biography.

4 MARITAL SELECTION

Lawrence Stone

Marriage Among the English Nobility[1]

In this paper an attempt is made to study the marriage customs and family relationships of the titular peerage and the 500 or so leading county families who together formed the dominant political and social grouping of Tudor and Stuart England. Generalizations here made apply only to this restricted class and not necessarily to those below it. When it comes to be investigated, the behavior of the lesser gentry, the yeomanry, the peasantry and the merchants may well show significant differences from the model set by their betters.

Marriage in England today is usually the result of the free choice of the individual man and woman, united primarily on the basis of romantic and sexual attraction, and a harmony of tastes and interests. The two distinct features of this situation are choice by the individuals concerned rather than by their parents, and selection mainly—though not necessarily exclusively—for personal reasons rather than for social or financial advancement. Thanks to the economic independence of young people under conditions of full employment and to the massive circulation of

1. In the interests of compression, this paper is confined to an outline of the main conclusions. The great bulk of the supporting evidence and the footnote documentation has been omitted, and will appear in my book on *The Nobility of England, 1558–1642*. I am very grateful to Mr. Keith Thomas and Mr. Christopher Hill for having read and criticized this paper in draft. Their comments, particularly those of the former, have saved me from many errors of judgment, though I have no doubt that they believe that many more remain.

literature exclusively devoted to the theme of romantic marriage, the image is probably a fair approximation to the truth in a majority of cases. But despite the rise of notions of romantic love in the twelfth century, the medieval popularity of stories like that of Tristan and Iseult, and the later success of *Amadis of Gaul* and similar romances, their impact upon the practice of the European landed classes was until very recently of negligible importance. There are two main reasons for this remarkable time-lag. Firstly there persisted very strongly that suspicion and dislike of passionate love between the sexes which was shared both by the Ancient World and the medieval church. Secondly there was the firm belief in the subjection of children to parental control which was natural to a society in which family discipline was the main guarantee of public order, and to a class in which young men were not expected to work and were therefore dependent for their living upon allowances from their fathers. This subordination was emphasized by outward forms of respect, upon which England was particularly insistent. As Donne pointed out "Children kneele to aske blessing of Parents in England, but where else?"[2]

The most severe parental pressure was inevitably exercised on daughters, who were most dependent and sheltered, who were regarded as members of an inferior sex, and who had little alternative to obedience since celibacy was even less attractive than an unwanted husband. Parents felt themselves morally obliged to see their daughters married off, and daughters were both unwilling and unable to resist. Fathers in their wills commonly made their bequests of marriage portions for their daughters conditional upon approval of the groom by guardians or executors, such clauses continuing with diminishing frequency, and perhaps with diminishing effect, in the early seventeenth century. Sometimes parents actually went so far as to nominate a particular husband for their daughters in their wills, though not always successfully. In the early sixteenth century wills and marriage contracts by which small children were bartered in advance like cattle were fairly common in all classes and all areas, and they were still being made by the lesser squires of the north at the end of the century.[3] In the more sophisticated circles of the upper gentry and aristocracy of the south, however, these extreme measures were now very rare, though they were still occasionally practiced. When in 1614 the King of Sumatra wrote to ask for an English wife, there was not lacking "a gentleman of honourable parentage" who, like the *Bourgeois Gentilhomme* of Molière, was prepared to sacrifice his daughter.[4]

2. *The Sermons of John Donne*, ed. E. M. Simpson and G. R. Potter, IX (Los Angeles, 1958), p. 59.
3. Boughton House, Buccleuch MSS, U.W. 27/63. *History of Northumberland*, IV, p. 415; X, p. 285. R. Surtees, *The County Palatine of Durham*, 1816–40, II, p. 7 n. 1, P.C.C., 12 Welles.
4. Cal. S. P. *Colonial, East Indies*, 1513–1616, p. 335.

It was only through bitter family struggles, some successful, some less so, that acceptance of woman's right of veto came to be accepted. Fathers began to realize that unwilling marriages tended to lead to quarrels and scandals that could be very harmful to family prosperity. As Fuller remarked "so many forced Matches make fained Love and cause real unhappinesse" with a consequent temptation to adultery.[5] Of course conditions varied from family to family according to the temperament of the father, and daughters continued to be under heavy parental pressure for several centuries, but on the whole contemporary comment suggests that this significant advance in the history of the emancipation of women took place between 1540 and 1640. Concrete proof of this shift in opinion is provided by changes in the nature of testamentary bequests. By the third decade of the seventeenth century many parents in their wills were leaving their daughters portions free from any strings at all, and which had to be paid at a certain age, whether the girl was married or not. With few exceptions, the age varied from 17 to 21, with 18 as the most common, though this did not mean that girls were legally free thereafter since the Canons of 1603 made marriage of children under 21 dependent on the consent of parents or guardians.[6] Nevertheless, fierce testamentary dispositions were now exceptional, and the farthest that most parents were willing to go was to offer a reward for obedience in addition to the basic portion. Finally, with the introduction of the "strict settlement" in the late seventeenth century, the portions of all future children were usually laid down at the time of their parents' marriage. A girl was at last in a position to defy her parents without depriving herself of her marriage portion. It should be emphasized, however, that this new freedom did not mean that women were now likely to ignore the old social and economic bases for selection, nor even that the traditional moral obligation to defer to parental wishes was very much less effective. Most girls would for centuries continue to obey their parents since this was what they had been taught to regard as their Christian duty. All that had been established was the moral right and the economic power to exercise a veto in the last resort.

For sons freedom of choice was almost as restricted as it was for daughters. The desire to prevent the marriage passing out of the family control because of wardship and the financial importance of the settlement prompted the father to marry his son and heir during his own lifetime to a woman he had chosen for him. The son was usually at the mercy of his father, since he depended on him for an allowance during the latter's lifetime and for the provision of a jointure for his widow, without either of which marriage was virtually impossible. Nevertheless, the early

5. T. Fuller, *The Worthies of England,* 1662, p. 234.
6. See, for example, P.C.C., 22 Nevill, 51 Stafforde, 23 Dorset, 54 Saville, 91 Ridley, 70 Seager. For the 1603 Canons, see E. Gibson, *Codex Juris Ecclesiastici Anglicani,* 1761, p. 421.

seventeenth century saw a softening of opinion, and by the middle of the century most parents had in practice conceded to their eldest sons the right of veto. When in 1633 Sir Owen Wynn remarked that his son was "a free man, to be disposed of as God Almighty and his parents think fittest for him," he was doing no more than express the current, muddled doctrine.[7]

To support these ancient habits of mind that disapproved of love and insisted on strict parental control, there was added a further, institutional, factor. By feudal law the King enjoyed rights over the lands and the disposal in marriage of any of his tenants in chief who inherited his estates while still a minor. The Tudors revived this authority as a fiscal device, the Court of Wards being set up to sell to individuals the Crown's rights over the minor's person and one third of his lands. The child could be bought from the Court, either to be married to one of the purchaser's own children, or to be auctioned to the mother, or to another. It was rare for a ward to refuse to marry his guardian's choice, since if he did he would merely be resold to the highest bidder. The will of the 1st Lord Rich, drawn up in 1567, provides a striking example of the cynical detachment with which such slave trading was still regarded in the mid-sixteenth century. Among other offspring Lord Rich left an illegitimate son, Richard, for whom he now made provision. Among other bequests, he instructed his executors to "provide or buy one woman warde or summe other woman having Mannors londes and tenements in possession of the Cler yerely value of Two hundreth pounde by yere over all chardges of the leaste for mariage to be had and solempnised to the said Richard." If Richard should refuse to marry the girl, the executors were "to sell the saide warde . . . to the uttermost advantage." The possibility that the ward might refuse Richard was not even thought worth considering.[8]

The notorious abuses of the system were coming under increasing criticism at the end of the sixteenth and the beginning of the seventeenth century. Though the distinction should not be pressed too hard, in the sixteenth century the main objection was that the traffic in wards both undermined the natural authority of parents and relatives by giving the power of marriage to strangers, and endangered the long-term family fortunes by placing a third of the property at the mercy of rapacious guardians. If natural rights were offended, at this stage they were more the natural rights of parents to authority than of children to freedom of choice. But in the early seventeenth century, the emphasis shifted from criticism of abuses of the system to direct attacks on the system itself. In 1607 George Wilkins devoted a whole play to illustrating the injustice and cruelty of wardship—a work performed, curiously enough, by the King's Players—while Marston went straight to the issue of personal liberty. By

7. *Cal. of Wynn Papers*, 1926, no. 2011.
8. P.C.C., 12 Babington.

the 1650's even an arch-conservative like the Duke of Newcastle was advising Charles II "that wardes may notte bee baughte and solde like Horses in Smithfield." [9]

When one discusses this extraordinary institution, it must be remembered that it was not out of keeping with the ideas of the sixteenth century, and that there was often little reason to suppose that the mother would prove a more responsible or less imperious guardian of her children than a stranger appointed by the Court. The Court of Wards was tolerated as long as the society upon which it preyed had itself little respect for individual freedom of choice. Only when that freedom began to win a grudging acceptance did its anachronistic character become obvious.

On the basis of the surviving evidence it would seem that freedom of choice for women was largely restricted to those with the opportunities of casual association with males afforded by life at Court. Under the watchful parental eye in the country manor-house, things were much more difficult. For men the least free were the heirs male of the greatest families. Nevertheless the doctrine of the absolute right of parents over the disposal of their children was slowly weakening in the late sixteenth and early seventeenth centuries. King James himself declared that "parents may forbid their Children an unfitt Marriage, but they may not force their Consciences to a fitt," and by 1638 Lord North was writing of the need to persuade "parents to leave their Children full freedome with their consent in so important a case." [10]

When one looks for the cause of this change of attitude, it seems likely that a preponderant part was played by the puritan ethic. Various tendencies were at work to stimulate the growth of individualism, not merely in man's relation to God, but also in economics and in politics. But superimposed upon them there was the strong working of moral and religious enthusiasm for a Christian society based on secure family relationships. The most advanced parents, like Mildmay or Montagu, were men of deep religious conviction, and an examination of puritan pamphlet and sermon literature shows criticism of the two basic presuppositions underlying the arranged marriage. It should be emphasized, however, that most puritans had no express intention of undermining parental authority, and indeed were positively anxious to reinforce it. For example in 1589 the Rev. John Stockwood published a book entirely devoted to the thesis that children should not marry without parental consent, the Bible and the great Protestant divines like Calvin and Beza being ransacked for suitable supporting evidence. But his desire for a happy and Christian marriage made him come down firmly against

---

9. G. Wilkins, *The Miseries of Inforst Marriage*, 1607 and 1611. J. Marston, *The Scourge of Villainy*, bk. I, Satyre ii. S. A. Strong, *A Catalogue . . . of Documents at Welbeck*, 1903, p. 195.

10. B. M. Harl. MSS 7582 f. 53v. Dudley Lord North, *A Forest of Varieties*, II (1645), p. 141.

parents who force marriage where there is no love for the sake of material gain, a practice which he regarded as being particularly prevalent among the nobility. Criticism of the manipulation of marriage for material ends had certainly always existed, but its volume seems to have been increasing in the early seventeenth century. Although most critics wanted to preserve parental control of marriage, their argument in fact destroyed the main incentive for such control. Secondly, there developed a vigorous popular controversy over the position of women in society, which, despite some determined rearguard action, nevertheless "quickened the process leading to the so-called freedom of woman in modern society." In the course of this debate the old tradition of the double standard of sexual morality for men and women came under heavy criticism, one of the features of puritanism being a refusal to accept the normal tolerant attitude toward adultery by the male.[11] This tightening of sexual *mores* made forced marriage to an unloved partner insupportable to men, and was a powerful influence in encouraging sons to assert themselves. The double standard is essential to the arranged marriage, and any attack on the one must lead to an undermining of the other.

A principal motive behind the arranged marriage was undoubtedly financial gain and we must therefore examine with care the mechanics of the legal transactions that preceded and accompanied the ceremony.

The father of the bride had to provide a substantial cash portion, usually payable in several installments over one or two years. In addition he had of course to provide the bride's trousseau and jewels, and usually the marriage feast as well, which was often an orgy of gargantuan proportions. In return for these straightforward payments the father of the groom had to undertake a far wider set of obligations. The most important was the provision of a future jointure, or annual allowance for support of the bride during her widowhood, and the ratio between it and the cash portion was the main issue around which negotiations turned. It usually took the form of physical ownership of land, though occasionally families preferred to retain the estates under unified management and to pay the widow a fixed annuity instead.

Second in importance to the jointure, and particularly significant if the bride's father had his daughter's present comfort at heart, was the allowance made to the groom in his father's lifetime. This also might take the form either of an annuity, or of a direct transfer of property and a house, often the same as the jointure. In either case, the father of the groom usually undertook to give the pair lodging in his own house for the first few years, the idea being to train them in the art of housekeeping and to give them time for the accumulation of furniture. As a result most

11. J. Stockwood, *A Bartholmew Fairing*, 1589, p. 76. L. B. Wright, *Middle-Class Culture in Elizabethan England* (Chapel Hill, 1935), pp. 208–9, 217–23, 484, 505–7. K. Thomas, "The Double Standard," *Journal of the History of Ideas*, XX (1959).

young couples had to start their married life under the interfering eyes of a mother or a mother-in-law. A further obligation written into an increasing number of settlements after about 1620 was that of settling on trustees an annual sum as a personal allowance for the bride. This was a new development, and is symptomatic of the increasing economic independence of women at this period.

Fourthly the father of the groom was expected to make clear the proportion of his estate which he proposed to leave to his eldest son after his death. This settlement of the estate was in some ways the crucial issue in the stability of the family inheritance, and important changes occurred in the late sixteenth and early seventeenth centuries. A father was faced with two separate problems, how to provide adequately for his younger sons in the event of his early death, and how to ensure that the eldest son did not dissipate the estate in an orgy of land sales to pay for extravagant living. In the early sixteenth century all he could do was to make a simple entail of the bulk of his estates, dividing the rest among the other children or leaving them life annuities in his will. By the middle of the century lawyers had invented the alternative of giving himself and his son life tenancies in the estate with reversion to the heirs male. But at any rate in the late sixteenth century an entail could usually be overthrown at any time after the father's death merely by suffering a recovery, and a life tenancy was only watertight after the birth of a son to the marriage, and before he reached his majority. The efficacy of the life tenancy thus depended in some measure on a continuing sense of family responsibility, and it was not proof against the maneuvers of the spendthrift waster or of the heir determined to defraud his younger brothers. On the other hand it certainly made it more difficult for estates to be dispersed, and an examination of Royalist Composition Papers shows conclusively that by 1642 the great bulk of aristocratic property was now held on life tenancy. The final solution of the "strict settlement," by which the father gave himself and his son an unbreakable life interest by the device of settling the reversion on trustees for contingent remainders, did not become current practice until the second half of the seventeenth century.[12]

In the early seventeenth century there are signs of a growing attachment to land and a growing emphasis on family aggrandizement. There are several causes of this change of attitude. In the Elizabethan period a good deal of the family property was but newly acquired, often from the sale of monastic estates, and there had not been time for it to acquire a sentimental value. By the early seventeenth century, however, it had taken on the prestige of antiquity and was more carefully cherished. Moreover increasing familiarity with alternative professional occupations

12. H. J. Habakkuk, "Marriage Settlements in the Eighteenth Century," T.R.H.S., 4th Series, XXXII (1950); and his preface to M. E. Finch, *Five Northamptonshire Families*, 1956, pp. 15–18.

for younger sons made fathers more ready to give cash allowances rather than landed estates. Lastly the growth of the life tenancy was accompanied by devices for facilitating the making of these monetary provisions. In the early seventeenth century the younger son could expect either cash or an annuity, or occasionally land specifically bought for the purpose by his father, but only rarely a slice of the ancient family estates. The result of these various developments was to increase the amount of property settled on the eldest son at marriage, and to make it much more difficult for the arrangement to be evaded. The father of the bride could rest assured that his daughter's jointure was safe and that the eldest son of the marriage would inherit the estate intact.

A further problem with which the settlement began to deal was the contingency of the birth of daughters but no sons. If the mother then died, there would be every probability that the groom would remarry in order to provide an heir male, which would leave the daughters of the first marriage at the mercy of a step-mother. The growing reluctance of landowners to break up their inheritance, together with their increasing inability to do so thanks to previous settlements, forced fathers in the early seventeenth century to make this provision for heirs general of a first marriage take the form of a cash sum.

Such were the obligations undertaken by parents on the marriage of their children in the sixteenth and seventeenth centuries, obligations which were enforced by the expanded equitable jurisdiction of the court of Chancery. There remains to be discussed the significance of these arrangements, and of changes in them, in affecting family fortunes. The first problem is to establish the relationship of the size of the portion to the annual income of the father of the bride. It is clear from the variation in the amounts left by fathers in their wills to individual daughters, that the natural element of favoritism not infrequently played its part. Again, many marriages were made with an eye to political or social advancement, and both these considerations had a cash value. Fathers with many daughters were perforce obliged to offer less than those with only one or two. And lastly the physical and mental defects of a girl had to be compensated for by a proportionally increased portion if she was to be married off at all, whereas a virtuous beauty could manage with rather less. Nevertheless sufficient evidence is available for these deviations from the norm to be taken into account, and some judgment made about the average size of portions. On the basis of some 230 examples, it appears that between the second quarter of the sixteenth and third quarter of the seventeenth centuries, portions given with daughters of the aristocracy increased approximately ten times. Though the rise more or less kept in step with the general increase of prices due to inflation up to about 1600, thereafter it soared far ahead; between 1600 and 1700 prices increased by about 50 percent, and portions by about 300 percent.

Aristocratic incomes were probably lagging behind the price rise in the late sixteenth century, and advancing ahead of it in the early seventeenth, though not to this degree. We must therefore conclude that by the late seventeenth century parents were devoting a substantially higher proportion of their incomes to marrying off their daughters than were their great-grandfathers in the early sixteenth. By the early seventeenth, few fathers, and then only those with numerous children, were offering less than the equivalent of one year's income as portions for their daughters.

One explanation of this remarkable rise in the size of portions is the simple factor of the laws of supply and demand. For a girl to remain single was certainly a disgrace to her family, and increasingly to herself as well, and as a result nearly all daughters of peers who reached maturity got married. The suppression of nunneries by Henry VIII had exacerbated the situation by closing the one honorable avenue of escape, for they had been used by aristocracy as "convenient stowage for withered daughters," to use Milton's rasping phrase.[13] Though not always cheap, these establishments at any rate avoided the necessity of finding large capital sums in a hurry. To this increased pressure from the abolition of nunneries in the mid-sixteenth century, was added competition from daughters of the rising gentry in the late sixteenth, and from daughters and widows of City Aldermen in the early seventeenth. But the supply of eligible husbands of good social standing had failed to keep pace with this rising demand. Daughters of peers had always been ready to marry heirs male of the greater gentry, so there was little compensatory social breakthrough here to ease the strain. It was still not considered decent to marry your daughter to a mere merchant's son, even though your son and heir might at a pinch marry a merchant's daughter. Younger sons, even of the peerage, were hardly in the running since the limited size of their inheritances made it impossible for them to provide jointures that could begin to match the portions their sisters were offering. (Under these circumstances the increased size of families which must have accompanied the remarkable growth of population of the late sixteenth century would itself have upset the balance, by producing a larger number of marriageable daughters, but relatively few more heirs male with whom to match them. This factor alone would go far to explain the increase in the size of portions.)

The size of the jointures was a matter of no less importance than the size of the portions, and the natural toughness and longevity of women once they had finished with the child-bearing cycle made jointures a regularly recurrent burden to aristocratic families rather than an occasional cross to be borne for a few years at infrequent intervals. Taking all peerage families which endured from 1560 to 1640 we find that on an

---

13. Quoted by C. Hill, *Puritanism and Revolution,* 1958, p. 35.

average jointures were being paid to widows for rather over half the time. It was quite common for families to be burdened with two jointures at the same time, and very occasionally with even three. By late medieval common law widows were granted a dower of one third of their late husband's real property, a figure which was about the maximum a family could bear. But the replacement of dower by jointure in the sixteenth and seventeenth centuries meant that the amount devoted to this purpose was freed from any rigid rules. The jointure could be whatever proportion of his landed income the bridgegroom's father chose to assign, and there is reason to think that, at any rate among the aristocracy, it now tended to be less than a third of the rental. It is self-evident that the striking rise in portions and the stagnation or decline of jointures in relation to income must involve a shift in the portion/jointure ratio. In demonstrating this shift we have included the wealthy squirearchy as well as the peerage, on the reasonable assumption—which seems to be borne out by the facts —that the ratio would be the same in classes as closely interlocked as these two. The resultant figures, based on about 130 examples, suggest that the current norm probably moved from about 4/1 or 5/1 in the early and mid-sixteenth century, to 6.33/1 or 6.66/1 in the first half of the seventeenth. In the third quarter, families hesitated between two norms, the old one of between 6/1 and 7/1 and the new one of 10/1, but in the last quarter of the century 10/1 finally emerged as the most commonly accepted ratio.

Why did the portion/jointure ratio change in this remarkable way? It must be admitted that part of the shift in the late sixteenth and early seventeenth century is illusory, and merely reflects the contemporary method of calculating jointures. These were assessed in terms of bare rental and ignored casualties such as fines for beneficial leases and the profits of sales of wood. But since during the inflation a larger and larger proportion of income tended to be taken in the form of fines rather than rents, land in the early seventeenth century was worth far more than its nominal rental. And so whereas the portion remained a finite cash sum, the jointure came to mean a real income in excess, and possibly a good deal in excess, of that state in the contract. For this reason the shift in the portion/jointure ratio, at any rate before about 1620, is probably some-what exaggerated by a change in the relationship between the nominal and the real value of the jointure.

But there can be no doubt that there was a real change as well. By 1640 a given portion could buy far less future jointure than it could in 1560. The primary cause for this must undoubtedly be the increase in the supply of eligible women on the marriage market which failed to meet an equal expansion in the number of eligible men. This not only caused the rise in the size of portions, but also the rise in the portion/jointure ratio which accompanied it. The second important factor was that growth in the range and importance of the obligations undertaken by the father of the groom which has already been examined. Thanks to these new provisions, the father of the bride was assured that the portion he paid would purchase substantial advantages for his daughter and her children, and would not run the risk of being largely wasted.

There are also other possibilities. The reduction of the standard rate of interest from 10 percent to 6 percent between 1624 and 1651 may have helped to stimulate the rise in the ratio by altering the price of a life annuity. Moreover, in many cases, though certainly not always, or even usually, landowners borrowed money in order to provide the portion, and the cheapening of the price of money would therefore increase the size of the portion they could afford to offer.

Such are the facts of the situation and possible explanations for them. It remains to be discovered how far the rise both in the size of portions and in the portion/jointure ratio affected for good or ill the fortunes of landed families. The fact that jointures rarely exceeded and often dropped below the one third of the estate laid down for dower at Common Law must have made it rather easier for a family to endure the burden of a series of long-lived widows. But the really important change was the rise in the size of portions, the most obvious consequence of which was to increase the gambling element in procreation. In financial terms sons became rather more desirable and daughters substantially less. The element of chance loomed so large because in the sixteenth and early seventeenth centuries the portion was paid direct to the father of the groom to be used for his own purposes. The marriage of a son, especially an eldest son, was a means of raising ready capital, often on advantageous terms, and this was consequently a frequent and well-recognized means of clearing off debts or paying for current expenditure.

In the sixteenth and early seventeenth centuries, therefore, the portion contributed nothing to the long-range stability or increase of family fortunes. Moreover, on the other side, the money was quite often found by breaking into family capital by the sale of lands. This was especially common in the sixteenth century, when entails and life interests could fairly easily be broken and when moral sanctions against sale of the family estates as an act of impious sacrilege had not yet developed very strongly. Borrowing was also a fairly frequent recourse, but a dangerous one when interest rates were at 10 percent and mortgages liable to absolute forfeiture for non-payment. And so there developed, particularly in the seventeenth century, a much safer method, which was to convey parts of the family estates to trustees for a period of years to raise the money out of the profits. At its worst the system increased the ability of and temptation to the holder of the estate to raise money for current needs by selling his son for profit. Nor did he hesitate to sell land or run up debt on very unfavorable terms in order to secure rich marriages for his daughters. The cost of the operation fell most heavily on the next generation, who would have to pay off the debts and live off an estate permanently truncated by land sales or temporarily reduced by jointures and trusts to raise portions.

It was not till the last half of the seventeenth century that these evils were overcome, thanks to four significant changes. Firstly the strict settlement made it impossible to raise portions by the sale of land, a fact which greatly encouraged the setting up of trust deeds well in advance. Secondly it at last became safe and even reasonably economical to borrow, thanks to the 40 percent reduction in the rate of interest and the security afforded to the mortgagee by the equity of redemption. Thirdly, the burden of the jointure was eased by the further rise in the portion/jointure ratio; and fourthly the long-term family assets were increased by the insertion into the marriage contract of the stipulation that the portion had to be used to purchase more land. Portions were no longer either raised by sale of land or squandered by the bride's father on current consumption. From being a cause of family decay in the late sixteenth and early seventeenth centuries, by the late seventeenth century the financial arrangements of marriage had become a cause of family growth; in its perfected form the system enabled the aristocracy to hoist themselves up by their own bootstraps.[14]

Having examined in detail the financial obligations that accompanied marriage, we must now ask whether there was any change in the emphasis parents placed on this mercenary factor. Contemporary attitudes are best revealed in the "Letters of advice to a son" which fathers were in the habit of composing for the edification of their children. These documents made it clear that the main objects of marriages were firstly companionship; secondly the avoidance of fornication, which is sinful, brings scandal, and—in the days before contraception—is likely to lead to embarrassing and expensive consequences; thirdly, the production of an heir male to carry on the family line and property; and fourthly direct financial gain. The first three objectives tended to be taken for granted, as too obvious to require much comment, but the fourth was always examined with care. The most extreme position was stated in the middle of the seventeenth century by Francis Osborne who, in a printed "Advice" which ran to seven editions in two years, was prepared to defend the position that "as the fertilitie of the ensuing yeare is guessed at the height of the river Nilus, so by the greatness of a Wive's portion may much of the future conjugall Happinesse be calculated."[15]

Relatively few seventeenth century parents or children were willing to go as far as this. The most famous letter of advice in the early seventeenth century and one which had great influence on current

14. See H. J. Habakkuk, *op. cit.*
15. F. Osborne, *Advice to a Son*, 5th ed. (1656), pp. 50–51, 66.

thought, was that of Lord Burghley to his son Robert. His counsel was a good deal more subtle and judicious than that of Osborne. "Enquire diligently of her Disposition & how her Parents have been inclined in their Youth. Let her not be poor how generous soever. For a Man can buy nothing in the Market with Gentility. Nor chuse a base & uncomely creature altogether for Wealth; for it will cause contempt in others and Loathing in thee." [16] In the late sixteenth century religious factors began to influence the choice of partners. After about 1570 the great Catholic families began increasingly that practice of religious *apartheid* that was to cut them off from the main stream of the English landed classes for four hundred years. The growth of puritanism further emphasized this tendency, and an inevitable consequence was the greater stress laid on the personal qualities of both bride and bridegroom. This concern with personal qualities was emphasized by several middle-class writers inspired by puritan ideals, and from them it spread to the upper classes, the most categorical of whom was Sir Edward Montagu, the future first Lord Montagu, who in 1621 succinctly advised his son: "In your marriage looke after goodnes rather than goodes." Edward Waterhouse was expressing an increasingly common opinion when he wrote in 1665 that "one of the greatest mistakes and mischiefs of our Age is dis-esteem of wives, and that upon conceit that any thing, if woman, serves for a wife, if she have but money." [17] Although there had always been some criticism, there is nevertheless some reason to believe that marriages exclusively, or even primarily, for money were coming under increasing popular disapproval during the seventeenth century.

Such were the theories: but what of the facts? It is perfectly possible for the swelling chorus of theoretical disapproval to be no more than a symptom of the increasing occurrence of these evils in practice. We have seen that wills, correspondence and contemporary comment strongly suggest that the negative right of veto was more freely conceded during the late sixteenth and early seventeenth centuries. The degree to which parents or children put money before other considerations in making their initial selection of final choice is, however, another matter altogether. So far as the aristocracy is concerned it is possible to give an answer to this question in statistical terms. Among the families elevated before 1603, some 20 percent of the marriages between 1540 and 1599 of holders of heirs apparent of titles were with heiresses. Thereafter there is a sudden jump to 35 percent for the next sixty years. It is thus evident that around the turn of the century the growing financial embarrassment of the peerage drove them into a far more single-minded pursuit of wealthy marriages than had previously been their custom. The new peers, created

16. F. Peck, *Desiderata Curiosa*, I, i, pp. 63–66.
17. L. B. Wright, *op. cit.*, ch. VII. Boughton House Buccleuch MSS, N.C. 13/2. E. Waterhouse, *The Gentlemans Monitor*, 1665, p. 383.

between 1603 and 1641, had always had a sharp eye to the main matrimonial chance, and indeed this was often an important cause of their advancement. During the late Elizabethan period 32 percent had bettered themselves by marriage to heiresses and they stepped up the process in the next thirty years to a figure equal to that of the older peerage. Taking the peerage as a whole, one of every three marriages was with an heiress in the early seventeenth century. When it is considered that these figures exclude marriages to women with huge portions but who were not heiresses, it is evident that wealth was the most important single consideration in very many early seventeenth century marriages, and that its supremacy seems to have been increasing. Whereas social and political factors had influenced many earlier marriages, the growing fluidity of society inevitably led to a growing emphasis upon more strictly financial considerations. Nevertheless the significance of this trend should not be exaggerated. Aristocratic marriages may have been more mercenary in the seventeenth century than in the fifteenth, but the difference is one of degree rather than of kind.

The consequences of this pursuit of heiresses were contradictory. In the first place it is likely that at least some of the girls brought with them an hereditary tendency to produce feeble children with a low expectation of life, and were therefore responsible in a few cases for the failure of the male line. But marriages with heiresses were of the greatest importance both in bringing new wealth into the peerage, and in preserving within the peerage class much of the estates of families which had thus failed in the male line. Since so many peers married within the aristocracy and since they so diligently pursued heiresses, a good deal of the dismembered property fell into the hands of other noble families. As a result the net loss of wealth and influence to the class as a whole was substantially reduced.

Part cause and part effect of the growing pursuit of wealthy marriages was the development of a nation-wide marriage market centered on London. In the sixteenth century, non-courtier families confined their alliances almost exclusively to the local nobility and gentry, often within the country. Even near London the same was often true, and investigation of the family connections of M.P.s of the Long Parliament has revealed interlocking ramifications within the country squirearchy of bewildering complexity. During the first two thirds of the sixteenth century in the north of England even the aristocracy was limited in its geographical range. For example, with only two exceptions all the Ogle and Wharton children married exclusively in the north to the end of the century. With the southern aristocracy there was usually a rather greater geographical range. The proximity of London, the better roads, the less ferocious winters, all made communication easier and reduced parochialism, but even so the evidence of these noble families shows a strong tendency to regional emphasis at least up to the third quarter of the sixteenth century.

It was the growth of London as a matrimonial clearing-house in the late sixteenth century which finally broke down this regionalism, not merely among the aristocracy but also among the gentry. Under Elizabeth some thirteen earls or future earls and five barons found their brides at Court among the Maids of Honor of the Queen, while for the squire-archy the contacts provided by the increasingly popular London "season" offered similar opportunities. At the same time the concentration of knowledge about settlements in the chambers of a few highly skilled London conveyancers must also have increased the importance of the capital. For the peerage the marriage-market had become nation-wide before the middle of the seventeenth century and even took Ireland into its scope.

If the geographical spread of aristocratic marriage was steadily widening to the limits of the kingdom, the social range followed no such regular curve. Between 1540 and 1569, 54 percent of the marriages of titular peers and their heirs male were within the peerage class, but between 1570 and 1599 the proportion fell to 33 percent. Intermarriage within the peerage had declined sharply, no doubt for the reasons offered by the Earl of Huntingdon to his son in about 1613: "Being allied to most of the nobility, match with one of the gentry, where thou mayest have a great portion, for there is a satiety in all things and without means honour will look as naked as trees that are cropped." Many of the gentry were well aware of this mercenary attitude among the peerage and a few of them tried to guard against it, Francis Osborne pointing out to his readers that "leane Honour, like Pharo's Kine, devour the Gentry with whom they match, by multiplying the quantity of their Expenses." [18]

By the time Osborne was writing, these counsels were perhaps beginning to prevail on the gentry, and the peerage was also voluntarily withdrawing again within itself. Between 1600 and 1629 the picture is blurred by the rapid elevation of large numbers of the upper gentry into the peerage, with the result that the aristocracy doubled in size. In the succeeding period from 1630 to 1659, when the new peerage may be said to have been absorbed, the nobility as a whole had reverted to its pre-1570 position of marrying rather more than 50 percent within itself. But since there were now twice as many families, this did not represent quite that strict exclusiveness that had characterized the mid-sixteenth century.

Apart from successful lawyers, who usually came from gentry stock and were rapidly re-absorbed into it at a higher level, the only other wealthy class in England was that of the London merchants. The marriage of a nobleman into a mercantile family was to the sixteenth century a distinct *mésalliance*, and the degree to which it was practiced throws a significant light on changing financial conditions and social attitudes. In the late fifteenth and early sixteenth century there was a

18. F. Osborne, *op. cit.*, p. 67. *H.M.C. Hastings MSS*, IV, p. 332.

trickle of aristocratic marriages with the daughters and widows of London Aldermen. After 1520 the older peerage abandoned this practice, though in the later years of Henry VIII there were very close links between the City and the high government officials, some of whom were soon to be ennobled. Once arrived, however, the Elizabethan aristocracy severed all ties with the merchant class and for thirty years after 1561 there was only one case of intermarriage between the two groups. The erection of this barrier is as interesting as its weakening in the 1590s. It was built partly on an urge by the newly elevated to cut themselves off from their more humble background, partly on a general sharpening of social distinctions, and partly on the temporary removal of the financial necessity for such alliances thanks to the rich booty of monastic estates.

For various reasons the peerage in the late Elizabethan period entered into a phase of grave economic crisis, one result of which was that a few bolder or more desperate spirits began to leap across this barrier that for thirty years had divided peers from merchants. After three of these alliances or attempted alliances in the 1590s, however, there was a gap of almost twenty years, due partly to the easing of the financial pressure thanks to King James's reckless generosity, and partly to the ample supply of gentry heiresses. Meanwhile it was the gentry who swallowed their pride and were courting the merchants. Several of the new nobility had married into the merchant class before their elevation, and in doing so they were merely following the tide. By 1618 the example set by the gentry, the decay of old standards of morality and propriety in the age of the Duke of Buckingham, and the soaring fortunes and ambitions of the Aldermen, all conspired to bring about a spate of matrimonial projects and alliances between titular peers and their heirs male and the daughters and widows of merchants. In all there were nine such alliances or attempted alliances in the thirteen years between 1618 and 1630, compared with six in the seventy years between 1548 and 1617 and three in the thirty years between 1631 and 1660. It is clear, therefore, that the third decade of the century witnessed a degree of mingling between the peerage and the City that was without parallel both before and after, and it was not till the 1670s that the flow began again in earnest.

The time has now come to examine the effects of these various developments upon the two individuals who were the subject of so much careful scheming and plotting. On the wedding day, the pair were often still more or less strangers to one another, for it was quite usual for them to have been permitted no more than a few hours in each other's company before the marriage ceremony. Some prospective bridegrooms thought even this formality superfluous. Sir Nicholas Pointz could hardly bring himself to be civil to a widow he was pursuing. "Lett me not wyn her love like a foole, nor spend long tyme like a boy. As God shall help, I am moch trobled to think I must speake to any woman won loving word." [19] But the importance of these brief encounters should not be minimized, for we have seen how fathers in the early seventeenth century became readier to allow their children the right of refusal, an agonizing decision that had to be based upon these short and formal interviews. It was on the basis of the indifference or even the mild dislike aroused by a little polite conversation that many, perhaps most, noble marriages were concluded.

The marriage ceremony itself was of course a public affair, followed by a huge dinner for the wedding guests. The long day of feasting and jollity ended not infrequently in the public bedding of the couple, with all the ancient ceremonies of casting off the bride's left stocking and sewing into the sheets. [20] And there, within the drawn curtains of the great four-poster, the room still echoing with the parting drunken obscenities of the wedding guests, the two strangers were left to make each other's acquaintance. Nor was this always the end of the publicity, for if either bride or groom was a royal favorite, King James would cross-question them closely the next morning to extract the last salacious details of the events of the night.

It was not at all unusual, however, for the contract, the marriage and the consummation to be widely spaced in time. Sometimes, though more commonly in the middle ages and the early sixteenth century than later, the ceremony itself occurred before one or both parties reached the age of consent. These premature arrangements were usually made to seal a political alliance or to secure an heiress, though all great landowners felt the temptation in order to prevent their children's marriages being disposed of by the Crown under its power of wardship. After all, the risk of annulment of the marriage was slight. In view of the extremely early age at which the decision had to be made, and the enormous power of parental pressure, it is hardly surprising that few boys or girls of 14 and 12 respectively had the strength of mind to reject the union.

Although the age of consent was so early, in fact very few of the nobility and gentry were married the moment it became legally possible. Taking the peerage as our statistical sample, only 6 percent married at 15 or under in the late sixteenth century, and only 5 percent in the early seventeenth. Moreover there was a significant trend towards the post-ponement of marriage to a more reasonable age. In the earlier period 21 percent of the peers were married at 17, but in the later only 12 percent, whereas at 25 the figure was virtually the same, at 78 percent and 76 percent. The shift was thus confined to a movement out of the middle 'teens into the early twenties. While not enough dates of birth of girls are known to make reliable statistical calculations, there is every reason to

19. *H.M.C. Finch MSS*, I, p. 21.
20. R. Winwood, *Memorials of Affairs of State*, 1725, II, p. 43. Cf. S. Pepys, *Diary*, 31 July, 1665.

suppose that the average age of brides also rose. This change, which occurred both in England and abroad, was due partly to the slow and hesitant introduction of humanist ideas about individual freedom of choice, whose effect has been observed in other spheres, and partly to views about the right age for consummation. At this period consummation by no means always coincided with the wedding day, even though prolonged failure to fulfil this condition after the husband was eighteen years old could be a ground for a nullity suit. Once consummation had taken place, however, full divorce *a vinculo* was much more difficult. In the middle ages the Papacy had been notoriously ingenious, at a price, in discovering impediments that justified annulments. Whether English ecclesiastical courts after the Reformation were equally amenable seems very doubtful. There is an isolated case of the legalization by Parliament of a second marriage after separation in 1551, but aristocratic divorce by Act of Parliament did not properly begin until 1669.[21]

The main reason in favor of early consummation was thus the issue of legality. Against it, however, there were three arguments whose weight was increasingly recognized as time went on. The first was that very young boys and girls produce stunted children. Secondly, it was believed, following Plato, Galen, and Avicenna, that the sperm was a vital fluid that governed all growth, and that immoderate discharge in adolescence would therefore impair a man's physical and intellectual development.[22] Lastly, there was some feeling that parturition by a girl below the age of sixteen or so was immediately dangerous and permanently damaging.[23] This consensus of medical advice finding its way into the consciousness of the aristocracy and gentry through popular manuals about health certainly had great influence, and brought about by the end of the sixteenth century an almost unanimous opinion against early consummation of marriage. John Smyth of Nibley could not stifle his disgust when he discovered that a medieval Lady Berkeley had given birth before she was 14. Not even the assurance of the Fathers that the Virgin Mary gave birth to Christ at the age of fifteen could satisfy him.[24]

By the end of the sixteenth century parents found themselves in a very awkward situation. To avoid interference from the Court of Wards, to snap up heiresses, to be able to dispose of children at their pleasure, they wanted to marry them off early. To be legally watertight the ceremony needed to be consummated, and yet they were assured that early consummation was bad for both parties, and was likely to produce

21. For the legal position, see E. Gibson, *op. cit.*, 1, pp. 445–7. The Peer was the Marquis of Northampton.

22. *Advice to his Son, by Henry ninth Earl of Northumberland*, pp. 55–6. T. Cogan, *The Haven of Health*, 1589, pp. 242, 249. *H.M.C. Hastings MSS*, IV, p. 333. See also A. Niccoles, "A discourse of Marriage and Wiving," 1615 (*Harl. Misc.*, II, p. 148).

23. J.O. Halliwell, *Autobiography of Sir Simonds D'Ewes*, I, p. 319.

24. J. Smyth, *Lives of the Berkeleys*, I, pp. 224–5.

sickly children. Caught on the horns of this dilemma, they tried three methods of getting themselves off. The first was to put medical advice first and to delay marriage, the result being, as we have seen, a tendency for the age of marriage for men to move from the late 'teens to the early twenties. Secondly the marriage was allowed to take place early but consummation was postponed, sometimes until several years later, the girl continuing to live with her parents and the boy proceeding with his education. Thirdly marriage was accompanied by a unique or even token consummation followed by prolonged separation. It was very common in the early seventeenth century for the marriage to take place a day or two before the young man set out for a year or more of travel on the Continent to finish his education. By this means full cohabitation—apart from the wedding night, as a result of which conception was thought unlikely—was effectively postponed, and the young man was prevented from getting trapped into an unsuitable marriage abroad.

The great object of marriage among the aristocracy was the provision of a male heir in order to maintain the continuity of the title and of the family estates. But a boy was not easily come by in the sixteenth and seventeenth centuries. It has been estimated that in 1925 7 to 8 percent of married women in England were sterile, and a more recent study has suggested that 12 percent of all marriages are likely to be infertile.[25] Fecundity is affected by disease and ill-health, by inherited propensities and by age of marriage. The earlier marriage age of the sixteenth and seventeenth centuries might be expected to have reduced modern figures for sterility, but in reality other factors raised it to a much higher level. Ill-balanced diet, tight corseting, lack of fresh air and exercise, liability to infection, psychological stresses all seriously impaired female health and led to miscarriages and still-births. As a result 19 percent of all first marriages among the nobility between 1540 and 1640 were childless, and no less than 29 percent produced no male children. These figures are undoubtedly exaggerated by failure to record many children who died soon after birth, but since only two children out of three survived at this period,[26] they are if anything an optimistic estimate of the proportion of first marriages which produced an adult male of marriageable age to carry on the line.

This emphasis on the frequency of childessness should not obscure the fact that there was a large number of very prolific marriages. If one third of first marriages produced one child or none at all, one third also produced more than six. As a result the recorded average of children per fertile marriage was as high as five, while unrecorded early deaths in the

25. *Papers of the Royal Commission on Population,* 1950, IV, pp. 35–8. *Family Doctor,* September, 1959.
26. S. Peller, "Studies in Mortality since the Renaissance," *Bull. Hist. Med.,* XIII (1943), p. 457.

first weeks of life should probably raise the average per married man nearer 6.1, which is the figure for the European nobility at this time. All too often the wife gave birth annually with monotonous regularity until the cycle was ended only in death. If wives disliked this biological slavery, husbands equally deplored it on financial grounds. Sir Patience Ward records that he was given his name because "his father began to think the family increased too fast for his estate, and made a vow that if there were another son, he would call him Patience."[27] There can be no doubt whatever about the force of these objections, and it is possible to ascribe part of the blame for the economic decline of more than one family to an excess of children who reached maturity. The rise in the size of portions made girls peculiarly expensive and unwanted, though boys were still welcomed so as to protect the direct male succession against the ravages of accident and disease. After three boys had been born, however, which was a situation which developed in at least one family in every five, there was a strong incentive to call a halt. It is therefore curious that there are few signs at this period of any practical steps being taken to prevent conception.

It seems likely that mechanical methods of contraception were virtually unknown to the nobility before the end of the seventeenth century, though contraceptive preparations were certainly mentioned in one of two medical treatises. Information about Dr. Fallopius' sheath had been published in 1564, but its purpose was as a protection against syphilis in casual extra-marital relations rather than as a contraceptive for use within marriage, and in any case, so far as we know, it did not come into general use in London society until the late seventeenth century. As for natural means, we are totally ignorant whether or not there was any knowledge of the female fertility cycle. There remains the possibility of abortion, which was as dangerous physically as it was considered reprehensible morally. Although the effects were certainly known of galloping on horseback, severe blood-letting, and even "venemous drenches," it cannot have been general practice, even at Court. Failing all this, the only effective methods of damming the flow of children were therefore *coitus interruptus* or total abstention. It has recently been argued that these restrictions, practiced for economic reasons, were powerful and possible determinant factors in governing peasant fertility even in the middle ages and the sixteenth and seventeenth centuries. Moreover the substantial decline in the average number of children per married man among the European nobility from 6.1 in the sixteenth and seventeenth century to 4.5 in the eighteenth and nineteenth can only be attributed to a change from a policy of letting nature take its

27. J. Hunter, South Yorkshire, II, p. 143, n. 1.

course to one of deliberate planning.[28] But substantial though the financial incentive was becoming, the large number of really enormous families suggests that very few of the English nobility before the middle of the seventeenth century were willing to resort to these heroic measures in order to reduce the burden of children. Whether this policy of laissez faire was due to technical ignorance, to the inadequate urgency of the incentive, or to moral or theological objections to interference in the biological process, we are not at present in a position to say.

We have seen that marriage at this period took place very early, that the partners were often virtually strangers to each other and were chosen by their parents, that the first years of their married life were usually spent in the house of the parents, that consummation tended to occur in a blaze of embarrassing publicity, or else some years after the marriage ceremony itself, and that it was followed more often than not either by total sterility or by an infinitely repetitive cycle of child-bearing. We must now consider how successfully marriage stood up to the physical and psychological strains imposed by these arrangements. There can be no doubt that the majority of these marriages survived without open and serious breakdown, and that in many cases there developed genuine affection and trust. In a very large number of aristocratic wills husbands refer to their wives in terms, leave them bequests, and saddle them with responsibilities, which make it clear beyond doubt that at the very least the unions provided satisfactory working partnerships.

Nevertheless in view of the tremendous religious, social, legal and economic pressures directed at holding the family unit together, it is remarkable how many marriages publicly and completely broke up. Disregarding entirely the evidence of illegitimate children, in the ninety years between 1570 and 1659 I know of 48 cases of annulment, separation *a mensa et thoro* or notorious marital quarrels among the peerage, which is nearly 10 percent of all marriages. The worst period seems to have been between 1595 and 1620, when something like one third of the older peerage was involved in serious marital difficulties. Why this generation should have been a particularly unhappy one is hard to tell. It is possible that thereafter friction was reduced by the growing reluctance of parents to press children too hard to marry against their inclinations; it may be that the spread of the puritan conscience damped down these public displays of temper; but it is unlikely to be an illusory product of imperfect evidence, though this may be the explanation of the modest level recorded in the early Elizabethan period.

28. J. T. Krause, "The Implications of Recent Research into Demographic History," *Comparative Studies in Society and History,* I (1958–9). J. Huarte Navarro, *The Examination of Men's Wits,* 1594, pp. 296, 319. A. B. Grosart, *Lismore Papers,* 2nd Ser., IV, p. 83. Bodl Rawlinson MSS Poet. 26 f. lv (I owe this reference to Mr. Julian Mitchell). S. Peller, *op. cit.,* XXI (1947), pp. 57–8.

To what extent were these matrimonial discords accompanied by scandal? In the sixteenth century the provision in wills for illegitimate children indicates that the maintenance by a peer of a lower-class mistress was compatible with a stable marriage, and that it was a fairly frequent occurrence, but between 1610 and 1660 the evidence becomes more rare, apart from notorious cases like that of Emmanuel, the last Lord Scrope. There is no very obvious explanation of this fact, though the following hypothetical model at any rate provides a possible solution. In the middle ages and the early sixteenth century, the arranged marriage was often accompanied and made tolerable by the mistress and the illegitimate children. This was a situation accepted by the wife and openly admitted by the husband, and as a result marriages held together as working business arrangements. But impressed by Calvinist criticism of the double standard, in the late sixteenth century wives began to object to their husbands openly maintaining a mistress, which would explain the increasing number of breakdowns of marriages, and the reluctance to mention bastards in wills. The arranged marriage was unable to stand the strain of the shutting down of this safety valve and the scale of separations became so alarming that parents began relaxing the pressure and giving their children some limited right of veto over the choice of marriage partners. As a result the number of open breakdowns of marriage and the number of illegitimate children declined after the first decade of the seventeenth century, though there may well have been an increase in both after the Restoration.

At the same time as there was a tightening up of the sexual *mores* of the nobility and gentry as a whole in the early seventeenth century, a small minority was moving swiftly in exactly the opposite direction. One of the most striking features of Early Stuart society was the growing cleavage in outlook and behavior between Court and Country. One of the aspects of this development which attracted most contemporary attention and criticism was the sexual license at the Jacobean court which may well have rivaled the more notorious conditions at the court of Charles II. Although behavior at court under Henry VIII appears to have been fairly lax, in the middle and late sixteenth century peers had taken lower-class mistresses but had jealously guarded the honor of their wives. Now there developed general promiscuity among both sexes at Court, where as early as 1603 Lady Anne Clifford noted that "all the ladies . . . had gotten such ill names that it was grown a scandalous place."[29] Accustomed to the exercise of power, with little training in self-control, and with all the time in the world on their hands, the aristocracy has probably always been substantially more free in sexual behavior than the gentry, yeomen or merchants. When the general atmosphere of the day is tolerant, however,

29. V. Sackville–West, *Diary of Lady Anne Clifford*, 1923, p. 17.

no harm is done to the prestige of the class and it is only in times like the early seventeenth or the mid-nineteenth centuries that trouble is likely to arise. It was very unfortunate, therefore, that the behavior of a minority—but a spectacular and much publicized minority—of the aristocracy was declining after 1590 as fast as general disapprobation of loose conduct was rising.

Even more damaging was the association in the public mind of the Court, and particularly the aristocracy, with homosexuality, an abnormality which aroused deep horror in the ever-widening circles of puritanism. With the accession to the throne of a king who made no attempt to disguise his tastes, the Court became a haunt of homosexuals. From his behavior in public the worst was assumed—probably rightly—of James's relations with his favorites, and scandalous rumors circulated about men like Bacon, Sir Anthony Ashley, Lords Roos and Stanhope.

Public attention was finally riveted on the sexual behavior of the aristocracy by a series of sensational scandals that found their way into the law-courts. The first was the annulment in 1613 of the marriage of the Earl and Countess of Essex in order to leave her free to marry her lover, the Earl of Somerset, on the grounds that she was *virgo intacta*—a hypothesis to the falsity of which a number of men about town could testify. Two years later there exploded the news that the Earl and Countess of Somerset were on trial on a charge of murdering Sir Thomas Overbury, a former friend of the Earl and a dangerous witness to the true facts of the divorce. At the trial the whole sordid story came out, embellished with obscene letters of the Countess and highly incriminating ones of the late Earl of Northampton. Hardly had the public recovered from the shock of these revelations than a new scandal broke out, in which Lady Roos first accused her husband of impotence, and then charged the Countess of Exeter with "adulterie, incest, murther, poison, and such like peccadillos." In the end Lady Roos's accusations were exposed as lies, and she herself convicted of incest with her brother.

Nor did it help the reputation of the King or the peerage that while the minor executants in these crimes were severely punished, the principals escaped with little more than loss of office and royal favor. It looked as if the aristocracy had reason to think themselves immune from both the dictates of conventional morality and the penalties of the law. It was well that Charles did something in 1630 to restore confidence in royal justice by declining to interfere in the death sentence imposed by his peers on the Earl of Castlehaven for a series of outrageous sexual offenses.

Although the court of King Charles was a far more respectable place than that of his father, the situation could not be restored overnight, and the puritan gentry, brooding in their country manor-houses upon the evils of the day, continued to be regaled with news of aristocratic scandal, most of it associated with the court group. As a result of this flood of gossip, sexual depravity became ineradicably associated in the public mind with the aristocracy and with the Court. Impacting on the puritan conscience, this was a powerful factor in undermining the moral authority of the peerage.

There can be little doubt that the institution of marriage among the landed classes underwent very considerable changes during this period. In the last thousand years ideas about the proper method of arranging marriage have passed through four successive phases. In the first, marriage was arranged by parents with relatively little reference to the wishes of the children; in the second, parents continued to arrange the marriage, but granted the children the right of veto; in the third, the children made the choice, but the parents retained the power of veto; and in the fourth, which was only reached in this century, the children arrange their own marriages with little reference to the opinions of the parents. In the late sixteenth and early seventeenth centuries, England passed from the first to the second of these phases. Though fairly successful efforts were made to maintain the moral authority of parents and guardians, their power was now tempered by the need for at least the passive consent of the children, and sometimes even for evidence of positive affection. The development of the London season, the widening of the marriage market, the use of the coach, all increased the range of social contacts of the children and thus encouraged them to assert themselves, while at the same time legal changes in the nature of family settlements made successful rebellion possible.

There was also a change in the theoretical approach. Due partly to the growth of puritan opposition to the double standard and of puritan emphasis on contented Christian partnership in marriage, partly to the development of ideas about economic and political liberty, it was slowly recognized that limits should be set not merely to the powers of King or Church, but also to those of parents and husbands. Supporters of kingship had constantly compared the authority of the monarch over his subjects with that of a father over his children. Any weakening in the position of the one thus led to a questioning of that of the others. And so in the first half of the seventeenth century Stuart monarchical claims were rejected, Wardship was abolished, and the arranged marriage itself was modified and humanized. Clarendon commented bitterly upon the consequences of the new ideas thrown up by the upheavals of the Interregnum: "Children asked not the blessing of their Parents . . . Parents had no manner of authority over their Children." [30] This is, of course, a gross exaggeration, but it contains a germ of truth. There was a modification in the relationship of parents and children which was an important—and still largely unrecognized—step in the growth of the freedom of the individual

30. Quoted by Keith Thomas, *Women and the Civil War Sects,* Past and Present, 13 (1958), p. 57.

in Western Europe, an aspect of what David Riesman would call the shift from a tradition-directed to an inner-directed society.

Changes also occurred in the financial aspects of marriage. The size of portions rose very much faster than that of jointures as eligible daughters increasingly outnumbered eligible husbands, and as the obligations of the father of the groom became more onerous. The old practice of raising portions by saving or sale of land and of spending them on current consumption gave way to a system by which portions were raised on deeds of trust or by borrowing, and were used to buy land. Since the growing social fluidity of the age encouraged an increase in the emphasis placed upon financial motives for marriage, this drastically affected the trend of family fortunes. As a result a hundred years of attrition was followed by a hundred years of growth of aristocratic property-holding, off-set in part by some increase in aristocratic debt.

At the same time there was a widening of the range of marriage. As new waves of self-made men were admitted to the peerage under Henry VIII and under James I, they first cut themselves off from the classes below them, and then, as financial pressure increased, began wooing them for their money. By the beginning of the seventeenth century the pattern of regional marriage was dissolving as London became the clearing house for a nation-wide marriage market.

Under pressure of medical opinion the age of marriage and of consummation was postponed to the early twenties. Novel objections by wives to the open maintenance of mistresses, and novel demands of compatibility of temperament and taste led to very large numbers of breakdowns of marriage in the later years of Elizabeth followed by a period of extreme sexual license at Court under James, the result of which was to help to discredit the aristocracy as a whole in the eyes of an increasingly puritan public. Already, however, the great majority were settling down fairly peacefully with the partner they had accepted if not chosen, and the number of notorious separations was declining, if only temporarily.

In almost every respect the nobility had adapted the institution of the arranged marriage as they had inherited it from the middle ages, and fitted it to suit the new social, political and intellectual conditions of the modern world. In this modified form it survived in the landed classes almost to within living memory.

Ellen Moers

Money, the Job,
and Little Women

*There are so many ways of earning a living and most of them are
failures.*   —GERTRUDE STEIN, *Ida*

All of Jane Austen's opening paragraphs, and the best of her first
sentences, have money in them; this may be the first obviously feminine
thing about her novels, for money and its making were characteristically
female rather than male subjects in English fiction. The wonderfully rude
blare that starts *Emma*—"Emma Woodhouse, handsome, clever, and
rich"—is as it happens imitation Mme. de Genlis (the French novelist
who meant much to Jane Austin), but the particular Austen touch is
precision. While the Genlis heroines, like Richardson's and Fanny
Burney's, are merely vaguely, gloriously rich, Emma has precisely 30,000
pounds. From her earliest years, Austen had the kind of mind that
inquired where the money came from on which young women were to
live, and exactly how much of it there was. In *Love and Freindship* [sic],
her classic spoof of the hippie heroine who scorns parental support
(written for the ages when Austen herself was fifteen), the money comes
from stealing, although Sophia is "most impertinently interrupted" as she
is "majestically removing the 5th Bank-note from the Drawer to her own
purse."

Marriage makes money a serious business in Austen's fiction; her
seriousness about money makes marriage important, as in fact it was in
the England of her day. In the last decades of the 18th century and the
first of the 19th, England moved from an aristocratic to a middle-class
orientation without any of those vulgar revolutions that convulsed the
Lesser Nations of the Continent. New people, with new money and new
kinds of power, engaged in that remarkable British enterprise of grafting
themselves onto the old aristocratic stock, essentially through intermarriage—Austen's subject. A title like *Pride and Prejudice* denotes
less of her conformity to the old 18th-century way of thinking in
personalized abstractions, than her 19th-century concern with social fact:
social class, social values, and money. "It is a truth universally acknowledged," runs the celebrated opening sentence of the novel, "that a single

man in possession of a good fortune must be in want of a wife." Of all its crystalline phrases, the one about money can least be dispensed with; it conveys the sharp point of Austen's very feminine wit.

Hard facts, with Austen, come first and are swiftly stated. Most of what we need to know about Mr. Bingley, for example, the single man about whom Mrs. Bennet is bursting to tell Mr. Bennet (so that he may get down to the serious business of matchmaking on behalf of their five daughters) is conveyed in her gossipy rattle on the first page of the novel. "Mrs. Long says that Netherfield is taken by a young man of large fortune from the north of England." That is, Bingley resides on an estate he has not inherited but merely "taken" or rented, and his wealth comes out of the North, region of industry and commerce; it is new money. This is the point of the whole comedy of snobbery that Austen spins out of Bingley's hateful sisters: "they were of a respectable family in the north of England; a circumstance more deeply impressed on their memories than that their brother's fortune and their own had been acquired by trade."

The Bingley girls are bitterly opposed to their brother's marriage to Jane Bennet, not because of her relative poverty but because of her middle-class connections. For what the family needs is not more wealth but aristocratic shadings to what they have; only land ownership, that sign of old money, can remove the stain of trade. That is why Bingley's sisters are desperate for him to purchase an estate, as their self-made father had intended but "did not live to do." And they have cause to fear that Bingley may have inherited dilatoriness and indecision, as well as a fortune, from their father: "it was doubtful to many of those who best knew the easiness of his temper, whether he might not spend the remainder of his days at Netherfield, and leave the next generation to purchase." Happily for all, marriage to Jane Bennet, and her aversion to remaining in the neighborhood of her vulgar mother, force Bingley at the end of the novel to purchase land himself, in another county.

Austen placed Bingley and all the other characters of *Pride and Prejudice* on a financial scale arranged with geometric precision. Her hero Darcy is at the top of the scale, with an income of 10,000 pounds a year, and a fortune twice the size of that of his friend Bingley, who has inherited "nearly an hundred thousand pounds" from which he derives an income of four to five thousand. Each of the Bingley sisters has a fortune of 20,000 pounds, or five times the sum that Mrs. Bennet brought in marriage to her husband. Mr. Bennet's income is 2,000 pounds a year, a fifth of Darcy's and somewhat less than half of Bingley's. He should be thought of as a rich man, nonetheless, by the standard provided by what we know of the novelist's own circumstances: the Austens managed with precarious gentility on about 600 pounds a year.

The Bennet family's socioeconomic position is complicated, however, and not only by that business of the entail which, as Mrs. Bennet is too stupid to understand but Jane Austen is not, deprives the children, simply because they are daughters, of a share in their father's estate. Mr. Bennet's fortune is in land, but Mrs. Bennet's is of less respectable provenance. Her father was a country attorney, and her sister, Aunt Phillips (whose indiscretion begins Lydia's ruinous course), married their father's clerk, who took over the law business. Mrs. Bennet's brother Gardiner, the girls' uncle, is a more significant figure in the novel; though kept to the background, he serves to point the moral of Austen's economic design. Mr. Gardiner is first mentioned in a shadowy way as "settled in London in a respectable line of trade"—but these shadows cast a smoky pall over the Bennet girls' prospect for social advancement. The Bingleys and Darcy have heard that their uncle "lives somewhere near Cheapside," revolting name; this alone—something like having relatives in the Bronx—"must very materially lessen their chance of marrying men of any consideration in the world."

When Mr. and Mrs. Gardiner take solider shape in the second half of *Pride and Prejudice,* they turn out to be the most sympathetic adults in the novel, the only ones in fact who combine intelligence, style, character, and fortune; not coincidentally, they are also the only happily married adult pair and the only good parents. The Bingley girls never get over their snobbish difficulty in "believing that a man who lived by trade, and within view of his own warehouses, could have been so well-bred and agreeable," but Darcy conquers both pride and prejudice where Gardiner is concerned.

Darcy himself, Austen's earliest conceived and most glamorous hero, is the least precisely imagined character in the novel. With his Norman name and accompanying ancient credentials (his first name is Fitzwilliam); with his splendid estate complete with ancestral portraits, Darcy is actually an improbable close friend for such as Bingley, and an even less probable catch for Elizabeth Bennet. Austen seems to have lifted Darcy, in all his stiff elegance, from Fanny Burney's *Cecilia,* one of her favorite novels; and he stands alone in her work (she would never do such a character again) as a reminder of her 18th-century formation. Like Richardson's Sir Charles Grandison, Darcy personifies the benefits that stream down, a sort of gilded rainfall, from landed wealth and power when held by a man of high moral character who, past the age and perils of libertinage, marries the right girl.

"How many people's happiness were in his guardianship!" Elizabeth ponders as she tours Pemberley, the Darcy estate. "—How much of pleasure or pain it was in his power to bestow!—how much of good or evil must be done by him!" These are the old ideas about aristocracy of the century of Austen's birth and juvenile reading, ideas emanating from a society securely ruled by a landed aristocracy; but Austen herself belonged to another era, of shifting class values and alignments. The happy ending of *Pride and Prejudice*—Elizabeth's marriage to Darcy

—brings together the uppermost and the shabbiest elements of the country gentry, as they were brought together in Austen's own family history. But not part of her family experience, and not, so far as I can tell, part of the stock of ideas she drew from novel-reading, is her original breeding of old Norman blood with new commercial money from Cheap-side, which Elizabeth's marriage also represents. Her uncle and aunt Gardiner are revealed finally to be, in Austen's design, the new kind of people whose benevolent power smooths the working of society, and gilds the happy ending comedy guarantees. The last paragraph of *Pride and Prejudice* is given to them:

> With the Gardiners they were always on the most intimate terms. Darcy as well as Elizabeth, really loved them; and they were both ever sensible of the warmest gratitude towards the persons who, by bringing her into Derbyshire, had been the means of uniting them.

"Now I will try to write of something else," Austen wrote in a letter announcing the publication of *Pride and Prejudice* in 1813, "& it shall be a complete change of subject—ordination": that is, the taking of clerical orders, the decisive step by which an Englishman enters upon a life's work in the church. No one has ever been happy with this statement of intention—the only one of such sharpness that Austen wrote down—and few have been able to eke out its application to the novel in question, *Mansfield Park*. In the best criticism of the novel that we have, Lionel Trilling looks seriously at "the ideal of professional commitment" as a moral, a religious, and a cultural phenomenon, and what he writes goes far to dignify Austen's intention. But Trilling's ignoring of her concern with the economic aspect of a man's professional choice—to put it bluntly, the question of his income—is, if I may say so, a sign of the masculinity of the critic; it certainly bypasses the essentially feminine quality of Austen's realism.

Because she cared deeply and primarily about young women, be-cause she suffered from a rooted disrespect for parents, especially fathers, because she saw the only act of choice in a woman's life as the making of a marriage upon which alone depended her spiritual and physical health,[1] Austen turned a severe and serious eye (for here she was rarely satirical) on the economic life of her heroes. Heroes were potential husbands, a momentous role. What I am suggesting is that Austen's realism in the matter of money was in her case an essentially female phenomenon, the result of her deep concern with the quality of a woman's life in marriage.

It may be in point here to mention another woman novelist who

1. The thought that a respectable woman might earn her own living never crossed Austen's mind except to fill it with revulsion. No more violent antipathy to the idea of woman's work can be found in English fiction than in Jane Fairfax's outburst in *Emma* against "governess-trade"—so-called in invidious comparison to the slave trade—until George Eliot's *Mill on the Floss*, where the heroine prefers prolonging an illicit flirtation to taking up the reviled work of schoolteaching.

seems to me to exhibit the same kind of realism for the same reason, because she was as different as possible from Austen in everything but sex: Harriet Beecher Stowe. *Uncle Tom's Cabin* is Austen-like in its precision on money matters (in nothing else), and as much at variance in this regard with the male-written fiction of its day as were Austen's novels. The brilliance of Stowe's attack on slavery was her success in associating it with the cash nexus of mid-century American society. She demonstrated that the true horror of the institution was not its inhumanity but its very human, very easy-going alignment with the normal procedures of the marketplace.

Those who know Stowe's novel only by reputation will be surprised by the level and domestic tone of its first chapter, one of the most important in the book. There Tom is sold to trader Haley, because he "will bring the highest sum," over the dinner table of Mr. and Mrs. Shelby, a pleasant, respectable Kentucky couple whose treatment of their slaves is remarkably civilized. Mr. Shelby is not at all a vicious man but an ordinary husband, who, unbeknownst to his wife, has gone seriously into debt. He must raise money quickly to pay for the amenities of their plantation establishment, amenities which include Mrs. Shelby's piety, her high moral code, her tender care of her slaves. Stowe's point is that Mrs. Shelby's genteel ignorance of the financial realities of her married life is, just as much as the sinister trade that Haley plies, a cause of the perpetuation of slavery. "How can I bear," the woman cries when she learns the truth of Tom's sale, "to have this open acknowledgment that we care for no tie, no duty, no relation, however sacred, compared with money?" But that is just the lesson Stowe wanted her readers, in both North and South, to carry away from *Uncle Tom's Cabin,* which she pointedly addressed to "the mothers of America."

Jane Austen, a spinster, was harsher on unmarried girls who, for good or evil reasons, ignore financial realities, than on those who think of nothing else. Mary Crawford, in *Mansfield Park,* is particularly disagreeable when she expresses astonishment that Edmund Bertram is to be a clergyman: "there is generally an uncle or a grandfather to leave a fortune to the second son." "A very praiseworthy practise," Edmund replies, "but not quite universal. I am one of the exceptions, and *being* one, must do something for myself."

Doing something for oneself, economically speaking, is hard for Edmund and Miss Crawford to conceive; it was also hard for Jane Austen. To the genteel classes of her time, a man should ideally be something and have something, but not *do* anything in order to be or to have. The point of Edmund's taking orders is in fact to place him in a position for someone to give him a *living,* that special British term familiar to readers of Austen and Trollope, signifying a clergyman's benefice; at once the sphere of his responsibility and the attached means of his livelihood, his income. A *living* was something one inherited, was given, took, or bequeathed, according to ancient and complicated systems of secular and clerical ownership of the land; the familiar modern phrase, *to make a living,* may have been, for all I know, in origin an Americanism. (The idiom was clearly well-established in mid-century America. "I never thought on 't;" says trader Haley of the rights and wrongs of Slavery. ". . .I took up the trade just to make a living; if 't an't right, I calculate to 'pent 't in time, *ye* know.")

Even today the Oxford English Dictionary takes as little notice of *to make a living* as it does of the word *job,* in the current sense of a man's major, daily, serious employment. I am not suggesting that Jane Austen concerned herself with Edmund Bertram's getting, holding, or executing anything that could remotely be called a job; that subject waited on the significantly later generation of Charlotte Brontë. But I think we must take seriously her intention to write in *Mansfield Park,* however unsuccessfully, a book about a man's practical and active choice of his life's work, and the role that women play in that choice. I think we must believe in her concern here with man's field.

Certainly the subject dominates, and far more brilliantly and successfully, her next published novel, *Emma*. Mr. Knightley, her finest male character, is more than the hero of the novel, more than the man Emma marries; he represents, as his name intentionally does, Austen's ripe thinking on the ideal of English manhood. Mr. Knightley has no elegance, hardly any surface, though he has great wealth in the form of ownership of vast and ancient lands—the sole form, for he is short of the cash which marriage to Emma is to provide. But the quality of the man lies not in his mere "possession of a good fortune," but in his active work to preserve it. For, in his rough gaiters and long stride, his loud forthright voice, his industrious outdoor life, and his interminable colloquies indoors, to Emma's irritation, on crops and prices, Mr. Knightley is and is proud to be a working farmer. Only as such has he been able to preserve in fruitful prosperity and ever-widening extent the beautiful green and spreading lands of his estate. Austen calls it Donwell Abbey to underline her view of Mr. Knightley as the English Knight who has Done Well.

Mr. Knightley is an unusual male character in Austen, not only in his responsible discharge of the landlord's obligations to his society, but also in his free and unencumbered possession of the land: no living parent to await the death of, no indigent brothers or sisters to support, no distant relative to truckle to. More typical, and closer to the reality Austen knew, in her own family, is Frank Churchill in the same novel, who cuts himself off from his amiable father Captain Weston, dropping even his name, in order to attach himself to his maternal relations, the hateful but rich and childless Churchills. What is a man to do, what can a man do in Austen's world? Austen seems strongly to have disapproved a man's establishing himself by marriage to an heiress, but she appears not to have been much troubled by the scramble after patronage. Any amount of servility, embarrassment, and dependence within the family circle seems in her novels to be worth the hero's prize: to end "in possession of a good fortune,"

That Frank Churchill or Henry Tilney or Edward Ferrars (the last two, the heroes of *Northanger Abbey* and *Sense and Sensibility*) should defy domestic tyranny, strike out on their own, and take a job seems beyond Austen's imagining. So rare indeed is the subject in 19th-century English fiction generations after Austen that one might think—what is not true—that job-holding simply did not exist as a viable possibility for the middle classes: that is, hiring one's services out for money, performing set tasks during fixed hours, surrendering control of the major share of one's waking hours to an employer, in return for the means of existence. The shadow of Great Expectations, long after the idea had become a myth, blackened out for even Victorian novelists the subject of the job.[2]

Most of Austen's young men follow a profession, that uncertain midpath between servile dependence and independent industry, for success in all the professions in Austen's day (and even in our own) rested to a degree on access to patronage; for example, that "living" in the church, in the gift of family or near acquaintance. The army was in the same sense a profession: witness Darcy's purchase of a commission for Wickham, which raises him in social class and readies him for marriage to an heiress.

Medicine was not then a middle-class profession; when it became one, later in the century, George Eliot wrote her brilliantly original study of the professional man as Lydgate in *Middlemarch*. And the law, for a rootedly country novelist like Austen, was a profession only when performed mysteriously in far-off London by someone like John Knightley. Geographical limitations also deprived Austen of the subject of politics and place-hunting. That she had heard of the new class of commercial entrepreneur, and was inclined to admire it, we know from her sketch of Mr. Gardiner in *Pride and Prejudice*, but she was prevented by ignorance from showing anything of the working life of a man engaged

2. Dickens is a case in point. He himself began his adult life with a job: he was employed by a newspaper as a parliamentary reporter, expert in shorthand. But this matter does not enter into his self-portrait as David Copperfield, who moves from a professional apprenticeship in the law direct to triumphs as an independent author.

Trollope worked most of his life as a clerk in the Postal Service, but his dozens of novels deal with the patronage-ridden professions of the church and the law, with politics and inherited wealth, not with the Civil Service. Johnny Eames, Trollope's one attempt to "do" the small clerk (*The Last Chronicle of Barset, The Small House at Allington*) is among those male characters who justify Bradford Booth's comment that "too many of Trollope's heroes [are] indefatigably concerned with who is going to give him some money"—as someone does for Johnny at the last.

Thackeray, who was unusually honest about his own fall from genteel status, tried in *Pendennis* to capture something of the working life of the hack writer he had been himself, from necessity. But posterity better remembers the comic brilliance of the chapters of *Vanity Fair* in which Thackeray wrote of Living on Nothing a Year.

in industry, manufacture, commerce, business—all summed up, by 19th-century England, as "trade." Austen does however provide a good deal of information about independent industry, risk-taking, and financial success in the navy, the profession she knew best; it claimed two of her brothers, who rose to be admirals.

The navy and trade might seem worlds apart; *Persuasion* tells us otherwise. The last and most unguarded of her novels, *Persuasion* begins with the driving of Sir Walter Elliot from his beautiful ancestral estate, for he is a merely ornamental snob who provides neither benevolent leadership nor sound economic management for the county of which he is a principal landowner. Sir Walter's improvidence makes residence at Kellynch impossible and rental necessary to Admiral Crofts and his wife: simple, unfashionable navy people of sterling worth and patriotic utility, but no refinement, who represent Austen's final ideal.

To Sir Walter, who is stupid, nasty, and wrong, the naval career is "offensive," for it is "the means of bringing persons of obscure birth into undue distinction, and raising men to honours which their fathers and grandfathers never dreamt of." Austen's own view, as presented by her heroine Anne, is otherwise: "she could not but in conscience feel that they were gone who deserved not to stay, and that Kellynch Hall had passed into better hands than its owners." Only when one considers that Kellynch is Anne's own home, and its dispossessed owner her father, can one gauge the measure of Austen's revulsion against the idle and worthless landlord, and of her admiration for "new people" in the navy. But then *Persuasion* is entirely, as the other Austen novels are only partly, the story of a daughter's moral, emotional, and socioeconomic rejection of her own family.

Austen's account of the naval profession, from which Anne Elliot at last takes a husband, includes little about danger and war (though the navy she knew defeated Napoleon under Nelson) but a great deal about the possibilities it offers of middle-class domestic felicity and middle-class economic success. The plot of *Persuasion* hinges on the economic fact that capture of an enemy vessel, a "prize" in naval parlance, meant direct financial reward to the naval captain of Austen's day. It is the foundation of Captain Wentworth's self-made success. Anne Elliot had been persuaded not to accept Wentworth as a suitor, because, though a fine and intelligent young man, he had "nothing but himself to recommend him, and no hopes of attaining affluence, but in the chances of a most uncertain profession." Anne follows at a distance Wentworth's rise to Captain in the navy: he "must now, by successive captures, have made a handsome fortune. She had only navy lists and newspapers for her authority, but she could not doubt his being rich."

The great names of Trafalgar and St. Domingo echo in the background of *Persuasion,* but what one hears in the foreground is naval reminiscence perhaps only a woman novelist would write, for it is full of money rather than glory. "Ah, those were pleasant days when I had the *Laconia,*" sighs Captain Wentworth. "How fast I made money in her! A friend of mine and I had such a lovely cruise together off the Western Islands. Poor Harville, sister! You know how much he wanted money; worse than myself. He had a wife. Excellent fellow!"

Austen was by temperament a realist, Charlotte Brontë by nature a romantic of passionate strain, who remained all her life in awe of the call of her own imagination, both to genius and to madness. When Brontë wrote as a realist, therefore, it was with deliberation, and from conviction. Thus it was as a Christian, as a modern (i.e., a Victorian), as a native of industrial Yorkshire, as an adult (a status painfully won by the children of her family), and finally as a woman that she committed herself to the sober portrayal of the realities of everyday modern life at the outset of her career as a novelist. The results were interestingly original. "I had adopted a set of principles," she later wrote of her first novel. "I said to myself that my hero should work his way through life as I had seen real living men work theirs—that he should never get a shilling he had not earned—. . . that whatever small competency he might gain, should be won by the sweat of his brow. . . ."

She held so firmly to these principles, and discharged so scrupulously her portrait of a man with a job—a middle-class man working routinely for a living—that no one would publish the book. "Indeed," she added drily, "until an author has tried to dispose of a manuscript of this kind, he can never know what stores of romance and sensibility lie hidden in breasts he would not have suspected of casketing such treasures. Men in business are usually thought to prefer the real"—but publishers, she had found, harbor a "passionate preference for the wild, wonderful, and thrilling." The latter preference a Brontë could easily satisfy; and so, against her principles, but forced by commercial necessity as well as inclination, she wrote her second novel, the romance called *Jane Eyre,* and thus entered history.

Charlotte Brontë's first novel, *The Professor,* was published only after her death, and barely entered history at all except as a literary curiosity to those concerned with the development of the Brontë masterpiece *Villette,* which deals wholly, as *The Professor* deals in part, with Charlotte Brontë's experience as teacher in a Brussels school. In *Villette,* her last novel, Brontë provides one of the best literary accounts ever written of what it is like to face a classroom of the disagreeable, stupid, and intractable young. But her first novel, especially the opening six chapters, has an interest of its own, for *The Professor* is truly the sober, unromantic story of a man intended as a hero, and as at least the social equal of his readers, who works for a living. I do not know any previous work of English fiction carried out upon such principles.

William Crimsworth is well-born and well-educated but penniless, and driven by various necessities to forget family patronage and consider "engaging in trade." He works as second clerk in a textile manufacturing establishment in ——shire, charged with translating and copying the firm's foreign correspondence. (Clerk then meant secretary, man's work before the late-Victorian invention of the typewriter, and the ensuing opening of office employment to women.) No exciting incident, no upsweep of fortune, no romance, no amusement other than reading and walking, and very few social encounters break the routine of his office life. He lives on his meager salary in lodgings, a rented bedroom where the sluttish servant regularly lets the fire go out. The interest of the opening chapters is the peculiar atmosphere Brontë evokes—a kind of sooty, acrid, coldness—and the peculiar character of her hero. For sensibility, refinement, youth, and individuality, the qualities with which her hero is endowed at birth, are swallowed up by the character of the job-holder.

Crimsworth is dry, bitter, and taciturn. He is punctual, diligent, tidy in his work, austere and thrifty in habit. He is obsessed with neatness, and a teetotaler who drinks a good deal of coffee as well as tea in the novel. In appearance he is "only a counting-house clerk, in a grey tweed wrapper." He likes to look at women, but has strong views about what might be called the "single standard." When threatened with violence by his insufferable employer, he threatens in return merely to summon the magistrate. Altogether, Crimsworth has a very good hold on his passions and his imagination—something which distinguishes him from the Brontë heroines.

Crimsworth hates his job, in fact hates working. His refusal to romanticize his employment is one of the more original touches in the character. And when a fight with his employer ends the job, and throws Crimsworth loose in the wide world, he reacts very differently from Jane Eyre or Lucy Snowe (of *Villette*): they revel in being free spirits, they dream of independence and mysteriously new experience, while Crimsworth grimly faces the fact of job-hunting. "I, a bondsman just released from the yoke, freed for one week from twenty-one years of constraint, must, of necessity, resume the fetters of dependency. Hardly had I tasted the delight of being without a master when duty issued her stern mandate: 'Go forth and seek another service.' " Subservience and self-denial are here the essentials of the white-collar working character. Whatever the defects of *The Professor*—whatever its conscious drabness of atmosphere, which I for one like to savor—the novel does not belong to the self-improving, success-worshiping genre of popular fiction.

The only burst of enthusiasm for work in itself that Brontë permits herself is, interestingly enough, in her delineation of the happy marriage that ends the novel. For an essential ingredient in its happiness is the working wife: it is she (a lace-mender turned schoolteacher) who craves employment for its own sake, she who finds fulfillment in work for pay. Crimsworth accedes to his wife's need, though at the end his income, amassed through school-managing and careful investing, makes her earnings a spiritual rather than an economic necessity.

> I put no obstacle in her way; raised no objection; I knew she was not one who could live quiescent and inactive, or even comparatively inactive. Duties she must have to fulfil, and important duties; work to do—and exciting, absorbing, profitable work; strong faculties stirred in her frame, and they demanded full nourishment, free exercise, mine was not the hand ever to starve or cramp them. . . .

Here and throughout the elaboration in the last chapters of *The Professor* of the ideal of work for married women—something of a landmark in that area, I imagine, for 1846—Brontë lets down her guard and reveals herself a woman novelist, whistling in the Victorian dark.

Charlotte Brontë's most important propaganda for work for women makes a strong feature of *Shirley,* the ambitious, brilliant, and also seriously flawed novel set in industrial Yorkshire that she wrote after *Jane Eyre,* with conscious intention to bridle the latter's melodrama and dampen its romance. These violent alternations between romance and realism mark all of her published work and fill her most interesting correspondence, where she argued more fully than any other English Victorian novelist the debate between Romanticism and Realism, not in the theoretical Continental manner, but in a practical, and very feminine style. The issue of working for a living was always present in her thinking about the literary real. "If you think . . . that anything like a romance is preparing for you, reader," she writes in the celebrated introduction to *Shirley,* "you never were more mistaken. Do you anticipate sentiment, and poetry, and reverie? Do you expect passion, and stimulus, and melodrama? Calm your expectations; reduce them to a lowly standard. Something real, cool, and solid lies before you; something unromantic as Monday morning, when all who have work wake with the consciousness that they must rise and betake themselves thereto."

Most of what made up popular knowledge of Victorian commerce and industry—for all that they were dominant features of the age—came from the writings of women novelists: Charlotte Brontë, Elizabeth Gaskell, Frances Trollope, Geraldine Jewsbury, Charlotte Tonna, and Harriet Martineau.[3] C. P. Snow must have forgotten all about the Victorian women writers when, in *The Two Cultures,* he denounced literary intellectuals as "natural Luddites" who always, starting in the

---

3. The one important male novelist associated with the so-called "factory novel" was Benjamin Disraeli, exceptional in many ways. In a later generation, this particular feminine tradition was continued by George Eliot's *Felix Holt, a Radical,* and, in America, by Rebecca Harding Davis's *Life in the Iron Mills,* which has just been reprinted by the Feminist Press with an introduction by Tillie Olsen.

Victorian age, turned their back on the Industrial Revolution. Oddly enough, Snow chose button-making as his example of the kind of productive process of which he said intellectuals have always been obdurately ignorant. He thus passed over Harriet Martineau's article, "What There Is in a Button," which gave readers of *Household Words* a very full account indeed of the production of metal, pearl, needle-wrought, engraved, and cloth-covered buttons, as it was carried on in Birmingham in 1852. Miss Martineau wrote it as part of a highly successful series she did for Dickens's periodical. She also covered the production of nails, needles, textiles, screws, matches, and glass.

Harriet Martineau, like Charlotte Brontë and most of the women writers I have named for their commitment to commercial realities, was a native of the industrial North. But most of these women, too, were daughters, wives, or sisters of clergymen, the one class that worked hardest on Sunday, and rested the following morning. Their gift of Monday realism to Victorian literature was the result of conscious deliberation bred from feminine experience; and in these degenerate times the gift looks particularly precious. Women again, perhaps, may see to its renewal. The one recent novel of quality that I have read which presents the ultimate rewards of a man's life as deriving from his working days and not his sexual nights is by a woman. It is a book positively obsessed with the idea of the job and, in probably unconscious tribute to an old female tradition, it is called *The Monday Voices*.[4]

The homely, unendowed spinster in Victorian England knew she had to work to live respectably, and, unlike her male counterpart, she could indulge no "great expectations" of something other than a job turning up. The realistic choice forced upon such women was that between paid employment and unpaid domestic servitude. That the intelligent Victorian woman should prefer the former for herself is no surprise, and hardly a new story; what is interesting, and what has rarely been commented upon, is that the enforced realism of her life led the woman writer to a commitment to the job, to paid employment, for everyone, man and woman alike. This is the original contribution of *The Professor*, which celebrates the job as a reality, not as an ideal, and expounds Charlotte Brontë's belief that a man without inherited wealth has to work to live—which sounds like, but is not at all like, Margaret Fuller's notorious acceptance of the universe. For Brontë had before her eyes an example of the reverse of her kind of feminine realism in the person of her brother Branwell. His unemployment, as much as her own and her sisters' employment, was the source of *The Professor*.

She was living at home when Branwell returned in disgrace to the Haworth parsonage to begin the long ordeal of self-pitying dissipation that

4. By Joanne Greenberg (Holt, Rinehart & Winston, 1965). Under the name of Hannah Green, she wrote the better known *I Never Promised You a Rose Garden*, also a title, as it is a novel, of feminine realism.

ended in his death three years later. Frustrated in his great, unfounded expectations of literary, artistic, and marital glory, Branwell was a drunkard and a drug-addict. His threats of suicide, arson, and murder were so genuine and unremitting that he required constant surveillance in that tiny household, when Charlotte began to write *The Professor*. "Branwell stays at home and degenerates instead of improving," she wrote. "He refuses to make an effort; he will not work—and at home he is a drain on every resource—an impediment to all happiness."

Branwell's Byronic outbursts in the role of social outcast and vindictive failure were also closely observed by his sister Emily, who was also writing her first novel at the same time. But Emily's attitude to her brother was one of tolerant fascination, even fellow-feeling, and her genius had nothing whatsoever to do with Monday-morning realism. As different as one sister was from the other, so different is *The Professor* from *Wuthering Heights*, but both are in their way strikingly original productions. It would be inaccurate to take as an easy commonplace, and to miss the fervent and feminine conviction in what Charlotte Brontë wrote, long after *The Professor*, about "earning one's subsistence." "Most desirable," she said, "is that all, both men and women, should have the power and the will to work for themselves—most advisable that both sons and daughters should early be inured to habits of independence and industry."

Habits of independence and industry were bred in the American bone, religion, history, and continental destiny all conducing to a native faith in hard work as the practical foundation of personal worth. Nothing so clearly separates American writers of the 19th century from their English contemporaries than their attitude toward work—and here, as in so much else, the Americans seem beside the English at once childishly naive and wearily sophisticated, at once behind and ahead of the times. For by mid-century, American "literary intellectuals," to use Snow's phrase, were sick of the work ethic and disgusted with moneymaking. While Charlotte Brontë was writing *The Professor*, and nervously exploring the new subject of genteel man at work for his living, Henry David Thoreau was living at Walden Pond, to which he moved on the 4th of July, 1845, to declare his independence of his hard-working, moneymaking Concord neighbors. "I am convinced," Thoreau wrote, "that to maintain one's self on this earth is not a hardship but a pastime, if we will live simply and wisely. . . . It is not necessary that a man should earn his living by the sweat of his brow, unless he sweats easier than I do."

Transcendental improvidence we now know to have been a source of much literary industry on the part of American women. The father, brother, or husband who could not or would not work, and left the entire or major support of a large household to their womenfolk (Harriet

Beecher Stowe had seven babies) was responsible for the writing of many best sellers by American women, and a few masterworks. Thoreau of course never married; it was a maiden aunt of his who paid those taxes in defiant nonpayment of which he went to jail in "civil disobedience." Not Thoreau, but his Concord neighbor and friend. Bronson Alcott, made literary history—female literary history—for Alcott, the most improvident of all transcendental philosophers, had a daughter to support him named Louisa May, who wrote forty books to that end in about thirty years.

Beside *Little Women,* she wrote dozens of "juveniles," many thrillers, and a few books intended in all seriousness for adult readers. In the last category, the one I have read that strikes me as most interesting is her first long fiction. She began to work on it only fifteen years after Charlotte Brontë wrote *The Professor*, but, for reasons similar to those that hindered publication of Brontë's first novel, it was not published till long afterward, in 1873. It is called *Work: A Story of Experience,* and it opens with a reference to American Independence very different from any to be found in *Walden*:

> "Aunt Betsey, there's going to be a new Declaration of Independence."
> "Bless and save us, what do you mean, child?"
> "I mean that, being of age, I'm going to take care of myself, and not be a burden any longer. . . . I don't intend to wait . . . but, like the people in fairy tales, travel away into the world and seek my fortune. . . . I'm old enough to take care of myself; and if I'd been a boy, I should have been told to do it long ago."

Under the jaunty tone, which came naturally to Alcott (it is all over her journals as well as her juvenile fiction), the author is quite in earnest. She wrote *Work* mainly about and primarily for women. The hero is a girl named Christie, closely modeled after Alcott herself, who goes jauntily out into the world to make what turns out to be a very scanty fortune. Too poorly educated to be a governess, she goes to a Boston employment agency to apply for a job as a housemaid. "I'll begin at the beginning, and work my way up. I'll put my pride in my pocket, and go out to service. Housework I like, and can do well. . . . I never thought it degradation to do it for [Aunt Betsey], so why should I mind doing it for others if they pay for it? It isn't what I want, but it's better than idleness, so I'll try it!" And a live-in housemaid she becomes, in cap and apron, at $2.50 a week, in an establishment where the cook, soon Christie's fast friend, is black.

All this is quite extraordinary for an American or English girl of Christie's type in the 1860's. Like everything else in *Work*—sewing for pay, or working as an actress—it was based on Alcott's real experience, but that did not make it less out of the run of normal American experience. Louisa May Alcott was of the Brahmin class, her father from a good if decayed old New England family, her mother a member of the distinguished, prosperous Boston clan of the Mays, the source, as few people realize, of Alcott's life-long snobbery, as well as her middle name. The March girls in *Little Women* are presumably month-named for the same reason.

A special gift Alcott had as a writer, and which accounts, I think, for much of her distinctive charm, was her ability to see her own experience—her weird father, her poverty-line childhood, the strange Concord ambience, her unique working life—as the sunshiny norm, which it was not, and in so doing to transform what she knew into a practical ideal. One result is the curious modernity of Alcott's fiction. It is hard to believe, when reading *Little Women,* that it was written in the 1860's, while Dickens and George Eliot were still writing; that the War which conveniently abstracts the father from the female household of *Little Women* (and even more conveniently kills off Christie's husband in *Work*) is the contemporary Civil War. For the working girls in Alcott, Jo or Meg or Christie, seem more like the American college girl of today, working at pickup jobs without loss of respectability or class status, than like the Jane Eyres and Lucy Snowes who were their nearer contemporaries.

In all of Alcott's books that I have read, the kind of work she describes with most conviction, with most imaginative and moral zeal, is humble work, lower in intellectual content and social status than the family atmosphere that produces her girls. *Hospital Sketches,* the first of her published books to capture the public's serious attention, deals with her service as a nurse—unskilled, ill-fed, backbreaking service under the worst conditions—in a Washington hospital during the Civil War. Meg works as a governess in *Little Women,* Amy as a companion; Jo does childcare and sewing for the mistress of a New York boarding house. All the girls are unfitted for the work they do and dislike doing it as much as they dislike the housework—cooking, sewing, cleaning—that, just as much as games, romances and dreams, makes up the texture of a girl's life in *Little Women.* Work is handled playfully in the novel, but it is not confused with play. It is something real, lasting, serious, necessary, and inescapable as Monday morning, to be shouldered manfully—by women, little and big. In fact, the importance of work in America's favorite girl-child's classic is worth **pondering.** A very different message, for boys, can be found in *Tom Sawyer,* published in the following decade. There work is presented as something to be avoided at all costs and with all ingenuity, whether through the swindle, the ruse, or flight.

To move from *Work* and *Little Women* to *La Condition Ouvrière* is to pass through mind-reeling distances of place and time, and yet to remain, I think, within a solid feminine tradition. For Simone Weil's book, often called the most profound writing produced by this century about the working condition, issues from a woman's desire to make contact with real life. That was Weil's motive, she wrote, for taking off a year (1935) from her normal career of philosophy teacher in a French lycée to work on the Renault assemblyline. Alcott, Brontë, and the rest would have understood her pride in the moral self-sufficiency she derived from the experience; she learned, she wrote, to accept perpetual humiliation without becoming humiliated in her own eyes. The feminine issues in *La Condition Ouvrière* are particularly clear in Weil's original language, where the play of genders sharpens her expressed resolve to stick with factory work until she could learn to support it in a way that conserved her dignity as a human being (*"Je me suis juré de ne pas sortir de cette condition d'ouvrière avant d'avoir appris à la supporter de manière à y conserver intact le sentiment de ma dignité d'être humain"*).

Simone Weil was a Jew drawn to Catholicism, a Marxist opponent of Marxism, a religious philosopher who was both a mystic and an analyst of the working class, and a sophisticated French modernist. Louisa May Alcott was a daughter of 19th-century New England transcendentalism, who wrote books for children. Yet their sense of the real word as a working world was in some ways the same, and in different ways equally religious. The fairy tale which underlies Alcott's *Work* is *The Pilgrim's Progress,* most revered of Puritan fantasies, and it makes a structure far too solid for Alcott's unpretentious tale of a middle-class girl who waits on table, runs after children, and sews seams for her livelihood. Yet there is something impressive, too, about Alcott's naive attempt to make a latter-day Christian, a pilgrim on the dangerous journey to the desired country, out of her little Christie, the working girl.

There is also an interest to Alcott's salute to a special kind of women's solidarity, with which she brings Christie's pilgrimage to a close. Widowed almost immediately after marriage, the mother of a little girl, Christie at forty is wealthy but occupied. She goes among working women to shake their hands ("roughened by the needle, stained with printer's ink, or hard with humbler toil") and arouse their enthusiasm for "the new emancipation" with the sort of simple, earnest speech that only she among the feminists can make, "for I have been and mean to be a working-woman all my life." The novel ends with a scene of hand-clasping all around the table, charmingly illustrated in the Victorian edition I have: Mrs. Wilkins the fat motherly laundress, Bella the elegant young society matron, Letty the fallen woman, Hepsey the black cook, Mrs. Powers the elderly Quaker lady, Christie, and her daughter Ruth—who "spread her chubby hand above the rest: a hopeful omen, seeming to promise that the coming generation of women will not only receive but deserve their liberty, by learning that the greatest of God's gifts to us is the privilege of sharing His great work."

Bronislaw Malinowski

Avenues to Marriage Among the Trobrianders

To us marriage appears as the final expression of love and the desire for union; but in this case we have to ask ourselves why, in a society where marriage adds nothing to sexual freedom, and, indeed, takes a great deal away from it, where two lovers can possess each other as long as they like without legal obligation, they still wish to be bound in marriage. And this is a question to which the answer is by no means obvious.

That there is a clear and spontaneous desire for marriage, and that there is a customary pressure towards it, are two separate facts about which there can be not the slightest doubt. For the first there are the unambiguous statements of individuals—that they married because they liked the idea of a life-long bond to that particular person—and for the second, the expression of public opinion, that certain people are well suited to each other and should therefore marry.

. . . Young people want to marry, even when they already possess each other sexually, and the state of marriage has real charm for them. But before I could entirely understand all the reasons and motives for this desire, I had to grasp the complexities and deeper aspects of the institution, and its relation to other elements in the social system.

The first thing to be realized is that the Trobriander has no full status in social life until he is married. . . . A bachelor has no household of his own, and is debarred from many privileges. There are, in fact, no unmarried men of mature age, except idiots, incurable invalids, old widowers and albinos. Several men were widowed during my stay in the Islands, and others were deserted by their wives. The former remarried almost as soon as their mourning was over, the latter as soon as their attempts at reconciliation had proved fruitless.

The same applies to women. Provided she is at all sexually tolerable, a widow or divorcée will not have long to wait. Once released from mourning, a widow again becomes marriageable. She may sometimes delay a little, in order to enjoy the sexual freedom of her unmarried state, but such conduct will ultimately draw on her the censure of public opinion, and a growing reputation for "immorality"—that is disregard of tribal usage—will force her to choose a new mate.

Another very important reason for marriage, from the man's point of view, is economic advantage. Marriage brings with it a considerable yearly tribute in staple food, given to the husband by the wife's family. This obligation is perhaps the most important factor in the whole social mechanism of Trobriand society. On it, through the institution of rank and through his privilege of polygamy, rests the authority of the chief, and his power to finance all ceremonial enterprises and festivities. Thus a man, especially if he be of rank and importance, is compelled to marry, for, apart from the fact that his economic position is strengthened by the income received from his wife's family, he obtains his full social status only by entering the group of *tovavaygile* [married men].

There is, further, the natural inclination of a man past his first youth to have a house and a household of his own. The services rendered by a woman to her husband are naturally attractive to a man of such an age; his craving for domesticity has developed, while his desire for change and amorous adventure has died down. Moreover, a household means children, and the Trobriander has a natural longing for these. Although not considered of his own body nor as continuing his line, they yet give him that tender companionship for which, when he reaches twenty-five or thirty, he begins to crave. He has become used . . . to playing with his sister's children and with those of other relatives or neighbors.

These are the reasons—social, economic, practical and sentimental—which urge a man towards marriage. And last, though not least, personal devotion to a woman and the promise of prolonged companionship with one to whom he is attached, and with whom he has sexually lived, prompt him to make certain of her by means of a permanent tie, which shall by binding under tribal law.

The woman, who has no economic inducement to marry, and who gains less in comfort and social status than the man, is mainly influenced by personal affection and the desire to have children in wedlock.

This personal motive comes out very strongly in the course of love affairs which do not run smoothly, and brings us from the reasons for marriage in general to the motives which govern the individual's particular choice.

In this matter it must first be realized that the choice is limited from the outset. A number of girls are excluded completely from a man's matrimonial horizon, namely those who belong to the same totemic class. . . . Furthermore, there are certain endogamous restrictions, though these are by no means so precisely defined as those imposed by exogamy. Endogamy enjoins marriage within the same political area, that is within some ten to twelve villages of the same district. The rigidity of this rule depends very much on the particular district. For instance, one area in the north-west corner of the island is absolutely endogamous, for its inhabitants are so despised by the other Islanders that the latter would not dream either of marrying or of having sexual relations within it.

Again, the members of the most aristocratic province of Kiriwina seldom marry outside their own district, except into the neighbouring island of Kitava, or into certain eminent families from one or two outside villages. . . .

Even within this limited geographical area, there are further restrictions on the choice of a mate, and these are due to rank. Thus, members of the highest sub-clan, the Tabalu, and more especially their women, would not marry into a sub-clan of very low caste, and a certain correspondence in nobility is considered desirable even in marriage between less important people.

It follows that choice must be made from among persons who are not of the same clan, who are not widely different in rank, who reside within the convenient geographical area, and who are of a suitable age. In this limited field, however, there is still sufficient freedom of selection to allow of *mariages d'amour, de raison, et de convenance.* . . .

The Consent of the Wife's Family

Permanent liaisons which are on the point of ripening into marriage become known and are talked about in the village, and now the girl's family, who, so far, have taken no interest in her love affairs, who have, indeed, kept ostentatiously aloof, must face the fact about to be accomplished, and make up their minds whether or no they will approve it. The man's family, on the other hand, need show little interest in a matter in which they have practically no say. A man is almost entirely independent with regard to matrimony, and his marriage, which will be a matter of constant and considerable effort and worry to his wife's family, will continue to lie completely outside the sphere of his own people's concerns.

It is remarkable that, of all the girl's family, the person who has most to say about her marriage, although legally he is not reckoned as her kinsman (*veyola*), is her father. I was astonished when this information was given to me early in the course of my field work, but it was fully confirmed later on by observation. This paradoxical state of affairs becomes less incomprehensible, however, if we bring it into relation with certain rules of morals and etiquette, and with the economic aspect of marriage. One would naturally expect a girl's brothers and maternal kinsmen to take the most important part in deliberations concerning her marriage, but the strict taboo which rules that the brother must have nothing at all to do with the love affairs of his sister, and her other maternal kinsmen but little, debars them from any control over her matrimonial plans.

Thus, although her mother's brother is her legal guardian, and her own brothers will in the future occupy the same position with regard to her own household, they must all remain passive until the marriage is an accomplished fact. The father, say the natives, acts in this matter as the spokesman of the mother, who is the proper person to deliberate upon her daughter's love intrigues and marriage. It will also be seen that the father is closely concerned in the work of his sons from the economic standpoint, in that after the marriage of their sister, these will have to divide the fruits of their labour between her and their mother, instead of, as previously, giving them all to the parental household. When two lovers have decided on marriage, the young man becomes assiduous in his attentions to his sweetheart's family, and perhaps her father will, on his own initiative, say: "You sleep with my child: very well, marry her." As a matter of fact, if the family are well disposed to the youth, they will always take this initiative either by such a direct declaration or else by asking him for small gifts, an equally unambiguous indication that he is accepted. . . .

Marriage Gifts

This simple declaration of marriage is followed by that exchange of gifts which is so typical of any social transaction in the Trobriands. Each gift is definite in nature and quantity, each has to take its proper place in a series and each is reciprocated by some corresponding contribution. . . .

The girl's family have to make the first offering to signify their consent to the marriage. Since their agreement is absolutely essential, this gift, in conjunction with the public declaration of the union of the partners, constitutes marriage. It is a small gift, a little cooked food brought in baskets and offered by the girl's father to the boy's parents. It is set down in front of their house with the words *kam katuvila*, "thy *katuvila* gift." It must be given on the day on which the two remain together, or on the morning of the next day. As we have seen, when the consent of the girl's family is doubtful the two partners often abstain from food till this gift is brought.

Soon afterwards, usually on the same day, the girl's relatives bring a bigger present. Her father, her maternal uncle, and her brothers who now for the first time emerge from the inaction imposed on them by the specific brother-sister taboo, each bring a basket of uncooked yam food, and offer it to the boy's parents. This gift is called *pepe'i*. But even this is not enough. A third offering of food is brought to the boy's parents, cooked this time and carried on large platters. . . . This gift is called *kaykahoma*.[1]

---

1. The reader who has grasped the complex psychology of ceremonial gifts in the *kula* and in associated activities will understand the great importance of the exchanges which accompany so many social transactions in the Trobriands. Cf. *Argonauts of the Western Pacific,* especially chs. iii and vi.

The boy's family must not delay long before they reciprocate. The last gift, cooked food on trays, is returned almost immediately and in exactly the same form as it was received. A more important gift follows. The boy's father has already prepared certain valuables of the *vaygu'a* type, that is to say, large, polished axeblades of green stone, necklaces of polished spondylus shell discs, and armlets made of the *conus* shell; also, when the second gift of uncooked food was brought to him by the girl's family, he made a small distribution of it among his own relatives, and they in turn now bring him other valuables to add to his own. All these he presents to the girl's family; he has kept the baskets in which the food was brought to him; he puts the valuables into these, and they are carried by himself and his family to the girl's house. This gift is called *takwalela pepe'i*, or "repayment in valuables of the *pepe'i* gift."

The reader is perhaps weary of all these petty details, but this meticulous absorption in small gifts and counter-gifts is highly characteristic of the Trobrianders. They are inclined to boast of their own gifts, with which they are entirely satisfied, while disputing the value and even quarrelling over what they themselves receive, but they regard these details as most important and observe them scrupulously. In the exchange of marriage gifts, as a rule, they are less cantankerous than on other occasions, and a more generous and friendly spirit prevails. After the *takwalela pepe'i* there is a long pause in the exchange of gifts, which lasts until the next harvest. During this time and while the couple's own dwelling is being built, the wife usually remains with her husband in his father's house. At harvest time they will receive the first substantial gift due from the girl's family, and of this they will themselves make a distribution by way of payment to those who have helped in the building of their new home.

To resume, then, the girl's family give a present of considerable value at the next harvest, and from then on at every harvest they will have to help the new household with a substantial contribution of fresh yams. The first present of this sort, however, has a special name (*vilakuria*), and is surrounded by a ceremonial of its own. Prism-shaped receptacles (*pwata'i*) are constructed of poles, in front of the young couple's yam-house. . . , and the girl's family, after selecting a large quantity, a hundred, two hundred, or even three hundred basketfuls of the best yams, arrange them in these receptacles with a great amount of ceremony and display.

This gift also must be repaid without any too great delay. Fish is considered a proper counter-offering. In a coastal village, the husband will embark with his friends on a fishing expedition. If he lives inland, he has to purchase the fish in one of the coastal villages, paying for them in yams.

The fish is laid in front of the girl's parents' house, with the words "*Kam saykwala*" (thy *saykwala* gift). Sometimes, if the young husband is very rich, or else if he and his family were not able previously to repay the *pepe'i* present, a gift of *vaygu'a* (valuables) will be given at this point in answer to the first harvest offering. This is called *takwalela vilakuria* (repayment by valuables of the *vilakuria* present), and closes the series of initial marriage gifts.

This series of gifts appears at first sight unnecessarily complicated. But, if we examine it more closely, we find that it represents a continuous story, and is no mere disconnected jumble of incidents. In the first place it expresses the leading principle in the economic relation which will subsequently obtain for the whole duration of the marriage: that the girl's family provide the newly established household with food, being occasionally repaid with valuables. The small initial gifts . . . , express the consent of the girl's family, and are a sort of earnest of their future and more considerable contributions. The return offering of food . . . , made immediately by the boy's family, is a characteristically Trobriand answer to a compliment. And the only really substantial gifts from the bridegroom's family to the bride's . . . exert a definitely binding force on the husband, for if the marriage be dissolved, he does not recover them save in exceptional cases. They are about equivalent in value to all the other first year's gifts put together. But this present from the husband must emphatically not be considered as purchase money for the bride. This idea is utterly opposed both to the native point of view and to the facts of the case. Marriage is meant to confer substantial material benefits on the man. These he repays at rare intervals with a gift of valuables, and it is such a gift that he has to offer at the moment of marriage. It is an anticipation of the benefits to follow, and by no means a price paid for the bride.

. . . It is necessary, as I have already said, to enter into such minute details as these if we would approximate to the savage point of view. Closely observing the care and anxiety with which the gifts are gathered and given, it is possible to determine the psychology of the acts themselves. Thus Paluwa, the father of Isepuna, worried good-humouredly as to how he might collect sufficient food to offer to a chief's son, his daughter's future husband; and he discussed his troubles with me at length. He was faced by the difficulty of having three daughters and several female relatives, and only three sons. Everybody's working power had already been taxed to provide food for the other married daughters. And now Isepuna was going to wed Kalogusa, a man of high rank in his own right, and also a son of To'uluwa, the paramount chief. All his people exerted themselves to the utmost to produce as big a crop as possible that season, in order to be able to give a fine *vilakuria* present. And To'uluwa, the bridegroom's father, on his side, revealed to me his own anxiety. Could he provide a worthy counter gift? Times were hard, and yet something fine had to be given. I inspected several of the chief's valuables, and discussed their respective suitability with him. There was an undercurrent of suggestion, in the conversation of both parties, that some tobacco from the white man would be a much appreciated addition to either gift.

Infant Betrothal and Cross-Cousin Marriage

There is another way of arranging marriages in the Trobriands besides the ordinary method of courtship, and in many respects the two are in sharp contrast to each other. Normal marriage is brought about by free choice, by trial, and by the gradual strengthening of bonds which assume a legal obligation only after marriage. In marriage by infant betrothal, a binding agreement is made by the parents in the children's infancy: the boy and girl grow up into the relationship, and find themselves bound to each other before they have had an opportunity to choose for themselves.

The great importance of this second type of marriage lies in the fact that infant betrothal is always associated with cross-cousin marriage. The two people who, according to native ideas, are most suited for marriage with each other—a man's son and the daughter of his sister—are betrothed in infancy. When the father's sister's daughter is too old to be betrothed to her male infant cousin, her daughter may replace her. By the native legal system the two are equivalent, for the purposes of this marriage.

The significance of this institution can be understood only if we return to a consideration of the compromise between father-love and matriliny.[2] Cross-cousin marriage is an arrangement whereby both tribal law, which enjoins matrilineal succession, and the promptings of paternal love, which incline the father to bestow all possible privileges on his son, find equitable adjustment and adequate satisfaction.

Let us take a concrete instance. A chief, a village headman—or, indeed, any man of rank, wealth, and power, will give to a favorite son all that he can safely alienate from his heirs; some plots in the village lands, privileges in fishing and hunting, some of the hereditary magic, a position in the *kula* exchange, a privileged place in the canoe and precedence in dancing. Often the son becomes in some sort his father's lieutenant, performing magic instead of him, leading the men in tribal council, and displaying his personal charm and influence on all those occasions when a man may win the much-coveted *butura* (renown). . . . But . . . privileged positions are invidious and insecure, even while they last, as the rightful heirs and owners in matriliny resent being pushed aside during the lifetime of the chief; and, in any case, all such benefits cease with the father's

2. Cf. also *Crime and Custom*.

death. There is only one way by which the chief can establish his son permanently in the village with rights of full citizenship for himself and his progeny, and secure possession of all the gifts until death; and that is by contracting the son in paternal cross-cousin marriage, marriage with his sister's daughter or with this daughter's daughter. The following diagram will help to make the genealogy of the relation clear.

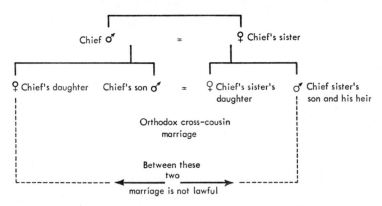

Diagrammatic Genealogy of Cross-Cousin Marriage

Our diagrammatical chief has a sister; and she has a son, the chief's heir and successor, and a daughter, the chief's niece by his sister, a girl who will continue the aristocratic line. The husband of this girl will enjoy a very privileged position, into which he will step on the day of his marriage. By native law and custom he will have a definite claim on his wife's brother or brothers and other male relatives, who will be obliged to give him annual tribute of food, and will be considered his *ex-officio* allies, friends, and helpers. He also acquires the right to live in the village if he chooses, and to participate in tribal affairs and in magic. It is clear, therefore, that he will occupy practically the same position as that enjoyed by the chief's son during his father's lifetime, and from which he is ousted by the rightful heir at his father's death. This type of marriage differs from the ordinary one also in that the husband comes to live in his wife's community. Cross-cousin marriage is thus matrilocal in contradistinction to the ordinary patrilocal usage.[3]

The obvious and natural solution, therefore, of the chief's difficulty is to marry his son to his niece or grandniece. Usually all parties benefit by the transaction. The chief and his son get what they want; the chief's niece marries the most influential man in the village, and in so doing

3. I think that any man could settle in his wife's community if he wished. But by doing so, he would both degrade himself and suffer disabilities. A chief's son, however, is an exception owing to his position in the village and his vested interests.

confirms this influence; and an alliance is established between the son of the chief and his lawful heirs which frustrates the potential rivalry between them. The girl's brother cannot oppose the marriage, because of the taboo; nor, as it is contracted in the chief's son's infancy, would he normally be in a position to do so.

Matrimonial Alliances in a Chief's Family

Whenever there is a possibility of it, a cross-cousin marriage will always be arranged. . . . Cross-cousin marriage is, undoubtedly, a compromise between the two ill-adjusted principles of mother-right and father-love; and this is its main *raison d'être*. The natives are not, of course, capable of a consistent theoretical statement; but in their arguments and formulated motives this explanation of the why and wherefore of the institution is implicit, in an unmistakable though piecemeal form. Several points of view are expressed and reasons given by them which throw some further light on their ideas, but all, if pushed to a conclusion, point to the same ultimate reason for cross-cousin marriage. Sometimes, for instance, it will be stated as a rider to the principle of exogamy that "the marriage between brother and sister is wrong" ("brother and sister" in the extended sense, all people of opposite sex and of the same generation related through the mother). "To marry a *tabula* (cross-cousin) is right; the true *tabula* (the first cross-cousin) is the proper wife for us."

Let us make clear one more point: among all the marriages possible between cousins, only one is lawful and desirable for the Trobriander. Two young people of opposite sex, . . . whose mothers are sisters, are, of course, subject to the strict sexual taboo which obtains between brother and sister. A boy and a girl who are the children of two brothers stand in no special relation to each other. They may marry if they like, but there is no reason why they should; no special custom or institution is connected with such a relationship, since in a matrilineal society it is irrelevant. Only a boy and a girl, descendants of a brother and sister respectively, can conclude a marriage which is lawful and which, at the same time, stands out from mere haphazard alliances; for here, as we have seen, a man gives his own kinswoman to his son for a wife. But an important point must here be noted: the man's son has to marry the woman's daughter, and not the man's daughter the woman's son. Only in the former combination do the two people call each other *tabugu,* a term which implies lawfulness of sexual intercourse. The other couple joined by a dotted line on the diagram . . . stand in a different relation according to native ideas of kinship. . . . A girl calls the son of her father's sister *tamagu* "my father.". . . Marriage with the *tama* ("father" = father's sister's son) is not incestuous, but it is viewed with disfavour and happens only rarely.

Such a marriage offers few inducements. A chief might like his daughter to be married to another chief or to a man of rank in his own family, but she would not thus acquire any specially high or privileged position. On the other hand, as his daughter will have to be supported by the same men who now work for her mother, the chief's wife, he may prefer for his own sake to marry her to a humbler and less exacting person than his heir. It all depends on his relations with his heir, which are, as we have seen, by no means so uniformly friendly and intimate as those with his own son.

The advantages of cross-cousin marriage were put to me from another point of view by Bagidou, when I asked him why he had wanted his little son Purayasi to marry Kabwaynaya. "I wanted a daughter-in-law who would be my real kinswoman," he said. "I wanted, when I got old, to have someone of my family to look after me; to cook my food; to bring me my lime-pot and lime-stick, to pull out my grey hairs. It is bad to have a stranger to do that. When it is someone of my own people, I am not afraid." His fear was, of course, of sorcery. It should be realized that since marriage is patrilocal, and since the son, in the case of important people, often remains near the father, this latter has good reasons to be interested in his daughter-in-law. Since she is his kinswoman there is yet another justification for his son's residence in the father's community. Thus we are brought back to cross-cousin marriage as the reconciling compromise between the claims of father-love and matriliny.

Peter Dobkin Hall

Marital Selection and Business in Massachusetts Merchant Families, 1700–1900

In order to understand the significance of marital selection in Massachusetts merchant families, it is necessary to examine the economic and social context in which marriage took place and the function it had in the relation between family life and business activity.

It is in the area of economic enterprise that the family assumed particular importance. Indeed, it was because of the family's involvement in economic enterprise that it was able to perform that multitude of tasks imposed upon it by the state. In order to understand the significance of this fact it is necessary to recall the two fundamental requirements of economic enterprise: capital and manpower. The family-business nexus supplied both to colonial mercantile enterprises.

New England society before 1780 was a society almost totally lacking in formal organizations for the performance of basic economic and social welfare activities. In the economic realm, there were no banks, no insurance companies, and no corporate enterprises. Nonetheless, business was carried on to so great an extent that the elite in Massachusetts was a *mercantile* elite. In the delivery of social services there were no hospitals, asylums, or orphanages. The church in the eighteenth century had not yet taken up a social gospel mission of performing charitable activities. Nonetheless, orphans were cared for, the sick were healed (within the capacities of eighteenth century physick), and the poor were not left to starve. There were no organizations responsible for vocational education or the training of professionals. Although Harvard College was an important institution, it provided only an unspecialized classical education. Nonetheless, professionals and artisans were trained in their various fields and skills.

The fact that social and economic activities of a fairly high order could be carried on rested on the integration of family and economic enterprise—together with a civil polity that depended explicitly on the family and "family government" to take on responsibilities that went far beyond simple internal regulation. The family was the unit through which virtually all major social and economic activities were mediated. It provided basic welfare services: not only through caring for kin, however distantly related, but also by caring for those who did not have families. Orphans, widows, the insane, and others in need of care or supervision were lodged by the towns with families. Vocational training, whether professional or manual, took place under a system of apprenticeship. Under this system a trainee took up residence for a number of years with his instructor's family. He became, in effect, a member of that family, learning his profession or trade in exchange for a sum of money and his day-to-day labors. Finally, and most important, the family was almost indistinguishable from economic enterprises and the conduct of economic activities.

Given the absence of formal economic organizations such as banks and insurance companies, colonial merchants had great difficulty in ensuring adequate capital for investment and trading activities. The problem of capital was made more difficult because Massachusetts had, from its foundation, adopted a system of partible inheritance whereby a testator's estate was, after a double portion had been given to the eldest son, divided equally among all children, both male and female. Needless to say, this partition tended to prevent the accumulation of capital and interfered with the ability of Massachusetts merchants to conduct business transgenerationally—as they might have been able to do under a system of primogeniture.[1] Inability to accumulate capital interfered seriously with the carrying on of commercial activities—and certainly tended to inhibit the ability of merchants to build up capital either for purposes of prestige and power or for purposes of more effective trade positions in world markets.

There were two possible ways for merchants to deal with this situation. Since sons tended to be taken into family firms, it was possible to make *inter vivos* transfers of capital from parents to sons in the context of businesses. This was analogous to the practices of Massachusetts farmers during this period as described by Philip Greven in *Four Generations: Population, Land, and Family in Colonial Andover, Massachusetts.*[2] As Greven describes it, a farm would often be given by a parent to one of his sons during his lifetime in exchange for the son's labor and an agreement to care for the father in his old age. This helped prevent

1. It is difficult to understand the reasons for the adoption of partible inheritance by the Massachusetts Puritans. It may well have involved their hostility to commerce and, by extension, to inherited wealth. After all, if the ability to earn wealth was an evidence of God's grace, it seems sensible that the transference of that grace along with *inherited* wealth would have been something of a travesty. For an interesting discussion of points bearing on this, *vide* Bernard Bailyn, *The New England Merchants in the Seventeenth Century* (Cambridge, 1955).
2. Austin Wakeman Scott, *The Law of Trusts*, 4 vols. (Boston, 1939), 1.0,3.

the fragmentation of agricultural capital into portions so small that they could no longer sustain economical agriculture—as occurred in France during the eighteenth century. The use of such *inter vivos* transfers of property by merchants to their partner-sons had a similar intent—to circumvent the total partition of family-business capital at a merchant's death and facilitate a rudimentary form of transgenerational capital accumulation.

This arrangement, however, had serious shortcomings. In the first place, it was inherently unfair to children who were not their fathers' business partners, particularly daughters and sons who became partners in firms other than their fathers'. Secondly, a merchant could not afford to transfer too much of his capital during his own lifetime. For to do so would have diminished his control not only over his children, but over his business as well. And this would have violated the mandates of patriarchal family government by removing authority from the head of the family to one of its younger members.

There were other possibilities, however, both involving selective intermarriage. The first possibility was the marriage of first cousins. In order to understand the relevance of such kin-marriage to problems of capital accumulation it is necessary to set forth a model of partible testamentary division and the potential effects of cousin marriage within it. Visualize a family with four children, each of whom married non-kin spouses and each of whom had, at their father's death, two children. In such a situation, the possible divisions of the paternal estate would be four within the generation of the testator's children, and eight within the generation of his grandchildren. If two of the grandchildren—first cousins—married, the number of possible testamentary divisions would be reduced from eight to seven—since the shares of the two grandchildren would be recombined. If four grandchildren intermarried, combining first-cousin marriage with sibling exchange, the number of possible divisions of the grandparent's estate would be reduced from eight to six. To put it another way, rather than splitting the grandparental estate into eight portions—each representing 12.5 percent of the whole—a combined cousin-marriage-sibling exchange would reconcentrate four portions, representing 50 percent of the grandparental estate.

The second method of avoiding capital vitiation through kin-marriage would involve sibling exchanges with non-consanguineous families. Unlike cousin marriage, this kind of alliance would be more directed at *consolidating* and *combining* the fortunes of two unrelated families rather than merely recombining the divided capital of a single one. Visualize two families, each with four children, each child having produced two children at the deaths of their parents. The number of possible estate divisions would be eight in the first generation and sixteen in the second. However, if a sibling exchange took place, with two children from one family marrying two children in the other, the number of possible divisions would be reduced from eight to six within the first generation—double the reduction possible through first-cousin marriage. By the second generation, a sibling exchange would reduce possible divisions from sixteen to fourteen that would be possible with simple first-cousin marriage. Clearly, with partible testamentation, sibling exchange was a more advantageous form of marital exchange than cousin marriage. Not only did it present the possibility of combining two fortunes—one from each set of parents—but it also permitted capital concentration within a much shorter span of time than would be possible through cousin marriage.

If the hypothesis that marital selection served particular purposes of capital concentration is true, one should expect to find two prominent features in the marriages of the Massachusetts merchant families under study. First, kin-marriage, whether of the cousin or the sibling exchange type, should occur with greatest frequency during the periods preceding the introduction of formal credit organizations and corporate business —that is, the periods during which the family would have been the only means of capital concentration. Secondly, one should expect to find a greater incidence of sibling exchange than of first-cousin marriage. This would be so because of the greater capital concentration possible through sibling exchange than through first-cousin marriage.

Table 1 shows the proportion of eligible males and females per birth cohort in a selected group of merchants who married and the percentage of kin-marriage that took place (combining both cousin and sibling exchange). "Eligible" is defined for both men and women as having lived past the age of twenty-one, the age of legal capacity. While this somewhat arbitrary definition of eligibility may distort the figures to a certain extent, it is defensible on the grounds that twenty-one is, almost without exception, the minimum age at which marriage took place in these families regardless of sex and throughout the period 1680–1859.

Table 1, which shows the percentage of kin-marriage among the children of the eight merchant families, reveals three important features. First, kin-marriage occurs with considerable frequency for both males and females throughout the period under study. Second, it occurs with the greatest frequency during the periods in which the family merchant partnership was the primary form of business organization—that is, for the cohorts born before 1800. Third, there appears to be differential between male and female kin-marriage. It is most important for the males born between 1720 and 1799. It is most important for the females born between 1740 and 1819.

The first feature, involving the overall frequency of kin-marriage among the merchant families, cannot be intelligently discussed without examining the other points. For the fact that kin-marriage occurs with considerable frequency in these group means nothing in itself. A behavior

TABLE 1. Percentage of Eligible Males and Females Who Married and Kin Marriage in the Amory, Cabot, Codman, Higginson, Jackson, Lawrence, Lee, Lowell, and Peabody Families, 1680–1859, by Birth Cohort and Sex

MALES

Birth Cohort	N	% of Cohort Married	% Kin Marriage
1680–1699	4	100.0	25.0
1700–1719	11	91.1	30.0
1720–1739	11	70.3	44.5
1740–1759	22	80.2	66.6
1760–1779	31	77.5	40.0
1780–1799	43	67.4	41.4
1800–1819	83	63.5	32.1
1820–1839	110	68.2	26.0
1840–1859	136	67.7	20.6
N = 451			

FEMALES

Birth Cohort	N	% of Cohort Married	% Kin Marriage
1680–1699	3	100.0	——
1700–1719	13	92.3	41.7
1720–1739	11	91.1	20.0
1740–1759	13	53.9	38.4
1760–1779	25	72.0	33.3
1780–1799	40	67.5	33.3
1800–1819	67	68.7	41.3
1820–1839	81	77.8	23.8
1840–1859	112	52.7	21.0
N = 365			

Total Males + Females = 816

of a certain type can take place for a variety of reasons. Kin-marriage can serve different purposes at different points in time. In order to ascertain the function of kin-marriage at various times between 1680 and 1859, it is necessary to examine it in relation to other behaviors.

The most important assertion about kin-marriage to be proved is that it took place with greatest frequency during the period preceding the broad adoption of corporate enterprise and the creation of forms of testamentation which circumvented the partible division of capital. These two innovations are related. Corporate enterprise involves the separation of capital from immediate family concerns. A corporation must, since it deals in funds invested by non-family persons, operate with concerns that are not identical with those of merchant families. Unlike a partnership, in which the business capital is identical with the personal funds of the partners, corporate capital is legally distinct from the personal property of the investors. While investors own their shares in corporate enterprises, they cannot take money from corporate funds for personal or family purposes. Nor can a corporate enterprise be made to serve the social welfare purposes of a family business. Employment takes place according to criteria of competence, not according to criteria of consanguineal obligation. While it is true that the personal concerns of shareholders and administrators may affect employment practices to the extent of hiring personnel from their own families, consanguinity is really a subsidiary factor. For such an employee will only be kept on as long as he performs well.

Historically, the growth of importance of corporate enterprise is parallelled by the growth of testamentary trusts. This latter legal device permits a circumvention of strict partible inheritance while satisfying traditional mandates of sharing family fortunes. Essential to the idea of a trust is the division of ownership of property into two types, legal and equitable.[3] It is possible for these two types of ownership to exist simultaneously and for one person to hold the legal title and for another to hold the equitable title. In testamentation this means that a testator can leave the legal title of his estate to one person, a trustee, and the equitable title to his children. The holder of the legal title can exercise the rights of ownership over the property. He can buy and sell with it, bring suit on behalf of it, and do all the things that an individual can do with a piece of property. However, the equitable title represents a claim on the property by its possessors. It imposes on the holder of the legal title certain personal duties towards the holders of the equitable title. Usually these duties involve the distribution of the income of a piece of property among certain beneficiaries.

In terms of testamentation and capital accumulation, this trust arrangement means that it is possible for an estate to remain intact while the income resulting from it is distributed among a testator's heirs. The result is that capital remains undivided—and separated from the demands of heirs. And in the hands of the trustee it can be allocated into the economic system through investment in corporate enterprises. In terms of families, it means that marriage no longer necessarily serves a capital accumulation function.

Following the American Revolution, pressures were brought to bear on the merchant families to reconsider the close relation between family and business. Freed from the trading restrictions of British mercantilism,

3. Bernard Farber, *Guardians of Virtue, Salem Families in 1800* (New York, 1972), 124.

Massachusetts merchants were in a position to engage freely in global trade. To do so, however, required larger amounts of capital than could easily be raised through family means alone. Moreover, global trade greatly increased commercial risk and made insurance much more imperative. Insurance operations required pools of capital sufficient to reimburse merchants for large losses—and such capital pools could not exist as long as capital was too closely tied to family interests. Finally, global trade required expansion of the geographical scope of operations to the point that employees and partners would have to travel abroad and would, as a result, be out of the sphere of control of co-partners and family members. Not only did this increase the necessity for responsible commercial decisions on the part of individual businessmen, but it made businesses much more vulnerable to errors in judgment and irresponsibility by firm members. For increased responsibility, it became increasingly necessary to choose employees according to criteria of competence rather than according to the needs of family members for employment.

It was one thing to contemplate the necessity for separating family concerns from business activities and quite another thing to accomplish it. To do so required basic changes in family patterns—particularly in the occupational choices of sons. For if family were to be separated from business, it was necessary to concentrate the activities of family members in fields other than business. While it would obviously be necessary for a portion of family manpower to remain in business—in order to retain control over economic life in the society—it was no longer desirable for businesses to carry on an employment function for merchants' sons. If sons could be directed into non-business pursuits, it would be possible to separate business activities from the familial obligation to care for children. Moreover, if sons could be directed out of business, they would no longer need control of family capital. The capital could remain intact in trust devices which allocated it into business activities, while the personal needs of merchant children were attended to in their roles as trust beneficiaries.

If actions of the sort described above were taken, they should be clearly visible in the occupational choices of merchants' sons. Further, they should be identifiably the product of parental decisions. *Table 2* shows the occupational choices of sons in the eight merchant families by birth cohort of fathers.

Table 2 indicates a rather sudden change in occupational choices for sons of fathers born after 1740. The fact that the change is away from business into the professions suggests strongly that these choices were made by parents for their children. For professional education demands a financial commitment that exceeds the resources of sons alone and could only be made by willing fathers. In other words, it would appear that the merchants born after 1740 increasingly determined that not all their sons

TABLE 2. Occupational Choices of Sons of Fathers Born in Birth Cohorts 1680–1839, in the Amory, Cabot, Codman, Higginson, Jackson, Lawrence, Lee, Lowell, and Peabody Families

Birth Cohorts of Fathers	N	1680–99	1700–19	1720–39	1740–59	1760–79	1780–99	1800–19	1820–39
Business	221	91.7%	85.6%	83.3%	73.2%	54.9%	51.6%	40.5%	29.5%
Law	55	—	14.4%	8.3%	11.5%	9.8%	11.9%	12.8%	18.2%
Medicine	34	8.3%	—	—	1.4%	11.6%	6.3%	11.9%	8.0%
Clergy	10	—	—	—	3.8%	2.0%	1.1%	1.8%	4.5%
Arts	12	—	—	—	—	2.0%	4.3%	1.8%	6.8%
Engineering	6	—	—	—	—	3.9%	—	1.8%	2.3%
Education	10	—	—	—	—	—	—	1.8%	9.1%
Nothing	46	—	—	—	10.1%	7.8%	21.5%	22.9%	13.7%
Misc.	13	—	—	4.2%	—	—	1.1%	4.6%	6.8%
Unknown	8	—	—	4.2%	—	7.8%	2.2%	—	1.1%
Total %		100.0	100.0	100.0	100.0	100.0	100.0	100.0	100.0
N	436	12	7	24	52	51	93	109	88

would enter business—as had been the case in the past, when the percentage of sons entering business ranged between 91.7 to 83.3 percent.

The trend indicated in *Table 2* is supported by evidence on the involvement of members of the merchant families in the governance of Harvard College from 1780. In the course of the Revolution there was a takeover of the College's governing board by merchants—several of them from the families under study. This was followed by an alteration in the educational goals of the institution—particularly in the introduction of a medical course in 1782. Complementing the increasing role of Harvard as a credentials-granting institution for the professions was the development of charitable institutions funded with endowments given by merchants and staffed by the latter's sons. These institutions made it possible for merchants to ensure the status and economic security of their non-business sons and to carry on traditional mandates of kin-support. At the same time, such institutions had an economic function very similar to that of trusts. The institutions' endowments were invested and hence reallocated into the economic sector. At the same time, the income yielded by them benefited the children of the donors who served as staff.

If it is true that the merchants acted to disengage families from business in order to free capital for expanded economic activities by altering the occupational choices of their sons, they ought to have behaved in similar manner in regard to marital selection. For if the concentration of capital was to be increasingly achieved through formal organizations —through banks, trusts, insurance companies, and incorporated businesses—*inter vivos* transfers among kin-partners and selective inter-marriage would be no longer necessary. *Table 3* shows the association between occupational choice and kin-marriage for males born between 1680 and 1859.

Table 3 shows the association between the decline in the entrance of sons of the merchant families into business and the decline in kin-marriage by sons. From 1760 on, both show a steady decline, reflecting the apparent decisions made by merchant parents to separate family concerns from business concerns and to turn to the creation of formal organizations for capital accumulation and entrepreneurial activity.

The preceding discussion has skirted the fundamental question raised by Farber and others with regard to the purposes of kin-marriage. Was it, as Farber asserts, an attempt to build "a single dominating class" based on kinship and motivated by a generalized drive for power in merchant families? Or was it a much more specific and instrumental behavior, oriented to mercantile needs for capital accumulation? If Farber is correct, the pattern of selection in kin-marriage should be towards certain kinds of kin. As Farber writes in *Guardians of Virtue*,

> The high sex differentiation and strong sibling solidarity in the Hebraic social structure suggest that in Salem society, which followed the Hebraic model,

TABLE 3. Occupational Choice and Kin-Marriage Among Sons in the Amory, Cabot, Codman, Higginson, Jackson, Lawrence, Lee, Lowell, and Peabody Families, 1680–1859, by Birth Cohort of Sons

Birth Cohorts	% Sons in Business	% Sons Marrying Kin
1680–1699	100.0	25.0
1700–1719	66.6	30.0
1720–1739	100.0	44.5
1740–1759	90.1	66.6
1760–1779	81.2	40.0
1780–1799	69.1	41.4
1800–1819	57.5	32.1
1820–1839	54.2	26.0
1840–1859	40.0	20.6
N = 451		

> ties between same-sex siblings would be firmer than those for cross-sex siblings. Accordingly, we would anticipate that in the Salem of 1770–1820, first-cousin marriages would tend to occur more often with father's brother's daughter and with mother's sister's daughter than with children of cross-sex siblings. This strong sibling solidarity also suggests that a major way for exchange to occur between families would be for the two sets of siblings to intermarry with one another. In that manner, alliances could be maintained from one generation to the next with multiple family ties. Thus we would anticipate that not only would marriage between parallel cousins tend to occur, but also marriages denoting sibling exchange.[4]

And, as he continues,

> In relating first-cousin marriage to the social structure, it is important to note whether a man marries his cousin on his mother's side or his father's side. The uncle or aunt who provides him with a wife apparently maintains a close tie with his parents. In a society where male kinship ties are emphasized, if the children of two sisters marry, they are in effect tying together the previously unrelated families of the sisters' husbands. Such an arrangement would denote the creation of unstable alliances, which might not persist through future generations. On the other hand, if the children of two brothers married, the marriage would merely multiply previously existing male bonds to perpetuate and strengthen an existing alliance.[5]

Restated somewhat, different kinds of kin-marriage are conducive to different kinds of social integration. If the purpose of kin-marriage is to create a consanguineally cohesive *family* group, one would expect to find a predominance of marriages of sons to their fathers' brothers' daughters. Such marriages would tie together the children of two brothers, reinforcing the bond between the two male siblings. If the purpose of kin-marriage is to create a consanguineally cohesive *group of several families*, one

4. *Ibid.*, 125.
5. *Ibid.*, 128.

would expect to find a predominance of sons marrying their mothers' brothers' daughters. Such marriages would establish a system of exchange of women between several families which would be highly stable—for every woman ceded by one family in the group would be replaced by a woman from one of the other families in the group. On the other hand, if the purpose of kin-marriage is merely to promote short-term gains—such as capital concentration and partner reliability—one would expect to find first-cousin marriages of various types coexisting without any special emphasis on any type and a high incidence of sibling exchanges. The lack of systematic prescription in such kin-marriages would indicate that the goals of the families did not involve the creation of a kin-defined dominant group—but merely emphasized the more directly instrumental economic capital and manpower needs resulting from the nature of colonial testamentation and business practice.

Table 4 shows the distribution of types of kin-marriage for sons in the merchant families by year of marriage. In this tabulation, "other" denotes all kin-marriages other than sibling exchanges and those within the first degree of consanguinity.

Table 4 would seem to demonstrate that the most favored forms of kin-marriage were those that promoted short-term instrumental alliances—particularly those that provided the economic advantages of capital concentration without the creation of on-going kin-systems. For the period before 1820—which was the period before the broad adoption of corporate business and testamentary trustmaking in Massachusetts —the most consistently favored form of kin-marriage was sibling exchange. These amounted to 13 out of 31 kin-marriages, or 41.9 percent. In the same period, the next most favored form was marriage by sons to their

TABLE 4. Percentage of Types of Kin-Marriage Engaged in by Sons in the Amory, Cabot, Codman, Higginson, Jackson, Lawrence, Lee, Lowell, and Peabody Families, by Year of Marriage, 1700–1899

Year of Marriage	Types of Marriage						
	FaBroDa	MoBroDa	FaSiDa	MoSiDa	Sib-Ex	Other	N
1700–19	—	—	—	—	—	—	0
1720–39	—	—	—	—	100.0	—	1
1740–59	—	—	—	25.0	25.0	50.0	4
1760–79	—	18.2	9.1	9.1	18.2	45.5	11
1780–99	—	—	—	40.0	20.0	40.0	5
1800–19	—	10.1	—	—	70.0	20.0	10
1820–39	7.1	14.2	21.4	—	14.3	41.9	14
1840–59	8.3	—	24.9	—	16.7	50.1	12
1860–79	—	7.1	—	7.1	14.2	71.6	14
1880–99	—	8.3	—	—	16.7	75.0	12

N = 84

mother's sister's daughter. This type account for 4 of 31 kin-marriages, or 12.9 percent. Of the types of marriage that would tend to promote kin-cohesion of either the family or family-group type, only 3 out of 31, or 9.7 percent.

The data in *Table 4* seem to suggest that no effort was made to create the kind of kin-defined elite structures discussed by Farber in *Guardians of Virtue*—at least by the families in this study. Indeed, the only periods in which the types of kin-marriage which Farber considers most conducive to strong kinship structures (FaBroDa and MoBroDa) occur after kin-marriage has been reduced to a very small proportion of the total number of marriages entered into by the merchant families. To say that these data refute Farber would, however, be incorrect. For the two research populations were differently structured. Farber studied all kin-marriages taking place in Salem between 1770 and 1820 and broke them down by SES. In so doing, Farber made no judgments about the ultimate economic or social success of particular families engaging in kin-marriage. He merely studied the range of kin-marriages in high-SES families and concluded that they failed to make the kind of alliances which would have promoted a "single dominating class."

This study took a different approach. It was, at the outset, a study of the development of the Boston Brahmins—the elite which began to form at Boston after the Revolution and which persists to this day. It was thus necessarily a study of a select group—a study of winners, rather than a study of a general population. Fortunately, five of the eight families studied came from Salem and appear to have been included in Farber's study of that area. Thus it is possible to compare the importance of marital selection among the "winners" as against marital selection in the inclusive high-SES group of Salem studied by Farber. Such a comparison yields interesting conclusions about the formation of the Massachusetts mercantile-capitalist elite and the role of marital selection in that process.

Table 5 presents a comparison of Farber's figures on first-cousin marriage by SES in Salem between 1770 and 1820 with cousin marriage among the eight Boston "Brahmin" families during the same period—a period during which five of the eight were in Salem.

If one views the data in *Table 5* as presenting the relation between marital selection and ultimate economic success, one sees some rather interesting features. The "Boston Brahmin" category consists exclusively of families who experience ultimate and lasting economic success. The "Salem High SES" category is a mixed group, composed of some families who succeeded economically and became "Boston Brahmins" (such as the Cabots, Ropeses, Higginsons, and Crowninshields) and some who did not (the Sparhawks, Kings, and Pierces). The "Salem Middle SES" category consists of persons whose ultimate economic success or failure is unknown. It is assumed, however, that none joined the Brahmin group.

TABLE 5. Comparison of Types of First-Cousin Marriages in General Population of Salem, by SES During the Period 1770–1820, with Marriages in the Amory, Cabot, Codman, Higginson, Jackson, Lawrence, Lee, Lowell, and Peabody Families

Wife's Relation to Husband	Boston Brahmins	Salem High SES	Salem Middle SES
FaBroDa	0 (0%)	7 (28%)	9 (53%)
MoBroDa or FaSiDa	5 (71%)	8 (32%)	7 (41%)
MoSiDa	2 (29%)	10 (40%)	1 (6%)
Total	7 (100%)	25 (100%)	17 (100%)

This breakdown of first-cousin marriage would seem to explain why certain families were able to migrate from Salem to Boston and were able to make major alterations in their family lives and business activities during a fairly short period of time. The most successful group, the Boston Brahmins, were the least prone to FaBroDa marriages. Indeed, they did not practice them at all. This meant that when presented with the need for economic change after the Revolution, they were *most* able to make those changes since they were not tied into a closed system of kinship. The moderately successful group, the Salem High SES, engaged in FaBroDa marriages, but to a far less extent than the Salem Middle SES, the least successful group.

The reasons for the relative successfulness of these groups does not lie in the marriages themselves, but in the purposes for different types of marriages. The FaBroDa marriage is, as Farber states, the most suited to marginal activities— to mutual aid and support. However, while it helps economically marginal families to survive, it limits their ability to be mobile, for all human resources tend to be reconcentrated into the narrow family group. They tend, in sum, to limit their ability to make alliances with other families by which resources might be combined and expanded—rather than being merely reconcentrated.

The kinds of marriages involving the more successful groups tend to be more conducive to *alliances* rather than to mutual support. While it is true that the Boston group more closely resembles the Salem Middle SES group than the Salem High SES group during the 1770–1820 period, this can probably be accounted for by the fact that Farber mixes his MoBroDa and FaSiDa marriages into a single category. If broken down, the Middle SES group would probably consist primarily of FaSiDa marriages—another form of closed-kin consolidation in which the husband and wife share all four grandparents (a double first-cousin marriage). In the Boston group, however, the MoBroDa-FaSiDa category of cousin marriages consists almost entirely of MoBroDa marriages, the type most conducive to groupings of several families into cohesive groups. The Salem High SES group would probably contain both types.

Finally, the type of first-cousin marriage most conducive to generalized alliances is the MoSiDa type, which links two unrelated husbands. This type is least suited to mutual support, but most suited to generalized alliances and to capital combination. Not surprisingly, it occurs least among the Middle SES group. The results for the High SES and Boston Brahmin group are ambiguous. However, *Table 4* shows that marriages of this type took place among the Boston group *before* the 1770–1820 period and that, in fact, MoSiDa marriages are the most common type of first-cousin marriage engaged in by the Boston group. This implies that if one expanded the temporal scope of Farber's study, one would find a simple progression in which the Boston group would have most MoSiDa marriages, the High SES the next most frequent, and the Middle SES, the least frequent.

These patterns of marital selection take on great importance when one seeks to understand the composition of the Boston elite—particularly in clarifying why some families were able to effect major alterations in their businesses and families, separating them in order to free capital for corporate investment and large-scale capital pooling. For those families who were most dependent on mutual support through kinship and who concentrated their resources through FaBroDa and FaSiDa marriages, would be least able to respond to the economic challenges presented by the post-Revolutionary era. Even if they had not been poor families to begin with, they would have been limited in their ability to grow and become socially and economically mobile because the types of kin-marriage in which they engaged precluded the making of alliances and involved too great a dependence on the reconcentration of family resources. The families who were least dependent on mutual support and most dependent on alliances would be in the best position to face the new economic problems. Because they emphasized short-term and instrumental marital selection—sibling exchanges and MoSiDa first-cousin marriages—they would have a number of important advantages. First, the short-term qualities of their alliances would give them maximum flexibility in the face of challenges. Because the bond of sentiment between two unrelated husbands (MoSiDa) is weaker, it can be broken more easily and with less serious consequences than other bonds. Secondly, the concentration of the more successful groups on sibling exchange would have created a larger concentration of capital in their hands than in the hands of those who had depended primarily on first-cousin bonds. For sibling exchange emphasized capital *combination* rather than mere reconcentration. In sum, the group most likely to make the most successful transition into the post-Revolutionary world was the group whose criteria for marital selection were the least particularistic. The Middle SES group tended to emphasize and depend on particularistic bonds between same sex siblings and to exploit them for mutual support. The high SES and Boston Brahmin groups tended to emphasize more universalistic criteria in regard to mate selection. They married along lines of economic and political advantage rather than placing a value on consanguinity *per se*. As a result, when economic challenges presented themselves that required abandonment of the traditional family-business nexus, these families were in a far better position to do so than other groups.

This approach would appear to explain the patterns of marital selection shown in *Table 1*—involving both the overall decline kin-marriage and its continuance at a fairly low level to the end of the nineteenth century. For even after the adoption of corporate business and testamentary trustmaking, alliances continued to be important insofar as the elite structure necessarily limited the pool of potential marriage partners. In addition, there were still economic advantages to kin-marriage. Even though testamentary trusts tended to keep family capital intact, the combined incomes of two testamentary trusts were greater than one. Moreover, the adoption of the Rule Against Perpetuities by the Massachusetts courts in the 1830s meant that such concentrated capital would be ultimately distributed among residuary legatees and remaindermen.[6] And it was unquestionably advantageous for these ultimate recipients of their forebears' thrift and luck to become allied. Nonetheless, while such alliances were economically sensible, alliances with other non-related wealthy merchant families in Boston were equally or more sensible. So while kin-marriage was still an option which made economic sense, it was an option increasingly less taken.

In conclusion, both marital selection and occupational choice were part of a powerful and compelling social alteration in which dominance in society and in the economy is contingent on the adoption of increasingly universalistic criteria for functioning. Those who are able to adopt those criteria are the most able to survive and continue their dominance. Those who are not are left behind in the Salems, Newburyports, and other minor ports—reminding one of Hawthorne's description of Salem in the middle nineteenth century:

> The pavement round about the above-described edifice—which we may as well name at once as the Custom House of the port—has grass enough growing in its chinks to show that it has not, of late days, been worn by any multitudinous resort of business. In some months of the year, however, there often chances a forenoon when affairs move onward with a livelier tread. Such occasions might remind the elderly citizen of that period before the last war with England, when Salem was a port by itself; not scorned, as she is now, by her own merchants and shipowners, who permit her wharves to crumble to ruin, while their ventures go to swell, needlessly and imperceptibly, the mighty flood of commerce at New York or Boston. . . .[7]

6. *15 Pickering's Reports* 104 (1833).
7. Nathaniel Hawthorne, *The Scarlet Letter* (New York, 1955), 3–4.

ROLE
DISTRIBUTION

Just as the choice of marital partners is a link between the kinship system and other aspects of social structure, differentiation of roles and distribution of authority within the family are articulated with the values of the society, its system of stratification, and its economy. Parsons discusses the integration with the occupational structure of familial roles based on sex and age, and the conflicts to which those roles are subjected.

In examining universal and variable aspects of the distribution of roles within the family, Morris Zelditch posits a universal basis for role differentiation between the parental figures. He finds that the father's role in most societies—especially in the patrilineal kinship system—is primarily *instrumental,* i.e., serves to adapt the family to the outside system, while the mother's is primarily expressive, i.e., serves to maintain the internal system.

If Zelditch should be right in his empirical generalization, it does not follow that such role distribution must be eternal. After all, many features of modern Western society are first-time occurrences—such as work away from home, a high level of literacy and mass education, not to speak of the latest technical advances. Philip Slater challenges the point of view that role differentiation between marital partners along an *instrumental-expressive* axis is a universal phenomenon, holding that such conceptualization is not applicable to modern society. He argues that in a society characterized by a high rate of mobility, a rigid role differentiation would in fact prevent rather than facilitate adequate personality molding of the young. And according to Judith Blake, the holding on to the traditional procreative function of the family, with the traditional prescription for the role of mother that this implies, is contrary to the present-day view that population ought to be drastically controlled for the sake of survival of future generations.

The next four papers examine differences in role distribution in modern society. Elizabeth Bott's findings indicate that where interaction with neighbors and extended kin is frequent, roles are more sharply segregated than in families that have only ephemeral relationships with neighbors and kin. While she does not claim that the differences she describes coincide with differences in social class, subsequent research has shown that, especially in this country, there is more role segregation and at the same time closer interaction with neighbors in the lower and in the working classes than in the middle and upper classes. Melvin Kohn shows that such differences are accompanied by different values governing the socialization of children. And the last paper, by the editor, calls attention to different types of authority—that is, different expectations of conformity which the parental figures held for their children in the past—and to the changes in differential expectations in the present. All these changes point in the direction of de-differentiation of roles in the present-day middle-class family, about which more will be said in the last part of this book.

5 FAMILY STRUCTURE IN THE MODERN UNITED STATES

Talcott Parsons

Age and Sex in the Social Structure

In our society age grading does not to any great extent, except for the educational system, involve formal age categorization, but is interwoven with other structural elements. In relation to these, however, it constitutes an important connecting link and organizing point of reference in many respects. The most important of these for present purposes are kinship structure, formal education, occupation and community participation. In most cases the age lines are not rigidly specific, but approximate; this does not, however, necessarily lessen their structural significance.[1]

In all societies the initial status of every normal individual is that of child in a given kinship unit. In our society, however, this universal

---

1. The problem of organization of this material for systematic presentation is, in view of this fact, particularly difficult. It would be possible to discuss the subject in terms of the above four principal structures with which age and sex are most closely interwoven, but there are serious disadvantages involved in this procedure. Age and sex categories constitute one of the main links of structural continuity in terms of which structures which are differentiated in other respects are articulated with each other; and in isolating the treatment of these categories there is danger that this extremely important aspect of the problem will be lost sight of. The least objectionable method, at least within the limits of space of such a paper, seems to be to follow the sequence of the life cycle.

starting point is used in distinctive ways. Although in early childhood the sexes are not usually sharply differentiated, in many kinship systems a relatively sharp segregation of children begins very early. Our own society is conspicuous for the extent to which children of both sexes are in many fundamental respects treated alike. This is particularly true of both privileges and responsibilities. The primary distinctions within the group of dependent siblings are those of age. Birth order as such is notably neglected as a basis of discrimination; a child of eight and a child of five have essentially the privileges and responsibilities appropriate to their respective age levels without regard to what older, intermediate, or younger siblings there may be. The preferential treatment of an older child is not to any significant extent differentiated if and because he happens to be the first born.

There are, of course, important sex differences in dress and in approved play interest and the like, but if anything, it may be surmised that in the urban upper middle classes these are tending to diminish. Thus, for instance, play overalls are essentially similar for both sexes. What is perhaps the most important sex discrimination is more than anything else a reflection of the differentiation of adult sex roles. It seems to be a definite fact that girls are more apt to be relatively docile, to conform in general according to adult expectations, to be "good," whereas boys are more apt to be recalcitrant to discipline and defiant of adult authority and expectations. There is really no feminine equivalent of the expression "bad boy." It may be suggested that this is at least partially explained by the fact that it is possible from an early age to initiate girls directly into many important aspects of the adult feminine role. Their mothers are continually about the house and the meaning of many of the things they are doing is relatively tangible and easily understandable to a child. It is also possible for the daughter to participate actively and usefully in many of these activities. Especially in the urban middle classes, however, the father does not work in the home and his son is not able to observe his work or to participate in it from an early age. Furthermore many of the masculine functions are of a relatively abstract and intangible character, such that their meaning must remain almost wholly inaccessible to a child. This leaves the boy without a tangible meaningful model to emulate and without the possibility of a gradual initiation into the activities of the adult male role. An important verification of this analysis could be provided through the study in our own society of the rural situation. It is my impression that farm boys tend to be "good" in a sense in which that is not typical of their urban brothers.

The equality of privileges and responsibilities, graded only by age but not by birth order, is extended to a certain degree throughout the whole range of the life cycle. In full adult status, however, it is seriously modified by the asymmetrical relation of the sexes to the occupational structure. One of the most conspicuous expressions and symbols of the underlying equality, however, is the lack of sex differentiation in the process of formal education, so far, at least, as it is not explicitly vocational. Up through college differentiation seems to be primarily a matter on the one hand of individual ability, on the other hand of class status, and only to a secondary degree of sex differentiation. One can certainly speak of a strongly established pattern that all children of the family have a "right" to a good education, rights which are graduated according to the class status of the family but also to individual ability. It is only in post-graduate professional education, with its direct connection with future occupational careers, that sex discrimination becomes conspicuous. It is particularly important that this equality of treatment exists in the sphere of liberal education since throughout the social structure of our society there is a strong tendency to segregate the occupational sphere from one in which certain more generally human patterns and values are dominant, particularly in informal social life and the realm of what will here be called community participation.

Although this pattern of equality of treatment is present in certain fundamental respects at all age levels, at the transition from childhood to adolescence new features appear which disturb the symmetry of sex roles while still a second set of factors appears with marriage and the acquisition of full adult status and responsibilities.

An indication of the change is the practice of chaperonage, through which girls are given a kind of protection and supervision by adults to which boys of the same age group are not subjected. Boys, that is, are chaperoned only in their relations with girls of their own class. This modification of equality of treatment has been extended to the control of the private lives of women students in boarding schools and colleges. Of undoubted significance is the fact that it has been rapidly declining not only in actual effectiveness but as an ideal pattern. Its prominence in our recent past, however, is an important manifestation of the importance of sex role differentiation. Important light might be thrown upon its functions by systematic comparison with the related phenomena in Latin countries where this type of asymmetry has been far more sharply accentuated than in this country in the more modern period.

It is at the point of emergence into adolescence that there first begins to develop a set of patterns and behavior phenomena which involve a highly complex combination of age grading and sex role elements. These may be referred to together as the phenomena of the "youth culture." Certain of its elements are present in pre-adolescence and others in the adult culture. But the peculiar combination in connection with this particular age level is unique and highly distinctive for American society.

Perhaps the best single point of reference for characterizing the youth culture lies in its contrast with the dominant pattern of the adult male role. By contrast with the emphasis on responsibility in this role, the orientation of the youth culture is more or less specifically irresponsible. One of its dominant notes is "having a good time" in relation to which there is a particularly strong emphasis on social activities in company with the opposite sex. A second predominant characteristic on the male side lies in the prominence of athletics, which is an avenue of achievement and competition which stands in sharp contrast to the primary standards of adult achievement in professional and executive capacities. Negatively, there is a strong tendency to repudiate interest in adult things and to feel at least a certain recalcitrance to the pressure of adult expectations and discipline. In addition to, but including, athletic prowess the typical pattern of the male youth culture seems to lay emphasis on the value of certain qualities of attractiveness, especially in relation to the opposite sex. It is very definitely a rounded humanistic pattern rather than one of competence in the performance of specified functions. Such stereotypes as the "swell guy" are significant of this. On the feminine side there is correspondingly a strong tendency to accentuate sexual attractiveness in terms of various versions of what may be called the "glamor girl" pattern.[2] Although these patterns defining roles tend to polarize sexually—for instance, as between star athlete and socially popular girl—yet on a certain level they are complementary, both emphasizing certain features of a total personality in terms of the direct expression of certain values rather than of instrumental significance.

One further feature of this situation is the extent to which it is crystallized about the system of formal education.[3] One might say that

2. Perhaps the most dramatic manifestation of this tendency lies in the prominence of the patterns of "dating," for instance among college women. As shown by an unpublished participant-observer study made at one of the Eastern Women's colleges, perhaps the most important single basis of informal prestige rating among the residents of a dormitory lies in their relative dating success—though this is by no means the only basis. One of the most striking features of the pattern is the high publicity given to the "achievements" of the individual in a sphere where traditionally in the culture a rather high level of privacy is sanctioned—it is interesting that once an engagement has occurred a far greater amount of privacy is granted. The standards of rating cannot be said to be well integrated, though there is an underlying consistency in that being in demand by what the group regards as desirable men is perhaps the main standard.

It is true that the "dating" complex need not be exclusively bound up with the "glamor girl" stereotype of ideal feminine personality—the "good companion" type may also have a place. Precisely, however, where the competitive aspect of dating is most prominent the glamor pattern seems heavily to predominate, as does, on the masculine side, a somewhat comparable glamorous type. On each side at the same time there is room for considerable difference as to just where the emphasis is placed—for example as between "voluptuous" sexuality and more decorous "charm."

3. A central aspect of this focus of crystallization lies in the element of tension, sometimes a direct conflict, between the youth culture patterns of college and school life, and the "serious" interests in and obligations toward curricular work. It is of course the latter which defines some at least of the most important foci of adult expectations of doing "good" work and justifying the privileges granted. It is not possible here to attempt to analyze the interesting, ambivalent attitudes of youth toward curricular work and achievement.

the principal centers of prestige dissemination are the colleges, but that many of the most distinctive phenomena are to be found in high schools throughout the country. It is of course of great importance that liberal education is not primarily a matter of vocational training in the United States. The individual status on the curricular side of formal education is, however, in fundamental ways linked up with adult expectations, and doing "good work" is one of the most important sources of parental approval. Because of secondary institutionalization this approval is extended into various spheres distinctive of the youth culture. But it is notable that the youth culture has a strong tendency to develop in directions which are either on the borderline of parental approval or beyond the pale, in such matters as sex behavior, drinking and various forms of frivolous and irresponsible behavior. The fact that adults have attitudes to these things which are often deeply ambivalent and that on such occasions as college reunions they may outdo the younger generation, as, for instance, in drinking, is of great significance, but probably structurally secondary to the youth-versus-adult differential aspect. Thus the youth culture is not only, as is true of the curricular aspect of formal education, a matter of age status as such but also shows strong signs of being a product of tensions in the relationship of younger people and adults.

From the point of view of age grading perhaps the most notable fact about this situation is the existence of definite pattern distinctions from the periods coming both before and after. At the line between childhood and adolescence "growing up" consists precisely in ability to participate in youth culture patterns, which are not for either sex, the same as the adult patterns practiced by the parental generation. In both sexes the transition to full adulthood means loss of a certain "glamorous" element. From being the athletic hero or the lion of college dances, the young man becomes a prosaic business executive or lawyer. The more successful adults participate in an important order of prestige symbols but these are of a very different order from those of the youth culture. The contrast in the case of the feminine role is perhaps equally sharp, with at least a strong tendency to take on a "domestic" pattern with marriage and the arrival of young children.

The symmetry in this respect must, however, not be exaggerated. It is of fundamental significance to the sex role structure of the adult age levels that the normal man has a "job" which is fundamental to his social status in general. It is perhaps not too much to say that only in very exceptional cases can an adult man be genuinely self-respecting and enjoy a respected status in the eyes of others if he does not "earn a living" in an approved occupational role. Not only is this a matter of his own economic support but, generally speaking, his occupational status is the primary source of the income and class status of his wife and children.

In the case of the feminine role the situation is radically different. The majority of married women, of course, are not employed, but even of those that are a very large proportion do not have jobs which are in basic competition for status with those of their husbands.[4] The majority of "career" women whose occupational status is comparable with that of men in their own class, at least in the upper middle and upper classes, are unmarried, and in the small proportion of cases where they are married the result is a profound alteration in family structure.

This pattern, which is central to the urban middle classes, should not be misunderstood. In rural society, for instance, the operation of the farm and the attendant status in the community may be said to be a matter of the joint status of both parties to a marriage. Whereas a farm is operated by a family, an urban job is held by an individual and does not involve other members of the family in a comparable sense. One convenient expression of the difference lies in the question of what would happen in case of death. In the case of a farm it would at least be not at all unusual for the widow to continue operating the farm with the help of a son or even of hired men. In the urban situation the widow would cease to have any connection with the organization which had employed her husband and he would be replaced by another man without reference to family affiliations.

In this urban situation the primary status-carrying role is in a sense that of housewife. The woman's fundamental status is that of her husband's wife, the mother of his children, and traditionally the person responsible for a complex of activities in connection with the management of the household, care of children, etc.

For the structuring of sex roles in the adult phase the most fundamental considerations seem to be those involved in the interrelations of the occupational system and the conjugal family. In a certain sense the most fundamental basis of the family's status is the occupational status of the husband and father. As has been pointed out, this is a status occupied by an individual by virtue of his individual qualities and achievements. But both directly and indirectly, more than any other single factor, it determines the status of the family in the social structure, directly because of the symbolic significance of the office or occupation as a symbol of prestige, indirectly because as the principal source of family income it determines the standard of living of the family. From one point

4. The above statement, even more than most in the present paper, needs to be qualified in relation to the problem of class. It is above all to the upper middle class that it applies. Here probably the great majority of "working wives" are engaged in some form of secretarial work which would, on an independent basis, generally be classed as a lower middle class occupation. The situation at lower levels of the class structure is quite different since the prestige of the jobs of husband and wife is then much more likely to be nearly equivalent. It is quite possible that this fact is closely related to the relative instability of marriage which Davis and Gardner (*Deep South*) find, at least for the community they studied, to be typical of lower class groups. The relation is one which deserves careful study.

of view the emergence of occupational status into this primary position can be regarded as the principal source of strain in the sex role structure of our society since it deprives the wife of her role as a partner in a common enterprise. The common enterprise is reduced to the life of the family itself and to the informal social activities in which husband and wife participate together. This leaves the wife a set of utilitarian functions in the management of the household which may be considered a kind of "pseudo-" occupation. Since the present interest is primarily in the middle classes, the relatively unstable character of the role of housewife as the principal content of the feminine role is strongly illustrated by the tendency to employ domestic servants wherever financially possible. It is true that there is an American tendency to accept tasks of drudgery with relative willingness, but it is notable that in middle class families there tends to be a dissociation of the essential personality from the perform-ance of these tasks. Thus, advertising continually appeals to such desires as to have hands which one could never tell had washed dishes or scrubbed floors.[5] Organization about the function of housewife, however, with the addition of strong affectional devotion to husband and children, is the primary focus of one of the principal patterns governing the adult feminine role—what may be called the "domestic" pattern. It is, how-ever, a conspicuous fact, that strict adherence to this pattern has become progressively less common and has a strong tendency to a residual status—that is, to be followed most closely by those who are unsuccessful in competition for prestige in other directions.

It is, of course, possible for the adult woman to follow the masculine pattern and seek a career in fields of occupational achievement in direct competition with men of her own class. It is, however, notable that in spite of the very great progress of the emancipation of women from the traditional domestic pattern only a very small fraction have gone very far in this direction. It is also clear that its generalization would only be possible with profound alterations in the structure of the family.

Hence it seems that concomitant with the alteration in the basic masculine role in the direction of occupation there have appeared two important tendencies in the feminine role which are alternative to that of simple domesticity on the one hand, and to a full-fledged career on the other. In the older situation there tended to be a very rigid distinction between respectable married women and those who were "no better than they should be." The rigidity of this line has progressively broken down through the infiltration into the respectable sphere of elements of what may be called again the glamor pattern, with the emphasis on a specifi-

5. This type of advertising appeal undoubtedly contains an element of "snob appeal" in the sense of an invitation to the individual by her appearance and ways to identify herself with a higher social class than that of her actual status. But it is almost certainly not wholly explained by this element. A glamorously feminine appearance which is specifically dissociated from physical work is undoubtedly a genuine part of an authentic personality ideal of the middle class, and not only evidence of a desire to belong to the upper class.

cally feminine form of attractiveness which on occasion involves directly sexual patterns of appeal. One important expression of this trend lies in the fact that many of the symbols of feminine attractiveness have been taken over directly from the practices of social types previously beyond the pale of respectable society. This would seem to be substantially true of the practice of women smoking and of at least the modern version of cosmetics. The same would seem to be true of many of the modern versions of women's dress. "Emancipation" in this connection means primarily emancipation from traditional and conventional restrictions on the free expression of sexual attraction and impulses, but in a direction which tends to segregate the element of sexual interest and attraction from the total personality and in so doing tends to emphasize the segregation of sex roles. It is particularly notable that there has been no corresponding tendency to emphasize masculine attraction in terms of dress and other such aids. One might perhaps say that in a situation which strongly inhibits competition between the sexes on the same plane the feminine glamor pattern has appeared as an offset to masculine occupational status and to its attendant symbols of prestige. It is perhaps significant that there is a common stereotype of the association of physically beautiful, expensively and elaborately dressed women with physically unattractive but rich and powerful men.

The other principal direction of emancipation from domesticity seems to lie in emphasis on what has been called the common humanistic element. This takes a wide variety of forms. One of them lies in a relatively mature appreciation and systematic cultivation of cultural interests and educated tastes, extending all the way from the intellectual sphere to matters of art, music and house furnishings. A second consists in cultivation of serious interests and humanitarian obligations in community welfare situations and the like. It is understandable that many of these orientations are most conspicuous in fields where through some kind of tradition there is an element of particular suitability for feminine participation. Thus, a woman who takes obligations to social welfare particularly seriously will find opportunities in various forms of activity which traditionally tie up with women's relation to children, to sickness and so on. But this may be regarded as secondary to the underlying orientation which would seek an outlet in work useful to the community following the most favorable opportunities which happen to be available.

This pattern, which with reference to the character of relationship to men may be called that of the "good companion," is distinguished from the others in that it lays far less stress on the exploitation of sex role as such and more on that which is essentially common to both sexes. There are reasons, however, why cultural interests, interest in social welfare and community activities are particularly prominent in the activities of women in our urban communities. On the one side the masculine occupational role tends to absorb a very large proportion of the man's time and energy and to leave him relatively little for other interests. Furthermore, unless his position is such as to make him particularly prominent his primary orientation is to those elements of the social structure which divide the community into occupational groups rather than those which unite it in common interests and activities. The utilitarian aspect of the role of housewife, on the other hand, has declined in importance to the point where it scarcely approaches a full-time occupation for a vigorous person. Hence the resort to other interests to fill up the gap. In addition, women, being more closely tied to the local residential community are more apt to be involved in matters of common concern to the members of that community. This peculiar role of women becomes particularly conspicuous in middle age. The younger married woman is apt to be relatively highly absorbed in the care of young children. With their growing up, however, her absorption in the household is greatly lessened, often just at the time when the husband is approaching the apex of his career and is most heavily involved in its obligations. Since to a high degree this humanistic aspect of the feminine role is only partially institutionalized it is not surprising that its patterns often bear the marks of strain and insecurity, as perhaps has been classically depicted by Helen Hokinson's cartoons of women's clubs.

The adult roles of both sexes involve important elements of strain which are involved in certain dynamic relationships, especially to the youth culture. In the case of the feminine role marriage is the single event toward which a selective process, in which personal qualities and effort can play a decisive role, has pointed up. That determines a woman's fundamental status, and after that her role patterning is not so much status determining as a matter of living up to expectations and finding satisfying interests and activities. In a society where such strong emphasis is placed upon individual achievement it is not surprising that there should be a certain romantic nostalgia for the time when the fundamental choices were still open. This element of strain is added to by the lack of clear-cut definition of the adult feminine role. Once the possibility of a career has been eliminated there still tends to be a rather unstable oscillation between emphasis in the direction of domesticity or glamor or good companionship. According to situational pressures and individual character the tendency will be to emphasize one or another of these more strongly. But it is a situation likely to produce a rather high level of insecurity. In this state the pattern of domesticity must be ranked lowest in terms of prestige but also, because of the strong emphasis in community sentiment on the virtues of fidelity and devotion to husband and children, it offers perhaps the highest level of a certain kind of security. It is no wonder that such an important symbol as Whistler's mother concentrates primarily on this pattern.

The glamor pattern has certain obvious attractions since to the woman who is excluded from the struggle for power and prestige in the occupational sphere it is the most direct path to a sense of superiority and importance. It has, however, two obvious limitations. In the first place, many of its manifestations encounter the resistance of patterns of moral conduct and engender conflicts not only with community opinion but also with the individual's own moral standards. In the second place, it is a pattern the highest manifestations of which are inevitably associated with a rather early age level—in fact, overwhelmingly with the courtship period. Hence, if strongly entered upon serious strains result from the problem of adaptation to increasing age.

The one pattern which would seem to offer the greatest possibilities for able, intelligent, and emotionally mature women is the third—the good companion pattern. This, however, suffers from a lack of fully institutionalized status and from the multiplicity of choices of channels of expression. It is only those with the strongest initiative and intelligence who achieve fully satisfactory adaptations in this direction. It is quite clear that in the adult feminine role there is quite sufficient strain and insecurity so that wide-spread manifestations are to be expected in the form of neurotic behavior.

The masculine role at the same time is itself by no means devoid of corresponding elements of strain. It carries with it to be sure the primary prestige of achievement, responsibility and authority. By comparison with the role of the youth culture, however, there are at least two important types of limitations. In the first place, the modern occupational system has led to increasing specialization of role. The job absorbs an extraordinarily large proportion of the individual's energy and emotional interests in a role the content of which is often relatively narrow. This in particular restricts the area within which he can share common interests and experiences with others not in the same occupational specialty. It is perhaps of considerable significance that so many of the highest prestige statuses of our society are of this specialized character. There is in the definition of roles little to bind the individual to others in his community on a comparable status level. By contrast with this situation, it is notable that in the youth culture common human elements are far more strongly emphasized. Leadership and eminence are more in the role of total individuals and less of competent specialists. This perhaps has something to do with the significant tendency in our society for all age levels to idealize youth and for the older age groups to attempt to imitate the patterns of youth behavior.

It is perhaps as one phase of this situation that the relation of the adult man to persons of the opposite sex should be treated. The effect of the specialization of occupational role is to narrow the range in which the sharing of common human interests can play a large part. In relation to his wife the tendency of this narrowness would seem to be to encourage on her part either the domestic or the glamorous role, or community participation somewhat unrelated to the marriage relationship. This relationship between sex roles presumably introduces a certain amount of strain into the marriage relationship itself since this is of such overwhelming importance to the family and hence to a woman's status and yet so relatively difficult to maintain on a level of human companionship. Outside the marriage relationship, however, there seems to be a notable inhibition against easy social intercourse, particularly in mixed company.[6] The man's close personal intimacy with other women is checked by the danger of the situation being defined as one of rivalry with the wife, and easy friendship without sexual-emotional involvement seems to be inhibited by the specialization of interests in the occupational sphere. It is notable that brilliance of conversation of the "salon" type seems to be associated with aristocratic society and is not prominent in ours.

Along with all this goes a certain tendency for middle-aged men, as symbolized by the "bald-headed row," to be interested in the physical aspect of sex—that is, in women precisely as dissociated from those personal considerations which are important to relationships of companionship or friendship, to say nothing of marriage. In so far as it does not take this physical form, however, there seems to be a strong tendency for middle-aged men to idealize youth patterns—that is, to think of the ideal inter-sex friendship as that of their pre-marital period.[7]

In so far as the idealization of the youth culture by adults is an expression of elements of strain and insecurity in the adult roles it would be expected that the patterns thus idealized would contain an element of romantic unrealism. The patterns of youthful behavior thus idealized are not those of actual youth so much as those which older people wish their own youth might have been. This romantic element seems to coalesce with a similar element derived from certain strains in the situation of young people themselves.

The period of youth in our society is one of considerable strain and insecurity. Above all, it means turning one's back on the security both of status and of emotional attachment which is engaged in the family of orientation. It is structurally essential to transfer one's primary emotional attachment to a marriage partner who is entirely unrelated to the previous family situation. In a system of free marriage choice this applies to women as well as men. For the man there is in addition the necessity to face the hazards of occupational competition in the determination of a career. There is reason to believe that the youth culture has important positive functions in easing the transition from the security of childhood

6. In the informal social life of academic circles with which the writer is familiar there seems to be a strong tendency in mixed gatherings—as after dinner—for the sexes to segregate. In such groups the men are apt to talk either shop subjects or politics whereas the women are apt to talk about domestic affairs, schools, their children, etc., or personalities. It is perhaps on personalities that mixed conversation is apt to flow most freely.

7. This, to be sure, often contains an element of romantization. It is more nearly what he wishes these relations had been than what they actually were.

in the family of orientation to that of full adult in marriage and occupational status. But precisely because the transition is a period of strain it is to be expected that it involves elements of unrealistic romanticism. Thus significant features in the status of youth patterns in our society would seem to derive from the coincidence of the emotional needs of adolescents with those derived from the strains of the situation of adults.

A tendency to the romantic idealization of youth patterns seems in different ways to be characteristic of modern western society as a whole.[8] It is not possible in the present context to enter into any extended comparative analysis, but it may be illuminating to call attention to a striking difference between the patterns associated with this phenomenon in Germany and in the United States. The German "youth movement," starting before the first World War, has occasioned a great deal of comment and has in various respects been treated as the most notable instance of the revolt of youth. It is generally believed that the youth movement has an important relation to the background of National Socialism, and this fact as much as any suggests the important difference. While in Germany as everywhere there has been a generalized revolt against convention and restrictions on individual freedom as embodied in the traditional adult culture, in Germany particular emphasis has appeared on the community of male youth. "Comradeship" in a sense which strongly suggests that of soldiers in the field has from the beginning been strongly emphasized as the ideal social relationship. By contrast with this, in the American youth culture and its adult romantization a much stronger emphasis has been placed on the cross-sex relationship. It would seem that this fact, with the structural factors which underlie it, have much to do with the failure of the youth culture to develop any considerable political significance in this country. Its predominant pattern has been that of the idealization of the isolated couple in romantic love. There have, to be sure, been certain tendencies among radical youth to a political orientation but in this case there has been a notable absence of emphasis on the solidarity of the members of one sex. The tendency has been rather to ignore the relevance of sex difference in the interest of common ideals.

The importance of youth patterns in contemporary American culture throws into particularly strong relief the status in our social structure of the most advanced age groups. By comparison with other societies the United States assumes an extreme position in the isolation of old age from participation in the most important social structures and interests. Structurally speaking, there seem to be two primary bases of this situation. In the first place, the most important single distinctive feature of our family structure is the isolation of the individual conjugal family. It is impossible to say that with us it is "natural" for any other group than husband and

8. *Cf.* E. Y. Hartshorne, "German Youth and the Nazi Dream of Victory," *America in a World at War, Pamphlet,* No. 12, New York, 1941.

wife and their dependent children to maintain a common household. Hence, when the children of a couple have become independent through marriage and occupational status the parental couple is left without attachment to any continuous kinship group. It is, of course, common for other relatives to share a household with the conjugal family but this scarcely ever occurs without some important elements of strain. For independence is certainly the preferred pattern for an elderly couple, particularly from the point of view of the children.

The second basis of the situation lies in the occupational structure. In such fields as farming and the maintenance of small independent enterprises there is frequently no such thing as abrupt "retirement," rather a gradual relinquishment of the main responsibilities and functions with advancing age. So far, however, as an individual's occupational status centers in a specific "job," he either holds the job or does not, and the tendency is to maintain the full level of functions up to a given point and then abruptly to retire. In view of the very great significance of occupational status and its psychological correlates, retirement leaves the older man in a peculiarly functionless situation, cut off from participation in the most important interests and activities of the society. There is a further important aspect of this situation. Not only status in the community but actual place of residence is to a very high degree a function of the specific job held. Retirement not only cuts the ties to the job itself but also greatly loosens those to the community of residence. Perhaps in no other society is there observable a phenomenon corresponding to the accumulation of retired elderly people in such areas as Florida and Southern California in the winter. It may be surmised that this structural isolation from kinship, occupational, and community ties is the fundamental basis of the recent political agitation for help to the old. It is suggested that it is far less the financial hardship[9] of the position of elderly people than their social isolation which makes old age a "problem." As in other connections we are here very prone to rationalize generalized insecurity in financial and economic terms. The problem is obviously of particularly great significance in view of the changing age distribution of the population with the prospect of a far greater proportion in the older age groups than in previous generations. It may also be suggested, that through well-known psychosomatic mechanisms, the increased incidence of the disabilities of older people, such as heart disease, cancer, etc. may be at least in part attributed to this structural situation.

---

9. That the financial difficulties of older people are in a very large proportion of cases real is not to be doubted. This, however, is at least to a very large extent a consequence rather than a determinant of the structural situation. Except where it is fully taken care of by pension schemes, the income of older people is apt to be seriously reduced, but, even more important, the younger conjugal family usually does not feel an obligation to contribute to the support of aged parents. Where as a matter of course both generations shared a common household, this problem did not exist.

Morris Zelditch

Role Differentiation in the Nuclear Family

In the distribution of instrumental tasks, the American family maintains a more flexible pattern than most societies. Father helps mother with the dishes. He sets the table. He makes formula for the baby. Mother can supplement the income of the family by working outside. Nevertheless, the American male, by definition, *must* "provide" for his family. He is *responsible* for the support of his wife and children. His primary area of performance is the occupational role, in which his status fundamentally inheres and his primary function in the family is to supply an "income," to be the "breadwinner." There is simply something wrong with the American adult male who doesn't have a "job." American women, on the other hand, tend to hold jobs *before* they are married and to quit when "the day" comes; or to continue in jobs of a lower status than their husbands.[1] And not only is the mother the focus of emotional support for the American middle-class child, but much more exclusively so than in most societies (as Margaret Mead has pointed out in her treatment of adolescent problems). The cult of the warm, giving "Mom" stands in contrast to the "capable," "competent," "go-getting" male. The more expressive type of male, as a matter of fact, is regarded as "effeminate," and has too much fat on the inner side of his thigh.

The distribution of authority is legitimized on a different basis in the "democratic" family than in the so-called "traditional" one; but the father is "supposed" to remain the primary executive member. The image of the "henpecked" husband makes sense only on this premise. His "commands" are validated on the basis of "good judgment," rather than *general* obedience due a person in authority. But when the mother's efforts at "disciplining" fail, she traditionally tells the errant child, "Wait till daddy gets home."

In generalizing this pattern, of instrumental leadership focused on the achievement of tasks and expressive leadership focused on emotionally supportive behaviors, the most difficult problem of interpretation lies in

---

1. See pp. 3–33 of *Family, Socialization and Interaction Process*.

clearly distinguishing the nuclear family from the descent groups which in some cases took precedence as solidarities over them. This may be discussed in terms of two rather unique cases. The Nayar (who do not appear in this sample) so completely incorporate the mother-child system in the matrilineage that no husband-father status *exists* in the sense usually given to this term. The males of the matrilineage take over the husband-father's functions, and to all intents and purposes *no nuclear family exists*. This is the limiting case in the incorporation of nuclear families in larger descent groups. It is, in a sense, the mirror opposite of the American isolated conjugal family; the same principle, applied in different ways, is at stake. The question is simply the relative solidarity of two cross-cutting systems. In our society the nuclear family is clearly a stronger solidarity than any other kinship-based group and no *corporate* descent group exists. Among the Nayar, the matrilineage was the clearly dominant solidarity to the unusual extent of destroying the nuclear family as a continuously functioning group entirely. Somewhere in between these poles lie most of the cases known. The Trobriands approach the uniqueness of the Nayar, however, in giving the mother's brother more extensive obligations to and responsibility over the nuclear family of his sister than is common even in matrilineal societies. (It may someday turn out that many of these obligations are primarily symbolic and do not in fact take up as much of the mother's brother's productive activity as has been supposed.) The effect of this is to reduce the husband-father's role in the nuclear family, since he is a mother's brother in someone else's nuclear family and is occupied in task-functions *outside* his own nuclear family. Again, the basis of this is clearly the relative emphasis on the *lineage* as a solidarity.

Ordinarily, however, the solidarity of the lineage does not completely obscure the husband-father's instrumental role in his own nuclear family. The Trobriands, that is, is *not* the paradigmatic matrilineal case, any more than the Nayar is. And where the husband-father spends any time at all in his own nuclear family even in the matrilineal case he takes on significant de facto instrumental authority. To the extent, that is, that the nuclear family *does* function as a system, it differentiates in the direction expected.

In dealing with the allocation problem, it is apparent that the initial relation of mother and child is sufficiently important so that the mother's expressive role in the family is largely *not* problematical. . . .

The allocation of instrumental leadership to the father, on the other hand, is only problematic in the sense that the interrelation of the nuclear family and the descent group may, in one class of cases, obscure the husband-father's role. And this we have already discussed. In the patrilineal cases, in which this particular problem raises fewer interpretative issues in concrete systems (except that, of course, there *are* important problems in the relations of a husband-father to *his* father) the role is reasonably clear. This is true also for bilateral systems.

On the whole, therefore, when the nuclear family can be clearly distinguished from incorporating solidarities, it differentiates in the direction expected and allocates the relevant roles to the persons expected. And the problems which are raised in interpreting the data do not arise so much from whether or not this is true, but rather from what effect the precedence of obligations to corporate descent groups may have. This becomes, stated in a general form, a problem of the relative authority of the husband-father compared to that of some person in the superordinate descent group; where this descent group is matrilineal, the problem is one of the relative authority of father vs. mother's brother. The effect on patrilineal systems is to confine the difficulties in this relationship *within* the corporate descent group; and eventually the husband-father achieves a role of dominance in the descent group as well as the nuclear family. The effect in matrilineal systems is different, since the father can never become a member of the matrilineage. He must validate his position through his contribution to the everyday life of the household group, and his position is much less stable. In a great many cases, nevertheless, he *does* become the significant instrumental figure in the household group; and *always,* relative to *mother* this is the case. From the point of view of this legal status in the system, he is at the same time freed from certain obligations to his own family and denied certain rights in control of his own family; from the point of view of the general conditions for the existence of social systems as systems, however, he *must* accept some of these obligations and be allowed certain of these rights.

Philip Slater

Parental Role Differentiation[1]

Some of the most confused segments of psychoanalytic theory are those which attempt to deal differentially with intra-familial relationships. The difficulties seem due largely to a failure to isolate the effects of formal, structural properties, based solely on variables such as the age and sex of family members. This defect has recently been remedied to a considerable extent by the work of Parsons, who attempts to integrate a formal analysis of this kind with classical psychoanalytic theory.[2] One of the more valuable products of this effort is a considerable clarification of the difficult concept of identification.[3]

At several points, however, the conceptual scheme advanced by Parsons encounters both theoretical and empirical difficulties. These involve the problem of role differentiation in the nuclear family. They may be stated as three hypotheses:

1. Role differentiation along an "instrumental-expressive axis" is a universal characteristic of the nuclear family.

2. Role differentiation between parents facilitates the child's identification with the same-sex parent.

3. Role differentiation between parents is essential to normal personality development in the child.

The position taken in this article is that parental differentiation along the "instrumental-expressive axis" is an optional feature of nuclear family structure and that under some conditions, notably those obtaining in large segments of our own society, it may actually impede identification with the same-sex parent and affect adversely the personality development of the child.

The Universality of Differentiation

In the concluding chapter of *Family, Socialization and Interaction Process*, Parsons and Bales refer to "the universal presence of two axes

1. Revision of a paper read at the 1960 annual meeting of the American Sociological Association.
2. See Talcott Parsons and Robert F. Bales, *Family, Socialization and Interaction Process* (New York: Free Press 1955), chap. ii.
3. *Ibid.*, pp. 91–94.

of differentiation, namely, an hierarchical axis of relative power and an instrumental-expressive axis."[4] The first difficulty we encounter in attempting to evaluate this statement is the lack of an adequate criterion for determining when differentiation is present and when it is not. If role differentiation is to be conceived as a quantitative variable—and it is difficult to see how it could be viewed otherwise—then the chance of finding a negative case is one divided by the square of the number of points on the scale used. If, of course, all that is meant by the statement of universality is that no two people exhibit a given type of behavior to exactly the same extent, then it cannot be questioned.

More than this is meant, however. Basic to the entire discussion of familial role differentiation is the notion that, in a family characterized by sharp differentiation of roles, it should be grossly apparent that the majority of the instrumental functions are being performed by one parent—the father—and the majority of the expressive functions by the mother.[5]

But now a second difficulty arises, for this formulation ignores the problem of parental salience. In many cultures one parent, usually the mother, is both more expressive (nurturant) and more instrumental (demanding). Thus in Pukapuka, "the child is mainly cared for by its mother. The father has no specific duties to perform. He is sympathetic and lavish in his affection for his child, caring for it, however, only when it is necessary or convenient. . . . Authority over the infant is largely focused in the mother. Love, dependence, and affection on the other hand tend to diffuse themselves among many members of or visitors to the household."[6] This description, a negative instance not included in Zelditch's cross-cultural survey,[7] could be applied to a large number of societies, including (save for the final sentence) our own middle class. Considering each parent alone, one may see a marked emphasis on instrumental or expressive behavior, but this should not lead us to ignore the fact that one parent plays a distinctly secondary role in the performance of both functions.

This problem is not considered by either Parsons or Zelditch, perhaps because of the apparent assumption that instrumental and expressive behavior are negatively related, so that if one is stressed the other must be minimized. This idea is implicit in the use of the term "axis" with regard to the relationship between the two roles. But there is

4. *Ibid.*, p. 355.
5. *Ibid.*, pp. 45, 80.
6. Ernest and Pearl Beaglehole, "Personality Development in Pukapukan Children," in W. E. Martin and Celia B. Stendler (eds.), *Readings in Child Development* (New York: Harcourt, Brace & Co., 1954), p. 161.
7. Morris Zelditch, Jr., "Role Differentiation in the Nuclear Family," in Parsons and Bales, *op. cit.*, chap. vi. [See pp. 256–58 in this volume.]

no way in which such an assumption of a negative relationship can be justified. In small-group studies, to which analogical appeals are often made in the Parsons and Bales volume, there is actually a positive correlation between the two roles.[8]

The argument for a negative relationship receives its ultimate expression in the following quotation from Zelditch: "Why after all, are *two* parents necessary? For one thing, to be a stable focus of integration, the integrative-expressive 'leader' can't be off on adaptive-instrumental errands all the time."[9]

We must be forgiven our pedantry for stressing, along with Briffault,[10] that the only time in a child's existence when two parents are "necessary" is when it is conceived. Passing over this issue, however, we note that the main weight of Zelditch's argument rests on the notion that role differentiation occurs because two discriminable types of behavior cannot be performed at the same time. One cannot, for example, work and play at once,[11] although the universality of work songs suggests that even this statement must be qualified. But it is not at all clear why differentiation should be limited to the instrumental-expressive "axis." If a special person is required to lead the laughing and playing, as Zelditch suggests, then it follows that still another person will be required to lead the weeping and mourning, since clearly a person cannot laugh and mourn at the same time. On the instrumental side, this role fragmentation becomes even more complicated. According to Zelditch's view, the farm family must at all times send two persons to the well, one to lower the bucket and one to raise it up, since the bucket cannot be raised and lowered at the same time.

We must not, however, overlook the grain of truth in Zelditch's statement. It would undoubtedly be possible to find persons so incompetent as to be capable only of lowering or only of raising a bucket. Similarly, many persons are too rigid or limited in their interpersonal repertory to shift easily from the performance of instrumental to the performance of expressive functions, and vice versa.[12] This was originally suggested as the basis of role differentiation in experimental groups,[13] and there is no reason to assume a different foundation in the

8. Parsons and Bales, *op. cit.*, p. 286.

9. Zelditch, *op. cit.*, p. 312.

10. Robert Briffault, *The Mothers* (New York: Macmillan Co., 1931), *passim*.

11. Zelditch, *op. cit.*, p. 311.

12. Philip E. Slater, "Psychological Factors in Role Specialization" (unpublished Ph.D. dissertation, Harvard University, 1955), pp. 205–13. Particularly interesting in Zelditch's argument is the implicit assumption that whereas it is possible for persons in subordinate positions to make this transition, it is not possible for those in positions of leadership (Zelditch, *op. cit.*, pp. 311–12).

13. Parsons and Bales, *op. cit.*, pp. 290–96; Philip E. Slater, "Role Differentiation in Small Groups," *American Sociological Review*, XX (June, 1955) pp. 308–10.

family. From this viewpoint, role differentiation could be characterized as a mechanism which takes nothing for granted with regard to the personalities of the incumbents.

It would be a rare society, however, which left such matters to chance, and we would expect societies characterized by sharp differentiation of parental roles to encourage role rigidity in individuals. In our own society the reverse is true, as the use of the word "role" and our fascination with Goffmanesque modes of analysis might suggest. The ability rapidly to alternate instrumental and expressive role performances is highly valued, and we have developed concepts such as "interpersonal flexibility" and "role-playing ability" to express this value. We must therefore be cautious in our inferences about personality, since societal pressures may have caused the ability to shift roles to have atrophied in the first instance and to have hypertrophied in the second, perhaps at the expense of other capacities.

Unidimensional Differentiation

The "human-limitations" theory of role differentiation assumes bidimensionality, that is, it is based on the assumption that instrumental and expressive roles are roughly independent of each other. The theory could not be maintained, however, if in some way it could be demonstrated that instrumental and expressive behavior were in fact incompatible, that is, opposite poles of a single dimension, as Parsons and Zelditch seem at times to imply. While we expect an adequate individual to be capable of varying his behavior over time—to be able, in Zelditch's terms, both to call for a coffee break and eventually to terminate it without having to call in a back-to-work specialist—we do not ask of him that he behave in a truly self-contradictory manner. If a parent, for example, is alternately indulgent and depriving *in identical situations* we call him inconsistent rather than flexible. Knowing the situation, we expect to be able to predict his response with some accuracy on the basis of his previous behavior. If one parent is consistently depriving, it will be necessary, if we desire for the child a wide range of behavior on the depriving-indulgent axis, to have the other parent behave in an indulgent manner.

But if instrumental and expressive behavior were incompatible and differentiation were "built into" the family to avoid personal inconsistency, the incompatibility would simply have been externalized, so that in place of a whimsical individual we would now have quarreling parents, one saying "be lenient," the other saying "be strict."

It is usually argued, of course, that differentiation does not involve a conflict of aims but simply an agreement to specialize in different directions, with complementarity binding rather than separating the participants. But this distinction breaks down whenever there is the slightest contradiction between the two directions of specialization. Vogel and Bell, for example, present cases in which unidimensional parental differentiation is utilized to institutionalize internal conflicts.[14]

Consider, for example, Parsons' statement that "the mother-figure is always the *more permissive* and supportive, the father the *more denying* and demanding."[15] In a family strongly differentiated along these lines, if the child wishes something which he fears might be denied him, he will probably go to the mother for it. If the mother grants the child what the father would have denied, does the father nonetheless support her in the performance of her differentiated function, since they are, after all, in a "coalition"? The notion of collaborative differentiation in socialization assumes, if the differentiation is unidimensional, that there is no relationship between personality and role behavior. Yet if the father is "denying," the chances are rather great that it is not simply because he feels it is something that *he* should do, but because he thinks it is something that should *in general* be done to the child, in which case he will not support the mother's indulgence at all, but will instead probably accuse her of subverting his authority or "spoiling" the child.[16] The maintenance of a "coalition" under conditions of sharp unidimensional differentiation assumes that the differentiated parents *will never interact with the child at the same time,* since it would obviously be impossible to do so and still support each other. The idea of collaborative differentiation is therefore relevant primarily to the large and formal upper-class households of an earlier era, when mother, father, and child were rarely together at one time under circumstances which were disciplinarily problematic. It was easy under those conditions to "agree" that the child going from parent to parent and room to room should encounter different responses to the same behavior, and that when all were together the mother should place herself in a totally subordinate position. But in the less formal, more intimate middle-class household of today, any such arrangement would be an occasion for mirth. Major differences between parents in beliefs about what is "good" for the child can no longer be masked by drawing a kind of 38th parallel between the front and back of the house.

Often, as in the beautiful example given by Vogel and Bell,[17] unidimensional differentiation may serve to keep a conflict at a covert level, with the parents expressing their disagreement only through their

14. Ezra F. Vogel and Norman W. Bell, "The Emotionally Disturbed Child as the Family Scapegoat," in Norman W. Bell and Ezra F. Vogel (eds.), *A Modern Introduction to the Family* (Glencoe, Ill.: Free Press, 1960), pp. 389–90 (cf. also Ezra F. Vogel, "The Marital Relationship of Parents and the Emotionally Disturbed Child" [unpublished Ph.D. dissertation, Harvard University, 1958]).

15. Parsons and Bales, *op. cit.,* p. 80. This statement also seems to imply that Parsons' model of differentiation is unidimensional, although the underlying theory would suggest a bidimensional model.

16. Cf. A R. Radcliffe-Brown, *Structure and Function in Primitive Society* (Glencoe, Ill.: Free Press, 1952), p. 20.

17. Vogel and Bell, *op. cit.,* pp. 390–91.

orders and remarks to the child and never directly to each other. In such a case it might be correct to speak of "collaboration," since the parents are co-operating to avoid an open clash. But as Vogel and Bell point out, while such a technique may serve to keep the family "intact," it effectively prevents any ultimate airing and resolution of the conflict, and "keeps the peace" only at the cost of impairing the emotional health of the child. [18]

In short, while bidimensional differentiation (i.e., role differentiation in which the required performances are not incompatible) is obviously functional for all parties concerned under certain conditions specified below, unidimensional differentiation (i.e., in which the required performances are incompatible) seems to be primarily a mechanism for the ritual expression of intrapsychic and interpersonal conflicts in and between the marital partners and is usually dysfunctional for the child and for the society as a whole.

Differentiation and Identification[19]

Parsons' position on the relationship between differentiation and identification is cleary stated: "If the boy is to 'identify' with his father in the sense of sex-role categorization there must be a discrimination in role terms between the two parents." [20] For the sake of simplicity let us follow Parsons' example and concentrate on the identification of the male child with the father.

Since Parsons has defined the differentiated role of the father as being "more denying and demanding," we would expect identification to be a function of the father's strictness. That being "denying" is inherently paternal is problematic, in view of findings such as that of Payne and Mussen, 87 percent of whose adolescent male subjects saw their fathers as more rewarding than their mothers, [21] but let us disregard this issue for the moment. That identification is a function of parental frustration is also a hoary psychoanalytic concept. [22] Empirically, however, the reverse

18. *Ibid.*, pp. 394–97.

19. "Identification" is here defined as any tendency for an individual to seek to maximize his similarity to another person in one or more respects. The studies I have cited in support of my position would not all serve as adequate evidence, were other definitions of identification to be used. I have elsewhere distinguished between "personal" and "positional" identification, the former based on a desire to assimilate the valued personal qualities of a loved object, the latter based on a desire to assume the position or role of an envied and hated object. See my "Toward a Dualistic Theory of Identification," *Merrill-Palmer Quarterly*, VII (April, 1961). It is to "personal" identification that this section is devoted.

20. Parsons and Bales, *op. cit.*, p. 80.

21. D. E. Payne and P. H. Mussen, "Parent-Child Relations and Father Identification among Adolescent Boys," *Journal of Abnormal and Social Psychology*, LII (1956), 358–62.

22. Otto Fenichel, *The Psychoanalytic Theory of The Neuroses* (New York: W. W. Norton & Co., 1945).

seems to be the case. Chronic punitiveness seems actually to impede identification, while an underlying nurturant attitude toward the child seems to facilitate it.[23]

There is some evidence, moreover, which is in more direct contradiction to Parsons' statement. Beier and Ratzeburg found that males identified preferentially with whichever parent was least extreme in the performance of his or her sex role, while the author found that the more denying and strict the father and the more supportive and lenient the mother, the more the son identified preferentially with the latter.[24] These findings suggest that in our society at least, unidimensional parental role differentiation, and perhaps also an extreme degree of bidimensional differentiation, may actually inhibit the son's identification with the father, and Parsons' statement should therefore be qualified to that extent.

The reason for this is implicit in Parsons' discussion of the process of identification in the family. Parsons argues that the child forms several identifications, the first being with the mother.[25] Once this maternal identification is formed, the male child must at some point extend his identification to the father. If, however, the parents are highly differentiated with respect to their socialization behavior, and particularly if the father is primarily a source of frustration for the child, the transition will be a difficult one. There will be no inducement for the child to adopt this entirely new frame of reference. Parsons states that "before he has internalized the father as an object the child cannot be fully sensitive to his attitudes as sanctions. He can, however, be motivated to do things *which please both mother and father* and be rewarded by mother's love and nurturance. By some such process he comes to cathect the father—*because mother loves father and backs him up*—and from this generalized parental object then a qualitatively different object can be differentiated out."[26] This process will only take place, however, if the parents are not differentiated to such an extent that (*a*) it is impossible to please both at the same time, and (*b*) it is impossible, either emotionally or

23. Cf. I. L. Child, "Socialization," in Gardner Lindzey (ed.) *Handbook of Social Psychology* (Cambridge, Mass.: Addison-Wesley, 1954), Vol. II; Susan W. Gray and R. Klaus, "The Assessment of Parental Identification," *Genetic Psychology Monographs,* LIV (1956), 87–114; Payne and Mussen, *op. cit.*; Pauline Sears, "Child-rearing Factors Related to Playing of Sex-typed Roles," *American Psychologist,* VIII (1953), 431 (abstract); J. W. M. Whiting and I. L. Child, *Child Training and Personality: A Cross-cultural Study* (New Haven, Conn.: Yale University Press, 1953).

24. E. G. Beier and F. Ratzeburg, "The Parental Identifications of Male and Female College Students," *Journal of Abnormal and Social Psychology,* XLVIII (1953), 569–72; Slater, "Psychological Factors in Role Specialization," p. 120.

25. Parsons and Bales, *op. cit.,* pp. 91–94; cf. also J. Kagan. "The Concept of Identification," *Psychological Review,* LXV (1958), 302; O. H. Mowrer, *Learning Theory and Personality Dynamics* (New York: Ronald Press Co., 1950) p. 608; R. R. Sears, Eleanor E. Maccoby, and H. Levin, *Patterns of Child Rearing* (Evanston, Ill.: Row, Peterson & Co., 1957).

26. Parsons and Bales, *op. cit.,* p. 81. (Italics mostly mine.)

conceptually, to form a "generalized parental object." For it should be emphasized that a major aspect of identification is "taking the role of the other" in G. H. Mead's sense, that is, adopting the viewpoint of the other with respect to oneself. The importance of paternal identification is that it makes possible the development of a "generalized other" from the perceived viewpoints of the two parents. If the parents' attitudes toward the child are reasonably similar, such generalization is possible, but if they clash, the child is thrown back on a particularistic orientation toward them. He may be able momentarily to empathize with first one and then the other, but he cannot easily form a generalized self-concept from these conflicting perceptions.

Differentiation and Personality Development

Since Parsons argues that the human personality is a structure composed of internalized systems of social objects,[27] and that this structure develops through an internal differentiation which reflects a differentiation among the social objects,[28] it is clear that parental differentiation is not seen, on the whole, as pathogenic.

Empirical studies, however, show a consistently negative relationship between degrees of parental role differentiation and the emotional adjustment of the child. Lazowick found greater "semantic similarity" between the parents of his less anxious subjects than between those of his more anxious subjects.[29] Manis found that his adjusted subjects saw their parents as more alike than did the maladjusted subjects.[30] A study by the author showed significant positive correlations between degree of perceived parental role differentiation and most of the pathological scales in the Minnesota Multiphasic Personality Inventory.[31] Wechsler found that subjects who perceived a high degree of role differentiation between father and mother also experienced conflict in their self-perceptions.[32] At the very least, one would be forced to conclude from these data that for the child parental role differentiation is not always an unmixed blessing.

One cannot, of course, generalize these findings beyond the specific context of the American middle class. In a society characterized by extended families, for example, the effects of sharp differentiation

27. Parsons and Bales, *op. cit.*, p. 54.
28. *Ibid.*, p. 27.
29. L. M. Lazowick, "On the Nature of Identification," *Journal of Abnormal and Social Psychology*, LI (1955), 175–83.
30. M. Manis, "Personal Adjustment, Assumed Similarity to Parents, and Inferred Parental Evaluations of the Self," *Journal of Consulting Psychology*, XXII (1958), 481–85.
31. Slater, "Psychological Factors in Role Specialization," pp. 133–35.
32. H. Wechsler, "Conflicts in Self-perceptions" (unpublished Ph.D. dissertation, Harvard University, 1957).

between the parents may be diluted by the presence of substitute figures. Our own society is remarkable in the extent to which it concentrates the socialization process in the nuclear family. Furthermore, in a social system predicated upon parental role differentiation, the healthy offspring of undifferentiated parents might feel himself constricted while the less healthy child of differentiated parents might find himself fulfilled.

The studies cited above deal primarily with college students, a segment of the population in which parental differentiation is traditionally less marked,[33] so that the children of differentiated parents have developed in a family environment which was in some sense "deviant." The apparent adverse "effects" of differentiation may be entirely due to this deviant position of the family, or to its antecedents and correlates. But they are even more likely to be a simple function of the child himself being ill-suited to the society in which he later finds himself, a possibility suggested by a finding of the author's. In small experimental laboratory groups, subjects showing the greatest tendency toward role specialization, whether in a task or social-emotional direction, also tended to report that one parent (more often but not necessarily the father) was denying and demanding and the other permissive and rewarding.[34]

When we consider the high degree of specialization in occupations in our society, however, we might well wonder why the development of specialized children should be anything but functional for both individual and society. Is there, nevertheless, some sphere in which role differentiation is discordant with American society?

Differentiation and Isolation

While it is impossible to do justice to a question of this magnitude within the scope of this paper, a promising hypothesis is suggested by Bott's study of the relationship between the degree of differentiation and segregation of conjugal roles and the kind of social matrix in which the marital couple finds itself. Bott distinguishes between "loose-knit net-

---

33. "The husbands who had the most segregated role-relationships with their wives had manual occupations, and the husbands who had the most joint role-relationships with their wives were professional or semi-professional, people" (Elizabeth Bott, "Conjugal Roles and Social Networks," in Bell and Vogel [eds.] *op. cit.*, p. 251 [this book, p. 319]). While Bott is primarily concerned with conjugal roles here, the type of differentiation, with its de-emphasis of shared activities, is one we would expect to be highly correlated with differentiation of socialization roles.

It is the middle-class parents, moreover, who are the principal consumers of the child-training manuals, which often specifically oppose such practices as deferring punishments for the father to administer, and which argue, in general, for an undifferentiated pattern of parental behavior (cf., e.g., Benjamin Spock, *The Pocket Book of Baby and Child Care* [New York: Pocket Books, 1956], pp. 14–15, 242–43).

34. Slater, "Psychological Factors in Role Specialization," pp. 207–9.

works" in which friends, neighbors, and relatives of the couple tend not to know each other, and "close-knit networks," in which the people known by a couple tend more often to interact also with one another.[35] She finds:

> Couples in close-knit networks expected husbands and wives to have a rigid division of labor. There was little stress on the importance of shared interests and joint recreation. It was expected that wives would have many relationships with their relatives, and husbands with their friends. Both parents could get help from people outside the family, which made the rigid division of labor between husband and wife possible. Successful sexual relations were not considered essential to a happy marriage.
>
> In contrast, families in loose-knit networks had a less rigid division of labor, stressed the importance of shared interests and joint recreation, placed a good deal of emphasis on the importance of successful sexual relations. They were more self-conscious about how to bring up their children than couples in close-knit networks. They were aware that the people they knew had a great variety of opinions on this subject and they were worried about which course they themselves should follow.[36]

Note that Bott associates this lack of differentiation with conjugal solidarity. She goes on further to suggest that the relationship is a causal one—that couples who cannot rely upon a stable and supportive external social context must develop a more intimate relationship with each other than a rigid division of labor permits. This is achieved through an increase in joint, shared activities.[37]

Bott also associates loose-knit networks with social and geographical mobility.[38] This suggests the hypothesis that couples will tend to decrease

35. See Bott, *op. cit.*, p. 252.
36. *Ibid.*, p. 439.
37. It would seem that the sharper the differentiation of conjugal roles in a society, the greater the reliance which will be placed upon sex segregation in the training of children for these roles. For while segregation of the sexes in the youth peer group may be universal, as Parsons suggests ("The Incest Taboo in Relation to Social Structure and the Socialization of the Child," *British Journal of Sociology*, Vol. V [June, 1954]), the degree and duration of such segregation may have important consequences. In some societies (and in some segments of the American lower class) it becomes something of a Frankenstein monster, inasmuch as the individual who has spent most of his youth in one-sex groups only feels truly at ease in such groups as an adult. The stress that this creates for marital relationships, even in the mildly segregated American middle class, is the bread-and-butter of cartoonists and comedians across the nation (note the ubiquity of poker, golf, and bridge-club jokes). The consequences of the more severe forms of sex segregation are discussed by Bettelheim in his *Symbolic Wounds* (Glencoe, Ill.: Free Press, 1955).

In wartime sex segregation is sharply increased, and the resulting stresses overload the usual mechanisms. This perhaps accounts for the temporary rash, during World War II, of psychiatric papers dealing with penis envy and other forms of sex antagonism (cf. e.g., *Psychiatry*, 1940–46). While each sex experiences severe deprivation and suffering during wartime, neither is in a position fully to understand or appreciate the different nature of the sufferings of the other. The resulting resentment finds its ultimate expression in fantasies of single-sex societies (cf., e.g., Bernice S. Engle, "Lemnos, Island of Women," *Psychoanalytic Review*, XXXII [1945], 353–58).

38. Bott, *op. cit.*, p. 256.

role differentiation whenever the welfare of the family is predicated upon a high degree of non-commitment to (or lack of dependence upon) external social relationships.[39] This degree of commitment, furthermore, may vary not only from couple to couple, but also within the same couple over time. De-differentiation typically occurs with a family whenever it is removed from its usual social context, such as during a vacation or a change in residence.[40]

Such a situation obtains in large segments of the American middle class and is particularly marked in families in which the husband works for an organization whose offices are widely distributed, so that advancement requires frequent changes of residence; or when such advancement necessitates the formation of new relationships at each status level.[41] But it seems clear that if a couple living in this kind of context does show a rigid division of labor it is much more likely to be associated with conflict and strain within the family than would be the case if both husband and wife could turn for support, friendship, and tension release to stable lifelong relationships outside the nuclear family. Furthermore, if a pattern of behavior appropriate to close-knit networks is formed in the absence of such networks, it would seem reasonable to expect that some of the burden of filling this vacuum would be placed upon the child, thus generating the negative relationship found above between parental differentiation and the emotional adjustment of the child.[42]

But apart from any considerations of emotional health, is there any more universal effect of parental role differentiation upon the child—one which might be functional in some social contexts and dysfunctional in others? Does parental role differentiation help foster, for example, a personality trait or constellation which is maladaptive for children growing up in a fluid social environment but necessary for life in a stable one?

39. Although animal sociology is not sufficiently advanced to enable us to generalize with much confidence, J. P. Scott implies that this relationship extends to the other primates, when he contrasts the relative lack of sex role differentiation among the gibbons, who live in isolated nuclear families, with the strong differentiation among baboons, who show more extended social groupings (*Animal Behavior* [Chicago: University of Chicago Press, 1958], p. 187).

40. Observation made to author by Theodore Mills.

41. Riesman and Roseborough, e.g., refer to the "young married proto-executives" who "become very adept at pulling up stakes, and at being at home everywhere and nowhere" (David Riesman and Howard Roseborough, "Careers and Consumer Behavior," in Bell and Vogel [eds.], *op. cit.,* pp. 143–62, esp. pp. 152, 155, 158). The academic world is so characterized to an almost equal extent. One reason that the de-differentiation of parental roles is a useful preparation for this kind of transient adult life is that it teaches the child at an early age that his human sources of gratification are more or less interchangeable.

42. Although loose-knit networks are, as noted before, less frequent among lower-class families, we might expect to find them in mobile or newly acculturated families. Vogel and Bell's "scapegoated" children were largely from families undergoing one or both types of transition, and there may have been a particularly strong need in such cases for the parents to place emotional demands upon the child which had previously been directed outside the nuclear family (see Vogel and Bell, *op. cit.,* pp. 384–85).

One possibility is suggested by a study of the Gusii by LeVine. Testing a prediction by Whiting that authoritarian sanctioning would develop with parental role differentiation, LeVine found that among the Gusii, who tend to violate cultural norms when authority figures are absent, the father is a non-nurturant and punitive disciplinarian, while the mother tends to specialize in the nurturing role, using the threat of paternal punishment as a principal means of control. "The child thus learns to fear the father's painful ministrations and to avoid them by being obedient and performing his tasks; but he does not internalize the father's evaluation of his behavior." [43]

It is not difficult to see why this is so. To the extent that the father is non-rewarding he will tend to appear as an alien ruler to the child. His demands will be acceded to when he is present, for the same reason that other forms of reality command obeisance, but when he is not present and cannot exert his authority, nothing is to be gained by obedience. To the extent that he is rewarding, however, much is to be gained by being a "good boy" even when the father is away. In other words, the internalization of parental values tends to occur to the degree that nurturance and discipline come from the same source. This point, which seems to be fairly well established today, is stressed by Eleanor Maccoby in an analysis of the effects upon children of the mothers working. She cites Solomon's work with dogs, noting that "punishment by a stranger, or a person who has been primarily cold and restrictive toward the animal in puppyhood, does not seem to last very well in its effects when the trainer's back is turned," and even goes so far as to recommend that "if nurturant caretaking is divided between two people . . . then discipline should be similarly divided." [44]

43. R. A. LeVine, "Social Control and Socialization among the Gusii" (unpublished Ph.D. dissertation, Harvard University, 1958), p. 358. The shallowness of internalization in the differentiated family is also shown in a study by Hazel Hitson ("Family Patterns and Paranoidal Personality Structure in Boston and Burma" [unpublished Ph.D. dissertation, Harvard University, 1959]). See also Stanley H. King and Andrew F. Henry, "Aggression and Cardiovascular Reactions Related to Parental Control over Behavior," *Journal of Abnormal and Social Psychology*, L (March, 1955), 206–10. Henry reported that "reluctance to blame the other person as well as willingness to blame the self both increase the likelihood that the mother will be viewed as principal disciplinarian" ("Family Role Structure and Self-blame," in Bell and Vogel [eds.], *op. cit.*, p. 542).

44. Eleanor E. Maccoby, "Effects upon Children of Their Mother's Outside Employment," in Bell and Vogel, *op. cit.*, pp. 528–29 (cf. also Urie Bronfenbrenner, "Socialization and Social Class through Time and Space," in Eleanor E. Maccoby, T. M. Newcomb, and E. L. Hartley [eds.], *Readings in Social Psychology* [New York: Henry Holt & Co., 1958], p. 419).

Maccoby is here assuming, of course, the desirability of internalization in American society, an assumption roundly rejected, along with the undifferentiated middle-class marital relationship, by Arnold Green ("The Middle-Class Male Child and Neurosis" and "The 'Cult of Personality' and Sexual Relations," both reprinted in Bell and Vogel [eds.], *op. cit.*, pp. 563–72, 608–15, see esp. pp. 564 ff. and 614–15).

But accustomed as we are to the serious consequences of a severe failure of internalization in our own society, it should perhaps be emphasized that in a society with a less fluid social structure a high degree of internalization is not only unnecessary to insure social control, but may in some instances be actually disruptive—if, for example, the society is heavily committed to a complex system of external controls with regulated violation, as in the case of chaperonage, or if such intensive internalization tends to erode other personality characteristics valued by the society, as Bronfenbrenner suggests.[45]

At the same time, an additional reason for the importance of internalization in our own society is suggested by this analysis. When large numbers of individuals spend their lives in shifting loose-knit networks, social control cannot be based on external sanctions to the extent that is possible with a stable and integrated social context; the need then is for a family structure that promotes the internalization of parental values.

The de-differentiation of parental roles also tends to palliate one of the major strains besetting the mobile nuclear family, that is, the potentially fragile relationship between child and father due to the latter's absence from the home during most of the child's waking hours. For as the burden of socialization has become increasingly concentrated in the nuclear family, the availability of the father to share this burden has remained unchanged and in many instances (e.g., the suburban commuter) actually decreased. Assuming that the importance of such sharing is nonproblematic, it seems clear that in the mobile nuclear family a great deal of pressure exists to soften and familiarize the paternal role. The specialized disciplinarian of other times and places, in an immobile and "connected" nuclear family, was in a sense the immediate representative of a like-minded community of persons well known to the child; if the child did not fully internalize his values, he at least developed a sense of respect for them as a consequence of their apparent universality. If the father was too extreme in his role, furthermore, there were often substitute males with whom the child could form a more complete and adequate relationship.

In the isolated mobile nuclear family, however, the father does not represent a known community of adults, and there are no permanent substitutes. A specialized disciplinarian role loses any semblance of a universalistic response and takes on the appearance of malicious caprice. The father who attempts it becomes an alien intruder to his children, a state of affairs which, while tolerable in the "connected" family, is severely disruptive in the isolated mobile family.

45. Urie Bronfenbrenner, "The Changing American Child—a Speculative Analysis," *Merrill-Palmer Quarterly,* VII (April, 1961), 73–84.

Perhaps the most dramatic expression of the difference between the two systems is the fact that while in the de-differentiated family[46] a great deal of effort is devoted to bringing the father closer to the children (often through his adoption of a tolerant, easy-going, occasional-playmate role), one of the principal mechanisms used to handle hostility in the differentiated family was distancing. This was effected not only by the general aloofness assumed by the father in the performance of his disciplinary function, but also by the mediator role played by the mother—a role which generally purports to be self-dissolving, but which in practice usually proves to be self-perpetuating.

In the most extreme case the father may play a kind of scapegoat role. If an individual is specialized in a non-rewarding direction, it is convenient to have him become the recipient of the hostile feelings occasionally aroused by more rewarding individuals. This is particularly likely to occur in a highly patriarchal family system, in which the mother may compensate for her inferior status and power in the society at large by using her strategic position as mediator to control family relationships. By a combination of public indorsement and private subversion of the father's authority she indicates to the child that the father is the source of all discomfort and she the source of all good. It should be clear that internalization of parental values under such circumstances is rather unlikely. The German *Hausfrau* who supports the father's disciplinary measures in his presence with verbal exhortations to the child to obey him, and then hustles the child off to the kitchen for candy and sympathy, is making a rather sharp distinction between what is necessary in the way of public behavior in the presence of authorities and what one may do and feel privately in their absence.

This point is sometimes misunderstood. It is assumed that because a mediator attempts to prevent conflict by establishing distance, he will ultimately be able to establish solidarity, and thus eliminate the need for his existence. But just as insulation keeps out heat as well as cold, so distance forestalls affection as well as hostility. As Simmel once pointed out, "although a bridge connects two banks, it also makes the distance between them measurable."[47] When the mother teaches her son how to please and placate the father, how to "deal with" and occasionally "get

46. The terms "differentiated family" and "de-differentiated family" are not intended to imply a pair of discrete types, or even a bimodal distribution of families along the differentiation continuum. In talking of such modal changes, furthermore, it should not be forgotten that they are always exaggerated in popular belief, since individual variation is overwhelming in any era. That such a de-differentiation has taken place in comparatively recent times, however, and that it has been associated with an increase in internalization, is demonstrated by a number of recent studies (cf. Bronfenbrenner, "The Changing American Child," *op. cit.,* pp. 75, 79; and Wanda C. Bronson, Edith Ṣ. Katten, and N. Livson, "Patterns of Authority and Affection in Two Generations," *Journal of Abnormal and Social Psychology,* LVIII (1959), pp. 143–52.

47. Kurt H. Wolff, *The Sociology of Georg Simmel* (Glencoe, Ill.: Free Press, 1950), p. 129.

around" him, she is creating a gap between father and son which will operate effectively even in her absence, since the two will always feel a little strange with each other. This perhaps accounts for the brittleness of paternal identification in the German family—a brittleness brilliantly manipulated by Hitler. For the mother's teaching, while it establishes the superior power and status of the father and sets him up as a person worthy of imitation, does not really permit the son enough closeness to the father, or the father enough affectionate behavior toward the son, for a full internalization of paternal values to take place. Instead, she teaches the son her own role of submission, placation, and deception, thus inculcating an identification with herself. To an extent the yearning for a powerful authority which gave rise to the Nazi era may be seen as an attempt to complete the semi-identification with the father while at the same time maintaining identification with the submissive mother.

The mechanism of the maternal mediator, reasonably adequate to the task of moderating strains in a family system which had liberal access to paternal substitutes, is out of the question in a system desperately bent on intensifying the intimacy of the child-father relationship as a way of lessening the otherwise unwieldy burden on the mother produced by the relative absence in the mobile family of alternative socializing agents.

A Problem in
the Comparison of Mechanisms

In an analysis of marital interaction, James March has argued that "specialization, by reducing the area of joint activity, would appear to reduce at the same time the possibility of conflict within the group." [48] It seems surprising that an otherwise perceptive author could ignore the fact that "reducing the area of joint activity" will reduce solidarity as well as conflict. It reveals the bias, common to sociologists, in favor of distancing mechanisms and raises a serious problem in the comparative analysis of social institutions.

Ambivalence is a profoundly difficult emotional state for human beings to handle. Often they are able to cope with contradictory feelings only through rigid and awkward intrapsychic and interpersonal mechanisms. When this is the case the raw material is provided for a social institution which "builds in" those components which are neglected or distorted by the individual. In order words, if the individual cannot find direct ways of expressing, in his most significant interpersonal relationships the ambivalence of his feelings, this ambivalence is likely to reappear in social structural form.

48. "Political Issues and Husband-Wife Interaction," in Bell and Vogel (eds.), *op. cit.*, p. 202.

Parental role differentiation, while it may serve many different functions in many different societies, is at one level this kind of externalizing mechanism. It tends to focus one kind of feeling toward one parent and a contrasting feeling toward the other. It facilitates displacement and dilutes the emotional intensity of the family situation by "reducing the area of joint activity" and **thus** increasing the psychological distance between members. In this **way it displays** a certain formal elegance which is lacking in the de-differentiated system; but we should bear in mind that the apparent structural simplicity of a family pattern in which both parents are equally loving and constraining serves to mask the complexity and subtlety of the interpersonal responses of the participants.

As sociologists, it is natural for us to see more clearly the function of institutions which neutralize human emotions with distancing mechanisms, as opposed to those which permit more idiosyncratic solutions to ambivalent feelings. But there is a danger in this preference—the danger that we will underestimate both the importance and the complexity of structural patterns such as we find in the de-differentiated family. In using the phrase "apparent structural simplicity" with reference to this institution, I have the uneasy feeling that this apparent simplicity may be simply a function of the inadequacy of our traditional modes of analysis. Is it not possible that we are fascinated with institutional forms such as parental role differentiation, joking relationships, and puberty rites precisely because they are simple and crude enough for us to understand? Are we not continually exposed to the risk of overrating the functional efficacy of the institutions of primitive societies because they are more transparent than our own?[49]

It may be that the more highly differentiated family, despite its prevalence, is simply too unsophisticated a structure for a technologically advanced industrial society such as ours. Its apparent dependence on a stable social context imparts to it a rigidity analogous, in its effects on the family system, to the greater rigidity of inherited as opposed to learned

49. A good example of this tendency to disregard more complex and subtle methods of articulating personality and social system may be found in the remarks often made by xenocentric anthropologists regarding the lack, in our society, of institutions designed to bridge the gap between childhood and adulthood. The role of the school system in this regard is generally ignored, yet one may ask if this institution—with its increasing separation of child from mother, its finely tuned system of age grading, its increasing acquaintance of the child with the adult world and adult roles, its provision of a long series of tasks and tests of gradually increasing difficulty and complexity, its careful training of internal controls through a gradual shift from minute-by-minute supervision of work to a system in which work-planning and work habits are left almost entirely in the hands of students, and its machinery for the actual training of students in adult roles—does not go a little way toward filling the appalling void posited by Benedictine observers of the contemporary scene, who seem at times to imply that a primitive adolescent, having been, in a single pubertal ceremony, tortured, isolated, and generally frightened to death, is in some magical fashion better prepared for adult life in his society than is an American graduate of high school or college.

responses in the individual organism. It is in part this very rigidity which aids us in studying its structure and function, while the mechanics of the more undifferentiated family remain somewhat obscure.

That greater attention has been devoted to the older pattern[50] is therefore natural and appropriate, but one cannot help hoping that an analysis such as Parsons' might now be extended to the de-differentiated family. The rapidity of social change, both subtle and violent, in our own era raises the fascinating possibility that a clear understanding of the functions of emergent as well as decadent institutions might enable us to anticipate the institutional arrangements of tomorrow.

50. This is not meant to imply, of course, that de-differentiation is "new," but only that at the present time there seems to be a trend toward the particular form discussed here.

Judith Blake

Coercive Pronatalism and American Population Policy

The achievement of zero population growth implies that American childbearing be limited to an average of approximately two children per woman. Since women who are currently approaching the end of the reproductive age span have borne an average of three children, advocates of population stabilization are concerned about the mechanisms for achieving a two-child average.[1] The search for measures to insure us a reproductive level that is both low and non-fluctuating is intensified by a growing recognition of the lead-time required to achieve zero population growth. For example, the two-child average will afford us zero growth only *after* the age structure of the population has become less favorable to reproduction than is currently the case. Until the baby-boom babies, who have grown up to be mothers and potential mothers, move out of the reproductive ages, the achievement of zero growth implies fewer than two children per woman.[2] It is clear, therefore, that long-run population stability will require either that Americans, in general, restrict themselves to micro-families, or that a substantial share of the population remain childless (and/or have only one child) while others have the moderate-sized families to which we are now accustomed.

It is perhaps not surprising that such a major change in our reproductive behavior would seem to call for the introduction of state-imposed coercions on individuals—an abrogation of the "voluntary" character of childbearing decisions.[3] This popular view of what must be done in order to achieve population stability is, of course, both shocking

1. *Vital Statistics of the United States,* Vol. I—Natality, 1968, pp. 1–15. By January 1, 1969, women aged 35–39 had borne 3,124 children per 1,000 women. If it were possible to relate this cumulative cohort fertility to *ever-married* women only, we would find that births per ever-married women (what we think of as "family size") were considerably higher.

2. Tomas Frejka, "Reflections on the Demographic Conditions Needed to Establish a U.S. Stationary Population Growth," *Population Studies,* Vol. 22 (November 1968), pp. 379–397.

3. See, for example, Garrett Hardin, "The Tragedy of the Commons," *Science,* Vol. 162, pp. 1243–1248; Paul R. Ehrlich and Anne H. Ehrlich, *Population, Resources, Environment* (San Francisco: W.H. Freeman & Co., 1970), pp. 254–256 and 272–274; and Kenneth Boulding, *The Meaning of the 20th Century* (New York: Harper and Row, 1964).

and frightening to government officials. In the face of suggestions regarding state "control" over reproduction, programs that promise population stability through the elimination of "unwanted" fertility alone seem reassuringly inoffensive. Understandably, they are embraced with relief regardless of how unlikely it is that they will be effective.[4] Their selling point is "the right to choose" one's family size and this "right" is celebrated as an ultimate end. In the words of Frank Notestein:[5]

> . . . Family planning represents a new and important freedom in the world. It will surely be a happy day when parents can have and can avoid having children, as they see fit. . . . It is a matter of major importance that this kind of new freedom to choose, now existing for the bulk of the population, be extended to its most disadvantaged parts. If it were extended, reproduction would be brought fairly close to the replacement level. However, I would advocate the right to choose even if I thought the demographic consequences would be highly adverse, because it will always be possible to manipulate the environment in which the choice is made.

However, both the coercion approach and the laissez-faire approach ("the right to choose") suffer from a serious empirical flaw. They each assume that free choice and voluntarism now exist and that they are marred only by incomplete distribution of contraceptives. One approach says that voluntarism must be curtailed, the other claims that it must be preserved at all cost. Neither recognizes that it does not exist right now. Neither takes into account that at present, reproductive behavior is under stringent institutional control and that this control constitutes, in many respects, a coercive pronatalist policy. Hence, an effective antinatalist policy will not necessarily involve an increase in coercion or a reduction in the "voluntary" element in reproduction, because individuals are under pronatalist constraints right now. People make their "voluntary" reproductive choices in an institutional context that severely constrains them not to choose non-marriage, not to choose childlessness, not to choose only one child, and even not to limit themselves solely to two children. If we can gain insight into the coercions and restraints under which we currently operate, it may become more obvious that an antinatalist policy can be one that is *more* voluntary—allows a wider spectrum of individual choice— than is presently the case. Let us first examine why individuals may be said to be under constraint and suffer coercion, in any society,

4. Bumpass and Westoff have calculated a "medium" estimate of the number of "unwanted" births in the United States for the period 1960–1965 as 19.1 percent of all births. Larry Bumpass and Charles F. Westoff, "The 'Perfect Contraceptive' Population," *Science*, Vol. 169 (September 18, 1970), pp. 1177–1182. For a demonstration that the current level of "unwanted" births in the United States is much lower than the Bumpass and Westoff estimate, see Judith Blake, "Reproductive Motivation and Population Policy," *BioScience*, Vol. XXI (March 1, 1971), pp. 215–220. This paper also shows that the inoffensiveness of the family planning approach is overrated. "Unwanted" births occur most frequently among politically sensitive sub-groups in our population.

5. Frank W. Notestein, "Zero Population Growth," *Population Index*, Vol. 36 (October–December 1970), p. 448.

regarding reproduction. We may then turn to the main body of our paper—the actual nature of some important existing reproductive coercions in American society.

The Sociology of the Family and the Reproductive Function

In order to understand the long-run determinants of birth rates, insofar as these relate to motivational and not conditional factors, one must translate birth rates into the operational context of reproduction.[6] People do not have birth rates, they have children. Their willingness to bear and rear children—to expend their human and material resources in this manner—cannot be taken for granted. Rather, childbearing and childrearing take place in an organizational context which influences people strongly to do one set of things—reproduce, and not do other sets of things—activities that would conflict or compete with reproduction. The bearing and rearing of children thus represents one kind of allocation and organization of human and material resources. In all viable societies social control has operated to organize human beings into childbearing and childrearing groups—families—that, by definition, have proven to be highly efficient reproductive machines. Reproductively inefficient societies have not survived for historical man to study.

As with other forms of social control, that responsible for the support of the family as an institution rests in informal and formal (legal) rules of behavior. These will range from behavior that must be performed—prescribed—to behavior that is forbidden—proscribed. Large areas of behavior are simply permitted or preferred. What leads us to abide by these rules? Clearly, the same mechanisms of social control that lead us to abide by any rules. First of all, we are socialized from the beginning both to learn the rules and to believe they are right. Second, the everyday process of interaction with others puts us in constant contact with the norm-enforcement process, since other people have a stake in how we behave. They can reward us with approval, or punish us with rejection. If these informal sanctions are not effective, then formal ones may be invoked such as, for example, the law. Finally, the master control of all is what might be called the "sociological predicament." This is that any existing social organization represents a selection of possible roles and statuses, goals and activities, etc., available to individuals. Not only are persons with certain characteristics allocated to particular roles and statuses and proscribed from others, but all individuals in a given society

6. Conditional factors affecting birth rates are, for example, involuntary infecundity or the inability to find a mate because of an imbalance in the sex ratio due to migration. Conditional factors are those over which the individual has no control—his efforts cannot affect them, hence, his motives are not relevant to the outcome.

typically have available to them, as the outer perimeter of their expectations, what the society has to offer from a role and status point of view. Such limitation of role alternatives obviates the need for many more direct coercions. Individuals are usually not afforded role options that might be deviant. This fact is abundantly documented by the social sciences. An illustration of particular relevance to this paper is Burgess and Wallin's criticism of Waller's well-known theory of the function of romantic love. Waller presupposed that the idealization and euphoria of being "in love" are necessary to propel people into marriage. He reasoned that a powerful force is needed to overcome the attractions of alternative ways of life. Burgess and Wallin's point is simple—such attractive alternatives do not exist.[7]

> ... The woman who does not marry is likely to be judged a failure, the implication generally being that she was not chosen, she was not desired. Apart from the injury to her self-esteem, nonmarriage imposes difficulties and frustrations. Adult social life tends to be organized around married couples. Sexual satisfaction is not easily obtained without risk by the unmarried female who desires it, and the experience of motherhood is denied her. . . .
>   [As for men,] . . . to marry is to be normal, and from childhood on we are exposed to the idea of marriage as something to be desired, the risk of divorce notwithstanding. Although some men can secure their sexual satisfaction outside of the matrimonial relationship, most of them are strongly attracted by the promise of sexual gratification with the regularity, convenience and comfort which marriage affords.

In sum, reproduction and replacement, like other societal functions, require an organized allocation of human and material resources. Societies have resolved this problem of resource allocation by means of diffused control mechanisms (rather than a government planning board, for example), but the mechanisms are nonetheless quite palpably there. And they involve the individual in an articulated and coercive set of constraints. He has some choice among fixed alternatives, but, as we shall see, even his "choices" are deeply influenced by his past social experience and the kind of person he has been influenced to become. His behavior is "voluntary" only in a restricted sense—not in the sense of being unpatterned, uncontrolled, or unrestrained. In effect, regardless of whether a typical birth cohort of individuals contains a large proportion of persons who might be unsuited to family life, human societies are so organized as to attempt to make individuals as suited as possible, to motivate them to want to be suited, and to provide them with little or no alternative to being suited as they mature. By fiction and by fiat, parenthood is the "natural" human condition, and to live one's life as a

7. Ernest W. Burgess and Paul Wallin, "Idealization, Love, and Self-Esteem," reprinted in *Family Roles and Interaction*, Jerold Heiss (ed.), (Chicago: Rand McNally, 1969), pp. 121–122.

family member is the desideratum. In this context, individuals make their reproductive "choice."

The present paper will concentrate on two such diffused and implicit pronatalist coercions in modern American society—the prescribed primacy of parenthood in the definition of adult sex roles and the prescribed congruence of personality traits with the demands of the sex roles as defined. I believe it can be shown that there is, in American society, not only an absence of legitimate alternatives to sex roles having parenthood as a primacy focus, but that change is particularly difficult to effect because those individuals who might aspire to such alternatives are suppressed and neutralized. My thesis is that unless we realize that we have been locking pronatalism into both the structure of society and the structure of personality, the problem of fertility control will appear to be the reverse of what it actually is. We will continue to believe that our principal policy problem is one of *instituting* antinatalist coercions instead of *lifting* pronatalist ones. We will see fertility reduction as involving *more* regimentation than presently exists, when, in fact, it should involve *less,* since individuals will no longer be universally constrained to forsake other possible interests and goals in order to devote themselves to the reproductive function.

Role Differentiation by Sex and the Primacy of Parenthood

Role differentiation by sex in American society makes actual or anticipated parenthood a pre-condition for all other aspects of men's and women's roles. The content of sex roles—men's and women's "spheres"—uses as a bench mark the sexually differentiated relation to childbearing and rearing. The feminine role is normatively maternal and, hence, intra-familial, "integrative," emotionally supportive, and "expressive." The masculine role is normatively paternal and, as a result, primarily the complement of the maternal role—extra-familial, protective, economially supportive, and "instrumental" (or "task-oriented").[8] By according primacy to the kinship statuses of "mother" and "father" these role expectations thus assume that parenthood is implicit in the very definition of masculinity and femininity. Moreover, not only does the identification of masculinity and femininity with parenthood mean that

8. Although the primary focus of the typical masculine role might seem to be occupational in modern societies, the structural basis for the man's claim on an occupational role relates very clearly to his family obligations. Indeed, as will be seen later in this paper, a man's prior claim, over a woman, to a job has rested on his role of provider for a family. A married man who is a father has a similar prior claim to a job (or to a promotion) over a bachelor. From the man's subjective point of view, except in a few independently attractive occupations, the economic role is merely instrumental to the private (usually familial) existence.

reproduction is implicitly prescribed for everyone but, as might be expected, it means that alternative role definitions for the sexes are, at best, tolerated, and, at worst, proscribed.

Since we have been speaking of the United States, it is worth asking whether the identification of gender with parenthood is unusual in human societies. Are Americans odd? The answer is, of course, negative. We share this linkage of sex roles and parenthood functions with a large number of primitive and technologically backward peoples, as well as with some more modern ones.[9] Indeed, it is probably true that, insofar as men and women engage in reproduction in families, this division of labor will be subject to only minor modifications. What is open to question, however, is the demographic appropriateness for a low-mortality society of rigidly identifying, for *everyone,* the sexual with the parental role. Since sex is an aspect of a person's identity that begins its influence from birth, we appear to be locking ourselves into reproduction through sex-role expectations that ceased to be demographically necessary for our entire population before most of us were born.

What is the evidence for the identification of sex roles with traditional parental functions in American society? Is such an identification really normative? One significant way of answering this question is to see what happens when the norm is challenged, or when there is some large-scale defection from the sex-role expectations as defined. If the norm is operative, we would expect to discover that a variety of sanctions are invoked to bring behavior back into line. Additionally, we might expect to see an effort to label the deviation as not merely contra-normative but pathological as well.

In the remainder of this section on sex roles, we shall examine a number of challenges to the traditional expectations for the sexes in American society. These challenges are: the labor force participation of

9. For a cross-cultural analysis (based on almost 50 societies) of sex-role differentiation, see Morris Zelditch, Jr., "Role Differentiation in the Nuclear Family: A Comparative Study," in Talcott Parsons and Robert F. Bales (eds.), *Family, Socialization and Interaction Process* (Glencoe, Ill.: The Free Press, 1955), pp. 309–351. [See this book, pp. 256–58.] Although of great value, Zelditch's analysis was not designed to bring out some of the variability among societies in the availability of alternative sex roles. For example, one contrast between many European countries and the United States is the existence, in the former but not in the latter, of an established religion having a celibate clergy. Additionally, European countries have suffered from numerous unintended antinatalist constraints —devastating wars on their own territories, acute housing shortages, and, as compared with overseas European countries, fewer opportunities for upward social mobility and more parental control over the means to marry. It is of some interest that, in the mid-1960's, only 10 percent of American women remained single in the age group 20–29. Among European countries, in the same period for the same age group, percentages single among women were, on the average, approximately double that of the United States. For a discussion of contrasts between Europe and the United States, see Judith Blake, "Demographic Science and the Redirection of Population Policy," in Mindel C. Sheps and Jeanne Clare Ridley, *Public Health and Population Change* (Pittsburgh: University of Pittsburgh Press, 1965), pp. 41–69; and "Parental Control, Delayed Marriage, and Population Policy."

women, higher education for women, feminism, and male homosexuality. We shall find, in all cases, widespread opposition to the recognized threat to sex-role expectations. Furthermore, in the case of the first three, we shall see that adjustment to this opposition has taken place so effectively as to substantially neutralize these sources of change in sex-role expectations. In the case of the last example, the deviancy is regarded as an aberration (a pathology) for which diverse causes and cures are sought. There is systematic refusal to recognize that *intra*-sex variability in temperament, personality traits, and physical and mental capability may, in actuality, be fully as important as *inter*-sex variation, if one but excludes the difference in reproductive capacity.

The Working Woman and the Primacy of Parenthood for Both Sexes. Nothing better illustrates the absence of genuine options to parental roles in our society than the nature of the opposition to having women work outside the home. The most salient and enduring objections to a genuine career role for women—a commitment to outside work—have been two: First, that no women—even unmarried women—should be allowed to challenge men's prior claim on jobs since men must support families; and second, that outside work is unsuited to women physically and mentally since their natural fulfillment lies in another sphere entirely— motherhood. In effect, the opposition to work-commitment by women has reaffirmed *both* the male's role as father and family supporter and the female's role as mother and housewife. Smuts documents legal and public concern along these lines since the 1870's.[10] Although, as he shows, the emphasis on the physical inappropriateness of outside work for women has disappeared, the "psychological" and temperamental uniqueness of women is still emphasized strongly. Hence, jobs are sex-typed, women are "protected" by legislation and both hiring and firing take advantage of the typical women's marginal commitment to full-time, long-term employment. Through an analysis of articles on women's labor force participation in major American popular magazines since 1900, Betty Stirling has shown that the dual considerations of concern for protecting the man's family-supporting job and concern for protecting the woman's motherhood role has characterized opposition to female employment outside the home from the beginning.[11] Public opinion polls have demonstrated the same anxieties.[12] Religious opposition to women working has been particularly vocal in the Catholic press and marriage manuals —specifically on the bases of threats to the supporting role of men and the motherhood role of women.[13]

10. Robert W. Smuts, *Women and Work in America* (New York: Columbia University, 1959), pp. 110–155.
11. Betty R. Stirling, "The Interrelation of Changing Attitudes and Changing Conditions with Reference to the Labor Force Participation of Wives," unpublished Ph.D. dissertation, University of California, Berkeley, 1963, pp. 6–72.
12. *Ibid.*, pp. 73–81.
13. *Ibid.*, pp. 180–183.

In effect, although economic opportunities might have led us to expect the emergence of a career role for a numerically important group of unmarried, and married but childless, women, in actual fact the immense increase in labor force participation by women took a different tack entirely. Women's labor in the market has been utilized and tolerated only on condition that it supported and enhanced the traditional parental roles for both sexes. In the words of the National Manpower Council:[14]

> ... Americans view the man in the family as the primary breadwinner and, when jobs are scarce, are inclined to believe that women workers should not compete with men who have families to support. Americans also believe that mothers should personally care for their children during their early formative years. Consequently, even though there are today over 2.5 million mothers in the labor force whose children are under six, there is still little sympathy with the idea of mothers holding full-time jobs when their children are of preschool age, unless they are compelled to do so by economic necessity. . . .

The difficulties women experienced who wished to challenge the identity of sexual and parental roles have not been simply "male dominance" or "male power," but rather the intense societal supports for the *family roles* of mother and father. The opposition to women working thus stemmed fully as much from the obligatory nature of family formation (and the sex differentiation of parents) as from a fear of the diminution of male authority generally. We shall see, moreover, in a later section, that, after World War II, when women's educational and economic opportunities could, objectively, have provided some challenge to the primacy of the parental role, the unmarried and married but childless women came under attack from "scientific" sources. In the face of declining religious influence, a breakdown of Victorian "traditions," and expanding career opportunities for women, "science" stepped in, in the guise of psychoanalysis, to provide an authoritative prescription of parenthood, and severe condemnation of the career women. Not surprisingly, few unmarried or childless females were available to re-define the role of the working woman along career lines. Women's labor force participation evolved as an adjunct, not an alternative, to motherhood.[15] The peculiar character of this participation—low wages, dead-end jobs, and sex-typing—tends moreover, to be self-perpetuating. Each generation of girls views the market and finds few

14. National Manpower Council, *Womanpower* (New York: Columbia University Press, 1957), pp. 15–16.
15. Oppenheimer's statistical analysis of the interaction of supply and demand in women's increased labor force participation between 1940 and 1960 illustrates this point. The supply of what had, historically, been the "typical" female worker, a young, unmarried woman, remained stationary or declined. Hence, the only mechanism whereby the observed increase in the female labor force could have taken place was through the participation of another category of women. This category was principally the older, married woman whose child-rearing obligations were either ended or greatly lessened. Valerie K. Oppenheimer, "The Interaction of Demand and Supply and Its Effect on the Female Labor Force in the United States," *Population Studies*, Vol. XXI (November 1967), pp. 239–259.

realistic career options therein. The primacy of men's and women's family roles has successfully absorbed what might have been a genuine alternative to reproduction for a number of women. As Smuts says:[16]

> . . . the woman who urgently wants to develop and utilize her abilities in work still has barriers to overcome. Employers tend to judge all working women on the basis of their experience with the majority who are content with modest rewards for modest efforts. . . .

Higher Education for Women: The Mother's Helper. Theoretically, the provision of higher education to women constituted a major challenge to the primacy of motherhood as *the* sex role for American females. Far more than the franchise, higher education seemed to imply that women *should* be given career avenues equal in all respects to the channels afforded to men. In this sense, it cast into doubt the norm that motherhood is the primary role for all but the unhappy few.

The initial efforts in the United States to provide higher education for women were met with much explicit verbalization concerning the possible undermining of the wife-mother role—the only proper feminine role. This history is well known and need not concern us here.[17] More important is the mounting evidence that genuine educational opportunities for women have been subtly infused by an implicit (occasionally even explicit) premise—the unchallenged assumption that the wife-mother role is a pre-condition for all other roles women might wish to play. As Mabel Newcomer has said:[18]

> The fact that homemaking is woman's most important role has never been seriously questioned either by those arguing in favor of college education for women or by those opposing it. Those opposing higher education for women have usually expressed the fear that it will encourage them to pursue independent careers, foregoing marriage; or if they marry, that it will make them dissatisfied with the homemaker's lot. Those promoting higher education have, on the contrary, insisted that college women make better wives and mothers than their less educated sisters. Even those who have been concerned with the rights and interests of unmarried women have never argued that higher education might encourage women to remain single, except as it occasionally offered a reasonably satisfactory alternative when the only available young men were not entirely acceptable.

Indeed, the women's colleges—in the vanguard of higher education for women—early learned to stress that their effect on diverting their charges from the path of wifehood and motherhood would be nonexistent. Defensively, they assured their trustees, their backers, the prospective parents of their tuition-paying student bodies that higher education for

16. Smuts, *op. cit.,* p. 109.
17. See, for example, Dorothy Gies McGuigan, *A Dangerous Experiment: 100 Years of Women at the University of Michigan* (Ann Arbor: Center for Continuing Education of Women, 1970).
18. Mabel Newcomer, *A Century of Higher Education for American Women* (New York: Harper & Brothers, 1959), p. 210.

women would leave unchallenged woman's *role* and women's *expectations*.[19]

The stated "aims" of the colleges, as reviewed by Newcomer in the late 1950's, were sufficiently vague concerning the purposes for which young girls were attending as to leave unthreatened either the classical feminine role definition, or the intellectual fantasies of the students.[20] Clearly, the educators of young women had learned the hard way that the uncomfortable resolution between the promise of "equality"—even for some—and the reality of motherhood for all was best left to each individual girl to resolve as best she could. The college was not to be the champion of the "odd-ball" girl.

The most obvious deviant among the college presidents and promoters of women's education was Lynn White, Jr. (then President of Mills College), who attempted to clarify and make explicit the hidden agenda behind women's education in America. Almost all women do marry, few women pursue systematic careers, and even these careers are typically "feminine" rather than masculine. Why not face it? Why not educate our daughters in the light of definitively sex-linked capabilities and the appropriate social roles that express these capabilities?[21] So eager was White to clinch his point, that he fell into the familiar position adopted by some of the feminists—the moral *superiority* of the traditional female virtues over the crasser male qualities. Thus, if women were constitutionally debarred from the more highly-regarded cultural pursuits, they should not feel badly. These pursuits have been overrated anyway.[22] White thus invoked the position that helped legitimate the downfall of feminism—women's battles were to be on higher ground as befits their universally more civilized, sensitive, and gentle natures. Of similar sentiments expressed by the feminists, O'Neill has written, "Definitions like this left men with few virtues anyone was bound to admire, and inspired women to think of themselves as a kind of super race condemned by historical accident and otiose convention to serve their natural inferiors."[23] In keeping with his effort to legitimate separate and unequal education for women, White celebrated motherhood as women's noblest pursuit.[24] He even deplored the anti-family bias that, he alleged, was being transmitted to men by the "celibate tradition" in higher education. For men as well as women, the family should come first, ". . . unless men as well as women can be given the conviction that personal

19. *Ibid.*, pp. 146–147.
20. *Ibid.*, p. 60.
21. Lynn White, Jr., *Educating Our Daughters* (New York: Harper & Bros., 1950), pp. 46–48.
22. *Ibid.*, pp. 46–47.
23. William O'Neill, *Everyone Was Brave: The Rise and Fall of Feminism in America* (New York: Quadrangle Books, 1968, p. 37.
24. White, *op cit.*, pp. 71–76.

cultivation and career are secondary to making a success of the family, and indeed that both are bleak satisfactions apart from a warm hearth, we shall not have found wisdom."[25] In a significant chapter that constitutes a paean to motherhood, he claimed that the American population was not replacing itself, that "the best" people were particularly remiss in their reproductive obligation, and that it was the duty of high-minded American women to devote themselves to maternity.[26] Repeatedly he emphasized the hopelessness of combining a genuine career with a family of sufficient size, and enjoined college women not to be inhibited by a college education from "flinging themselves with complete enthusiasm and abandon" into family life.[27]

Is the aim-inhibition that has suffused higher education for women, its absorption into the anticipated motherhood role, merely an intellectual preoccupation of the educators, or have young college women themselves received the message that their college experience must be adapted to their future role as mothers? Two studies of American college girls, one done by Komarovsky in the 1940's, and another done by Goldsen and others in the 1950's, show clearly that the pressures on women to remain undiverted from motherhood followed them into college.

Komarovsky, writing in 1953, expressed the concern of the educator over holding out to women impossible and contradictory goals.[28]

> . . . The very education which is to make the college housewife a cultural leaven of her family and her community may develop in her interests which are frustrated by other phases of housewifery. We are urged to train women for positions of leadership in civic affairs when, at the same time, we define capacity for decisive action, executive ability, hardihood in the face of opposition as "unfeminine" traits. We want our daughters to be able, if the need arises, to earn a living at some worth-while occupation. In doing so, we run the risk of awakening interests and abilities which, again, run counter to the present definition of femininity.

Her case studies of women students seemed to indicate to her that these young women were presented with "equally compelling" but "contradictory" pressures. Actually, the data seem to trace a temporal change in parental and peer pressure concerning academic and occupational achievement and the traditional female role. Parents and peers were encouraging of achievement until it seemed to stand in the way of marriage and motherhood. Then, for the girl who had not already received "the message" by means of less obvious cues, sanctions came into play. She was effectively told that she should not allow academic or professional achievement "to get in her way."[29] For example:

25. *Ibid.*, p. 76.
26. *Ibid.*, pp. 93–96.
27. *Ibid.*, p. 101.
28. Mirra Komarovsky, *Women in the Modern World* (Boston: Little, Brown & Company, 1953), pp. 66–67.
29. *Ibid.*, pp. 68–69, 69–71, 72. Italics mine.

All through grammar school and high school my parents led me to feel that to do well in school was my chief responsibility. A good report card, an election to student office, these were the news Mother bragged about in telephone conversations with her friends. *But recently they suddenly got worried about me: I don't pay enough attention to social life, a women needs* some *education but not that much.* They are disturbed by my determination to go to the School of Social Work. Why my ambitions should surprise them after they have exposed me for four years to some of the most inspired and stimulating social scientists in the country, I can't imagine. They have some mighty strong arguments on their side. What is the use, they say, of investing years in training for a profession only to drop it in a few years? Chances of meeting men are slim in this profession. Besides, I may become so preoccupied with it as to sacrifice social life. The next few years are, after all, the proper time to find a mate. But the urge to apply what I have learned, and the challenge of this profession is so strong that I shall go on despite the family opposition.

I . . . work for a big metropolitan daily as a correspondent in the city room. I am well liked there and may possibly stay as a reporter after graduation in February. I have had several spreads (stories running to more than eight or ten inches of space), and this is considered pretty good for a college correspondent. Naturally, I was elated and pleased at such breaks, and as far as the city room is concerned I'm off to a very good start in a career that is hard for a man to achieve and even harder for a woman. General reporting is still a man's work in the opinion of most people. *I have a lot of acclaim but also criticism, and I find it difficult to be praised for being clever and working hard and then, when my efforts promise to be successful, to be condemned and criticized for being unfeminine and ambitious.*

The 1952 study of both male and female Cornell students by Goldsen, Rosenberg, Williams, and Suchman shows that the coeds had almost universally accepted motherhood as a pre-condition for any other activity.[30]

A traditional middle-class idea that a woman's only career should be her family is rejected by almost all the students. Instead, they are neither unequivocally for nor unequivocally against the idea of women having careers. The attitude seems to be, "It's okay providing. . . ." Providing she is not married, or providing she has no children, or providing her children are "old enough"—a notion about which there is a wide range of opinion. Let the women have careers, indeed encourage them, but be sure it does not interfere with her main job of bearing and rearing children.

Interestingly, the young women in the Cornell study had adjusted their ideas of the proper jobs for women to the demands of their motherhood role. Unlike the new feminists of the 1960's and 1970's, these women assumed that their labor market activity would not be equal in demands or prestige with that of men.[31]

. . . Our data indicate that just about every college girl wants to marry and have children, and that she fully expects to do so. . . . Most of them see no

30. Rose K. Goldsen, Morris Rosenberg, Robin M. Williams, Jr., and Edward A. Suchman, *What College Students Think* (Princeton, New Jersey: Princeton University Press, 1960), pp. 46–47.
31. *Ibid.*, pp. 47–49.

essential conflict between family life and a career—the sort of career, that is, that they consider "suitable" for a woman. . . . The occupations women choose to go into are quite different from those chosen by men. They overwhelmingly select the traditional "women's occupations."

Why did they want to work at all? One reason was to keep occupied before marriage. Another was insurance—against the remote possibility of remaining single, and against adversity in their marriage. More significant, however, was ambivalence about the suitability of homemaking and motherhood to their interests and temperaments. A striking feature of these data is that these young women did not appear to be overwhelmingly *attracted* to maternity, they simply did not see any alternative role as realistic.[32]

> There is no question that college girls count on building up equity in family life, not in professional work. A dedicated career-girl is a deviant: in a real sense she is unwilling to conform to her sex-role as American society defines it. For professional work among women in this country (and the college-trained women agree) is viewed as an interlude, at best a part-time excursion away from full-time family life which the coeds yearn for, impatiently look forward to . . . and define as largely monotony, tedium, and routine.

The intention to work, the vision of personal realization through the use of the talents and capabilities they had come, through their college training, to know they possessed, represented the psychological life-preserver they promised themselves to keep at hand.[33]

By what mechanisms was the "career girl" role rendered so deviant? One mechanism was clearly the girls' perception of what men wanted in a woman. The Cornell study found, for example, that other than the condition that an ideal mate love her spouse, two-thirds of all college men in the sample cited "interested in having a family" as highly important in a mate.[34] To the young college woman, a way of life as deviant as a genuine and demanding career represented a journey toward an unknown, inappropriate, and potentially tragic destination. She might never meet *any* man who was interested in such a freak. Half of the Cornell men were quite clear in stating that they either did not approve of women having careers, or approved only if the woman was unmarried or, if married, had no children. Only 22 percent of the men approved of a woman having a career regardless of the age of her children, and most of the remainder approved only if the children were of high school age or older.[35] Finally, the young women's sense of constraint concerning pre-marital sexual relations made an indefinite postponement of marriage appear lonely and sexless. Even among girls who were interested in careers, sexual relationships were defined only in romantic, emotional terms, and close to 40

32. *Ibid.*, p. 58.
33. *Ibid.*, pp. 58–59.
34. *Ibid.*, p. 90.
35. *Ibid.*, p. 48.

percent felt that pre-marital sex relations were "never justified" for women. Among young women who ranked low on careerism, half felt that pre-marital relations were "never justified."[36]

Has it all changed by 1971? Obviously, there have been many external changes. The development of contraception—especially the pill—has greatly altered the conditions under which young college men and women may consider non-marital relationships. Public policy is increasingly concerned with equal educational and occupational opportunity for women, and the country has been literally deluged by antinatalist and neo-feminist propaganda. How have college women reacted? And what reactions must they cope with in college men? Is there yet a perceived alternative to marriage and a family, or simply a scaling down of family size desires? In an attempt to clarify this and other issues, I inserted a set of questions on family size preferences, preferred age at marriage, non-marriage, attitudes toward the pill and abortion in a special youth study conducted by the Gallup Poll in June 1971. The study included two samples of young people aged 18–24—one a college sample and one a representative national sample of persons in this age group. Table 1 presents some relevant data for the college sample.

The results indicate clearly that few men or women in this college sample would like to be childless, or have only one child. More than half of the men, and approximately half of the women would like to have a two-child family. A third of the men and almost 40 percent of the women want three or more children. Although these results show that family-size preferences are smaller than those expressed in the 1950's and 1960's, the desire for at least two children is clear and apparently firm.[37] A question on the family size considered "too small" demonstrates that an acceptable family size begins with two children. On the other hand, there seems to be no clear proscription against even a relatively large family. A question concerning the size family the respondent would consider "too large" shows that three children are tolerated by all but a minority of respondents—20 percent. Even at the level of five children, 27 percent of the men and 40 percent of the women have not yet designated the family as "too large."

Turning to age at marriage we see that, according to both men and women, women should definitely be married by age 25. Men believe that women should marry earlier than do women themselves, but there is consensus that age 25 is the upper limit. Although the best age at marriage

36. *Ibid.*, p. 53.
37. Although no exactly comparable data on a college-*attending* population are available for the earlier period, it is worth noting that among college-*educated* men and women under age 30 in the late 1950's mean *ideal* family size was 3.3–3.4, in contrast to 2.4–2.5 as the mean *desired* family size in this current sample of college students. Data for 1971 on *ideal* family size among college-educated respondents in the reproductive ages show means varying between 2.6 and 2.8. These recent data will be published shortly by the author.

for men is clearly older than for women, there is remarkable consensus between men and women concerning what this age should be. Not before age 21, not after age 30. Preferably between ages 21 and 25. However, although marrying and having a family are clearly the norm, the college

TABLE 1. Family-Size Preferences and Attitudes Toward Age at Marriage and Non-Marriage Among a National Sample of White American College Students, June 1971. Percentages.*

	College Men	College Women
How many children would you like to have?		
None	7	9
1	3	4
2	56	49
3 or more	33	38
Total	100	100
(N)	(548)	(348)
According to your personal tastes and preferences, what size family do you think is too small— a husband, wife, and how many children?		
No children	36	31
One child	53	58
Two children	7	6
Three or more	4	5
Total	100	100
(N)	(529)	(331)
And what size family do you think is too large—a husband, wife, and how many children?		
One child	1	0
Two children	1	1
Three children	19	16
Four children	25	21
Five children	25	23
Six children	11	15
Seven or more children	17	25
Total	100	100
(N)	(548)	(350)

* The difference between N's shown under the various questions and the total number of respondents (562 males and 355 females) constitute the NA/DK category in each case.

TABLE 1. (CONTINUED) Family-Size Preferences and Attitudes Toward Age at Marriage and Non-Marriage Among a National Sample of White American College Students, June 1971. Percentages.*

	College Men	College Women
What do you think is the best age for a girl to marry?		
Under 18	1	0
18–19	5	2
20	14	12
21	21	16
22	23	20
23–25	31	44
Over 25	5	6
Total	100	100
(N)	(529)	(343)
What do you think is the best age for a man to marry?		
Under 21	5	3
21–22	22	20
23–24	26	26
25	24	27
26–30	21	24
Over 30	2	1
Total	100	100
(N)	(533)	(344)
Do you think a woman can have a happy life even if she never marries?		
Yes	81	82
No	16	15
DK	3	3
Total	100	100
(N)	(562)	(355)
What about a man—do you think he can have a happy life if he never marries?		
Yes	87	84
No	12	13
DK	1	3
Total	100	100
(N)	(562)	(355)
Total Respondents	(562)	(355)

* The difference between N's shown under the various questions and the total number of respondents (562 males and 355 females) constitute the NA/DK category in each case.

men and women in this sample do not deny that either a man or a woman can have a happy life in the unmarried state. There is a clear recognition that at least *some* people can do this. Unfortunately, we do not know, from this single question, whether respondents believe the "average" or "normal" person can be happy unmarried, or whether they believe only an unusual person can so exist.

These results may seem surprising in today's context. Has neo-feminism had no effect? Why is there no clear break with the family role altogether among a substantial number of the college elite?[38] In order to understand their position, one must realize that no call has come to make such a break, no models have been presented, no champion of a genuinely alternative role has appeared. "Women's liberation," like higher educa-tion for women and women's labor force activity, has absorbed, in its turn, the norm that the American woman's adult role *includes* motherhood. To have done otherwise would have been to sacrifice its principal constituency, as we shall see. It, like higher education for women and jobs for women, has *accommodated* itself to maternity and even become its militant champion. Motherhood is, after all, one of "women's rights."

Feminism and the "Do Both" Syndrome. It is often assumed that the present-day "woman's liberation" movement is essentially antinatalist in ideology and that its effects will be antinatalist as well. Actually, however, the main thrust of the movement's stand is supportive of motherhood for all; what is decried is the relative disadvantage that women experience because of childbearing and rearing. In effect, women's liberation is concerned with lowering the exclusionary barriers for women in the labor force, opening up educational channels, elevating women's awareness of subtle forms of discrimination against them in the outside world *and* supporting women's right to have families as well. Rather than concerning itself with the atypical spinster, or childless woman, the movement has gained popularity through its recognition of the problems of women who already have made a choice to be mothers and who then are dissatisfied with their impaired occupational chances, or who find motherhood less than they expected it to be and wish to switch gears. Betty Friedan's book, *The Feminine Mystique*, was addressed primarily to this group of women—those suffering from "the problem that has no name." However, although the movement has pitched its appeal to women who have already made their reproductive choices and urged them to seek out an alternative identity as well, its general philosophy for *all* women is one of *combining* marriage and motherhood, on the one hand, with a non-familial role, on the other. Indeed, it is this militant

38. It should be noted that, as might be expected, the non-college sample of 18–24 year olds is more pronatalist in its attitudes than the college group.

statement that women should not *have* to make a choice that gives the movement wide appeal. For example, Friedan says,[39]

> When enough women make life plans geared to their real abilities, and speak out for maternity leaves or even maternity sabbaticals, professionally run nurseries, and other changes in the rules that may be necessary, they will not have to sacrifice the right to honorable competition *any more than they will have to sacrifice marriage and motherhood*.

The movement sees the major injustice toward women as inhering in the expenditure of time and effort on child-rearing, together with the loss of seniority and skills in the labor market due to interrupted career patterns. This philosophy is embodied in the Statement of Purpose of the National Organization for Women.

The modern liberationist position, which requires that women generally be enabled to forego choice in their dominant career roles and shift child-rearing onto outside agencies, has been elaborated by a number of sociologists.

Writing in 1964, Alice Rossi claims that:[40]

> . . . There is no sex equality until women participate on an equal basis with men in politics, occupations, and the family. . . . In politics and the occupational world, to be able to participate depends primarily on whether home responsibilities can be managed simultaneously with work or political commitments. Since women have had, and probably will continue to have, primary responsibility for child-rearing, their participation in politics, professions or the arts cannot be equal to that of men unless ways are devised to ease the combination of home and work responsibilities.

Rossi goes on to outline the need for mother-substitutes, child-care centers, less sexual demarcation in personal traits, and a less demanding definition of the mother's role in socialization. However, she accepts the parental roles for both sexes. Rather than recognizing that men and women may be variably suited to parenthood, she assumes that all are suited and all could be androgynous. Thus they could reconcile the demands of child-care and the desire of the woman to excel outside the home by having both parents play the "inside" and "outside" roles.[41]

Epstein sees the primacy of motherhood obligations for women as the principal barrier to occupational commitment and success. Yet, like Rossi, she does not question the basic premise of the universal desirability of motherhood. As she notes, being single or childless is being a "nonconformist." Thus, the basic inequality lies in the fact that although

39. Betty Friedan, *The Feminine Mystique* (New York: Dell Publishing, 1963), pp. 381–382. Italics mine.
40. Alice S. Rossi, "Equality Between the Sexes: An Immodest Proposal," *Daedalus* (Spring, 1964), p. 610.
41. *Ibid.*, pp. 639–646.

women are normatively held to child care and the home, men can ignore their families with impunity. She says:[42]

> The man who spends too much time with his family is considered something of a loafer. . . . In extreme cases of neglect, wives may be permitted to complain, but clearly the absorption of the man in his work is not considered intolerable. Professors who prefer their work to their wives or children are usually "understood" and forgiven. A similar absorption in work was reported by Stanley Talbot in *Time* magazine; he found that the business tycoon (not surprisingly) clearly preferred his work to his family. There is no comparable "lady tycoon" with a husband and children to neglect; and the lady professional who gives an indication of being more absorbed in work than in her husband and family is neither understood nor forgiven. The woman, unlike the man, cannot spend "too much time" with her family; her role demands as mother and wife are such that they intrude on all other activities. She remains on call during any time spent away from the family and, if she works, many of her family tasks must be fitted into what usually would be working time.

We thus see that, far from questioning the basic premise that all women *should* be mothers, or for that matter that all men should be fathers, the woman's liberation movement accepts the goal of reproduction for all as a basic "good." Childlessness is regarded as an inherent deprivation for all, rather than a socially-induced deprivation for some (perhaps even many). Women who cannot share equally with men in ignoring and neglecting their children are "disadvantaged." Unquestioned is the notion of why persons of *either* sex who have such a marginal commitment to child-rearing should be pressed into having children. If a man wishes to spend virtually his entire time on occupational achievement, travel, and golf, why should the parental status be socially supported as obligatory, or his way of life condemned as self-centered and hedonistic? At present, he has to buy his way out of censure by having a family as "window-dressing" even though he may not change his way of life as a result.[43] Similarly, if a woman wishes to enjoy an externally-oriented way of life, it is intensely pronatalist to specify that nominal parenthood—shored up by maids, nurseries, and child-care centers—be required as a badge of respectability, normality, or conformity.

The woman's liberation movement thus parts company with antinatalism by failing to recognize that it is not in society's interest to

42. Cynthia Fuchs Epstein, *Woman's Place* (Berkeley and Los Angeles: University of California Press, 1970), pp. 99–100 [this book, pp. 473–89].

43. According to Whyte, the good executive's wife is one who accedes to and abets the husband's total commitment to the organization. The company views the man's family as instrumental to its ends and tolerates it only insofar as this proves to be the case. For this reason, the executive's wives are screened in order to see whether they are willing to play the required role. In this manner, many large corporations endeavor to hire men who are, effectively, domesticated bachelors. See William H. Whyte, "The Wife Problem," *Life* (January 7, 1952), reprinted in Robert F. Winch, Robert McGinnis, and Herbert R. Baringer (eds.), *Selected Studies in Marriage and the Family* (New York: Holt, Rinehart, Winston, 1962), pp. 111–126.

encourage the emergence of families in which *neither* parent is committed to parenthood. Rather, a genuine antinatalist policy would be aimed at the *indiscriminate* nature of the family-building vortex that now exists. At present, marriage and parenthood are almost ascribed statuses. They are not really chosen, they happen to people, as the Burgess and Wallin quotation cited earlier states admirably. Moreover, the state takes an essentially frivolous attitude toward the *contracting* of the marital obligation, far more carefree than the attitude it takes toward business contracts. This point is well made by Robert Kingsley in an article on the grounds for granting annulments in the United States.[44]

> A few courts have said that the issue was whether or not the party was mentally capable of entering into an ordinary commercial contract; but the later cases have held that there is no necessary connection between the capacity to make commercial contracts and the capacity to become married. The test today is usually put as requiring the mental ability to "understand the nature of the marriage-relation and the duties and obligations involved therein." So put, it is clear that the capacity to enter into business relations has no bearing on the capacity to marry. . . . For the numerically considerable group of mentally weak persons, whose estates are controlled by guardians but who are permitted to go at large in the community, a legal prohibition on marriage would simply result in fornication, temporary liaisons, and similar socially undesirable practices. Consequently, the law wisely has permitted such persons to marry if it appeared that, concerning that particular kind of relationship, they had a reasonably intelligent attitude.

Clearly, the state has, as a matter of public policy, viewed marriage not as the licensing of parental responsibility, but as a sop to Mrs. Grundy. Yet, the modern interest of the state concerning a marriage lies in the quality of the children produced, not in the prevention of premarital fornication. Nonetheless, the law of marriage is still geared to a time when it was important to use sex as a means of enticing people into marriage and childbearing. In this regard we may suggest that a significant control over reproductive motivation in the future could be the further development of the legal personality of the child, and a diminution of his being treated, at law, as the property of his parents. The "rights" of parents to "choose" parenthood, and the number of offspring they will have could be tempered by the rights of children to certain legal guarantees from their parents.[45] If fathers have already been "liberated" from many parental obligations, and mothers are on the way to "libera-

44. Robert Kingsley, "What Are the Proper Grounds for Granting Annulments?" *Law and Contemporary Problems,* Vol. 18 (1953), pp. 40–41.
45. For a discussion of American family law and the shift "from a patriarchal family structure to one in which the spouses are more nearly equal as between themselves but dominant in their legal relations with their children," see Herma H. Kay, "The Outside Substitute for the Family," reprinted in John N. Edwards (ed.), *The Family and Change* (New York: Knopf, 1969), pp. 261–269. Kay also documents indications that "the future path of legal development will be directed toward the emergence of the child as a person in his own right" (p. 266).

tion," then obviously the rights and welfare of children must come under far more detailed legal and social scrutiny.

It is of some interest that the origins of the acceptance of (even insistence on) universal motherhood were clearly visible in the suffragette movement. As O'Neill points out:[46]

> . . . Having already taken the economic context of American life as essentially given, feminists went on to do the same thing for the marital and domestic system, accepting, for the most part, Victorian marriage as a desirable necessity. In so doing they assured the success of women suffrage while guaranteeing that when women did get the vote and enter the labor market in large numbers, the results would be bitterly disappointing.
> . . . while feminism was born out of a revolt against stifling domesticity . . . by the end of the century most feminists had succumbed to what Charlotte Perkins Gilman called the "domestic mythology." . . . The original feminists had demanded freedom in the name of humanity; the second generation asked for it in the name of maternity. What bound women into selfless sisterhood, it was now maintained, was their reproductive capacity.
> . . . So the effort to escape domesticity was accompanied by an invocation of the domestic ideal—woman's freedom road circled back to the home from which feminism was supposed to liberate her. In this manner feminism was made respectable by accommodating it to the Victorian ethos which had originally forced it into being.

Charlotte Perkins Gilman, however, recognized the logical problems inherent in the motherhood emphasis and presaged the feminist movement of the 1960's and 1970's by a formula that is now familiar to us: Women, generically, should both have families and take an equal place with men, in the non-familial world. In order to enable them to do this, the society must provide mechanisms to relieve them of their homemaking burdens.[47]

The assumption was made then, as it is now, that men—most or all men—find self-expression and fulfillment in the labor market, and that parenthood (and the economic obligations it involves) essentially leaves men's, but not women's, life chances untouched. Since the movement is a special pleading device, it could not be expected to recognize that those differential social and economic advantages that men experience as patriarchs have constituted an incentive for them to undertake the economic obligations of domesticity and parenthood. In many cases, men's chances for social and personal mobility, for education, for promotion, etc., may be impaired by parenthood, although these personal losses may be concealed or dulled by the satisfactions of conforming and the lesser social approval attached to bachelors and the childless. As with women, so with men, the society has many mechanisms for obscuring the costs of parenthood. The fact that men's story of frustration and despair

46. O'Neill, *op cit.*, pp. 30–36.
47. Carl N. Degler, "Revolution Without Ideology: The Changing Place of Women in America," *Daedalus* (Spring, 1964), p. 668.

has found expression in a context different from women's—that of liberation from external economic exploitation—should not obscure the relevance of this story for our concern with pronatalist coercions. The dominant, powerful male of the feminist, woman's liberation script, the male in whose interest and for whose pleasure the society appears to exist, is clearly not the same character who appears in the Marxist-New Leftist script. In the latter, modern man is enslaved by a "system," forced to labor at meaningless tasks from which he is totally alienated, an "un-person," a "nothing." As Marcuse has said:[48]

> Men do not live their own lives, but perform pre-established functions. While they work, they do not fulfill their own needs and faculties but work in *alienation*. Work has now become *general*, and so have the restrictions placed upon the libido: labor time, which is the largest part of the individual's life time, is painful time, for alienated labor is absence of gratification, negation of the pleasure principle. Libido is diverted for socially useful performances in which the individual works for himself only in so far as he works for the apparatus, engaged in activities that mostly do not coincide with his own faculties and desires.

Although neither the feminist nor the New Left movements can be taken as unbiased observers of the social scene, the quotation from Marcuse cautions us not to forget that men undergo both direct and opportunity costs in meeting their economic obligations to their families. It is possible, indeed probable, that many men would choose a different way of life were it both honored and accessible.

Taboo on Homosexuality: A Reinforcement of the Family's Sexual Monopoly. Given the polarization of male and female sex roles in terms of a division of labor that is congruent with parenthood, it is hardly surprising that American society should taboo homosexuality. Although this taboo is doubtless supported by the Judeo-Christian tradition of emphasizing the procreative, as against the purely hedonistic, aspects of sexual intercourse, the religious values do not explain the homosexual taboo but rather covary with it. Both the Judeo-Christian doctrines and the taboo on homosexual relations are part of a pronatalist normative structure that we have inherited.[49]

The function of the homosexual taboo as a support for the normative identity of sex roles with parental roles has been stated explicitly by Parsons:[50]

> . . . the prohibition of homosexuality has the function of reinforcing the differentiation of sex roles, the earliest and hence in one sense the most

48. Herbert Marcuse, *Eros and Civilization* (New York: Vintage Books, 1962), p. 41.
49. Noonan has traced the development of pronatalist doctrine as expressed in Christianity, but dating from the Romans and Jews. See John T. Noonan, Jr., *Contraception* (Harvard University Press, 1965).
50. Talcott Parsons, "Family Structure and the Socialization of the Child," in Talcott Parsons and Robert F. Bales, *op cit.,* pp. 103–104.

fundamental qualitative differentiation of role and personality. Put a little differently, seen structurally the taboo on homosexuality is the obverse of the intra-familial incest taboo, in that it protects the monopoly by the parties to the marriage relationship over erotic gratifications within the family. From the societal point of view it serves to prevent competing personal solidarities from arising which could undermine the motivation to marriage and the establishment of families. In the case of individual psychology it reinforces sex-role identification very strongly. The relation of any erotically bound pair must be to some important degree analogous with the marriage relationship, given the immense importance of the latter in the social structure and in the socialization process. Then at least implicity the question must always arise, which partner plays which role? This means, if it is a homosexual relationship, that *one* of the partners must be radically denying his sex role, while the other does so less drastically by admitting erotic attraction to the same rather than the opposite sex. Put very generally, homosexuality is a mode of structuring of human relationships which is radically in conflict with the place of the nuclear family in the social structure and in the socialization of the child. Its nearly universal prohibition is a direct consequence of the "geometry" of family structure.

The same point is made by Kingsley Davis:[51]

> Homosexual intercourse is obviously incompatible with the family and the sexual bargaining system. The norms and attitudes required to support these institutions as a means of getting the business of reproduction and sexual allocation accomplished tend to downgrade homosexuality . . . . Homosexual devotion . . . directly competes with male-female relationships; it may even mimic heterosexual love, as when the pair pretend to be "married," set up "housekeeping" together, demand mutual fidelity, and distinguish between the dominant (masculine) and the subordinate (feminine) mate.

Thus, by placing a whole class of possible sexual partners beyond the pale, the taboo on homosexuality has the same social effect as the constraint on pre-marital intercourse, or the pariah status of prostitution. It helps to channelize sexual motivation and activity into the narrow range of legitimated marital-parental roles. What is condemned in the cases of deviance from sexual norms is not a specific item of behavior, or even a specific motive, but rather that the behavior and/or the motive are antithetical to the primacy of the family as a goal and the subordination of sexual bargaining to the family's interest. Speaking of the condemnation of the prostitute, Kingsley Davis has said:[52]

> Her willingness to *sell* her favors and her feeling of emotional indifference are also condemned, but . . . a wife who submits dutifully but reluctantly to intercourse is often considered virtuous for that reason, although she is expected to cherish her husband in a spiritual sense. The trading of sexual favors for a consideration is what is done in marriage, for in consenting to get married a woman exchanges her sexual favors for economic support. As long as the bargain struck is one that achieves a stable relationship, especially a marriage, the mores offer praise rather than condemnation for the trade. The prostitute's affront is that she trades promiscuously.

51. Kingsley Davis, "Sexual Behavior," in *Contemporary Social Problems* (New York:
52. *Ibid.*, p. 342.

In spite of the taboo, the homosexual alternative is seized upon by a sizeable proportion of men in the United States (and elsewhere).[53] The pervasive public concern about increased "conversion," should the legal bans on homosexual acts be lifted, is doubtless not unrealistic.[54] Like prostitution, homosexual relationships are very convenient. They do not require that a man either make long-term commitments, or engage in complex and expensive courting merely to achieve sexual satisfaction. Male homosexuality, as Cory points out, takes place between two individuals who are, physiologically and by social expectation, promiscuous. The inhibiting and restraining influence that women are expected and constrained to exert, and in fact to exert in the high proportion of cases where they are attempting to utilize the man's sexual interest for precipitating a marriage, does not exist. As Cory says:[55]

> The key to the puzzle and problem of homosexual promiscuity is therefore quite simple: the promiscuous (heterosexual) male meets the discriminating (heterosexual) female. She acts as the restraining factor. He cannot indulge indiscriminately without her, but she will not permit him to do so with her. But, the promiscuous (homosexual) male meets the promiscuous (homosexual) male, and the restraints are entirely removed. . . .

However, it is important that homosexuality differs from prostitution in not axiomatically involving inequality of social status between partners. Two homosexuals may be of the same socio-economic class and, although *both* would be under a cloud if their proclivities were made public, it is not true that one is a pariah and the other a respected citizen, as is the case with the prostitute and her client. Hence, homosexual relations are not, by definition, ephemeral, promiscuous, or segmental.[56]

---

53. Alfred C. Kinsey, *et al., Sexual Behavior in the Human Male* (Philadelphia: W. B. Saunders, 1948), pp. 650–651. It is generally believed that the Kinsey figures showing that 37 percent of white males had had a homosexual experience, and that 4 percent were exclusively homosexual, are now too low for the United States.

54. The Parliamentary debate on the Wolfenden Report in England involved explicit concern over the influence on "conversion" of abolishing the legal restraints on homosexuality. See, for example, "The Wolfenden Report," *The Lancet,* Vol. ii (December 6, 1958), pp. 1228–1230. See, also, Lawrence J. Hatterer, *Changing Homosexuality in the Male* (New York: McGraw-Hill, 1970).

55. Donald Webster Cory, *The Homosexual in America* (New York: Greenberg, 1951), p. 141.

56. It is not without interest that a high proportion of the occupations in which overt homosexuals engage—hairdressing, interior decorating, the arts—involve them in constant contact, as part of their work, with the most respected, and presumably respectable, *women* in the society. The willingness of millions of husbands to allow their wives to associate freely, and often on a basis of friendly intimacy, with men who, by law and tradition, are vilified as the most unnatural degenerates requires some explanation. Presumably, this permissiveness reflects a widespread social recognition of the range of behaviors and social relationships involved in homosexuality, as well as the belief that the homosexual male is "harmless" in the same sense as the eunuch in a harem. Given the fact that wives will meet some men in the course of the day, the homosexual seems far less threatening to husbands than men like themselves and, therefore, represents a lesser of evils. Obviously, in a changing, mobile society taboos and segregation are hard to maintain.

Since homosexuality offers a range of alternatives, from the casual to the mimicking of stable marriage, it is far more threatening to the traditional definition of sex roles in terms of marriage and parenthood than are other transgressions. Understandably, societies requiring relatively high and stable fertility have exercised strong coercion against homosexuality. As we shall see in the next section, the challenge that *de facto* homosexuality presents to traditional sex role expectations has been met in modern American society by relegating the homosexual to the realm of pathology. His way of life does not represent an alternative but rather an illness.

Social Science and the Law: The Reaffirmation and Legitimation of Pronatalist Sex Roles

Implicit in our description of how challenges to traditional sex roles have been neutralized is the existence of powerful sources of legitimation for the identity of masculinity and femininity with parental functions. Meeting the challenges required reaffirmation and revalidation of the norm. However, the traditional legitimations would not do for moderns who had rejected a fundamentalist interpretation of Genesis, on the one hand, and a blind faith in natural law, on the other. What did it mean that women were working under the same conditions as men, competing with men in universities, demanding the right to vote? What did the psychiatric cases in World War I, the ineffective soldiers of World War II, the increasingly obvious manifestation of "effeminacy" in men portend? Where were we going? Where was there a model of society—a successful, functioning society (not, like Rome, on the road to ruin)—in which the obligations and rights of the sexes were in such a muddle? Were there other principles of organization more suited to modern life? If so, what were they?

To such questions no novel answers were forthcoming. Yet people had to make decisions, to act, to see themselves and their children as living in and moving toward some way of life that was predictable and socially validated. The answers they found re-connected them with the past. These answers came primarily from the social sciences—from psychology, sociology, and anthropology. They came directly, through the popularization of social science, and, indirectly, through the educational system, social welfare, the ministry, clinical medicine and psychology, and the courts. With few exceptions, the social sciences served to reaffirm the validity of identifying sex roles with parental functions. In the case of psychoanalysis this legitimation involved an elaborate biologistic psychology. With regard to sociology and anthropology the legitimation came about not because the research itself was necessarily biased or contaminated, but because the questions that were asked virtually assumed the consequence. Rather than regarding the identity of sex role with parental role as an *object* for research, sociology and anthropology have, by and large, taken this identity as given. The research questions that have been raised related to possible differences in sex role definitions *given* the assumption of almost universal parenthood, and to an investigation of child-rearing by means alternative to the nuclear family. There has been a notable lack of interest in, even recognition of, sex roles apart from the family and kinship. With tradition seemingly validated by scientific expertise, it is hardly surprising that legal reaffirmations of the identity of sexual and parental roles should seem legitimate as well. Let us look at the record.

Psychoanalysis and Prescriptive Parenthood. One of the strongest sources of legitimation for parenthood as the only "normal" adult sexual role comes from psychoanalytic psychology. Psychoanalysis views parenthood as the natural culmination of "normal" development to adulthood and insists that sex role differentiation should be congruent with the basic psycho-biological substratum. The natural predispositions should not be thwarted or by-passed by inappropriate social demands, activities, or expectations. Indeed, it is regarded as mandatory that the sex *roles* properly *express* what is believed to be the normal psycho-biological given. The only "normal" woman is heterosexual and a mother, the only "normal" man is heterosexual and a father.

Freud's writings on the diverse characters of the sexes, particularly his unabashed denigration of women under the guise of "scientific" description, have already been criticized in a voluminous literature.[57] Our concern here, however, is not with Freud's misogyny, but with the pronatalism which the psychoanalytic view of female psycho-biology has prescribed.

As is well known, in the Freudian scheme the basic determination of female psychology is negative. Freud believed that women were highly motivated to compensate for the lack of a penis by having children. Indeed, in Freudian psychology, the only way for women to achieve a "normal" (i.e., not cripplingly neurotic) existence is to accept their

57. Dr. Clara Thompson, a psychiatrist writing in the 1940's, was one of the first to question systematically and objectively the Freudian description of female psychology. See her "Cultural Pressures in the Psychology of Women," reprinted in Patrick Mullahy (ed.), *A Study of Interpersonal Relations* (New York: Hermitage Press, 1949), pp. 130–146. Mirra Komarovsky has also analyzed the effect of Freudianism on sex role definitions. In particular, she has noted the influence on the mass media of the Freudian characterization of the neurotic, unfulfilled career woman (the "Lady in the Dark") who loses by being successful. See Mirra Komarovsky, *op cit.*, pp. 31–52. Philip Rieff also analyzed and criticized Freud's feminine psychology in *Freud: The Mind of the Moralist* (Garden City, New York: Doubleday, 1961), pp. 191–204. This book was first published in 1959. The woman's liberation movement of the 1960's has engaged in far more detailed criticisms of Freudian psychology. Among the more penetrating are those of Betty Friedan and Kate Millet. See Betty Friedan, *op cit.*, Chapter 5; and Kate Millet, *Sexual Politics* (Garden City, New York: Doubleday, 1970), pp. 176–220.

passive and denuded condition and seek their fulfillment in childbearing. Freudian psychology, from Freud to Deutsch to Erikson, is invariant in its insistence that the reproductive capacity must be actualized for the woman to approach mental health. Motherhood is what women do and they should not be encouraged to embark on social roles that conflict with the realization of their basic psycho-biological needs.[58]

One might, of course, argue that Freudian psychology has had little popular influence, that Freud's depiction of the "normal" feminine role (updated by Erikson and others) has exerted no moral pressure on women to pursue reproduction as a career, and to eschew social roles that might label them as neurotic "masculine protesters." I believe, however, that the burden of such an argument rests with its proponent. Not only has Freudian psychology been popularly absorbed throughout the Western world, but its influence on mediating agencies of society—on schools, welfare agencies, the medical profession, and the arts and mass media, to say nothing of the social sciences—has been demonstrably profound.[59] In the words of Philip Rieff:[60]

> In America today, Freud's intellectual influence is greater than that of any other modern thinker. He presides over the mass media, the college classroom, the chatter at parties, the playgrounds of the middle classes where child-rearing is a prominent and somewhat anxious topic of conversation; he has bequeathed to many couples a new self-consciousness about their marriages and the temperature of their social enthusiasms.

Indeed, as will be readily apparent, the Freudian influence on other social sciences has contributed what might be called "back up" legitimation for the emphasis on motherhood as the primary lifetime role for women. For example, Parsons says:[61]

> . . . By and large a "good" marriage from the point of view of the personality of the participants, is likely to be one with children; the functions as parents reinforce the functions in relation to each other as spouses. . . . The most important part . . . is the contingency of sexual love on the assumption of

58. See Sigmund Freud, *New Introductory Lectures on Psychoanalysis,* translated by J. H. Sprott (New York: W.W. Norton & Co., Inc., 1933); *Three Contributions to the Theory of Sex,* translated by A. A. Brill, (New York and Washington, D.C.: Nervous and Mental Disease Publishing Company, 1920); "Analysis Terminable and Interminable," *The International Journal of Psychoanalysis,* Vol. XVIII (October 1937), pp. 373–405; "Some Psychological Consequences of the Anatomical Differences Between the Sexes," in *Collected Papers of Sigmund Freud,* Joan Riviere (ed.), (New York: Basic Books, 1959, Vol. IV); and "Female Sexuality," *Collected Papers,* Vol. V. For post-Freudian works in the same vein of fulfillment-through-motherhood, see Helene Deutsch, *The Psychology of Women* (New York: Grune and Stratton, 1945, 2 vols.); and Erik H. Erikson, "Inner and Outer Space: Reflections on Womanhood" *Daedalus,* Vol. 93, (1964), pp. 582–606.
59. The pro-motherhood bias in modern erotic literature has been noted by many. The unmistakable "message" of modern sexually uninhibited literature is that most women's problems can readily be solved by copulation and impregnation—a primal fix. For a discussion of Freud's influence on some important literary figures, see Kate Millett, *op. cit.,* pp. 237–313 and Betty Friedan, *op cit.,* pp. 174–196 and 247–270.
60. Philip Rieff, *op cit.,* p. xxi.
61. Talcott Parsons and Robert F. Bales, *op. cit.,* pp. 21–22.

fully adult responsibilities in roles other than that of marriage directly. Put very schematically, a mature woman can love, sexually, only a man who takes his full place in the masculine world, above all its occupational aspect, and who takes responsibility for a family; conversely, the mature man can only love a woman who is really an adult, a full wife to him and mother to his children. . . .

The "experts" thus appear to agree. And, indeed, the more the dogma is paraphrased and embellished by sources at some remove from psychoanalysis, the more pervasively "right" it seems to be.

Perhaps the best evidence of the normative influence of psychoanalytic thinking concerning sex-role differentiation is the allegedly disastrous effect on child-rearing if the parents do not adhere to traditional, polarized sex roles. In effect, a person who does not exemplify the Freudian sex role definitions will not only suffer himself but, if he has children, will warp their personalities as well. The following quotation exemplifies the psychoanalytic belief in the overriding importance of the early years; the emphasis on parents playing highly differentiated, traditional sex roles; and the attribution to parental "failure" of diseases of unknown etiology like schizophrenia (that is, the clear formulation of a terrible punishment for non-conformity).[62]

> The maintenance of the appropriate sexual roles by parents in their coalition plays a major role in guiding the child's development as a male or female. Security of sexual identity is a cardinal factor in the achievement of a stable ego identity. *Of all factors entering into the formation of personality characteristics, the sex of the child is the most decisive.* Confusions and dissatisfactions concerning sexual identity can contribute to the etiology of many neuroses and character defects as well as perversions. Probably all schizophrenic patients are seriously confused in this area. . . .
>
> Clear-cut role reversals in parents can obviously distort the child's development, both when they are marked in the sexual sphere, as when the father or mother is an overt homosexual, or when they concern the task divisions in maintaining the family. A child whose father performs the mothering functions both tangibly and emotionally while the mother is preoccupied with her career can easily gain a distorted image of masculinity and femininity. . . . While the sharing of role tasks has become more necessary and acceptable in the contemporary family, there is still need for the parents to maintain and support one another in their primary sex roles.

Not only has psychoanalysis provided a "scientific" rationalization for prescriptive motherhood, it has attempted to consign to the realm of abnormality and mental illness any deviation from patriarchal masculinity for men. Thus psychoanalysis views male homosexuality as axiomatically indicating mental illness. In Bieber's words:[63]

All *psychoanalytic* theories assume that adult homosexuality is pathologic

62. Theodore Lidz, "Family Organization and Personality Structure," reprinted in Norman W. Bell and Ezra F. Vogel (eds.), *A Modern Introduction to the Family,* revised edition (New York: Free Press, 1969). Italics mine.

63. Irving Bieber, *Homosexuality. A Psychoanalytical Study* (New York: Vintage Books, 1962), p. 18.

and assign differing weights to constitutional and experiential determinants. All agree that the experiential determinants are in the main rooted in childhood and are primarily related to the family.

Indeed, psychoanalytic studies of homosexuals, based invariably on those who have psychological problems serious enough to bring them to an analyst, turn up pathological syndromes.[64] Data such as these are used to question controlled studies of homosexuals and heterosexuals who are functioning adequately in the community without psychoanalytic help.[65]

It may be noted that the psychoanalytic view of homosexuality, which equates deviation from a social norm as equivalent to mental illness, is not shared by biologically oriented students of sexual behavior.[66] Both the Kinsey study and the study by Ford and Beach present evidence indicating that human beings, like other animals, are normally capable of indiscriminate sexual responsiveness. In their view, the rejection of homosexuality is culturally conditioned rather than indicative of the only "normal" psychological development for the human male.[67]

Finally, we must emphasize that the doctrine of the libidinal causes of neurosis promulgated by psychoanalysis has rendered a sexually active way of life prescriptive for all. Within this framework there is no place, except as a deviant, for the person of relatively low-keyed sexual interests. Thus, the social role of the unattached bachelor or spinster has been denigrated as psychologically abnormal.

In sum, in a century of massive social change (and accompanying personal uncertainty and anxiety), Freud reaffirmed for modern man the family roles of a people whose customs long antedated the Christian era. Freudianism, whether applied to women or to men, decreed that any deviation from the ideal of the tribal Jewish patriarch be an object of

64. Such as the Bieber study cited in the previous footnote.
65. See Bieber's discussion of the studies by Hooker, and Chang and Block. *Ibid.*, pp. 17–18, and 305–36. A recent study by Evans replicates the Bieber study using individuals who had never sought psychotherapy. Evans' results are similar to Bieber's in showing disturbed or pathological parental relationships among the homosexuals. However, as Evans points out, the nature of the relationship with parents does not demonstrate a cause and effect sequence of parental disturbance leading to homosexuality. Equally plausible is that the son's homosexuality and traits unacceptable to the father *lead to* parental rejection and maternal devotion (as is often the case with a retarded or handicapped child). See Ray B. Evans, "Childhood Parental Relationships of Homosexual Men," *Journal of Consulting and Clinical Psychology,* Vol. 33 (1969), pp. 129–135. For a discussion of Evans' findings and a methodological critique of existing research on the psychoanalytic interpretation of homosexuality, see the discussion by Evelyn Hooker, "Parental Relations and Male Homosexuality in Patient and Non-Patient Samples," following the Evans' article, pp. 140–142.
66. The ban on suicide is another example of a norm that has, in the Judeo-Christian tradition, become "natural law." A person attempting suicide is regarded as unbalanced mentally, by definition. Every effort is supposed to be made to stop him from succeeding in his "irrational" act of self-destruction.
67. Alfred C. Kinsey *et al., op. cit.,* and Clellan S. Ford and Frank A. Beach, *Patterns of Sexual Behavior* (New York: Harper, 1951).

clinical contempt. At best, psychoanalysis could guide human beings who did not measure up to the ideal from "hysterical misery" to "common unhappiness" as a way of life.

The Reproductive Function and Sex Role Differentiation in Sociology. Psychoanalysis has viewed traditional role differentiation by sex— differentiation in terms of wife-mother and husband-father roles—as a reflection of human psycho-biology in its "normal" form. By contrast, sociology has studied masculinity and femininity in cross-cultural per- spective and come to the conclusion that the relative invariance in sex role definitions among human societies relates to the functionality of these definitions for the family—that is, for reproductive efficiency. The conclusion reached by sociology is, however, essentially very similar to that of psychoanalysis—there is not much variability possible in the masculine and feminine roles. Why? Not because of a psycho-biological substratum but because of the need for role differentiation within the family (as with other small groups) along the lines of internally versus externally oriented activities and functions, "task-oriented" as against "emotionally supportive" behavior.[68] The internal, familially-oriented role goes to women because of their biological connection with childbear- ing and child-rearing (particularly nursing and feeding), the external role goes to men pretty much *faute de mieux*.[69] It is frequently noted that efforts to vary this pattern of sex differentiation within the reproducing family have not, to date, proven very successful.[70] In the United States, Parsons now believes that American women no longer suffer from the "role conflict" he once postulated as resulting from the option to work outside the home. They have adjusted to the "functional demands" of their wife-mother role—adjusted better than he believed they would when he first started writing about American women.[71] Recently, he has said:[72]

> It seems quite safe in general to say that the adult feminine role has not ceased to be anchored primarily in the internal affairs of the family, as wife, mother and manager of the household, while the role of the adult male is primarily anchored in the occupational world, in his job and through it by his status-giving and income-earning functions for the family. Even if, as seems possible, it should come about that the average married woman had some

68. Robert F. Bales and Philip E. Slater, "Role Differentiation in Small Decision- Making Groups," in Talcott Parsons and Robert F. Bales, *op. cit.*, pp. 259–306.
69. Morris Zelditch, Jr., "Role Differentiation in the Nuclear Family: A Comparative Study," in Talcott Parsons and Robert F. Bales, *op. cit.*, pp. 309–351. Zelditch's data on the similarities of sex role differentiation are based on almost 50 primitive and modern societies [this book, pp. 256–58].
70. See, for example, Melford E. Spiro, *Kibbutz, Venture in Utopia* (New York: Schocken Books, 1963), and, by the same author, *Children of the Kibbutz* (New York: Schocken Books, 1965), especially Chapters 4 and 5.
71. Talcott Parsons, "Age and Sex in the Social Structure of the United States," in Talcott Parsons (ed.), *Essays in Sociological Theory Pure and Applied* (Glencoe, Illinois: The Free Press, 1949), pp. 218–232 [this book, pp. 243–55].
72. Talcott Parsons, "The American Family: Its Relations to Personality and to Social Structure," in Talcott Parsons and Robert F. Bales, *op. cit.*, pp. 14–15.

kind of job, it seems most unlikely that this relative balance would be upset; that either the roles would be reversed, or their qualitative differentiation in these respects completely erased.

In a footnote to the passage just quoted, Parsons makes the point that, even when women do attain "higher-level jobs," the latter typically mirror the "expressive" components of the "normal" female role.[73]

The distribution of women in the labor force clearly confirms this general view of the balance of the sex roles. Thus, on higher levels typical feminine occupations are those of teacher, social worker, nurse, private secretary and entertainer. Such roles tend to have prominent expressive components, and often to be "supportive" to masculine roles. Within the occupational organization they are analogous to the wife-mother role in the family. It is much less common to find women in the "top executive" roles and the more specialized and "impersonal" technical roles. Even within professions we find comparable differentiations, e.g., in medicine women are heavily concentrated in the two branches of pediatrics and psychiatry, while there are few women surgeons.

Consequently, in interpreting the relevance of sociological thinking to possible changes in sex roles, we must be aware that such thinking is about men and women viewed as actual and potential parents. The sociological questions that have been asked about sex roles have never strayed far from the basic presupposition that most, or all, persons will and should form families of procreation. Indeed, modern sociology has typically assumed that no structural deviations from parentally defined sex roles can be tolerated (except perhaps in pariah form), since they detract from individual motivation to marry and have children.

Yet, this definition of sex roles is "functional" for the society only insofar as the number of children so produced is actually needed. If the society needs fewer children, far fewer, than will be forthcoming from sex role differentiation on the basis of parenthood, then such differentiation, in its traditional form, is no longer functional. The logic of sociological analysis concerning sex roles may well be correct. However, the conclusions are based on a long-outdated demographic assumption—that the country's problem is to secure itself an abundance of children. If the same logic is applied to our current demographic needs, the conclusion is that role differentiation by sex must be released from its total dependency on kinship, if the country is to achieve fertility low enough to match its highly favorable mortality.

The Legal Identification of Sex Roles with Parental Functions. In a recent review of sex discrimination and the law in the United States, Kanowitz traces the ways in which the law explicitly and implicitly considers issues of sex differentiation in terms of parental roles.[74]

73. *Ibid.*, p. 15.
74. Leo Kanowitz, *Women and the Law* (Albuquerque: University of New Mexico Press, 1969).

Although his study was undertaken to expose the "injustice" of sex-based legal discrimination and its presumed reinforcement of male dominance, Kanowitz acknowledges that it would be a mistake to assume that all (or even most) sex-based legal differentiation disadvantages women in the sense of restricting their rights or elaborating their obligations. On the contrary, such discrimination in many cases defines the obligations of men as husbands and fathers.[75] Indeed, what comes through most consistently in Kanowitz's presentation of American sex-discrimination laws and the philosophy behind them is not a dimension of social stratification, of "advantage" or "disadvantage" of one sex over the other, as much as an explicit legal affirmation of and concern for the differential *family* roles of the sexes, particularly their *parental* roles. The law sees men and women primarily in terms of the reproductive arrangement, and draws its conclusions accordingly. Given the assumption, the conclusions cannot be regarded as affording one sex an advantage—the assumption is that the sex roles are incommensurable and complementary. There is also the assumption that *intra*-sex variability in physique, temperament, or actual achievement of the ideal sex role in society is negligible. Hence, the application to all men and all women of a legal philosophy that assumes universal parenthood seems to be only logical.

However, from a demographic point of view, such legal philosophy clearly represents a strong pronatalist coercion since the basic assumptions are applied to cases in which role *alternatives* might emerge were it not for the precedent of reaffirming the primacy of marital and parental roles. For example, Kanowitz notes that some of the language used by the United States Supreme Court in the famous case of *Muller* v. *Oregon* "was unnecessary to the decision."[76] As a result, this case has often been invoked by the courts in upholding a wide variety of sex-discrimination laws. Indeed, when one realizes that the case involved no more than a consideration of the validity of Oregon's law limiting women's hours of work to 10 a day, the language clearly indicates that the Supreme Court had a larger issue in mind—the issue of reaffirming and elaborating on the sexual division of labor implied by parenthood.[77]

> . . . The two sexes differ in structure of body, in the functions to be performed by each, in the amount of physical strength, in the capacity for long-continued labor, particularly when done standing, the influence of vigorous health upon the future well-being of the race, the self-reliance which enables one to assert full rights, and in the capacity to maintain the struggle for subsistence. *This difference justifies a difference in legislation*, and upholds that which is designed to compensate for some of the burdens which rest upon her. . . .

The success of the Supreme Court's effort at legitimation is measured by

75. *Ibid.*, p. 3.
76. *Ibid.*, p. 152.
77. *Ibid.*, p. 153.

the fact that this language has affirmed the principle that "sex is a valid basis for classification." This principle, as Kanowitz says, ". . . is often repeated mechanically without regard to the purposes of the statute in question or the reasonableness of the relationship between the purpose and sex-based classification." [78] With forgivable sociological naiveté, Kanowitz puzzles over and condemns the influence and immortality that this legitimation has achieved.

> . . . The subsequent reliance in judicial decisions upon the *Muller* language is a classic example of the misuse of precedent, of later courts being mesmerized by what an earlier court had *said* rather than what it had *done*. For though *Muller* was concerned only with a protective labor statute which took account of the general physical differences between the sexes, it has been cited, as Murray and Eastwood point out, in cases "upholding the exclusion of women from juries, differential treatment in licensing various occupations and the exclusion of women from state supported colleges."

The language of Mr. Justice Brewer in *Muller* v. *Oregon* is so archaic that we may be moved to dismiss its substance as outmoded as well. We may believe that the *operating* norms of modern Americans do not prescribe either men's or women's roles in such polarized terms —protector and economic supporter of the family at one pole, mother and gentle housewife at the other. However, we have seen that potential challenges to the primacy of motherhood for all women have, so far, been neutralized by prescriptive reproductive norms. Even today, Brewer could be cited as an accurate observer of the "real" norms governing the modern woman—more correct than those who believe that higher education, labor force participation, and feminism have effective "basic changes."

The Imprint of Sex Roles
on Personality

The magnitude of pronatalist coercions in human societies, ours included, is far from encompassed by the fact that sex roles are so closely identified with the division of labor according to parental functions. As an added precaution, human societies (and American society is no exception) have built the perpetuation of pronatalist sex roles into the structure of personality through socialization "for" personality traits that are congruent with these sex roles, and "against" traits that could produce conflict with them. Such rigid sex-typing of personality traits doubtless explains, in part, why a change in sex role expectations is so difficult to effect. Intra-sex variability is, as we shall see, systematically suppressed by the socialization process which can, in the case of sex-typing, begin to take place from the moment of birth.

78. *Ibid.*, p. 154.

Research concerning socially prescribed, preferred, permitted, and proscribed personality traits for the sexes has not been extensive. However, since the explicit research of Komarovsky (on college populations) in the 1940's, it has continued systematically. Hence, we have a long-range body of data concerning the views of college students with regard to the normatively appropriate traits for men and women. Other data on socialization practices generally indicate that the norms expressed among college populations correspond to differential childrearing practices for the sexes and that, if anything, college students are more permissive concerning a blurring of sex-typed personality traits than are less advantaged groups in the population.

Komarovsky's work on the inconsistent role expectations by parents for their daughters has already been discussed. We saw that the college girls studied by Komarovsky were encouraged to play a "modern" role of achievement in sports and academic life up to the point when this role (if taken seriously by the girl) clearly began to interfere with courtship. At that point, many of the parents (and even male siblings) of the girls began to lecture concerning the advisability of not allowing the modern role to be carried "too far." In effect, the girls were frequently advised to modify their goals and their behavior so as to be in line with anticipated wifehood and motherhood.

The Komarovsky research also showed, as might indeed be expected, that the traditional sex-role, expectations were accompanied by expectations that the young womens' personality traits would be congruent with the sex role. In Komarovsky's research, the young women perceived young men as the principal enforcers of such traits since, of course, the men were the active agents in initiating dates and marriage. Girls who did not exemplify the appropriate traits risked being sanctioned by unpopularity with the opposite sex and endured the threat of nonmarriage. Komarovsky points out that the desired female personality is "often described with reference to the male sex role as 'not dominant, or aggressive as men' or 'more emotional, sympathetic.' "[79]

One of the principal findings of the Komarovsky study was the extent to which her subjects felt called upon to dissimulate their real personalities, to "fake" traits that they did not have and did not evaluate highly—traits of helplessness, dependency, lesser intelligence relative to men, etc. Such deprecating presentations of self were seen by these women as catering to their escorts' need to live up to the role expectation of males—higher dominance, security, and intelligence than that of females. Clearly conveyed to these young women was the fact that existing social roles for the sexes presupposed that males would typically have the personality traits that are congruent with occupational achievement and the demonstration of superior physical strength. Since, in

79. Mirra Komarovsky, "Cultural Contradictions and Sex Roles," *American Journal of Sociology*, Vol. LII (November 1946), pp. 184–189 [this book, pp. 512–19].

actuality, a high proportion of men may not have these traits in as great abundance as a high proportion of women, maintenance of the male image requires collusion by women. These young women, although at the outer reach of "modernity" for American girls, nonetheless were impressed that "success" for a woman, namely the achievement of the wife-mother role, meant subordinating their personality traits to the personality requirements of sex-role differentiation on the basis of parenthood. The following quotations from Komarovsky illustrate the problem as perceived by her subjects:[80]

> When a girl asks me what marks I got last semester I answer, "Not so good—only one 'A'." When a boy asks the same question, I say very brightly with a note of surprise, "Imagine, I got an 'A!'"
>
> On dates I always go through the "I-don't-care-anything-you-want-to-do" routine. It gets monotonous but boys fear girls who make decisions. They think such girls would make nagging wives.
>
> I am a natural leader and, when in the company of girls, usually take the lead. That is why I am so active in college activities. But I know that men fear bossy women, and I always have to watch myself on dates not to assume the "executive" role. Once a boy walking to the theater with me took the wrong street. I knew a short cut but kept quiet.

Later research has served to substantiate and elaborate Komarovsky's roster of personality traits normatively expected of each sex. The work of McKee and Sherriffs in the 1950's clearly documented that women believe men demand traits of them that are exclusively feminine and restrict them from masculine virtues.[81] And McKee and Sherriffs found that men actually do wish to restrict women from such "male-valued" traits as being "aggressive," "courageous," "daring," "deliberate," "dominant," "forceful," "independent," "rugged," and "sharp-witted." On the other hand, women are found to desire more of a combination of both masculine and feminine traits in men than men consider ideal for themselves. That is, women would be more tolerant of a less polarized male than men would be of a less polarized female.[82] This result may well be because, in general, the traits chosen as appropriately "feminine" by both sexes are *evaluated* by both sexes less positively than are the masculine traits.[83] Although women select the more highly-valued feminine traits as being also desirable for men (gentleness, sympathy, etc.), men apparently wish to avoid the roster of traits listed as feminine since, on the average, these carry relatively low esteem.

80. *Ibid.*, pp. 27–28.
81. John P. McKee and Alex C. Sherriffs, "Men's and Women's Beliefs, Ideals, and Self-Concepts," *American Journal of Sociology*, Vol. LXIV (January 1959), pp. 356–363.
82. *Ibid.*, pp. 359–361.
83. J. P. McKee and A. C. Sherriffs, "The Differential Evaluation of Males and Females," *Journal of Personality*, Vol. XXV (1957), pp. 356–371; and A. C. Sherriffs and J. P. McKee, "Qualitative Aspects of Beliefs about Men and Women," *Journal of Personality*, Vol. XXV (1957), pp. 451–464.

More recently, Rosenkrantz, Bee, Vogel, Broverman and Broverman have also studied college students and found that even in the late 1960's there is clearly defined recognition of personality traits expected of men and women, and that agreement on these traits is very great by both sexes.[84] Moreover, men and women agree that a greater number of traits typically associated with masculinity are socially desirable than those associated with femininity. The list runs as follows:[85]

STEREOTYPIC TRAITS

Male-valued traits

Aggressive	Knows the way of the world
Independent	Feelings not easily hurt
Unemotional	Adventurous
Hides emotions	Makes decisions easily
Objective	Never cries
Easily influenced	Acts as a leader
Dominant	Self-confident
Likes math and science	Not uncomfortable about
Not excitable in a minor crisis	being aggressive
Active	Ambitious
Competitive	Able to separate feelings from ideas
Logical	Not dependent
Worldly	Not conceited about appearance
Skilled in business	Thinks men are superior to women
Direct	Talks freely about sex with men

Female-valued traits

Does not use harsh language	Interested in own appearance
Talkative	Neat in habits
Tactful	Quiet
Gentle	Strong need for security
Aware of feelings of others	Appreciates art and literature
Religious	Expresses tender feelings

The authors also examined whether the self-concepts of their subjects correspond to the stereotypes. The self-concepts and the stereotypes were found to be very similar. The authors say:[86]

> . . . The self-concepts of men and women are very similar to the respective stereotypes. In the case of the self-concepts of women this means, presumably, that women also hold negative values of their worth relative to men. This implication is particularly surprising when it is remembered that the data producing the conclusion were gathered from enlightened, highly selected

84. Paul Rosenkrantz, Helen Bee, Susan Vogel, Inge Broverman, and Donald Broverman, "Sex-Role Stereotypes and Self-Concepts in College Students," *Journal of Consulting and Clinical Psychology,* Vol. 32 (1968), pp. 287–293.
85. *Ibid.*, p. 291.
86. *Ibid.*, p. 293.

college girls who typically more than hold their own vis-à-vis boys, at least in terms of college grades. The factors producing the incorporation of the female stereotype along with its negative valuation into the self-concept of the female Ss, then, must be enormously powerful.

Although the results of these studies are not placed by the authors in the context of Komarovsky's older work on dissimulation by women, the data suggest that women find themselves in a situation in which personality traits are expected of them that they do not particularly admire, and that they are inhibited from manifesting traits that they do admire. The generally less-admired traits are those that are judged to be congruent with wifehood and motherhood—concern for appearances, concern for the feelings of others, gentleness, quietness, expressivity of succorant and nurturant emotions. The generally more-admired traits are those making for success in the outside world, but incompatible with the wife-mother role as this is defined vis-à-vis the husband-father and the traits his role requires. A more recent study by Broverman, Broverman, Clarkson, Rosenkrantz, and Vogel brings out the double-standard of evaluation for male and female traits even more clearly.[87] The subjects in this study were 79 clinically trained psychologists, psychiatrists and social workers, all involved in clinical practice. They were given the questionnaire concerning bi-polar traits previously used on college students and asked to designate which pole would be closest to a mature, healthy, socially competent adult male, adult female, and adult of sex unspecified. The male, female, and adult instructions were given to separate groups of subjects. The traits these clinicians assigned the adult (sex unspecified) agreed closely with the traits deemed socially desirable by college students, and, as might be expected, male-valued traits were more commonly designated for the healthy male and female-valued traits for the healthy female. However, such designations when examined substantively meant that:[88]

> . . . clinicians are more likely to suggest that healthy women differ from healthy men by being more submissive, less independent, less adventurous, more easily influenced, less aggressive, less competitive, more excitable in minor crises, having their feelings more easily hurt, being more emotional, more conceited about their appearance, less objective, and disliking math and science. This constellation seems a most unusual way of describing any mature, healthy individual.

As a corollary of this finding, the researchers also discovered that the "adult" and "masculine" concepts of health do not differ significantly, but that a significant difference does exist between the concept of health

---

87. Inge K. Broverman, Donald M. Broverman, Frank E. Clarkson, Paul S. Rosenkrantz, and Susan R. Vogel, "Sex-Role Stereotypes and Clinical Judgments of Mental Health," *Journal of Consulting and Clinical Psychology,* Vol. 34 (1970), pp. 1–7.
88. *Ibid.*, pp. 4–5.

for "adults" versus "females." In effect, as they say, ". . . the general standard of health is actually applied only to men, while healthy women are perceived as significantly less healthy by adult standards." [89] Why do clinicians hold such double-standards of health for the sexes? Broverman *et al.* suggest that:[90]

> . . . the double standard of health for men and women stems from the clinicians' acceptance of an "adjustment" notion of health, for example, health consists of a good adjustment to one's environment. In our society, men and women are systematically trained, practically from birth on, to fulfill different social roles. An adjustment notion of health, plus the existence of differential norms of male and female behavior in our society, automatically lead to a double standard of health. Thus, for a woman to be healthy, from an adjustment viewpoint, she must adjust to and accept the behavioral norms for her sex, even though these behaviors are generally less socially desirable and considered to be less healthy for the generalized competent, mature adult.

We thus see that although the differentiation of sex roles based on parenthood is sociologically complementary and unstratified, the personality traits expected of the people who fill these roles differ greatly, on the average, in social esteem. The lower evaluation of feminine personality traits relative to "adult" traits generally, constrains men to attempt to achieve "masculine" traits at all costs (or to avoid feminine ones).[91] One might expect women to have the same reaction, and indeed Komarovsky has shown that many really do at some time in their lives, but such a reaction carries severe sanctions because such women run the risk of not being selected for marriage, or being unsuccessful within it. The absence of alternative sex roles for women forces conformity to the personality traits that are congruent with the parenthood roles and no other. As a result, most women are not psychologically equipped to seek out alternative sex roles, or to switch gears from motherhood to success in the outside world. By virtue of a trained incapacity, their personalities are geared to failure, or only very marginal achievement in the world of

89. *Ibid.*, p. 5.
90. *Ibid.*, p. 6.
91. The lower evaluation of feminine personality traits does not imply a disvaluation of motherhood, but rather reflects the necessity of motivating men to make the effort required for the masculine role. As has often been noted, if the feminine role is defined in terms of motherhood, then the social control problem for the society regarding women is simply to ensure that they allow themselves to be chosen and impregnated in a normatively approved fashion. After this, they must patiently and serenely await parturition. Deviance for them is chafing at the bit. The problem is quite different among men. The masculine achievement cannot be childbearing, but its complement. This takes "doing" rather than "being," and it is necessary to motivate men to make this relatively more extraordinary effort. It is worth noting that the recent professionalization of motherhood, the emphasis on gourmet cooking and the resurgence of handicrafts for the home (art needlework, etc.) serve to up-grade housewifery and the talents that are "needed." However, since there is no externally validated mechanism of quality control for housewives and mothers, no separation procedures that most probably result from poor performance, and no extraordinary rewards for excellence, the evaluation of female traits associated with the wife-mother role rests on minimum criteria.

business and professional competition. Consequently, most women are more permanently attached to motherhood as their primary status than might be expected given the economic opportunities in American society. It is thus simplistic and unrealistic to expect economic and career incentives to affect women in the same way that they affect men. Women's personalities have been "adjusted" to sex-role expectations that assume a lifetime of home-centered priorities.

By what mechanisms do the adult subjects of the research cited above acquire such sex-typed personality traits and the belief that these traits are appropriate to each sex? Such research as has been done on this subject—whether on parent-child socialization, social pressures by peers in high schools, or public treatment of individuals who do not conform to sex-typing of personality traits and behavior—all have a common theme. This is the theme of social coercion—of punishment, withdrawal of affection, ridicule, unpopularity, ostracism. Moreover, these sanctions are brought into play not only for major deviations from sex-typing (such as, for example, overt homosexuality), but for what might seem to be relatively minor variations such as being a brilliant and achieving female high-school student (in a coeducational school) instead of a cheerleader and fashionable dresser. One has to appreciate the social pressure leading to "adjustment" to reproductively-oriented adult sexual roles in order to understand that fertility behavior in American society is, at present, far from "voluntary."

Let us begin with a brief discussion of sex-typing by parents (and adults with whom a very young child is likely to be in contact). This process is documented widely in books on child development and indeed is tacitly accepted as part of what parents do "for" their children. Mussen, Conger and Kagan say:[92]

> . . . in general, overt physical aggression, dominance, competence at athletics, achievement, competitiveness, and independence are regarded as desirable traits for boys. On the other hand, dependence, passivity, inhibition of physical aggression, competence at language skills, politeness, social poise, and neatness are some of the characteristics deemed more appropriate for girls.
> Most parents reward behaviors that they view as appropriate to the sex of their child and punish responses that are considered inappropriate. . . . definite patterns of praise and punishment from both parents and playmates during the preschool and school years put pressure on the child to adopt sex-appropriate behaviors.

The authors point out that, in personal interviews, both boys and girls at ages as young as four to nine say that they feel their parents prefer them to adopt sex-typed behaviors.[93] Mussen, Conger, and Kagan go on to state

92. Paul H. Mussen, John J. Conger, and Jerome Kagan, *Child Development and Personality* (New York: Harper & Row, 1963), p. 261.
93. *Ibid.*, p. 263.

that the learning of "appropriate" sex-role behaviors in early childhood has its results in adulthood. The degree to which the authors accept as "appropriate" that women are socialized into a feeling of inability to cope with life is well-demonstrated by the following paragraph:[94]

> . . . A large group of young adults was presented with a list of adjectives and asked to select those attributes that they felt were most and least characteristic of themselves. In comparison to men, women felt less adequate, more negligent, more fearful, and less mature. These adult attitudes about the self may be traceable, to some degree, to sex-appropriate attitudes and characteristics inculcated in the preschool boy and girl.

More pressure is apparently required to enforce identification by girls with the feminine role than by boys with the masculine one, since studies have shown that children of both sexes regard fathers as more powerful and competent than mothers, are more likely to imitate a man than a woman, and that boys typically identify with the father but that girls identify about equally with the mother and father.[95]

Pressure for sex-typing occurs at a very early age not only through parental channels, but also it is strongly reinforced in childhood as the peer group takes over increasing control in the young person's life. Mussen, Conger, and Kagan point out that the child's "acceptance or rejection by his friends is determined in part by the degree to which he has adopted traits that are appropriate for his sex role." [96] They go on to point out how pervasive and primary in the child's life is the sex-type assignment by peers to most activities and behaviors.[97]

One of the largest-scale documentations of coercive sex-typing is in Coleman's study of 9 highly-diversified high schools in Northern Illinois.[98] Coleman found that, among adolescents of both sexes, the effect of high school as a scholastic system was neutralized, and even nullified, by the counter-effect of adolescent control over the operating daily goals and activities of the students. Since all of the high schools were coeducational, one aspect of adolescent control was extreme differentiation of sex roles in the school along the lines of physical (athletic) prowess for males and beauty coupled with "activity" (party giving) for females. To be a bright, scholarly student was the least desired "image" for both sexes, and indeed students answering to this description were simply ignored. As Coleman points out, the students were actually expressing in the school situation the real values and goals conveyed by most parents, in counterdistinction to the parental lip-service paid to educational achievement and sexually neutral but desira-

94. *Ibid.*
95. *Ibid.*, pp. 272–273 and 370–372.
96. *Ibid.*, p. 372.
97. *Ibid.*
98. James S. Coleman, *The Adolescent Society* (New York: Free Press, 1961).

ble character traits. For parents (and many teachers) as well as adolescents, the male athlete is the super-hero and the beautiful, popular girl (the athlete's choice) the super-heroine.

Clearly, in paying the enormous bill that it does for high school education, American society is buying, for most students, not intellectual stimulation and the acquisition of valuable cognitive skills, but rather, just the opposite. Being provided are expensive arenas for male athletes and female cheerleaders, together with their hopeful imitators. Compared with the all-important task of competing in the sexual jungle, school work is defined by adolescents as externally imposed and juvenile. Coleman has suggested that scholarly achievement could be stimulated by making inter-scholastic competitions as widespread as inter-athletic ones. Then the creative scholar could win for his school (like the athlete) instead of merely for himself (as is currently the case). However, Coleman's own data indicate that the situation will not yield to such a tactic. This is because, perhaps unwittingly, parents tend to regard the practice adolescents receive, in activities that are intensely differentiated by sex, as "good training" for adult adjustment. These sexual roles, and not the "new math," are typically what parents themselves understand, and it is to these that they can, by and large, relate. After all, it is in these images that they themselves were socialized.

In sum, although we may take it for granted that the process of socialization is a legitimate and necessary constraint on human freedom, research suggests that socialization for sex-typed personalities goes well beyond the constraint on individuals required for social order. It actually represents the enforcement of the society's commitment to a specific goal—reproduction. One may or may not agree with the goal, but it is hard to deny that the process of reaching it constitutes a mammoth feat of social engineering. Individuals, especially women, are channelled in the direction of reproductive activity, and diverted away from other activities, just as inexorably as if they were under orders from a master planning board. Under such circumstances, the notion of reproductive "choice" is an illusion. Indeed, it may always be an illusion, but there is nothing more voluntary about an illusory pronatalist choice than an illusory antinatalist one.

Conclusion

The formulation of explicit antinatalist policies requires an awareness of existing pronatalist ones. Lacking such awareness, action is side-tracked by a spurious controversy as to whether coercion should be instituted or voluntarism maintained. Actually, as this paper has tried to show, our society is already pervaded by time-honored pronatalist constraints.

Thus, I have argued, we cannot preserve a choice that does not genuinely exist, and, by the same token, it makes no sense to institute antinatalist coercions while continuing to support pronatalist ones. Insofar as we wish to move in the direction of stabilized zero population growth, the first job for policy would seem to be to eliminate coercive pronatalist influences in a manner that is minimally disruptive of social order.

The scope of this task reminds us that a demographic revolution has more profound implications than might appear from a mere consideration of birth, death, and growth rates. These are only indicators of a society's ability to cope with the survival problem in a particular way. Behind them lie the social organization and control mechanisms that channel resources into the production and rearing of offspring on the one hand, and the effort to avert death, on the other. Population policy, therefore, inevitably goes to the heart of our way of life. To move from one policy (albeit implicit) to another (perhaps explicit) raises issues that threaten many of our established norms and habits. We are bound to experience anxiety in even thinking about the changes that may lie ahead. On the other hand, to allow a diversion of resources from reproduction may help to resolve social problems that are currently engendered by pronatalist constraints. Certainly our increased reproductive efficiency does not, of itself, imply the need for greater regimentation but rather the opposite. It makes possible a fuller expression of human individuality and diversity. After all, each generation provides us with the raw materials for evolutionary adaptation. The problem of adapting to low mortality is, therefore, not one of browbeating biologically specialized individuals out of behavior that is "natural" for all. Rather, it is one of directing cultural and social institutions into the use of human variability for meeting the new functional demands of a modern, low mortality society. In this endeavor, freedom for the development of individual potential may be greatly enhanced. I seriously doubt that it will be curtailed.[99]

99. I gratefully acknowledge support by the Ford Foundation of the research presented in this article.

6

DIFFERENCES IN FAMILY STRUCTURES

Elizabeth Bott

Conjugal Roles and Social Networks

There was considerable variation in the way husbands and wives performed their conjugal roles. At one extreme was a family in which the husband and wife carried out as many tasks as possible separately and independently of each other. There was a strict division of labor in the household, in which she had her tasks and he had his. He gave her a set amount of housekeeping money, and she had little idea of how much he earned or how he spent the money he kept for himself. In their leisure time, he went to cricket matches with his friends, whereas she visited her relatives or went to a cinema with a neighbor. With the exception of festivities with relatives, this husband and wife spent very little of their leisure time together. They did not consider that they were unusual in this respect. On the contrary, they felt their behavior was typical of their social circle. At the other extreme was a family in which husband and wife shared as many activities and spent as much time together as possible. They stressed that husband and wife should be equals: all major decisions should be made together, and even in minor household matters they should help one another as much as possible. This norm was carried out in practice. In their division of labor, many tasks were shared or interchangeable. The husband often did the cooking and sometimes the washing and ironing. The wife did the gardening and often the household repairs as well. Much of their leisure time was spent together, and they shared similar interests in politics, music, literature, and in entertaining friends. Like the first couple, this husband and wife felt their behavior was typical of their social circle, except that they felt they carried the interchangeability of household tasks a little further than most people. One may sum up the differences between these two extremes by saying that the first family showed more segregation between husband and wife in their role-relationship than the second family. In between these two extremes there were many degrees of variation. This chapter attempts to interpret these differences in degree of segregation of conjugal roles.

. . . The husbands who had the most segregated role-relationships with their wives had manual occupations, and the husbands who had the most joint role-relationships with their wives were professional or semi-professional people, but there were several working-class families that had relatively little segregation, and there were professional families in which segregation was considerable. Having a working-class occupation is a necessary but not a sufficient cause of the most marked degree of conjugal segregation. . . .

The data suggested that the families with most segregation lived in homogeneous areas of low population turnover, whereas the families with predominantly joint role-relationships lived in heterogeneous areas of high population turnover. Once again, however, there were several exceptions.

. . . The external social relationships of all families assumed the form of a *network* rather than the form of an organized group.[1] In an organized group, the component individuals make up a larger social whole with common aims, interdependent roles, and a distinctive sub-culture. In network formation, on the other hand, only some, not all, of the component individuals have social relationships with one another.

. . . There was considerable variation in the *"connectedness"* of their networks. By connectedness I mean the extent to which the people known by a family know and meet one another independently of the family. I use the word *"close-knit"* to describe a network in which there are many relationships among the component units, and the word *"loose-knit"* to describe a network in which there are few such relationships. Strictly speaking, "close-knit" should read "close-knit relative to the networks of the other research families," and "loose-knit" should read "loose-knit relative to the networks of the other research families."

1. In sociological and anthropological literature, the term "group" is commonly used in at least two senses. In the first sense it is a very broad term used to describe any collectivity whose members are alike in some way; this definition would include categories, logical classes, and aggregates as well as more cohesive social units. The second usage is much more restricted. In this sense, the units must have some distinctive interdependent social relationships with one another; categories, logical classes, and aggregates are excluded. To avoid confusion, I use the term "organized group" when it becomes necessary to distinguish the second usage from the first.

The shorter terms are used to simplify the language, but it should be remembered that they are shorthand expressions of relative degrees of connectedness and that they are not intended to be conceived as polar opposites.

A qualitative examination of the research data suggests that the degree of segregation of conjugal roles is related to the degree of connectedness in the total network of the family. Those families that had a high degree of segregation in the role-relationship of husband and wife had a close-knit network; many of their friends, neighbors, and relatives knew one another. Families that had a relatively joint role-relationship between husband and wife had a loose-knit network; few of their relatives, neighbors, and friends knew one another. There were many degrees of variation between these two extremes. On the basis of our data, I should therefore like to put forward the following hypothesis: *The degree of segregation in the role-relationship of husband and wife varies directly with the connectedness of the family's social network.* The more connected the network, the greater the degree of segregation between the roles of husband and wife. The less connected the network, the smaller the degree of segregation between the roles of husband and wife.

Highly Segregated Conjugal Role-Relationship Associated with Close-Knit Network

The research set contained only one family of this type, the Newbolts. They had been married six years when the interviewing began and had three small boys. In the following discussion, I describe their actual behavior, indicating the points at which they depart from their norms.[2]

2. Although I am not primarily concerned here with whether the research families are typical of others, the literature suggests that there are many such families, chiefly in certain sections of the urban working class. (See T. Hopkinson, "Down Jamaica Road," *The Observer*, March 1954; A. P. Jephcott and M. P. Carter, *The Social Background of Delinquency*, unpubl. ms., University of Nottingham, 1955; M. Kerr, "Study of Personality Deprivation Through Projection Test," *Soc. Econ. Stud.*, Vol. 4, 1955; J. B. Mays, *Growing Up in the City*, Liverpool: Liverpool University Press, 1954; J. J. Mogey, *Family and Neighborhood*, London: Oxford University Press, 1956; E. L. Packer, "Aspects of Working-Class Marriage," *Pilot Papers*, Vol. 2, 1947; L. A. Shaw, "Impressions of Family Life in a London Suburb," *Sociological Rev.*, Vol. 2 (New Series), 1954; E. Slater and M. Woodside, *Patterns of Marriage*, London: Cornell, 1951.) There is some evidence of similar conjugal segregation in "lower-class" American families (A. Davis, "American Status Systems and the Socialization of the Child," *American Sociological Review*, Vol. 6, 1941; "Child Training and Social Class," in R. G. Barker *et al.*, Eds., *Child Behavior and Development*, New York: McGraw-Hill, 1943; "Socialization and Adolescent Personality," Forty-third Yearbook, Nat. Society Stud. Educ., Part I, Adolescence, 1946; A. Davis and R. Havighurst, "Social Class and Color Differences in Child Rearing," *American Sociological Review*, Vol. 11, 1946; *Father of the Man*, Boston: Houghton Mifflin, 1947; J. Dollard, *Caste and Class in a Southern Town*, New Haven: Yale University Press, 1937; E. F. Frazier, *The Negro Family in the United States*, Chicago: University of Chicago Press, 1940; H. S. Maas, "Some Social Class Differences in the Family Systems and Group Relations of Pre- and Early Adolescents," *Child Development*, Vol. 22, 1951).

The role of the husband-father in such families is often described as "authoritarian," implying that he has clear authority over his wife and children in most or all of their activities. Although I agree that the husband has the right to control the actions of his wife in certain activities, I think the characterization of his role as "authoritarian," is too sweeping. Male authoritarianism is often confused with segregation of conjugal roles; this comes about because authors assign to the financial and sexual arrangements of these families the same psychological meaning as they would have to families where husband and wife expected to have a joint relationship. This view is supported by the fact that authors also describe these families as "mother-centered," although this description is not usually put side by side with that of male authoritarianism because the two characterizations sound contradictory. But both are valid, for each partner has authority and responsibility in his own sphere.[3]

External Social Relationships. Mr. Newbolt had a semi-skilled manual job at a factory in Bermondsey. He and his wife lived in a nearby area of the same borough. He said that several other men in the local area had jobs at the same place as himself, and that others were doing similar jobs at other factories and workshops nearby. Mrs. Newbolt did not work, but she felt that she was unusual in this respect. Most of the neighboring women and many of her female relatives had jobs; she did not think there was anything morally wrong with such work, but she said that she had never liked working and preferred to stay at home with the children. Mr. Newbolt expressed the same view, and added that it was a bit of a reflection on a man if his wife had to go out to work.

The Newbolts used the services of a local hospital and a maternity and child welfare clinic. They expected to send their children to the local primary school. They were also in touch with the local housing authority because they were trying to find a new flat. These various service

---

3. Several studies show that not all working-class families have pronounced segregation of conjugal roles (Cf. A. P. Jephcott and M. P. Carter, *op. cit.*; M. Young and P. Willmott, *Family and Kinship in East London,* London: Routledge & Kegan Paul, 1957; J. J. Mogey, *op. cit.*; S. B. Hammond, "Class and Family (Part I)," Chapter XVIII of O. A. Oeser and S. B. Hammond, Eds., *Social Structure and Personality in a City,* London: Routledge and Kegan Paul, 1954).

Although I have found no studies analyzing conjugal segregation in terms of external relationships and network-connectedness, there are some suggestions in the literature that families like the Newbolts have many important relationships outside the family, especially with kin, and it is sometimes implied or can be inferred that these external people are well known to one another. (See F. Dotson, "Patterns of Voluntary Association among Urban Working-Class Families," *American Sociological Review,* Vol. 16, 1951; G. Gorer, *Exploring English Character,* London: Cresset Press, 1955; Jephcott and Carter, *op. cit.*; Kerr, *op. cit.,* Mays, *op. cit.,* Shaw, *op. cit.,* J. H. Sheldon, *The Social Medicine of Old Age,* London: Oxford University Press, 1948; P. Townsend, *The Family Life of Old People,* London: Routledge and Kegan Paul, 1957; M. Young, "The Planners and the Planned—The Family," *J. Tn. Plann. Inst.,* Vol. 40, 1954, and "The Extended Family Welfare Association," *Soc. Work,* Vol. 13, 1956; M. Young and P. Willmott, *Family and Kinship in East London, op. cit.*; F. Zweig, *Women's Life and Labor,* London: Gollancz, 1952.)

institutions were not felt to have any particular relationship to one another, except in the sense that they were all felt to be foreign bodies, not really part of the local life. Mrs. Newbolt was a little afraid of them. On one occasion, while waiting with her baby and myself in an otherwise empty hospital room for a doctor to attend to the baby, she said in a whisper, "My husband says that we pay for it (the hospital services, through National Health subscriptions) and we should use it, but I don't like coming here. I don't like hospitals and doctors, do you?"

To the Newbolts the local area was definitely a community, a place with an identity of its own and a distinctive way of life. They spoke of it with pride and contrasted it favorably with areas. "It has a bad name, they say we are rough, but I think it's the best place there is. Everyone is friendly . . . there is no life over the water up West. They drink champagne and we drink beer. When things are la-di-da you feel out of place." They took it for granted that the other inhabitants had similar feelings of local pride and loyalty. Trips outside the area were like ventures into a foreign land, especially for Mrs. Newbolt. Few informal social relationships were kept up with people outside the area, and physical distance was felt to be an almost insuperable barrier to social contact.

. . . The Newbolts felt their neighbors were socially similar to themselves, having the same sort of jobs, the same sort of background, the same sort of outlook on life. Because the Newbolts had grown up in the area, as had many of their relatives and neighbors, they knew a considerable number of local people, and many of these people were acquainted with one another. In other words, their social network was close-knit. There was overlapping of social roles; instead of there being people in separate categories—friend, neighbor, relative, and colleague—the same person frequently filled two or more of these roles simultaneously.

The Newbolts took it for granted that Mr. Newbolt, like other husbands in their social circle, would have some recreation with men away from home. In his case it was cycle-racing and cricket, although the most common form of recreation was felt to be drinking and visiting friends in the local pub where many husbands spent an evening or two a week; frequently some of these men were friends of long standing who had belonged to the same childhood gang; others were colleagues at work. Mr. Newbolt had kept in touch with one or two childhood friends; he also played cricket and went to matches with some of his work colleagues; several of his friends knew one another. Mrs. Newbolt knew a little about these men, but she did not expect to join in their activities with her husband. She had a nodding acquaintance with two or three of the wives, and occasionally talked to them when she was shopping.

Mrs. Newbolt had separate relationships in which her husband did not expect to join. She knew many female neighbors, just as they knew one another. She took it for granted that a friendly relationship with a neighbor would end if the woman moved away. Neighbors saw one another on the landings, in the street, in shops; they hardly ever asked each other inside the flat or house. They talked over their affairs and those of other neighbors. Neighbors frequently accused one another of something—betraying a confidence, taking the wrong side in a children's quarrel, failing to return borrowed articles, or gossip. One has little privacy in such a situation. But if one wants to reap the rewards of companionship and small acts of mutual aid, one must conform to local standards and one must expect to be included in the gossip. Being gossiped about is as much a sign of belonging to the neighborly network as being gossiped with. If one refuses contact with neighbors one is thought odd and eventually one will be left alone; no gossip, no companionship.

With the exception of visiting relatives and an occasional Sunday outing with the children, the Newbolts spent little of their leisure in joint recreation. Even though they could have asked relatives to mind the children for them, they rarely went out together. In particular, there was no joint entertaining of friends at home. From time to time Mr. Newbolt brought a friend home and Mrs. Newbolt made tea and talked a little. Female neighbors often dropped in during the evening to borrow something, but they did not stay long if Mr. Newbolt was there. There was no planned joint entertaining in which Mr. and Mrs. Newbolt asked another husband and wife to spend an evening with them. Such joint entertaining as existed was carried on with relatives, not with friends. Poverty does not explain the absence of joint entertaining, for the Newbolts considered themselves relatively well-off. It did not seem to occur to them that they might spend money on entertaining friends; they felt surplus money should be spent on furniture, new things for the children, or gatherings of relatives at wedding, funerals, and christenings.[4]

There was much visiting and mutual aid between relatives, particularly the women. The Newbolts had far more active social relationships with relatives than any other research family, and there was also a great deal of independent contact by their relatives with one another in addition to their contacts with the Newbolts themselves. Thus the network of kin was close-knit, probably more so than those of neighbors or friends. The women were more active than the men in keeping up contacts with relatives, with the result that the networks of wives were more close-knit than the networks of their husbands. Although husbands were recognized to be less active in kinship affairs than their wives. Mr. Newbolt paid occasional visits to his mother, both by himself and with his wife. Furthermore, there were some activities in which joint participation by

4. The absence of joint entertainment of friends made our technique of joint interviewing somewhat inappropriate for this family.

husband and wife was felt to be desirable. At weddings, funerals, and christenings, there were large gatherings of relatives and it was felt to be important that both husband and wife should attend. Such basic kinship ceremonies formed an important topic of discussion throughout the interviews with the Newbolts.

In a group discussion, a man living in the same local area as the Newbolts and having a similar sort of family life and kinship network summed up the situation by saying, "Men have friends. Women have relatives," succinctly describing the difference between men and women in external relationships, and implying segregation between husband and wife. Wives, through their close relationships with their children and with their parents, are deeply involved in activities with kin. Husbands are more concerned with jobs and friends. This man's epigram also suggests the overlapping of roles mentioned above. Mrs. Newbolt had no independent category of "friend"; friends were either neighbors or relatives. She had had a succession of girl-friends in her adolescence, but she said that she did not see so much of them since they were all married with children. She always described them as "girl-friends" not as "friends." Both Mr. and Mrs. Newbolt used the term "friend" as if it applied only to men. The term "neighbor," on the other hand, seemed to refer only to women. Mr. Newbolt looked rather shocked when I asked him if he saw much of the neighbors.

Later in the group discussion the same man observed, "Women don't have friends. They have Mum." In Mrs. Newbolt's case the relationship between herself and her mother was very close. Her mother lived nearby in the same local area, and Mrs. Newbolt visited her nearly every day, taking her children with her. She and her mother and her mother's sisters also visited Mrs. Newbolt's maternal grandmother. These women and their children formed an important group, helping one another in household tasks and child care, and providing aid in crises.[5]

Conjugal Segregation. The previous description reveals considerable segregation between Mr. and Mrs. Newbolt in their external relationships. There was a similar segregation in the way they carried out their internal domestic tasks. They believed there should be a clear-cut division of labor between them, and that all husbands and wives in their social circle organized their households in a similar way. One man said in a group discussion, "A lot of men wouldn't mind helping their wives if the curtains were drawn so people couldn't see," and this was how the Newbolts felt about it too.

Although the Newbolts felt that major decisions should be made jointly, in the day-to-day running of the household he had his jobs and she

5. See also Chapter V, *Family and Social Network,* Elizabeth Bott, London: Tavistock Publications Limited, 1957; and M. Young, "The Planners and the Planned," *op. cit.,* and "The Extended Family Welfare Association," *op. cit.,* Young & Willmott, *op. cit.*

hers. He had control of the money and gave her a housekeeping allowance of £5 a week. Mrs. Newbolt did not know how much money he earned, and it did not seem to occur to her that a wife would want or need to know this. Although the Newbolts said £5 was the amount given to most wives for housekeeping, Mrs. Newbolt had difficulty in making it cover the cost of food, rent, utilities, and five shillings' saving for Christmas. She told her husband whenever she ran short, and he left a pound or two under the clock when he went out next morning. She said he was very generous with his money and she felt she was unusually fortunate in being spared financial quarrels.

Mrs. Newbolt was responsible for most of the housework although Mr. Newbolt did household repairs and she expected him to do some of the housework if she became ill. This was usually unnecessary because her mother or sister or one of her cousins came to her aid. These female relatives helped her greatly even with the everyday tasks of housework and child care.

Like all the research couples, the Newbolts took it for granted that husband and wife should be jointly responsible for the welfare of their children. In practice, Mrs. Newbolt carried out most of the actual tasks of caring for the three boys, though Mr. Newbolt helped to entertain them in the evenings and on Sundays. Occasionally he put them to bed and sometimes he got up when they cried in the night. He bought them many presents. Mrs. Newbolt felt that he was a very good father. She said fathers took more of an interest in children nowadays than they used to, but that even allowing for this, Mr. Newbolt was exceptional.

Attitudes Towards the Role-Relationship of Husband and Wife. Mr. and Mrs. Newbolt took it for granted that men had male interests and women had female interests and that there were few leisure activities they would naturally share. In their view, a good husband was generous with the housekeeping allowance, did not waste money selfishly on himself, helped his wife with the housework if she got ill, and took an interest in the children. A good wife was a good manager, an affectionate mother, a woman who kept out of serious rows with neighbors and got along well with her own and her husband's relatives. A good conjugal relationship was one with a harmonious division of labor, but the Newbolts placed little stress on the importance of joint activities and shared interests.

Families Having Joint Conjugal Role-Relationship Associated with a Loose-Knit Network

There were five families of this type. The husbands had professional, semi-professional, and clerical occupations. Two of the husbands considered their occupations to be of higher social status than the occupations of their fathers. One husband had an occupation of lower social status. All five families, however, had a well-established pattern of external relationships; they might make new relationships, but the basic pattern was likely to remain the same. Similarly, all had worked out a fairly stable division of labor in domestic tasks.

External Social Relationships. The husbands' occupations had little intrinsic connection with the local areas in which they lived. All five husbands carried on their work at some distance from their areas of residence, although two did some additional work at home. In no case was there any feeling that the occupation was locally rooted.

Whether or not wives should work was considered to be a very controversial question by these couples. Unless they were very well-off financially—and none of them really considered themselves to be so —both husband and wife welcomed the idea of a double income, even though much of the additional money had to be spent on caring for the children. But money was not the only consideration; women also wanted to work for the sake of the work itself. It was felt that if she desired it, a woman should have a career or some special interest and skill comparable in seriousness to her husband's occupation; on the other hand, it was felt that young children needed their mother's care and that ideally she should drop her career at least until the youngest child was old enough to go to school. But most careers cannot easily be dropped and picked up again several years later. Two of the wives had solved the problem by continuing to work; they had made careful (and expensive) provision for the care of their children. One wife worked at home. The fourth had a special interest (shared by her husband) that took up almost as much time as a job, and the fifth wife was planning to take up her special interest again as soon as her youngest child went to school.

These husbands and wives maintained contact with schools, general practitioners, hospitals, and in some cases local maternity and child welfare clinics. Most of them also used the services of a solicitor, an insurance agent, and other similar professional people as required. Unlike the Newbolts, they did not feel that service institutions were strange and alien; it did not bother them when they had to go out of their local area to find such services. They were usually well informed about service institutions and could exploit them efficiently. They were not afraid of doctors. There was no strict division of labor between husband and wife in dealing with service institutions. The wife usually dealt with those institutions that catered for children, and the husband dealt with the legal and financial ones, but either could take over the other's duties if necessary.

These husbands and wives did not regard the neighborhood as a source of friends. In most cases the husband and wife had moved several times both before and after marriage, and none of them were living in the neighborhood in which they had grown up. Four were living in areas of such a kind that few of the neighbors were felt to be socially similar to the family themselves. The fifth family was living in a suburb which the husband and wife felt to be composed of people socially similar to one another, but quite different from themselves. In all cases these husbands and wives were polite but somewhat distant to most neighbors. One couple had found two friends in the neighborhood through their children. Another couple had friendly though rather formal and gingerly relations with three or four neighbors. In order to become proper friends, neighbors had not only to be socially similar to the family themselves, but also had to share a large number of tastes and interests. Establishing such a relationship requires exploratory testing, and it seems to be considered dangerous to approach neighbors since one risks being pestered by friendly attentions one may not wish to return. Since many neighbors probably had similar feelings, it is not surprising that intimate social relationships were not rapidly established. Since these families had so little social intercourse with their neighbors, they were less worried than the Newbolts about gossip and conformity to local norms. In the circumstances one can hardly say that there were any specifically local norms; certainly there was not a body of shared attitudes and values built up through personal interaction since childhood as was characteristic of the area inhabited by the Newbolts.

In marked contrast to the Newbolts' situation, nearly all of the husband's and wife's friends were joint friends. It was felt to be important that both husband and wife should like a family friend, and if he or she was married, then it was hoped that all four people involved would like one another. Exceptions were tolerated, especially in the case of very old friends, but both husband and wife were uncomfortable if there was real disagreement between them over a friend. Friendship, like marriage, requires shared interests and similar tastes, although there was some specialization of interests in this respect. For example, one couple might be golfing friends whereas others might be pub and drinking friends; still others were all-round friends, and it was these who were felt to be the most intimate.

Joint entertainment of friends was a major form of recreation. Even when couples did not have enough money to arrange dinners or parties, friends were still asked over jointly even if only for coffee or tea in the evening. It was considered "provincial" for husbands to cluster at one end of the room and wives at the other; everyone should be able to talk to everyone else. These husbands and wives usually had enough shared interests to make this possible.

After these couples had children, it became increasingly difficult for them to visit their friends, who often lived at a considerable distance. Since most friends were also tied down by young children, mutual visiting became more and more difficult to arrange. Considerable expense and trouble were taken to make such visiting possible. It was obvious that friends were of primary importance to these families.

There were usually other forms of joint recreation, such as eating in foreign restaurants, going to plays, films, concerts, and so forth. After children were born, there had been a marked drop in external joint recreation in favor of things that could be done at home. Going out became a special event with all the paraphernalia of a baby-sitter and arrangements made in advance. All these couples felt that it was not quite right for one partner to go out alone. It happened occasionally, but joint recreation was much preferred.

These five families had far less contact with their relatives than the Newbolts. Their relatives were not concentrated in the same local area as themselves. In most cases they were scattered all over the country and did not keep in close touch with one another, thus forming a loose-knit network. It was felt that friendly relations should be kept up with parents, and in several cases the birth of the children had led to a sort of reunion with parents. Becoming a parent seems to facilitate a resolution of some of the emotional tensions between adult children and their own parents, particularly between women and their mothers. Possibly the arrival of children may exacerbate such tensions in some cases, but none of these five families had had such an experience. There are obvious practical advantages in increased contact with parents; they are usually fond of their grandchildren so that they make affectionate and reliable baby-sitters and if they live close enough to take on this task their services are appreciated.

Among the families with loose-knit networks, there was not the very strong stress on the mother-daughter relationship that was described for Mrs. Newbolt, although women were usually more active than men in keeping up kinship ties. There were fewer conflicts of loyalty; it was felt that if conflicts arose between one's parents and one's spouse, one owed one's first loyalty to one's spouse. Unless special interests, particularly financial ties, were operating among relatives, there was no very strong obligation towards relatives outside the parental families of husband and wife. Even towards siblings there was often very little feeling of social obligation. These couples were very much less subject to social control by their relatives than the Newbolts, partly because they saw less of them, but also because the network of kin was dispersed and loose-knit so that its various members were less likely to share the same opinions and values.

In brief, the networks of these families were more loose-knit than that of the Newbolts; many of their friends did not know one another, it was unusual for friends to know relatives, only a few relatives kept in touch with one another, and husband and wife had very little contact with neighbors. Furthermore, there was no sharp segregation between the wife's network and the husband's network. With the exception of a few old friends and some colleagues, husband and wife maintained joint external relationships.

Conjugal Role-Segregation. As described above, these families had as little segregation as possible in their external relationships. There was a similar tendency towards joint organization in their carrying out of domestic tasks and child care. It was felt that efficient management demanded some division of labor, particularly after the children came. There had to be a basic differentiation between the husband's role as primary breadwinner and the wife's as mother of young children. In other respects such division of labor as existed was felt to be more of a matter of convenience than of inherent differences between the sexes. The division of labor was flexible and there was considerable sharing and interchange of tasks. Husbands were expected to take a very active part in child care. Financial affairs were managed jointly, and joint consultation was taken for granted on all major decisions.

Husbands were expected to provide much of the help that Mrs. Newbolt was able to get from her female relatives. The wives of the families with loose-knit networks were carrying a very heavy load of housework and child care, but they expected to carry it for a shorter time than Mrs. Newbolt. Relatives helped them only very occasionally; they usually lived at some distance so that it was difficult for them to provide continuous assistance. Cleaning women are employed by four couples and a children's nurse by one; all couples wanted to have more domestic help but could not afford it. In spite of their affection for their children, all five couples were looking forward to the time when they would be older and less of a burden. In so far as they could look ahead, they did not expect to provide continuous assistance to their own married children.

It seems that in the case of Mrs. Newbolt and other wives with close-knit networks, the burden of housework and child care is more evenly distributed throughout the lifetime of the wife. When she is a girl she helps her mother with the younger children; when she herself has children her mother and other female relatives help her; when she is a grandmother she helps her daughters.

Like all the research couples, those with loose-knit networks took it for granted that husband and wife should be jointly responsible for the welfare of the children. But the husbands were expected to help more than Mr. Newbolt. Mrs. Newbolt thought her husband was a very good father because he took an interest in the children; the wives of families with loose-knit networks took it for granted that husbands would take an interest in the children. Husbands had to help their wives because the wives got less help from relatives and neighbors. But it was more than that. Co-parenthood was considered to be a most vital part of the joint conjugal relationship. Even so, the wives carried most of the burden of child care because, with the exception of those who had full-time jobs, they were at home most of the day.

In spite of the great number of child-care activities that were shared by husband and wife, it was taken for granted that the relationship between mother and child was different from that between father and child. The difference was greatest when the children were infants. It was felt, although never explained in so many words, that the relationship between mother and infant was a special very close relationship, almost one of bodily union, that a father could never achieve. At most he could be an auxiliary mother, and if he tried to be more the wife felt he was poaching on her territory. When the children were older the gap between the mother-child relationship and the father-child relationship was less marked. As far as I could tell, these couples did not feel that fathers should be the final authorities and disciplinarians and that mothers should be more warm-hearted. They thought husband and wife should be more or less equal both in authority and in warm-heartedness.[6] But there was a recognized tendency for fathers to specialize in entertaining the children. Two of the five fathers also had closer relationships with the oldest child than with the others, although it was felt that favoritism by either parent was bad for the children and attempts were made to conceal it from the children.

Attitudes Towards the Role-Relationship of Husband and Wife. Among the families with loose-knit networks, there were frequent discussions as to whether there really were any psychological or temperamental differences between the sexes. These differences were not simply taken for granted as they were by the Newbolts. In some cases so much stress was placed on shared interests and sexual equality (which was sometimes confused with identity, the notion of equality of complementary opposites being apparently a difficult idea to maintain consistently) that one sometimes felt that the possibility of the existence of social and temperamental differences between the sexes was being denied. In other cases, temperamental differences between the sexes were exaggerated to a point that belied the couple's actual joint activities and the whole pattern of shared interests felt to be so fundamental to their way of life. Quite

6. This finding contradicts Parsons' ideal type of the elementary family, in which the father, the "instrumental leader," is feared and respected whereas the mother, the "expressive leader," is loved more warmly (Parsons and Bales, *Family, Socialization and Interaction Process*, New York: The Free Press of Glencoe, Ill., 1955). This discrepancy may be due to the fact that Parsons looks at the situation chiefly from the point of view of the child and I am looking at it from the point of view of the parents. But in general I think Parsons overestimates the difference in the roles of husband and wife in this respect, particularly for families with loose-knit networks. I agree that the basic division of labor between husband and wife, in which the husband supports the family financially while the wife cares for the house and children, is of fundamental importance, but I think Parsons underestimates the amount of variation in conjugal segregation.

frequently the same couple would minimize differences between the sexes on one occasion and exaggerate them on another. Sometimes these discussions about sexual differences were very serious; sometimes they were witty and facetious; but they were never neutral—they were felt to be an important problem. Such discussions may be interpreted as an attempt to air and resolve the contradiction between the necessity for joint organization with its ethic of equality, on the one hand, and the necessity for differentiation and recognition of sexual differences on the other. "After all," one husband said to conclude the discussion, *"vive la différence,* or where would we all be?"

It was felt that in a good marriage, husband and wife should achieve a high degree of compatibility, based on their own particular combination of shared interests and complementary differences. Their relationship with each other should be more important than any separate relationship with outsiders. The conjugal relationship should be kept private and revelations to outsiders or letting down one's spouse in public were felt to be serious offences. A successful sexual relationship was felt by those couples to be very important for a happy marriage. It was as if successful sexual relations were felt to prove that all was well with the joint relationship, whereas unsatisfactory relations were indicative of a failure in the total relationship. In some cases one almost got the feeling that these husbands and wives felt a moral obligation to enjoy sexual relations, a feeling not expressed or suggested by the Newbolts.

The wives in these families seemed to feel that their position was rather difficult. They had certainly wanted children, and in all five cases they were getting a great deal of satisfaction from their maternal role. But at the same time, they felt tied down by their children and they did not like the inevitable drudgery associated with child care. Some were more affected than others, but most complained of isolation, boredom, and fatigue. They wanted a career or some special interest that would make them feel they were something more than children's nurses and housemaids. They wanted more joint entertainment with their husbands and more contact with friends. These complaints were not leveled specifically at their husbands—in most cases they felt their husbands were trying to make the situation easier—but against the social situation and the conflict in which they found themselves. One wife summed it up by saying, "Society seems to be against married women. I don't know, it's all very difficult."

It may be felt that the problem could be solved if such a family moved to an area that was felt to be homogeneous and composed of people similar to themselves, for then the wife might be able to find friends among her neighbors and would feel less isolated and bored. It is difficult to imagine, however, that these families could feel that any local area, however homogeneous by objective criteria, could be full of potential friends, for their experience of moving about in the past and their varied social contacts make them very discriminating in their choice of friends. Further, their dislike of having their privacy broken into by neighbors was deeply rooted; it diminished after the children started playing with children in the neighborhood but it never disappeared entirely.

The Nature of the Relationship Between Segregation of Conjugal Roles and Connectedness of Networks

The data having been described, the nature of the relationship between conjugal segregation and network-connectedness may now be re-examined in general terms.

Close-knit networks are most likely to develop when husband and wife, together with their friends, neighbors, and relatives, have grown up in the same local area and have continued to live there after marriage. Many people know one another and have known one another since childhood. Women tend to associate with women and men with men. The only legitimate forms of heterosexual relationship are those between kin and between husband and wife. Friendship between a man and a woman who are not kin is suspect.

In such a setting, husband and wife come to marriage each with his own close-knit network. Each partner makes a considerable emotional investment in relationships with the people in his network. Each is very sensitive to their opinions and values, not only because the relationships are intimate, but also because the people in the network know one another and share the same norms so that they are able to apply consistent informal sanctions to one another. The marriage is superimposed on these pre-existing relationships. . . .

Because old relationships can be continued after marriage, both husband and wife can satisfy some personal needs outside the marriage, so that their emotional investment in the conjugal relationship need not be as intense as it is in other types of family. The wife, particularly, can get outside help with domestic tasks and with child care. A rigid division of labor between husband and wife is therefore possible. The segregation in external relationships can be carried over to activities within the family.

But although external people may help the elementary family, close-knit networks may also interfere with conjugal solidarity. A wife's loyalty to her mother may interfere with her relationship with her husband. Similarly her relationship with her husband may interfere with her relationship with her mother. A man's loyalty to his friends may interfere with his obligations to his wife and vice versa.

Networks become loose-knit when people move from one place to another or when they make new relationships not connected with their old ones. If both husband and wife have moved considerably before marriage, each will bring an already loose-knit network to the marriage. Many of the husband's friends will not know one another; many of the wife's friends will not know one another. Although they will continue to see some old friends after marriage, they will meet new people too, who will not necessarily know the old friends or one another. In other words, their external relationships are relatively discontinuous both in space and in time. Such continuity as they possess lies in their relationship with each other rather than in their external relationships. In facing the external world they draw on each other, for their strongest emotional investment is made where there is continuity. Hence their high standards of conjugal compatibility, their stress on shared interests, on joint organization, on equality between husband and wife. They must get along well together, they must help one another in carrying out familial tasks, for there is no sure external source of material and emotional help. Since their friends and relatives are physically scattered and few of them know one another, the husband and wife are not stringently controlled by a solid body of public opinion. They are also unable to rely on consistent external support. Through their joint external relationships they present a united front to the world and they reaffirm their joint relationship with each other. Joint relationships with friends give both husband and wife a source of emotional satisfaction outside the family without threatening their relationship with each other.

Melvin L. Kohn

Social Class
and Parental Values

We undertake this inquiry into the relationship between social class and
parental values in the hope that a fuller understanding of the ways in
which parents of different social classes differ in their values may help us
to understand why they differ in their practices.[1] This hope, of course,
rests on two assumptions: that it is reasonable to conceive of social
classes as subcultures of the larger society, each with a relatively distinct
value-orientation, and that values really affect behavior.

Sample and Method of Data Collection

Washington, D.C.—the locus of this study—has a large proportion of
people employed by government, relatively little heavy industry, few
recent immigrants, a white working class drawn heavily from rural areas,
and a large proportion of Negroes, particularly at lower economic levels.
Generalizations based on this or any other sample of one city during one
limited period of time are, of course, tentative.

Our intent in selecting the families to be studied was to secure
approximately two hundred representative white working-class families
and another two hundred representative white middle-class families, each
family having a child within a narrowly delimited age range. We decided
on fifth-grade children because we wanted to direct the interviews to

1. There now exists a rather substantial, if somewhat inconsistent, body of literature on
the relationship of social class to the ways that parents raise their children. For a fine
analytic summary see Urie Bronfenbrenner, "Socialization and Social Class through Time
and Space," in Eleanor E. Maccoby *et al., Readings in Social Psychology* (New York:
Henry Holt & Co. 1958). Bronfenbrenner gives references to the major studies of class and
child-rearing practices that have been done.

For the most relevant studies on class and *values* see Evelyn M. Duvall, "Conceptions
of Parenthood," *American Journal of Sociology,* LII (November, 1946), 193–203; David F.
Aberle and Kaspar D. Neagele, "Middle Class Fathers' Occupational Role and Attitudes
toward Children," *American Journal of Orthopsychiatry,* XXII (April, 1952), 366–78;
Herbert H. Hyman, "The Value Systems of Different Classes," in Reinhard Bendix and
Seymour M. Lipset (eds.), *Class, Status, and Power* (Glencoe, Ill.: Free Press, 1953), pp.
426–42; and Melvin Kohn, *Class and Conformity* (Homewood, Ill.: The Dorsey Press,
1969).

relationships involving a child old enough to have a developed capacity for verbal communication.

The sampling procedure[2] involved two steps: the first, selection of census tracts. Tracts with 20 percent or more Negro population were excluded, as were those in the highest quartile with respect to median income. From among the remaining tracts we then selected a small number representative of each of the three distinct types of residential area in which the population to be studied live: four tracts with a predominantly working-class population, four predominantly middle-class, and three having large proportions of each. The final selection of tracts was based on their occupational distribution and their median income, education, rent (of rented homes), and value (of owner-occupied homes). The second step in the sampling procedure involved selection of families. From records made available by the public and parochial school systems we compiled lists of all families with fifth-grade children who lived in the selected tracts. Two hundred families were then randomly selected from among those in which the father had a "white-collar" occupation and another two hundred from among those in which the father had a manual occupation.

In all four hundred families the mothers were to be interviewed. In every fourth family we scheduled interviews with the father and the fifth-grade child as well.[3] (When a broken family fell into this subsample, a substitute was chosen from our over-all sample, and the broken family was retained in the over-all sample of four hundred families.)

When interviews with both parents were scheduled, two members of the staff visited the home together—a male to interview the father, a female to interview the mother. The interviews were conducted independently, in separate rooms, but with essentially identical schedules. The first person to complete his interview with the parent interviewed the child.

Indexes of Social Class and Values

Social Class. Each family's social-class position has been determined by the Hollingshead Index of Social Position, assigning the father's

2. I owe a considerable debt of gratitude to Samuel W. Greenhouse, chief of the Section on Statistics and Mathematics, Biometrics Branch, NIMH, for his expert help in sample design, as well as for his advice on general statistical problems of the research.
3. The interviewing staff was composed of Eleanor Carroll, Mary Freeman, Paul Hanlon, and Melvin Kohn. We were aided from time to time by three volunteers from the NIMH staff: Leila Deasy, Erwin Linn, and Harriet Murphy. Field work was conducted between March, 1956, and March, 1957.
We secured the co-operation of 86 percent of the families where the mother alone was to be interviewed and 82 percent of the families where mother, father, and child were to be interviewed. Rates of non-response do not vary by social class, type of neighborhood, or type of school. This, of course, does not rule out other possible selective biases introduced by the non-respondents.

occupational status a relative weight of 7 and his educational status a weight of 4. We are considering Hollingshead's Classes I, II, and III to be "middle class," and Classes IV and V to be "working class." The middle-class sample is composed of two relatively distinct groups: Classes I and II are almost entirely professionals, proprietors, and managers with at least some college training. Class III is made up of small shopkeepers, clerks, and salespersons but includes a small number of foremen and skilled workers of unusually high educational status. The working-class sample is composed entirely of manual workers but preponderantly those of higher skill levels. These families are of the "stable working class" rather than "lower class" in the sense that the men have steady jobs, and their education, income, and skill levels are above those of the lowest socioeconomic strata.

Values. We shall use Kluckhohn's definition: "A value is a conception, explicit or implicit, distinctive of an individual or characteristic of a group, of the desirable which influences the selection from available modes, means, and ends of action." [4]

Our inquiry was limited to the values that parents would most like to see embodied in their children's behavior. We asked the parents to choose, from among several alternative characteristics that might be seen as desirable, those few which they considered *most* important for a child of the appropriate age. Specifically, we offered each parent a card listing 17 characteristics that had been suggested by other parents, in the pre-test interviews, as being highly desirable. (These appear down the left margin of Table 1. The order in which they were listed was varied from interview to interview.) Then we asked: "Which three of the things listed on this card would you say are the *most* important in a boy (or girl) of (fifth-grade child's) age?" The selection of a particular characteristic was taken as our index of value.

Later in this report we shall subject this index to intensive scrutiny.

Class and Values

Middle- and working-class mothers share a broadly common set of values—but not an identical set of values by any means (see Table 1). There is considerable agreement among mothers of both social classes that happiness and such standards of conduct as honesty, consideration, obedience, dependability, manners, and self-control are highly desirable for both boys and girls of this age.

Popularity, being a good student (especially for boys), neatness and

4. Clyde Kluckhohn, "Values and Value Orientations," in Talcott Parsons and Edward A. Shils (eds.), *Toward a General Theory of Action* (Cambridge, Mass.: Harvard University Press, 1951), p. 395.

cleanliness (especially for girls), and curiosity are next most likely to be regarded as desirable. Relatively few mothers choose ambition, ability to defend one's self, affectionate responsiveness, being liked by adults, ability to play by one's self, or seriousness as highly desirable for either boys or girls of this age. All of these, of course, might be more highly valued for children of other ages.

TABLE 1. Proportion of Mothers Who Select Each Characteristic as One of Three "Most Desirable" in a Ten- or Eleven-Year-Old Child

Characteristics	For Boys		For Girls		Combined	
	Middle Class	Working Class	Middle Class	Working Class	Middle Class	Working Class
1. That he is honest	0.44	0.57	0.44	0.48	0.44	0.53
2. That he is happy	.44[a]	.27	.48	.45	.46[a]	.36
3. That he is considerate of others	.40	.30	.38[a]	.24	.39[a]	.27
4. That he obeys his parents well	.18[a]	.37	.23	.30	.20[a]	.33
5. That he is dependable	.27	.27	.20	.14	.24	.21
6. That he has good manners	.16	.17	.23	.32	.19	.24
7. That he has self-control	.24	.14	.20	.13	.22[a]	.13
8. That he is popular with other children	.13	.15	.17	.20	.15	.18
9. That he is a good student	.17	.23	.13	.11	.15	.17
10. That he is neat and clean	.07	.13	.15[a]	.28	.11[a]	.20
11. That he is curious about things	.20[a]	.06	.15	.07	.18[a]	.06
12. That he is ambitious	.09	.18	.06	.08	.07	.13
13. That he is able to defend himself	.13	.05	.06	.08	.10	.06
14. That he is affectionate	.03	.05	.07	.04	.05	.04
15. That he is liked by adults	.03	.05	.07	.04	.05	.04
16. That he is able to play by himself	.01	.02	.00	.03	.01	.02
17. That he acts in a serious way	0.00	0.01	0.00	0.00	0.00	0.01
N	90	85	84	80	174	165

a. Social-class differences statistically significant, 0.05 level or better, using chi-squared test.

Although agreement obtains on this broad level, working-class mothers differ significantly[5] from middle-class mothers in the relative emphasis they place on particular characteristics. Significantly fewer working-class mothers regard happiness as highly desirable for *boys*. Although characteristics that define standards of conduct are valued by many mothers of both social classes, there are revealing differences of emphasis here too. Working-class mothers are more likely to value obedience; they would have their children be responsive to parental authority. Middle-class mothers are more likely to value both consideration and self-control; they would have their children develop inner control and sympathetic concern for other people. Furthermore, middle-class mothers are more likely to regard curiosity as a prime virtue. By contrast, working-class mothers put the emphasis on neatness and cleanliness, valuing the imaginative and exploring child relatively less than the presentable child.[6]

Middle-class mothers' conceptions of what is desirable for boys are much the same as their conceptions of what is desirable for girls. But working-class mothers make a clear distinction between the sexes: they are more likely to regard dependability, being a good student, and ambition as desirable for boys and to regard happiness, good manners, neatness, and cleanliness as desirable for girls.

What of the *fathers'* values? Judging from our subsample of 82 fathers, their values are similar to those of the mothers (see Table 2). Essentially the same rank-order of choices holds for fathers as for mothers, with one major exception: fathers are not so likely to value happiness for their daughters. Among fathers as well as mothers, consideration and self-control are more likely to be regarded as desirable by the middle class; middle-class fathers are also more likely to value another standard of conduct—dependability. Working-class fathers, like their wives, are more likely to value obedience; they are also more likely to regard it as desirable that their children be able to defend themselves.[7]

5. The criterion of statistical significance used throughout this paper is the 5 percent level of probability, based, except where noted, on the chi-squared test.

6. Compare these results with Bronfenbrenner's conclusion, based on an analysis of reports of studies of social class and child-rearing methods over the last twenty-five years: "In this modern working class world there may be greater freedom of emotional expression, but there is no laxity or vagueness with respect to goals of child training. Consistently over the past twenty-five years, the parent in this group has emphasized what are usually regarded as the traditional middle class virtues of cleanliness, conformity, and (parental) control, and although his methods are not so effective as those of his middle class neighbors, they are perhaps more desperate" *(op. cit.)*.

7. A comparison of the values of the fathers in this subsample with those of the mothers in this same subsample yields essentially the same conclusions.

We do not find that fathers of either social class are significantly more likely to choose any characteristic for boys than they are to choose it for girls, or the reverse. But this may well be an artifact of the small number of fathers in our sample; Aberle and Naegele *(op. cit.)* have found that middle-class fathers are more likely to value such characteristics as responsibility, initiative, good school performance, ability to stand up for one's self, and athletic ability for boys and being "nice," "sweet," pretty, affectionate, and well-liked for girls.

TABLE 2. Proportion of Fathers Who Select Each Characteristic as One of Three "Most Desirable" in a Ten- or Eleven-Year-Old Child

Characteristics	For Boys		For Girls		Combined	
	Middle Class	Working Class	Middle Class	Working Class	Middle Class	Working Class
1. That he is honest	0.60	0.60	0.43	0.55	0.52	0.58
2. That he is happy	.48	.24	.24	.18	.37	.22
3. That he is considerate of others	.32	.16	.38	.09	.35[a]	.14
4. That he obeys his parents well	.12[a]	.40	.14	.36	.13[a]	.39
5. That he is dependable	.36[a]	.12	.29[a]	.00	.33[a]	.08
6. That he has good manners	.24	.28	.24	.18	.24	.25
7. That he has self-control	.20	.08	.19	.00	.20[a]	.06
8. That he is popular with other children	.08	.16	.24	.45	.15	.25
9. That he is a good student	.04	.12	.10	.36	.07	.19
10. That he is neat and clean	.16	.20	.14	.09	.15	.17
11. That he is curious about things	.16	.12	.10	.00	.13	.08
12. That he is ambitious	.20	.12	.14	.00	.17	.08
13. That he is able to defend himself	.04	.16	.00[a]	.18	.02[a]	.17
14. That he is affectionate	.00[a]	.04	.05	.18	.02	.08
15. That he is liked by adults	.00	.08	.00	.09	.00	.08
16. That he is able to play by himself	.00	.08	.05	.00	.02	.06
17. That he acts in a serious way	0.00	0.04	0.00	0.00	0.00	0.03
N	25	25	21	11	46	36

a. Social-class differences statistically significant, 0.05 level or better, using chi-squared test.

We take this to indicate that middle-class parents (fathers as well as mothers) are more likely to ascribe predominant importance to the child's acting on the basis of internal standards of conduct, working-class parents to the child's compliance with parental authority.

There are important differences between middle- and working-class parents, too, in the way in which their choice of any one characteristic is related to their choice of each of the others.[8]

We have already seen that parents of both social classes are very likely to accord *honesty* first-rank importance. But the choice of honesty is quite differently related to the choice of other characteristics in the two classes (see Table 3). Middle-class mothers[9] who choose honesty are more likely than are other middle-class mothers to regard consideration, manners, and (for boys) dependability as highly desirable; and those mothers who regard any of these as desirable are more likely to value honesty highly. Consideration, in turn, is positively related to self-control, and manners to neatness. Honesty, then, is the core of a set of

8. A logical procedure for examining these patterns of choice is to compare the proportions of parents who choose any given characteristic, B, among those who do and who do not choose another characteristic, A. But since a parent who selects characteristic A has exhausted one of his three choices, the a priori probability of his selecting any other characteristic is only two-thirds as great as the probability that a parent who has not chosen A will do so. (A straightforward application of probability considerations to the problem of selecting three things from seventeen when one is interested only in the joint occurrence of two, say, A and B, shows that we can expect B to occur 2/16 of the time among those selections containing A and 3/16 of the time among those not containing A.) This, however, can be taken into account by computing the ratio of the two proportions: p_1, the proportion of parents who choose B among those who choose A, and p_2, the proportion who choose B among those who do *not* choose A. If the ratio of these proportions (p_1/p_2) is significantly larger than two-thirds, the two are positively related; if significantly smaller, they are negatively related.

The test of statistical significance is based on the confidence interval on a ratio, originally given by Fieller, with the modification that we deal here with the ratio of two independent proportions whose variances under the null hypothesis (chance) are known and whose distribution we assume to be normal. The 95 percent confidence interval on the true ratio, R, of the two proportions, p_1 and p_2, that hold for any given A and B, is given by:

$$R = \frac{r \pm (1/8p_2)\sqrt{(28/n_1)+(39r^2/n_2) - [(28\times39)/64n_1n_2p_2^2]}}{[1 - (39/64n_2p_2^2)]}$$

where p_1 and p_2 are the observed sample proportions, $r = p_1/p_2$, n_1 = the number of persons selecting A, and n_2 = the number of persons who do not select A.

The logic of the testing procedure is as follows: If the interval contains the null hypothesis value of $R = 2/3$ implied by chance selection, then we assume no association between B and A. If the interval excludes 2/3 such that the lower limit is larger than 2/3, we conclude that the true R is greater than we expect on the basis of randomness and hence that B is positively associated with A. On the other hand, if the upper limit of the interval is smaller than 2/3, then we conclude that the true R is smaller than 2/3 and hence B and A are negatively related.

This procedure was suggested by Samuel W. Greenhouse. For the derivation of the test see E. C. Fieller, "A Fundamental Formula in the Statistics of Biological Assay, and Some Applications," *Quarterly Journal of Pharmacy and Pharmacology*, XVII (1944), 117–23; see also Pandurang V. Sukhatme, *Sampling Theory of Surveys with Applications* (Ames, Iowa: Iowa State College Press, 1954), pp. 158–60.

9. This analysis and those to follow will be limited to the mothers, since the sample of fathers is small. For simplicity, we shall present data separately for boys and for girls only where the relationship under discussion appears to differ for the two sexes considered separately.

TABLE 3. All Cases[a] Where Mothers' Choice of One Characteristic as "Desirable" Is Significantly Related to Their Choice of Any Other Characteristic as "Desirable"

		Proportion Who Choose B Among Those Who:		
Middle-Class Mothers				
			Do Not	
Characteristic		*Choose A*	*Choose A*	
A	B	(p_1)	(p_2)	p_1/p_2
Positive Relationships:				
1. Honesty	Consideration	0.42	0.37	1.14
2. Honesty	Manners	.22	.16	1.38
3. Honesty	Dependability (boys)	.33	.22	1.50
4. Consideration	Honesty	.47	.42	1.12
5. Manners	Honesty	.52	.43	1.21
6. Dependability	Honesty (boys)	.54	.41	1.32
7. Consideration	Self-control	.24	.22	1.09
8. Self-control	Consideration	.41	.39	1.05
9. Manners	Neatness	.24	.08	3.00
10. Neatness	Manners	.42	.16	2.63
11. Curiosity	Happiness	.58	.43	1.35
12. Happiness	Curiosity	.23	.14	1.64
13. Happiness	Ambition (boys)	.13	.06	2.17
Negative Relationships:				
1. Honesty	Popularity	.04	.24	0.17
2. Popularity	Honesty	.12	.50	0.24
3. Curiosity	Obedience	.03	.24	0.13
4. Obedience	Consideration	0.17	0.45	0.38

Working-Class Mothers

A	B	(p_1)	(p_2)	p_1/p_2
Positive Relationships:				
1. Happiness	Honesty	0.51	0.55	0.93
2. Popularity	Honesty	.62	.51	1.22
3. Honesty	Popularity	.20	.14	1.43
4. Honesty	Defend self	.07	.05	1.40
5. Consideration	Manners (girls)	.42	.30	1.40
6. Manners	Consideration (girls)	.31	.20	1.55
7. Consideration	Curiosity	.11	.04	2.75
8. Ambition	Dependability	.29	.19	1.53
9. Happiness	Consideration (boys)	.35	.27	1.30
10. Consideration	Happiness (boys)	.32	.25	1.28
11. Happiness	Popularity (girls)	.25	.16	1.56
Negative Relationships:				
1. Obedience	Popularity	.05	.24	0.21
2. Manners	Popularity	.00	.23	0.00
3. Consideration	Popularity	.02	.23	0.09
4. Popularity	Obedience	.10	.38	0.26
5. Popularity	Manners	.00	.29	0.00
6. Popularity	Consideration	.03	.32	0.09
7. Manners	Dependability (girls)	0.00	0.20	0.00

a. Where it is not specified whether relationship holds for boys or for girls, it holds for both sexes. In all the relationships shown, p_1 and p_2 are each based on a minimum of 20 cases.

standards of conduct, a set consisting primarily of honesty, consideration, manners, and dependability, together with self-control and neatness. As such, it is to be seen as one among several, albeit the central, standards of conduct that middle-class mothers want their children to adopt.

This is not the case for working-class mothers. Those who regard honesty as predominantly important are not especially likely to think of consideration, manners, or dependability as comparable in importance; nor are those who value any of these especially likely to value honesty. Instead the mothers who are most likely to attribute importance to honesty are those who are concerned that the child be happy, popular, and able to defend himself. It is not that the child should conduct himself in a considerate, mannerly, or dependable fashion but that he should *be* happy, *be* esteemed by his peers, and, if the necessity arise, *be* able to protect himself. It suggests that honesty is treated less as a standard of conduct and more as a quality of the person; the emphasis is on being a person of inherent honesty rather than on acting in an honest way.

Note especially the relationship of popularity to honesty. For middle-class mothers these are *negatively* related. To value honesty is to forego valuing popularity; to value popularity is to forego valuing honesty. One must choose between honesty "at the risk of offending" and popularity at the sacrifice of absolute honesty. The exact opposite obtains for working-class mothers: those who accord high valuation to either are *more* likely to value the other. The very mothers who deem it most important that their children enjoy popularity are those who attribute great importance to honesty. Honesty does not interfere with popularity; on the contrary, it enhances the probability that one will enjoy the respect of one's peers.

However, working-class mothers who value obedience, manners, or consideration are distinctly unlikely to value popularity, and vice versa. They do see each of these standards of conduct as inconsistent with popularity.[10] This further substantiates the view that working-class mothers are more likely to view honesty as a quality of the person, a desideratum of moral worth, rather than as one among several highly valued standards of conduct.

Happiness, in distinction to honesty, implies neither constraints upon action nor a moral quality; rather, it indicates a desired goal, achievable in several different ways. One way of specifying what is implied when happiness is regarded as a major value is to ascertain the

10. It may be that these three characteristics have more in common than that they are all standards of conduct. The fact that working-class mothers who value consideration for their *daughters* are especially likely to value manners, and the converse, suggests the possibility that consideration may be seen as a near-equivalent to manners by at least a sizable portion of working-class mothers. If so, all three values negatively related to popularity can be viewed as reflecting close conformance to directives from parents—as contrasted to directives from within. (Note, in this connection, that working-class mothers who would have their daughters be mannerly are distinctly unlikely to deem it important that they be dependable.)

other values most likely to be related to the choice of happiness.

The two choices positively related to the choice of happiness by middle-class mothers are curiosity and (for boys) ambition. Those middle-class mothers who deem it exceedingly important that their children aspire for knowledge or success are even more likely than are middle-class mothers in general to value their children's happiness highly.

Working-class mothers who value these, however, are no more likely to value happiness. Instead, curiosity is related to consideration, to the child's concern for others' well-being, and ambition to dependability, to his being the type of person who can be counted on. The values that are positively related to happiness by working-class mothers are honesty, consideration (for boys), and popularity (for girls). Not aspirations for knowledge or for success, but being an honest—a worthy—person; not the desire to outdistance others, but, for boys, concern for others' well-being and, for girls, enjoyment of the respect and confidence of peers: these are the conceptions of the desirable that accompany working-class mothers' wishes that their children be happy.

Still the perhaps equally important fact is that no choice, by mothers of either social class, is negatively related to the choice of happiness.

The final bit of information that these data provide concerns the conception of *obedience* entertained in the two classes. Middle-class mothers who value curiosity are unlikely to value obedience; those who value obedience are unlikely to value consideration. For middle-class mothers, but not for working-class mothers, obedience would appear to have a rather narrow connotation; it seems to approximate blind obedience.

Class, Subculture, and Values

In discussing the relationship of social class to values we have talked as if American society were composed of two relatively homogeneous groups, manual and white-collar workers, together with their families. Yet it is likely that there is considerable variation in values, associated with other bases of social differentiation, *within* each class. If so, it should be possible to divide the classes into subgroups in such a way as to specify more precisely the relationship of social class to values.

Consider, first, the use we have made of the concept "social class." Are the differences we have found between the values of middle- and working-class mothers a product of this dichotomy alone, or do values parallel status gradations more generally? It is possible to arrive at an approximate answer by dividing the mothers into the five socioeconomic strata delineated by the Hollingshead Index (see Table 4). An examination of the choices made by mothers in each stratum indicates that variation in values parallels socioeconomic status rather closely:

TABLE 4. Mothers' Socioeconomic Status and Their Choice of Characteristics as "Most Desirable" in a Ten- or Eleven-Year-Old Child

| Characteristic | Proportion Who Select Each Characteristic Socioeconomic Stratum (on Hollingshead Index) | | | | |
	I	II	III	IV	V
Obedience	0.14	0.19	0.25	0.35	0.27
Neatness, cleanliness	.06	.07	.16	.18	.27
Consideration	.41	.37	.39	.25	.32
Curiosity	.37	.12	.09	.07	.03
Self-control	.24	.30	.18	.13	.14
Happiness	.61	.40	.40	.38	.30
Boys	.48		.40		.27
Girls	.54		.40		.45
Honesty	0.37	0.49	0.46	0.50	0.65
N	51	43	80	128	37

a. The higher a mother's status, the higher the probability that she will choose consideration, curiosity, self-control, and (for boys)[11] happiness as highly desirable; curiosity is particularly likely to be chosen by mothers in the highest stratum.

b. The lower her status, the higher the probability that she will select obedience, neatness, and cleanliness; it appears, too, that mothers in the lowest stratum are more likely than are those in the highest to value *honesty*.

Mothers' values also are directly related to their own occupational positions and educational attainments, independently of their families' class status. (The family's class status has been indexed on the basis of the husband's occupation and education.) It happens that a considerable proportion of the mothers we have classified as working class hold white-collar jobs.[12] Those who do are, by and large, closer to middle-class mothers in their values than are other working-class mothers (see Table 5). But those who hold manual jobs are even further from middle-class mothers in their values than are working-class mothers who do not have jobs outside the home.

So, too, for mothers' educational attainments: a middle-class mother of *relatively* low educational attainment (one who has gone no further than graduation from high school) is less likely to value curiosity and more likely to value (for girls) neatness and cleanliness (see Table 6). A

11. The choice of happiness is, as we have seen, related to social class for boys only. Consequently, in each comparison we shall make in this section the choice of happiness for *girls* will prove to be an exception to the general order.

12. No middle-class mothers have manual jobs, so the comparable situation does not exist. Those middle-class women who do work (at white-collar jobs) are less likely to value neatness and cleanliness and more likely to value obedience and curiosity.

TABLE 5. Working-Class Mothers' Own Occupations and Their Choice of Characteristics as "Most Desirable" in a Ten- or Eleven-Year-Old Child

| Characteristic | Proportion Who Select Each Characteristic | | |
	White-Collar Job	No Job	Manual Job
Obedience	.26	.35	.53
Neatness, cleanliness	.16	.18	.42
Consideration	.39	.21	.05
Curiosity	.10	.04	.00
Self-control	.13	.14	.11
Happiness	.33	.40	.26
Boys	.32	.21	—
Girls	.36	.59	—
N	69	77	19

working-class mother of *relatively* high educational attainment (one who has at least graduated from high school) is more likely to value self-control for boys and both consideration and curiosity for girls. The largest differences obtain between those middle-class mothers of highest educational attainments and those working-class mothers of lowest educational attainments.

Even when we restrict ourselves to considerations of social status and its various ramifications, we find that values vary appreciably within each of the two broad classes. And, as sociologists would expect, variation in values proceeds along other major lines of social demarcation as well. Religious background is particularly useful as a criterion for distinguishing subcultures within the social classes. It does *not* exert so powerful an effect that Protestant mothers differ significantly from Catholic mothers of the same social class in their values.[13] But the combination of class and religious background does enable us to isolate groups that are more homogeneous in their values than are the social classes *in toto*. We find that there is an ordering, consistent for all class-related values, proceeding from middle-class Protestant mothers, to middle-class Catholic, to working-class Protestant, to working-class

13. The index here is based on the question "May I ask what is your religious background?"

Even when the comparison is restricted to Catholic mothers who send their children to Catholic school versus Protestant mothers of the same social class, there are no significant differences in values.

Jewish mothers (almost all of them in this sample are middle class) are very similar to middle-class Protestant mothers in their values, with two notable exceptions. More Jewish than Protestant mothers select popularity and ability to defend one's self—two values that are not related to social class.

TABLE 6. Mothers' Education and Their Choice of Characteristics as "Most Desirable" in a Ten- or Eleven-Year-Old Child

	Middle-Class Mothers Proportion Who Select Each Characteristic			
	Male Child		Female Child	
Characteristic	At Least Some College	High-School Graduate or Less	At Least Some College	High-School Graduate or Less
Obedience	0.11	0.22	0.13	0.29
Neatness-cleanliness	.03	.09	.03[a]	.23
Consideration	.47	.35	.41	.37
Curiosity	.31[a]	.13	.31[a]	.06
Self-control	.33	.19	.19	.21
Happiness	0.50	0.41	0.59	0.40
N	36	54	32	52

	Working-Class Mothers Proportion Who Select Each Characteristic			
	Male Child		Female Child	
Characteristic	At Least High-School Graduate	Less than High-School Graduate	At Least High-School Graduate	Less than High-School Graduate
Obedience	0.29	0.43	0.28	0.32
Neatness-cleanliness	.12	.14	.21	.35
Consideration	.32	.27	.33[a]	.14
Curiosity	.07	.05	.12	.00
Self-control	.22[a]	.07	.16	.08
Happiness	0.27	0.27	0.47	0.43
N	41	44	43	37

a. Difference between mothers of differing educational status statistically significant, 0.05 level or better, using chi-squared test.

Catholic (see Table 7). Middle-class Protestants and working-class Catholics constitute the two extremes whose values are most dissimilar.

Another relevant line of social demarcation is the distinction between urban and rural background.[14] As we did for religious background, we

14. We asked: "Have you ever lived on a farm?" and then classified all mothers who had lived on a farm for some time other than simply summer vacations, prior to age fifteen, as having had a rural background.

Ordinarily, one further line of cultural demarcation would be considered at this point —nationality-background. The present sample, however, is composed predominantly of parents who are at least second-generation, United States-born, so this is not possible.

TABLE 7. Mothers' Religious Background and Their Choice of Characteristics as "Most Desirable" in a Ten- or Eleven-Year-Old Child

	Proportion Who Select Each Characteristic			
Characteristic	Middle-Class Protestant	Middle-Class Catholic	Working-Class Protestant	Working-Class Catholic
Obedience	0.17	0.25	0.33	0.36
Neatness, cleanliness	.08	.15	.17	.27
Consideration	.36	.38	.26	.29
Curiosity	.24	.12	.07	.05
Self-control	.28	.15	.15	.09
Happiness	.47	.42	.38	.30
Boys	.48	.32	.35	.13
Girls	0.45	0.52	0.42	0.54
N	88	52	107	56

TABLE 8. Rural Versus Urban Background of Mothers and Their Choice of Characteristics as "Most Desirable" in a Ten- or Eleven-Year-Old Child

	Proportion Who Select Each Characteristic			
Characteristic	Middle-Class Urban	Middle-Class Rural	Working-Class Urban	Working-Class Rural
Obedience	0.19	0.24	0.29	0.42
Neatness, cleanliness	.11	.12	.17	.25
Consideration	.42	.27	.31	.18
Curiosity	.19	.12	.07	.04
Self-control	.20	.33	.15	.11
Happiness	.47	.42	.41	.25
Boys	.44	.47	.28	.25
Girls	0.50	0.37	0.57	0.26
N	141	33	110	55

can arrange the mothers into four groups delineated on the basis of class and rural-urban background in an order that is reasonably consistent for all class-related values. The order is: middle-class urban, middle-class rural, working-class urban, working-class rural (see Table 8). The extremes are middle-class mothers raised in the city and working-class mothers raised on farms.

Several other variables fail to differentiate mothers of the same social class into groups having appreciably different values. These include the mother's age, the size of the family, the ordinal position of the child in the family, the length of time the family has lived in the neighborhood, whether or not the mother has been socially mobile (from the status of her childhood family), and her class identification. Nor are these results a function of the large proportion of families of government workers included in the sample: wives of government employees do not differ from other mothers of the same social class in their values.

In sum, we find that it is possible to specify the relationship between social class and values more precisely by dividing the social classes into subgroups on the basis of other lines of social demarcation—but that social class seems to provide the single most relevant line of demarcation.

Adequacy of Index of Values

The form in which our major question was asked enabled us to set the same ground rules for all parents. No premium was put on imaginativeness or articulateness. But the fact that we limited their choice to these particular characteristics means that we denied them the opportunity to select others that they might have regarded as even more desirable. However, we had *previously* asked each parent: "When you think of a boy (or girl) of (child's) age, are there *any* things you look for as most important or most desirable?" Only three additional characteristics were suggested by any appreciable number of parents. The first, suggested by a significantly larger proportion of middle- than of working-class parents, was "self-reliance" or "independence"—a result entirely consistent with the rest of this study. The second, variously labeled "friendliness," "co-operativeness," or "ability to get along well with others" was also predominantly a middle-class concern. It indicates that we may have underrepresented the proportion of middle-class parents who value their children's ability to relate to others. Finally, several parents (of both social classes) said that they considered it desirable that the child not "act too old," "too young," or be effeminate (in a boy) or masculine (in a girl). There seems to be a certain concern, not adequately indexed by our major question, that the child conform to his parent's conception of what constitutes the proper age and sex role.

Of course, parents might have selected other characteristics as well, had we suggested them. These possible limitations notwithstanding, it appears that the index is reasonably comprehensive.

More important than the question of comprehensiveness is whether or not it is really possible for parents to select characteristics as desirable independently of the way that they rate their own children's behavior. Since each parent was later asked to rate his child's performance with respect to each characteristic, we can compare the ratings given by parents who chose a characteristic with those given by parents of the same social class who did not. Parents who chose each characteristic were no more and no less likely to describe their children as excelling in that characteristic; nor were they any more or less likely than other parents to feel that their children were deficient. The parents have not imputed desirability to the characteristics that they feel represent their children's virtues or their children's deficiencies.

The final and most important question: Is it wise to accept someone's assertion that something is a value to him? After all, assertions are subject to distortion.[15] To the degree that we can ascertain that parents act in reasonable conformity to the values they assert, however, we gain confidence in an index based on assertions.

This study does not provide disinterested observations of the parents' behavior. Our closest approximation derives from interviews with the parents themselves—interviews in which we questioned them in considerable detail about their relevant actions. Perhaps the most crucial of these data are those bearing on their actions in situations where their children behave in *disvalued* ways. We have, for example, questioned parents in some detail about what they do when their children lose their tempers. We began by asking whether or not the child in question "ever really loses his temper." From those parents who said that the child does lose his temper, we then proceeded to find out precisely what behavior they consider to be "loss of temper"; what they "generally do when he acts this way"; whether they "ever find it necessary to do anything else"; if so, what else they do, and "under what circumstances." Our concern here is with what the parent reports he does as a matter of last resort.[16]

Mothers who regard *self-control* as an important value are more likely to report that they punish the child—be it physically, by isolation, or by restriction of activities; they are unlikely merely to scold or to ignore his loss of temper altogether (see Table 9).

To punish a child who has lost his temper may not be a particularly effective way of inducing self-control. One might even have predicted that mothers who value self-control would be less likely to punish breaches of control, more likely to explain, even ignore. They do not, however, and we must put the issue more simply: mothers who assert the value are more likely to report that they apply negative sanctions in situations where the child violates that value. This response would certainly seem to conform to their value-assertion.

A parallel series of questions deals with the mother's reactions when

15. But inferring values from observed behavior may not be satisfactory either, for we cannot be certain that we are correctly distinguishing the normative from other components of action. As Robin Williams states: "No student of human conduct can accept uncritically, as final evidence, people's testimony as to their own values. Yet actions may deceive as well as words, and there seems no reason for always giving one precedence over the other" *(American Society: A Sociological Interpretation* [New York: Alfred A. Knopf, 1951], p. 378).

16. This comparison and those to follow are limited to parents who say that the child does in fact behave in the disvalued way, at least on occasion. (Approximately equal proportions of middle- and working-class mothers report that their children do behave in each of these ways.)

TABLE 9. Choice of "Self-control" as "Most Desirable" Characteristic and Most Extreme Actions That Mothers Report They Take when Their Children Lose Their Tempers

	Proportion					
	Middle Class		*Working Class*		*Both*	
	Choose Self-control	Don't Choose Self-control	Choose Self-control	Don't Choose Self-control	Choose Self-control	Don't Choose Self-control
Punish physically	0.26	0.20	0.44	0.26	0.32	0.23
Isolate	.20	.11	.11	.12	.17	.11
Restrict activities, other punishments	.06	.05	.17	.14	.10	.10
Threaten punishment	.06	.03	.00	.02	.04	.02
Scold, admonish, etc.	.31	.40	.17	.31	.26	.36
Ignore	0.11	0.21	0.11	0.15	0.11	0.18
	1.00	1.00	1.00	1.00	1.00	1.00
N	35	113	18	113	53	226

her child "refuses to do what she tells him to do." Mothers who assert that they regard *obedience* as important are more likely to report that they punish in one way or another when their children refuse.[17] There is also evidence that mothers who value *consideration* are more likely to respond to their children's "fighting with other children," an action that need not necessarily be seen as inconsistent with consideration, by punishing them, or at least by separating them from the others.[18]

In all three instances, then, the reports on parental reactions to behavior that seems to violate the value in question indicate that mothers who profess high regard for the value are more likely to apply negative sanctions.

17. The figures are 47 versus 29 percent for middle-class mothers; 36 versus 18 percent for working-class mothers.
18. The figures are 42 versus 29 percent for middle-class mothers; 61 versus 37 percent for working-class mothers.
There is also some indication that *working-class* mothers who value *honesty* have been more prone to insist that their children make restitution when they have "swiped" something, but the number of mothers who say that their children have ever swiped something is too small for this evidence to be conclusive. (The figures for working-class mothers are 63 versus 35 percent; for middle-class mothers, 38 versus 33 percent.)
The interviews with the children provide further evidence that parents have acted consistently with their values—for example, children whose mothers assert high valuation of dependability are more likely to tell us that the reason their parents want them to do their chores is to train them in responsibility (not to relieve the parents of work).

Interpretation

Our first conclusion is that parents, whatever their social class, deem it very important indeed that their children be honest, happy, considerate, obedient, and dependable.

The second conclusion is that, whatever the reasons may be, parents' values are related to their social position, particularly their class position.

There still remains, however, the task of interpreting the relationship between parents' social position and their values. In particular: What underlies the differences between the values of middle- and of working-class parents?

One relevant consideration is that some parents may "take for granted" values that others hold dear. For example, middle-class parents may take "neatness and cleanliness" for granted, while working-class parents regard it as highly desirable. But what does it mean to say that middle-class parents take neatness and cleanliness for granted? In essence, the argument is that middle-class parents value neatness and cleanliness as greatly as do working-class parents but not so greatly as they value such things as happiness and self-control. If this be the case, it can only mean that in the circumstances of middle-class life neatness and cleanliness are easily enough attained to be of less immediate concerne than are these other values.

A second consideration lies in the probability that these value-concepts have differing meanings for parents of different cultural backgrounds. For example, one might argue that honesty is a central standard of conduct for middle-class parents because they see honesty as meaning truthfulness; and that it is more a quality of the person for working-class parents because they see it as meaning trustworthiness. Perhaps so; but to suggest that a difference in meaning underlies a difference in values raises the further problem of explaining this difference in meaning.

It would be reasonable for working-class parents to be more likely to see honesty as trustworthiness. The working-class situation is one of less material security and less assured protection from the dishonesty of others. For these reasons, trustworthiness is more at issue for working-class than for middle-class parents.

Both considerations lead us to view differences in the values of middle- and working-class parents in terms of their differing circumstances of life and, by implication, their conceptions of the effects that these circumstances may have on their children's future lives. We believe that parents are most likely to accord high priority to those values that seem both *problematic,* in the sense that they are difficult of achievement, and *important,* in the sense that failure to achieve them would affect the child's future adversely. From this perspective it is reasonable that working-class parents cannot afford to take neatness and cleanliness as much for granted as can middle-class parents. It is reasonable, too, that working-class parents are more likely to see honesty as implying trust-worthiness and that this connotation of honesty is seen as problematic.

These characteristics—honesty and neatness—are important to the child's future precisely because they assure him a respectable social position. Just as "poor but honest" has traditionally been an important line of social demarcation, their high valuation of these qualities may express working-class parents' concern that their children occupy a position unequivocally above that of persons who are not neat or who are not scrupulously honest. These are the qualities of respectable, worthwhile people.

So, too, is obedience. The obedient child follows his parents' dictates rather than his own standards. He acts, in his subordinate role as a child, in conformity with the prescriptions of established authority.

Even in the way they differentiate what is desirable for boys from what is desirable for girls, working-class mothers show a keen appreciation of the qualities making for respectable social position.

The characteristics that middle-class parents are more likely to value for their children are internal standards for governing one's relationships with other people and, in the final analysis, with one's self. It is not that middle-class parents are less concerned than are working-class parents about social position. The qualities of person that assure respectability may be taken for granted, but in a world where social relationships are determinative of position, these standards of conduct are both more problematic and more important.

The middle-class emphasis on internal standards is evident in their choice of the cluster of characteristics centering around honesty; in their being less likely than are working-class parents to value obedience and more likely to value self-control and consideration; and in their seeing obedience as inconsistent wih both consideration and curiosity. The child is to act appropriately, not because his parents tell him to, but because he wants to. Not conformity to authority, but inner control; not because you're told to but because you take the other person into consideration —these are the middle-class ideals.

These values place responsibility directly upon the individual. He cannot rely upon authority, nor can he simply conform to what is presented to him as proper. He should be impelled to come to his own understanding of the situation.[19] He is to govern himself in such a way as

19. Curiosity provides a particularly interesting example of how closely parents' values are related to their circumstances of life and expectations: the proportion of mothers who value curiosity rises very slowly from status level to status level until we reach the wives of professionals and the more highly educated businessmen; then it jumps suddenly (see Table 4). The value is given priority in precisely that portion of the middle class where it is most appropriate and where its importance for the child's future is most apparent.

to be able to act consistently with his principles. The basic importance of relationship to self is explicit in the concept of self-control. It is implicit, too, in consideration—a standard that demands of the individual that he respond sympathetically to others' needs even if they be in conflict with his own; and in the high valuation of honesty as central to other standards of conduct: "to thine own self be true."

Perhaps, considering this, it should not be surprising that so many middle-class mothers attribute first-rank importance to happiness, even for boys. We cannot assume that their children's happiness is any less important to working-class mothers than it is to middle-class mothers; in fact, working-class mothers are equally likely to value happiness for *girls*. For their sons, however, happiness is second choice to honesty and obedience. Apparently, middle-class mothers can afford instead to be concerned about their sons' happiness. And perhaps they are right in being concerned. We have noted that those middle-class mothers who deem it most important that their sons outdistance others are especially likely to be concerned about their sons' happiness; and even those mothers who do not are asking their children to accept considerable responsibility.

Bernard Farber

Kinship and Class

Affinity Versus Consanguinity

Among lower status populations, there tends to be a strong emphasis on interaction with relatives.[1] Such interaction is understandable in that relatives are more readily trusted and counted upon for assistance in time of need. The heightened degree of interaction among kin would increase the proportion of marriages between persons who are already related. This phenomenon can be observed in various contexts. For instance, in *stetl* life in Tsarist Russia, there was a high proportion of first-cousin marriages in Jewish families. The same phenomenon can be seen in Tennessee mountain communities. Matthews[2] reports that in one community south of Nashville intermarrying between indigenous families has persisted for five or more generations. As a result, "though first-cousin marriages are still not uncommon and even continue to be the mode for several families' lines . . . valley mates today are not as often first cousins and first cousins once removed as they are second cousins, second cousins once removed and third cousins" (pp. 23–24). This continual intermarriage of individuals already related may blur the distinction between affinal and consanguineous kin when little importance is attached to symbolic family estates. Further, when marriages are unstable, this blurring creates problems in identifying descent groups.

In genealogies obtained in the course of my study, it was not unusual for the respondents to point out that certain kin were related to one another in two or more ways. Among poor whites, whose family background extended to the southeast United States, marriage of two brothers to two sisters was not uncommon. There were also instances in which relatives of different generations married. In a white slum area, respondents continually indicated that almost everyone whose family had lived in that area over a period of time was related to the other inhabitants in some way. Mr. W. tried to clarify his relationships to neighboring kin to

1. Bert N. Adams, *Kinship in an Urban Setting,* Chicago: Markham, 1968; Michael Aiken and David Goldberg, "Social Mobility and Kinship: A Reexamination of the Hypothesis," *American Anthropologist,* 71 (1969), 261–270.
2. Elmora Messer Matthews, *Neighbor and Kin in a Tennessee Ridge Community,* Nashville: University of Vanderbilt Press, 1965.

the interviewer, but in doing so became confused himself toward the end.

> I would have a cousin, I believe [living] over here. Louis Heller and, I think, Jimmy Winthrop lives in the little house that I used to live in. And that Jimmy would be another cousin, or a half-brother to Helen, which is Louis Heller's wife. And Ellen Cothran would be a cousin. I see Louis more than anybody. Oh, once a month maybe . . . and Ellen, I'll see her, oh maybe, once every three or four months—but of course they're both older than I am. We never did really neighbor a lot; they done most of their neighboring with their older brothers and sisters. Ellen and my oldest sister buddy around quite a bit. And of course as far as Louis and Helen goes, they never did neighbor, you know, too much—occasionally—there's just something different along there.
>
> Jimmy Winthrop is Uncle Claude and Aunt Rose's son, and Aunt Rose is in her second marriage to Uncle Claude, which makes him [Jimmy] a half-brother to Helen, which still is a full cousin to me—I guess you would call it—because it's on Claude's side. I don't dig this relationship bit. [Interviewer: Why did you say that?] Oh, something like this: here he's a half-brother to Helen but yet a full cousin to me. It don't seem quite right. Of course, I got the same thing with myself because my brother down here is also my uncle. [Interviewer: How does that work?] Well, Aileen's mother and Eddie's wife Sara is sisters. I married Aileen, which makes Sara . . . Aileen's mother of course by marriage. [Pause to recover composure.] But this way it comes out that he [Eddie] is either my uncle or my brother. And Alva in the same way—Aunt Alva or Sister Alva. So for some it's kind of crazy.

With the complexity of relationships described, relatives are grouped broadly as "cousins" or "uncles" and "aunts" without an attempt to demarcate the relationship clearly.

This complexity of relationships often existed in the Negro families studied. Sometimes, when respondents were asked to discuss the cousin best known to them, they chose a distant relative—at times in their own generation, at other times in another generation. A review of a number of interviews suggests that low status Negro respondents generally show little interest in precise relationships of kinsmen.

Findings described earlier have suggested that symbolic aspects of kinship are considered less important by lower-class populations than are domestic aspects. Consequently, the high intermarriage rates of consanguineous kin would accrue in this population not from a desire to form alliances between descent groups but from residential proximity and frequent interaction. The fact that a minority of marriages tend to occur with consanguineous kin may be interpreted as indicating that while there are few barriers or objections to such marriages, no special pressures exist to form alliances.

In itself the redundancy of kinship ties does not inhibit the symbolic incorporation of individuals into their spouse's descent group. Marriage between certain consanguineous relatives can be used to strengthen ties between descent groups in societies practicing prescribed or preferred marriage of (actual or classificatory) cross-cousins, or in which marital selection is based on membership in sections (or other corporate units), or in which (formally or informally organized) lineage segments are delineated by descent from common ancestors. The key is that, in lower-class kinship, marriage is not restricted to specific relatives but (outside the intimate-kin group where incest taboos are operative) to kinsmen of all distances and generations on the same basis as nonrelatives. Given this nonspecificity in marital selection, marrying consanguineous kin has little consequence for strengthening of kinship alliances. Hence, in contrast to the strong husband-wife coalition presupposed by incorporation into each other's descent group, in low socioeconomic families, the marital bonds tend to be fragile.[3]

In higher socioeconomic families, weddings are an occasion for drawing the relatives together and ritualistically accepting the bride and groom into the kindred. Similarly the naming ceremony (such as a christening or a *bris*) symbolically incorporates the newborn infant into the descent group. At low socioeconomic levels, however, as Mr. C. pointed out,

> if you marry a guy who's got a record or is a dishwasher down the street, not only is there the money problem in having a wedding but I mean—who cares? You don't want to make a big thing out of that. There's not going to be any star in your crown that your daughter is marrying this nobody.

In addition, if the woman already has at least one illegitimate child, or the bride and groom have been publicly living (or at least sleeping) together over a period of time, or the marriage represents a second or third try for the bride or groom (with a high probability of divorce or separation), there is little reason to emphasize the marriage as a change in status. Consequently, affinal ties are subordinated to consanguineous relationships. At least one generally can count on blood relatives for companionship, love, trust and assistance.

The fragility of man-woman relationships in low SES families results in a high rate of illegitimacy. Even though only a minority of the women may give birth to illegitimate children, the high prevalence of divorce and desertion means that all women in this segment of the population—and their daughters—at one time or another in their lives may face the prospect of an illegitimate child. Both the white and Negro slums in Champaign-Urbana contained some families with seven or eight children, in which most children had been fathered by different men. In these situations, it would be difficult to identify paternal descent groups in spite of a desire to do so. If individuals are to survive with any semblance of self-esteem in this situation, they must deemphasize the importance of the

3. Herbert Gans, *The Urban Villager,* New York: Free Press, 1962; Gerald Gurin, Joseph Verott, and Sheila Feld, *Americans View Their Mental Health,* New York: Basic Books, 1960; Lee Rainwater, Richard Coleman, and Gerald Handel, *Workingman's Wife,* New York: Oceana, 1959.

legitimacy functions of kinship and must tolerate illegitimacy. This tolerance may take various forms, all of which assume that acceptance of illegitimacy is making the best of an unfortunate situation, but that marriage itself is of minor importance.

> *Mrs. L.:* I would like my home life to be like Cynthia's—a married life—but we couldn't get along, that's all. Ain't no use for me to—I've got to work and take care of my kids so I don't need no husband. In a way, I would want my home life to be like hers, if I could get along. . . . I think my home life is like Dorothy's because we're both separated. [Dorothy has six illegitimate children.] She hasn't been married, and I've been married, and I just as well might not have been married. We couldn't get along.
>
> *Mrs. P.:* They went ahead and got a divorce, and she was pregnant. Now, who's to say that it was his or someone else's? Whose business is it, you know?
>
> *Mrs. K.* [referring to HuSi]: She has never been married, I think she has too many kids to get a husband.

Demarcation of Generations

Among low socioeconomic families the failure to incorporate the couple into their spouse's descent group (at least symbolically) seems to inhibit making distinctions by generation in family interaction. The vagueness of generations emerges especially through the complications of marrying across generations and through illegitimacy. Tolerance of illegitimacy alone requires a blurring of affinal relationships. At higher socioeconomic levels, symbolic incorporation of EGO into his spouse's descent group provides him with a new status which signifies his adulthood. At low socioeconomic levels, this affinal status does not carry the same significance, and EGO retains his old status as a basis for self-identity. Moreover, in an unskilled social stratum where almost everyone has similar personal and family problems, no one can claim special knowledge accrued with age. The older persons face the same kinds of problems of residence, courting, illegitimacy, childbirth, and childrearing, illness, job holding, and divorce as do younger persons. As a result of these factors, there does not seem to be a shift in self-concept from child to adult—the individual never fully emerges socially as an adult.[4]

The following interview excerpt illustrates some of the points in the previous paragraph. Mrs. S. is fortyish, with her own children approaching adulthood. However, her tale could just as easily have been told by an adolescent in that she refers in several places to "us kids" and muses, "But we sure miss going to Mom's." The story itself is about her mother's boyfriend and his efforts to monopolize her attentions.

> Larry Holden. He's the one who's really broke our family up. He was a

4. Philippe Ariès, *Centuries of Childhood*, New York: Knopf, 1962.

friend of my brother's, Lew and Sally, and they kind of felt sorry for the kid. I mean, he was married and his wife left him. Of course, he's got a little boy and has been having quite a problem with him because the boy won't live with Larry; he won't live with his mom. He lives with Larry's folks. But he seemed like a pretty nice guy when we first met him. . . . None of us like him, but he don't want us to go to Mama's. If we go to Mom's, and he happens to be coming over to Mom's, he'll either call her and ask her "Well, what are you doing tonight, Mabel?" And Mom will say, "Talking to Carol and Martin, John and Donna," whichever one might be coming over there. He'll say, "Well, get rid of them. I'm coming over." It makes us kids kind of left out because we have always been a close-knit family until just here lately. . . . Well, we've asked him, why don't he just stay out of our lives and I said, "As far as coming and visiting Mom, we don't mind it." We really and truly don't, and if he wants to come and take her to town, that's all right because lots of times us kids don't have a chance to or know when she's going. But I told Larry one time over there . . . I said, "It's my Mom, and I'll come and see my Mom any time I get ready to whether you like it or not." So, he don't hardly speak to me now. . . . But we sure miss going to Mom's. . . . Now when Larry took off for a while, why heck, us kids went home and we actually enjoyed ourselves over there. . . . He loves to break up families, because he tried it with my aunt and uncle. Sneaking around to see Aunt Ruth while Petey wasn't home. I guess Uncle Petey kind of caught on and then he [Larry] also caused a little bit of trouble between Danny and Laurene Peters, a cousin of mine. There ain't hardly anybody that likes Larry.

One consequence of the failure to organize family life on the basis of generational differentiation is a probable confusion in roles between a husband-wife relationship and a parent-child relationship, as among the lower-class Negroes studied by Liebow.[5]

Within very broad limits, a woman's chronological or relative age does not appear to be a crucial factor in assessing her potential as a sex partner. . . .The same man may be at once attracted to a girl in her middle teens and to a woman in her mid-forties, as evidenced for example, by the fact that the mother of one of Tally's children was a teen-age girl and the mother of another of his children was herself a grandmother in her forties. Conversely, one may also find a man in his early twenties and a man in his forties competing for the favor of, say, a twenty- or thirty-year-old woman. Actions and attitudes varied greatly from individual to individual.[6]

A similar situation exists among the low status families studied in Champaign-Urbana. It is not an oddity for a seventeen-year-old girl to marry a thirty-seven-year-old man or for a woman to be ten or eleven years older than her husband. In the interview just cited, the boyfriend Larry is thirty-five, while Mama is in her late fifties. Mrs. V. remarked about a neighbor:

And she was always attracted to old men. I've never seen a person like her, but I think that everybody she went with was old. Of course, I've got a lot of

5. Elliott Liebow, *Tally's Corner*, Boston: Little, Brown, 1967.
6. *Ibid.*, p. 41.

room to talk, but I don't think Martin's age and my age is quite as bad as her and Bob's. Ten years, four months, five days [between Martin and me], and I forget the minutes.

Failure to accord importance to age-grading clouds family status generally. The nonadult self-concept expresses itself in a variety of ways. One woman complains of her husband, "Just seems like here in the last five years, he's more jealous of the kids than I've ever seen him—since they got older." Another describes a relationship between her brother and stepmother, "Well, at the time she was sort of like a sex fiend, and they got to telling around that she was trying to get Ernie and all this and that, with him only fourteen." Yet another woman reports, "Dad is kind of a kid at heart; he would blow every cent he had." In general the attitude is, "I don't think age makes a difference. Age don't make a marriage or anything." . . .

Instrumental Orientation

The data on kinship revealed a diffuseness in erotic and affective relationships among low socioeconomic families. The pervasiveness of eroticism and affect as opposed to the maintenance of a symbolic family estate—in forming and maintaining relationships—seems to derive ulti- mately from the deemphasis on affinal relationships and from the lack of sexual exclusiveness as a basis for marriage.[7] The emphasis on eroticism and affect is viewed by "middle-class" society as a moral lapse from the self-restraint and self-discipline required to achieve success in education and occupation.

Among lower-class populations, the role of affect in evaluating work is heightened by the emptiness and insecurity of the unskilled, unstable jobs themselves. Rather, friendships and congeniality become important in weighing the desirability of a particular job. Liebow suggests that "there is no mystically intrinsic connection between 'present-time' orientation and lower-class persons."[8] Instead, the failure to delay gratifications derives from the fact that there is little expectation of later reward. The lack of generational differentiation is thus ultimately related to the fact that the *lumpenproletariat* has no future. . . .

. . . The basis for the perpetuation of lower-class kinship seems to reside in the structure of modern society. In highly industrialized societies, large-scale social networks develop to integrate the major institutions. Industrial and political bureaucracies require particular kinds of behavior for their operation. The educational system is necessarily connected with the industrial and political systems as well as with the

7. *Ibid.*, pp. 107–108.
8. *Ibid.*, pp. 68–69.

religious organization of the society. With the diffusion of literacy, forms of worship and belief systems change, the relationship between government and the individual is modified, and more complex economic organization becomes possible.[9] Consequently the emergence of integrative networks of institutions evokes the need for a public culture to facilitate integration.[10]

The public culture required to sustain the interdependence of large-scale organization consists of norms and skills associated with efficiency of communication, high technical sophistication, rational organization of personnel and machines, and effective planning of future operations. This culture is supported by the system of rewards in the society. In American society, the distribution of rewards is justified in terms of ability of persons to perform successfully in the complex of integrated institutions.[11] Intelligent action is then interpreted in terms of the incorporation of the individual into this public culture.

Coexisting with the integrated network of social relationships and its cultural paraphernalia are small, fragmented, somewhat autonomous groupings that have bases for existence outside the public culture. The family, for example, exists in almost all societies; but, in modern society, families do not have the particular political or economic production activities that would integrate directly into the public culture. Instead, families are incorporated this way only tangentially, through the fortuitous participation of individual members. There is, therefore, a great deal of variation in the extent to which families are integrated into the general public culture.

Those families and individuals whose way of life is incompatible with the public culture are a superfluous population; if anything, their private worlds generally inhibit the smooth operation of the economic, educational, and political institutions. The extent of integration into the public culture depends in part upon various other groupings with which the family is involved. For example, the father provides a major economic support in fostering family solidarity. Under certain conditions, his absence may produce disastrous effects on the children; the intelligence of lower-class children from fatherless homes continually declines throughout grade school.[12] In addition, some religious groupings have norms and patterns of conduct that are consistent with the public culture, while others are in conflict with it. To the extent that these religious

9. Talcott Parsons, *Societies: Evolutionary and Comparative Perspectives*, Englewood Cliffs, N.J.: Prentice-Hall, 1966.

10. Bernard Farber, *Mental Retardation: Its Social Context and Social Consequences*, Boston: Houghton Mifflin, 1968, pp. 103–118.

11. Talcott Parsons, "Analytical Approach to the Theory of Social Stratification," *American Journal of Sociology*, 45 (1940), 841–862.

12. Martin Deutsch and Bert R. Brown, "Social Influences in Negro-White Intelligence Differences," *Journal of Social Issues*, 20 (1964), 24–95.

groupings are consonant with the public culture, their members tend to act "intelligently" with respect to the dominant industrial and political systems. Similarly, ethnic groupings vary in the degree of their incorporation into the public culture. Some ethnic groups are characterized by norms and values that facilitate their members' successful participation in modern educational, political, and economic institutions. Others have norms and values that run counter to the norms of distributive justice of the public culture.

In those segments of the society which do not receive the major rewards of the institutions related to the public culture, other justifications must be sought for living. Mysticism, chance, and fate, which emphasize the anti-intellectual norms and values to be found in the society, must furnish explanations for events. This anti-intellectualism thus coexists with an intellectual tradition related to the dominant public culture. Since intellectual explanations do not provide a satisfactory reason for existence for the population segment that does not receive the major rewards, this segment is stimulated to rely on anti-intellectual justification for action.

In addition, public and private cultures are not subject to the same kinds of proof or the same kind of evaluation to justify their existence. The public culture is required to be coherent and rational; however, emphasizing expressiveness and social solidarity, the private culture can incorporate contradictory elements in its structure. Hence the social and cognitive processes that are basic to the continuity or persistence of the public culture need not be present in the private culture. In short, individuals immersed in deviant private cultures do not need to develop the capacity for intelligent judgment and action with respect to the public culture.

. . .The institutions forming the basis for the public culture deny support to kinship systems in which symbolic family estates are derogated, in which consanguineous relationships are emphasized, and in which affect and eroticism are important bases for determining ties in the family and community. People adhering to the latter forms of kinship organization are relegated to superfluous populations; they are the perennial adolescents, apparently destined to remain always outside the public culture.

Rose Laub Coser

Authority and Structural Ambivalence in the Middle-Class Family[1]

Among the research findings gradually accumulating on the family background of schizophrenics, the domineering mother has been singled out, perhaps more than any other factor, as a source of her child's personality disturbance. The descriptions of what is loosely known as the "schizophrenogenic mother," although they do not agree in many ways and they lack conceptual clarification, point to two characteristics: the mother's attempt completely to control the child, and her inconsistency both in her behavior toward the child and in her expectations of him. She is described as being punitive at the same time as overprotective, and as disapproving of behavior in the child that she herself calls forth. Clinicians and researchers generally agree on these two attributes of the "schizophrenogenic" mother: her domination of the child and her strong ambivalence.

Unlike the psychological focus on the personality dynamics involved in these traits, my attention will be turned to the ways in which mother-domination and mother-child ambivalence are built into the role structure of the modern American middle-class family.[2] Such an approach calls for examination of the meaning of authority in the middle-class value system and of the patterned distribution of authority within this type of family.

1. I am indebted to Robert K. Merton for his critical reading of an earlier and somewhat different version of this paper. The writing of the paper has also profited from discussions with my colleagues Richard Longabaugh and Robert Rapoport, as well as from the devoted assistance of Rachel Kahn-Hut.
2. Merton and Barber's concept of "sociological ambivalence" has helped me to formulate the problem that I am dealing with in this paper. See Robert K. Merton and Elinor Barber, "Sociological Ambivalence," in Edward A. Tiryakian, ed., *Sociological Theory, Values, and Sociocultural Change,* New York: The Free Press of Glencoe, 1963, pp. 91–120.

Class Differences in the Use of Authority

The research of Kohn and Clausen[3] on the "domineering mother" of schizophrenic patients and Kohn's research on class differences in child-rearing practices[4] will serve as a point of departure. By comparing the findings in Kohn's later work with some of his earlier research on the "domineering mother," it will be possible to clarify the concept of maternal authority in the middle class and to analyze its consequences for the maternal role.

In their paper on "Parental Authority Behavior and Schizophrenia," Kohn and Clausen[5] present data on the relation between schizophrenia and mother-domination in the family. Their schizophrenic subjects, more often than the controls, report having been dominated by the mother and having had a weak father. However, a breakdown of the data by socioeconomic status reveals that the correlation between perceived mother-domination and schizophrenia holds for higher and middle but not for lower socioeconomic strata. Both schizophrenics and controls in the lower strata tend to perceive mother as stronger than father.

Kohn's subsequent research on value differences in child training between the middle and working classes may well furnish a clue for understanding the differences in the perception of mother-domination in the different class settings. Here Kohn found that, in bringing up their children, working-class families are primarily concerned with "overt acts" while middle-class families are more interested in "motives and feelings."[6] The crucial difference in value orientation raises the question whether the different values in the two classes do not also include a differential conception of "domination" or "authority."

According to Kohn's findings, middle-class parents value the child's development of internalized standards of conduct, while working-class parents insist on the child's obeying behavioral prescriptions. The first focus on the actor's intent, the second on the act itself. This difference is reminiscent of the distinction formulated by Merton between attitude

3. Melvin L. Kohn and John A. Clausen, "Parental Authority Behavior and Schizophrenia," *American Journal of Orthopsychiatry*, XXVI (April 1956), 297–313.

4. I wish to acknowledge my debt to Melvin Kohn. It is his work on class differences in values that gave me the opportunity to develop the ideas set forth in the present paper; and my discussions and correspondence with him have further helped me clarify my thoughts. See his "Social Class and the Exercise of Parental Authority," *American Sociological Review*, XXIV (June 1959), 352–366; "Social Class and Parental Values," *American Journal of Sociology*, LXIV (January 1959), 337–351, [this book, pp. 334–53]; "Social Class and Parent-Child Relationships: An Interpretation," *American Journal of Sociology*, LXVIII (January 1963), 471–480; *Class and Conformity*, Homewood, Illinois: The Dorsey Press, 1969.

5. *Op. cit.*

6. *Op. cit.*

—inner disposition—and behavior, which may or may not be in accord with such inner disposition, and Merton's emphasis on their independent variability.[7] Consequently, Kohn's findings may be expressed as follows: the middle-class child tends to be trained primarily for attitudinal conformity while the working-class child tends to be trained primarily for behavioral conformity.[8] Expectations of attitudinal conformity are directed at the total personality of the child, i.e., at his very identity. This is what Arnold Green has called "personality absorption."[9] Expectations of behavioral conformity, in contrast, leave the person relatively free to maintain his own feelings and motives; the child in the working-class family can "do as mother says" without always agreeing with her. Personality molding is not necessarily involved. It follows that if mother's commands are not directed at the child's deeper feelings, her orders do not tend to be perceived as emanating from feelings of love or hostility. When the working-class mother says, "get out of the way," she means just what she says: "You're under foot when I have work to do." Such an order emanating from a middle-class mother would have overtones of maternal rejection.[10]

Domination would therefore seem to have a different meaning in the two social contexts. In the middle class, a *strong* mother would tend to be experienced as impinging on one's inner personality, whereas in the working class her *strength* would be seen as a mere behavioral attribute, such as an ability to run the household efficiently in spite of difficult circumstances. The fact that for middle-class patients Kohn and Clausen found an association between schizophrenia and reports of having had a *strong* mother, while for working-class patients there was no such association (a strong mother being reported more often than not by both patients and controls) would therefore seem to be explainable in part by the different meaning of discipline in the two environments.

This distinction between variant expectations of authority-holders makes it possible to reformulate Green's proposition about "personality-absorption"[11]: authority that expects attitudinal conformity is more likely to affect the inner organization of the personality and can therefore more readily be a source of personality disorganization than

7. See especially "Discrimination and the American Creed," in *Discrimination and National Welfare*, R. H. MacIver, ed., New York and London: Harper Bros., 1949, pp. 94–126.

8. On these different types of conformity, see Robert K. Merton, "Conformity, Deviation and Opportunity Structures," *American Sociological Review*, XXIV (April 1959), 177–188.

9. Cf. Arnold W. Green, "The Middle-Class Male Child and Neurosis," *American Sociological Review*, XI (February 1946), 31–41.

10. The distinction here is similar to that made by Maslow between the "intrinsic meaning" of deprivation and its "symbolic value." See Abram H. Maslow, "Deprivation, Threat and Frustration," *Psychological Review*, XLVIII (1941), 364–366.

11. Green, *op. cit.*

authority that calls only for behavioral conformity. There remains the task to specify the structural source of mother domination in the middle class, and the consequence of this domination for the mother-child relationship.

Authority, Observability and Expectations of Conformity

First let us examine a type of family in which a *strong* mother does not necessarily affect the personality growth of her children. The Eastern European Jewish family provides a convenient starting point for a structural analysis of the problem at hand. This type of family is in many respects mother-centered and mother-dominated,[12] yet it does not lead to a high incidence of schizophrenia. Mother exercises control over the daily run of affairs and over her children's behavior, as well as over most of the practical aspects of her husband's life. The father's authority tends to be so remote that it does not impinge much upon the details of the children's daily lives. Father may be, according to modern psychiatric concepts, a "dependent personality," and often is; but—and this is the decisive point—there is no stigma attached to his so-called dependency. He has well-defined privileges and rights, many of which are denied to the mother. His prestige is largely based on the religious value system.

To understand the authority structure in this type of family, the distinction between expectations of attitudinal and of behavioral conformity may again be useful. This distinction does not only apply to the use of authority in different social strata, but also to some extent to its distribution within the family. In the Eastern European Jewish family there would seem to be an allocation of different types of authority between the parental figures; they tend to expect different types of conformity and to differ in their socially patterned interest in the children, as well as in the extent to which they observe the children's behavior. Father is primarily concerned with the children's attitudes. He is in charge of their religious education and watches over the type of behavior that seems to manifest inner dispositions for becoming "a good Jew." Mother is concerned with the children's daily behavior in terms of its immediate consequences; she must supervise them for their own well-being and for the smooth functioning of the household. In addition—and this is perhaps more important than the socially patterned "division of interest" between the parents—the person who is mostly concerned with attitudes, i.e., with that aspect of the personality that lends itself more readily for "personality-absorption," does not observe the everyday

12. For a detailed description of the Polish Jewish family, see Mark Zborowski and Elizabeth Herzog, *Life is with People*, New York: International University Press, 1953, *passim* and pp. 131 ff.

details of the children's daily behavior, and the person who has greater access to these everyday details does not focus as much on attitudes. There is more than a simple distribution of authority between parental figures. There is a distribution of types of authority, of types of socially patterned interest in the children, and of the extent of observability of the children's behavior.

These differences in the relations between role-partners provide the social mechanisms for the articulation of roles that Merton has identified in his theory of role-set: the status-occupant's ability to articulate his role when facing the expectations of different role-partners is facilitated by the different degrees of interest these role-partners have in his behavior; by the fact that not all role-partners are equally powerful in shaping his behavior; and by the fact that not all role-partners are equally in a position directly to observe his behavior.[13]

The father's partial separation from the irritations of everyday family life permits him to judge his children's attitudes in terms of the criteria governing the religious value system. The Jewish father wants rules pertaining to the religious system rigorously observed, but he is willing to be permissive in regard to daily behavior concerning practical matters. In contrast, the mother supervises the children's daily behavior because she is primarily interested in its immediate consequences—health, appearance in public, etc. Hence, the child's personality is not much absorbed in his efforts to conform to his mother's demands; and in conforming to the religious prescriptions that prepare his identity as "a good Jew," he is not subjected to continuous supervision.[14]

Neither parent, of course, is indifferent to the primary interest of the other. The traditional Jewish mother would be quick to lament a son's abandonment of a religious orientation. And a Jewish father, no matter how far removed from practical concerns, would be seriously annoyed if his son were to defy mother's behavioral prescriptions. The system of complementary role allocation in the family (as in all groups) requires a degree of consensus between authority holders on all levels; yet, in spite of such consensus, there is leeway for the youngster in the presence of each of the parents: mother is more ready than father to overlook minor infringements of religious prescriptions, and father may smile good-naturedly at his son about some of the "petty details" of everyday behavior about which mother is so persistent. And when the child finds himself in the presence of both parents, tactful parents will try not to disturb the somewhat ceremonial quality of togetherness by insisting on demands

13. *Social Theory and Social Structure*, Glencoe, Illinois: The Free Press, 1957, pp. 371–79, *passim*. See also Rose Laub Coser, "Insulation from Observability and Types of Social Conformity," *American Sociological Review*, XXVI (February 1961), 28–39.
14. This puts mother in the position of a "mediator" in the dual sense of the term. She keeps father informed about the children, at the same time as, by not reporting minor infringements that have escaped his notice, she protects them from the harsh exercise of his authority.

that are peculiar to each. In this type of family, leeway is afforded the child to conform in somewhat different manner to the expectations of each parent; he is able to gain distance to organize these expectations for himself, i.e., to articulate his role.

Role Allocation and Role Involvement

The distinction between the parents' interest in types of conformity, the differential allocation of authority, and the extent of observability are presumably present where the mother acts mainly as the manager of the household and where the father acts as a representative of the family in the community and of the community in the family. In this sense the "community" need not be geographically based; it may be a religious collectivity sustained by a common value system. In such a social setting, whether or not father dominates family life, the respect he commands among its members is sustained by the values of the community.

This distinction between the father's role as mediator between the community and his family and the mother's role as "organizer" of family affairs within the unit is similar to Parsons's distinction between "external" and "internal" functions of the family system, i.e., between those functions that "concern relations outside the system" and those concerning "the internal affairs of the system."[15] However, this distinction has become blurred in modern industrial society, where mediation between the community and the family has not remained the exclusive domain of the father. It is not important whether or not it can be shown that the father's functions are still primarily external, while the mother's functions are still primarily internal; it is precisely the measure of "marginal de-differentiation" of familial roles which presents both the social and the theoretical problem with which I am concerned here.

One hardly need belabor the fact that the modern economic system has become differentiated in many ways. One important differentiation is that between what Max Weber has called the production unit and the budgetary unit, i.e., between the realm of production and the realm of consumption. This has resulted in a separation between the occupational sphere and the family abode. The middle-class father usually derives status for himself and his family from his occupational activities away from home. His main reference group consists of professional colleagues or business associates. These persons, however, even if known to the children through occasional visiting, are not very important in their lives. Much of their socialization takes place in the community, through school, scouts, sport groups, and other extracurricular activities. There might easily be a separation between the values governing the father's status

15. Talcott Parsons, *Family, Socialization and Interaction Process*, Glencoe, Illinois: The Free Press, 1955, p. 47.

aspirations and those governing the socialization of his children,[16] were it not for some integrating mechanisms. The choice of residence, as one of these mechanisms, often "accidentally" brings into the same neighborhood families whose adults belong to a similar professional world. Another at least equally important means of integration between the values governing the family and those governing the community is the modern role of the mother. Through her activities in the PTA, brownies, cub scouts, and the like, she helps both maintain the communal social network and integrate her children in it. Her community activities are not limited to those relating to her children; she also becomes concerned with values governing the political life of the community, if not the country at large, through political activities of all sorts. Membership in the League of Women Voters is one case in point. The status of the middle-class family is not only derived from the father's occupation but from mother's club affiliations as well. Hence, the modern middle-class American mother performs a large share of the mediation between the community and the family; to use Parsons's phrase, she helps to adapt the family to the "external system."

This is only one aspect, of course, of the measure of equality between men and women in modern society. Equalitarianism, which is part of the modern American value system, and which is derived from the emphasis on achieved rather than ascribed status, brings about a sharing of rights and obligations, of concerns and of tasks between husband and wife. Within the family, the wife claims her husband's participation in some of her tasks and, in turn, actively participates in preparing the children to become "good Americans" and in molding their character. It will be remembered that Kohn found that in the middle-class family both parents partake in their concerns for the children's inner dispositions.

While the middle-class mother does assume some of the rights and obligations that traditionally belonged to the father, she does not necessarily give up her obligations to maintain the "internal system." She may delegate some of her chores to members of the family or to paid help, but she remains in charge of "running the household." As far as the children are concerned, the modern middle-class mother would therefore seem to be overinvolved in their lives. She focuses on their inner dispositions for their personality development, and her efforts to integrate them in the community are meant to help them acquire its dominant values. She cannot, however, ignore the details of everyday behavior. It is her task to supervise all the children's activities, either to schedule most of them herself or at least to be informed of them. The modern middle-class mother occupies a position of control over her children that strongly tends

16. Cf. Philip Slater's point that in the modern family rigid role differentiation would make identification of children with parents difficult. "Parental Role Differentiation," *American Journal of Sociology*, LXVII (November 1961), 296–308, this book, pp. 259–75.

to outweigh any possible control that a busy and absent father may be able to have.

The combined interest in both behavioral and attitudinal conformity and the potentially weak position of the father may well lead the mother to be domineering. Her control can indeed be pervasive because the children can hardly be insulated from her observation. Being interested in the children's attitudes as well as in their behavior, her supervision makes it possible for her to weigh all their acts not only in terms of the immediate situation, but also in terms of their symbolic meaning in regard to attitudes and future development. The scolding phrase, "It's not that I mind you not doing the dishes—I do them faster myself anyway—it's your attitude that I object to," expresses criticism both of the youngster's inability to do the task as well as the mother and of his underlying disposition. Such control is aimed at both levels of the personality at the same time.

The most important consequence of her interest in both types of conformity is not merely her domination, but the fact that expectations directed at both immediate consequences of behavior and inner dispositions may be contradictory. Conflicts in time perspective may serve as a convenient example. Expectations of behavioral conformity involve a short time perspective, whereas expectations of attitudinal conformity presuppose a long time perspective: one must be able to overlook the concrete details of everyday life, and take everyday annoyances lightly for the sake of "more important matters," such as long-range character development. We saw how such divergent time perspectives of father and mother balanced each other in the Jewish family. However, in the modern middle-class family a mother is often called upon to make a quick choice between two conflicting modes of response to a child's action. Should a child who breaks an appliance while experimenting with its mechanics be scolded for the damage, or should he be commended for showing "initiative" and "scientific interest"? There is a danger that mother will expect both "initiative" and "care," and that she may scold him for failing in either one of these. Not only does she "dominate," she dominates in a special way, by having conflicting expectations.

The consequence is that any conflicts that may exist between attitudinal and behavioral expectations for the child do not emanate from two role-partners, father and mother, but stem primarily from one role-partner. If conflicting expectations emanate from *different* persons, the child can make use of the mechanisms ordinarily available to deal with different role-partners in the role-set: the difference in the amount of observability by his role-partners and in the type of interest that they have in him.[17] This would not only afford the child the opportunity to deal with

17. Cf. Merton, *Social Theory and Social Structure, op. cit.*

conflicting expectations but also to grow in his awareness of his own mastery.[18] If father would expect primarily "initiative" and mother would expect mainly "careful handling of household articles," the child could live up to the expectations of each in turn. He would, in addition, differentiate between these spheres of activities and learn about their meaning for him in his relationships to his role-partners. This is what is meant by "role articulation."

Hence, if contradictory expectations emanate from different role-partners, they can more easily be resolved because of the mechanisms available in the more complex relationship. If, however, the contradictory expectations emanate from the same person, we have what Merton has called a "core case of sociological ambivalence," i.e., one of "incompatible expectations incorporated in a *single* role of a *single* social status."[19] The ambivalence is here not traced to the personality attributes of mother or child, but to the social position of the modern middle-class mother.

Adjustment of Authority Patterns

The fact that the disturbance in the balance of authority that is endemic in the American middle-class family does not more frequently lead to personality disorganization in the children than it already does is due to some countertrends. Only two such trends will be identified here.

Actually, in most families the mother either tends to reduce her interest in attitudinal conformity, which re-establishes the traditional balance described earlier; or she, as well as the father, tends to be permissive in regard to behavioral conformity, which establishes a different kind of balance.

Although concerned with her children's inner dispositions, the mother may be led to relegate this interest because her daily behavior is primarily motivated by practical concerns. Though she may indeed, in conversations with her friends or in an interview with a researcher, emphasize her concern about her children's attitudinal development, in actual dealings with them she may be pressed to concern herself mainly with their not upsetting the order of daily routine; the demands of the

18. Jesse Pitts describes how the French child is able and expected to "manipulate" the various role-partners available in the extended family. He concludes: "The consequences for the child's development are to give the seal of legitimacy to his own search for gratification. The unique identity of the personality is entitled to its own satisfaction as long as its consequences are not destructive of the family. Thus the child learns the limits of value conformity and the complexity of life." ("The Family and Peer Groups," in *The Family*, Norman W. Bell and Ezra E. Vogel, eds., New York: The Free Press of Glencoe, 1960, pp. 266–286. See esp. pp. 271–273.) See also by the same author, "The Case of the French Bourgeoisie," in the first edition of this book, pp. 545–50.

19. Robert K. Merton and Elinor Barber, "Sociological Ambivalence," *op. cit.*

immediate situation may make the mother lose sight of her principles. She may not be very different from the nurse who said in an interview, "One ought to look at the patient as a person, not just a case," but was overheard saying to a student nurse: "You've got to teach those patients not to be too demanding; after all, we've got our work to do." This is not to accuse either nurse or mother of simply paying lip service to professed values, but rather to point out that the task at hand may induce a person not to be overly involved with professed ideals. In other words, though there is equal concern *expressed* with attitudinal conformity by both parents, in everyday practice the mother may feel forced to concentrate her immediate attention on the child's behavior. Thus in actual fact there could still be an implicit balance between father's and mother's expectations. Mother, who supervises the children's daily lives, focuses her interest on their everyday behavior, while father, who is not in a position to observe his children most of the day, concentrates his interest on their attitudes. The child has two role-partners with somewhat different expectations of conformity and different degrees of access to observe his behavior, and has the opportunity to articulate his role.

Another countertendency to the mother's domination of the child is her willingness to detach herself in some measure from her interest in his behavioral conformity. She mitigates the heavy combined impact of her demands for attitudinal and behavioral conformity by being permissive. Permissiveness is based on the principle that not every act has to be scrutinized. It means that observability is either deliberately restricted or, as when infringement of norms has occurred, that observation is ignored.[20] By limiting her observation of everyday behavior, the permissive mother can detach her concern from many details that otherwise would be disturbing and can thereby give up some of the control vested in her position.

In the equalitarian structure of the modern middle-class family, permissiveness is particularly appropriate,[21] for it allows the mother to gain distance at the same time as it allows the father to come closer. He no longer has to maintain the aloofness which was associated with the authority traditionally focused on attitudinal conformity. Indeed, it will be remembered that in the Jewish family described earlier, the distance the father maintained from the children permitted him not to let his

20. Merton anticipates this definition of "permissiveness" when, writing about "institutionalized evasions," he says: "The social function of permissiveness, the function of some measure of small delinquencies remaining unobserved or if observed, unacknowledged, is that of enabling the social structure to operate without undue strain." (*Social Theory and Social Structure, op. cit.*, p. 344.)

21. In regard to the greater measure of permissiveness in the middle class as compared with the working class, see Urie Bronfenbrenner, "Socialization and Social Class Through Time and Space," in *Readings in Social Psychology,* Macoby, Newcomb & Hartley, eds., New York: Henry Holt & Co., 1958, pp. 400–425.

concern with their inner dispositions be influenced by his possible irritation with everyday behavior. If, however, the father can be permissive, he can ignore the behavioral details that might otherwise interfere with his major interest and yet be able to maintain close touch with his children. Such redistribution of the authority of the significant role-partners affords the child the opportunity to relate to both of them and in this way to form a conception of his self.

In families in which permissiveness does not guide the parents' relationships with their children, or in which, alternately, the mother is not willing to give up her focus on the children's character development, the mother finds herself in a structural position that fosters an ambivalent relationship between her and her child.

The Domineering Mother

Not only does the mother who is always interested in both attitudinal and behavioral conformity interpret the numerous details of her children's behavior in terms of their inner dispositions, but her own inner dispositions also are deeply involved because she feels that her children's futures are at stake. Hence, through the lack of social distance between her and the child combined with her intense interest in him, her total personality is exposed to the irritations of everyday life.

The domineering mother may try to avoid the painfulness experienced in her close involvement by withdrawing some of her affect. The often observed "coldness" of the domineering mother can be seen as an attempt to compensate for the intense affective involvement inherent in her structural position.

Seen in this light, Bateson's concept of the *double bind* gains sociological significance. Bateson *et al*[22] see the schizophrenogenic mother as one who exposes her child to both love and hostility—to attraction and rejection. When the child comes close to the mother, she responds with a gesture that implies rejection, and yet she will be resentful if he keeps some distance between them. This is a situation in which the closeness of two role-partners intensifies for each of them both affective closeness and detachment, and where because of lack of permissiveness there are no institutionalized channels through which either the child or the mother can express their hostility directly.[23] The fact that the father's position is weakened makes the ambivalent mother-child relationship nearly paralyzing: neither of them can turn to him as a significant role-partner so that they are "bound" to each other.

22. Gregory Bateson, Don D. Jackson, Jay Haley, and John Weakland, "Toward a Theory of Schizophrenia," *Behavioral Science,* I (October 1956), 251–264.
23. About the positive function of institutional channels for the expression of hostility, see Lewis A. Coser, *The Functions of Social Conflict,* Glencoe, Illinois: The Free Press, 1956, pp. 63 ff.

The ambivalence is not merely a "state of feeling" of the participants, but is an attribute of a social relationship characterized by contradictory expectations. It would seem that one way in which ambivalence comes to be built into the structure of social roles is through the restriction of a person's role-set. If different (and often conflicting) expectations emanate from one and the same role-partner, the mechanisms of role-articulation can hardly operate.[24] These mechanisms depend on the existence of several role-partners; the status-holder can make use of their differential power over him, their different interest in him, and the difference in observability with which he is exposed to them to articulate his role.[25] Thus, in the family that does not provide a duality of significant role-partners, the child is likely to encounter serious difficulties in clarifying the meaning of his relationships and hence in gaining consciousness of his identity.

24. On some dysfunctional aspects of a restricted role-set, see my paper, "Alienation and the Social Structure," in E. Freidson, ed., *The Hospital in Modern Society*, New York: The Free Press of Glencoe, 1963, pp. 231–265.

25. Cf. Merton, *Social Theory and Social Structure, op. cit.*

FAMILY
AND SOCIETY

The papers in this part of the book examine several ways in which the norms governing the family have their effects on the structure of society and, conversely, in which the economic, political and occupational structure of the society significantly affects the relations among family members.

The manner in which property is passed on from parents to children has its consequences both for the society and for the relations between family members. Sussman, Cates and Smith examine the functions of testamentary freedom in modern industrial society. Habakkuk shows the differential effects of primogeniture and partible inheritance on two parts of the same country in the nineteenth century. The relations between family structure, the authority of the father, and testamentary freedom are explored, for one agrarian society, by Arensberg and Kimball. Finally, Jeff Rosenfeld examines the relations, as well as the distinction, between the passing on of property and the passing on of items of symbolic value.

As societies change, so does family life. Since, as an agent of socialization, the family is a conservative force, its importance is likely to be played down during periods of social revolution and to come into full force again during periods of social stability, as Lewis A. Coser shows with the example of Soviet Russia. The chapter from C. K. Yang's book on China affords a dramatic illustration of the result of an especially abrupt industrialization—the overthrow of the traditional age structure as a result of the overthrow of the old authority relations. Rapid social change creates conflicts for adolescents as well, as Kingsley Davis's analysis shows in some detail. Finally, Janet Zollinger Giele suggests that the increased differentiation of society leads to a dedifferentiation of sex roles—a topic which will be explored further in the last part of this book.

7 THE FUNCTIONS OF INHERITANCE

Marvin B. Sussman, Judith N. Cates,
and David T. Smith

The Concept
of Testamentary Freedom

Inheritance, in the broad sense, has existed in all civilizations and preliterate societies known to man. Intergenerational transfers are a common phenomenon in all societies, and the inheritance process is one major technique for effecting these transfers. There has been, and is, great variation, however, in the use of testamentary freedom. There appears to be a high correlation between its exercise and the rise in societal complexity. Parallel with this increase is a development and extension of society-wide systems of welfare, social security, insurance, and so forth, which are basically economic transfers (forms of inheritance) along generational lines. The existence of a multilineal family-descent system, a nuclear family structure voluntarily organized into kin networks, and a relatively high rate of social and geographical mobility of nuclear units are conditions that favor, and perhaps even require, testamentary freedom as part of any inheritance process. This is not to say that testamentary freedom came into being with industrialization, and there is some reason to believe that there are important exceptions to the correlation of modernization and testamentary freedom. There is historical evidence of the use of testamentary freedom in ancient Greece and

Rome and in Anglo-Saxon England before 1066, especially when the individual had no descendants. France, on the other hand, has severely prescribed distribution of an estate at death. With few exceptions, beneficiaries are immediate family members. The economy of France until very recently was built around family enterprises, and the restriction on testamentary freedom may be an accommodation to this economic condition. Present French economy, resembling more the corporate structure of the United States, may bring about changes in existing restrictions on testamentary freedom. Also, as the state itself assumes more responsibility for the care of the young and the old, conditions are increasingly conducive to the extensive exercise of testamentary freedom. The severe restrictions on testamentary freedom in France have not been conducive to the development of charitable foundations and agencies having the functions of public service and research. The government has control over research and social-betterment programs. The implications of this are worth a speculative essay. For the purposes of this study, the point is that testamentary freedom and its exercise are intricate parts of the economy, political ideology, and social systems of a society.

Testamentary freedom may be perceived by the testator as a way to "right a wrong" done to an individual, to improve the family's capability of surviving as a unit, to maintain a surviving member over time, to reward a deserving person, or to punish the undeserving. Testamentary freedom, in this sense, can function to support the family and social order and especially those values that undergird intimate relationships: affection, service, reciprocity, exchange, and identification. Extensive use of testamentary freedom to provide for nonfamily or kin members by disinheriting closely related family members, on the other hand, would raise serious questions about the functions of testamentary freedom in modern society. If, for example, it had been discovered in this study that there is widespread naming in wills of nonrelated persons in lieu of kin, particularly individuals who provided few services and little affection or friendship, then it would be necessary to question whether inheritance is intended to enhance intergenerational family continuity, provide for the smooth transition of power via intergenerational transfers, function as an important mechanism by which the older generation can maintain power within the family, or whether inheritance has a role in maintaining the social structure.

If inheritance provides survivors in this study with more than property, if inheritance symbolizes a transfer of love, affection, and identification, and if testamentary freedom is employed to name as beneficiaries nonfamily individuals or particular family members who provided emotional services, then it is possible to enumerate more systematically the conditions under which intergenerational family continuity can be maintained. Such a finding would suggest focusing on the family as an interaction system and studying the quality and character of interactions. The money involved in inheritance and the power and use it represents may be the least important variables in explaining intergenerational behavior.

Family Continuity

Intergenerational family continuity is one important linkage, perhaps the most important, of the nuclear family kinship network in American society. It pertains to ongoing relationships between parents, children, and grandchildren. Reciprocity, exchange, expectations, and services are some of the conditions, acts, and perceptions that determine continuity.[1] Data from this study of intergenerational transfers of property within kinship networks may provide clarification of the relationship between variables such as family size, occupation, education, ages of members, sex distribution and patterns of service, exchange, expectations, and reciprocities.

Reciprocity and exchange are fundamental to all social relationships. The bases of social relationships within the family are found in help patterns involving the exchange of unequal amounts and of different orders. Yet the giving and taking in meeting the needs of individual family members as well as the needs of whole families are basic for the continuity of nuclear family relationships, whether along generational or bilateral kinship lines. The anticipation of inheritance and the rightful claim to a large share of the inheritance precipitate the provision of services to those who have money to leave by relatives who expect to be compensated for providing care throughout the lifetime of the testator, but especially in his last years. Thus, within the family system it may be that inheritance is an important stimulus for making manifest reciprocity and exchange mechanisms that become the essential links in any viable social system.

In complex modern societies like ours, we have developed many other institutional systems and programs that materially support families. These range from welfare programs to outright subsidies and the pattern of intergenerational transfers that has already been discussed. The increasing program coverage and number of individuals involved in these society-wide generational economic transfers, a universal form of inheritance transmission, may condition the bases upon which individual

1. For a review of this position, see M. B. Sussman and L. G. Burchinal, "Kin Family Network: Unheralded Structure in Current Conceptualizations of Family Functioning," *Marriage and Family Living* 24 (1962): 231–240; M. B. Sussman and L. G. Burchinal, "Parental Aid to Married Children: Implications for Family Functioning," *Marriage and Family Living* 24 (1962): 320–332; M. B. Sussman, "Relationships of Adult Children with Their Parents in the United States," *Family, Intergenerational Relationships and Social Structure*, ed. Ethel Shanas and Gordon E. Streib (Englewood Cliffs, N.J.: Prentice-Hall, Inc., 1965), pp. 62–92.

dispositions are made. Inheritance transfers may be less a consequence of acts of serial reciprocity, based upon what specific individuals of one generation in a family do for others of another generation, but more a function of serial service.[2] Serial service involves an expected generational transfer that occurs in the normal course of events. It is expected that parents have to help their young children, and middle-aged children may be called upon to give care or arrange for care of an aged and often ailing parent. This is within the cycle of life, and services of this kind are expected and are not based upon reciprocal acts. Whatever parents have in the way of worldly possessions will in due course be passed on to lineal descendants.

The study of inheritance provides one opportunity to examine this issue of serial reciprocity versus serial service. Is the transfer of property within families and along generational and bilateral kin lines based upon notions of distributive justice (a person receives according to his contribution) or on another principle such as equal distribution to survivors, or on distribution to specifically named heirs and legatees on grounds other than acts of service?

A related issue is that with the growth of society-wide support programs, a longer life span, increasing inflation, and increased consumer spending, the dollar amounts to be inherited by the overwhelming majority of survivors will be relatively small. Consequently, inheritance for many families may turn out to be symbolically more important than the material aid it provides. Undoubtedly, where estates are large, it is impossible to overlook the material assistance given to selected takers. But in most cases, inheritance symbolizes what were at one time the love links and bonds between family members, most often those between marital partners, and between parents and children.

The juxtaposition of family continuity and testamentary freedom is not so incongruous as it first appears. Continuity implies order, succession, transfer, and identification; freedom suggests the right to act, the control of decision making, and (what is often forgotten) responsibility. The inheritance transfers discussed in this study provide the necessary behavior for the description of the conditions under which the normative requirements of testamentary freedom and family continuity are met and of the consequences of the exercise of testamentary freedom for family continuity.

. . .

Functions of Inheritance and Testamentary Freedom. Inheritance buttresses the activities of society-wide support systems in providing for the biological maintenance of the aged, the incapacitated, and other dependent family members. This is accomplished by two procedures: the

2. Wilbert E. Moore discusses this concept in Chapter 13 of *Order and Change* (New York: John Wiley & Sons, Inc., 1967), pp. 245–249.

testamentary provisions exercised by the will makers in behalf of needy spouses, parents, children, and so forth, and the redistribution of the estate by the heirs in intestate cases in order to care for needy kin, in most instances the surviving aged widow.

These patterns of distribution aid other family members who do not inherit part of the estate by freeing them of legal, emotional, and moral commitments for the financial support of surviving needy relatives. Community organizations, in turn, are also rewarded. When those persons least capable of being financially independent or semi-independent are provided for through inheritance, the pressure on general welfare and care systems to provide such support is lessened. . . .

Expectation, exchange, and reciprocity are characteristics endemic to organized groups and provide the bases for interaction among their members. Each group works out its own system of unequal exchange, and the expectation of reciprocation, although disparate in amount or in kind, provides the individual with the rationale and reward for continuing the interaction within the group. Inheritance furnishes a view of these reciprocities, exchanges, and expectations in the holder-heir relationship. Provisions made by testators to provide inheritances of different order, value, and kind according to the individual's position in the reciprocity system and the almost universal acceptance of this distribution by beneficiaries authenticate the notion that participation in interaction within any group is a function of the individual's acceptance of his position in the reciprocity system and the real or anticipated rewards resulting from such participation.

Serial service is another characteristic feature of both society-wide and individual transfer systems. Time accounts for generational transfers; a person gives service and support or receives it according to his position in the life cycle. He receives his due in payment for services already or yet to be rendered, and there is little affect in relation to giving or receiving such services. In situations of individual transfer such as inheritance, who receives and what is acquired depend upon exchanges in relation to the real or perceived needs of the testator or holder. Survivors use criteria embodying exchange and reciprocity in determining the justice of specific property distributions.

Inheritance provides the conditions for examining the relationships that existed between benefactor and heir. This ex post facto analysis of role relationships includes the symbolic meaning of interaction and the affective bases for family continuity. Measures of the symbolic meaning of heir-holder relationships are obtained by examining the transfer of mementos and other items cherished by the testator, such as a favorite chair or art object, and feelings expressed by beneficiaries about these items. The use made by heirs of intangible property in line with the descendent's wishes or expectations is another measure.

Inheritance provides one major source of funds for religious, welfare, and other charitable organizations and foundations in American society. Andrée Michel has suggested to the authors that one major reason why there is very little privately funded research in France (where research is controlled largely by the government) is the severe restrictions on testamentary freedom.[3] In contrast, the relatively healthy state of charitable institutions in the United States is in part due to philanthropic giving at death. The consequence is a division and sharing of power over such basic institutional systems as religion, medicine, education, and welfare; the state does not control all these basic systems. Although only a minority of testators make charitable provisions, if this study is representative of populations in other jurisdictions, the total given is reasonably large. It is important to state that these gifts do not deprive the families, since the givers have either already provided for family members or are without an immediate family. . . .

Inheritance functions to improve the status of women to the extent that women are not discriminated against by testators. Whereas will makers do select between kin on the basis of need and services, neither the intestate distribution nor testators discriminate on the basis of sex. Female children are as likely to inherit as male children, and given the greater longevity of women and the likelihood that they are younger than their husbands, female spouses are more likely to inherit than male spouses. Thus, although women may be disadvantaged in the occupational marketplace, they are not disadvantaged in matters of inheritance. The findings that women considered inheritance as their own and that many were successful in their investments of this nest egg have implications for role allocations, distribution of power, and control within the family.

Obtaining a windfall through inheritance may or may not act as an incentive or a damper on mobility and achievement. The societal vision of the effects of inheritance is stereotyped: we see the rich or almost rich passing on their fortunes to children who are willing to live on the income of the inheritance or even to fritter it away and who have little incentive to improve their status; and the less wealthy, those of the middle class, capitalizing on the inheritance and using it to improve the mobility of themselves and their families. The study data cannot support either view, and it is highly doubtful that inheritance functions as either a damper or a spur to achievement. Most beneficiaries in this study inherited too late in life for the windfall to affect their life style. Moreover, few inheritances were of sufficient size to make that kind of difference. Anticipation of an inheritance is clouded by unknown variables: the age at death of the holder, the amount in the will to be received, the testator's perception of

3. Professor Andrée Michel is on the Faculty of Social Sciences at the University of Ottawa. Private communication, January, 1967.

need of potential legatees, the beneficiary's position in the reciprocity system, changes in interaction patterns, and emergent but unpredictable situations requiring emergency and long-term care of the aged family member.

The fact that most individuals inherited so late and used what they received for maintenance of themselves and other family members suggests that inheritance is a negative incentive for potential inheritors. A person cannot anticipate any significant assist from inheritance in the mobility race; he has to achieve success by his own efforts. . . .

. . . . The functions of inheritance are to meet the maintenance needs of family members and to strengthen symbolic identification. This has relevance for the proposition that inheritance helps perpetuate the family through time. Although testamentary freedom permits the disinheritance of immediate or distant kin in favor of nonrelated persons, this rarely occurs. The continuity of the family is ensured by the setting up of reciprocities and expectations, taking care of family members and providing a symbolization of family continuity. The providing of symbolic meaning and identification cannot be achieved by society-wide generational transfers in effect today or by those to be created in the future. For this reason alone, there is little prospect that the inheritance system as we know it today will ever be abolished.

H. J. Habakkuk

Family Structure and Economic Change in Nineteenth-Century Europe

The scholars of continental Europe have devoted much attention to the social consequences of rules and customs of inheritance, and there exists a large body of work of this subject by lawyers and agricultural historians.[1] The purpose of this paper is to consider, in the light of this European evidence, the possible significance of such rules and customs for economic development in the nineteenth century.

The peasant families of western Europe had two conflicting aims: to keep the family property intact and to provide for the younger children. Families differed very widely, from region to region, both in the relative importance they attached to these two aims and in the methods they customarily adopted to achieve them. At one extreme, the ownership property descended intact to a succession of elder sons, who had complete discretion in what provision they made for the younger members of the family. At the other extreme, the ownership was divided between all the children in equal shares. The best example of the former limiting case is provided by England, where the owner had complete freedom to will his property as he pleased, and where, in the absence of a will (or a settlement), the entire property was inherited by the eldest son. Something like the latter limiting case is to be found in France under the Napoleonic Code, which severely restricted the share of property which an owner could leave by will to a single heir and in the absence of a will provided for equal division between the children.

---

1. There is a useful comparative account of inheritance systems in Ernest Roguin, *Traité de droit civil comparé*, III–VII (Paris, 1904–12). J. W. Hedelmann, *Die Fortschritte des Zivilrechts im XIX Jahrhundert* (Berlin, 1910–35), II, also contains relevant material on the law of the subject. The fullest source on the history of inheritance practices in Germany is the officially commissioned work, Max Sering (ed.), *Die Vererbung des ländlichen Grundbesitzes in Königreich Preussen* (Berlin, 1908). Of the volumes in this series, I have obtained most help from VII, *Erbrecht und Agrarverfassung in Schleswig-Holstein,* written by Sering himself; this also contains an account of inheritance in Norway. See also I, *Oberlandsgerichtsbezirk Köln*, by W. Wygodzinski. There is considerable historical material in the more recent work of Max Sering and C. von Dietze, *Die Vererbung des ländlichen Grundbesitzes in der Nachkriegszeit* (Munich, 1930). For a discussion of the effects of inheritance customs in a restricted area in the present century see Hans Bittorf, *Die Vererbungsgewohnheiten des bäuerlichen Grundbesitzes in Landkreis Hildburghausen* (Thesis, Jena, 1930), pp. 43–72.

The English case was exceptional; nowhere else in western Europe did the owner enjoy such freedom of testamentary disposition, and nowhere else were the younger children, in cases of intestacy, void of any claim on the family property; in other countries, the portion that a landowner could freely dispose of—the *quotité disponible*—was limited by law, and the children all had a claim to some share in the property. Among the continental countries, however, there were considerable differences in the size of the *quotité disponible,* that is, in the extent to which an owner could favor a single heir. The law was complicated; the *quotité* varied according to the number of surviving children, sometimes also according to the nature of the property involved, whether it had been inherited or acquired. Any precise generalization about the geography of these differences is therefore impossible. But, as a rough approximation, we can say that proprietors in most states of Germany and Italy could will a greater part of their property to a single heir than was the case in France, Russia, Spain and Portugal, Holland, Belgium, and the Rhine provinces.[2]

The law on this point did not invariably afford an adequate index of actual practice. Owners varied in the extent to which they availed themselves of their testamentary powers. The French sociologist Le Play argued that where an owner could not freely dispose by will of at least half of his property, the practice of making wills disappeared, and the property descended according to the rules on intestacy. If this was the case—and it is difficult to be sure, because very little systematic study has been made of habits of will-making—areas in which the *quotité disponible* was small would have had an even stronger bias towards equality. For the exercise of testamentary power was generally in favor of a single heir, while the rules on intestacy tended to have an equalitarian effect. The position was further complicated by the fact that in many areas the succession to the property was commonly settled during the life of the parents and that the substance as well as the timing of such settlements was subject to considerable variation. In some parts of Germany, for example, the parents customarily transferred ownership to a single heir, during their lifetime, on a valuation of the property, and left to his discretion the size of the provision for the younger children. In other areas, the succession and the provision for the children was specified in detail in a settlement made on the marriage of the parents.

Besides differences in the *extent* of provision for younger children, there were differences in the *form* in which the provision was made. Sometimes they took their share in land, sometimes in money; sometimes they had a choice between the two, and sometimes the choice was made for them by law or convention. When the younger children took their provision in the form of land, they might physically divide their share of

2. See the discussion in Rougin, *op. cit.,* IV, 389.

the property—that was the presumption in the countries to which the Napoleonic Code applied—or they might work their shares in common. If they took money, as was commonly the case in many parts of Germany, their shares might be calculated on the sale value of the property *(Verkehrswert)* or on lower valuation, its *Ertragswert,* the brother and sister valuation.[3] Broadly speaking, actual physical division of the property was most general in the countries of the Napoleonic Code. Over most parts of Germany, outside the Rhineland and Thuringia, the property descended intact to a single heir, who was charged with the payment of compensation *(Abfindung)* to his younger brothers and sisters. But there might be considerable variations within a single region: islands of inheritance by a single heir in areas where the predominant rule was division, and vice versa.[4] There were also changes over time in inheritance systems; in the prosperous years before 1914 there was, in middle Germany, some increase in the area over which the single-heir rule of inheritance prevailed.[5]

We are therefore not dealing with two sharply distinguished systems of inheritance, coinciding exactly with well-defined geographical areas, though within the limits of this paper I shall have often to assume that this was the case. We have, instead, a wide range of compromise between two principal aims of family policy. Nor did different inheritance systems, even when they differed widely, invariably produce widely different results. A farm left to an eldest son, but burdened with heavy payments to his younger brothers and sisters who remained living on the farm with him, might in appearance not differ greatly from the farm, the ownership of which was divided among heirs, but which was by agreement worked by them as a single unit. A farm divided among heirs, one of whom bought out the interests of the rest, might for many intents and purposes look like a farm left to a single heir, but burdened with compensation for his younger brothers and sisters.

Nevertheless, there were important differences in inheritance systems from one region to another, and these left permanent marks on the social and economic structure. The influence of an inheritance system was very widely diffused. It affected the distribution of property, and thus the nature of the market. It influenced the type of agriculture and the level of agricultural efficiency. It was not without importance for the supply of capital: I have sometimes suspected, for example, that the development in England of forms of marriage settlement that provided for daughters by assuring them capital sums contributed greatly to the development of the

3. Max Sering, *Deutsche Agrarpolitik* (Leipsig, 1934), pp. 46–49.
4. See, for example, the mixture of systems in middle Germany, described by Sering and von Dietze, *op. cit.,* I, 219ff. There is a good account of variations of custom within a single area in Fritz Elsas, "Zur Frage des Anerbenrechts in Württemberg," *Schmollers Jahrbuch* (1913), pp. 264–67.
5. Sering and von Dietze, *op. cit.,* I, 228.

English mortgage market in the seventeenth century. In particular, inheritance systems exerted an influence on the structure of the family, that is, on the size of the family, on the relations of parents to children and between the children; and it is with the economic significance of this fact that I am now concerned.

There are a number of interesting problems in this field. One might consider, for example, the effect of family structure on entrepreneurial decision. In the early stages of industrialization, the family was the commonest form of economic enterprise throughout western Europe, both where industrial development was rapid and where it was slow. How far was the success of its performance influenced by differences in internal structure? Were German entrepreneurial families more success- ful than the French simply because they worked in a more favorable external environment, or did it have something to do with differences in the legal rights of the father, and of the sisters and younger brothers, who were also the uncles and aunts and nephews and nieces? Is the wicked uncle the villain of the economic plot? How far do the legal relations of the family repeat themselves in the family concern? I meant originally to consider these questions, but, conscious of how much a novice I am in entrepreneurial history, decided to escape, under cover of the exigencies of space, to a ground more familiar to me. I propose, therefore, to consider the effect of the property relations between members of a family first on its demographic behavior and second on its geographic mobility.

Almost all the writers on this subject agree that rules of inheritance have a profound influence on population growth. But they differ as to the nature of this influence. French demographers have generally been inclined to argue that, in their country, the provision for equal division, in the Napoleonic Code, tended to retard population growth.[6] The peasant who worked to keep his property intact had a powerful incentive to limit the number of children between whom his property would be divided. Friedrich List, on the other hand, in his analysis of the migration from Württemburg in the early nineteenth century, suggested that the applica- tion of the Napoleonic Code in the Rhineland had stimulated marriages and hence births.[7] In eighteenth-century Bavaria, division of properties was advocated specifically as a means of encouraging population growth,

6. There is an interesting discussion in J. Bertillon, *La dépopulation en France* (Paris, 1911). Three reasons suggest that the low French birth rate should not be ascribed to the provisions of the Civil Code relating to succession. (a) The desire to avoid partition by limiting births could have operated with great force only among the more substantial peasantry. Were these numerous enough to have had a significant effect on the birth rate for the country as a whole? (b) Belgium and Baden, both areas of division, showed substantial population increases. (c) The French law of 1909, which allowed the creation of inalienable rural property and so obviated any necessity for a limitation of births to achieve this end, was rarely used.

7. Friedrich List, *Schriften, Reden, Briefe*, ed. Erwin von Beckerath *et al.* (Berlin, 1927–35), IV: *Die Ackerverfassung, die Zwergwirtschaft und die Auswanderung*.

and most German writers lean towards the view that the single-heir system tended to restrain the birth rate.[8] In a peasant society, so the argument runs, children did not marry until they could establish a home; equal division of the family property enabled all the children to acquire an establishment and therefore to marry, whereas inheritance by a single heir made it difficult in a rural society for younger children to set up on their own and therefore condemned many of them to celibacy.

Clearly, it is difficult to bring these views to the bar of empirical verification. Inheritance by a single heir meant one thing in an area where land was still sufficiently plentiful for younger sons to acquire new farms of their own and marry and something quite different where it persisted in a crowded area where the younger children were compelled to remain at home unmarried. A recent study of marriage in France shows that in the remoter regions where the traditional obligation to maintain the social standing of the family was generally recognized, the younger children were often voluntarily celibate, despite their legal ownership of the family property; whereas, in other areas where more "liberal" and modern ideas prevailed, equal division enabled the younger children to acquire their own establishments and marry. And the influence of equal division was not only modified by moral ideas; it had one consequence where properties were still substantial and quite different consequences where fragmentation had already proceeded far. It is therefore difficult in the extreme to disentangle the effects of the rules of succession from the many other circumstances that influence population growth. The general direction of the influence exerted by these rules can, however, be distinguished. In the single-heir areas the owner had relatively slight inducement to limit the number of his children; but his brothers and sisters tended to remain unmarried. In an area of equal division, on the other hand, it was easier for all the heirs to marry, though they may have had some incentive to limit the number of *their* children in order to avoid progressive fragmentation. The typical family in the single-heir region tended, therefore, to consist of the owner and his wife with a large number of children, surrounded by a penumbra of celibate uncles and aunts, younger brothers and sisters. The typical family in the equal-division regions tended to consist of man and wife with a smaller number of children, but with fewer celibates. My own belief—to state summarily what ought to be argued further—is that, other things being equal, the higher proportion of marriages under the latter system was likely to produce in the aggregate more children than the fewer but more productive marriages of the former. I suggest, that is, that the single-heir system tended to retard population growth and division to promote it.

The writers on inheritance systems also differed when they came to

8. Valentin Steinert, *Zur Frage der Naturalteilung* (Lucka, 1906), pp. 53–61; Ludwig Fick, *Die Bäuerliche Erbfolge in rechtsrheinischen Bayern* (Stuttgart, 1895), pp. 34, 276.

discuss the second question—the effect of different inheritance systems on the mobility of population. To this problem much more direct attention was paid, for it was relevant to one of the most controversial developments in the later nineteenth century, the flight from the land; and consequently a large body of evidence was assembled on the point. Little of this evidence is entirely unambiguous, for it is difficult to isolate the effects on mobility of inheritance systems from the effects, for example, of the distribution of property: all the more difficult because the distribution of property was influenced by inheritance systems. To take a specific case, it is not easy to decide whether large numbers migrated from East Prussia because it was an area of *Anerbensitte,* inheritance by a single heir, or because it was, for reasons that had not a great deal to do with rules of inheritance, an area of large estates.

But this much is clear, that a good deal of the discussion was cast in the wrong terms. The question was not one of mobility versus immobility, but of different types of mobility. Long-distance migration, for seasons or short periods, was common throughout Europe, whatever the prevailing rules of inheritance. There is something to be said for the view that equal division promoted such migration, which was the method by which the sons of a peasant household who enjoyed a certain expectation of a share in the patrimonial property could acquire money to enlarge their holdings and supplement their family income. But, in any case, this sort of migration was not of primary importance for economic change, for it was essentially temporary. Seasonal migration was not an escape from the peasant family but a condition of its survival. The peasant went, not to acquire a new occupation in a different society, but to improve his position in the old.

Of much greater importance were the permanent migrations, and where these migrations are concerned there is a reasonably evident distinction between the influence of different systems of inheritance. There are a number of instances of large-scale permanent migration from areas of division. Where division led to a considerable morselization of properties and to a rapid growth of population, a succession of poor harvests might break down the normal resistances and lead to a sudden, explosive, and permanent exodus. South Germany in the early nineteenth century is a case in point. But the inhabitants of division areas were not likely, in the absence of such severe pressure, to respond readily to demands for permanent industrial labor in regions distant from their homes. In the first place, not only was the peasant himself rendered immobile by his property; his sons were deterred from permanent migration by the certainty of succeeding to a share of their family property. Secondly, in these areas, the market in small parcels of land was more active, and the chances of even a landless laborer acquiring some property were brighter than they were in areas where farms descended to a single heir. The retentive effect of property was thus very widely diffused. Finally, though in these areas the peasants often found ways, by agreement, to circumvent the worst excesses of morselization, the division of property did tend to create a class of peasants too poor to find their living outside the village, even had they wished to do so. The poverty of areas of division, as well as the wide diffusion of property rights, might hinder mobility.[9]

By comparison, the inhabitants of single-heir regions responded more easily to a demand for permanent industrial labor. The typical peasant families of these regions tended to contain a higher proportion of celibates, and single men were more likely than families to leave their villages permanently. It was only when there was a breakdown of social morale, such as there was in Ireland in the 1840's, that whole families migrated in large numbers. Moreover, the fact that the share of the younger children was under this system provided in the form of money facilitated their permanent movement away from the family holding. Generally speaking, moreover, the younger children in these areas were not debarred from compounding for their expectations during the lifetime of their parents. This was in Germany a recognized institution—the *Erbverzichtsvertrag*—and it gave the younger members of German families much greater freedom to leave the family home early in their life than was available in France, where the prohibition of the *pacte de renonciation* was one of the main principles of the law relating to succession.

There is, thus, a broad contrast. The one system provided for the younger children usually on a more generous scale but in a form that tethered them to peasant society; the other generally provided less generously but in a form that allowed the younger children to leave that society for good. The division areas may have tended to have the densest populations in relation to their capacity, but they were populations which it was difficult in normal times to induce permanently to leave the area. The population in single-heir areas may have been less dense, but it was more capable of permanent movement.

Czechoslovakia provides an example of the effect of inheritance systems on mobility. The west of Czechoslovakia—Bohemia, Silesia, and northern and western Moravia—belonged to the great East German *Anerbengebiete*; property went to a single heir. The east of Czechoslovakia—southwestern Moravia, Slovakia, and Ruthenia—was an area of division. In Slovakia, where division had created extremely small holdings, it was common for the sons of a peasant household, after

9. For the view that *Anerbensitte* favored migration, see Adolph Buchenberger, *Agrarwesen und Agrarpolitik*, I, 442–45; Fick, *op. cit.*, and von der Goltz, *Die agrarischen Aufgaben der Gegenwart* (Jena, 1894). The contrary view was taken by Sering and Wygodzinski in the works already cited, but the method by which they arrived at their conclusions was statistically faulty; see R. Kuczynski, *Der Zug nach der Stadt* (Stuttgart, 1897), pp. 235–50.

marriage, to leave their homes and wives and emigrate. In the 1930's, in one district of 45,000 inhabitants, 3,000 worked as miners outside the district, 3,000 as seasonal agricultural laborers, and 1,500 as building workers. But their intention was not permanent settlement away from the district; it was to earn enough money to set themselves up as farmers or to supplement the family earnings at home. "In many parts of Slovakia this type of emigration was so widespread that the existence of whole villages was based upon it."[10] But *permanent* migration from the family seems to have been commoner in the western parts of Czechoslovakia. Before the development of industry, the younger sons remained unmarried and worked with the lord of the manor or became agricultural wage-earners. With the development of an industrial and urban society they found new employments. Some of them entered the professions, for since the parental holdings in this region remained undivided, the peasant was often wealthy enough to educate his younger sons. "Thus the Historical Provinces, where estates are passed on to a single heir, unlike the Slovak regions, where estates are divided among the heirs, provided a heavy quota of peasants for the liberal professions calling for a secondary university education."[11]

Now for the effects of these differences in mobility on economic change, on the form and speed of industrial development. In early industrial society, labor was probably a higher proportion of total costs than, in general, it is today, and, in societies that were still predominantly peasant and where transport facilities were few, geographical mobility of labor was certainly lower. The terms on which labor was ,available to industry were therefore a more decisive influence on the location of industry than it is in modern Europe. Where the peasant population was relatively dense but immobile, industry tended to move to the labor; where the peasant population was more mobile, even if less fertile, the industrialist had much greater freedom to choose his site with reference to the other relevant considerations.

But it is a question not only of the location of industry but of its type. The practice of division of property was favorable to the development of local industry in the home or small workshop, for it tended to create a population with time for by-employments. The relation between division and domestic industry was not indeed a one-way relation. In some areas it was not so much that division facilitated industrial by-employments, as that the independent existence of domestic industry diminished resistance to division; because nonagricultural by-employments were available, properties could be divided and still be capable of maintaining families. Such a case was Schleswig Holstein, predominantly an area of the single

10. H. Boker and F. W. Von Bulow, *The Rural Exodus in Czechoslovakia* (I. L. O. Studies and Reports, Series K [Agriculture], No. 13 [Geneva, 1935]).
11. *Ibid.*

heir, in which the practice of division was concentrated in the fishing villages along the western coast. In most cases, however, the practice of division appears to have arisen independently of the customs of local domestic industry, and it is a reasonable conjecture in some cases that it directly promoted the development of such industry. It is, for example, perhaps not entirely a coincidence that the medieval woolen textile industry should have flourished in East Anglia, a region of partible inheritance.[12]

Whether or not inheritance customs had much to do with the early distribution of local domestic industry, division did greatly influence the capacity of that type of industry to resist the competition of the factory in the nineteenth century. To attract labor permanently from peasant families in areas of division the factory had to offer a wage sufficiently high to compensate them for renouncing their prospects of rising in peasant society; this fact limited the range of operations over which the factory could successfully compete with domestic industry, decentralized in the small workshop and the home and drawing its labor from local peasant families of the neighborhood.

The clearest example of the effect of labor immobilities is Russia in the later nineteenth century where, largely because of the existence of the *mir,* the factory failed to make headway against the village industry. The persistence of old forms of industry in France and the wide geographical diffusion of French industry are also, in considerable measure, to be ascribed to immobilities arising from the structure of the French family. It is significant that England, the country of the earliest factories and regions of industrial concentration, was the country where, with a few minor exceptions, younger children had no claim at common law to any share of their father's estate, that is, had only such claims as might be specifically granted them my special agreement—for example, at the time of their parents' marriage. And if space allowed, I think it could be shown that the prevalence of *Anerbensitte* over most of nineteenth-century Germany outside the Rhineland and Thuringia was a significant influence in the rapid development of German industry.

The two features I have been discussing—the mobility of a population and its capacity to increase—are closely related. I have argued that a peasant community in which the single-heir system prevails is likely —with the important proviso of other things being equal—to be mobile but unprolific in comparison with one in which division prevails. But because of its capacity to send forth its younger sons to become part of a permanent industrial labor force, the single-heir system made a powerful

12. G. C. Homans, *English Villagers of the Thirteenth Century* (Cambridge, Mass.: Harvard University Press, 1941) contains a discussion of inheritance customs in medieval England.

indirect contribution to population increase. It retarded population increase in the country but accelerated it, and to a greater extent, in the towns and areas of industrial concentration. For in all the western European countries, the industrial wage-earners were the most prolific class. They were not restrained by traditional views, which in peasant societies subordinated marriage to the purposes of the maintenance of the family; a higher proportion of them married, and they married younger. And once the initial stages of industrialization had got under way, the natural increase from this source very greatly diminished the extent to which the further expansion of industry needed to depend upon continued migration from the countryside.

In the years before 1914, a large amount of writing was devoted to a discussion of a third consequence of inheritance systems for economic change—their influence on the efficiency of agriculture. It was argued by the opponents of equal division that it starved the land of capital. Regions of division were regions of land hunger; small peasants, anxious to add acre to acre, bid up the price of land to an excessively high level and often mortgaged in order to buy. As a result, the savings of the peasants were not applied to improving their properties but to extending them; in substance, that is, the savings of the fortunate peasants went in absorbing the fragments thrown on the market by the less fortunate members of their own class. Moreover, the flow of outside capital into agriculture was impeded because the high price of land made capitalists reluctant to buy. On the other hand, it was argued by the defenders of division that the single-heir system often had equally bad effects on agricultural efficiency; where the property descended to a single heir who was charged with an obligation to compensate the younger children with sums of money calculated on the market value of the property, it might become heavily burdened with debt and so starved of capital.[13]

Wherever the truth of this argument about the effect of inheritance systems on productivity may lie,[14] it is probable that any given increase in productivity in the regions of equal division tended to exhaust itself in an increase in population, and to accelerate the process of division; whereas an equivalent increase in the single-heir areas was more likely to increase the surplus available for sale to the nonagricultural population. The

13. In Austria, between 1868 and 1892, 958,876 cases of inheritance resulted in 543,747 new mortgages, incurred to compensate heirs, which averaged 25 percent of the value of the land. E. H. Kaden, "The Peasant Inheritance Law in Germany," *Iowa Law Review,* XX (1934–35), 350–88.

14. That question of the effect of inheritance customs on productivity is difficult to resolve because the fertility of an area may have helped to determine its inheritance system. In Bavaria, according to the study of Fick, the harvest yield was greatest in areas where division was the ruling custom, but this may well have been due to the fact that it was the more fertile land that was the most suitable for division. In any case, in Bavaria the differences do not appear to have been significant.

agriculture of a single-heir region was therefore more capable of responding to the increased demands for food which arose in the course of industrialization.

I have described three ways in which a feature of family structure influenced economic development. I am very conscious not only of having restricted myself to one feature only but also of not having assessed the magnitude, as opposed to the direction, of the influences which flowed from it. I would only say that most of the models produced by the economists who observed the early stages of European industrialization assigned an important place to population and food supply, and that, since inheritance systems had an influence on both these, they ought to be considered among the factors that determined the rate at which industrialization got under way in the different parts of Europe and the forms it assumed.

Conrad M. Arensberg and Solon T. Kimball

Family and Community in Ireland

Of the demographic phenomena the small farmers present, the decline of population is most easily isolated. The facts are as follows: There has been a continuous and characteristic decline since the great famine of 1845. Numbers have fallen from 6,548,000 in 1841 to 2,963,000 in 1926. With the exception of Dublin, the whole of the country has suffered in this decline. On the whole, however, the country districts have suffered at a greater rate than have the towns. In 1841, 80 percent of the population was rural; today only 63 percent. In other words, since 1841 there has been an almost continuous increase in the town population at the expense of the rural, though the two have shared a common decline. Put in terms of percentages: since 1841, the country districts have lost 64 percent of their population, towns from 200 to 500, 49 percent, towns from 5,000 to 10,000, 25 percent, and towns other than Dublin over 10,000, 13 percent. Dublin, on the other hand, has gained 47 percent. That the enormous emigration associated with this decline is a matter of the contemporary generation is evident when it is recognized that 30 percent of the native-born Irish were living in other countries in 1926.

The closest approach among European countries is the case of Norway, where 15 percent live outside. Italy, which has provided so many citizens for the United States and the Argentine, has only 4 percent of its natives residing in foreign countries. Since 1911 there has, however, been a check in the decrease; only 5 percent of the population was lost between 1911 and 1926. The region of our investigation, County Clare, shares in this general loss, falling in population from 250,000 in 1841 to 95,000 in 1926. Since 1911 it has lost only 8 percent. . . .

Clearly connected with the decline in population are other demographic statistics, particularly those of marriage. They present features which are unique among civilized peoples. Inasmuch as they are again indications of an underlying uniform social pattern whose occurrences they record, it is necessary to analyze them in terms of the behavior patterns of rural Ireland. Like emigration, they are more characteristic of the country people. Springing from marriage, they are thus directly indicative of social forces within the small farmers' family economy.

Briefly stated, they present the following characteristics: In Saorstat Eireann in 1926, according to the census then conducted, there was a larger proportion of unmarried persons of all ages than in any other country for which records are kept. Marriage, furthermore, did not take place until a comparatively late age. Thus 80 percent of males between twenty-five and thirty years of age were unmarried in 1926, 62 percent of males thirty to thirty-five, 50 percent of males thirty-five to forty, and 26 percent of males fifty-five to sixty-five. The significance of these figures springs from their comparison with other countries. In the United States only 39 percent of males twenty-five to thirty are unmarried, 24 percent between thirty and thirty-five, and only 10 percent between fifty-five and sixty-five. Denmark, an agricultural country similar in many ways to Ireland, had only 49 percent, 25 percent, 15 percent, and 8 percent of these age groups not yet benedict, respectively. In England the percentages were 45 percent, 25 percent, 16 percent, and 10 percent, a great contrast to the sister island. Indeed, in the Free State the percentages of unmarried among the males of each age group are usually double those of other countries. . . .

The kernel of the problem lies, of course, in the behavior of the country people. Marriage brings both dispersal of the farm family and change of status for boys and girls. The marriage of one of the sons brings re-formation of the whole family group upon the farm. The crux of the matter lies in this reorganization of the farm family and the mechanism of the change and continuity it provides.

The nearly universal form of marriage in the Irish countryside unites transfer of economic control, land ownership, reformation of family ties, advance in family and community status, and entrance into adult procreative sex life. It is a central focus of rural life, a universal turning point in individual histories. This form of marriage is known as matchmaking. It is the usual, in fact until recently the only respectable, method of marriage and usually too of inheritance. . . .

A match (Gaelic, *cleamhnas*, marriage, and *spré*, a match) is a contractual marriage made by the parents or families of the marrying parties and involving the disposal of properties. Generally it begins with a farmer's casting round for a suitable girl for one of his sons who is to inherit his farm. The choice of the heir from among the sons rests in the father's hands. Historically, all the sons and daughters were provided for on the land, and, where possible, this is still the ideal situation, but the closer identification of family with one particular plot of land and the difficulty of land division fostered through three generations of agrarian agitation and land reform have prevented this. One son, then, is ordinarily to be "settled on the land." Typically today only one son remains, and he gets the farm. . . .

. . . With the transfer of land at the marriage of the son who remains to work the farm, the relations of the members of the farm family to each other and to the farm they work undergo a drastic change. In the first place, the headship of the old couple under whom the family group worked undergoes change. The old couple relinquish the farm, they enter the age grade of the dying, and direction of the enterprise of the group passes from their hands to those of the young people. . . . From the view of the father, it means the abandonment of the ownership he has long enjoyed; from the point of view of the old woman it means she is no longer the "woman of the house." Her place is taken by the incoming daughter-in-law. Naturally, this change is accomplished in effect only with difficulty and with considerable reluctance upon the part of the old couple. . . .

. . . The internal reorganization of the family consequent on the marriage of one of their number produces a marked change in the situation of the as yet unprovided-for brothers and sisters. The other members of the family broken up by the marriage of one of their number on the home farm must be provided for elsewhere. They feel themselves entitled to portions, either in the form of dowries to marry into another farm or of some other means of establishing themselves. . . .

. . . The sons and daughters who are not to be portioned at home, in the words of the Luogh residents, "must travel." To that end both the savings of the family, created through their united efforts under the headship of father and mother, and the incoming dowry, are devoted. In Luogh there had been only four marriages in ten years; two of them were the usual farm-transferring matches, one a returned emigrant who married a boyhood sweetheart and bought a farm, and one a widower who took a second wife and a second fortune. . . .

Marriage, property transfer, and the dispersal of the family members derive their character from family relationships. The immediate family of father, mother, and children form a corporate group engaged in agriculture upon a small farm. The roles of the father and mother make them superordinate to the children. Theirs is the direction of the group enterprise. Within the group, technological roles correspond with family status. Economic endeavor, both upon the individual farms and in the form of cooperation between farms, is controlled through the operation of social forces springing from the family. In the testimony of the farmers themselves, that effort is but part of a larger constellation of behavior patterns, obligations, and sentiments governing the individual in other fields by virtue again of his place in the family group. In total, Irish small farm agriculture presents a picture, not of isolated individuals or units pursuing a course of the greatest economic gain, amassing material objects in response wholly to individual desires and selling labor as a commodity, but of a way of life, only a small part of which we have examined, in which the relations between individuals, the soil, productive work, and the material goods of the household constitute a web of social ties, bearing their own incentive and reward and determining the part of the individual in the labor and the goods of the group.

At marriage and at death, as we have seen, this web of relationships is disturbed. New individuals are introduced, old ones lost. The match brings a re-formation of the family involving a dispersal of former members and an introduction of a new set of component individuals into the relationships between land, goods, labor, and human beings.

In the light of this system and of the internal changes which are brought about within it, the Irish population statistics now may become interpretable. Late marriage and the high incidence of bachelorhood are associable with the reluctance of the old couple to renounce their leadership, the necessity of acquiring sufficient means to portion children, and the delay in dispersing the closed corporation of the family group until it is possible to establish the new one. The practical self-sufficiency of the family group makes it difficult to destroy. The identification of a single immediate family with the individual farm prevents the setting up of more than one new such group upon the land.

As we pointed out, subdivision of holdings practically ceased after 1852. Since then the struggle for land and legal reforms in land tenure have prohibited any great further division. The matchmaking system is very old in Ireland. The works of such Gaelic writers as Canon O'Leary describe it explicitly for the pre-famine period. With the cessation of subdivision of holdings came the necessity of providing for children elsewhere than on the land. From that same cessation of subdivision dates the high incidence of bachelorhood. In 1841, at the time of greatest population, age of marriage was normal. Then only 43 percent of males between twenty-five and thirty-five were unmarried, not 72 percent, as at present. Then only 15 percent of males between thirty-five and forty-five were celibate, not 29 percent as today. Figure 1 represents the percentages of unmarried males and females at each age in each subsequent census from 1841 to 1926.

Viewed in the light of this family structure, the decline of population becomes interpretable not as a flight from intolerable conditions, though economic distress had a powerful effect, not as a political gesture, though political disturbance took its toll, but rather as a movement arising from the effect of all these causes upon a family system whose very nature predisposed it to disperse population and which could, therefore, accommodate itself to that dispersal when it occurred. Emigration, no new thing in 1845, appears as the logical corollary of this dispersal. It derives much of its character, such as assisted passages and remittances, from the social forces at work in the family. It can become a traditional movement like the movement from country to town without destroying the family structure or the rural culture whose members it takes away.

Figure 1
Percentage of Unmarried Persons, Irish Free State

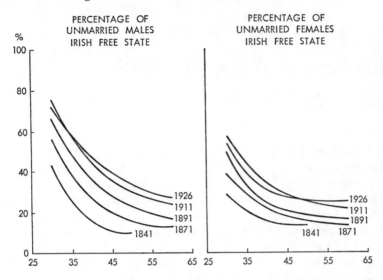

The authors do not mean to imply that anything within the social forces of the family as it exists in Ireland has had direct causal effect upon the peculiar statistics of Irish population. The authors would rather point out that the forces operative within that structure are of such a nature as to allow the society of which they are a part to continue to function in essentially similar fashion through the welter of economic, political, and other events which have impinged upon the human beings who have successively filled the structure. Likewise, the structure is capable of continued and virile existence in the present, governing the lives of its component individuals and modifying itself to take in new influences.

Jeffrey P. Rosenfeld

Inheritance: A Sex-Related System of Exchange

One of the most interesting aspects of inheritance, from a sociological point of view, is that it can provide a framework for studying the passage of social standing and the reallocation of status positions.

In order to grasp the social dimensions of inheritance, it is necessary to go beyond the allocation of real property, and to examine the impact of symbolic bequests upon individuals and groups. In American society, it appears that restrictions in access to monetary bequests have been countered by greater valuation of hereditary matrilineal statuses. Symbolic bequests seem to have become increasingly meaningful for women especially where they represent an important exchange value for the purpose of social mobility and marital selection.

Inheritance as a Type of Exchange

Exchange theory provides a viable means of interpreting inheritance once it is understood that wills or similar formalized gifts represent the expressed wish of a donor to pass items or statuses to specified donees. This approach relates inheritance to the more general concept of reciprocity.[1]

Exchange theory emphasizes the *quid pro quo* aspect of social relationships. Mauss noted the part played by exchange in interactive relationships more than half a century ago,[2] and recently Sussman, Cates and Smith incorporated the notion in their theory of inheritance, considering that death is one of a number of situations that call for an exchange of statuses and roles. Their discussion of inheritance as a form of gift-giving concentrates on the social consequences of a bequest rather than on the attributes of the donor.[3]

Peter Blau deals with the social consequences of what he terms

1. Cf. Claude Lévi-Strauss, this book, pp. 3–12.
2. Marcel Mauss, *The Gift*, New York: W. W. Norton & Co., Inc., 1967.
3. Marvin B. Sussman, Judith N. Cates and David T. Smith, *The Family and Inheritance*, New York: Russell Sage Foundation, 1970, this book, pp. 377–83.

"indirect exchange": "Donations are exchanged for social approval," and they must be understood in terms of group norms, not monetary value. Although Blau here refers to philanthropic donations, his point applies to testatory practices because the making of a will, like a philanthropic donation, establishes a claim for being admired and remembered favorably, i.e., a claim for social approval, in this case after death.[4]

Wilbert Moore contributes to this discussion by suggesting that much interaction is motivated not by passing action back to the initiator, but rather by passing it on to others in the group. He develops the concept of serial service to underscore the importance of services rendered to those who are "still later in the sequential pattern."[5] Moore insisted that the concept of serial service would help explain the part played by inheritance in the intergenerational distribution of statuses and values.

Inheritance, Kinship, and Normative Values

Inheritance helps regulate the exchange of status, although the part it plays varies directly with the social class of the testator, and with the importance of land ownership as a stratification variable.[6] Before the American Revolution, when land tenure was the major indicator of social position, a set of highly formalized inheritance laws developed which insured that land, and the social status that was associated with its ownership, would inhere with a minimum of dispute. The system of primogeniture guaranteed that an entire estate, or *fee*, would automatically pass to the oldest son of the testator. This left the land holdings intact. Yet, with industrialization, this system of inheritance impeded the acquisition of status through social mobility.[7] The development of voluntaristic testation brought with it changes in the social and legal definitions of property and hence affected kinship patterns and the distribution of property from one generation to the next.

As long as primogeniture relied upon birth order to determine who would receive the lion's share of the decedent's estate, social-psychological and sociological factors such as parental preferences, services rendered by siblings, and interpersonal relationships could not be

4. Peter M. Blau, *Exchange and Power in Social Life*, New York: John Wiley & Sons, 1964, p. 92.

5. Wilbert E. Moore, *Order and Change*, New York: Russell Sage Foundation, 1967, p. 245.

6. Daniel Bell, "The Break-up of Family Capitalism," *The End of Ideology*, New York: The Free Press, 1962: "Property sanctioned by law and reinforced by the coercive power of the state, meant power," p. 39.

7. *Ibid.*, pp. 39–40. On the dysfunctional aspects of *entail* in the United States, and in New England in particular, see Bernard Farber, *Guardians of Virtue: Salem Families in 1800*, New York: Basic Books, 1972, pp. 69 ff.

important criteria for inheritance and exchange. Once the fundamental definitions of property and succession had changed, the inheritance of non-monetary items gained salience in intergenerational distributions.[8]

As a result of the widespread popularity of property ownership in *fee simple* near the end of the eighteenth century, it became possible to give or to bequeath items with high monetary worth but little sentimental value, like sums of money or stocks, bonds and insurance policies. It also became possible to bequeath highly symbolic items that were monetarily worthless. Although control increased over the distribution of property to family members, little control was placed upon the passage of sentimental or monetarily worthless items.[9]

As monetary bequests became more closely regulated, the passing on of items symbolizing group norms and values took on added meaning. It became possible, therefore, to conceptualize testation as influencing group cohesion and property distribution independently for this period, in a society that witnessed the differentiation between financial and non-financial concerns within the family unit.[10] Although the passage of money and group norms is likely to be interrelated, there is merit to the argument that in the system of inheritance that developed during the latter part of the eighteenth century, normative and monetary distributions often occurred independently of each other.

It is a familiar fact that inheritance of property is important for maintaining a system of stratification. What is less familiar is that the inheritance of monetarily worthless items serves a similar function. The manifest function of inheritance may be the orderly distribution and partition of a testator's estate, but one of its latent functions is the creation or alteration of social relationships among the survivors. In this respect, the symbolic meaning of a bequest may be at least as relevant to the sociologist as its monetary value.

Sentimental or highly prized items perpetuate statuses and relation-

8. Bernard Farber, *op. cit.,* pp. 68–69. Farber notes that entailed estates were legally abolished after the American Revolution, but suggests that they had lost their utility and their popularity long before their legal abolition.

9. Peter Dobkin Hall, Ph.D. dissertation, History Department, State University of New York at Stony Brook, 1973. Hall shows that partible inheritance practices in the latter part of the eighteenth century began to pose a threat to family partnerships and similar enterprises that were dependent upon the concentration, not the dissipation of capital. This threat ultimately contributed to the creation of testamentary trusts designed to retain capital within the family group.

10. Max Weber distinguished between class and status, using the former term to refer to economic criteria in a stratification system, and employing the latter to stand for socially determined or honorific criteria. Recently, Bendix suggested that class and status are empirical opposites, but that on a more abstract level they are mutually reinforcing. The development of partible inheritance, which resulted in normative and monetary distributions, provides a useful example for Weber's approach to the complexity of social standing. See Reinhard Bendix and Bennett Berger, "Images of Society and Problems of Concept Formation in Sociology," Reinhard Bendix, ed., *Embattled Reason,* New York: Oxford University Press, 1970, pp. 124–127.

ships that were cherished during the lifetime of the testator. A grandfather's clock, inherited as a bequest or gift, may lead to little or no financial gain. Its importance lies in the fact that the clock symbolizes its previous owner and is retained as a symbolic bequest that gives status.

Symbolic inheritance became increasingly important for women who frequently were excluded from the benefits of financial windfalls. In fact, restrictions on patrilateral sources of monetary wealth seem to have been countered by increased emphasis on matrilateral distributions of a sentimental or symbolic nature.

Hereditary Associations: An Illustrative Example

The existence of hereditary associations, whose memberships are based on lineal descent, suggests that normative distributions have implications for social relations among family members as well as for the continuity of organizations in the community. Peter Blau observes, for example, that "special institutions" occasionally arise to insure "the survival of a legitimate social order beyond the life span of individuals."[11] It would appear that hereditary associations are examples of such special institutions because they provide mechanisms for the intergenerational passage of group norms and values.

The number of hereditary associations has increased steadily since 1775 (Table 1), and over seventy of them exist today. The smallest, Sons of Sherman's March to the Sea, has only one hundred members. But the largest and probably the most well-known, Daughters of the American Revolution, is supported by 193,345 women in 2939 chapters throughout the United States. In fact, the mean size of the total membership for hereditary associations is 19,518 members.

TABLE 1. Hereditary Associations in the United States, by Date of Founding

Date	Number of Organizations Founded	Cumulative Frequency
1775–1800	1	1
1801–1825	3	4
1826–1850	6	10
1851–1875	8	18
1876–1900	15	33
1901–1925	16	49
1926–1950	13	62
1951–1972	8	70
N = 70		

11. Peter Blau, *op. cit.*, p. 273.

At first blush it might seem paradoxical that the number of organizations based on lineal descent has proliferated in a society that abolished entailed estates and made primogeniture illegal. But their increasing popularity becomes more understandable when one moves beyond the strictures of the law and examines the social implications of partible inheritance.

Peter Hall, studying the wealthy merchants of Boston, contends that the manner in which testamentary practices developed is related in some way to the decline of merchant family partnerships and to the tendency for larger segments of the merchant class to pool capital for business ventures. He cites the year 1819 as the benchmark for tracing the development of perpetuities and trusts, but suggests that such legislation culminated in social and economic changes that had already affected marriage practices and the distribution of property and capital.

Cross-cousin marriage had been frequent during periods when family partnerships were common among the merchant families of Boston. As family partnerships declined, and the mode of doing business broadened to include individuals, mainly from the same social stratum, who were once competitors, the older form of endogamous cross-cousin marriage was in large part supplanted by exogamous patterns, first by sibling exchanges (1800–1819) whereby business partners married each other's sisters, then increasingly by non-kin marriages (from 1820 onwards).[12] It seems that the rate of exogamy increased when the support among affines became less important than it had been for the partnerships in the mercantile period. What became important now was the extension of the network through alliances.[13] At the same time it became necessary to prevent capital from being siphoned off through bequests or partitions of an estate. The legislation that began placing restraints on testatory practices, starting in 1819, represented a response to changes in the emergent capitalist system that had left nascent corporations vulnerable to capital depletions resulting from partible inheritance.

The exogamous system of marital alliances was in tune with changes in business practices, but should also have lowered the exchange value of women by depleting the resources that they could bring into marriage, due to increasingly stringent limitations on a daughter's access to her share of the family estate. Lévi-Strauss insists that marriage is a system of exchange predicated on the high social value of women, ". . . that most precious of items . . ."[14] as objects of exchange. Indeed, these upper-class women, though they were deprived of much monetary inheritance,

---

12. Peter Dobkin Hall, *op. cit.*, pp. 63, 64. [See also this book, p. 236 (Table 4).]
13. On the difference between marriage as a means for alliance, and marriage as a means of social support, see Bernard Farber, *Kinship and Class*, New York: Basic Books, 1971. [Also see this book, p. 354.]
14. Claude Lévi-Strauss, *op. cit.*

continued to be worthy objects of exchange. This is because social worth is not determined by money alone. Wills and gifts *causa mortis* convey more than simply financial wealth. It seems reasonable to suppose that the high exchange value of women could be maintained, in spite of the social and economic changes that have been mentioned, by accentuating the value of normative distributions.

The second half of the 19th century, a time when exogamous marriages increased among Boston's upper-class families, marks a period of capitalist development with concomitant social mobility. Exogamous marriages meant that there was a strong likelihood that upper-class women married men below them in social standing, who, because they came from wealthy mercantile families, could become allied with the upper-class families through marriage.[15] Although a relatively small number of upper-class women married "down," thus helping extend the network of capitalists some steps down the ladder, hypergamy, i.e., cases of women marrying upward, became a pattern of marital selection in the country as a whole that has been maintained unto our day.

In the middle class, the problem of the daughter's "worth" was, of course, more acute under conditions of social mobility and the consequent desirability of hypergamy. This was conceivably difficult under conditions of limited wealth at best, and was impeded by the partitioning of estates among siblings and by laws that permitted the establishment of testatory trusts. But not all mechanisms of status enhancement depended upon monetary wealth, or even upon the patrilineal estate. Normative attributes that were symbolic of status became resources to be increasingly mobilized as monetary resources were channeled into business.

Normative Distributions and Hereditary Associations

Normative distributions provided a functional equivalent of the "family name" for upwardly mobile middle-class women. In fact, one type of voluntary association even helped establish a kind of pedigree for its members that was similar in many ways to the "family name." This was the hereditary association, whose criterion for membership was lineal descent. It was through membership in organizations of this type that an increasing number of persons sought to legitimate their claims to community status.

The data presented in Tables 2 and 3 would seem to suggest that membership in associations based on lineal descent has become increas-

15. On such compensatory features of marital exchange, see Robert K. Merton, "Inter-marriage and the Social Structure: Fact and Theory," in Rose Laub Coser, ed., *The Family, Its Structure and Functions*, New York: St. Martin's Press, 1964, pp. 128–52.

TABLE 2. Hereditary Associations in the United States, by Sex of Membership

	1775–1800	1801–1825	1826–1850	1851–1875	1876–1900	1901–1925	1926–1950	1951–1972
Males Only	1.00	.66	.66	.37	.37	.31	.15	.13
Females Only				.49	.44	.50	.46	.28
Males and Females		.33	.33	.12	.18	.19	.38	.57
	1.00	.99	.99	.98	.99	1.00	.99	.98
	n = 1	n = 3	n = 6	n = 8	n = 16	n = 16	n = 13	n = 7

N = 70

TABLE 3. Brother-Sister Hereditary Associations According to Membership Size in 1972*

Brother Organization	Number of Members	Sister Organization	Number of Members
1. Sons of the American Legion	18,091	American Legion Auxiliary	100,000
2. Sons of Confederate Veterans	2,500	United Daughters of the Confederacy	35,000
3. General Society of the War of 1812	1,216	National Society of the Daughters of 1812	4,500
4. Sons of the American Revolution	20,000	Daughters of the American Revolution	193,345
5. Sons of Utah Pioneers	1,150	Daughters of Utah Pioneers	40,000
6. Polish Legion of American Veterans	15,000	Polish Legion of American Veterans Ladies Auxiliary	8,000

* Data on membership size was taken from listings in the *Encyclopedia of Associations,* Gage Research Co., 1972 edition, "Veterans, Hereditary and Patriotic Associations."

ingly popular among women, and that they currently attract a disproportionately larger female following. Hereditary associations began to be founded at roughly the time at which, according to Hall's study of Boston's elite, endogamous kin-marriage began declining in importance; that is, for males after 1799 and for females after 1819[16] (Table 2).

Although Table 2 reveals the increase in popularity of these organizations chronologically, it says little about the relative importance placed upon membership either by men or by women. Only after examining Table 3 does it become apparent that enrollment in such associations was

16. Peter Dobkin Hall, *op. cit.,* p. 55.

hardly an elitist phenomenon. When associations of the brother-sister variety, like Daughters of the American Revolution and Sons of the American Revolution, are compared, the differences are striking. Table 3 contrasts membership size for these sibling associations. It should be noted that in five out of the six cases presented below, females greatly outnumber male constituents (the one exception being an ethnic organization).

In fact, the membership of the Daughters of the American Revolution, the largest of all hereditary associations, today exceeds the total enrollment in associations that are exclusively male. The DAR has 193,345 members, as compared to approximately 86,500 members in all twenty-four associations that are exclusively male, and the nearly 65,000 members of organizations open to males and females. Membership size supports the contention that associational membership is largely a middle- rather than an upper-class phenomenon.

Nearly all hereditary associations venerate heroic acts like fighting in the American Revolution, or migrating to a new area, as in the case of the Sons of the Utah Pioneers. In order to join these organizations, applicants must prove that they are lineal descendants of these national heroes. In short, members associate themselves with events that are of historical significance for the community and pass these memberships, and their concomitant social status, to others in the family. Bernard Farber suggests that most families have "biographies" of events and of famous or infamous ancestors that are passed from one generation to the next: "Family heroes and villains, family secrets and skeletons in the closet . . . provide a symbolic content to the family estate."[17]

He notes that family biographies are often called upon to help legitimate the place of a family in the community.[18] Although he does not specifically cite membership in hereditary associations as datum for a family biography, it is clear that being a member of the Sons of Sherman's March to the Sea or the National Society of Colonial Daughters of the Seventeenth Century is a symbolic status that contributes to the social value of the family name. Passing of lineally-determined memberships from one generation to the next serves to perpetuate the memory of an ancestor's participation in a venerable event and, at the same time, continues to associate family status with community history.

That middle-class women would want to be associated with organizations that venerate community history becomes more understandable in light of the fact that claims to status became increasingly difficult to prove, for all but entrenched elites, as America industrialized. Geographic mobility and the growth of towns and cities posed a problem for

17. Bernard Farber, *Kinship and Class*, San Francisco: Basic Books, 1971, p. 106.
18. *Ibid.*, p. 101.

upwardly mobile middle-class women who were intent upon proving that they were solid community citizens. Informal evaluative criteria that are effective in small, cohesive communities, like knowledge of others' kinsmen and local reports on a woman's reputation, lose their effectiveness when families move frequently. Peter Berger contends that informal social controls like gossip, that were powerful in ". . . small communities, where most people live their lives in a high degree of social visibility and inspectability by their neighbors . . .,"[19] are not nearly so powerful when individuals and families can remain anonymous.

But chapters of national voluntary associations provide informal rating criteria. They are enclaves of ascribed status for mobile families, and perpetuate the symbolic value of family biographies. Although families like the Cabots and the Dodges did not have to resort to hereditary associations to maintain their family biographies, families that were lower on the social scale did indeed resort to such mechanisms. Membership in the hereditary association provided an opportunity for competitive advantage[20] and was a means of legitimating one's claims to social status in a society where the upper strata generally demand that those who wish to associate with them prove that they have the right to do so. Associational membership became a resource for demonstrating one's social standing and for accomplishing hypergamy, since it could be used to attest to one's social pedigree. In this sense, hereditary associations contribute to mobility according to Pareto's use of the term. Pareto viewed mobility as the recruitment of eligibles by the elite, and hereditary associations appear to provide a criterion for such recruitment to occur.[21]

When hereditary associations are studied in terms of degree and extent of social organization, it becomes evident that associations that are exclusively female have more highly developed networks of local chapters than do their male counterparts. For example, an examination of number of chapters, controlling for organization size, shows that the exclusively female associations have considerably more chapters than male, or male-female associations of the same size (Table 4).

It is not possible to compare organizations with memberships greater than 3,000 because most of the associations in that category are exclu-

19. Peter L. Berger, *Invitation to Sociology,* Garden City, New York: Doubleday, 1963, p. 72.

20. Philip Slater's interpretation of the function of collectivities further helps explain why the hereditary association became a particularly popular form of participation for middle-class women. It provides "the competitive advantage in natural selection enjoyed by those organisms which participate in collectivities, and the still further advantage held by collectivities which are highly organized and integrated." Following Slater, an individual appears to gain a competitive edge and enhances his survival value by participating in collectivities. When the collectivity derives status by identifying with community history, it provides additional social leverage for its members.

21. S. E. Finer, ed., *Vilfredo Pareto: Sociological Writings,* New York: Frederick Praeger, 1966, p. 249: ". . .families rising from the lower classes, bring with them the energy . . . necessary for maintaining [the elite] in power."

TABLE 4. Mean Number of Local Chapters of Hereditary Associations by Organizational Size and Gender of Members

Number of Members in the Organization	Males Only	Females Only	Males and Females	
100–1000	5.72	14.60	4.33	n=21
1001–2000	9.50	31.50	2.00	n=10
2001–3000	5.43	11.00	6.37	n=6

sively female. But when two larger organizations of roughly the same size, Sons of Union Veterans of the Civil War (8,000 members) and Daughters of American Colonists (10,400 members), are compared, there is a glaring difference in the number of their local chapters. The male association has 21 local chapters as compared with 250 for the female one.

Farber's comparison of differential and integrated kinship systems helps explain why female associations have broader networks of local chapters and higher enrollment rates. Contrasting families at the higher socioeconomic levels of American society with families near the bottom of the social scale, Farber suggests that the latter tend to rely upon integrative alliances which "maximize the number of marital liaisons" [22] and de-emphasize the maintenance of an enduring family culture. In contrast, family culture is more important to families with higher social status, and it is generally preserved by limiting marriage to "individuals from families or descent groups with identical norms and values." [23] The emphasis placed upon family culture by members of the social elite is also noted by Blau who says that powerful families are likely to adhere to traditional criteria in mate selection because "the institutional structure embodying these values is the one on which their dominant position rests." [24] By utilizing lineal descent as a criterion in determining who will marry whom, marriage is carefully prescribed, but at the same time it is possible to strengthen one's alliances with other members and ultimately widen the family network.

Concluding Remarks

It is important to note that other statuses besides membership in hereditary associations are passed through lines of lineal descent. For example, matriculation at certain academic institutions is an American tradition that is passed from one generation to the next. Whether it be a college education at a state school or at an Ivy League university, it is

22. Bernard Farber, *Kinship and Class, op. cit.*, p. 9.
23. *Ibid.*, p. 8.
24. Peter Blau, *op. cit.*, p. 276.

regarded as a family *mos* for many children to attend the academic institutions where their parents studied. Stephen Birmingham, writing about wealthy Jewish families in New York, described the schooling of financier Jacob Schiff's son:

> Morti had never wanted to go to Groton; all he wanted to do was to go to Harvard. . . . Harvard had already become something of a tradition in the family. Solomon Loeb's boys had gone there. . . . Harvard's president was a close personal friend of Schiff's. . . .[25]

Similarly, the fictional Oliver Barret of *Love Story* was expected to follow in his family's footsteps and study at Harvard:

> ". . .I answered and then confessed that my entire name was Oliver Barret."
> ". . .Barret like the Hall?"
> ". . .It is my special albatross to be related to the guy that built Barret Hall, the largest and ugliest structure in Harvard Yard, a colossal monument to my family's money, vanity and flagrant Harvardism."[26]

Despite his lament, Segal's novella implied that if Oliver Barret had had any sons, they too would have attended Harvard.

Associations based on lineal descent, and alma maters that encourage generations from the same family to apply for admission, represent a broader, but by no means less effective, application of inheritance. The concepts of monetary and normative distributions are not vitiated by broadening the term to include organizational or institutional statuses that inhere through lines of lineal descent. This is particularly true for American society, where associational membership and academic pedigree still play important parts in the process of mobility.

A scrutiny of last wills and testaments reveals that groups do not only rely on prescribed rituals of mourning to maintain social cohesion after the death of one or more members. Such cohesion is not only brought about by short-range mechanisms, as when the mourning period, as we know ever since Durkheim, helps draw group members together to share the immediate tragedy of death, and to affirm that the group itself is still intact. There are long-range mechanisms as well, and inheritance is one of them. Bequests help insure that the normative framework of intragroup relations will continue long after the shock of death has worn off and mourning family members have dispersed.

Sussman *et al.* indicate that inheritance of money is no longer the primary means by which large sums pass to the survivors in a group.[27] But it would be incorrect to assume that inheritance in a broader sense is declining in importance in American society. Older forms of testation that

25. Stephen Birmingham, *Our Crowd: The Great Jewish Families of New York,* New York: Harper and Row, 1967, p. 186.
26. Erich Segal, *Love Story,* New York: Harper and Row, 1970, p. 4.
27. Marvin B. Sussman *et al., op. cit.,* p. 356.

were based on primogeniture and impartible property may be obsolete, but this in no way detracts from the fact that inheritance still gives many individuals the potential for mobility. Memberships or items that are bequeathed today often enhance the social value of the donee by providing resources for access to community elites that may be, for this purpose, the functional equivalent of material goods.

An examination of wills and testaments may reveal how power is concentrated and redistributed among survivors who are named in, or omitted from, a bequest. The content of a will can be taken to indicate a testator's appraisal of how faithfully others in the group have performed their roles. Normative and monetary distributions present opportunities for the restructuring of social relationships, using the stipulations of the bequest as a source of legitimation for role modification. In short, the probating of a will can lead to new definitions of status and new opportunities for exchange. Popular phrases like "Mama would have wanted it this way" and "The dead are more powerful than the living" indicate the extent to which the death of a family member is seen as a continuing influence on the living. It is hoped that future studies of wills and testaments, as well as of gifts of *inter vivos* and gifts *causa mortis*, will profit from the tenets of exchange theory.

8 THE FAMILY AND SOCIAL CHANGE

Lewis A. Coser

Some Aspects of Soviet Family Policy

Present-day family legislation in Russia reveals a purposeful attempt on the part of the Russian policy-makers to strengthen the family as a social institution. This paper purports to outline a few of the social consequences of this legislation for various strata in the population and for the total societal system. Research in this area will provide considerably more useful information on the Russian social structure than some of the current attempts to explain the Russian regime in terms of the child-rearing practices of its citizens.[1]

The family as an institution is being strengthened in the Soviet Union because of three factors.

1. The decision-makers desire an increase in the birth rate. Russian industry is still very imperfectly mechanized, and the sheer quantity of

1. Soviet society exhibits a continual shift toward more rigid stratification and the solidification of a ruling class which disposes collectively of the means of production and tends increasingly to erect social barriers between itself and the underlying population; vertical social mobility decreases, and ascent into the ruling class becomes more and more difficult (see Alex Inkeles, "Stratification and Mobility in the Soviet Union," *American Sociological Review*, XV [1950], 465–79; N. S. Timasheff, "Vertical Social Mobility in a Communist Society," *American Journal of Sociology*, L [July, 1944], 9–21; David Dallin, *The Real Soviet Russia* [New Haven: Yale University Press, 1944]; Leon Trotsky, *The Revolution Betrayed* [Garden City, N.Y.: Doubleday, Doran & Co., 1937]).

labor must make up for low productivity of the individual worker. Productivity is so low, indeed, that even forced labor yields economical results, so that squandering of labor power brings about ever present hunger for more labor.[2] Military demands are also compelling in this respect.

2. The family can act as an effective counterweight against social mobility, as a stabilizer of status. The family, through transmission of skills, connections, and wealth, serves to insure inheritance of social status from parents to children.

3. The Russian policy-makers now realize that the authoritarian family acts as a "transmission belt" for the inculcation of the authoritarian norms of the total society. They apparently feel that this task was not sufficiently well performed by the extrafamilial institutions for socialization.

These purposeful actions on the part of the policy-makers serve to strengthen the ruling strata while simultaneously they create strains and stresses in the social system which they did not foresee. At the same time the functional consequences of many recent policy decisions create new areas of conflict within the system.

The Birth Rate, Womanpower, and the Social Structure

Official Nazi ideology in the early years of the Hitler regime stressed the need to rebuild the traditional paternalistic structure of the German family. The ideology of the "three K's" *(Kueche, Kinder, Kirche)*, which relegated the woman to the household and made her a good breeder, could in part be implemented in practice during the first years of absorption of unemployment.[3] In later years the demands of war production led to the gradual disappearance of this slogan, owing to a conflict between the needs of production and the subservient role of the woman in the household. Some Nazis then argued very logically that the family should be broken up completely. Furthermore, the Nazis also experienced great difficulty in reconciling their official family policy with the overriding aim of total control of the individual by the state. As Max Horkheimer states very well: "Although [the National Socialists] exalted the family in ideology as indispensable to a society based on the 'blood' principle, in reality they suspected and attacked the family as a shelter

2. See David J. Dallin and Boris Nicolaevsky, *Forced Labor in Soviet Russia* (New Haven: Yale University Press, 1944).

3. For Nazi family policies see, among others, Clifford Kirkpatrick, *Nazi Germany: Its Women and Family Life* (Indianapolis and New York: Bobbs-Merrill Co., 1938); Alfred Meusel, "National Socialism and the Family," *Sociological Review* (British) XXVIII (1936), 166–86, 389–411; Max Horkheimer (ed.), *Autoritaet und Familie* (Paris: Librairie Alcan, 1936).

against mass society. They looked on it as a virtual conspiracy against the totalitarian state."[4] The attempt of the Nazi state to claim a monopoly of loyalty conflicted with official family ideology. As a rapid increase in the birth rate was one of the key objectives of Nazi policy, the state attempted to remove the taboo on illegitimate children, thus contradicting the officially stressed sanctity of the family which was supposed to serve the same end. Reichsminister Frank revealed this contradictory attitude in one and the same speech, when he first defended the illegitimate child by stating that "everything is legal that is beneficent for the German people," only to continue: "National Socialism will surround the primary cell of the community of the people with all kinds of guarantees and legal protections."[5]

The situation faced by the Russian decision-makers is in many respects similar to that of the Nazis. Breeding is highly encouraged. Taxes for spinsters, bachelors, and families with less than three children are exceedingly steep, whereas mothers receive a nonrecurring government payment of 400 rubles upon the birth of the third child, 1,300 upon the birth of the fourth, with the premium gradually increasing to a premium of 5,000 upon the birth of the eleventh child. Furthermore, monthly allowances of 80 rubles for the fourth child to 300 rubles for the eleventh and subsequent children are paid by the government. There are also various decorations for "good breeders"—the "Motherhood Medal" for mothers with five to six children, the "Order of Motherhood Glory" for mothers of seven to nine children, and the title of "Heroine Mother" for mothers who have given birth to ten children.[6]

Yet Russia cannot permit the labor power of half the population to be "wasted." Every conceivable effort is made, on the contrary, to use as much womanpower as possible within industry and agriculture. The curve of employment of women has been going up virtually without interruption since 1929. In 1934 almost 32 percent of the Soviet labor force were women. During the war women comprised the majority of the labor force. More recent data indicate that 47 percent of wage- and salary-earners in all spheres of labor in 1947 were women.[7]

The living standard of the Russian workers has considerably decreased since 1928. The simplest way to increase the family's total wage income so as to offset the effect of falling real wages was to have more members of the worker's family join the labor force. According to official

4. In Ruth N. Anshen (ed.), *The Family, Its Function and Destiny* (New York: Harper & Bros., 1949), p. 374.

5. Quoted by Meusel, *op. cit.*, p. 186.

6. Text of the Family Law of July 8, 1944, in Rudolf Schlesinger (ed.), *The Family in the USSR* (London: Routledge & Kegan Paul, Ltd., 1949), pp. 367 ff.

7. *Pravda*, March 8, 1948, quoted by Solomon M. Schwarz, "The Living Standard of the Soviet Worker," *Modern Review*, II (June, 1948), 285. Cf. Judith Grunfeld, "Women's Work in Russia's Planned Economy," *Social Research*, IX (1942), 22–45.

Russian statistics, the number of dependents per gainful worker in workers' families decreased from 2.46 in 1927 to 2.05 in 1930, to 1.75 in 1932, and to 1.59 in 1935.[8] The legal working day, which was six to seven hours until 1940, is now considerably longer. Moreover, one to three hours of overtime are permitted; the standard work week is forty-eight hours; a working woman, therefore, stays away from her home for at least ten hours a day.[9]

While *Kueche, Kinder, Kirche* are perfectly compatible ideals, the three K's plus *Fabrik* are not.[10] The attempt to reconcile the rival demands upon the woman's time by building crèches, day camps for children, etc., is not made to overcome the contradictions stemming from rival definitions of the woman's role. Public child care keeps the child away from the family and thus weakens traditional family ties.

The new emphasis on the family also clashes with general economic conditions within Russia. To establish a stable family life, housing conditions must be such that they make possible at least a minimum of family privacy. Yet, Russian housing conditions always have been appalling and have further deteriorated since the war. In spite of this, construction of houses has received a relatively low priority in all five-year plans because of the primary concern with a rapid expansion of a modern productive apparatus. In 1932 the average urban dweller had only 20 square feet of living space. In Moscow in the same year a family of five had, on the average, two rooms, with not over forty square feet. All recent reports stress that housing conditions have considerably deteriorated since.[11]

The objection that members of the Russian family spend more time outside the house—in clubs, cafeterias, etc.—may be valid, but this would be only an added reason why the Russian planners will find it difficult to legislate a stable family into existence. The Western urban family, though no longer a productive unit, has maintained—in part, at least—its character as a unit of common consumption.

Housekeeping also is a quite different affair for the Russian housewife than for her American sisters. Efficient cooking and housekeeping devices are almost completely lacking except in the small upper stratum. A Russian study of time required for housekeeping which was conducted in the thirties showed that a woman wage-earner can devote less than a

8. Schwarz, *op. cit.*, pp. 272–85.

9. *Ibid.*, p. 278; see also R. Maurer, "Recent Trends in the Soviet Family," *American Sociological Review*, IX (1944), 242 ff.

10. At least not in a society which is characterized by low productivity and low standard of living. For a suggestive statistical treatment of similar problems in the United States see John D. Durand, "Married Women in the Labor Force," *American Journal of Sociology*, LII (November, 1946), 217–23.

11. Mildred Fairchild, "The Family in the Soviet Union," in Bernhard J. Stern (ed.), *The Family, Past and Present* (New York: D. Appleton–Century Co., 1938).

quarter of the time to the care of children than a full-time housewife can. The former spent 470 hours in preparing food; the latter, 997. The former spends 110 hours mending the family clothes; the latter, 228.[12]

One arrives at the startling conclusion that the economic basis for a stable family life, such as is required by the new Soviet ideology, can be found only among the families of the upper strata. The top bureaucrat can allow himself the luxury of a stable family life and of a Victorian morality. He has enough housing space, his wife does not have to work full time, his household equipment is more adequate and modern, and he can engage domestic help. To maintain a family that comes up to the official standards is a leisure-class activity.[13]

Establishment of a stable family unit as required by the Russian decision-makers encounters difficulties within the social structure, arising from the contradictory pressures of other institutions. Since Soviet legislators, propagandists, and ideologists generally belong to the upper socioeconomic strata, they tend to ignore the socioeconomic context in which the "common man," or, in this context, the "common woman," must move.

The Russian decision-makers seem to suffer from a contradictory attitude toward illegitimacy similar to that of the Nazis. Early legislation had done away with all legal distinctions between legitimate and illegitimate children,[14] thereby departing from the almost universal habit of discrimination against illegitimate children. With the strengthening of the family, the attitude toward illegitimate children has changed. Children of unmarried adults must now carry the mother's, not the father's, name, and the unmarried mother can no longer hold the father responsible for the support of the child. The new Soviet code has adopted the principle of the Code Napoléon: "La recherche de la paternité est interdite."

On the other hand, in order to foster an increase in the birth rate, the Soviet state now assumes support of children of unmarried mothers until the age of twelve and, in addition, allocates to them the regular assistance granted mothers with three or more children. Thus, childbearing out of wedlock might become a regular "profession," and the unmarried mother will be, under certain circumstances, definitely better off economically than her married sister.[15] We have here another instance in which measures primarily designed to boost the birth rate actually contradict the aim of stabilizing family relations and also interfere with the supply of "womanpower." This case is all the more startling, since measures for support to unmarried mothers and measures to stabilize marriage were

12. Dallin, *op. cit.*, p. 193.
13. Data on domestic services in the occupational statistics would be a most revealing index of the newly acquired privileges of the upper strata—if they were published. But Russian statistics included these data only for very few years, and each year showed an increase in domestic workers, whereupon these records were discontinued (*ibid.*, p. 174).
14. Fannina W. Halle, *Women in Soviet Russia* (New York: Viking Press, 1933), p. 154.
15. Schlesinger, *op. cit.*, esp. pp. 402 ff.

enacted in the same law of July 8, 1944. The "Heroines of Socialist Motherhood," even if their children are born out of wedlock, may make a significant contribution to the rise of the birth rate; but they will tend not to enter the labor force. If motherhood becomes a profession and if the legislator makes no discrimination between motherhood in or out of wedlock, one of the main props under the new family-strengthening legislation would seem to be removed at the same time as it was built.

The official explanation for the decree banning abortion in 1936[16] was that *(a)* it was to combat the "light-minded attitude toward the family and toward family obligations" and that *(b)* abortion was detrimental to the health of the women undergoing the operation. A Russian author defending the new law probably comes closer to the truth when he states: "Mass abortions resorted to for egoistic reasons are not to be tolerated. The Soviet state cannot countenance the fact that tens of thousands of women ruin their health and delay the growth of a new generation for socialist society."[17]

Apologists of the Russian regime suddenly discovered that the rate of abortions during the years when abortion was legal was such that it seriously threatened the birth rate. A few years before, they were diligently engaged in defending the then official attitude which legalized abortion and adduced facts to the contrary. They were right *then*. Legal abortions did not threaten to reduce the birth rate to the western European level,[18] but a further increase would, of course, be realized if abortion was outlawed.

Abortion is the most uneconomical means of preventing birth. If it was so widely resorted to by Russian women, at least in the cities, this was probably because contraceptives were not easily available. We do indeed learn from various authors that this is the case.[19] No wonder, then, that abortion, when legal, was extensively practiced at least among

16. This decree was the only law in the recent history of the Soviet Union that was submitted to public discussion before promulgation. Test votes were taken in factories and women's meetings, and the official press carried a number of letters pro and con. They showed heavy majorities against the law, at least in urban centers—whereupon the discussion was called off and the law promulgated by decree of December 27, 1936. For the text of the law, as well as the text of some of the published discussion, see Schlesinger, *op. cit.*, pp. 251–79; cf. Maurer, *op. cit.*

17. S. Wolfson in an article in *Pod Znamenem Marxisma*, quoted by Schlesinger, *op. cit.*, p. 310.

18. The annual birth rate in those years was about 37 per thousand, while it was considerably lower in most European countries. In Moscow there were between 20 and 30 abortions to every 100 births in the early twenties, while the number in Berlin in those same years was estimated at 54 (see Halle, *op. cit.*, pp. 143–44; Schlesinger, *op. cit.*, p. 175). The population of European Russia increased from 112 million in 1914 to 129 million in 1936, despite the exceedingly heavy losses during World War I, civil war, and the great famines.

19. Halle (*op. cit.*, p. 134) states: "For the time being preventatives are short in the Soviet Union; the demand for them considerably exceeds the supply." Milton Hindus, writing about a later period (in Ashen [ed.], *op. cit.*, p. 119), says: "Birth control remained legal but was frowned upon. Literature on the subject vanished. . . . Physicians were not forbidden to impart the necessary information to patients, but they were urged to use their influence to dissuade women from preventing childbirth."

urban women; no wonder either that after the imposition of the ban the number of registered births in nineteen sample cities increased from 33,796 for July–November, 1935, to 68,511 for the same period of the following year.[20]

In a totalitarian society in which mechanical means of contraception are scarce or unavailable, the birth rate will respond much more directly to the abolition of legal abortion than it will in a society in which contraceptives are accessible and where, moreover, the police system is less equipped to prevent illegal abortion on a mass scale.

The relatively high abortion rate in the cities during the twenties and thirties could easily be brought down by increased popularization of birth-control measures, if the aim had been the preservation of women's health. But Schuman is correct when he states: "Chronic labor shortage calls for more babies. Children are most numerous and most likely to grow into productive citizens where family life is stable."[21] He might have added that the upper strata are accustomed to the use of contraceptives and have the means to practice it; but the lower classes in this planned society are denied the means of planned parenthood. The law against abortion is indeed a rank example of what the Communists used to call "class legislation."

An American reporter overheard girls who were discussing the publication of the new family legislation say to each other: "Well, the new slogan means for women: children and not careers."[22] One wonders whether these girls and many like them are as loyally attached to the regime now as they may have been before.

The Social Position of Soviet Women

The Russian press still proclaims that the Soviet Union is the only country in which equality of the sexes has been realized. But such equality becomes a myth once a woman is called upon to become a breeder of as many children as possible without the means of restricting the number of births. Under such conditions, equality of opportunity in employment must also become a myth.

In this connection a far-reaching change in the system of education must be mentioned. Many observers have reported the great achievements of the Soviet educational system during the first years of the regime. This coeducational system was in great part responsible for helping millions of Soviet women to reach intellectual equality with men.

20. *Izvestia,* December 5, 1936, quoted by Frederick L. Schuman, *Soviet Politics at Home and Abroad* (New York: A. A. Knopf, 1946), pp. 338–39.
21. *Op. cit.,* pp. 338–39.
22. Richard E. Lauterbach, *These Are the Russians* (New York: Harper & Bros., 1945), p. 249.

But since 1943 coeducation no longer exists in the urban schools of the Soviet Union. Professor Eugene Medynsky of the Lenin Pedagogical Institute, writing in the *American Sociological Review*,[23] attempted a rather lame rationalization by stating that coeducation hinders the adaptation of the school program to the differences of physiological development of boys and girls; but he lets the cat out of the bag by adding that it also hinders the differentiation for the training of boys and girls for practical activity. As Lauterbach points out, *Izvestia* is considerably more frank when it states that, though boys and girls must have access to all professions and should be trained for them, girls must be educated to be loving and capable mothers and rearers of children, and that schools for girls must also develop femininity, modesty, and a sense of the great worthiness and honor of women.

The abolition of coeducation may also be connected with the emphasis on military training for boys, but the main reason seems to be the desire to have "a system by which the school develops boys who will be good fathers and manly fighters . . . and girls who will be intelligent mothers competent to rear the new generation."[24]

Once women are regarded primarily as mothers of future Soviet fighters, it is indeed inevitable that the standard of girls' schools will gradually be lowered, so that women will be handicapped in their attempts to compete with men in professional and other better-paid careers. The state still needs womanpower in industry but seems to have decided that, while the upper-class woman does indeed belong in the home, the lower-class woman does not belong, at least, in the better-paid positions.

The abolition of coeducation is an attempt to strengthen the upper-class family by removing the element of competition for occupational status between husband and wife. The gradual introduction of clearly defined sex roles is intended to remove all "invidious comparison" between husband and wife and to make the wife subservient to the husband. The woman cannot be dispensed with in the labor force, but at least she seems no longer needed in the prestigeful and economically rewarding professions. In the lower classes, on the other hand, the difference in education for men and women gives the men a slight chance of social mobility, in a society in which upward mobility becomes increasingly difficult.[25]

23. IX (1944), 287–95.

24. M. Tsulmer in *Soviet War News*, quoted by Schlesinger, *op. cit.*, p. 393.

25. It is certainly not accidental that in recent years such magazines as the *Soviet Woman*—a kind of Russian *Ladies Home Journal*—have made their appearance. These magazines feature articles on such topics as "Wrinkles Are Appearing—How Can I Prevent Them?" This is evidently an appeal to upper-class women; but it would have been horribly unthinkable twenty years ago, when the ethos of work still completely dominated all appeals to women (Waclaw Solsky, "The Soviet Press," *Modern Review*, II [June, 1948], 288).

Divorce legislation is a crucial index for evaluating the changing social position of women in Soviet society.

We can assume the facts of the case to be fairly well known. The earlier Soviet legislation, especially the Code of Laws on Marriage, Family, and Wardship, adopted in November, 1926,[26] established complete juridical equality between factual nonregistered marriage and registered marriage and made dissolution of the latter very easy. The state merely registered the dissolution of marriage, which was based on the free decision of the partners according to the decision of the supreme court that "for a court to concern itself with the conduct of either party in a divorce case would imply an utterly false interpretation of Soviet law." When no mutual agreement was reached, the fact of the dissolution was communicated to the other spouse within three days; if the address was unknown, notice in the pages of *Izvestia* at a nominal fee was all that was required.

The new Family Laws of July, 1944—published without any previous discussions—abolished the institution of *de facto* marriage and stated that thereafter only registered marriages would be recognized by the law. The new procedures for divorce are equivalent to the medieval pillory. The notice of divorce action must be advertised in a local newspaper at considerable expense. Compulsory entry of divorce is made in the home passports of man and woman. The proceedings take place in an open court, the People's Court, whose only task is to attempt to reconcile the couple, and where both parties must appear before proceedings can begin. The claimant has the right of appeal to the next higher court, which may or may not dissolve the marriage; and subsequent appeals to still higher courts are possible. But the fees are such that a divorce has become a luxury which the average citizen cannot possibly afford. It varies from 600 to 2,100 rubles (the average monthly earnings of the Soviet wage-earner have been estimated around 500 rubles at the beginning of 1948,[27] and many unskilled workers earn considerably less).

In August, 1944, the Russian press reported that, during the first month following promulgation of the new law, not a single petition for divorce had been filed throughout the whole U.S.S.R.;[28] according to a Russian author quoted by Schlesinger, statistics "show a rapid fall in the number of divorces."[29] One can well understand Monsignor Fulton Sheen's appreciation that "the family is higher in Russia than in the United States, and God, looking from heaven, may be more pleased with Russia than with us."[30]

26. For the text of the code and Russian discussions of its principles see Schlesinger, *op. cit.*, pp. 81–168; cf. Halle, *op. cit.*

27. Schwarz, *op. cit.*, p. 281.

28. Arthur Koestler, "Soviet Myth and Reality," in *The Yogi and the Commissar* (New York: Macmillan Co., 1945), p. 169.

29. Schlesinger, *op. cit.*, p. 380.

30. Quoted by Lauterbach, *op. cit.*, p. 248.

I know of no reports on the reception of the new divorce laws among the Russian population and especially among women; it would seem safe, however, to assume that the reaction of the Russian girls overheard by Lauterbach and quoted earlier is not untypical. It is superfluous to comment in detail on the consequences for the social position of women brought about by the practical impossibility of getting divorced. Any textbook on the family contains all the requisite arguments and data.[31]

Yet in this sphere also it seems that the Russian planners have been unaware of some of the consequences of their recent moves. The new laws will almost automatically lead to a significant increase in "free love" and concubinage, that is, the very things that the new legislation intended to combat. As divorce becomes almost impossible, many prospective couples will postpone marriage, preferring nonlegalized sex activities, especially since the state assumes the financial burden for illegitimate offspring. Had the Russian planners studied the sad experience of the Catholic church in Latin America, for example, they might have been wiser.

Moreover, in a country like the Soviet Union, where there is a high rate of enforced geographical mobility, where sudden transfers of workers from Moscow to the Urals are a frequent occurrence, easy divorce seems to be almost inescapable. If it is nevertheless impossible, the separation of partners will lead to customs which must conflict with the law. While such a conflict may have serious consequences even in a democratic society, it might lead to intolerable difficulties in a totalitarian society which is precisely built on the assumption that all activity of the individual must be controlled by the state. If the individual develops a "private sphere" outside of legislative and police control, this amounts to the weakening of one of the keystones of totalitarian structure.[32]

The Disruptive Effects of Sex

Uncontrolled sex relations deprive the ruling strata of society of important means of social control. A society which moves toward rigid hierarchical organization will therefore be concerned seriously with regulating and channeling sex relations.

The history of the Soviet state shows an uninterrupted line of development from a minimum of interference with sex relations to an almost puritanical horror of unregulated sexual activity. The parallelism

31. Hindus (*op. cit.*, p. 124) excellently summarizes the situation, at least as far as the legal norm is concerned: "For the present . . . freedom of action in sex and family life in Russia is as dead as the private ownership of the means of production."

32. It is not true that easy divorce procedures before the 1944 law led to significantly higher divorce rates than in the United States today. William Henry Chamberlin reports in his *Soviet Russia* (Boston: Little, Brown & Co., 1931), pp. 381–82, that there was in 1927, e.g., a ratio of about 1:4 in the proportion of divorces granted to marriages registered; this is roughly the ratio in this country today.

between this changing attitude toward sex and the increasing concern with rigid stratification need be no further elaborated.

The theories on "free love" of the first years of the Russian revolution are sufficiently well known not to require special elaboration here.[33] Lenin himself was concerned over the disruptive effects of "free love" as it was then preached and practiced among the younger generation, especially during the civil war period; other Bolsheviks shared this concern. Thus Kalinin, addressing the Comsomol in 1928, says: "Is it really permissible . . . that a man should marry six or seven times in the course of ten years? Mustn't there be responsibility between man and woman?"[34] Yet William Henry Chamberlin reports in 1929: "Despite these occasional admonitions from comrades of the older generation, 'free love' is still the rule rather than the exception among the city youth. Sex in Russia is a matter-of-fact affair, equally removed from the traditional sanctities and inhibitions of monogamous marriage and from artificial voluptuousness."[35]

However, since the middle thirties all media of mass communication in Russia try to instill strict sex mores. Russian spokesmen stress that "love is an act very different from simple biological relationship. Free love is a revolting practice, unworthy of Soviet society. 'Variety' must be provided by the wife herself, not by changing partners. Promiscuity leads to degradation. The monogamous family has a better chance under socialism than under capitalism. Successful physical relationships between partners are not the most important thing. Under full communism, the family will even grow stronger and more stable. . . . The sanctity of family ties is a fundamental bond which knits society into an invisible whole. . . . Sound society is unthinkable without a sound, economically secure family."[36]

Free love not only creates fortuitous associations which, by their very nature, are not subject to police control; it also may foster spontaneity in human relationships and human personality which is incompatible with the discipline demanded in a totalitarian society.

Just as all other family legislation, so the restrictions on sex activity serve to strengthen the authoritarian family. It is not possible here to go into a social-psychological analysis of the contributions that the authoritarian family structure with its accompanying sex restrictions can make to the authoritarian society,[37] but it seems fairly well established that this contribution is considerable.

33. See, e.g., Halle, *op. cit.*, pp. 109–37.
34. Quoted by Chamberlin, *op. cit.*, p. 327.
35. *Ibid.*
36. See, e.g., Alexander Werth, "Love and Marriage in Russia," *Nation*, April 24, 1948; Schlesinger, *op. cit.*; cf. Alex Inkeles, "Family and the Church in the Postwar USSR," *Annals of the American Academy of Political and Social Science*, CCLXIII (1949), 33–44.
37. For discussion of this relation see especially Horkheimer, *op. cit.*, and the work of Erich Fromm, especially *Escape from Freedom* (New York: Farrar & Rinehart, 1941).

However, the Russian decision-makers are unable to make the facts of the situation fit the desired objectives. Stringent legislation to insure the sanctity of marriage ties will in actual fact lead to an increase of free love. The state, by its very interference in the life of its citizens, must necessarily undermine a parental authority which it attempts to restore. Merton has pointed out that "social structure exerts a definite pressure upon certain persons in the society to engage in non-conformist rather than conformist conduct." [38] Will the Russian decision-makers be able to come to grips with the unanticipated consequences of their actions?

The Soviet Child and the Social Order

Reports—both nonfiction and fiction—on the earlier periods of the Soviet regime are replete with accounts of revolt of son against father, of the shaking-off by the young of the authority of the parents. In the early years of the regime the authority of the state and of the party decidedly took the side of the young against the old generation. Children were commended for denouncing the "counterrevolutionary tendencies" of their parents; parades of children against excessive drinking and other "antisocial" behavior of their fathers were common occurrences. The Communist movement fought the family as an enemy of the new social order, a bulwark against change, a seedbed for antistate tendencies.

In the middle thirties this policy also was completely revised. Trotsky's quip that the stabilization of the Russian family runs parallel with the stabilization of the ruble is indeed quite perceptive. As the hierarchical structure of society became stabilized, the child also had to be fitted more rightly into the social framework. The family is still considered a "bulwark against change" as before, and as such it is being strengthened now. The control function of parental authority and the strategic position of the parents for the inculcation of authoritarian norms are recognized and officially supported. [39] The legislator now sides with the parents, approving their attempts to uphold their authority.

Yet this strengthening of parental authority meets with serious obstacles, and a conflict between different forms of social control tends to arise. The totalitarian state aims at direct control over the individual from cradle to grave, from kindergarten via Comsomol and school to job. Only in this way can it hope to ascribe status directly to every individual in the system. On the other hand, no complete equivalent for the parental inculcation of authoritarian norms seems to be available, and the role of authority in the family is officially being stressed again. But then authority

38. Robert K. Merton, *Social Theory and Social Structure* (Glencoe, Ill.: Free Press, 1949), pp. 125–26.

39. For an excellent discussion of this problem in Western society see Kingsley Davis, "The Sociology of Parent-Youth Conflict," *American Sociological Review*, V (August, 1940), 523–35.

of the family must clash in many areas with the authority of the state. The Nazis also glorified the family, at least in the earlier period of their regime, yet they also competed with the parents for the loyalty of the children; they approved only a family in which all members were subservient to the state. This finally led to a situation graphically depicted in a joke then current in Germany: "What is the ideal German family? It's a family in which the father is a member of the party, the mother member of the Association of Nazi Women, the daughter belongs to the Association of German Girls and the son is in the Hitler Youth—they meet once a year at the Nazi congress in Nürnberg."[40] Nazi policies for family and youth attempted to strengthen the paternalistic family and at the same time attacked and weakened it. We see no reason why the Russian policy-makers should find it easier to escape these contradictions.

In totalitarian society, as Meusel says, all authority finally derives from the highest political power; the head of the family possesses authority over the children not because he is their father but because he is their leader. Whereas in feudal society political power was patterned on a family model, an exact reversal takes place in totalitarian society. Totalitarian regimes intensify the dependence of the family father upon the coercive power of the state and impress awareness of this dependence on the consciousness of the child as he enters very early into direct contact with the coercive forces of the state which shape the father's life.[41] The Russian child will find it difficult to accept a parental authority which—at least in the lower strata—seems so completely devoid of actual power of decision.

The Russian state makes an effort to synchronize a revived paternalistic family with a revival of a paternalistic school system. A new Code of Rules for Soviet Schools was adopted in 1943.[42] Some of the rules are: "Obey without question the orders of school principal and teacher. . . . Sit erect during the lesson period. . . . Rise as the principal or teacher enters or leaves the room. . . . Be polite to elders, respectful to school director and teacher. . . . Obey parents and assist in care of little brothers and sisters. . . . For violation of these rules, the pupil is subject to punishment, even to expulsion from school."

But what if "the care of brothers and sisters" interferes with Comsomol activites? Who is to be obeyed—the parent or the Comsomol leaders? If it is true, as Maurer states, that "increasingly the Soviets have come to regard the family as the hub where all other spokes of activity tie in,"[43] it would seem, however, that Comsomol, Young Pioneers, and

40. Quoted by Meusel, *op. cit.*
41. *Ibid.*, esp. p. 406. Our discussion at this point is essentially an application of Meusel's brilliant analysis to Russian conditions.
42. See William M. Mandel, *A Guide to the Soviet Union* (New York: Dial Press, 1946), p. 226.

Little Octobrists are equally if not more important hubs. If Russia wants to build up the authority of the family and yet does not relinquish direct state control over the child, the child must be torn between conflicting demands and cannot have the secure position that either predominant familial or predominant state authority could provide.

So far we have not considered the effects of class position on the position of the child in the Russian social structure. As Russian society moved farther away from an initial relative equality in class position, as the hierarchical structure of society hardened and vertical mobility decreased, the educational system had to be transformed. In early Soviet society free public education at all educational levels prevented rigidity in stratification. But free public education no longer exists in the Soviet Union.

Since 1940 a fee of 50 rubles ($10.00) a year is required in high schools. The fee for secondary schools amounts to from 150 to 200 rubles; for universities, from 300 to 500 rubles.[44] If we remember that the average monthly income of a wage-earner is 500 rubles—it was about 340 rubles in 1940, when free public education was abandoned—it is easily apparent that the social and economic status of the family again has become a crucial determinant of the future of the child. Higher education becomes the privilege of people who can afford it. There are scholarships and stipends, of course, but these are awarded upon conditions that often are harsher than in capitalist countries. Moreover, they are granted only to students in technical or specialized secondary schools; students in academic secondary schools—normal gateways to higher education—are granted no stipends. Hence students from poorer families tend to gravitate toward technical schools, while the upper-class child has a considerably better chance to pursue a higher education.

The decree of 1940 only further reinforced a trend which began earlier. Schwarz gives the following percentages showing the decline of the proportion of manual workers and their children in higher education:[45]

	1933	1935	1938
Universities	50.3	45.0	33.9
Secondary schools	41.5	31.7	27.1

The percentages for industrial colleges, gateways to key managerial positions, are even more revealing:

	1938
Manual workers and their children	43.5
Peasants and their children	9.6
Bureaucracy—specialists and their children	45.4

43. Maurer, *op. cit.*
44. Mandel, *op. cit.*, esp. pp. 224 and 234; cf. Inkeles, "Stratification and Mobility in the Soviet Union," *op. cit.*, pp. 473–76.
45. Solomon M. Schwarz, "Heads of Russian Factories," *Social Research,* IX (1942), 323–24.

Up to one million children whose parents cannot afford the fees for secondary schools, on the other hand, are annually conscripted to four years of compulsory labor service.[46] They are given vocational training for six months to two years and are then required to work four more years wherever directed.

Hence, the degree of authority of the parent depends upon his social position: if the father is made to pay for the schooling of the son, the latter will be less inclined to disregard the father's authority. The children of lower-class families, on the other hand, are taken away from the family into the custody and control of the state.

The limiting of educational opportunities means a shift away from an open class system to a structure in which ascribed status gains over achieved status. This may be adequate for stabilizing a hierarchical social system, but the price to be paid may be very high. Can a society as poor in qualified human resources as the Soviet Union afford to waste potential human resources in order to assure status to its ruling strata?

The new educational policy serves to assure inheritance of social status through transmission of skills and connections. This is in tune with the revival of the principle of inheritance, as laid down in the Soviet Constitution of 1936, which assures transmission of wealth from parents to children, thus canceling the early Soviet measures which abolished inheritance by law or will and all life insurance.[47] The 1936 constitution legally re-established inequality at birth. Inheritance has been legalized again, life insurance reinstalled, and the right of unrestricted disposal of property by last will guaranteed to each individual. Well-to-do citizens are encouraged to buy policies from the State Insurance Trust, the minimum premium being fixed at 5,000 rubles.[48]

The upper-class family has assumed again a most important status-ascribing function. But what repercussions will this have on the attitudes of millions of lower-class youngsters whose loyalty was in part due to the open opportunities which the regime provided in its first period?

In conclusion, we may say that the family policy in Soviet Russia serves to stabilize the upper class. But in other strata it meets with stresses and strains which may well prove to impair the smooth functioning of the total system.

Postscript 1962

Post-Stalinist Russia has witnessed a number of changes in family policy. Most of these represent measures of "liberalization" in tune with the

46. Inkeles, "Stratification and Mobility in the Soviet Union," *op. cit.,* pp. 473–75.
47. After the death of a person, his mobile and immobile property became state property, with certain exceptions in the case of farm property.
48. Koestler, *op. cit.,* pp. 148–49.

general orientation of Khrushchev's Russia. The two major reform measures concern areas that I considered likely to produce high amounts of strain among Soviet women:

1. The attempt to separate the sexes in the educational system——never fully applied in the first place except in big cities—has been given up. The school system is again coeducational.

2. A law of November 23, 1955, repealed the law of 1936 and provided that abortions, if performed by a doctor in a hospital, are lawful.

It would seem that in both cases the reasons for this reform are to be sought in the need to utilize female labor power to the full and hence in some measure to take account of the wishes and desires of women.

Many other reforms of the family law have been heatedly discussed in the Soviet press. But the promised revision has still not been forthcoming. This might be an indicator of the high degree of tension stemming from contradictory functional requirements in this area, to which I referred in my paper. Two reforms have been especially called for:

1. The divorce laws are being liberalized, with lower fees and the legalization of *de facto* divorces and of separation agreements between the spouses. The main justification advanced for such a reform stresses, as I had predicted, that the stringent divorce laws have led to a multitude of *de facto* unions and to an increase in the number of technically illegitimate children.

2. The demand is being made that the discriminations against illegitimate children which the 1944 Family Law created be abolished. A number of Soviet authors now stress that children whose birth certificates leave the name of the father empty are being discriminated against in occupational and social life. They also stress that this legislation discriminates against unmarried mothers and puts them into an inferior position vis-à-vis the father.[49]

The post-Stalinist decision-makers have not given up the aim of strengthening the Russian family, but they have made concessions—and might be prepared to make further concessions—whenever the need to utilize manpower to the full and to mobilize the maximum popular support requires "liberalization."

Postscript 1974

During the last decade a number of significant parallels between developments in the family sphere in the United States and the USSR have become apparent:

1. There has been a striking increase in Soviet divorce rates; they are

49. Cf. R. Schlesinger, "Proposed Changes in Family Law," *Soviet Studies*, VIII, 4 (April, 1957) 453–57.

now among the highest in the world and only slightly below American rates. While in 1950 the U.S. rate was 2.6 (per thousand population) and the Soviet rate was only 0.4, the Soviet rate for 1969 was 2.6 as against a U.S. rate of 3.2.

2. Similarly, contraceptive devices now being easily available in the Soviet Union, and abortion again being legal, Soviet birth rates have significantly declined over the past decade and now approximate American rates. The Soviet rate was 31.2 (per thousand population) in 1940 and 26.7 in 1950. It declined to 17.2 by 1968, thus being slightly lower than the U.S. rate of 17.5 that same year.

3. Although Soviet ideology continues to stress Communist commitment to equality between the sexes, and although the expansion of women's participation in the occupational world and in educational institutions as well as the increase in day-care centers and maternity benefits represent positive steps in this direction, there remains a very wide gap between the goal of full equality and the actual status of women. Currently women are over half the wage- and salary-earners in the Soviet Union, but they form but a fifth of Communist Party members, 5 percent of those holding ministerial posts in the various Soviet republics, 1 percent of the Council of Ministers of the USSR, and zero percent of the summit in the Politbureau. Similarly, while over 75 percent of the physicians in the USSR are women, 50 percent of all chief physicians and medical executives are men. Women constitute about four-fifths of all schoolteachers, but less than 30 percent of all school principals. Thirty-nine percent of all scientific workers are women, but they form 50 percent of the assistants, 26 percent of the research associates, 21 percent of the professors, and but 10 percent of the members of the prestigious Academy of Science. While women make up one-half of the industrial labor force, they serve as supervisors, shop chiefs, etc., one-sixth to one-seventh as frequently as men.

In addition, though most Soviet women are fully employed, they continue to carry the main burden of household work. These burdens are accentuated by the fact that modern household appliances are still relatively rare in the Soviet Union. Among working class families, 15 percent have washing machines, 17 percent refrigerators, and 20 percent vacuum cleaners. Now Soviet sociologists have recently begun to admit that the "double burden" of being a housewife and a breadwinner is still typically imposed on Soviet women. Writes G. Rowina: "Research has convinced us that the possibilities for liberating women from the 'double burden' are being realized only in small degree. As a result of women's entry into production, negative consequences have accompanied the positive ones: worsened physical and psychological conditions, lowered general tone of conjugal and family life, restriction of social and cultural contacts." Since household work is not typically shared between men and women, Soviet women have considerably less free time (and even sleep less) than Soviet men. Soviet men and women may be formally equal, but the men are considerably more equal than the women. In the Soviet Union sexual stratification is at least as pronounced as general social stratification.[50]

50. The above data are mainly derived from Soviet publications as quoted in Seymour Martin Lipset and Richard B. Dobson, "Social Stratification and Sociology in the Soviet Union," *Survey* (London) III (Summer, 1973), 114–84, and Paul Hollander, *Soviet and American Society* (New York: Oxford University Press, 1973), pp. 245–99.

C. K. Yang

The Chinese Family:
The Young and the Old

The struggle for freedom of marriage and divorce represented a rebellion of the young against parental authority over the arrangement of the children's marriage and their married life, but the ascendance of the young and the retreat of the old resulting from this rebellion concerned more than parental authority over children's marriage. These influences undermined the structure of traditional family authority in general. If the change in the form of marriage mainly affected the roles of the married sons in relation to the roles of the parents and other family members, the undermining of family authority by the rise of the young affected the general structure of the entire traditional family organization, for it altered the role of practically every member in the family and changed the mode of family integration. There is hardly a more significant aspect of the Communist revolution than the attempt to shift the foci of power from the old to the young in the family as well as in society in general.

The Traditional Age Hierarchy and the
System of Family Status and Authority

In the traditional structure of family status and authority age was a leading factor. The Five Cardinal Relations, the basic principles of family organization, taught that family members should be arranged into "proper order by their age." The importance of age was clearly pointed out by Mencius' statement: "In the Kingdom there are three things that command universal respect. Nobility is one of them; age is one of them; virtue is one of them. In courts nobility is first of the three; in local communities age is first; but for helping one's generation and presiding over the people the other two are not equal to virtue."[1] The organization of the local community was centered upon the kinship group, hence the supremacy of age. Elsewhere in Confucian teachings, upon which generations of Chinese down through the centuries have been reared, the importance of

---

1. Meng Tzu, Book II, Part II, ch. 2. The quotation represents a slight alteration by the author from James Legge's translation, *The Works of Mencius*, pp. 213–214.

age as a factor in family status and authority was elaborated and emphasized with tireless repetition. A modern middle-aged Chinese today still retains vivid childhood memories of being ceaselessly reprimanded for not having observed the age line and for showing disrespect to those senior to him. Such reprimands are so much a part of an individual's upbringing that he finds it difficult later in life to address even older friends and senior colleagues by their first name, preferring to call them by their surnames with the prefix of *sen sheng* (the English equivalent of mister), literally meaning "born earlier," or *hsiung,* meaning elder brother.

This "proper order by age" formed the foundation for hierarchy of status and authority in the traditional Chinese family. In its kinship connotation age implied two factors, generation and chronological age. The generational structuring of Chinese kinship members has been analyzed by H. Y. Feng in his *Chinese Kinship System.* He says, "The architectonic structure of the Chinese kinship system is based upon two principles: lineal and collateral differentiation, and generation stratification. The former is a vertical and the latter a horizontal segmentation. Through the interlocking of these two principles every relative is rigidly fixed in the structure of the whole system."

The status and authority of family members were defined first by the stratified successive generational layers[2] . . . and, second, by chronological age. Thus all members in a senior generation enjoyed higher status and authority than those in a junior generation, and, among members in each differentiated group of relatives of the same generational level (as represented by each square in the chart), older members took precedence over younger ones. A third factor in the situation was the proximity of biological relatedness or kinship. This was what Feng calls vertical segmentation based on lineal and collateral differentiation. . . . Ego was under heavier pressure from the status and authority of members closer to him in kinship and senior to him in both generation and physical age than with members of the same generational and age seniority but more distant to him in kinship. Ego's status and authority over members junior to him in generation and chronological age was also graduated by the proximity or distance of kinship. Thus Ego's relation to lineal relatives was closer than to collateral relatives, and the closeness of Ego's relation to collaterals was in inverse proportion to the number of collateral degrees. Ego's relation to a patrilineal relative was closer than to a corresponding matrilineal relative. It was an important part of a child's education to learn to recognize and distinguish the degree of *ch'in* (closeness) and *su* (distance) in his contacts with his kinsmen as a basis for the proper amount of deference or obedience to be shown to them. In this respect, kinship relations take on the form of a series of concentric circles with

2. See Han-yi Feng, "The Chinese Kinship System," *Harvard Journal of Asiatic Studies,* II (July, 1937), pp. 141–275 [Ed.].

Ego as the center—hence the foremost place for parents-children and sibling relationships in the Confucian system of family ethics.

The interlocking operation of these three factors, generation, age, and proximity of kinship, resulted in a system of status and authority that assigned to every person in the kinship group a fixed position identified by a complex nomenclature system.[3] The identification of status for distant relatives was facilitated by giving the same middle name to all sons born into the same generational level so that the kinship position of a person could be readily identified by the generational name whenever distant members met. An important feature of this system was that it could fit a kinship group of any size, from a small conjugal family to a vastly extended family like a clan with ten thousand or more members, thus giving the small family a ready organizational framework for expansion whenever economic conditions permitted.

This hierarchy of status and authority imposed strong compulsion on the individual to observe his own place in the group through, among other factors, the operation of the mores of filial piety and veneration of age. Filial piety demanded absolute obedience and complete devotion to the parents, thus establishing the generational subordination of the children. In traditional society an individual from childhood to the end of his life was completely immersed in an atmosphere which compelled the observation of filial piety. The lesson of filial piety was carried in nursery stories, in daily exhortations and reprimands, in tales and novels, in textbooks from the first primer to the most profound philosophical discourse, in the numerous "temples of filial sons and chaste women" (chieh hsiao tz'u) which studded the land, in dramatized living examples of extremely filial children.

The requirement of obedience to parents, fully supported by formal law in the Ching dynasty before 1912,[4] is still supported by the informal coercive instrument of clan regulations in the rural communities and even by "unregenerated" local officials in the Communist government, whose judgment of civil cases is frequently based more on social institution than on the already changed formal law. Under traditional social order it took exceptional courage and imagination to be an unfilial son.

To be sure, coercion was not the only means by which filial piety was instilled into the individual's mind. Equally important was the emphasis upon parental affection, parent-children interdependence, the children's

3. Feng's study gave 41 groups of relatives each with a distinct category of kinship terminology. Ch'ing Wei Lu (A Collection of Nomenclature) in volumes 1 to 8, gave 160 different kinship terms, with each term capable of further subdivision by the ranking of physical age. As Feng did not use the Ch'ing Wei Lu in his research, there may be some disagreement between his results and the listing in the Ch'ing Wei Lu. Nevertheless, both works show vast numbers of people that could be included in the traditional hierarchy of status and authority based primarily on the factors of generation, age, and proximity of kinship.

4. See Ch'ü T'ung-tsu, Chung-kuo fa-lu yü Chung-kuo sheh-hui (Law and Chinese Society), Kunming, 1944.

moral obligation to repay parental care and affection by observing filial piety. Parental affection and feelings of gratitude were very active factors, for Chinese parental affection toward the children is traditionally both genuine and strong. In the old family institution the parents depended upon the children for their old-age security; hence their deep devotion to the care and upbringing of the children. Where the parents belonged to a humble station, they pinned their hopes of social and economic advancement on the future development of the children, particularly the son, another basis for the strong traditional affection toward children. Consequently, the old family structure and ethics did not permit a son to leave his parents in a humble social position when he himself had gained social and economic advancement, the basis for the automatic granting of honorific titles by the imperial government to parents of sons who had won social distinction by passing the traditional civil service examinations.

Dependence upon the children, especially the sons, was particularly strong with the mother. Since her status in the family depended upon the bearing of male heirs, it was not uncommon in traditional society for a mother to sacrifice her health, at times even her life, for the benefit of the children, especially the sons. The writer was told in his boyhood that an aunt contracted tuberculosis and finally died from it on account of her sacrifice for and worry over her son. It matters little whether that was the real cause of her illness and death; what is important was the significance the story had for inducing a feeling of filial piety among the young. The poor family selling property and undergoing extreme sacrifice to give the son an education reflected the same principle.

In recent decades, the once strong parent-children interdependence has been steadily diminished by the increasingly individualistic development of children, the elevation of the social and economic status of the young, the separation of married sons from the parental household through the new form of marriage, the decreasing significance of the family as a basic unit of economic production, and the gradual shifting of the individual's center of loyalty away from the family. These factors, which have an adverse effect on the value of children as an asset to the parents, plainly tend to dilute traditional parental devotion. In addition, the rise of democratic and individualistic trends in the Republican period resulted in widespread resentment against the oppressive features of filial piety which required absolute obedience, devotion, and sacrifice on the part of children. Thus filial piety, once the most emphatically stressed value in the traditional social order for over two thousand years, was subjected to open challenge in the 1920's, gradually lost its sacred and binding character among the modern intellectuals by the 1930's, and, by the time the Communists became the ruling power, was publicly discredited by them as feudalistic, designed for the exploitation of the young.

While the functioning of filial piety was limited to relationships between parents and children, the veneration of age was traditionally a means of inspiring respect and obedience by the young toward all the other senior members of the family and society as a whole. To demonstrate the glory and prestige of age, an individual's sixtieth birthday and every subsequent tenth birthday were celebrated with a feast and ceremony as elaborate and impressive as the family and close relatives could possibly afford. This ritualistic glorification symbolized increased respect for the person's status and authority and implied a greater consideration of his personal needs by others.[5] In vital matters of the family and community his advice was heeded, although he might no longer have the heavy family responsibilities or the actual compelling power of his younger days. The old grandfather and, to a lesser degree, the old grandmother were frequently the only ones in the family who could restrain a despotic or wayward father, relying upon the support of the mores and law for their authority. The seat of honor on family and community occasions was for the old man. Not only did the family try to give him the best material benefits in food and clothing; the clan also accorded him honor. In the southern provinces of Kwangtung and Kwangsi, where the distribution of pork to male clan members was a token of clan membership and status, he was given a double share. He was at the pinnacle of the age hierarchy.

The social logic for this practice was the consideration of old people as a symbol of wisdom. In a society of empirical knowledge and predominant illiteracy the old person had the advantage of experience. He had traversed the greater part of a life cycle and so had seen the operation of major crises in life from routine matters of birth, marriage, and death to other happenings such as major clashes between family members, devastation of wars, visits of natural calamities such as flood and droughts, or the appearance of a portentous star in the skies. When younger people were stunned by a happening, an older person remained calm and knew what to do. He knew the procedure for handling the birth of a baby, the marriage of the young, the burial of the dead, the settlement of a dispute in accordance with the traditional sense of justice, and the safe direction in which to flee when calamity struck. His stock of common sense even included the administration of medicine to the sick. An "old man of worldly affairs" was the guiding hand of the family and the community. His "I have lived longer than you" was the ready and effective reminder to the occasionally disrespectful young.

Where empiricism and illiteracy prevailed, age was also an asset in technical fields. In every traditional craft, the "old master" was most respected, not the brilliant and vigorous young worker. In agriculture his experience was similarly valued by the community. In 1949 the writer

5. See the presentation of this point in Marion J. Levy, Jr.'s *The Family Revolution in Modern China*, Cambridge, 1949, pp. 127–133.

tried to introduce into a village an improved weeder which worked much more effectively than hand weeding or hoeing. The younger peasants tried it and liked it very much, but a few days later nobody wanted to use the new instrument because "the old people concluded that it will hurt the root system of the plant." The writer challenged the younger peasants to experiment with the instrument by offering to pay for any damage resulting from it, but to no avail. Confucius' advice of learning to farm from an "old farmer" still stood firm.[6] From handicraft to farming, the "old master" was the model of skill and knowledge. There were few books and no school of technical training in traditional society. The old master taught and advised and laid down rules for the young to follow. He led the family and the community in economic matters.

Thus old people in traditional society were far from being decrepit seniles living off the kindness of society on empty prestige, for age had very practical significance for both the family and the community. The veneration of age not only compelled respect for the aged but also lent prestige to all senior members in the hierarchy of age.

Functioning through the strength of filial piety and veneration of age, the hierarchy of age served to provide a status system for the operation of family authority, to firmly initiate the young into the institution of family life until they reached full maturity, to establish security for the old, and to impress upon the individual the dominance of the family as a corporate body. The long stability of the traditional family institution was due in no small measure to the successful operation of this factor.

But such stability was achieved at the price of strenuous repression of the young and was weakened when it came under fire from modern ideologies and social movements that advocated equality and freedom, particularly freedom for the young. Under the weight of the age hierarchy, the status of the young was indeed low, at times helpless. The authority of parents over the child was absolute. Infanticide, approved by the community, was an expression of it; and even as the child grew older, the parents' threat against his life was by no means completely eliminated. The proverb "The son must die if so demanded by the father" was a means of compelling obedience from the young in traditional China, especially in rural communities, although the carrying out of the threat was extremely rare. A childhood that passed without frequent physical punishment was an exception rather than the rule. When a child reached his mid-teens, his increased physical strength and his ability to run away bolstered his security, but the requirement of filial piety kept a tight rein on him. The necessity of observing this moral code was not merely impressed upon him in the operation of the family institution and group pressure of the community; it was also enforced by formal law. In the

6. Fan Tz'u asked Confucius how to farm, and the reply was, "I do not know as much as an old farmer." See Confucius, *Analects,* Book XIII, ch. 4.

Ch'ing period sons were flogged or banished by the court merely on the charge of disobedience brought by the father.[7]

In the Republican period few such cases came to public attention, but the rigid enforcement of filial piety by the clans was not much relaxed in places where the clan organization was strong, such as in rural communities in the Central-South provinces. It is interesting to note that P'eng Teh-huai, a prominent Communist general, was once close to being condemned to death by his clan on the charge of being unfilial to his stepmother.[8] In the writer's own boyhood in the 1920's there was still the frequent verbal threat of being taken back to the ancestral village "to be drowned in a pig's cage by the clan elders" in case of gross disobedience to the parents—although he lived in the city, where the clan wielded no direct influence. Such legal and social pressures drove fear and a feeling of rigid subordination deep into the mind of the young individual.

Although less absolute and rigid than parental dominance over the children, the pressure of status and authority of senior members over junior members in the age hierarchy was by no means light. This was especially so with members of one's own superior generation having a close degree of kinship tie, such as one's grandparents and older uncles. Before them one behaved only with great respect, and one did not argue with or talk back to them. In material rights and privileges their share undisputably came first. On ceremonial occasions one stood or sat in an inferior position to them. They were the "respected elders" even though some of them might not actually be chronologically older. They were held up to the young as models of good conduct, as masters of arts and skills. Before a person reached the age of thirty his words had little weight; his conduct and his work were under constant criticism by senior kinsmen around him. Not until the fourth decade in one's life would one begin to gain serious consideration from senior members in the age hierarchy.

Rise of the Young Under the Republic

The practical value of age as a major basis for the great respect of the age hierarchy began to be challenged with the impact of revolutionary currents early in this century. The dominant note of the modern times has been the acquisition of Western knowledge and technological skills and the development of new institutions to implement Western-inspired ideas in an effort to save China in the struggle for national existence; and these could not be acquired simply by experience in the traditional social environment. The only means of acquiring them were through learning

7. See *Ch'ing-ch'ao Hsu Wen-hsien T'ung-k'ao* (Compendium of Documents of the Ch'ing Dynasty), Shanghai, 1934, ch. 242, p. 9861.
8. Edgar Snow, *Red Star Over China*, New York, 1944, p. 292.

and training in schools and through new sources of information; and the required method of developing them, in China as elsewhere, was through science, not empiricism enriched by age.

In the acquisition of new knowledge, new skills, and new ideas the young (those from families capable of affording a modern education) had a distinct advantage over the old. The young had plasticity of mind, eagerness for the new and the adventurous, fewer obstacles in the consciousness of vested interests and entrenched traditional social relationships. Above all, rigid repression of the young by the hierarchy of age gave them an eagerness to alter their old status by acquiring new knowledge and skills and by promoting the adoption of new institutions. Hence, the modern educated young Chinese formed a nucleus from which new influences germinated and gradually developed into leading forces in political, economic, and social trends. The young were no longer bowing to the old at every turn, and age was no longer always a mark of personal prestige and social authority.

Over the past half century every political revolution and social development has acted as a new force in expanding the number and influence of the modern educated young. In the course of its limited success in encouraging revolutionary ideas championed by the young the Republican revolution of 1911 put a larger number of young elements into prominent political positions than there ever had been under the old imperial government. In the turbulent years of 1917 to 1919 the young were presented to the nation as a distinctive age group under the term "new youth" by the rising crescendo of the youth movement, culminating in the May 4th Movement of 1919, which placed the educated young in a position of new importance in political and cultural fields. Led by the historic periodical, *Hsin Ch'ing-nien* (The New Youth), tons of literature in the form of magazines, press articles, and pamphlets poured forth on the subject of the new youth and its problems, forcing the new age group to the nation's attention. Political and economic crises of the period, the necessity of new means for their solution, together with the impotent traditionalism of the old and the general illiteracy of the common people, created a new role for the modern educated youth and led them to demand revision of the subordinate status of the young. For the first time a powerful social and political movement put up a young group in opposition to the old and the institutions the latter stood for.

When the Second Revolution swept the country in the mid-1920's, the revolutionary regime based in Canton was marked by the youthfulness of the personnel that staffed it. Every branch of the new political machine that baffled and at times frustrated the old was led and manned mainly by young men and colored by the outlook of youth. The occasional presence of an old man over sixty in their midst was a spectacle, for here was "an old dog that had learned new tricks." When the seat of political power, the center of formal social control, was captured by the young, the sanctity of the age hierarchy could not be expected to remain intact.

In the cultural field the "Renaissance" of the May 4th Movement was a product of the young, and by the mid-1920's it had made deep inroads into the educational system of the country, particularly in the storm center of the South. The quantity of "New Culture" publications in all fields had by that time distinctly pushed Confucian classical works to the side, at least in the cities. The new literature, particularly in works of fiction, clearly steered away from the traditional motif of fairy tales and from Confucian themes and drew its inspiration from Western ideas that concerned the special problems of the young. Its undisputed literary dominance together with its modern theme of romantic love led the educated young and indirectly the younger generation in general, toward an outlook of life and love which retained little respect for the age hierarchy and frequently held little consideration at all for the old.

In the economic field accelerated industrial development after World War I gave increasingly responsible positions to the young, who alone commanded modern technical qualifications. Technical dreams of the young set the blueprints for the nation's economic development. The "old master's" prestige declined with the diminishing importance of the traditional crafts under the crushing superiority of modern technology. The old master still held sway in the vast pre-industrial sector of the country's economic structure, but his technical competence no longer commanded the moral respect of the educated young, and his outmoded technical role could no longer support the age hierarchy in that modernized segment of the population which was leading the trend of economic development. The social and economic plight of the growing army of unemployed old craft masters was hardly conducive to the effective maintenance of age as a criterion of technical competence.

The older generation watched in bewilderment the making and unmaking of governments, the waging of the unending civil wars, the ever-rising prestige of new commodities and new economic organizations, the unfamiliar events that occupied increasing space in the newspapers and in the people's daily conversations, the untraditional ways of training and educating the young—all these changes staged by a group that had hitherto been in an inferior position in the age hierarchy forced society to grant more consideration to the young. In the family, if the young still paid a measure of respect to parents and senior members in the age hierarchy, it was done with a tinge of begrudging formality and seldom with the spontaneous sincerity and voluntary devotion formerly developed by filial piety and veneration of age.

The vital change of attitude toward age was limited largely to the modern educated young, the new youth, but the new youth were an articulate group playing a stategic role in the shaping of social trends. The facilities of modern education were rapidly expanding, with its middle and primary levels steadily extending to members of the lower middle class, and the mass education movement which started after the May 4th Movement of 1919 served as another vehicle for the diffusion of the new attitude into a small part of the working class and the peasantry. Largely centered in urban areas, the change affected also the young elements of the richer portion of the rural population as they took to the cities for better educational facilities, where their attitude toward the traditional age hierarchy was altered by absorbing new ideas and by insulation from the immediate pressure of parents and senior kinsmen at home.

When the great upheaval of the 1920's settled down to a divided course in the 1930's, with the Kuomintang dominating the nation and the Communist Party setting up red areas in the South, the traditional Chinese attitude toward the age hierarchy had already been substantially diluted. The two decades that followed saw the continued extension of the new influence to growing numbers of the young, aided by the increased absence of the young of all social classes from home in a period of increasing population mobility, which freed the younger generation from the immediate pressure of the age hierarchy in the kinship system. In the early 1930's such mobility was mainly a consequence of the accelerated development of urbanism, which set many of the young on the move from home for jobs or educational opportunities. After 1937 the Japanese invasion drove millions far from their local communities, and the young were left free to develop the new attitude toward age with a minimum of immediate interference from older kinsmen. Thus, long before 1949 the ground had been prepared for the developments under communism.

Status of the Young Under the Communist Regime

The triumph of the Communist revolution carried the exaltation of the young to a new height. If youth furnished the vital force of China's previous revolutions, it certainly did so even more emphatically with the Communist revolution. Its radical ideological departure from tradition first found acceptance only in the more plastic young minds, and the Communists possessed great skill in organizing the young for the service of the revolution.

The elevation of the status of the young under the Communist regime has been, first of all, a highly organized movement, not a spontaneous development. Secondly, that movement has spread from the hitherto confined circle uf upper- and middle-class young intelligentsia to the numerically large group of young workers and peasants. For some three decades before Communist accession to power youth organizations had had a steady growth, but they were comparatively small in membership and poorly integrated. Under the Communist regime youth organizations have been vastly expanded in membership, centrally directed, and well-disciplined.

The New Democratic Youth League is an example. According to statistics of September 1951, its national membership had reached 5,180,000—twenty-seven times the membership figure of 190,000 of April 1949. There were 24,200 branches in various parts of the country. Classification of the membership was as follows: workers, 33.88 percent; peasants, 51.18 percent; students, 11.44 percent; others, 2.5 percent. Females accounted for about 30 percent of the total. By 1957 the League membership had leaped to 23,000,000, "accounting for 19.17 percent of the total number of young people in China."[9]

It is notable that students who monopolized the youth movement in the pre-Communist period now comprise only a little over one-tenth of the membership of the most important organization of the young under the Communist regime. In this respect, the Democratic Women's League, with its vast network of affiliated organizations, also has a fast expanding membership, the majority of whom are now women peasants and workers, not intellectuals. Above all, the Chinese Communist Party itself, which has experienced a phenomenal growth in membership since 1949, is dominated numerically by the young, who are drawn mainly from the peasantry and the workers, only a minority coming from the urban intelligentsia.

Young organizations and other organizations containing a majority of young members serve a variety of purposes, among which is the conscious and unconscious function of advancing the power and status of the young. In this sense, these organizations have the significance of representing a formally organized struggle, aided by political power, to alter the status of the young in the traditional age hierarchy.

Organized struggle for status by the young is actively advanced by the publication of literature on the subject of youth in unprecedented quantity. Let us consider the publishing activities of the New Democratic Youth League in 1951 alone: "For the purpose of propaganda and education, the Youth League publishes 61 newspapers and periodicals for its general membership throughout the nation. The Youth Publication Company under the Central Committee of the Youth League, which was established in 1950, has published 14 categories and 260 kinds of book series and periodicals, which total 8,800,000 copies. *Chung-kuo Ch'ing-nien pao* (Chinese Youth), the daily newspaper serving as the official organ of the Central Committee of the Youth League, will be published on April 27 of this year (1951). *Chung-kuo Ch'ing-nien Shuang-chou-k'an* (Chinese Youth Biweekly), also an organ of the Youth

9. Feng Wen-pin, "Present Conditions and Work of the Youth League," *Ch'ang-chiang Daily*, January 8, 1952, p. 4; New China News Agency, Peking, May 12, 1957.

League's Central Committee, is among the most widely circulated periodicals in the country." [10]

If the youthfulness of the personnel of the Southern revolutionary regime in the mid-1920's had the effect of elevating the status of the young, the same is even more true of the present Communist regime. Although the top leaders of this regime are generally older than their counterparts in the mid-1920's, Mao Tse-tung and the majority of the leading party figures started their political career in close connection with youth organizations. [11] The three decades of struggle for power advanced their age, but it did not lessen their identification with the cause of youth.

As for the middle- and lower-ranking party members who form the lower echelon of the Communist regime, the average age level is lower than that of corresponding personnel in any previous Chinese government. A government announcement on the recruitment of young men and women for training to be junior officers in police work listed an age limit of eighteen to twenty-three. [12] Similar age limits for other types of political work can be seen in other recruiting announcements. Young men in their twenties and thirties head local government departments that concern the vital interests of tens of thousands of people. In urban neighborhood and village indoctrination and propaganda meetings it is the young leaders who do the talking and lay down the line, and it is the older people who have to do the listening and following. In enforcing policies, be it a bond sales campaign, suppression of counterrevolutionaries, mass trial of landlords and local bullies and the redistribution of land, the Five-Anti movement against businessmen committing bribery, evasion of taxes, theft of state property, cheating on state contracts and theft of confidential state economic information, or a score of other major and minor movements that have disorganized the traditional pattern of life under Communist rule, it is the young leaders, ranging in age from the teens to the thirties, who have been running the show.

The amount of political power and responsibility vested in the hands of young local leaders is certainly without precedent in China's history; and it is shared by young men and women belonging to public organizations which are regularly mobilized to participate in current movements and to help enforce government policies. Members of the Youth League, the Democratic Women's League, the student union, and many other organizations work side by side with party officers in carrying out major government policies.

The young have come to possess not only coercive power but also social prestige under the new standards set up by the regime. To the

10. Feng Min-pin, "The Chinese New Democratic Youth League as the Standard Bearer of the Tradition of Revolutionary Struggle of the Chinese Youth," *Hsin Chung-kuo yueh-k'an* (New China Monthly), no. 19, May 1951, p. 52.

11. *Hsin Chung-kuo jen-wu chih* (Who's Who in New China), 1950 Hong Kong, pp. 2–3.

12. *Nan-fang jih-pao*, Canton, April 19, 1950, p. 3.

young go the large proportion of awards for "model workers," "model farmers," winners in production emulations; they are the recipients of many other honors symbolizing new values[13] that are foreign to the old generation. The leading "model workers" held up as examples of production efficiency for the rest of the workers, from Ma Heng-chang in mining to Nan Chien-hsiu in the textile industry, the counterparts of Stakhanovites in the Soviet Union, are young men and women, most of them in their twenties. The influence of youth begins to invade even the old empirical field of agriculture wherever improvements of agricultural methods are being vigorously introduced.

> In the patriotic production movement in the villages, members of the Youth League are vigorous shock brigades. They not only participate in agricultural production but also actively propagandize the agricultural policy of the People's Government among the people. They lead in organizing mutual-aid teams, in popularizing new agricultural methods. For example, Kuo Yu-lan in Heilung-kiang Province and Wang ching-mei in Hopei Province, both female members of the Youth League, have won the title of model agricultural workers. They both have popularized seed-selection, the soaking of seeds before sowing, and other new agricultural methods in their own communities, and the yields from their fields are higher than the average of other farmers. In the irrigation project of controlling the Huai River, members of the Youth League inhabiting the banks of the river mobilized large numbers of young people to participate in the work. Last winter (1951), in the northern part of Anhwei Province alone, one-third of the 600,000 labor conscripts were young people. Among these young workers were 16,000 members of the Youth League who formed the leading force of the labor conscripts. In the county of Pu-yang, Youth League members accounted for 30 per cent of the model irrigation workers.[14]

If it was the young technical men of the modern bourgeois intelligentsia who dimmed the prestige of the traditional "old craft masters" in the pre-Communist period, now the progressive young workers and peasants are doing the same thing on a more extensive scale. In traditional days a brilliant and successful young man might be held up as an example for members of his own generation, but never for his senior members in the age hierarchy or the old masters of the trade, who might regard him with benign approval but always considered him immature, with more to learn from older people. Now in every factory, every neighborhood, and in the villages young models of production and revolutionary conduct are glorified with fanfare and honored with material rewards. Ended is the sanctity of the time-honored rule that the old teach and the young learn, the old lead and the young follow. A student leader told his professor in 1951: "You and your generation are too beset with considerations and worries for decisive action, so we young ones should lead in changing the nation's way of life."

13. Feng Wen-pin, in *Chang-chiang jih-pao*, January 8, 1952, p. 4.
14. *Hsin chung-kuo yueh-k'an*, no. 19, May 1951, p. 52.

Change of Status of the Old in the Family

It is clear that the traditional older generation with its conservatism is regarded as an obstacle to progress. Even though there is no substantiation to rumors of summary gross mistreatment of all old people as an age group, such rumors reflect the general decline in status and power of the older generation. This change has inevitable effects on the status of the older generation within the family organization.

The political struggle in which the young are playing a leading part is carried into the family. From the time the Communists took control of the nation, and through the successive crises of the suppression of counter-revolutionaries, the Five-Anti and the Three-Anti movements, and the "thought reform" of the intellectuals, every progressive young person has been increasingly under group pressure to disregard kinship ties and the prestige of age and ferret out dissenters and recalcitrants for correction and, at times, even for elimination.[15] Since parents and uncles and elder brothers have been openly accused or secretly reported by junior members in the age hierarchy for offenses leading to police surveillance, fines, labor correction, imprisonment, or even death, the progressive young person is as much feared at home as in public. It is common to find older people suddenly stop talking about public matters, particularly political affairs, as soon as a progressive young family member comes home, especially if he comes home from school, where ideological indoctrination has been vigorously carried on. While the exact proportion of progressives among the young will remain unknown for some time, there is little doubt of the widespread effect of the new ideology on young minds and the rapid extension of this effect from the bourgeois intelligentsia to the much wider circle of young workers and peasants, as seen in the membership growth of the Youth League. Sharp is the contrast between this situation and the traditional order when family mores were in complete harmony with the nation's political ideology, when a successful and prominent son paid homage to his socially humble parents and other senior kinsmen.

Communist law and political principles no longer provide any support for the superiority and rights of an individual over another based on age. On the contrary, they tend to limit traditional authority and the rights of the old over the young. The prohibition of mistreatment of children limits what the parents can do with the young.[16] Elaborate legal stipulations on the protection of children's interests in the family have the same effect.[17] The single legal requirement of children is that they must support

15. The Five-Anti movement, aimed at the business class, has been explained before. The Three-Anti movement is aimed at correcting corruption, wastefulness, and bureaucratism among government officials and employees.
16. Marriage Law, Article 13.
17. *Ibid.*, Articles 13, 14, 15, 16, 20, 21, 22.

the parents and must not mistreat or abandon them.[18] In stipulations of the Marriage Law responsibilities of parents are much heavier than their rights over children—a reversal of the requirements of traditional filial piety which compelled almost one-sided devotion by the children.

There are no stipulations in Communist law governing the relationship of the older generation to the young aside from that of parents to children. However, since the parent-child relationship is stronger than the relationship between other members in the age hierarchy, when the parents' position is greatly weakened the position of other senior members in the family over the young deteriorates more rapidly. For a young progressive the traditional authority of an uncle or an aunt carries little weight, and that of more distant seniors in the age hierarchy means even less. Published documents show more political accusations by the young against other relatives than against parents.[19]

If the older generation finds no protection for their traditional status from politics and law in the revolution, it finds the safeguards also weak in other directions. Wherever modern economic development prevails, older people are finding it difficult to retain positions of leadership in family production. The replacement of numerous family businesses in trade and industry by state enterprises and the development of collectivized agriculture have had serious effects in this respect. The tendency of increasing economic qualifications and rights of the younger family member and the growing system of free education lessen the dependence of the young and reduce the economic authority of the older generation as a factor in maintaining its traditional status in the age hierarchy.

The development of centers of activity outside the home for the young adds another difficulty to the maintenance of the age hierarchy as a system of family status and authority, both because of the lack of time to teach the traditional ideas to the young at home and because of the conflicting ideology being instilled into the minds of the young in outside centers of activity. The development of modern schools during the past half century and the rapid growth of membership of youth organizations under the Communist regime are examples of this development. Under the Communists young men and women are recruited in large numbers as paid workers or volunteers for a great variety of public activities which take them away from home part time or full time at an age from the early teens to the twenties, an age in which they would have remained very close to home in the traditional system. The following is illustrative of the increasing separation of the young from family influence.

> In Feng Ch'i village near the city of Canton over forty young men and women, led by some twenty Youth League members, cultivated an acre of

18. *Ibid.*, Article 13.
19. Of the 73 cases in which young family members brought public accusation against relatives from March 1 to September 25, 1951, in the province of Kwangtung, 26 were against parents. See *Wah-kiu yat-po*, Hong Kong, September 25, 1951, p. 4.

"tabooed" land (land that the villagers would not till for superstitious fear of bringing misfortune). They sold the rice yielded from it, bought lumber with the money, built a house, and called it "The Home of Youth." They used the house for ideological classes, meetings, and activities. It has become the youth center in the village.[20]

The establishment of a center of organized activities exclusively for the young as an age group in the rural community is a new phenomenon, for all activity of the young except school was traditionally centered in the home. It is interesting to note the name of the center, "The Home of Youth," still using the word "home" which has a connotation of strong social affinity for the Chinese. At this "home" the older generation can no longer exercise discipline and control over the young.

With the superiority of age being seriously undermined, with the young tending to move out of the range of family education and discipline, with the legal support of filial piety gone, with the basic concept of the marriage of the children being changed, the welfare and security of the old becomes a weighty consideration in this transitional period. True, Communist law requires children to support their parents. In Shanghai, for example, an old woman abandoned by her son obtained support from him by order of the "people's court."[21] But the law does not prosecute such cases unless brought to court. In spite of increased accessibility to the law, there is a question whether every neglected or abandoned parent will bring the case to court in a situation where rule by law is still unfamiliar to common people. There is little doubt that such legal support is incomparably weaker than the guarantee provided by the traditional family for the welfare and security of the old.

The spectacular rise of the young and the decline of the old in power and prestige are plainly products of that stage of revolution which needs plastic young minds to accept the novel ideology, to practice the new standards, and to effect a drastic break with the traditional past. As the revolutionary situation settles down to an established order, with its new institutions and tradition sufficiently developed, age as a factor affecting the status and authority of individuals will undoubtedly resume some degree of importance, and accumulated knowledge and experience through age will again bear weight in the social evaluation of an individual. But it is doubtful whether age will ever resume the former traditional importance which summarily subjected the young to an inferior position in disregard of his other qualifications. The development of industrialization, which emphasizes technical competence, not age, and the popularization of science, which discounts empiricism, are both major goals of the present Communist revolution. Should the revolution successfully set up its institutions and traditions, these two factors among others will preclude a full return to the former Chinese consideration for age.

20. *Jen-min Jih-pao*, May 5, 1951, p. 6.
21. *Hun-yin fa hsin-hua* (New Talks on the Marriage Law), pp. 29–30.

Kingsley Davis

The Sociology
of Parent-Youth Conflict

It is in sociological terms that this paper attempts to frame and solve the sole question with which it deals, namely: Why does contemporary western civilization manifest an extraordinary amount of parent-adolescent conflict?[1] In other cultures, the outstanding fact is generally not the rebelliousness of youth, but its docility. There is practically no custom, no matter how tedious or painful, to which youth in primitive tribes or archaic civilizations will not willingly submit.[2] What, then, are the peculiar features of our society which give us one of the extremest examples of endemic filial friction in human history?

Our answer to this question makes use of constants and variables, the constants being the universal factors in the parent-youth relation, the variables being the factors which differ from one society to another. Though one's attention, in explaining the parent-youth relations of a given milieu, is focused on the variables, one cannot comprehend the action of the variables without also understanding the constants, for the latter constitute the structural and functional basis of the family as a part of society.

The Rate of Social Change

The first important variable is the rate of social change. Extremely rapid change in modern civilization, in contrast to most societies, tends to

1. In the absence of statistical evidence, exaggeration of the conflict is easily possible, and two able students have warned against it. E. B. Reuter, "The Sociology of Adolescence," and Jessie R. Runner, "Social Distance in Adolescent Relationships," both in *Amer. J. Sociol.*, November 1937, 43:415–16, 437. Yet sufficient nonquantitative evidence lies at hand in the form of personal experience, the outpour of literature on adolescent problems, and the historical and anthropological accounts of contrasting societies to justify the conclusion that in comparison with other cultures ours exhibits an exceptional amount of such conflict. If this paper seems to stress conflict, it is simply because we are concerned with this problem rather than with parent-youth harmony.

2. Cf. Nathan Miller, *The Child in Primitive Society*, New York, 1928; Miriam Van Waters, "The Adolescent Girl Among Primitive Peoples," *J. Relig. Psychol.*, 1913, 6:375–421 (1913) and 7:75–120 (1914); Margaret Mead, *Coming of Age in Samoa*, New York, 1928 and "Adolescence in Primitive and Modern Society," 169–188, in *The New Generation* ed. by V. F. Calverton and S. Schmalhausen, New York, 1930; A. M. Bacon, *Japanese Girls and Women*, New York and Boston, 1891 and 1902.

446

increase parent-youth conflict, for within a fast-changing social order the time-interval between generations, ordinarily but a mere moment in the life of a social system, becomes historically significant, thereby creating a hiatus between one generation and the next. Inevitably, under such a condition, youth is reared in a milieu different from that of the parents; hence the parents become old-fashioned, youth rebellious, and clashes occur which, in the closely confined circle of the immediate family, generate sharp emotion.

That rapidity of change is a significant variable can be demonstrated by three lines of evidence: a comparison of stable and non-stable societies;[3] a consideration of immigrant families; and an analysis of revolutionary epochs. If, for example, the conflict is sharper in the immigrant household, this can be due to one thing only, that the immigrant family generally undergoes the most rapid social change of any type of family in a given society. Similarly, a revolution (an abrupt form of societal alteration), by concentrating great change in a short span, catapults the younger generation into power—a generation which has absorbed and pushed the new ideas, acquired the habit of force, and which, accordingly, dominates those hangovers from the old regime, its parents.[4]

The Birth-Cycle, Decelerating Socialization, and Parent-Child Differences

Note, however, that rapid social change would have no power to produce conflict were it not for two universal factors: first, the family's duration; and second, the decelerating rate of socialization in the development of personality. "A family" is not a static entity but a process in time, a process ordinarily so brief compared with historical time that it is unimportant, but which, when history is "full" (i.e., marked by rapid social change), strongly influences the mutual adjustment of the generations. This "span" is basically the birth-cycle—the length of time between the birth of one person and his procreation of another. It is biological and inescapable. It would, however, have no effect in producing parent-youth conflict, even with social change, if it were not for the additional fact, intimately related and equally universal, that the sequential development of personality involves a constantly decelerating rate of socialization. This deceleration is due both to organic factors (age—which ties it to the birth-cycle) and to social factors (the cumulative character of

3. Partially done by Mead and Van Waters in the works cited above.
4. Soviet Russia and Nazi Germany are examples. See Sigmund Neumann, "The Conflict of Generations in Contemporary Europe from Versailles to Munich," *Vital Speeches of the Day,* August 1, 1939, 5:623–28. Parents in these countries are to be obeyed only so long as they profess the "correct" (i.e., youthful, revolutionary) ideas.

social experience). Its effect is to make the birth-cycle interval, which is the period of youth, the time of major socialization, subsequent periods of socialization being subsidiary.

Given these constant features, rapid social change creates conflict because *to* the intrinsic (universal, inescapable) differences between parents and children it adds an extrinsic (variable) difference derived from the acquisition, at the same stage of life, of differential cultural content by each successive generation. Not only are parent and child, at any given moment, in different stages of development, but the content which the parent acquired at the stage where the child now is, was a different content from that which the child is now acquiring. Since the parent is supposed to socialize the child, he tends to apply the erstwhile but now inappropriate content (see Diagram). He makes this mistake, and cannot remedy it, because, due to the logic of personality growth, his basic orientation was formed by the experiences of his own childhood. He cannot "modernize" his point of view, because *he* is the product of those

Figure 1

The Birth-Cycle, Social Change, and Parent-Child
Relations at Different Stages of Life[a]

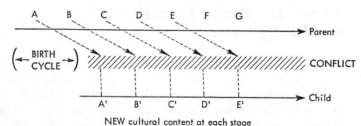

a. Because the birth-cycle interval persists throughout their conjoint life, parent and child are always at a different stage of development and their relations are always therefore potentially subject to conflict. E.g., when the parent is at stage D, the child is at stage B. But social change adds another source of conflict, for it means that the parent, when at the stage where the child now is, acquired a different cultural content from that which the child must now acquire at that stage. This places the parent in the predicament of trying to transmit old content no longer suited to the offspring's needs in a changed world. In a stable society, B and B' would have the same cultural content. In a changing society, they do not, yet the parent tries to apply the content of A, B, C, etc., to the corresponding stages in the child's development, A', B', C', etc., which supposedly and actually have a different content. Thus, a constant (the birth-cycle) and a variable (social change) combine to produce parent-youth conflict.

Though the birth-cycle remains absolutely the same, it does not remain relatively the same, because it occupies, as time goes on, a successively smaller percentage of the total time lived. Furthermore, because of the decelerating rate of socialization, the difference in the total amount of cultural content as between parent and child becomes less pronounced. After the period of adolescence, for example, the margin is reduced to a minimum, which explains why a minimum of conflict is achieved after that stage.

experiences. He can change in superficial ways, such as learning a new tune, but he cannot change (or *want* to change) the initial modes of thinking upon which his subsequent social experience has been built. To change the basic conceptions by which he has learned to judge the rightness and reality of all specific situations would be to render subsequent experience meaningless, to make an empty caricature of what had been his life.

Although, in the birth-cycle gap between parent and offspring, astronomical time constitutes the basic point of disparity, the actual sequences, and hence the actual differences significant for us, are physiological, psychosocial, and sociological—each with an acceleration of its own within, but to some degree independent of, sidereal time, and each containing a divergence between parent and child which must be taken into account in explaining parent-youth conflict.

Physiological Differences

Though the disparity in chronological age remains constant through life, the precise physiological differences between parent and offspring vary radically from one period to another. The organic contrasts between parent and *infant,* for example, are far different from those between parent and adolescent. Yet whatever the period, the organic differences produce contrasts (as between young and old) in those desires which, at least in part, are organically determined. Thus, at the time of adolescence the contrast is between an organism which is just reaching its full powers and one which is just losing them. The physiological need of the latter is for security and conservation, because as the superabundance of energy diminishes, the organism seems to hoard what remains.

Such differences, often alleged (under the heading of "disturbing physiological changes accompanying adolescence") as the primary cause of parent-adolescent strife, are undoubtedly a factor in such conflict, but, like other universal differences to be discussed, they form a constant factor present in every community, and therefore cannot in themselves explain the peculiar heightening of parent-youth conflict in our culture.

The fact is that most societies avoid the potential clash of old and young by using sociological position as a neutralizing agent. They assign definite and separate positions to persons of different ages, thereby eliminating competition between them for the same position and avoiding the competitive emotions of jealousy and envy. Also, since the expected behavior of old and young is thus made complementary rather than identical, the performance of cooperative functions is accomplished by different but mutually related activities suited to the disparate organic needs of each, with no coercion to behave in a manner unsuited to one's organic age. In our culture, where most positions are *theoretically* based on accomplishment rather than age, interage competition arises, superior organic propensities lead to a high evaluation of youth (the so-called "accent on youth"), a disproportionate lack of opportunity for youth manifests itself, and consequently, arrogance and frustration appear in the young, fear and envy, in the old.

Psychosocial Differences: Adult Realism Versus Youthful Idealism

The decelerating rate of socialization (an outgrowth both of the human being's organic development, from infant plasticity to senile rigidity, and of his cumulative cultural and social development), when taken with rapid social change and other conditions of our society, tends to produce certain differences of orientation between parent and youth. Though lack of space makes it impossible to discuss all of these ramifications, we shall attempt to delineate at least one sector of difference in terms of the conflict between adult realism (or pragmatism) and youthful idealism.

Though both youth and age claim to see the truth, the old are more conservatively realistic than the young, because on the one hand they take Utopian ideals less seriously and on the other hand take what may be called operating ideals, if not more seriously, at least more for granted. Thus, middle-aged people notoriously forget the poetic ideals of a new social order which they cherished when young. In their place, they put simply the working ideals current in the society. There is, in short, a persistent tendency for the ideology of a person as he grows older to gravitate more and more toward the status quo ideology, unless other facts (such as a social crisis or hypnotic suggestion) intervene.[5] With advancing age, he becomes less and less bothered by inconsistencies in ideals. He tends to judge ideals according to whether they are widespread and hence effective in thinking about practical life, not according to whether they are logically consistent. Furthermore, he gradually ceases to bother about the *untruth* of his ideals, in the sense of their failures to correspond to reality. He assumes through long habit that, though they do not correspond perfectly, the discrepancy is not significant. The reality of an ideal is defined for him in terms of how many people accept it rather than how completely it is mirrored in actual behavior.[6] Thus, we call him, as he approaches middle age, a realist.

The young, however, are idealists, partly because they take working

5. See Footnote 11 for necessary qualifications.
6. When discussing a youthful ideal, however, the older person is quick to take a dialectical advantage by pointing out not only that this ideal affronts the aspirations of the multitude, but that it also fails to correspond to human behavior either now or (by the lessons of history) probably in the future.

ideals literally and partly because they acquire ideals not fully operative in the social organization. Those in authority over children are obligated as a requirement of their status to inculcate ideals as a part of the official culture given the new generation.[7] The children are receptive because they have little social experience—experience being systematically kept from them (by such means as censorship, for example, a large part of which is to "protect" children). Consequently, young people possess little ballast for their acquired ideals, which therefore soar to the sky, whereas the middle-aged, by contrast, have plenty of ballast.

This relatively unchecked idealism in youth is eventually complicated by the fact that young people possess keen reasoning ability. The mind, simply as a logical machine, works as well at sixteen as at thirty-six.[8] Such logical capacity, combined with high ideals and an initial lack of experience, means that youth soon discovers with increasing age that the ideals it has been taught are true and consistent are not so in fact. Mental conflict thereupon ensues, for the young person has not learned that ideals may be useful without being true and consistent. As a solution, youth is likely to take action designed to remove inconsistencies or force actual conduct into line with ideals, such action assuming one of several typical adolescent forms—from religious withdrawal to the militant support of some Utopian scheme—but in any case consisting essentially in serious allegiance to one or more of the ideal moral systems present in the culture.[9]

A different, usually later reaction to disillusionment is the cynical or sophomoric attitude; for, if the ideals one has imbibed cannot be reconciled and do not fit reality, then why not dismiss them as worthless? Cynicism has the advantage of giving justification for behavior that young organisms crave anyway. It might be mistaken for genuine realism if it were not for two things. The first is the emotional strain behind the "don't care" attitude. The cynic, in his judgment that the world is bad because of inconsistency and untruth of ideals, clearly implies that he still values the ideals. The true realist sees the inconsistency and untruth, but without emotion; he uses either ideals or reality whenever it suits his purpose.

7. See amusing but accurate article, "Fathers Are Liars," *Scribner's Magazine*, March, 1934.

8. Evidence from mental growth data which point to a leveling off of the growth curve at about age 16. For charts and brief explanations, together with references, see F. K. Shuttleworth, *The Adolescent Period*, Monographs of the Society for Research in Child Development, III, Serial No. 16 (Washington, D.C., 1938), Figs. 16, 230, 232, 276, 285, 308.

Maturity of judgment is of course another matter. We are speaking only of logical capacity. Judgment is based on experience as well as capacity; hence, adolescents are apt to lack it.

9. An illustration of youthful reformism was afforded by the Laval University students who decided to "do something about" prostitution in the city of Quebec. They broke into eight houses in succession one night, "whacked naked inmates upon the buttocks, upset beds and otherwise proved their collegiate virtue. . . ." They ended by "shoving the few remaining girls out of doors into the cold autumn night." *Time*, October 19, 1936.

The second is the early disappearance of the cynical attitude. Increased experience usually teaches the adolescent that overt cynicism is unpopular and unworkable, that to deny and deride all beliefs which fail to cohere or to correspond to facts, and to act in opposition to them, is to alienate oneself from any group,[10] because these beliefs, however unreal, are precisely what makes group unity possible. Soon, therefore, the youthful cynic finds himself bound up with some group having a system of working ideals, and becomes merely another conformist, cynical only about the beliefs of other groups.[11]

While the germ of this contrast between youthful idealism and adult realism may spring from the universal logic of personality development, it receives in our culture a peculiar exaggeration. Social change, complexity, and specialization (by compartmentalizing different aspects of life) segregate ideals from fact and throw together incompatible ideologies while at the same time providing the intellectual tools for discerning logical inconsistencies and empirical errors. Our highly elaborated burden of culture, correlated with a variegated system of achieved vertical mobility, necessitates long years of formal education which separate youth from adulthood, theory from practice, school from life. Insofar, then, as youth's reformist zeal or cynical negativism produces conflict with parents, the peculiar conditions of our culture are responsible.

Sociological Differences: Parental Authority

Since social status and office are everywhere partly distributed on the basis of age, personality development is intimately linked with the network of social positions successively occupied during life. Western

10. This holds only for expressed cynicism, but so close is the relation of thought to action that the possibility of an entirely covert cynic seems remote.

11. This tentative analysis holds only insofar as the logic of personality development in a complex culture is the sole factor. Because of other factors, concrete situations may be quite different. When, for example, a person is specifically trained in certain rigid, other-worldly, or impractical ideals, he may grow increasingly fanatical with the years rather than realistic, while his offspring, because of association with less fanatical persons, may be more pragmatic than he. The variation in group norms within a society produces persons who, whatever their orientation inside the group, remain more idealistic than the average outsider, while their children may, with outside contacts, become more pragmatic. Even within a group, however, a person's situation may be such as to drive him beyond the everyday realities of that group, while his children remain undisturbed. Such situations largely explain the personal crises that may alter one's orientation. The analysis, overly brief and mainly illustrative, therefore represents a certain degree of abstraction. The reader should realize, moreover, that the terms "realistic" and "idealistic" are chosen merely for convenience in trying to convey the idea, not for any evaluative judgments which they may happen to connote. The terms are not used in any technical epistemological sense, but simply in the way made plain by the context. Above all, it is not implied that ideals are "unreal." The ways in which they are "real" and "unreal" to observer and actor are complex indeed. See T. Parsons, *The Structure of Social Action*, 396, New York, 1937, and V. Pareto, *The Mind and Society*, III: 1300–1304, New York, 1935.

society, in spite of an unusual amount of interage competition, maintains differences of social position between parent and child, the developmental gap between them being too clearcut, the symbiotic needs too fundamental, to escape being made a basis of social organization. Hence, parent and child, in a variety of ways, find themselves enmeshed in different social contexts and possessed of different outlooks. The much publicized critical attitude of youth toward established ways, for example, is partly a matter of being on the outside looking in. The "established ways" under criticism are usually institutions (such as property, marriage, profession) which the adolescent has not yet entered. He looks at them from the point of view of the outsider (especially since they affect him in a restrictive manner), either failing to imagine himself finding satisfaction in such patterns or else feeling resentful that the old have in them a vested interest from which he is excluded.

Not only is there differential position, but also *mutually* differential position, status being in many ways specific for and reciprocal between parent and child. Some of these differences, relating to the birth-cycle and constituting part of the family structure, are universal. This is particularly true of the super- and subordination summed up in the term *parental authority*.

Since sociological differences between parent and child are inherent in family organization, they constitute a universal factor potentially capable of producing conflict. Like the biological differences, however, they do not in themselves produce such conflict. In fact, they may help to avoid it. To understand how our society brings to expression the potentiality for conflict, indeed to deal realistically with the relation between the generations, we must do so not in generalized terms but in terms of the specific "power situation." Therefore, the remainder of our discussion will center upon the nature of parental authority and its vicissitudes in our society.

Because of his strategic position with reference to the new-born child (at least in the familial type of reproductive institution), the parent is given considerable authority. Charged by his social group with the responsibility of controlling and training the child in conformity with the mores and thereby insuring the maintenance of the cultural structure, the parent, to fulfill his duties, must have the privileges as well as the obligations of authority, and the surrounding community ordinarily guarantees both.

The first thing to note about parental authority, in addition to its function in socialization, is that it is a case of authority within a primary group. Simmel has pointed out that authority is bearable for the subordinate because it touches only one aspect of life. Impersonal and objective, it permits all other aspects to be free from its particularistic dominance. This escape, however, is lacking in parental authority, for since the family includes most aspects of life, its authority is not limited, specific, or impersonal. What, then, can make this authority bearable? Three factors associated with the familial primary group help to give the answer: (1) the child is socialized within the family, and therefore knowing nothing else and being utterly dependent, the authority of the parent is internalized, accepted; (2) the family, like other primary groups, implies identification, in such sense that one person understands and responds emphatically to the sentiments of the other, so that the harshness of authority is ameliorated;[12] (3) in the intimate interaction of the primary group control can never be purely one-sided; there are too many ways in which the subordinated can exert the pressure of his will. When, therefore, the family system is a going concern, parental authority, however, inclusive, is not felt as despotic.

A second thing to note about parental authority is that while its duration is variable (lasting in some societies a few years and in others a lifetime), it inevitably involves a change, a progressive readjustment, in the respective positions of parent and child—in some cases an almost complete reversal of roles, in others at least a cumulative allowance for the fact of maturity in the subordinated offspring. Age is a unique basis for social stratification. Unlike birth, sex, wealth, or occupation, it implies that the stratification is temporary, that the person, if he lives a full life, will eventually traverse all of the strata having it as a basis. Therefore, there is a peculiar ambivalence attached to this kind of differentiation, as well as a constant directional movement. On the one hand, the young person, in the stage of maximum socialization, is, so to speak, *moving into* the social organization. His social personality is expanding, i.e., acquiring an increased amount of the cultural heritage, filling more powerful and numerous positions. His future is before him, in what the older person is leaving behind. The latter, on the other hand, has a future before him only in the sense that the offspring represents it. Therefore, there is a disparity of interest, the young person placing his thoughts upon a future which, once the first stages of dependence are passed, does not include the parent, the old person placing his hopes vicariously upon the young. This situation, representing a *tendency* in every society, is avoided in many places by a system of respect for the aged and an imaginary projection of life beyond the grave. In the absence of such a religio-ancestral system, the role of the aged is a tragic one.[13]

Let us now take up, point by point, the manner in which western civilization has affected this *gemeinschaftliche* and processual form of authority.

---

12. House slaves, for example, are generally treated much better than field slaves. Authority over the former is of a personal type, while that over the latter (often in the form of a foreman-gang organization) is of a more impersonal or economic type.

13. Sometimes compensated for by an interest in the grandchildren, which permits them partially to recover the role of the vigorous parent.

1. *Conflicting norms*. To begin with, rapid change has, as we saw, given old and young a different social content, so that they possess conflicting norms. There is a loss of mutual identification, and the parent will not "catch up" with the child's point of view, because he is supposed to dominate rather than follow. More than this, social complexity has confused the standards *within* the generations. Faced with conflicting goals, parents become inconsistent and confused in their own minds in rearing their children. The children, for example, acquire an argument against discipline by being able to point to some family wherein discipline is less severe, while the parent can retaliate by pointing to still other families wherein it is firmer. The acceptance of parental attitudes is less complete than formerly.

2. *Competing authorities*. We took it for granted, when discussing rapid social change, that youth acquires new ideas, but we did not ask how. The truth is that, in a specialized and complex culture, they learn from competing authorities. Today, for example, education is largely in the hands of professional specialists, some of whom, as college professors, resemble the sophists of ancient Athens by virtue of their work of accumulating and purveying knowledge, and who consequently have ideas in advance of the populace at large (i.e., the parents). By giving the younger generation these advanced ideas, they (and many other extrafamilial agencies, including youth's contemporaries) widen the intellectual gap between parent and child.[14]

3. *Little explicit institutionalization of steps in parental authority*. Our society provides little explicit institutionalization of the progressive readjustments of authority as between parent and child. We are intermediate between the extreme of virtually permanent parental authority and the extreme of very early emancipation, because we encourage release in late adolescence. Unfortunately, this is a time of enhanced sexual desire, so that the problem of sex and the problem of emancipation occur simultaneously and complicate each other. Yet even this would doubtless be satisfactory if it were not for the fact that among us the exact time when authority is relinquished, the exact amount, and the proper ceremonial behavior are not clearly defined. Not only do different groups and families have conflicting patterns, and new situations arise to which old definitions will not apply, but the different spheres of life (legal, economic, religious, intellectual) do not synchronize, maturity in one sphere and immaturity in another often coexisting. The readjustment of authority between individuals is always a ticklish process, and when it is a matter of such close authority as that between parent and child it is apt to

14. The essential point is not that there are other authorities—in every society there are extrafamilial influences in socialization—but that, because of specialization and individualistic enterprise, they are *competing* authorities. Because they make a living by their work and are specialists in socialization, some authorities have a competitive advantage over parents who are amateurs or at best merely general practitioners.

be still more ticklish. The failure of our culture to institutionalize this readjustment by a series of well-defined, well-publicized steps is undoubtedly a cause of much parent-youth dissension. The adolescent's sociological exit from his family, via education, work, marriage, and change of residence, is fraught with potential conflicts of interest which only a definite system of institutional controls can neutralize. The parents have a vital stake in what the offspring will do. Because his acquisition of independence will free the parents of many obligations, they are willing to relinquish their authority; yet, precisely because their own status is socially identified with that of their offspring, they wish to insure satisfactory conduct on the latter's part and are tempted to prolong their authority by making the decisions themselves. In the absence of institutional prescriptions, the conflict of interest may lead to a struggle for power, the parents fighting to keep control in matters of importance to themselves, the son or daughter clinging to personally indispensable family services while seeking to evade the concomitant control.

4. *Concentration within the small family.* Our family system is peculiar in that it manifests a paradoxical combination of concentration and dispersion. On the one hand, the unusual smallness of the family unit makes for a strange intensity of family feeling, while on the other, the fact that most pursuits take place outside the home makes for a dispersion of activities. Though apparently contradictory, the two phenomena are really interrelated and traceable ultimately to the same factors in our social structure. Since the first refers to that type of affection and antagonism found between relatives, and the second to activities, it can be seen that the second (dispersion) isolates and increases the intensity of the affectional element by sheering away common activities and the extended kin. Whereas ordinarily the sentiments of kinship are organically related to a number of common activities and spread over a wide circle of relatives, in our mobile society they are associated with only a few common activities and concentrated within only the immediate family. This makes them at once more instable (because ungrounded) and more intense. With the diminishing birth rate, our family is the world's smallest kinship unit, a tiny closed circle. Consequently, a great deal of family sentiment is directed toward a few individuals, who are so important to the emotional life that complexes easily develop. This emotional intensity and situational instability increase both the probability and severity of conflict.

In a familistic society, where there are several adult male and female relatives within the effective kinship group to whom the child turns for affection and aid, and many members of the younger generation in whom the parents have a paternal interest, there appears to be less intensity of emotion for any particular kinsman and consequently less chance for severe conflict.[15] Also, if conflict between any two relatives does arise, it may be handled by shifting mutual rights and obligations to another relative.[16]

5. *Open competition for socioeconomic position.* Our emphasis upon individual initiative and vertical mobility, in contrast to rural-stable regimes, means that one's future occupation and destiny are determined more at adolescence than at birth, the adolescent himself (as well as the parents) having some part in the decision. Before him spread a panorama of possible occupations and avenues of advancement, all of them fraught with the uncertainties of competitive vicissitude. The youth is ignorant of most of the facts. So is the parent, but less so. Both attempt to collaborate on the future, but because of previously mentioned sources of friction, the collaboration is frequently stormy. They evaluate future possibilities differently, and since the decision is uncertain yet important, a clash of wills results. The necessity of choice at adolescence extends beyond the occupational field to practically every phase of life, the parents having an interest in each decision. A culture in which more of the choices of life were settled beforehand by ascription, where the possibilities were fewer and the responsibilities of choice less urgent, would have much less parent-youth conflict.[17]

6. *Sex tension.* If until now we have ignored sex taboos, the omission has represented a deliberate attempt to place them in their proper context with other factors, rather than in the unduly prominent place usually given them.[18] Undoubtedly, because of a constellation of cultural conditions, sex looms as an important bone of parent-youth contention. Our morality, for instance, demands both premarital chastity and postponement of marriage, thus creating a long period of desperate eagerness when young persons practically at the peak of their sexual capacity are forbidden to enjoy it. Naturally, tensions arise—tensions which adolescents try to relieve, and adults hope they will relieve, in some socially acceptable form. Such tensions not only make the adolescent intractable and capricious, but create a genuine conflict of interest between the two generations. The parent, with respect to the child's behavior, represents morality, while the offspring reflects morality *plus* his organic cravings. The stage is thereby set for conflict, evasion, and

15. Margaret Mead, *Social Organization of Manus,* 84, Honolulu, Bernice P. Bishop Museum Bulletin 76, 1930. Large heterogeneous households early accustom the child to expect emotional rewards from many different persons. D. M. Spencer, "The Composition of the Family as a Factor in the Behavior of Children in Fijian Society," *Sociometry* (1939) 2:47–55.

16. The principle of substitution is widespread in familism, as shown by the wide distribution of adoption, levirate, sororate, and classificatory kinship nomenclature.

17. M. Mead, *Coming of Age in Samoa,* 200 ff.

18. Cf., e.g., L. K. Frank, "The Management of Tensions," *Amer. J. Sociol.,* March 1928, 33:706–22; M. Mead, *op. cit.,* 216–217, 222–23.

deceit. For the mass of parents, toleration is never possible. For the mass of adolescents, sublimation is never sufficient. Given our system of morality, conflict seems well nigh inevitable.

Yet it is not sex itself but the way it is handled that causes conflict. If sex patterns were carefully, definitely, and uniformly geared with non-sexual patterns in the social structure, there would be no parent-youth conflict over sex. As it is, rapid change has opposed the sex standards of different groups and generations, leaving impulse only chaotically controlled.

The extraordinary preoccupation of modern parents with the sex life of their adolescent offspring is easily understandable. First, our morality is sex-centered. The strength of the impulse which it seeks to control, the consequent stringency of its rules, and the importance of reproductive institutions for society, make sex so morally important that being moral and being sexually discreet are synonymous. Small wonder, then, that parents, charged with responsibility for their children and fearful of their own status in the eyes of the moral community, are preoccupied with what their offspring will do in this matter. Moreover, sex is intrinsically involved in the family structure and is therefore of unusual significance to family members *qua* family members. Offspring and parent are not simply two persons who happen to live together; they are two persons who happen to live together because of past sex relations between the parents. Also, between parent and child there stand strong incest taboos, and doubtless the unvoiced possibility of violating these unconsciously intensifies the interest of each in the other's sexual conduct. In addition, since sexual behavior is connected with the offspring's formation of a new family of his own, it is naturally of concern to the parent. Finally, these factors taken in combination with the delicacy of the authoritarian relation, the emotional intensity within the small family, and the confusion of sex standards, make it easy to explain the parental interest in adolescent sexuality. Yet because sex is a tabooed topic between parent and child,[19] parental control must be indirect and devious, which creates additional possibilities of conflict.

Summary and Conclusion

Our parent-youth conflict thus results from the interaction of certain universals of the parent-child relation and certain variables the values of

19. "Even among the essentially 'unrepressed' Trobrianders the parent is never the confidant in matters of sex." Bronislaw Malinowski, *Sex and Reproduction in Savage Society*, 36 (note), London, 1927, p. 36n. Cf. the interesting article, "Intrusive Parents," *The Commentator*, September 1938, which opposes frank sex discussion between parents and children.

which are peculiar to modern culture. The universals are (1) the basic age or birth-cycle differential between parent and child, (2) the decelerating rate of socialization with advancing age, and (3) the resulting intrinsic differences between old and young on the physiological, psychosocial, and sociological planes.

Though these universal factors *tend* to produce conflict between parent and child, whether or not they do so depends upon the variables. We have seen that the distinctive general features of our society are responsible for our excessive parent-adolescent friction. Indeed, they are the same features which are affecting *all* family relations. The delineation of these variables has not been systematic, because the scientific classification of whole societies has not yet been accomplished; and it has been difficult, in view of the interrelated character of societal traits, to seize upon certain features and ignore others. Yet certainly the following four complex variables are important: (1) the rate of social change; (2) the extent of complexity in the social structure; (3) the degree of integration in the culture; and (4) the velocity of movement (e.g., vertical mobility) within the structure and its relation to the cultural values.

Our rapid social change, for example, has crowded historical meaning into the family time-span, has thereby given the offspring a different social content from that which the parent acquired, and consequently has added to the already existent intrinsic differences between parent and youth, a set of extrinsic ones which double the chance of alienation. Moreover, our great societal complexity, our evident cultural conflict, and our emphasis upon open competition for socioeconomic status have all added to this initial effect. We have seen, for instance, that they have disorganized the important relation of parental authority by confusing the goals of child control, setting up competing authorities, creating a small family system, making necessary certain significant choices at the time of adolescence, and leading to an absence of definite institutional mechanisms to symbolize and enforce the progressively changing stages of parental power.

If ours were a simple rural-stable society, mainly familistic, the emancipation from parental authority being gradual and marked by definite institutionalized steps, with no great postponement of marriage, sex taboo, or open competition for status, parents and youth would not be in conflict. Hence, the presence of parent-youth conflict in our civilization is one more specific manifestation of the incompatibility between an urban-industrial-mobile social system and the familial type of reproductive institutions.[20]

20. For further evidence of this incompatibility, see the writer's "Reproductive Institutions and the Pressure for Population," *(Brit.) Social. Rev.* July 1937, 29:289–306.

Janet Zollinger Giele

Changes in the Modern Family: Their Impact on Sex Roles

We have just passed through an era, lasting roughly from 1920 to 1960, in which women were extraordinarily satisfied with and optimistic about their status. There was, in some circles, a derisive attitude toward the feminists of an earlier era who had been aggressive in the cause of winning equal political rights for themselves. During that recent period it took an intellectual effort to remember that female suffragists had to *fight* against considerable *opposition* to accomplish their goal.

In 1971 the mood has changed. College students who five years ago showed no interest in the status of women (although they were very much interested in the problems of blacks) are today demanding and getting courses on the history, sociology, psychology, and literature of women. Betty Friedan's *The Feminine Mystique*[1] commands more attention now than when it first appeared in 1963. The women's movement is a topic of interest even to the mass media. And since *Sexual Politics*[2] appeared, more women are wary of "patriarchal" domination by men. Furthermore, some people are now broadening the question of sex roles to take issue with the whole structure of the nuclear family, particularly with the division of labor that makes the husband the sole provider and keeps the wife at home in charge of the children.

The Problem

The question I wish to pose is this: Why do we find this new *consciousness* emerging, critical of women's status and the relationship between the sexes?

The easy answer is that women have been converted to the feminist cause. Such an explanation assumes that the ideology of a Kate Millet, once it has been developed and propagated, is irresistible. But this is hardly satisfying, for it fails to account for the relative lack of response to

1. New York: Norton, 1963.
2. K. Millet, Garden City, N.Y.: Doubleday, 1970.

Simone de Beauvoir's powerful statement, *The Second Sex*, which appeared in America in 1952.[3]

A more satisfying approach looks to deeper changes in process in the society, which have laid a foundation for a change of consciousness in those born since 1930. It is in these generations that we see budding interest in the new feminism and in possible new forms of family life.

Some Alternative Theories

Previous explanations of the relation between the sexes have generally been of three sorts, ascribing the main cause of change or stability to technology, ideology, or the division of labor. Each provides elements of an explanatory theory, but any one, taken alone, cannot satisfactorily account for the current burst of consciousness.

The technological theory of change, long associated with the name of W. F. Ogburn[4] in sociology, points to labor-saving devices, improved contraception, better health and longer life span as some of the important factors that have freed women from the family and contributed to the rise in their labor force participation. Such a theory explains a gradual increase in percent of women working, but it explains neither the quiescence of the 1950s nor the angry outburst of the late 1960s.

The ideological theory of change represented by Friedan or Millet points to subtle attitudes that allow men to dominate women. But taken alone, it cannot account for the emergence of a new consciousness which rejects patriarchy and the feminine mystique.

Parsons and Bales[5] have developed a more complete theoretical position that could encompass both technology and values by focusing on the division of labor. According to their theory, American men and women together value equality of opportunity and achievement, but their roles are different: Men achieve in work outside the home; women cultivate the opportunity of the child to realize his full potential by staying inside the home. Though this theory provided an adequate interpretation for the 1950s, it did not foresee the turmoil we now observe.

Consciousness and the Universalization of Sex Roles

The fault of Parsons and Bales' analysis was that it froze men's and women's roles at one point in time, while in fact those roles were

3. New York: Modern Library.
4. W. Ogburn and M. Nimkoff, *Technology and the Changing Family*, Boston: Houghton-Mifflin, 1953.
5. T. Parsons and R. Bales, *Family, Socialization, and Interaction*, Glencoe, Ill.: The Free Press, 1955.

changing with the increasing complexity of the surrounding social structure.[6]

When a society becomes more complex, roles become more specialized, or differentiated. That is, a job is broken down into several different operations, some of which may be performed by the person who originally did the whole job, some of which may be taken over by experts who perform only newly specialized functions.

When a job is broken up like this (*i.e.*, differentiated), two other things happen at the same time. First, parts of the job can now be performed by persons who under the old rule were not qualified. Second, the very fact of breaking up the job into component parts has an effect on the consciousness of all the people involved: they become aware that certain qualifications they once thought intrinsically necessary to the performance of the job are not in fact so, at least not for certain parts of the operation. As a result the original role, which was seen to be segmentally related to others around it, is now seen as an *integral* made up of several components, a number of which are like the components in other units. Thus is built the possibility of a *shared consciousness*—a sense of commonality or of universal qualities in persons and roles that were initially felt to be totally different from each other.[7] It was a similar process that Marx and Engels described when they observed the relation between the introduction of the factory system and the emergence of class consciousness.

If the change in men's and women's roles is a process of differentiation with its greater potential for recognizing human qualities that are shared across the sexes, then it should be possible to identify forces in the larger society that have served to split up traditional sex roles into several component parts, allowing some previously performed by only one sex to be carried out by persons with requisite qualifications without regard to sex.

It is my thesis that such a process of differentiation has been going on in men's and women's roles. Women's work such as cooking or washing has been routinized and rationalized to a point that a man can put a load of laundry in the dryer or a frozen dinner in the oven as well as any woman. Similarly, men's work is less and less tied to physical strength in which presumably males excel, and women are therefore able to do many of the manual, clerical, or intellectual operations that men do. The upshot is that a cross-over is possible in many aspects of role performance that were formerly linked to sex. Consequently, a shared consciousness is possible in which men and women can perceive more clearly each other's problems and satisfactions, and as a result identify with each other.

6. Had they applied the theory of their Chapter VII to the evolution of adult sex roles, they would have avoided this difficulty.

7. My analysis of the differentiation process owes much to a theoretical formulation by Talcott Parsons in *Societies* (Prentice-Hall, 1966), pp. 21–24.

Institutional Changes

Such an outcome is not due to changed technology alone. If it were, we would be hard pressed to explain why sex roles received so little attention only a few years ago, when admittedly technology had already made great strides. Important changes have also been occurring in more subtle aspects of the sexual division of labor such as child care and the nature of family life. I shall argue that, roughly since the 1930s, relevant changes have occurred in four major institutional areas of the society that have had a formative influence on the generations born since then and have laid the foundations for a revolution of consciousness about sex roles that is just beginning to emerge.

These changes occurred in 1) the relation of the individual to the accepted moral code; 2) the relation of the individual to the family; 3) the relation of family to government; and 4) the relation of the family to the economy.

In each of these areas, I shall describe two phases of functional differentiation that have set the stage for change in attitudes about sex roles. The first phase is a process of *specialization* in which one primary concern is selected. The second phase is a process of *inclusion* in which other necessary functions are also identified as worthy of attention. As a result of both these processes *universalization of consciousness* becomes possible.

Changes in the Moral Code

The first important institutional change was based on discovery of a new basis for morality, initially apparent in sexual conduct, later in other moral issues. Moral changes were significant for family and sex roles because they could transform general assumptions about the boundaries between behavior appropriate to youth and adults, to single and married people, and to men and women.

Specialization of the Sexual Function as Expression of Individuality. The central theme of the sexual revolution has been a change in standards of premarital chastity. As Reiss[8] has pointed out, the rates of non-virginity at marriage have changed little since the 1920s. What has changed is the acceptance of premarital intercourse if it occurs within the context of affection.[9]

Sexual mores changed because sexuality came to be regarded as *the* means of individual self-expression and gratification if it occurred in the

8. I. Reiss, "Premarital Sexual Standards," in *The Individual, Sex, and Society*, C. Broderick and J. Bernard, eds., Baltimore: Johns Hopkins Press, 1969.
9. F. Wood, *Sex and the New Morality*, New York: Association Press, 1968.

context of a continuing relationship. As such, sexual intercourse gained legitimacy outside marriage and apart from its reproductive aspect. It was available to youth as well as to adults. Its exercise was regulated not by traditional authority but by consideration for the feelings of the individuals involved.[10]

Inclusion of Self-Expression and the New Morality in Moral Transformation. Once the sexual function had been differentiated from the total married adult state, it became apparent that performance of other aspects of adult life might also be subjected to redefinition. In the 1960s, young people began to experiment with other than sexual forms of expression—drugs and the hippie style. Youth also gave expression to a new kind of moral concern for war, peace, and responsible exercise of authority in universities, industry, and the military. SNCC, the Peace Corps, and Vista all voiced a moral purpose in areas once thought the sole province of adults.

Universalization of Sexual and Moral Consciousness. The consequence of moral transformation was the emergence of youth as a distinct stage in the life cycle, a period when boys and girls could, as Keniston[11] has said, "acknowledge both self and society, personality and social process, without denying the claims of either." By such a standard, sexuality could occur outside marriage; responsible moral positions could be argued by persons who are not yet adults.

Significantly, at each stage of the moral revolution, *both men and women have been involved.* Women have been allowed to become as sexually expressive as men had earlier been. Young men have become as morally concerned with peace and community well-being as were women of Jane Addams's era. The result has been new consciousness of universal qualities shared between the sexes.

Psychology and Family Life

While the sexual revolution and the emergence of youth clarified the nature of responsible moral and sexual behavior *outside* the family, new attitudes about child-rearing clarified the central activities occurring *within* the family. Later still came concern with the development of adult personality. The outcome of these changes was a new sensitivity to the question of whether the family as it is presently constituted can serve the needs of individual men and women.

Specialization of the Family in Child Care. Following as they did the loss of important productive functions from the home, the decades of the

10. Of course technical improvements in contraception facilitated this change, but they alone do not account for it.
11. K. Keniston, *Young Radicals,* New York: Harcourt Brace, 1968.

1920s and 1930s saw a concentration on the child-rearing functions of the family. The goal was to bring up children able to live in a peaceful and democratic world, capable of cooperation and self-direction, and not merely obedient to authority. To this end the whole child development movement was oriented.[12] By the end of the depression, nursery schools, permeated by these ideas and linked to efforts at parent education, had spread across the country. The new ideas were followed most closely by the middle classes, but by the late 1950s there was evidence that even working class parents had felt the effects.[13]

Initially the mother was seen as the expert in child-rearing. She was more open to the new ideas, while the father might revert to being "heavy-handed." Gradually, however, the importance of the father's role was also recognized. In 1939, L. K. Frank wrote,

> While the mother is largely responsible for the child's patterns of intimacy, the father is primarily responsible for the child's ideals of social conduct and his major aspirations and ambitions toward the social world.[14]

Thus eventually *both* mother and father were seen as important in child-rearing.

Inclusion of Concern for Development of Adults. While at first the special function of the family was seen as child-rearing, in recent years the marital role has been singled out for increased attention.[15] Perhaps it is because child-rearing is bunched in the early years of marriage that more attention is given the needs of adults who continue in the family. Perhaps, also, husband and wife now need to find greater satisfaction in each other because their high mobility has uprooted them from single sex social networks that supported them in the past.

Whatever the dynamics of this development, its consequences have been more striking for women than for men. Women are now demanding that the home serve their individual needs for self-realization as much as it appears to serve the husband (by letting him do his work in peace and providing rest and recreation at the end). They protest the "shitwork" that constantly serves others' needs and not their own.[16] In their demand is the belief that the home should be a place that facilitates women's personal growth rather than a prison of stagnation.

Universalization of Parental and Marital Roles. If child-rearing and

12. L. Frank, "The beginnings of child development and family life education in the twentieth century," *Merrill-Palmer Quart.*, 8 (July 1962), 207–227.
13. U. Bronfenbrenner, "Socialization and social class through time and space," in *Readings in Social Psychology*, 3rd ed., E. Maccoby, T. Newcomb, and E. Hartley, eds., New York: Holt, 1958.
14. L. Frank, "The father's role in child nurture," *Child Study*, 16 (March 1939), 135–136.
15. J. Galbraith, *The Affluent Society*, Boston: Houghton-Mifflin, 1958.
16. "How We Live and With Whom," *Women: A Journal of Liberation, Inc.*, Winter 1971.

stabilization of adult personality are identified as the special functions of the family, the structure of the family has to become more flexible. During the early years of married life child-rearing will predominate and sex roles may diverge sharply. Later a couple may devote themselves to common interests such as travel or life in a retirement village in which their roles become more similar. Such flexibility is not unknown to us now. It may eventually result in more widespread questioning of traditional family patterns. Today among the avant garde, alternative forms of child care (day care, etc.) and marriage (serial or communal) are already being considered and tried out.

Government Policy Toward the Family

Simultaneous with the evolution of a new sexual ethic and deepening awareness of the psychological significance of the family, there has been a gradual and at times painful effort to formulate government policy toward the family. Initially, in the 1930s, the concern of government was to ensure support of children under conditions of depression and unemployment. During the 1960s, however, government concern broadened to consider the problem of maintaining incentive for work, and proposals for a negative income tax and family allowances were put forward. Despite considerable resistance to these proposals, I believe we are on the threshold of an era when the family's crucial contribution to the formation and maintenance of responsible citizens in a free society will be publicly recognized.

Specialization of Family Support to Aid Dependent Children. The crisis of the depression created a distinction in the public mind between adults' economic roles and their family responsibilities. It was recognized that persons might be unemployed through no fault of their own and yet have families whose lives depended on their work. A patchwork of insurance, pension, and Social Security programs developed to provide for the young, the old, and the infirm.[17] Of these the most relevant to family change was AFDC, Aid to Families with Dependent Children, established under Title IV of the Social Security Act.

During the 1930s, governmental support of the family identified the child-rearing function as being of special importance. And again, as in the child psychology of the era, the mother was seen as the specialist who could carry on this activity more or less alone if she and her children were provided with support.

Inclusion of the Incentive Problem in Family Support. In the 1960s, however, with the discovery of poverty in the midst of an affluent society,

17. J. Vadakin, *Family Allowances: An Analysis of Their Development and Implications,* Miami: University of Miami Press, 1958.

and the recognition that a disproportionate number of draft rejects were children who had received AFDC, there was a new willingness to recognize the hazards of father absence and the self-perpetuating cycle of dependence. The Moynihan Report and ensuing proposals for a negative income tax and family allowances pointed to the necessity of assuring fathers jobs (or compensation commensurate with their family responsibilities) so that they would not desert and would instead maintain incentive to support their families and fulfill the important paternal role.[18]

In 1968, Moynihan wrote, "Men are paid for the work they perform on the job, not for the role they occupy in the family."[19] But his point was that they should be paid for that too. He had earlier argued that it would save the government money to ensure fathers jobs and foster stable family life, rather than later have to rehabilitate disadvantaged children by expensive government programs.[20]

Universalization of Family Consciousness Across Sex and Class Lines. It is easy to see conditions for one kind of universalization of consciousness emerging that recognizes that *both* men and women are important to family life and that children can suffer from *pa*ternal deprivation as well as *ma*ternal deprivation.

But the storm that the Moynihan Report raised suggests that another kind of universalization is also occurring—albeit haltingly and painfully. This is a sharing of consciousness across class, ethnic, and racial groups. Blacks bitterly protested the Moynihan Report because they thought it was saying that one kind of family, the white, middle-class, "intact" family was best. Actually their protest may point to an enlarged consciousness of the future that will assert that it is not important which person (mother, father, or other family member) performs the provider role, or performs the parental function. What may instead be the crucial question in the future is simply, are these functions being performed adequately?

The Family in an Affluent Economy

Government policy toward the family is gradually moving away from an implicitly anti-natalist policy that gives only minimal support to the poor, to a policy of universal family allowances that would be neither pro-natalist nor anti-natalist but would give compensation for performance of parental functions. This still leaves open the question of population

18. D. Moynihan, "A family policy for the nation," in *The Moynihan Report and the Politics of Controversy*, L. Rainwater and W. Yancey, eds., Cambridge: M.I.T. Press, 1967.
19. J. Vadakin, *Children, Poverty, and Family Allowances*, New York: Basic Books, 1968.
20. Moynihan, *op. cit.*

control. In the 1950s, women chose to have a third or fourth child to fill the time left free by diminishing household tasks. In the 1960s there is growing awareness that women may better use their leisure by taking a job outside the home, thereby making not only a productive contribution to the economy but also a step toward control of population.

Specialization of the Household in Consumption. The striking achievement of the affluent society has been elimination of toil within the household. Seeley[21] and Whyte[22] in their accounts of suburbs in the 1950s both note the acquisition of new household appliances and the kind of "managerial" role the housewife performed as she coordinated the purchase and serving of packaged foods, the care of household and clothing, and the scheduling of her own and her family's activities. Gone is the 19th century pattern of hours spent sewing, cleaning, baking or gardening.[23] These activities are now done by *choice,* for ready-made articles are easily bought. The modern household's specific function is to consume rather than to produce. And it is the woman who is seen as the expert in home management.

Her life is not always satisfying, however. Seeley found that "many a Crestwood mother, while 'accepting' the culturally approved maternal role, reveals an underlying resentment." One "creative" solution was to have more children.[24] Another was to invest more time in their care. Van Bortel[25] found in 1953 that homemakers used about as many hours in cooking and housework as they had in the late 1920s. But they spent nearly twice as many hours in "caring for the family."

Inclusion of Occupation in the Choice of Alternatives. By the beginning of the 1960s, however, there were indications that the baby boom would not last forever and that the choice of outside employment was an increasingly accepted alternative. In an affluent society where the ideal is to do work that is interesting and satisfying, not tiring or boring,[26] it is understandable that women would frequently choose the satisfactions of employment over the sometimes less satisfying routines of housework. But, in addition, women's work might bring extra money into households, not as in the past to cover the bare necessities, but to further new and higher goals of consumption.

Universalization of Family Planning and Commitment to Occupation. As the household conveniences of the affluent society have grown, women have had more choice in how they will spend their time, and they have

21. J. Seeley, R. Sim, and E. Loosley, *Crestwood Heights,* New York: Wiley, 1956 (Science Editions, 1963).
22. W. Whyte, *The Organization Man,* New York: Simon and Schuster, 1956.
23. R. Smuts, *Women and Work in America,* New York: Columbia University Press, 1959.
24. L. Hoffman and F. Wyatt, "Social change and motivations for having larger families: some theoretical considerations," *Merrill-Palmer Quart.,* 6 (July 1960), 235–244.
25. D. Van Bortel, *Homemaking: Concepts, Practices and Attitudes in Two Social Class Groups,* unpublished Ph.D. dissertation, University of Chicago, 1954.
26. J. Galbraith, *op. cit.*

come into more control of consumer decisions than they have ever had before. Among all such decisions, perhaps the most far-reaching has to do with family size. The number and spacing of children determines the time and resources that will be available for other uses. Women liberationists currently emphasize the right of women to control their own bodies and their right to easy contraception and abortion. But generally, I believe, our emerging desire for population control implies that not just the woman but each couple will engage in rational planning about family size, and that the outcome will be the result of a *joint decision*. Thus the issue of family planning is universalized to touch the consciousness of both men and women.

As more women enter paid employment, the possibility arises for another kind of exchange of consciousness between men and women. On the one hand, women may learn to share with men the frustrations and demands, as well as the stimulations, of occupation. On the other hand, women may be able to teach men how better to integrate work and family by arguing for part-time work, more flexible hours, parent leaves—all of which can relieve some of the strain on the working man as well as on the working woman.

Demographic Trends

Recent changes in rates of marriage, child-bearing, and employment of women all suggest that parental and marital roles have been differentiated so that they are no longer seen as coterminous with women's lives. Since the 1940s, more women are free to combine activities that were once thought to be mutually exclusive. Like men, they are free to do several things at once: marry, have children, *and* work.

A key factor in this change has been the shortening of the child-bearing period. Beginning with the 1920s the average number of children per family dropped to 3.5.[27] This factor, combined with earlier marriage, resulted in the average woman bearing her last child by the age of 26. Clearly a great deal of her time was set free for other activities.

A second key development has been the drop in number of people who remain single. The change was most striking during the 1940s among highly educated women for whom the rate of change was twice that of the general population.[28] Given that a higher proportion of college-educated women work than those with less education, the combined effect of these trends was to bring more married women into the labor force.[29]

A third significant shift was in the employment rate of mothers with

27. R. Thomasson, "Why has American fertility been so high?" in *Kinship and Family Organization*, B. Farber, ed., New York: Wiley, 1966.

28. P. Glick, *American Families*, New York: Wiley, 1957.

29. However, it was probably this same increase in marriage rate that also accounted for the drop in percent in women receiving advanced degrees after 1940 (U.S. Women's Bureau, *Trends in Educational Attainment*, 1969).

young children, which more than doubled in the years between 1948 and 1967.[30] That such an increase could occur during a period of general affluence suggests a remarkable reorganization of marital and parental roles. Women had time, energy, and motivation to fulfill several kinds of obligations at once, perhaps because housework, child-rearing, marriage, and occupation were all specific and limited enough in their demands to permit such integration.

Conclusion

Change in the family, demographic trends, and new consciousness about sex roles are linked. Institutional change impinging on the family facilitated women's entry into the labor force. At the same time, actual changes in men's and women's behavior undoubtedly influenced the mores of family life. But this two-way relationship does not in itself explain the *sudden* rise of consciousness about sex roles in the late 1960s.

The fact that the great majority of women in the current liberation movement were born since 1930 is suggestive here. Perhaps it was only when these generations had come of age that a concerted assault on traditional family roles could take place. These younger people had been steeped in the new morality, the new psychology, the experience of mechanization and the interchangeability of personnel. It took only a small step to extend these principles to sex roles.

Change will require a much larger step from older generations and people unfamiliar or unsympathetic with these trends. The elements of a stereotyped sex role ideology are still very much with us. Nevertheless, it is not amiss to suggest that there may be a more rapid acceptance of sex equality *in principle* (as distinguished from all aspects of behavior) than is presently supposed. For it is after all not only the generation under forty that has experienced post-depression changes, but the whole society. If poeple can be shown that liberation of men and women is not a wild idea but an extension of reasonable principles they have already accepted, and in fact *lived,* then it is only a matter of time until we shall see further change of remarkable proportions.

30. U.S. Department of Labor, Bureau of Labor Statistics, *Handbook of Labor Statistics,* Bulletin no. 1630, 1969.

CHANGING ROLES OF AMERICAN WOMEN

With the separation between the home and the place of work in modern society, women have been deprived to a large extent of participation in the world of work. In our achievement-oriented society, however, a person's occupation is the main source of status; woman, in general, derives her status from her husband's occupation.

Women who want to be achievers in the occupational world have to reconcile contradictory expectations. Our educational system has taught them that their achievement is measured in the same way as that of men; yet this is no longer the case after education has been obtained. If they want to work outside the home, they must reconcile the expectations for equal achievement with those concerning their role in the family. Cynthia Epstein examines in great detail the problems and conflicts underlying such reconciliation and the mechanisms, insufficient as they are, for bringing it about.

The problems women encounter when entering the occupational world—such as exclusion or inequality in rewards—are due in large part to the assumption that occupational commitments conflict with the woman's cultural mandate that she, and she alone, be responsible for the care of the family. This is linked with the man's cultural mandate that he, and he alone, be responsible for the family's support and status placement, even where the wife supplements the family income. The paper by the editor with Gerald Rokoff examines the consequences of these cultural mandates.

Mirra Komarovsky's analysis of the contradictions in women's roles is followed by her examination of attitudes thirty years later of both men and women. It turns out that while much has changed in regard to expectations of women in the occupational sphere, ambiguities remain, the main one concerning the potential superiority of women over men within the same interactional system.

If women's roles change, so will the structure of the family. Some people believe that the nuclear family cannot continue to exist if husband and wife are fully equal. In the last chapter some alternative living arrangements are explored. It will turn out that freedom and full equality are not easy to obtain under communal arrangements either. If, in American society, equality is a guiding value, much effort has to be spent for its realization; and whether the change will be effected within the family, or by eliminating it, remains to be seen. In my considered opinion, the family has changed before, and it can change again.

9 CONFLICT AND CONTRADICTION IN WOMEN'S ROLES

Cynthia Fuchs Epstein

Reconciliation of Women's Roles

. . . Women face the problem of being the wrong sex in professional life because there are expectations in society and in the professions about the compatibility of different statuses in status sets.[1] "Status-set typing" occurs when a class of persons shares statuses (that is, certain statuses tend to cluster) *and when it is considered appropriate that they do so*. The upper stratum of the legal profession, for example, is status-set typed because it is commonly expected and preferred that lawyers will share not only their common occupational status (the "functionally relevant"[2] status conferred by admission to the bar), but other statuses—for example, white, male, and Anglo-Saxon—some of which are irrelevant to the practice of law. (The latter statuses are believed to complement the occupational status, although they may not be necessary for performance of the professional task.) The configuration of statuses encountered in any case of status-set typing is the one found most frequently in

---

1. A status set is defined by Merton as the complement of social statuses of an individual; "Reference Groups and Group Structure" in his *Social Theory and Social Structure*, p. 370. The dynamics of status sets, including the consequences of status sets which occur infrequently and which do not conform to cultural expectations, is a subject which has been dealt with extensively by Professor Merton in lectures at Columbia University over the past few years. This analysis draws upon his conceptualization of many of these questions.
2. Functionally relevant in Merton's sense of being *task*-linked.

combination. When statuses occur in a combination not typically found, the situation is considered "news" and it makes people feel uncomfortable. Both of these reactions are illustrated by the way in which the rigid status-set typing of the British legal profession recently created a Chaplinesque protocol crisis when confronted with the appointment of a woman judge, Mrs. Elizabeth Lane, to the High Court of Justice. The Lord Chancellor's Office, charged with resolving the matter, decreed that, for reasons of protocol, the lady should be referred to as a man. According to *Time* magazine's account of the crisis and its resolution:

> Only four women barristers have yet earned the elite title of Queen's Counsel (senior barrister). Only one woman Q.C. has yet become a judge in one of Britain's nearly 400 county courts. Not surprisingly, the elevation of that same woman to the country's No. 3 tribunal, the High Court of Justice, has touched off a splendidly British protocol crisis.
>
> Visually, Mrs. Elizabeth Lane, 60, will look little different from her male colleagues when she dons her gown and wig and joins four other new appointees as the first woman among the High Court's 62 justices. But the problem is: what should lawyers call her. "My Lord" seemed confusing at best, while traditionalists cringed at the sound of "Mrs. Justice." After grave deliberation, the Lord Chancellor's office has duly issued its decision: henceforth, Mrs. Lane will be Mr. Justice Lane, and may indeed be called "My Lord." "There simply isn't any precedent for calling a woman anything different," argued a harassed official. "We've taken what seems the least absurd decision."
>
> His Lordship, Mr. Justice Lane, is also entitled by ancient judicial tradition to a bachelor knighthood. . . .[3]

The major consequence of a person's acquisition of a status which "should" not fit in with the others he holds is that irrelevant statuses will be focused upon, or activated. In such deviant cases, the irrelevant status is the *salient* status.[4]

. . . Robert Merton has pointed out that some statuses are more "dominant" than others in that they may limit or facilitate the acquisition of other statuses. For example, if I know that someone is a middle-class woman, I can feel safe in predicting that she does *not* also hold the status of corporation manager. The salient status in a status set is the one activated by the individual and his role partners and becomes the object of focus in interaction. The salient status may be the irrelevant one (often because it is not normally found in combination with the other statuses with which it appears) in any given context. (If we are at a business meeting and the lady has indeed turned out to be a corporation manager, I will be most conscious of the fact that she is a woman even though I ought to keep my mind on whether she is a good "businessman" or not.) The salient status then may draw the attention of the members of one's various role sets to

---

3. *Time* (August 27, 1965), p. 40.
4. This follows Merton's definition of salience in his analysis of the dynamics of status sets (definitions from unpublished lectures).

the exclusion of other statuses which may be more relevant. Certain ascribed statuses—sex status and racial status, for example—are central in controlling the choices of most individuals. The status of "woman" is one such dominant and often salient status. For a woman, sex status is primary and pivotal and it inevitably determines much of the course of her life, especially because of rigid cultural definitions which limit the range of other statuses she may acquire. . . .

Hierarchy in the Status Set

Why must the woman who aspires to a professional career be a noncon-formist? Why have so many been single? What barriers has society stacked against her? Most fundamentally, the woman professional must face a conflict in the hierarchy of status priorities in Western society. For women, the obligations attached to family statuses are first in priority, while for men the role demands deriving from the occupational status ordinarily override all others. The woman's duties as a mother override most other role obligations, her duties as a wife are second, and other status obligations are usually a poor third.

The woman who acquires the status of professional acquires with it a seemingly insurmountable problem of role strain: Should she conform to the demands imposed on her because she is a mother or wife, or should she give priority to those demands which come as a result of being a doctor or scientist? What must she do when, as often occurs, the two conflict?

The role strain experienced by the woman professional can easily become constant and enervating, aggravated by the ambiguity that makes necessary a new decision for each minor conflict, and by the often conflicting positions taken by other people in her role network.

The man is to a great extent shielded from conflict "by the existence in his environment of a hierarchy of values which preclude, for the most part, the necessity of conscious decision. Unless family needs reach crisis proportion, the demands of his work come first. And neither he nor his wife is faced with problems of choice in a condition of crisis."[5]

Persons engaged in professional activity are especially expected to channel a large proportion of their emotional and physical energies to work. Not only is achievement a positive good, but in the tradition of the Protestant ethic, work itself is good and often its own excuse. The man who spends too much time with his family is considered something of a loafer.

Furthermore, a man's duties and obligations *as a husband* fall

5. Lotte Bailyn, "Notes on the Role of Choice in the Psychology of Professional Women," pp. 706–707.

primarily in the occupational sphere. If he earns an adequate living for his family, he has nearly fulfilled society's demands on him and, depending on his social rank, he has a wide range of acceptable behavior within which he may fulfill his other husband-father roles. For example, he is admired if he likes to putter around the house, but if he can afford it he can pay a handyman to do home repairs with little loss of esteem. If he likes sports he can play ball with his son, but if he prefers sedentary activities no one will hold it against him if he instead plays chess or checkers or builds model airplanes with his child. He must, of course, show some interest in his child to be considered a good father in our society, but a little is often enough. It is not even as onerous to be labeled a poor father as it is to be called a poor mother. Expectations about what is an adequate amount of time for a man to be with his wife are also imprecise; a man's other activities, starting with work obligations but including clubs, hobbies, politics, and informal male social get-togethers, all are legitimate reasons for cutting down on this time. Assuming that the husband is not spending time away from home to be with another woman, the wife is given little legitimation for objecting to his absence. The wife who does object and who demands that her husband remain home is likely to be labeled a "nag." In addition, the husband may feel free to be away from home and family, knowing that his wife is there to take care of things, to supervise the children's activities, to manage the house. In extreme cases of neglect, wives may be permitted to complain, but clearly the absorption of the man in his work is not considered intolerable. Professors who prefer their work to their wives or children are usually "understood" and forgiven.[6] A similar absorption in work was reported by Stanley Talbot in *Time* magazine; he found that the business tycoon (not surprisingly) clearly preferred his work to his family.[7] There is no comparable "lady tycoon" with a husband and children to neglect; and the lady professional who gives any indication of being more absorbed in work than in her husband and family is neither understood nor forgiven. The woman, unlike the man, cannot spend "too much time" with her family; her role demands as mother and wife are such that they intrude on all other activities. She remains on call during any time spent away from the family and, if she works, many of her family tasks must be fitted into what usually would be working time.[8]

Since the woman who works must deal with two conflicting priority systems (occupational demands are not lowered for the woman though she may consider them second in importance), she may often find herself under strain to perform both roles adequately.

6. See Jessie Bernard's comments in "Wives and Mothers," chapter 15 of *Academic Women*, pp. 215–241.

7. *Time* (November 10, 1952), p. 109.

8. Bryan and Boring, "Women in American Psychology: Factors Affecting Their Professional Careers," *American Psychologist* 2 (January 1947), 3–20.

It is often assumed that a woman's professional commitments deflect her from home obligations and vice versa. A man may find that being a husband supports his occupational roles.[9] Edwin Boring and Alice Bryan have observed, in a study of factors affecting the professional careers of women psychologists, that "Women averaged 14.1 hours per week on familial or domestic activities as compared with 10.6 hours for the men. Three or more hours per week were spent on child-training and guidance by 29.4 percent of women, on physical care of children by 24.5 percent, and on special problems of children by 10.2 percent."[10]

In a later study, Boring also noted that nearly all the male psychologists are married, and "a married man usually manages to make his marriage contribute to his success and prestige. Most of the married women do not receive the same professional support from their husbands and the unmarried women have no husbands."[11] Riesman has pointed to the married male professor's advantage in having a wife, "who even if she does pursue a part-time career, guards her husband's productivity and performance in obvious and in subtle ways, just as her husband's secretary or the woman librarian . . . speeds him on his way."[12] The man's status set is complementary and reinforcing and the woman's is not. The professional woman who marries and permits proliferation of her family statuses must early face the fact that she has no wife at home.

Family Roles

What are the role demands on the wife which lead to conflict with her possible or actual occupational roles?

To begin with, the American conjugal family system heavily weights the obligations of the woman's roles in the family—far beyond those of the man. The obligations of the mother-wife role are rigorously demanding of the woman. Indeed, they have typically constituted a full-time occupation in spite of the observations of Talcott Parsons[13] and other sociologists who claim that the American woman has little to do. Although many share his view that the "utilitarian aspect of the role of the housewife . . . has declined in importance to the point where it scarcely approaches a full-time occupation for a vigorous person,"[14] it is obvious to all that most middle-class women do fill their days in a myriad of household activities.

9. See William J. Goode's analysis of the interlocking of role obligations, "A Theory of Role Strain," *American Sociological Review* 25 (August 1960), 483–496.
10. Bryan and Boring, *op. cit.*, pp. 17–18.
11. Boring, "The Woman Problem," p. 681.
12. David Riesman, in his introduction to Jessie Bernard, *Academic Women*, p. xxiv.
13. In "Age and Sex in the Social Structure of the United States," pp. 89–103.
14. *Ibid.*, p. 98.

Unlike the extended family, in which a division of household labor is possible among numbers of kin, in the conjugal family the primary responsibility for managing the household falls to the wife. Even though some paid domestic help often is feasible, she must administer the household and as a manager is responsible for a very large number of tasks. These responsibilities become more numerous with income, class position, and number of children. They also seem to proliferate in middle age. Whether or not all these tasks are essential or could be eliminated does not mitigate the fact that they demand decision and are usually not easy to delegate to others.

Note, too, that the burden of these tasks is nearly constant and repetitive; food must be planned daily, children's activities occur throughout each day, and in the evening the husband wants and expects his wife to be a good companion or just to "be around." In clear conflict with this schedule, which demands that the wife be "on tap" from time to time, are the needs of the professional for large blocks of uninterrupted time. Snatches of time taken here and there are not additive,[15] and snatches of time are often all that the housewife can muster.

Limitations of the Institutional Structure

. . . The American woman faces her major impediment to a career in obligations she has and feels as a result of her statuses as wife and mother. Another important barrier lies in the power, authority, and ranking structure of the American social system, today more simplistically known as the Establishment. Women may be involved in the Establishment and essential to its smooth functioning, but only rarely do they occupy positions of power and authority within it. The problems they face in reaching such positions arise because vested interests fight to maintain the status quo and social pressures act to maintain the system as it has been.

Although some institutions change easily with the times, others seem more resistant to change. Women who respond to progress in the occupational world may find that the institution of the family is slower to change. Reconciling the disharmonies becomes a problem which the individual must face alone.

One can gain some insight by application of the "power" terminology so popular today.

---

15. Bailyn, *op. cit.*, p. 706. Goode, too, has commented on the great amount of administrative work handled by the women, also suggesting that this capacity could be tapped for managerial work in business and the professions.

Vested Interests in the Role Network

Goode is one social analyst who has indicated that men are loath to grant women opportunities to challenge their power positions.[16] Their opposition is not ideologically based but "interest" based. Because men typically have more power, they suspect and fear encroachment on that power. The situation is, of course, analogous to the fears of whites about retaining job priorities in the face of advancing opportunities for Negroes.[17] Hacker has claimed that discrimination against women arises from the "present contravention of the sexes," and outlines a number of types of opposition men display in the face of their "doubts and uncertainties concerning women's character, abilities and motives."[18] Many working women have firsthand knowledge of the responses of the threatened male, husband or employer, responses such as restraining, hindering, and upsetting their plans in managing work and home, often with the excuse that it is in the best interests of the woman. In fact, both the men and women in role network of the career-seeking woman may have interests in keeping her out of the occupational sphere and will put pressure on her to remain occupied with her home.

Let us examine the sources of negative pressures which arise from women's role networks and those which are culturally built in.

Husbands who may stand to lose on a number of levels if their wives work. The husband may need his wife to be available to promote his own success. As we have seen, she must be ready for business entertaining or to free him from time-consuming tasks (shopping for clothes, planning trips, maintaining links with his kin, and administering the home).

The husband may also feel threatened by the possibility that a working wife could outrank him in occupation or level of success. In American society the man whose wife is more prominent than he is, is usually pitied.[19] His position may be threatened even within the home. Most men are in an economically dominant position as breadwinner in the household and are usually the final decision-makers.

There seems to be a curvilinear relationship between male dominance in the household and class position. It is lowest among the lower classes and increases with class level until it drops as it approaches the upper class, where the woman may command independent economic resources by inheritance. Thus, particularly in the middle class, the wife may in fact make most household decisions but most concede the right of

16. Goode, *The Family,* p. 74.
17. For a further comparison see Helen Mayer Hacker, "Women as a Minority Group," *Social Forces* 30 (1951–52), 60–69.
18. *Ibid.,* p. 67.
19. The problems of rank disequilibrium and some mechanisms women lawyers use for coping with it in situations where they outrank their husbands are dealt with in my dissertation, "Women and Professional Careers," chapter 7.

the husband to a final veto. An index to the normative mandate requiring the wife's deference to the husband in important matters is the many jokes and folk wisdoms which instruct the wife how to "get around" her husband. The husband may demand his "rights"; the wife must wheedle. But a number of studies have indicated that where the wife also has command over economic resources, that is, if she works, her decision-making power in the household increases.[20] Her income, especially if it is greater than his, can undermine the basis for his authority over both her and the family as a whole.

The husband of a working wife may feel genuinely deprived compared to other husbands he knows and may well be absolutely deprived (he may, for example, have more household tasks to do). Practically, the husband requires a wife-surrogate when his wife is not present or is only a part-time wife, just as the child needs a surrogate for an absent mother. But the wife will usually be unwilling to find herself substituted for. The surrogate-wife is hardly an institutionalized role in the United States (those substitutes the husband picks usually are given other names). Thus the husband may make do with less by choice or by becoming resigned to it even though it is hardly in his interest to do so. And, although they might not be willing to admit it, some husbands may feel threatened by sexual competition from the men their wives encounter in the course of their work. Keeping women home-bound; segregating them in suburbia where their only companionship is obtained from women in the same straits is as good a social structural device as India's purdah for keeping them locked into marriage. Though the housewife may meet many men in the course of a day, they are not typically from her own class. The husband faces real competition only when his wife is in contact with men from her own class who share her interests and tasks. The middle-class woman might run away with a corporate vice president, but she is not likely to run away with the laundry man. (A wife may also feel threatened by her husband's contacts with women in the work world. His daily association with a secretary who is either from a different social class and/or age category may not threaten too much because the relationship is normatively defined as necessary to the work. But like it or not, wives are in no position to do much about their feelings of insecurity.)

On the other hand, there may be, of course, considerable payoff in terms of shared interests, the "halo effect" to the husband of his wife's success, and the luxuries that added income may buy. The husband may also feel no loss if his wife performs all her roles with deep commitment and high energy but, as yet, such perfectly balanced relationships are rare.

20. For example, Robert O. Blood, "The Husband-Wife Relationship," in F. Ivan Nye and Lois Wladis Hoffman, *The Employed Mother in America* (Chicago: Rand McNally & Co., 1963), p. 294.

Housewives who see the working woman as a threat to themselves.[21] The threat is varied. Career women are seen as competitors for their husbands (the working woman, through deprecated, also seems more glamorous—and often is, because she usually takes care of her appearance and is more interesting). The career also provides an alternate model to the domestic life and may cause the housewife to question her own choice of life style.

Parents, who may feel uncomfortable at having a career-minded daughter. Although parents usually derive satisfaction from the mobility of a son, they may feel more ambivalent about their daughter's occupational success. The career-woman/daughter sometimes must be explained away or apologized for, lest friends believe they have produced an unfeminine daughter. Success is measured by the daughter's performance of the more traditional female roles. But parents may demonstrate considerable after-the-fact recognition because they do not assume their daughter will be successful. Once she has "arrived" they feel a deep sense of pride and forget having put emotional obstacles in her way or having chosen to assist their son in preference to their daughter.

Children, who more than any other group cannot perceive any personal advantage in the career of their mother. This attitude tends to vary, however, with the social environment of the child. We would expect youngsters who are reared with other children of working mothers to experience a lesser sense of relative disadvantage. However, those who grow up in communities where only a small percentage of mothers work might be expected to exert strong pressures on their mothers not to work.

Problems Caused by Stratification

Mechanisms which support stratification deter women's participation in high-ranking careers. Women derive rank first from their fathers and later from their husbands. This process works to keep families unified and is useful and necessary for the socialization of the children. Another consequence, however, is that it makes for a closed caste system for the married woman. Given our system, in which work is one of the prime determinants of rank position, it would indeed be "bad" if the woman achieved a high-ranking job, one higher than her husband's. Confusion would arise over her proper social niche. This is true to some extent also for the woman who outranks her husband socially by birth. A husband can raise a lower-ranking wife to his level without much disturbing the

21. Arnold Rose, in "The Adequacy of Women's Expectations for Adult Roles," makes an analogy between these women and those who opposed women's suffrage.

stratification system, provided, of course, that she can assume social graces appropriate for the rank.[22]

But when the husband is of lower social rank than the wife, he will rise only with difficulty and will experience and cause distress in social relations. There are few norms which guide the higher-ranking network in dealing with the lower-ranking aspirant: women may be absorbed; it is far more difficult to accept a man.

Institutions–The Pressures and Their Needs

A striking social obstacle to the utilization of woman-power in the occupational sphere comes from their participation in other institutions. The most obvious demands are, of course, those made by the family, described above. But changes in the economic structure of American society also have engaged women's time in other restrictive ways by enlarging the scope of the female role.

That women are probably the main agents of consumption in American society is an observation that social philosophers (including those on the left) fail to decry but that the advertising experts of Madison Avenue know well. Betty Friedan examined the implications of feminine spending in a chapter of *The Feminine Mystique* that never evoked popular excitement. She asked:

> Why is it never said that the . . . really important role that women serve as housewives is *to buy more things for the house?* In all the talk of femininity and women's role, one forgets that the real business of America is business. But the perpetuation of housewifery, the growth of the feminine mystique, makes sense (and dollars) when one realizes that women are the chief customers of American business.[23]

Of course there is a "chicken-or-the-egg" question involved here: Do American women, because of greater leisure time, devote themselves to perusing the marketplace, or are there important pressures which direct them to devote more time to it because the economy, built on consumption, obsolescence, and replacement, depends on this essentially feminine activity? There is no doubt that, whether or not this activity is an intended or an unanticipated consequence of our economic system, prosperity and production would probably falter if women were to spend more time with ideas rather than with furniture, clothing, and the popular media.

It is also part of the wife's role to adorn herself and her home as an attestation of the husband's rank. We can expect that activity in this area increases with socio-economic level.

It is not necessary to our analysis to consider the dynamics of the

22. Elinor Barber describes the phenomenon for another historical period in *The Bourgeoisie in 18th Century France* (Princeton, N.J.: Princeton University Press, 1955).
23. Betty Friedan, *The Feminine Mystique*, pp. 206–207.

economic system, or even to question whether or not alternative modes of consumption could guarantee the United States an equally high standard of living; we need only point out its implications for the woman's time budget and life style.

Consider some implications of the fact that in American society woman's primary economic role has come to be that of a consumer.

In the sex division of labor, women have been allocated the purchasing role in the United States, important because a large part of the culture is built around consumption. Shopping is a popular activity, legitimized by the value attached to intelligent shopping—getting good value and bargains. The value of clever shopping seems to be rated higher than the value of the time spent on it, which, in the case of housewives, is rarely calculated in the total cost. Of course, the shopping syndrome is made possible by the large amount and variety of goods available in the society and the money and credit available for purchases.

In contrast, Soviet and Chinese society are not consumer societies. Perhaps they will become so in time, but they do not now have an array of goods to consume. Therefore the consumer's role does not have to be filled by persons of any particular social category. In a sense, women in the Soviet Union gain from their society's deprivation. Even the Russian counterpart of the corporation wife cannot ordinarily buy a large house and devote herself to decorating it. Though people wish to have consumer goods, their acquisition is still sharply limited by availability, time, money, and space in which to put them. Families live in cramped quarters, and apartments often shelter several generations of a family or even several families.[24] Women living in these conditions can hardly reinforce each other's addiction to home improvements. For the Soviet woman truly to express herself, she must follow the male pattern —through work.

To the extent to which business acknowledges and encourages women's institutionalized role as consumers, it has a vested interest in keeping the costs of women's professional activity high. Professional women are less consumer-oriented; they have less time to buy and be pre-occupied with purchasing, and they have not generally been a target group for advertising. We do not know whether working women in fact spend less than housewives of the same class. Women lawyers interviewed for my study did not report spending a significant percentage of their time on shopping; they did make substantial purchases and used personal services such as professional laundries and caterers, and, of course, they often bought expensive clothing. As yet, however, business has not produced specifically for the market oriented to the career woman and therefore appears to be not interested in selling to it.

24. See David Granick, *Red Executive* (New York: Doubleday, 1963), for a description of how middle-managerial people in the Soviet Union live.

The Economics of Working

American society finds its rationale for work in the Protestant ethic: work is a means of livelihood rather than an avenue for self-expression or self-realization. So the case against the middle-class married woman who works is often put in economic terms: "Does it *pay* her to work?" Only rarely will it go beyond, to "Does it benefit society?" "Does she want to work?" or some similar question. The reply is expected to be measured in terms of the high expenses incurred by the woman for child-care services, added clothing, daily work expenses, domestic help, expenditure for high-cost convenience foods, and the difference between the cost of her convenience shopping and the full-time housewife's comparison shopping.

The incomes of working women are taxed at the same rate as men's and often at higher rates if they are added to the husbands', as they are on most family tax returns. Although the cost of child care is the most fundamental of a working mother's business expenses, tax relief for child care is available only to those women in the very lowest economic strata. Child care alone can consume a considerable portion of the working mother's salary. (Although much has been said publicly on this issue, including a recommendation of the President's Commission on the Status of Women to liberalize existing provisions for tax exemptions,[25] no implementing legislative action has been taken. This suggests a rather low priority given to it by society.)

Thus, work pays only those women who must work (and perhaps depend on free baby-sitting from kin) and the relatively rare highly paid woman professional. When the family's books are balanced, the typical woman's work is not likely to show a sizeable economic return, at least when compared to that of her husband. Further, the weighing of potential economic return is usually applied to the woman early in her life, when the possibility of substantial financial gain seems—and is—remote. It seems a reasonable assumption that many lower-income families will strain their budgets to help a son through college while declining to pay any part of a girl's expenses; it is further likely that many girls from poorer families, realizing the difficulty of earning all their own expenses, never seriously consider college.[26]

In addition, girls do not ask for financial help even when it is available. In James Davis's *Great Aspirations* study of bright students going on to graduate schools, only 18 percent of the men but 41 percent of

25. *Report of the Commission on the Status of Women* (Washington, D.C.: U.S. Government Printing Office, 1963).

26. Ernest Havemann and Patricia West, *They Went to College: The College Graduate in America Today* (New York: Harcourt Brace & Co. 1952), p. 15; and Goode, *World Revolution and Family Patterns*, p. 14.

the women did not apply for stipends. Of those who did not apply, 47 percent of the brightest men were not going on to graduate school for financial reasons; 38 percent of the brightest women did not go on.[27]

In a discussion of the work of President's Committee on Education Beyond High School, Anna Hawkes has commented: "Very few girls will mortgage their future for the present education. They will not saddle their husbands-to-be with the cost of their education, and they are fearful they will not be able to repay the debt before they marry. For boys, borrowing for their education is a definite investment in their future."[28] Girls who go to college generally depend on their parents for financial support; Havemann and West report that of the girls in their sample only one in six earned one-half or more of their own expenses as opposed to five-sixths of the boys who partially or entirely paid for their own education.[29]

The evidence suggests that while the daugher of the upper-stratum family has the same access to higher education that her brother has (although not to professional training), the goals of the daughter of the lower-strata family will be sacrificed as a matter of course to give her brother the opportunity at college training.

It is likely that where the family is under financial strain it will find ways to pay for a boy's medical or other professional education, and then will elicit assistance from other kin to buy equipment to put him in practice. This is probably not true for the girl, even if her feelings of commitment are strong, except in a markedly better family economic situation. (One governing factor may be the girl's marriage prospects at the time she enters her profession. If her prospects are poor, she may have a better chance for aid, but if she is about to be married her family may refuse to help her.) Parents who expect to reap benefits in their old age from investment in a son may not feel they can count on such support from a daughter's success.

This type of economic reasoning is a strong element in the sequence of decisions that leads most girls to liberal arts programs in college. Training in a technical specialization is not considered a good investment for a girl. Technical training is specific training, and the more specific the training, the more real the sense of impending waste—if a woman marries and does not work, the specialized training is unusable. (Women lawyers who leave law often claim their training in logical thinking is useful in everyday life, but none is able to use her specific knowledge of the law in more than peripheral ways.)

27. James A. Davis, *Great Aspirations*. Volume I: "Career Decisions and Educational Plans During College," p. 499.
28. Anna L. Rose Hawkes, "Factors Affecting College Attendance," in Opal D. David (ed.), *The Education of Women*, p. 31.
29. Havemann and West, *op. cit.*, p. 18.

Many assume that the woman will not practice in the field in which she has been trained, or if she does that her career will lack continuity. It is true that this career pattern is followed by many professionally qualified women. But the pattern, though the understandable result of many pressures, cannot reasonably be held to be inevitable or to be a justification, on economic grounds, for a veto of effective career planning. The failure to plan effectively is often a result of cultural attitudes toward the value of time and money and priorities for spending which are economically nonrational.

It is true that usually little or no thought is given to the investment necessary early in many women's careers for child and household care, even though this is an investment likely to be returned with interest as the woman advances in her work. Thus, while a male doctor expects to go into debt to buy equipment for an office or to pay for his training, a woman doctor may not feel as free to borrow in addition to pay a housekeeper, an essential part of what she requires to build a practice. It is also probably true that if her family did not have resources, a bank would not give a loan for this specific purpose, though perhaps this has not been tested. Even when women are given fellowship aid for studies, they are reluctant to use it for child care or other household help. Very likely she will drop or delay her work because she cannot afford to be free to work. (Hanna Papenek suggests[30] that because there is not enough work in the modern American home to keep a housekeeper busy full time, it is not considered worthwhile to pay her to be around in case she is needed, *even if one can afford it*.)

The problem varies, however, with the type of work. Doctors can count on a good income in the early years of practice; attorneys, however, usually do not reach a comparable level until their practices are well established, perhaps not until late middle age. Thus the woman doctor may have far better economic reasons to stick to her practice than the woman lawyer who knows that economic reward still is far away. This may also be the reason why women lawyers, far more than men, seek salaried positions.

It is precisely in the years in which a woman most needs household help that she is also most apt to make the least money. Unless she plans well ahead and has vision and confidence, she may be unable to succeed. (Many professional women I interviewed did not face this problem because they married late and had children after their careers were well established.)

But there is no doubt that the professional woman who does make the early investment can make work pay. We would expect, therefore, that those women who have families and also build successful professional

---

30. As quoted by Lotte Bailyn, *op. cit.*, p. 706.

lives do not fall prey to the dominant attitudes concerning the economics of women's work. Almost any professional makes more money than a domestic employee, and each additional year of practice means an increased income.

Vested Interests of the Middle-Class Woman

. . . The American middle-class woman has a substantial interest in the status quo. This commitment is clearly linked to the secondary gains that have accrued to her, seemingly as rewards for service to her class, her husband, and her society. Consider the wide range of these gains.

Rank. To the extent that her husband is successful, the American woman need not concern herself with building or maintaining rank in society. She simply takes as her own the rank achieved through her husband's success. (Of course, it is no gain to her if her husband does not achieve respectable rank, but nevertheless she rides tandem with him on the road to success *or* failure.)

Public Attention. To the extent that her husband is successful, the wife will gain attention irrespective of her own qualities (although these can, of course, enhance the demand for her presence). Mrs. Richard Nixon, for example, recently was the recipient of an honorary Doctor of Laws degree from Finch College, although she had not participated notably in any occupational or artistic activities. As wife of the the Republican candidate for president, she had achieved "fame." Hers is but one of the numerous cases of women who rise to public attention when their husbands attain success; they become subjects for feature articles in women's magazines and national magazines such as *Life* or *Time.*

Leisure Time. If the woman chooses to use domestic help to care for her home and children, she has considerable freedom to pursue individual interests in the arts, athletics, and social activities. However, her freedom is somewhat limited, and should a hobby develop into a vocational interest she may encounter considerable opposition. She may, however, schedule her time as she pleases and is limited only by the schedules of her children and husband.

Lack of Economic Pressure to Work. The woman is freed from pursuing a vocation and, short of a family economic crisis, she is not expected to contribute to the joint finances. Should she want to work, she need not make a great deal of money. Thus, because she doesn't have to, the woman has a choice of either voluntary work or work for pay.

Lowered Standards. The middle-class woman is required to operate at only minimum capacity. So far as achievement is concerned, it is likely that anything she does outside of the home—from P.T.A. and charity work to a part-time job or participation in politics—will be regarded as extra and evidence that she is a superior person. (Although standards for housekeeping performance have undoubtedly gone up, it is doubtful that a plain cook will suffer criticism; rather, a gourmet cook will be praised.)

If the middle-class woman enters the occupational world, she is not judged by the same standards as her husband. Working women receive more praise and notice at a lower rank in the occupational hierarchy than a man would, and for a lower level of performance as well.[31] This gain has a clear drawback. She gets more for doing less, but is more satisfied with less and has less incentive to aim higher. George Homans describes this phenomenon as "occupational justice," since "by the standards current in American industry, the female sex is considered to have made a lower investment than the male, and so by distributive justice, to deserve a less good job than the male."[32]

The Pattern of Revocability. As we pointed out earlier, American women have cultural approval to "cop out." Those women who choose to leave an occupation or profession at any level, from training to practice, may do so with society's full approval and will be given credit for having reached whatever level they have attained, though a man in a similar situation would be considered a failure. We found that women ex-lawyers were eagerly sought after in their communities as P.T.A. presidents and club leaders. Male ex-lawyers who retire to a job with lower status would probably be ignored by community organizations.

Devotion to Self. The middle-class woman may have the freedom to devote a major portion of her time to personal adornment and attention to herself. Though some may criticize such narcissistic behavior, it is expected that a wife of a successful man should look her best, much in the same way that a man's efforts to improve his position are not seen as ego adornment but as an effort on behalf of his family. The woman need not work hard at adornment either; she needs only the taste and money to pick her beauticians and couturiers. In another culture this style of life might be considered parasitic, but to the extent that the woman enjoys it and can afford it, it is condoned in American society.

Money. Middle-class and upper-class women can depend on income that bears no direct connection to their efforts, ability, or output. They have achieved, in effect, a guaranteed annual wage. They receive it because of their ascriptive status—wife. This definition is upheld by the social system; for example, in divorce actions, alimony for the wife is often calculated on the basis of the style of life her husband has provided

---

31. *Time* (March 6, 1964), p. 48, reporting on women in law, notes that "Many Portias admit with a touch of asperity that they are often overpraised by men for a performance that would be regarded as merely competent in another male."

32. *Social Behavior: Its Elementary Forms* (New York: Harcourt, Brace, and World, 1961), pp. 236–237.

her with before the separation.

       .   .   .

Suburban shopping centers have made it unnecessary for women to come to the central city where there are libraries, art museums, lectures, and, most important, stimulating events and people. Suburban women live in a kind of solitary confinement with those of their own kind.

Child-care services of all kinds are more available in the city. Domestic workers usually prefer to work in the city; probably more emergency child care is available through agencies and neighbors who are sympathetic to the needs of the working mother. In addition, many more private and public nurseries and schools operate in the city.

Though smaller communities offer less anonymity and one can know and depend on one's neighbors more, personal involvements and the requirements of reciprocity can consume more time and energy than they would in a city.

Women and Careers

Much of the strain experienced by the woman who attempts to work is structured strain, caused by a combination of an over-demanding set of role obligations, lack of consensus as to the hierarchy of obligations, and the clash of obligations from home and occupational statuses.

However, there are women who manage to fulfill a difficult combination of statuses. At the very least, they perform the basic role demands of each, though levels of efficiency and competence vary.

       .   .   .

Where the burdens people face in fulfilling status obligations are highly visible, and society places a high priority on them, the institutional structures in which the tasks need to be done will bend to meet personal needs.

When shortages of manpower occur, for example, institutions which must employ women adjust their occupational demands to permit women to meet the demands of their home lives simultaneously. Examples are all-day nurseries attached to factories, more common in Europe than in the United States. In response both to their needs and to public notice of the problem, some American institutions have begun making provision for the children of their professional women staffs. In meeting the needs of women doctors, New York Medical College (The Metropolitan Hospital Center) has initiated a new program permitting part-time residence at the Department of Psychiatry. . . .

Some of the obstacles to women's working come from traditional patterns of work hours and locations, habits usually not at all essential to the tasks involved. Many of these could be and are being changed to adapt to the needs of working mothers.

Rose Laub Coser and Gerald Rokoff

Women in the Occupational World: Social Disruption and Conflict*

The small representation of women in the professions and in high-status positions is a logical consequence of women's cultural mandate which prescribes that their primary allegiance be to the family and that men be its providers of both economic means and social status. Once the premise of this mandate is granted, women who have or wish to have careers are said to have a "conflict," and this conflict is seen as a source of disruption in the social order. The limitation of women's access to high-status positions and prestige professions can be seen as helping prevent disruption in both the occupational and the familial systems.

The conflict experienced by professional women who have a family, and anticipated by young women planning their future, stems not simply from participation in two different activity systems whose claims on time allocations are incompatible. The conflict derives from the fact that the values underlying these demands are contradictory: professional women are expected to be committed to their work "just like men" at the same time as they are normatively required to give priority to their family.

Normative Priorities and Their Routinization

The conflict is one of allegiance, and it does not stem from the mere fact of involvement in more than one social system. It is a conflict of normative priorities. After all, men are fully engaged in their occupations without fearing, and without being told, that they are not committed to their families. It can be said that it is precisely this commitment on the part of men which is the driving force for their hard work. Yet, one does not think of working men as having a conflict between family and occupational obligations. It is only when there is a normative expectation that

---

* Grateful acknowledgment goes to a number of colleagues, who read an earlier version of this paper and contributed to its formulation: Stephen Cole, Andrew Collver, Lewis Coser, Laurie Cummings, Hanan and Rhoda Selvin, Gaye Tuchman, and Harriet Zuckerman.

the family will be allocated resources of time, energy, and affect that cannot be shared with other social institutions that a conflict may arise.

Conflicts of allegiance between the family and other activity systems are not a uniquely modern phenomenon. Economic, political, or religious systems often compete with the family for the allegiance of its members. There always is some tension between society's need for the family as a transmitter of status and values to the next generation, and society's claim on its members for extra-family commitments.

In some societies or organizations that can be called "greedy" because they claim the total allegiance of their members, the importance of the family is played down or denied. It is in this way that we must understand the fact that the Catholic Church has prescribed celibacy for its priests, monks, and nuns. And, paradoxical as this may seem, some Bolsheviks tried to obtain the total allegiance of committed members through an opposite sexual pattern, that is, by extolling the virtues of "free love" and thereby preventing permanent unions. Similarly, in many Utopian communities, prescriptions of either sexual abstinence or sexual promiscuity helped prevent permanent unions and thus served to have the energies of their members concentrated on the well-being of the "community" or the furthering of the "cause."[1]

In modern society, total allegiance to one or the other activity system is rarely expected. Modern life is to a significantly greater extent than primitive or medieval life characterized by the individuals' ability to segment their roles. Modern man involves some of his dispositions in some of his roles, other dispositions in others. The most salient roles in modern American society are those of family and work.

Normative priorities for involvement are often assigned through prescribed separation of activities by time and place. Modern capitalism, as Max Weber has been one of the first to show, owes much of its tremendously rapid and forceful development to the fact that the place of work became separated from the home.[2] This has made possible the exclusion of personal needs and desires, of affective attractions and distractions, from the rational pursuit of the efficient enterprise.

Weber's notion of the separation between home and work is extremely important to understand the efficiency that comes with shutting out personal considerations from rational activities. By combining Weber's notion of the importance of the separation between activity systems with Merton's concept of *status-articulation,* it will become

1. Lewis A. Coser, *Greedy Institutions,* New York: The Free Press, 1974, esp. Chs. 1 and 8, and this book, pp. 532–40. Rosabeth Moss Kanter, "Commitment and social organization: A study of commitment mechanisms in utopian communities," *American Sociological Review* 33 (August 1968): 499–517.

2. A. M. Henderson and Talcott Parsons, eds. and trans., *Introduction to Max Weber, The Theory of Social and Economic Organization,* New York: The Free Press of Glencoe, 1947.

492   *Women in the Occupational World*

possible to spell out the mechanisms that facilitate dealing simultaneously with various status positions. This will also put into a new light the difference between men and women in our society in regard to their dealing with their involvements in multiple activity systems.

In each of his status positions, a person has a set of role-partners; and he usually deals separately with each of the sets. For a father, the family set includes his wife, his children, their teachers, his in-laws, and siblings, his children's friends and the latter's parents, as well as the pediatrician and sometimes the veterinarian. In his occupational set, the same person deals with his associates on the job, and his subordinates or superordinates on different levels of the hierarchy. The fact that the place of work is separated from the home makes it possible for the two role-sets, that of the family and that of work, not to overlap; if they accidentally do, as when an associate on the job is also a neighbor, they overlap less than would be the case if the two realms were not separated.

This separation of the different role-sets makes possible the operation of mechanisms that facilitate and, more importantly, routinize *status-articulation,* that is, the decision a person must make as to which of his role-sets he will give priority to. This is not to say that an individual will never experience contradictory demands in his different roles, but that he will face fewer of them than if these mechanisms were not at work.

We do not have to go far to investigate the mechanisms that facilitate status-articulation. They are the same as those outlined by Merton in regard to role-articulation, that is, in regard to the decision a person must make as to which of the multiple expectations facing him in his *single* role he will give priority to. Merton[3] shows that the fact that an individual is not in the presence of all of his role-partners at the same time helps reduce the burden of their incompatible or conflicting expectations; and so does the fact that the various role-partners have a different amount or type of power over him, as well as a different type of interest in his activities.

Here Weber's observation about the importance of the separation between home and work gains salience. Through the territorial and temporal separation of activities, the mechanisms of *insulation from observability, differential authority over,* and *differential interest* in the status-occupant on the part of his various role-partners operate more efficiently than if these activities were merged. In this arrangement the individual is not only insulated from the observability but also from the authority and the interest of his role-partners in the other set. A woman is not expected to tell her husband how to behave on the job, nor can his employer tell him how to behave at home. The fact that in both cases it can be said that "it is none of their business to care" bears witness to the normative limits of interest in the status-occupant's behavior in the other

3. Robert K. Merton, *Social Theory and Social Structure,* New York: The Free Press, 1968, pp. 425 ff.

system. If it will be objected that frequently men do try to tell their wives how to behave on the job, this confirms the point we are making: her being separated from him when she is at work makes the exercise of his authority less likely, if at all possible, in the occupational realm.[4]

The important fact about the operation of these mechanisms is that they reinforce the normative pattern of priorities which helps remove from the individual the burden of making his own decisions anew in most situations. Thus expectations concerning everyday behavior become largely routinized. Children learn early that there is no choice in the matter of leaving the home in the morning for school; no decision has to be made as to whether or not father is to go to work. This routinization accounts for the fact that the various activity systems operate relatively smoothly even as they demand criss-crossing allegiances from their participants.

It would seem that the mechanisms for dealing with multiple allegiance operate in the same way for men and women. Yet, this is not always the case. These mechanisms are a necessary but not a sufficient condition for routinizing status-articulation. They are likely to eliminate the conflict only when they help status-articulation become routinized, and this happens only under conditions of normative consensus about priorities. It is only because the expectations that father be at work during the day and children at school are shared by all that no decision has to be made about whether and when to take up these activities. Where normative consensus is lacking, or where there is normative ambiguity, the routine is likely to break down occasionally. Such is the case, among others, in emergency situations.

Emergency situations are a convenient example for showing the difference in normative priorities for men and women; these situations highlight the fact that the mechanisms for routinizing status-articulation fail to operate for women the way they do for men.

The Failure of Routines and Status Articulation

An emergency can be said to occur in the routinized distribution of activities when one activity system claims the time and effort that is

4. The rule of nepotism, which states that two members of the same family will not be permitted to work for the same employer, has its sources in the functional requirement for modern organizations that they remain protected from familial concerns and allegiances during working hours. This is not only to avoid distraction; it is a response to the fact that different norms regulate behavior in the different activity systems. If it is objected that the rule of nepotism is obsolete because of the complexity of modern organizations where the internal separation of offices and lines of command can insulate individual members of a same family, this confirms the point that is emphasized here. Separation between different areas of activities assures insulation from observability as well as involvement in a different authority structure, and this at least reduces, if it does not eliminate, the potential conflict.

normatively assigned to the other, as when a mother or father has to stay home from work to care for a sick child or has to work on a weekend instead of being available to the family. In such instances of unanticipated demands, i.e., when the demands cannot be dealt with through ordinary normative regulation, an individual has to articulate his status anew; he has to make his own decision about which of his role-sets will be given priority.

However, such a choice is not between equally weighted alternatives. In fact, the examples of mother or father staying home for a sick child, or working overtime on weekends, are hypothetical. In all likelihood it will be mother (and *not* father) who will stay home for the sick child, and it will be father (and *not* mother) who would give to the job the weekend time that is usually assigned to the family. Even where there is a choice to be made between two activity systems, it follows a preferential cultural pattern. The woman has the cultural mandate to give priority to the family. The fact that, even when working she is expected to be committed to her family first, her work second, helps prevent disruptions within the family.

Non-routinized status-articulation, even if it does not violate the norm, is potentially subversive. The working woman's expected commitment to her family is a source of disruption in the occupational sphere because "those involved in the role-set have their own patterned activities disturbed when [the status-occupant] does not live up to his obligations."[5] This is likely to happen even if the mechanisms operate, or are being manipulated, to maximize the status-occupant's insulation from the observability of his role-partners and from the exercise of their authority over and interest in him. Incompatible expectations force the individual to articulate his status anew, to give priority to some normative demands at the expense of others. The woman who remains absent from work in order to care for a sick child creates a disruption in her place of work; the father who cannot come home for dinner because of some emergency at work creates a disruption at home. *Implicit in the act of articulating one's status beyond the routine is a disruption within one role-set, whether or not the disruption is considered legitimate.*

Merton's distinction between role-articulation and status-articulation becomes especially useful when we examine the significance of social disruption as a result of contradictory expectations. Status-articulation involves the temporary abandonment of one role. Role-articulation, in contrast, usually is aimed at better performance of the role, even if it implies some disappointment for some role-partners within one role-set. And the sanctions for such disappointments are more easily avoided than if one role has been abandoned altogether.

Role-articulation is likely to be less disruptive than status-articulation

5. Merton, *op. cit.*, p. 436.

which involves a whole separate role-set that is going to be abandoned if he decides to devote himself to the other set. What is more, manipulation in this case is more difficult.[6] It turns out that the same arrangement that facilitates routinized status-articulation—that territorial and temporal separation between the activity systems—makes manipulation more difficult in case the status has to be articulated anew. Just because the two systems are separated in time and place it is harder to cheat, so to speak.

Status-articulation is, therefore, both easier and harder to achieve than role-articulation. It is easier because the mechanisms of insulation and of differential authority and interest favor the routinization of activities in the two activity systems. This happens when the cultural mandate concerning priorities is unequivocal. If, however, the cultural mandate is equivocal, that is, if a person is expected to give priority to his commitment at work at the same time as he is expected to be committed to his family, routinization breaks down and the separation between the two activity systems makes status-articulation most difficult.

It follows as a consequence that the act of status-articulation, when it is not routinized, produces role conflict. This is because individuals anticipate the disruptions they might create in situations that would demand repeated status-articulation. The conflict about priorities and about whether or how to manipulate the mechanisms for status-articulation is structural not only in the sense that it stems from incompatible or contradictory demands but in the sense that the individual anticipates that status-articulation will create some disruption in his relations with one of his role-sets. The conflict is not merely his own. It is between two activity systems that have legitimate demands on the actor's allegiance.

The social anxiety created by the anticipation of such structural role-conflict helps activity systems remain protected from disruptions. There is a fit between the perceived need of potential recruits to occupations to minimize the conflicts that would ensue from repeated demands for status-articulation, and the perceived need of occupations and professions to minimize disturbances resulting from such status-articulation. Hence, women tend to limit their options by "wanting to do what they have to do," and occupations narrow women's access to opportunities.

The Cultural Mandate

If women were to press for admission to medical schools and law schools and academic disciplines the way Jews used to, they would crash the gates. They do not. This is because they accept the cultural mandate in

6. In regard to "ego manipulation of his role structure," see William J. Goode, "A theory of role strain," *American Sociological Review* 25 (August 1960): 483–496.

defining their own priorities as belonging to the family.[7] The reason for this lies in the most familiar of all facts: that almost every woman is married, or hopes to be married to a man. The family is the locus of consensus regarding the cultural mandate.

The most salient value pertaining to women's cultural mandate is that they ought to expect men to be providers of economic means and of prestige.[8] All through their early lives at home and in school, and later in college, women learn that their value commitments differ from those of men,[9] and that the basic principle underlying these commitments is that women are not to have social prestige of their own. The woman is to be the caretaker of the family, whose prestige is determined by a man.[10]

Sex segregation in school in regard to physical activities and emphasis on masculine prowess are perhaps not as symbolically important in teaching women their "proper place" as the fact that it is the boys who will give public prestige to the school through their performance in games, and that the girls are to act as cheerleaders.[11] This is the general image of women's role: they are to cheer men on, i.e., they are to help men in *their* achievements.

The recent popular film, M.A.S.H., a nominee for the best movie of the year, offers a good example of this cultural message. The picture shows a professional military woman on a surgical ward of an army base. She is shown to overconform to military norms and to repress her sexuality. However, her sexuality emerges as a form of entertainment for the whole base as her awkward lovemaking is broadcast over the camp loudspeaker. Later, her nude body is exposed to the cheers of the professional male crew. At the end, when the conflict which is the main plot of the movie gets resolved through the all-American consensus-producing device of a ballgame, she finds true happiness as a cheerleader.

There is a negative connotation to the term "career woman." No such derogatory term exists for men, since their careers are taken for granted. It is acceptable, even commendable, if middle-class women take jobs to help children go to college. Their caring in this way for members of the family is seen as part of their cultural mandate. Their occasional

7. Davis and Oleson found in the study of nursing students that 87 percent of the students ranked first "devotion to the family" in their choice between this item and "attractiveness to men," "activity in community affairs," and "dedication to work and career." See Fred Davis and Virginia L. Oleson, "The career outlook of professionally educated women," *Psychiatry* 28 (November 1965): 334–345.

8. On the dysfunctional aspects of the "husband-provider role" see Erik Grønseth, "The dysfunctionality of the husband provider role in industrialized societies," paper for the VIIth World Congress of Sociology, 1970, mimeo.

9. The nature of the pressures deterring women from planning careers still awaits systematic investigation. This cannot be done here for lack of space.

10. Typically, the woman takes her husband's surname. The negative connotation attached to the term *spinster* in contrast to the lack of such connotation to the term *bachelor* is due to the fact that the unmarried woman tends to be wanting in social standing.

11. For this observation I am indebted to Steven Coser who, when still in grammar school, remarked sarcastically: "How do you like the way this high school is integrated? The boys are on the football team and the girls are the cheerleaders!"

working is even acceptable if it is to buy some extras for themselves, or for Christmas presents, just as children from well-to-do families are encouraged to engage in character-building by earning their own Christmas money. Just as for children, women's work is not meant to give them prestige. At best, it will earn recognition for being a good sport.

As a corollary, women are available to pick up the slack at times and places where an occupational system gets overloaded, when it does not want to allocate resources that are considered too costly for an activity that nevertheless has to be carried out. Women's availability for such jobs stems, of course, from the fact that home and family to which they are assigned do not need all the time at their disposal. They can fill in as saleswomen (typically called sales*girls* no matter what their age because of the low status of the activity) at Christmas time; be invited on the spur of the moment to teach introductory courses where an unexpected high number of freshmen enter a class; be called upon when a college department has to give service by teaching what is defined as "unessential" courses, say sociology to students in nursing, engineering or business; or be volunteers in understaffed hospitals where they are supposed to make up for the lack of nurturing services—implying that nurturing is an unessential activity which is nice when you can get it but to which we cannot afford to allocate time that is considered "valuable," namely that has to be paid for. Paradoxical as it may seem, women's time is considered cheap just because they live up to the highly prized cultural mandate. This is because, it will be remembered, it is the occupational role that gives prestige, and prestige-seeking is assigned to men.

What is at stake is that women are not supposed to be equal, much less superior in their talents and achievements to those of men. The mass media often show women to be "smarter," but if they are truly "smart," they will manipulate the situation so as to make men believe that they, and not the women, have ultimate control.[12] While in the privacy of the household her superiority can sometimes be tolerated or even command deference, what is important is that her achievements not be made public, as they would be if she were to gain her own occupational status.[13] As a

---

12. Girls learn this practice in college, when they tend to underplay their academic achievements in the presence of boys, as when they underreport their grades to their dates and boy-friends. (See Mirra Komarovsky, "Cultural contradictions and sex roles," this book, pp. 512–19.) A recent article in the *New York Times* reports that women seldom wear their Phi-Beta-Kappa keys. One interviewee, Mrs. Arpajolu, "remembered one way in which the key was regarded as a hindrance for women: it might frighten men. 'You'd better bury that down in the deepest corner of your trunk, or this will be the last date,' she was advised when she first wore the key as a pin." Although Mrs. Arpajolu "can remember no adverse reaction other than 'unflattering surprise,' . . . a number of women, even today, admit they would hesitate to let a man know they are members of the select society" (*New York Times* February 24, 1971, p. 46).

13. A mother reported proudly about her daughter: "She has her hands full. In addition to taking care of the house and the children, she writes book reviews for her husband." Asked who signs these reviews, she says: "He signs them, of course. *She is really very clever about that.*"

consequence, most educated and talented women do not even attempt to enter high-status professions or be trained for them.

The mass media show career women to be undesirable as both professionals and women. In a movie called "A Very Special Favor," starring Rock Hudson (symbolizing masculinity) and Charles Boyer, the latter's daughter is shown as a psychiatrist, a most unpleasant one who overconforms in so-called masculine behavior. Boyer considers this tragic and asks Rock Hudson to make his daughter "a woman" again. The bulk of the movie shows Hudson's tactics in getting her to fall in love with him. Of course, her femininity shows through in the end and they get married. She has seven children and is a housewife.

This is the image that is presented to the public, teaching the adolescent audience the "dangers" that threaten men and women alike if the latter were to become professionals. Television commercials abound with the same message, usually with two essential themes: One: there is the masculine, overconforming professional woman. There is a man, usually lower in status. There is a battle. In the end, "masculinity" wins out as she falls in love with him and becomes subordinate to him. The second theme is the implication that a woman's choice of an occupation is not compatible with her having a family. Only few men want to take the risk of being married to the "type" of domineering professional woman shown on the screen, and only few women want to take the risk of not getting married.

Career and family life are presented as mutually exclusive alternatives for women. It would seem as if modern women were not capable, as modern men are, to segment their various roles and statuses. The American family appears as a "greedy institution" which demands total allegiance of women. Those who choose permanent careers are expected to be likely to remain celibate, like Catholic priests.

As a consequence, women are hard put to avail themselves to the extent that men do of the mechanisms of status-articulation which make up the fabric of modern society. Status-articulation between two activity systems is rarely routinized for working women with children because the family too often claims time and energy from them that should be assigned to work. The normative priorities for working women who have a family are ambiguous: if they live up to the normative requirement of caring for their families in situations of unexpected demands (such as illness), they introduce a disruption in their place of work; if they do not live up to this normative requirement, they introduce a disruption in the family.

The anticipation of conflict which this creates in women is integrated with the desire on the part of occupations to prevent disruptions as they are socially defined. These two factors account in large part for the widespread absence of women in high-status positions and in the professions.

TABLE 1. Sex Distribution in Selected Professions/by Highest Degree: 1968[1] (Proportion of Women)

Highest Degree	Field				
	Dentistry	Medicine	Law	Physical Science	Social Science
B.A.	—	—	—	13.8	36.5
M.A.	—	—	—	11.5	31.5
Doctorate or 1st Professional	1.6	7.9	4.1	5.2	12.2

1. United States Department of Commerce, Bureau of the Census, *Statistical Abstracts of the United States: 1970* Washington, D.C. 1970.

The Opportunity Structure

In early 1970, working women accounted for nearly 40 percent of the entire labor force,[14] yet they comprised only eight percent of the nation's physicians, four percent of its lawyers, less than two percent of its dentists.[15]

The largest proportion of working women is to be found in lower-status occupations. This seems contrary to our claim that type of employment of women is related to their family commitments, i.e., it seems curious that women should be fairly well represented in occupations where the day is long and the hours are rigidly controlled, and that they are not well represented in the professions where they can more readily manipulate their allocation of time. Would it not seem that women would be less likely to cause disruptions in a type of work that does not so much depend on regular presence for the major part of the day? The woman physician could decide to practice only part of the day, or to have office hours at night; the woman college teacher could do much of her work evenings and weekends; her presence at school is not rigidly required except for meetings and scheduled classes. Yet women are more likely to be found in occupations that demand a full day's involvement

14. Helen B. Shaffer, "Status of women," *Editorial Research Reports,* Vol. II, pp. 565–585. According to Secretary of Labor Jas. D. Hodgson at his news conference on the job outlook for the 1970s (*New York Times,* November 11, 1970, p. 32), out of a total labor force of 85 million, 31 million or 36.5 percent are women.

15. According to the U.S. Bureau of the Census, women in 1960 comprised 19 percent of college faculty, 6.8 percent of physicians, 3.5 percent of lawyers, 0.8 percent of engineers, 2.1 percent of dentists, 9.9 percent of scientists, 4.2 percent of physicists. Even the proportion of women in social work, which was at its peak in 1930 with 68 percent, has been decreasing steadily to 57 percent in 1960. Apparently, as this profession is upgrading its status, a larger proportion of men are entering the field. See Cynthia F. Epstein, "Encountering the male establishment: Sex-status limits on women's careers in the professions," *American Journal of Sociology* 75 (May 1970): 965–982.

and where there is little flexibility for the manipulation of time, and are less likely to be in occupations in which they could follow a flexible schedule. This would seem to contradict our statement that the sex distribution in occupations is to be understood in terms of minimizing disruption resulting from competing allegiances. For it should stand to reason that occupations that can follow a flexible schedule can absorb the shock of disruption more easily than those that depend on rigid time keeping, and that women would be attracted precisely to occupations where they can manipulate their time and hence more easily articulate their status.

The difference between occupations in which women are well represented and those in which their participation is conspicuously rare seems to be that, irrespective of these requirements of schedule, women are in occupations in which each individual worker is *replaceable,* or *defined as replaceable,* and are not in occupations that are seen as demanding full commitment allegedly based on individual judgment and decision-making.

What is important here is not so much the technical nature of the task as the sociological fact of normative requirements. High-status positions are said to require the commitments necessary for exercising individual judgment. In these positions, people allegedly control their own work; they are said to be in charge of defining its nature so that hardly anyone can do it for them. One recognizes here the definition of unalienated labor. If Alice Rossi bemoans the fact that American women tend not to engage in *meaningful* work,[16] this is exactly the point: it is not that women are not expected to work; it is only that they are not expected to be commited to their work through their individual control over it; if they did, they would tend to subvert the cultural mandate, thereby allegedly causing disruption in the family system, and would risk disrupting the occupational system as well.

If purely sex-discriminatory employment practices rather than anticipated disruption as a result of family commitments (either on the part of employers or on the part of potential women employees) were the main reason for the small number of women among the faculties of colleges and universities, little difference should be observed between the proportion of unmarried and that of married women. That this does not tend to be the case has been shown by Simon *et al.,* in a study of women who are holders of Ph.D. degrees.[17] It would seem that family commitments account in large part for women's low representation in academic positions for it turns out that almost all unmarried Ph.D. holders are

16. Alice S. Rossi, "Equality between the sexes: An immodest proposal," *Daedalus* 93 (1964): 607–657.
17. Rita James Simon, Shirley Merritt Clark, and Kathleen Galway, "The woman Ph.D.: A recent profile," *Social Problems* 15 (1967–68): 221–236.

TABLE 2. Amount of Employment of Ph.D.s by Sex and Marital Status[1] (in percent)

Sex and Marital Status	Full Time	Part Time	Not Employed	Total
Men	99.2	——	.8	100 (492)
Women Unmarried	96.3	——	3.7	100 (886)
Women Married	87.2	3.5	9.3	100 (259)
Women Married with Children	59.3	24.5	16.2	100 (619)

1. From Simon *et al.*, 1967, p. 223.

TABLE 3. Proportion of Employed Ph.D.s in Academic Positions[1] (Percent in Academic Positions)

Men	78.3%
Unmarried Women	78.5
Married Women	63.0
Married Women with Children	45.1

1. From Simon *et. al.*, 1967, p. 222.

employed full time in contrast to only 60 percent of those who have children (Table 2).

The more family obligations accrued to women by virtue of the cultural mandate, the less likely are they to be employed full time even if they are holders of a higher degree. Moreover, among those employed, the more family obligations, the less likely are these women to be employed in academic positions (Table 3).

Unmarried women Ph.D.s and men Ph.D.s tend to be represented in equal proportions in academic positions; but as family obligations increase, the proportion of women Ph.D.s decreases in the academy.

When considering the academic rank of those who are employed, the difference between unmarried women and men, though significant at the higher ranks, is much smaller than the difference between married women and men.[18]

Married women with or without children are more likely to be found in the lower ranks, men and unmarried women are more likely to be found in the upper ranks. Although there is a difference that remains to be

18. Simon *et al., op. cit.*, p. 228.

explained between the proportion of men and that of unmarried women in the upper ranks, and can most probably be understood on the basis of women's lower status in the culture at large, the difference is not as striking as that between those who do and those who do not have family commitments.

There is, in our society, a widespread association for women between single marital status and higher occupational status. Epstein [19] shows that the incidence of unmarried women who rose to the top of their professions has been significantly greater than the incidence of those who were married. Two-thirds of the top women in federal civil service were unmarried in 1967. Epstein quotes Havemann and West's study,[20] which shows that a great majority of the career women never married. She also quotes Rossi[21] to the effect that in the scientific and engineering fields, two out of five women, as compared to four out of five men, are married. The trend is similar for women in other male-dominated professions.

That women who have families are not as likely as are single women to be found in high-status positions is a consequence of the fact emphasized earlier that the family is a "greedy institution" for women. Single women do not have, nor are they made to anticipate, a conflict between their two roles and hence are willing to dedicate themselves to their occupations.[22] Similarly, employers may more readily accept women from whom they do not expect disruptions caused by family commitments.

Married women and women with children are more likely to be represented in positions that are defined as being more easily replaceable, and this definition applies to lower ranks. This is supported by the fact that married women with children have the highest proportion of lecture-ships (Table 4), i.e., positions of undefined status which are likely not to require commitments other than scheduled lecturing. And in this task replacements are more easily made than in individual student-advising, research supervision and direction, or committee work, in which full-time faculty members, especially of higher rank, are expected to be more fully involved.

19. Epstein, *op. cit.*, p. 96.
20. Ernest Havemann and Patricia West, *They Went to College: The College Graduate in America Today*, New York: Harcourt Brace & Co., 1952.
21. Rossi, *op. cit.*
22. It is quite possible that women with children, once they are working, realize that the conflict is not as great as it seems in anticipation. In a study on women's work commitments in Austria, Haller and Rosenmayr found that among white-collar women, those who had children were more likely to want to continue working than those without children in the same age category. (Max Haller and Leopold Rosenmayr, "The pluridimensionality of work commitment," paper for the XIth International Family Research Seminar [September 1970], mimeo.)

TABLE 4. Professional Rank by Sex and Marital Status of Ph.D. Holders in the Natural and Social Sciences, Humanities, and Education[1]

	Instructor Assistant Prof.	Associate Professor Full Prof.	Lecturer
Men	42.4%	53.8	.9
Unmarried Women	44.3	47.1	1.6
Married Women	56.8	23.7	1.8
Married Women with Children	50.9	22.6	9.8

1. From Simon *et al.*, 1967, p. 228.

Replaceability and Commitment

The replaceability on jobs where women are or feel readily admitted, as well as the commitment to and individual control over work in which they are or feel unwelcome, are, to be sure, normatively defined, rather than necessarily inherent in the nature of work. That we deal here with *social definitions* of replaceability and commitment rather than with actual task requirements can be shown with two examples: the social definition of replaceability in school teaching, which is mainly done by women, and the social definition of individual control over patients in a hospital by the predominantly male house staff.

In schools, there is an institutionalized mechanism for allowing absenteeism. The prediction that there will be a high rate of absenteeism among its predominantly women teachers has led to the practice of substitute teaching.[23] This is so patterned that in many states a special diploma is needed to perform this task. Everyone knows, however, that substitute teaching is a very poor substitute for teaching. Notoriously the students are hostile to substitutes, and their hostility is patterned, in that it is tolerated by adults and expected by peers; and nobody expects that pupils will learn much while "their" teacher is off the job. Surely, if we examine the nature of teaching, we recognize that a grade school teacher is as much in control over his class as a college teacher, and should, therefore, be as irreplaceable as the latter. Yet, what seems to be important is to prevent disruption in the system which would occur if pupils were left unattended or if the already overloaded classrooms were required to "double up." Substituting in teaching does not serve to replace performance as much as it serves to avoid disruption.

23. In nursing, the equivalent is the "floater."

Let us consider, in contrast, a higher-status profession like medicine. Here, the work is defined as personal service to the patient. Although, as far as the nature of work is concerned, interns and residents on a hospital service could replace one another because they usually know one another's patients, the rare woman intern or resident will not make use of this *de facto* replaceability by giving priority to the demands of her family. The house staff is supposed to learn during training the importance of individual responsibility for and control over individual patients with all the commitment this entails. This explains at least in part the disproportionate demands made on the trainee's time and energies in teaching hospitals. Here, absences due to anything other than serious illness or death in the immediate family would not be tolerated. In this normative system the ethos is that there be no priority of commitment to the family on the part of man *or* woman. Consequently, there are few women in this profession.

Occupations differ in the measure of commitment, i.e., internal involvement they claim from their members; and this measure is directly related to prestige in the stratification system. The distinction Merton makes between behavioral and attitudinal conformity can be usefully applied here. He speaks of *behavioral* conformity when, whatever the individuals' dispositions, they *act* according to normative prescriptions; and of *attitudinal* conformity when individuals grant legitimacy to institutional values and norms.[24] In routinized occupations, performance requires mainly *behavioral* conformity to detailed prescriptions and little involvement of internal dispositions. In contrast, professionals are to be guided by *attitudes* and internal dispositions, and there exists leeway concerning behavioral details.[25] Individual decisions regarding courses of action are to be made; and if these are to conform to standards, they must be informed by internalized values on which to rest individual judgment. "Sanctions . . . [do not] attach to particular acts . . . but only to very general principles and attitudes."[26] Between the two extreme expectations of pure behavioral and pure attitudinal conformity there is a continuum of relative emphasis on either type, determined by the measure of routinization and the measure of individualization of judgment and control that allegedly are involved in the practice of a particular occupation. For example, grade-school teaching or nursing should require attitudinal involvement; yet to the extent that these occupations are

24. Robert K. Merton, "Conformity, deviation and opportunity structures," *American Sociological Review* 24 (April 1959): 177–188. Cf. Rose Laub Coser, "Insulation from observability and types of social conformity," *American Sociological Review* 26 (February 1961): 29–39.

25. Rose Laub Coser, "Role distance, sociological ambivalence and transitional status systems," *American Journal of Sociology* 72 (September 1966): 173–187.

26. Talcott Parsons, *The Structure of Social Action,* New York: The Free Press of Glencoe, 1937, p. 323.

socially defined as being routinized, there is less expectation of internal involvement and the practitioners are considered to be replaceable in their work.

Commitment can be defined as the positive involvement of internal dispositions, but we must make a second distinction, namely, between commitment to one's *work* and commitment to *other persons* engaged in the same work. A craftsman who has pride in his work can be said to be committed to it. But what distinguishes a craftsman from a professional is that the latter is committed *to his colleagues*.

In high-status occupations, commitment is expected to be not only to work but to one another. It is not only important that the work be done, but that it be done with the approval of colleagues with whom one shares basic values. Long years of training not only serve to teach technical skills but to instill the necessary attitudes and professional values.[27] The future commitment and the strength of the bonds of solidarity with co-professionals is to be commensurate with the investment of time, energy, and affect that such long years of intensive training require. Co-professionals are to become a most meaningful reference group toward whom the practitioners' internal dispositions will be oriented. All through their training, "the theme is mutual commitment, reinforced by students' auxiliaries sponsored by the professional associations, and by the use of such terms as 'student-physician,' which stress that the student is already in the professional family. One owes allegiance for life to a family."[28]

And thus allegiances are sex-typed: a man owes to his profession what a woman owes to her family. An occupation that requires the involvement of internal dispositions demands the kind of absorption of the mind that the family claims from mothers and wives. As the writer Marya Mannes rightly says, pointing to a woman's deep involvement, "No woman with any heart can compose a paragraph when her child is in trouble or her husband ill: forever they take precedence over the companions of her mind."[29]

The type of commitment that is ideally expected of the professional implies selflessness and devotion to a calling. It brings to mind the nostalgic stereotype of the traditional country physician who foregoes sleep and food to ride through the night in snow and mud in order to save lives; or the traditional priest who foregoes the comfort of a family to save souls; or the scientist who foregoes monetary gains for the love of his

27. Robert K. Merton, "Introduction" in *The Student-Physician*, R. K. Merton, G. Reader, and P. L. Kendall, eds., Cambridge: Harvard University Press, 1957.
28. Everett C. Hughes, "Professions," *Daedalus* 92 (Fall 1963): 655–668.
29. Marya Mannes, "The problem of creative women" in *The Potential of Women*, Seymour M. Farber and Roger H. L. Wilson, eds., New York: McGraw Hill Book Co., Inc., 1963, pp. 116–130.

work.[30] This kind of devotion commands prestige; and this is why, as a consequence, prestigeful positions are said to require commitment.

Since women are expected to give this kind of commitment to their families, they tend to be restricted to the type of work that is defined as requiring a larger measure of behavioral conformity and a smaller measure of attitudinal involvement; this designates them mainly for the type of employment where they are replaceable in case of disruption caused by their normative family commitment.

As a result, professions that are sex-typed as feminine will be accorded less prestige. A corollary of the principle of replaceability is that a profession in which women predominate will be defined as requiring less commitment, whether or not task performance could profit from it.[31] Although grade-school teaching or nursing could be defined as needing much attitudinal involvement, the premise of the cultural mandate depresses the commitment value of these occupations and hence depresses their prestige.[32]

The distinction between routinized tasks and professions also applies to the stratification system. The lower the status, the more it is associated with expectations for behavioral conformity; the higher the status, the more it is said to require the involvement of internal dispositions, and the less it is defined as being replaceable.[33]

It would seem that strong commitments are held to be incompatible

30. "[During the congressional hearings in 1945 and 1946, a characteristic] of scientists was their intense commitment to the ideals and pursuit of science. 'I have personal knowledge of several scientists who stayed in the work almost entirely because of the love of the work rather than the salary that they received' " (Harry S. Hall, 1966, quoting from Science Legislation, Hearings before the Subcommittee on Military Affairs, U.S. Senate, 79th Congress, 1st Session, Wash., D.C.: U.S. Government Printing Office, 1945, p. 845. From Harry S. Hall, "Scientists and politicians," *Bulletin of the Atomic Scientists* 12 (February 1956): 45–52. Reprinted in *Professionalization,* Howard M. Vollmer and Donald L. Mills, eds. Englewood Cliffs, N.J.: Prentice-Hall, Inc., 1966, pp. 310–321.)

31. About the lack of career commitment of nursing students, see Davis & Oleson, *op. cit.* These authors quote similar findings in regard to beginning women teachers. Ward S. Mason, Robert J. Dressel, and Robert K. Bain, "Sex role and the career orientation of beginning teachers." *Harvard Education Review* 29 (1959): 370–383.

32. This is, of course, only a restatement of the familiar fact that women have lower status than men in the culture at large, and that this is carried over to female occupations in the public image. As a consequence, professions try to protect themselves lest too many women in their ranks depreciate the prestige with the public. The reluctance of medical schools to admit women students is similar to their reluctance in an earlier day to admit Jews. At that time, for a profession to be typed "Jewish" was as derogatory as it still is today to be typed "a woman's occupation." The public, less able than colleagues to judge the ability of individual practitioners, makes a global assessment of the profession by relying more on the image perpetuated by the cultural mandate which assigns women to the home and high-status men to positions of competence and commitment.

33. In regard to commitment being associated with maleness and high status, see Fred Davis and Virginia L. Oleson, "Initiation into a woman's profession: Identity problems in the status transition of co-ed to student nurse," *Sociometry* 26 (March 1963): 89–101. On value orientation from, as well as occupational requirements for, behavioral conformity among blue-collar workers, see Melvin L. Kohn, "Social class and parent-child relationship: An interpretation," *American Journal of Sociology* 68 (1963): 471–480.

with disruption of activities. Yet it will be objected that professionals and other high-status occupants cause disruptions when their commitments take them away from their place of work. This raises the more general problem of legitimate and illegitimate disruptions.

Legitimate Disruptions, Role Flexibility, and "The Self Fulfilling Prophecy"

In high-status positions there exist provisions for disruptions and for flexibility of role performance. These provisions are not equally available to men and women.

If high-status occupants were to stay put at their desks, they would resemble employees at the lower levels of bureaucratic structure. These, however, are defined as being replaceable. In actual fact, high status is associated with demands emanating from many places. A chief of a teaching hospital, for example, has to go to meetings all over the city or region, participate in regional, national, and sometimes international meetings, not counting trips to Washington and elsewhere in the country where his council and consultation are sought. Professors travel to hold lectures elsewhere, take part in meetings and conferences, give consultations, and every so often take a leave of absence for a semester or a year. These absences create disruptions in their organizations. The hospital's chief is absent from rounds, staff meetings, and case conferences. A professor may have to cancel classes; if he goes away for a year, his advanced students may be left without a thesis advisor.

With rise in status, the number and diversity of obligations as well as the number of role-partners tend to increase, and this multiplies the number of expectations. Correlatively, the more complex the role-set, the more territory it covers; and this augments the demands for being in many places. For it will be remembered that commitment of professionals is not only to their work but to one another, and colleagues are scattered all over the country, if not all over the world. Consequently, the higher the status, the more likely that all obligations cannot be met. The rule enunciated earlier, that the *higher the status, the less is the position defined as being replaceable* must be supplemented with another rule: *the higher the status, the more frequently will demands upon its occupant cause disruptions in his place of work*.

It seems paradoxical that women should tend to be unacceptable in positions where commitments to the family might cause disruptions, when disruptions seem to be taken for granted in high-status occupations; more than that, status-occupants often are congratulated for bringing honor to the organization by being wanted elsewhere.

Here the distinction mentioned earlier between status-articulation and role-articulation is especially relevant. Although both role-articulation and status-articulation are likely to disrupt relationships in one role-set, what organizations and professions try to avoid in high-status positions is status-articulation. Disruptions caused by women are not considered legitimate because they are seen as being due to a *failure* to meet occupational role expectations. In contrast, disruptions caused by men in high-status positions are legitimate because they are seen as being due to *fulfillment* of occupational role expectations.

Yet, flexibility is built into the expectation of performance in high-status positions not only for role-articulation, but for occasional status-articulation also. More generally, high-status occupants are not only more easily given what has been called "idiosyncrasy credit,"[34] being permitted some deviance by showing otherwise prized qualities,[35] like the famous professor who can cancel classes more often than his less famous colleagues. It is not only that some measure of deviance is *tolerated* from high-status occupants; they often are being congratulated for showing that they take their status lightly by deviating from a strict adherence to its demands.[36] This raises the more general problem of legitimate and non-legitimate flexibility of role-performance.

Concern with extra-professional issues testifies to the fact that the status-occupant is not "narrow" in his interests. If a person of high status takes time out to show concern for his family, he gives evidence of being a "good family man," a trait highly prized for a responsible position. As long as the status-occupant's attitudinal conformity cannot be questioned—and the likelihood of not having it questioned is directly associated with the prestige his status commands—occasional status-articulation is permitted and may even call forth approving smiles from role-partners, e.g., when the executive announces in his office that he must take time off to buy his wife a valentine.[37] For professional women, however, it is risky openly to articulate their family status. The following conversations which actually took place between two faculty members illustrate this point:

Professor X to Professor Y:
   I think that Joan [who is now only giving an introductory course] should be

34. E. P. Hollander, "Conformity, status and idiosyncracy credit," *Psychological Review* 65 (1958): 17–27.
   35. Lewis A. Coser, "Deviant behavior and normative flexibility," *American Journal of Sociology* 68 (September 1962): 172–181.
   36. Cf. Erving Goffman, "Role distance," in *Encounters,* Indianapolis: Bobbs-Merrill Co., pp. 85–152; Rose Laub Coser, *op. cit.*
   37. This type of flexibility is especially welcome in bureaucratic organizations because it helps lower the status boundaries. If a person of high status deviates somewhat from his obligations, he implies that in return he will also renounce some claims on status prerogatives. In contrast to him, the lower-status occupant who has fewer prerogatives has fewer resources from which he can offer something in return for taking the license of deviating from the norm.

given a position in the Department. She is a good teacher and does good work.
Professor Y:
I don't think so. The other day after classes I said to her: "We should have a conference about our next year's program. Can we talk about it now?" And she said, "No, it's too late, I have to go home because the children are home from school." She is just not committed as a professional.
Two days later, Professor X to Professor Y:
We should have a meeting because the deadline for next year's curriculum is drawing close. How about meeting this afternoon, since there are no classes?
Professor Y:
I can't today, I have to go home to babysit.
Professor X:
That's good of you. Perhaps we can meet tomorrow.

Although both Joan and Professor Y have in turn disrupted the relationship with a role-partner by giving priority to parental obligations, only Joan is accused of lack of commitment to her work. What is at stake here is *legitimacy of status*.

Women's occupational status is never quite legitimate.[38] It is understood that if they have a family, this should command their major commitment, and this would cause a detriment to their occupation. Yet, if they are single, they are "deviant" and are looked down upon for not having been able to attract a husband. They are damned if they do and damned if they don't. If they are single and still young enough, they might yet succeed in finding a husband, in which case it is predicted that their career will be jeopardized. A faculty member from a high-prestige university, who prides himself on his liberal views, had this to say:

The chairman of my department refuses to give fellowships to women. He has a point. It's a bad investment. When they marry or have children, they drop out.

38. Since women, even if they are professionals, tend to share the values that assign them to the family, they often feel guilty about "intruding" in the world of men (Hans Strotzka, "Zur psychosozialen Lage berufs-taetiger Frauen," in *Soziologie-forschung in Oesterreich,* Leopold Rosenmayr and Sigurd Hoellinger, eds., Vienna: Verlag Hermann Boehlaus Nachf. 1969, 543–558). Whether they are actually considered to be intruders or merely fear to be so considered, this may lead them to a kind of overconformity (much emphasized in the mass media, it will be remembered) that is reminiscent of the lower-class person who insists on stressing his respectability. Those who are not fully accepted sense that they meet with much less tolerance than those who are. This explains Dittes and Kelley's findings in their small-group experiments that individuals who felt acceptable in a group were freer to express disagreements publicly, while those with a low sense of acceptance were much higher in their public conformity (J. E. Dittes and H. H. Kelley, "Effects of different conditions of acceptance upon conformity to group norms," *Journal of Abnormal and Social Psychology* 53 (1956): 100–107. See also Herbert Menzel, "Public and private conformity under different conditions of acceptance in the group," *Journal of Abnormal Psychology* 55 (1957): 399–402.) If people in secure positions make a display of flexibility or even nonconformity, they show permissiveness. In contrast, if people in insecure status positions want to be flexible, they arrogate for themselves a freedom to which they have no right. While women who insist on status prerogatives appear to be aggressive, they appear similarly aggressive if, by permitting themselves flexibility, they make a claim for a status they are not readily granted.

This is the process of the "self-fulfilling prophecy"[39] by which opportunities are so structured that women will be less likely to be trained, and if trained, less likely to be employed in high-status positions, than men with equal potentialities for achievement. This process also accounts for the fact that many women drop out before getting their degrees. In most cases, however, women are likely to anticipate much earlier in life that marriage and children will make it difficult to use the qualifications they could acquire, and are, therefore, likely to refrain from seeking the training that would be commensurate with their abilities.

Summary and Conclusions

Societies always have social definitions of desirable life goals. In modern American society, men are to get occupational status and women are to get men who will get such status. Achieved status is the salient one in American society in that it tends to determine position in the stratification system. Hence, while men are in charge of placing their families in that system, women's statuses remain vicarious. Women tend to be deprived of the opportunity of obtaining achieved statuses for themselves.

Equal education for women helps them compete with one another to attract the most "valued men" and makes women capable of helping their husbands in their careers. Yet, modern American society also values equality of opportunity for its members. Hence equal education also holds out for women the potential opportunity for careers for themselves. Up to and including college, middle-class women are as well prepared as are men to enter the occupational system and derive prestige from their participation in it.

However, as long as the premise of women's cultural mandate is accepted, women will be considered a potential source of disruption in high-status positions as a result of their expected status-articulation which interrupts routine. The mechanisms of status-articulation that operate in modern society to help routinize multiple status obligations and hence integrate the activity systems of family and occupations are not available to women to the extent they are for men.

In an industrial society whose operation depends on the distribution of status positions according to achievement, attempts to shut the gates of opportunity, or even to leave them merely ajar, for one-half of the educated population on the basis of ascribed status cannot be maintained without considerable strain and conflict. If there is to be a change to reduce or eliminate contradictory expectations for women, it will have to be in the definitions of desirable life goals in American society. Many of

39. Merton, *Social Theory and Social Structure*, pp. 475–490.

our young men and women, who at the present time object to the frantic pursuit of money and status on the part of men, are ready for a scrutiny of alternative life styles.[40]

This need not threaten the solidarity of the family but may actually increase its cohesion. Solidarity in the family implies sharing commitments in regard both to caring for family members and providing the financial means for its comfortable existence. If either spouse would spend a little more time in one of these activities than he or she does now, and a little less time in the other, children might grow up with the sense that both parents are committed to their vocation at work and to their calling at home as well; and that both these commitments can be deeply satisfying for adults of both sexes. This may help induce young men and women to want to grow up to become productive and committed adults. Nothing could foster solidarity and growth more than for parents to share the responsibility of providing for their children, of caring for them and for each other, at the same time as they are committed to their respective vocations outside the home.

Our analysis implies that incremental, short-run changes, though beneficial, would not suffice to alter the situation significantly. Although practical institutional changes are required and are clearly possible at this time, changes of a more radical nature are also required, that is, changes of values concerning the cultural mandate of the woman as the career of family and children, and of the man as provider of financial means and social status.

No doubt, these changes will not be easy, and it is probable that if they take place the generation that ushers them in will be particularly beset with problems and ambiguities. But simplicity is not always the best guide to action or inaction. Maintaining the status quo might be the easiest alternative, but not the wisest for the society, nor the most consistent with our values.

The understanding, with the help of sociological theory, of the structure, functions, and consequences of a particular social arrangement leads us to believe that changes are required that will move our society to adopt behavioral patterns consistent with ideas of freedom and achievement. Are we to make these changes, or are we to be trapped by the past, unwilling to sacrifice for the future?

---

40. As Gagnon has pointed out, equality of women would mean a truly revolutionary change because unlike other grants of equality to minorities, women's equality would affect the structure of the American family. See John H. Gagnon, "The woman's revolution," printed in *McCalls* under the title: "Is a woman's revolution possible?" October 1969, pp. 76, 126–27, 128–29.

Mirra Komarovsky

Cultural Contradictions
and Sex Roles

Profound changes in the roles of women during the past century have been accompanied by innumerable contradictions and inconsistencies. With our rapidly changing and highly differentiated culture, with migrations and multiplied social contacts, the stage is set for myriads of combinations of incongruous elements. Cultural norms are often functionally unsuited to the social situations to which they apply. Thus they may deter an individual from a course of action which would serve his own, and society's, interests best. Or, if behavior contrary to the norm is engaged in, the individual may suffer from guilt over violating mores which no longer serve any socially useful end. Sometimes culturally defined roles are adhered to in the face of new conditions without a conscious realization of the discrepancies involved. The reciprocal actions dictated by the roles may be at variance with those demanded by the actual situation. This may result in an imbalance of privileges and obligations or in some frustration of basic interests.

Again, problems arise because changes in the mode of life have created new situations which have not as yet been defined by culture. Individuals left thus without social guidance tend to act in terms of egotistic or "short-run hedonistic" motives which at times defeat their own long-term interests or create conflict with others. The precise obligation of a gainfully employed wife toward the support of the family is one such undefined situation.

Finally, a third mode of discrepancy arises in the existence of incompatible cultural definitions of the same social situation, such as the clash of "old-fashioned" and "radical" mores, of religion and law, of norms of conomic and familial institutions.

The problems raised by these discrepancies are social problems in the sense that they engender mental conflict or social conflict or otherwise frustrate some basic interest of large segments of the population.

This article sets forth in detail the nature of certain incompatible sex roles imposed by our society upon the college woman. It is based on data collected in 1942 and 1943. Members of an undergraduate course on the family were asked for two successive years to submit autobiographical

512

documents focused on the topic; 73 were collected. In addition, 80 interviews, lasting about an hour each, were conducted with every member of a course in social psychology of the same institution—making a total of 153 documents ranging from a minimum of five to a maximum of thirty typewritten pages.

The generalization emerging from these documents is the existence of serious contradictions between two roles present in the social environment of the college woman. The goals set by each role are mutually exclusive, and the fundamental personality traits each evokes are at points diametrically opposed, so that what are assets for one become liabilities for the other, and the full realization of one role threatens defeat in the other.

One of these roles may be termed the "feminine" role. While there are a number of permissive variants of the feminine role for women of college age (the "good sport," the "glamour girl," the "young lady," the domestic "home girl," etc.), they have a common core of attributes defining the proper attitudes to men, family, work, love, etc., and a set of personality traits often described with reference to the male sex role as "not as dominant, or aggressive as men" or "more emotional, sympathetic."

The other and more recent role is, in a sense, no sex role at all, because it partly obliterates the differentiation in sex. It demands of the women much the same virtues, patterns of behavior, and attitude that it does of the men of a corresponding age. We shall refer to this as the "modern" role.

Both roles are present in the social environment of these women throughout their lives, though, as the precise content of each sex role varies with age, so does the nature of their clashes change from one stage to another. In the period under discussion the conflict between the two roles apparently centers about academic work, social life, vocational plans, excellence in specific fields of endeavor, and a number of personality traits.

One manifestation of the problem is in the inconsistency of the goals set for the girl by her family.

Forty, or 26 percent, of the respondents expressed some grievance against their families for failure to confront them with clearcut and consistent goals. The majority, 74 percent, denied having had such experiences. One student writes:

> How am I to pursue any course single-mindedly when some way along the line a person I respect is sure to say, "You are on the wrong track and are wasting your time." Uncle John telephones every Sunday morning. His first question is: "Did you go out last night?" He would think me a "grind" if I were to stay home Saturday night to finish a term paper. My father expects me to get an "A" in every subject and is disappointed by a "B." He says I

have plenty of time for social life. Mother says, "That 'A' in Philosophy is very nice dear. But please don't become so deep that no man will be good enough for you." And, finally, Aunt Mary's line is careers for women. "Prepare yourself for some profession. This is the only way to insure yourself independence and an interesting life. You have plenty of time to marry."

A Senior writes:

I get a letter from my mother at least three times a week. One week her letters will say, "Remember that this is your last year at college. Subordinate everything to your studies. You must have a good record to secure a job." The next week her letters are full of wedding news. This friend of mine got married; that one is engaged; my young cousin's wedding is only a week off. When, my mother wonders, will I make up my mind? Surely, I wouldn't want to be the only unmarried one in my group. It is high time, she feels, that I give some thought to it.

A student reminisces:

All through high school my family urged me to work hard because they wished me to enter a first-rate college. At the same time they were always raving about a girl schoolmate who lived next door to us. How pretty and sweet she was, how popular, and what taste in clothes! Couldn't I also pay more attention to my appearance and to social life? They were overlooking the fact that this carefree friend of mine had little time left for school work and had failed several subjects. It seemed that my family had expected me to become Eve Curie and **Hedy Lamarr** wrapped up in one.

Another comments:

My mother thinks that it is **very** nice to be smart in college but only if it doesn't take too much effort. She always tells me not to be too intellectual on dates, to be clever in a light sort of way. My father, on the other hand, wants me to study law. He thinks that if I applied myself I could make an excellent lawyer and keeps telling me that I am better fitted for this profession than my brother.

Another writes:

One of my two brothers writes: "Cover up that high forehead and act a little dumb once in a while"; while the other always urges upon me the importance of rigorous scholarship.

The students testified to a certain bewilderment and confusion caused by the failure on the part of the family to smooth the passage from one role to another, especially when the roles involved were contradictory. It seemed to some of them that they had awakened one morning to find their world upside down: what had hitherto evoked praise and rewards from relatives, now suddenly aroused censure. A student recollects:

I could match my older brother in skating, sledding, riflery, ball, and many of the other games we played. He enjoyed teaching me and took great pride in my accomplishments. Then one day it all changed. He must have suddenly become conscious of the fact that girls ought to be feminine. I was walking with him, proud to be able to make long strides and keep up with his long-legged steps when he turned to me in annoyance, "Can't you walk like a lady?" I still remember feeling hurt and bewildered by his scorn, when I had been led to expect approval.

Once during her freshman year in college, after a delightful date, a student wrote her brother with great elation:

"What a wonderful evening at ———— fraternity house! You would be proud of me, Johnny! I won all ping-pong games but one!"

"For heaven's sake," came the reply, "when will you grow up? Don't you know that a boy likes to think he is better than a girl? Give him a little competition, sure, but miss a few serves in the end. Should you join the Debate Club? By all means, but don't practice too much on the boys." Believe me I was stunned by this letter but then I saw that he was right. To be a success in the dorms one must date, to date one must not win too many ping-pong games. At first I resented this bitterly. But now I am more or less used to it and live in hope of one day meeting a man who is my superior so that I may be my natural self.

It is the parents and not the older sibling who reversed their expectations in the following excerpt:

All through grammar school and high school my parents led me to feel that to do well in school was my chief responsibility. A good report card, an election to student office, these were the news Mother bragged about in telephone conversations with her friends. But recently they suddenly got worried about me: I don't pay enough attention to social life, a woman needs some education but not that much. They are disturbed by my determination to go to the School of Social Work. Why my ambitions should surprise them after they have exposed me for four years to some of the most inspired and stimulating social scientists in the country, I can't imagine. They have some mighty strong arguments on their side. What is the use, they say, of investing years in training for a profession, only to drop it in a few years? Chances of meeting men are slim in this profession. Besides, I may become so preoccupied with it as to sacrifice social life. The next few years are, after all, the proper time to find a mate. But the urge to apply what I have learned, and the challenge of this profession is so strong that I shall go on despite the family opposition.

The final excerpt illustrates both the sudden transition of roles and the ambiguity of standards:

I major in English composition. This is not a completely "approved" field for girls so I usually just say "English." An English Literature major is quite liked and approved by boys. Somehow it is lumped with all the other arts and even has a little glamour. But a composition major is a girl to beware of because she supposedly will notice all your grammar mistakes, look at your letters too critically, and consider your ordinary speech and conversation as too crude.

I also work for a big metropolitan daily as a correspondent in the city room. I am well liked there and may possibly stay as a reporter after graduation in February. I have had several spreads [stories running to more than eight or ten inches of space], and this is considered pretty good for a college correspondent. Naturally, I was elated and pleased at such breaks, and as far as the city room is concerned I'm off to a very good start on a career that is hard for a man to achieve and even harder for a woman. General reporting is still a man's work in the opinion of most people. I have a lot of acclaim but also criticism, and I find it confusing and difficult to be praised for being clever and working hard and then, when my efforts promise to be successful, to be condemned and criticized for being unfeminine and ambitious.

Here are a few of these reactions:

My father: "I don't like this newspaper set-up at all. The people you meet are making you less interested in marriage than ever. You're getting too educated and intellectual to be attractive to men."

My mother: "I don't like your attitude toward people. The paper is making you too analytical and calculating. Above all, you shouldn't sacrifice your education and career for marriage."

A lieutenant with two years of college: "It pleased me greatly to hear about your news assignment—good girl."

A Navy pilot with one year of college: "Undoubtedly, I'm old-fashioned, but I could never expect or feel right about a girl giving up a very promising or interesting future to hang around waiting for me to finish college. Nevertheless, congratulations on your job on the paper. Where in the world do you get that wonderful energy? Anyway I know you were thrilled at getting it and feel very glad for you. I've an idea that it means the same to you as that letter saying 'report for active duty' meant to me."

A graduate metallurgist now a private in the Army: "It was good to hear that you got that break with the paper. I am sure that talent will prove itself and that you will go far. But not too far, as I don't think you should become a career woman. You'll get repressed and not be interested enough in having fun if you keep after that career."

A lieutenant with a year and a half of college: "All this career business is nonsense. A woman belongs in the home and absolutely no place else. My wife will have to stay home. That should keep her happy. Men are just superior in everything, and women have no right to expect to compete with them. They should do just what will keep their husbands happy."

A graduate engineer—my fiancé: "Go right ahead and get as far as you can in your field. I am glad you are ambitious and clever, and I'm as anxious to see you happily successful as I am myself. It is a shame to let all those brains go to waste over just dusting and washing dishes. I think the usual home life and children are small sacrifices to make if a career will keep you happy. But I'd rather see you in radio because I am a bit wary of the effect upon our marriage of the way of life you will have around the newspaper."

Sixty-one, or 40 percent, of the students indicated that they have occasionally "played dumb" on dates, that is, concealed some academic honor, pretended ignorance of some subject, or allowed the man the last word in an intellectual discussion. Among these were women who "threw games" and in general played down certain skills in obedience to the unwritten law that men must possess these skills to a superior degree. At the same time, in other areas of life, social pressures were being exerted upon these women to "play to win," to compete to the utmost of their abilities for intellectual distinction and academic honors. One student writes:

I was glad to transfer to a women's college. The two years at the co-ed university produced a constant strain. I am a good student; my family expects me to get good marks. At the same time I am normal enough to want to be invited to the Saturday night dance. Well, everyone knew that on that campus a reputation of a "brain" killed a girl socially. I was always fearful lest I say too much in class or answer a question which the boys I dated couldn't answer.

Here are some significant remarks made from the interviews:

When a girl asks me what marks I got last semester I answer, "Not so good—only one 'A'." When a boy asks the same question, I say very brightly with a note of surprise, "Imagine, I got an 'A!'"

I am engaged to a southern boy who doesn't think too much of the woman's intellect. In spite of myself, I play up to his theories because the less one knows and does, the more he does for you and thinks you "cute" into the bargain. . . . I allow him to explain things to me in great detail and to treat me as a child in financial matters.

One of the nicest techniques is to spell long words incorrectly once in a while. My boy-friend seems to get a great kick out of it and writes back, "Honey, you certainly don't know how to spell."

When my date said that he considers Ravel's *Bolero* the greatest piece of music ever written, I changed the subject because I knew I would talk down to him.

A boy advised me not to tell of my proficiency in math and not to talk of my plans to study medicine unless I knew my date well.

My fiancé didn't go to college. I intend to finish college and work hard at it, but in talking to him I make college appear a kind of a game.

Once I went sailing with a man who so obviously enjoyed the role of a protector that I told him I didn't know how to sail. As it turned out he didn't either. We got into a tough spot, and I was torn between a desire to get a hold of the boat and a fear to reveal that I had lied to him.

It embarrassed me that my "steady" in high school got worse marks than I. A boy should naturally do better in school. I would never tell him my marks and would often ask him to help me with my homework.

I am better in math than my fiancé. But while I let him explain politics to me, we never talk about math even though, being a math major, I could tell him some interesting things.

Mother used to tell me to lay off the brains on dates because glasses make me look too intellectual anyhow.

I was once at a work camp. The girls did the same work as the boys. If some girls worked better, the boys resented it fiercely. The director told one capable girl to slow down to keep peace in the group.

How to do the job and remain popular was a tough task. If you worked your best, the boys resented the competition; if you acted feminine, they complained that you were clumsy.

On dates I always go through the "I-don't-care-anything-you-want-to-do" routine. It gets monotonous but boys fear girls who make decisions. They think such girls would make nagging wives.

I am a natural leader and, when in the company of girls, usually take the lead. That is why I am so active in college activities. But I know that men fear bossy women, and I always have to watch myself on dates not to assume the "executive" role. Once a boy walking to the theater with me took the wrong street. I knew a short cut but kept quiet.

I let my fiancé make most of the decisions when we are out. It annoys me, but he prefers it.

I sometimes "play dumb" on dates, but it leaves a bad taste. The emotions are complicated. Part of me enjoys "putting something over" on the unsuspecting male. But this sense of superiority over him is mixed with feelings of guilt for my hypocrisy. Toward the "date" I feel some contempt because he is "taken in" by my technique, or if I like the boy, a kind of a maternal condescension. At times I resent him! Why isn't he my superior in all ways in which a man should excel so that I could be my natural self? What am I doing here with him, anyhow? Slumming?
   And the funny part of it is that the man, I think, is not always so unsuspecting. He may sense the truth and become uneasy in the relation. "Where do I stand? Is she laughing up her sleeve or did she mean this praise? Was she really impressed with that little speech of mine or did she only pretend to know nothing about politics?" And once or twice I felt that the joke was on me: the boy saw through my wiles and felt contempt for me for stooping to such tricks.

Another aspect of the problem is the conflict between the psychogenetic personality of the girl and the cultural role foisted upon her by the milieu. At times it is the girl with "masculine" interests and personality traits who chafes under the pressure to conform to the "feminine" pattern. At other times it is the family and the college who thrust upon the reluctant girl the "modern" role.

While, historically, the "modern" role is the most recent one, ontogenetically it is the one emphasized earlier in the education of the college girl, if these 153 documents are representative. Society confronts the girl with powerful challenges and strong pressure to excel in certain competitive lines of endeavor and to develop certain techniques of adaptation very similar to those expected of her brothers. But, then, quite suddenly as it appears to these girls, the very success in meeting these challenges begins to cause anxiety. It is precisely those most successful in the earlier role who are now penalized.

It is not only the passage from age to age but the moving to another region or type of campus which may create for the girl similar problems. The precise content of sex roles, or, to put it in another way, the degree of their differentiation, varies with regional class, nativity, and other subcultures.

Whenever individuals show differences in response to some social situation, as have our 153 respondents, the question naturally arises as to the causes. It will be remembered that 40 percent admitted some difficulties in personal relations with men due to conflicting sex roles but that 60 percent said that they had no such problems. Inconsistency of parental expectations troubled 26 percent of the students.

To account for individual differences would require another study, involving a classification of personalities in relation to the peculiar social environments of each. Generally speaking, it would seem that it is the girl with a "middle-of-the-road personality" who is most happily adjusted to the present historical moment. She is not a perfect incarnation of either role but is flexible enough to play both. She is a girl who is intelligent enough to do well in school but not so brilliant as to "get all 'A's'"; informed and alert but not consumed by an intellectual passion; capable but not talented in areas relatively new to women; able to stand on her own feet and to earn a living but not so good a living as to compete with men; capable of doing some job well (in case she does not marry or, otherwise, has to work) but not so identified with a profession as to need it for her happiness.

A search for less immediate causes of individual reactions would lead us further back to the study of genesis of the personality differences found relevant to the problem. One of the clues will certainly be provided by the relation of the child to the parent of the same and of the opposite sex. This relation affects the conception of self and the inclination for a particular sex role.

The problems set forth in this article will persist, in the opinion of the writer, until the adult sex roles of women are redefined in greater harmony with the socioeconomic and ideological character of modern society. Until then neither the formal education nor the unverbalized sex roles of the adolescent woman can be cleared of intrinsic contradictions.

Mirra Komarovsky

Thirty Years Later:
The Masculine Case*

In a rapidly changing society, normative malintegration is commonly assumed to lead to an experience of strain. Earlier research (Komarovsky 1946) on cultural contradictions and the feminine sex role showed that women at an eastern college suffered uncertainty and insecurity because the norms for occupational and academic success conflicted with norms for the traditional feminine role.[1] A replication (Wallin 1950) at a western university reported agreement in the questionnaire data, but the interview material led the investigator to conclude that the problem was less important to the women than the earlier study had suggested.[2] However, Wallin pointed out that, in his replication, the respondents were oriented to marriage, while the Komarovsky study had included an appreciable number of women oriented to careers. This finding tended to support the view that women who were satisfied with the traditional female role would show less strain when confronted with contrary expectations than women who hoped to have both a rewarding career and a rewarding marriage.

Men are also confronted with contradictory expectations. For example, the traditional norm of male intellectual superiority conflicts with a newer norm of intellectual companionship between the sexes. This research investigated the extent of masculine strain experienced by 62 college males randomly selected from the senior class of an Ivy League male college. The study included a variety of status relationships, but the results reported here deal with intellectual relationships with female friends and attitudes toward working wives.

* This research is supported by NIMH grant MH 14618. Associated with the author in the interviewing were Mr. Wesley Fisher, Mrs. Susanne Riveles, and Dr. Edith Sanders. Mrs. Ana Silbert analyzed the scored psychological tests and prepared the 62 psychological profiles. The field work was done in 1969–70.

1. Mirra Komarovsky, "Cultural Contradictions and Sex Roles," *American Journal of Sociology* 52 (November 1946): 184–89; this book, pp. 512–19.
2. Paul Wallin, "Cultural Contradictions and Sex Roles: A Repeat Study," *American Sociological Review* 15 (April 1950): 288–93.

Methods

Each of the 62 respondents contributed a minimum of three two-hour interviews and also completed a set of five schedules and two psychological tests, the California Personality Inventory and the Gough Adjective Check List. The psychological tests were interpreted by a clinical psychologist. The 13-page interview guide probed for data on actual role performance, ideal role expectations and limits of tolerance, personal preferences, perception of role partner's ideal expectations, and relevant attitudes of significant others. Direct questions on strains came only at the end of this sequence. Extensive use was made of quasi-projective tests in the form of brief episodes. The total response rate of the original sample (*N*=79) was 78%.

Intellectual Relationships with Female Friends

When fewer women attended college, the norm of male intellectual superiority might have had some validation in experience. But today college women are more rigorously selected than men in terms of high school academic performance.[3] Nevertheless, social norms internalized in early childhood are resistant to change. The first question for this research was, How many men would show insecurity or strain in their intellectual relationships with women when confronted with both bright women and the traditional norm of male superiority?

The Troubled Third. Of the 53 men for whom the data were available (six did not date, three could not be classified reliably), 30% reported that intellectual insecurity or strain with dates was a past or current problem. This number included men who, having experienced stress, sought to avoid it by finding dates who posed no intellectual threat. The following excerpts from interviews illustrate the views of this troubled third:

> I enjoy talking to more intelligent girls, but I have no desire for a deep relationship with them. I guess I still believe that the man should be more intelligent.

> * * *

> I may be a little frightened of a man who is superior to me in some field of knowledge, but if a girl knows more than I do, I resent her.

> * * *

> Once I was seeing a philosophy major, and we got along quite well. We shared a similar outlook on life, and while we had some divergent opinions, I seemed better able to document my position. One day, by chance, I heard her discussing with another girl an aspect of Kant that just the night before she described to me as obscure and confusing. But now she was explaining it

3. *Princeton Alumni Weekly,* February 23, 1971, p. 7.

to a girl so clearly and matter-of-factly that I felt sort of hurt and foolish. Perhaps it was immature of me to react this way.

The mode of strain exemplified by these men might be termed "a socially structured scarcity of resources for role fulfillment." Apart from the ever-present problem of lack of time and energy, some social roles are intrinsically more difficult to fulfill, given the state of technical skills, the inherent risks, or other scarcities of facilities. The strain of a doctor called upon to treat a disease for which modern medicine has no cure is another case in point.

Selective dating and avoidance of superior women solved the problem for some troubled youths, but this offered no solution for six respondents who yearned for intellectual companionship with women but dreaded the risk of invidious comparisons. The newly emerging norm of intellectual companionship with women creates a mode of strain akin to one Merton and Barber termed "sociologic ambivalence." [4] Universalistic values tend to replace sex-linked desiderata among some male undergraduates who now value originality and intelligence in female as well as in male associates. The conflict arises when, at the same time, the norm of masculine intellectual superiority has not been relinquished, as exemplified in the following case: "I am beginning to feel," remarked one senior about his current girl friend, "that she is not bright enough. She never says anything that would make me sit up and say, 'Ah, that's interesting!' I want a girl who has some defined crystal of her own personality and does not merely echo my thoughts." He recently met a girl who fascinated him with her quick and perceptive intelligence but this new girl made him feel "nervous and humble."

The problem of this youth is to seek the rewards of valued attributes in a woman without arousing in himself feelings of inferiority. It may be argued that in a competitive society this conflict tends to characterize encounters with males as well. Nonetheless, if similar problems exist between two males, the utility curve is shaped distinctively by the norm of male intellectual superiority because mere equality with a woman may be defined as a defeat or a violation of a role prescription.

The Adjusted Majority. The 37 students who said that intellectual relationships with dates were not a problem represented a variety of types. Eleven men felt superior to their female friends. In two or three cases, the relationships were judged equalitarian with strong emphasis on the rewards of intellectual companionship. In contrast, several men—and their dates—had little interest in intellectual concerns. In a few instances the severity of other problems overwhelmed this one. Finally, some eight men were happily adjusted despite the acknowledged intellectual

4. Robert K. Merton and Elinor Barber, "Sociological Ambivalence," in *Sociological Theory, Values and Socio-cultural Change,* E. A. Tiryakian, ed., New York: Free Press, 1963.

superiority of their women friends. What makes for accommodation to this still deviant pattern?

In seven of the eight cases, the female friend had some weakness which offset her intellectual competence, such as emotional dependence, instability, or a plain appearance, giving the man a compensating advantage. A bright, studious, but relatively unattractive girl may be acceptable to a man who is not as certain of his ability to win a sexually desirable female as he is of his mental ability. In only one of the eight cases the respondent admitted that his steady girl was "more independent and less emotional, actually a little smarter than I. But she doesn't make me feel like a dunce." Her superiority was tolerable because she provided a supportive relationship which he needed and could accept with only mild, if any, emotional discomfort.

Another factor which may account for the finding that 70% of the sample reported no strain is the fact that intellectual qualities are no longer considered unfeminine and that the imperative of male superiority is giving way to the ideal of companionship between equals. This interpretation is supported by responses to two standard questions and by the qualitative materials of the interviews. A schedule testing beliefs on 16 psychological sex differences asked whether the reasoning ability of men is greater than that of women. Only 34% of the respondents "agreed" or "agreed somewhat," while 20% were "uncertain"; almost half "disagreed" or "disagreed somewhat."

Another question was put to all 62 respondents: what are for you personally the three or four most desirable characteristics in a woman (man) who is to be close to you? Of all the traits men desired in a woman, 33% were in the "intellectual" cluster, in contrast with 44% of such traits if the friend were male. The fact that the sex difference was not larger seems significant. The major difference in traits desired in male and female intimates (apart from sexual attractiveness and love) was the relative importance of "social amenities and appearance" for women.

The qualitative data amply document the fact that the majority of the respondents ideally hoped to share their intellectual interests with their female as well as their male friends. To be sure, what men occasionally meant by intellectual rapport with women was having an appreciative listener: "I wouldn't go out," declared one senior, "with any girl who wasn't sharp and perceptive enough to catch an intellectual subtlety." But for the majority a "meaningful relationship" with a woman included also a true intellectual interchange and sharing. As one senior put it, "A guy leaving a movie with his date expects her to make a stimulating comment of her own and not merely echo his ideas." Another man wanted a date with whom he could "discuss things that guys talk about," and still a third man exclaimed: "What I love about this girl is that she is on my level, that I can never speak over her head."

It is this ideal of intellectual companionship with women, we suggest, that may explain the relative adjustment of the men in this sphere. As long as the expectation of male superiority persisted, anything near equality on the part of the woman carried the threatening message to the men: "I am not the intellectually *superior* male I am expected to be." But when the ideal of intellectual companionship between equals replaces the expectation of male superiority, the pressure upon the man eases and changes. Now he need only reassure himself that he is not inferior to his date, rather than that he is markedly superior to her. Once the expectation of clear superiority is relinquished, varieties of relationships may be accommodated. Given a generally similar intellectual level, comparative evaluations are blurred by different interests, by complementary strengths and weaknesses, and occasionally by rationalizations ("she studies harder") and other devices.

One final explanation remains to be considered. May the intellectual self-confidence of the majority be attributed in part to women's readiness to play down their intellectual abilities? That such behavior occurs is attested by a number of studies.[5]

When respondents were asked to comment upon a projective story about a girl "playing dumb" on dates, the great majority expressed indignation at such "dishonest," "condescending" behavior. But some three or four found the behavior praiseworthy. As one senior put it, "Her intentions were good; she wanted to make the guy feel important."

Although we did not interview the female friends of our respondents, a few studies indicate that such playing down of intellectual ability by women is less common today than in the 1940s. Questionnaires filled out in 1970 and 1971 by 87 members of two undergraduate classes in sociology at an eastern women's college duplicated earlier studies by Wallin and Komarovsky. The 1970 class was a course on the family, and the 1971 class probably recruited a relatively high proportion of feminists. Table 1 indicates that the occasional muting of intellectual competence by women may have played some role in the adjustment of the men, but it would appear to be a minor and decreasing role.

The hypothesis that the emerging ideal of intellectual companionship serves as a buffer against male strain needs a test which includes (as our study did not) some index of intellectual ability as well as indices of norms and of strain. Of the 27 men who disagreed with the proposition that the reasoning ability of men is greater than that of women, only five reported intellectual insecurity with women, whereas of the 34 men who believed in masculine superiority or were uncertain, nine experienced strain. Most troubled were the 12 men who were "uncertain"; four of them were insecure with women. Case analyses suggest that the interplay between a

5. Komarovsky, *op. cit.*, 182–89; Wallin, *op. cit.*

TABLE 1. Readiness of Women to Play Down Intellectual Abilities (%)

	Wallin 1950 (N = 163)	Sociology Class 1970* (N = 33)	Advanced Sociology Class 1971* (N = 55)
When on dates how often have you pretended to be intellectually inferior to the man?			
Very often, often, or several times	32	21	15
Once or twice	26	36	30
Never	42	43	55
In general, do you have any hesitation about revealing your equality or superiority to men in intellectual competence?			
Have considerable or some hesitation	35	21	13
Very little hesitation	39	33	32
None at all	26	46	55

* Mirra Komarovsky, unpublished study.

man's experience, personality, and beliefs is complex. For example, one traditional man, having confessed feelings of intellectual insecurity on dates, clung all the more tenaciously to the belief in superior male reasoning ability.

Some men took the "liberal" position on sex differences as a matter of principle. Of the nine black students, eight rejected the belief in male superiority, perhaps because they opposed group comparisons in intelligence. Again, in some cases, the direction of the causal relation was the reverse of the one we posited: men who felt in fact intellectually superior were hospitable to the "liberal" ideology. In view of these complexities, our suggestive results as to the positive association between egalitarian norms and the absence of strain remain to be tested in larger samples.

Attitudes Toward Future Wives' Occupational Roles

The ethos on the campus of this study clearly demanded that men pay at least lip service to liberal attitudes toward working wives. If the initial responses to structured questions were accepted as final, the majority would have been described as quite feminist in ideology. But further probing revealed qualifications which occasionally almost negated the original response. For example, an affirmative answer to a proposition,

"It is appropriate for a mother of a preschool child to take a fulltime job," was, upon further questioning, conditioned by such restrictions as "provided, of course, that the home was run smoothly, the children did not suffer, and the wife's job did not interfere with her husband's career." The interview provided an opportunity to get an assessment of normative expectations, ideal and operative, as well as of actual preferences. The classification of attitudes to be presented in this report is based on the total interview. Preferences reported here assume that a wife's paycheck will not be an economic necessity. The overwhelming majority were confident that their own earnings would be adequate to support the family. Throughout the discussion of working, only two or three men mentioned the temptation of a second paycheck.

Four types of response to the question of wives' working may be identified. The "traditionalists," 24% of the men, said outright that they intended to marry women who would find sufficient fulfillment in domestic, civic, and cultural pursuits without ever seeking outside jobs. "Pseudofeminists," 16% of the men, favored having their wives work, at least when the question was at a high level of abstraction, but their approval was hedged with qualifications that no woman could meet.

The third and dominant response included almost half (48%) of the respondents. These men took a "modified traditionalist" position which favored a sequential pattern: work, withdrawal from work for child rearing, and eventual return to work. They varied as to the timing of these stages and as to the aid they were prepared to give their wives with domestic and child-rearing functions. The majority saw no substitute for the mother during her child's preschool years. Even the mother of school-age children, were she to work, should preferably be at home when the children return from school. Though they were willing to aid their wives in varying degrees, they frequently excluded specific tasks, for instance, "not the laundry," "not the cleaning," "not the diapers," and so on. Many hoped that they would be "able to assist" their wives by hiring maids. The greater the importance of the wife's work, the more willing they were to help her. (One senior, however, would help only if his wife's work were "peripheral," that is, not as important to her as her home.)

The last, the "feminist" type, was the smallest, only 7% of the total. These men were willing to modify their own roles significantly to facilitate their future wives' careers. Some recommended a symmetrical allocation of tasks—"as long as it is not a complete reversal of roles." In the remaining 5% of the cases, marriage was so remote that the respondents were reluctant to venture any views on this matter.

The foregoing summary of types of male attitudes toward working wives fails to reveal the tangled web of contradictory values and sentiments associated with these attitudes. We shall presently illustrate a variety of inconsistencies. But underlying them is one basic problem. The ideological support for the belief in sharp sex role differentiation in marriage has weakened, but the belief itself has not been relinquished. Increasing skepticism about the innate character of psychological sex differences and some convergence in the ideas of masculinity and femininity[6] have created a strain toward consistency. The more similar the perceptions of male and female personalities,[7] the more universalistic must be the principles of evaluation applied to both sexes. "If you could make three changes in the personality of the girl friend who is currently closest to you, what would they be?" we asked the seniors. Universalistic values were reflected in the following, as in many other responses: "I would like her to be able to set a goal for herself and strive to achieve it. I don't like to see people slacking off." Earlier cross-sex association in childhood and early adolescence has raised male expectation of enjoying an emotional and intellectual companionship with women.[8] These expectations, however, coexist with the deeply rooted norm that the husband should be the superior achiever in the occupational world and the wife, the primary child rearer. One manifestation of this basic dilemma is the familiar conflict between a value and a preference. "It is only fair," declared one senior, "to let a woman do her own thing, if she wants a career. Personally, though, I would want my wife at home."

More interesting are the ambivalent attitudes manifested toward both the full-time homemaker and the career wife. The image of each contained both attractive and repellent traits. Deprecating remarks about housewifery were not uncommon, even among men with traditional views of women's roles. A conservative senior declared, "A woman who works is more interesting than a housewife." "If I were a woman," remarked another senior, "I would want a career. It must be boring sitting around the house doing the same thing day in, day out. I don't have much respect for the type of woman whom I see doing the detergent commercials on TV."

But the low esteem attached by some of the men to full-time homemaking coexisted with other sentiments and convictions which required just such a pattern for one's wife. For example, asked about the disadvantages of being a woman, one senior replied, "Life ends at 40. The woman raised her children and all that remains is garden clubs and that sort of thing—unless, of course, she has a profession." In another part of the interview, this young man explained that he enjoyed shyness in

6. John P. McKee and Alex C. Sherriffs, "The Differential Evaluation of Males and Females," *Journal of Personality* 25 (March 1957): 356–63. John P. McKee and Alex C. Sherriffs, "Men's and Women's Beliefs, Ideals, and Self-Concepts," *American Journal of Sociology* 64 (1959): 356–63.

7. Kenneth Kammeyer, "The Feminine Role: An Analysis of Attitude Consistency," *Journal of Marriage and the Family* 26 (August 1964): 295–305.

8. J. Richard Udry, *The Social Context of Marriage*, Philadelphia: Lippincott, 1966.

a girl and detested aggressive and ambitious women. He could never be attracted to a career woman. It is no exaggeration to conclude that this man could not countenance in a woman who was to be his wife the qualities that he himself felt were necessary for a fulfilling middle age.

A similar mode of contradiction, incidentally, was also disclosed by some seniors with regard to women's majors in college. "There are no 'unfeminine' majors," declared one senior: "I admire a girl who is premed or prelaw." But the universalistic yardstick which led this senior to sanction and admire professional goals for women did not extend to the means for their attainment, as he unwittingly revealed in another part of the interview. Questioned about examples of "unfeminine" behavior, this senior answered: "Excessive grade consciousness." If a premed man, anxious about admission to a good medical school, should go to see a professor about a C in chemistry, this senior would understand although he would disapprove of such preoccupation with grades. But in a woman premed he would find such behavior "positively obnoxious."

If the image of the full-time homemaker contained some alienating features, the main threat of a career wife was that of occupational rivalry, as illustrated in the following excerpt from the interviews. A senior speaks:

> I believe that it is good for mothers to return to fulltime work when the children are grown, provided the work is important and worthwhile. Otherwise, housewives get hung up with tranquilizers, because they have no outlet for their abilities. . . . Of course, it may be difficult if a wife becomes successful in her own right. A woman should want her husband's success more than he should want hers. Her work shouldn't interfere with or hurt his career in any way. He should not sacrifice his career to hers. For example, if he is transferred, his wife should follow—and not vice versa.

In sum, work for married women with grown children is approved by this young man, provided that the occupation is of some importance. But such an occupation is precisely one which carries a threat to the husband's pride.

The expectation that the husband should be the superior achiever appears still to be deeply rooted. Even equality in achievement of husband and wife is interpreted as a defeat for the man. The prospect of occupational rivalry with one's wife seems intolerable to contemplate. "My girl friend often beats me in tennis," explained one senior. "Now, losing the game doesn't worry me. It in no way reduces my manhood. But being in a lower position than a woman in a job would hurt my self-esteem."

Another student, having declared his full support for equal opportunities for women in the occupational world, added a qualification: "A woman should not be in a position of firing an employee. It is an unpleasant thing to do. Besides, it is unfair to the man who is to be fired.

He may be a very poor employee, but he is still a human being and it may be just compounding his unhappiness to be fired by a woman."

In sum, the right of an able woman to a career of her choice, the admiration for women who measure up in terms of the dominant values of our society, the lure but also the threat that such women present, the low status attached to housewifery but the conviction that there is no substitute for the mother's care of young children, the deeply internalized norm of male occupational superiority pitted against the principle of equal opportunity irrespective of sex—these are some of the revealed inconsistencies.

Such ambivalences on the part of college men are bound to exacerbate role conflicts in women. The latter must sense that even the men who pay lip service to the creativity of child rearing and domesticity reserve their admiration (if occasionally tinged with ambivalence) for women achievers who measure up in terms of the dominant values of our society. It is becoming increasingly difficult to maintain a system of values for women only.[9]

Nevertheless, to infer from this account of male inconsistencies that this is an area of great stress for them would be a mistake. It is not. By and large, the respondents assumed that the women's "career and marriage" issue was solved by the sequential pattern of withdrawal and return to work. If this doomed women to second-class citizenship in the occupational world, the outcome was consistent with the conviction that the husband should be the superior achiever.

Men who momentarily worried about the fate of able women found moral anchorage in their conviction that today no satisfactory alternative to the mother's care of young children can be found. Many respondents expressed their willingness to help with child care and household duties. Similarly, many hoped to spend more time with their own children than their fathers had spent with them. But such domestic participation was defined as assistance to the wife who was to carry the major responsibility. Only two or three of the men approved a symmetrical, rather than a complementary, allocation of domestic and occupational roles. An articulate senior sums up the dominant view:

> I would not want to marry a woman whose only goal is to become a housewife. This type of woman would not have enough bounce and zest in her. I don't think a girl has much imagination if she just wants to settle down and raise a family from the very beginning. Moreover, I want an independent girl, one who has her own interests and does not always have to depend on me for stimulation and diversion. However, when we both agree to have children, my wife must be the one to raise them. She'll have to forfeit her freedom for the children. I believe that, when a woman wants a child, she must also accept the full responsibility of child care.

9. Mirra Komarovsky, *Women in the Modern World, Their Education and Their Dilemmas,* Boston: Little, Brown, 1953.

TABLE 2. College Women's Attitudes Toward Work and Family Patterns (%)

	Random Sample of Sophomore Class at Women's Liberal Arts College 1943 (N = 78)	Class in Introductory Sociology Same College 1971 (N = 44)
Assume that you will marry and that your husband will make enough money so that you will not have to work unless you want to. Under these circumstances, would you prefer:		
1. Not to work at all, or stop after childbirth and decide later whether to go back.	50	18
2. To quit working after the birth of a child but definitely to go back to work.	30	62
3. To continue working with a minimum of interruption for childbearing.	20	20

Source—Mirra Komarovsky, unpublished studies.

When he was asked why it was necessarily the woman who had to be fully responsible for the children, he replied:

> Biology makes equality impossible. Besides, the person I'll marry will want the child and will want to care for the child. Ideally, I would hope I'm not forcing her to assume responsibility for raising the children. I would hope that this is her desire and that it is the happiest thing she can do. After we have children, it will be her career that will end, while mine will support us. I believe that women should have equal opportunities in business and the professions, but I still insist that a woman who is a mother should devote herself entirely to her children.

The low emotional salience of the issue of working wives may also be attributed to another factor. The female partners of our respondents, at this particular stage of life, did not, with a few exceptions, force the men to confront their inconsistencies. Apparently enough women will freely make the traditional-for-women adjustments—whether scaling down their own ambitions or in other ways acknowledging the prior claims of the man's career. This judgment is supported by the results of two studies of female undergraduates done on the same campus in 1943 and 1971 (Table 2). The big shift in postcollege preferences since 1943 was in the decline of women undergraduates who opted for full-time homemaking and volunteer activities. In 1971, the majority chose the sequential pattern, involving withdrawal from employment for child rearing. The proportion of committed career women who hope to return to work soon after childbirth has remained constant among freshmen and sophomores.

If women's attitudes have not changed more radically in the past 30 years, it is no doubt because society has failed to provide effective supports for the woman who wishes to integrate family life, parenthood, and work on much the same terms as men. Such an option will not become available as long as the care of young children is regarded as the responsibility solely of the mother. In the absence of adequate child care centers, an acceptance of a symmetrical division of domestic and work responsibilities, or other facilitating social arrangements, the attitudes of the majority of undergraduates reflect their decision to make some kind of workable adjustment to the status quo, if not a heroic struggle to change it.

Summary

Role conflicts in women have been amply documented in numerous studies. The problem underlying this study was to ascertain whether recent social changes and consequent malintegration with regard to sex roles have created stressful repercussions for men as well as for women. In a randomly selected sample of 62 male seniors in an eastern Ivy League college, nearly one-third experienced some anxiety over their perceived failures to live up to the norm of masculine intellectual superiority. This stressful minority suffered from two modes of role strain: scarcity of resources for role performance and ambivalence. The absence of strain in the majority may be explained by a changed role definition. Specifically, the normative expectation of male intellectual superiority appears to be giving way on the campus of our study to the ideal of intellectual companionship between equals. Attitudes toward working wives abounded in ambivalences and inconsistencies. The ideological supports for the traditional sex role differentiation in marriage are weakening, but the emotional allegiance to the modified traditional pattern is still strong. These inconsistencies did not generate a high degree of stress, partly, no doubt, because future roles do not require an immediate realistic confrontation. In addition, there is no gainsaying the conclusion that human beings can tolerate a high degree of inconsistency as long as it does not conflict with their self-interest.

10 ALTERNATIVES TO THE PRESENT-DAY FAMILY

Lewis A. Coser

The Sexual Requisites of Utopia

We are justly punished for those exclusive attachments which cause us to become blind, unjust, and restrict our universe to the person we love.

Jean Jacques Rousseau[1]

The hopeful settlers who, in the late eighteenth and the nineteenth centuries, went out to the frontier in order to build a New Jerusalem of community and fraternity, rejected the increasing differentiation and segmentalization of life which they suffered from in the United States or in Europe. They wished to curb within their own nature excessively individualistic tendencies and to immerse themselves in an active community of their fellows.

If, as Frank E. Manuel argued, "the utopia may well be a sensitive indicator of where the sharpest anguish of an age lies,"[2] then we can assert with some confidence that the anguish of these settlers was caused to a large degree by the differentiation and segmentalization of modern urban and industrializing society. Their urge to build a utopia was rooted in a desire for a comprehensive de-differentiation, a deep immersion of

1. *Correspondence Générale*, Paris: Collin, 1924–34, Vol. IV, p. 82, October 13, 1758.
2. Frank E. Manuel, "Toward a Psychological History of Utopia," in his *Utopias and Utopian Thought*, Boston: Houghton Mifflin, 1966, p. 70.

hitherto fragmented souls in a great brotherhood that would make man whole again.

The motives of individuals are never sufficient to explain the functioning of the organizations and institutions they fashion. "Between the idea and the reality," writes T. S. Eliot, in *The Hollow Men,* "between the notion and the act falls the shadow." The successful functioning of these utopias depended upon strict control over the allegiance of their members. Whatever facilitated such controls maximized the chances of success. Hence, religiously oriented communities were considerably more enduring than secular ones because religion served as a binding force. Similarly, communities with strong charismatic leaders provided for the followers that sense of mission which served to harness their energies. In all instances of successful utopian communities, the complete elimination, or at the very least the decided de-emphasis, of dyadic sexual relations provided that form of organization in which commitments would not be diverted from the one central purpose of fashioning an ideal all-encompassing community.

"All successful communities," writes John Humphrey Noyes, the founder of Oneida and one of the earliest and most sophisticated historians of Utopian communities, "[. . .] exercise control more or less stringent, over the sexual relation; and this principle is most prominent in those that are most successful."[3] All the materials I have been able to examine seem fully to support this seminal statement. What, then, can help account for this correlation?

Organizations that set themselves off from the larger society can thrive only if they are able to absorb their members fully and totally within their confines. Whatever draws the member away from the community threatens it. A de-differentiated brotherhood, an egalitarian community of believers, must be concerned with minimizing any individualistic attachment.[4] As Philip Slater has written, "If we assume a finite quantity of libido in every individual, then it follows that the greater the emotional involvement in the dyad, the greater will be the cathectic withdrawal from objects."[5] Hence, as Slater documents, there has been fear and suspicion of dyadic intimacy in all social life. It stands to reason that such hostility is likely to be greatly accentuated in small, closed organizations. The dyad is the nemesis of such groups.

Whatever draws the member away from total cathexis of the community poses a threat to its existence. Since sex harbors perhaps the most powerful potential for particularized and privileged relations between

3. John Humphrey Noyes, *History of American Socialism*, New York: Hillary House, 1961 (first published in 1870), p. 147.
4. The point is discussed in detail in Rosabeth Moss Kanter's fine work on utopias, *Commitment and Community*, Cambridge: Harvard University Press, 1972.
5. Philip Slater, "On Social Regression," *American Sociological Review* 28 (1963), pp. 339–64.

individuals, it needs to be stringently controlled if the utopian community is to be successful. This seems to account, by the way, for the strong anti-familistic bias of many literary utopias from Plato's to Campanella's.

Even if one agrees that regulation and control of sexual relations is a functional imperative for these collectivities, it will be objected that the character of these regulations vary widely even among the relatively successful utopian communities. Many instituted celibacy; others, while valuing celibacy more, nevertheless permitted endogamous marriages. Noyes' Oneida, on the other hand, instituted a controlled form of promiscuity. This apparent difficulty can be easily overcome if it is realized that the problem those communities faced was not sex as such but rather dyadic withdrawal into a private—hence, non-communal —world. Once this is understood, an important sociological truth alluded to earlier comes again into view: *Celibacy and promiscuity, though opposed sexual practices, fulfill identical sociological functions*. From a structural point of view, they are but variants on the same theme—the prevention of particularistic, dyadic attachments. Whether members refrain from all sexual relations, as among the Shakers, or whether there is Complex Marriage as in Oneida, where men and women within the community may and do cohabit for short periods of time, turns out upon inspection to be sociologically unimportant. The true enemies of community are those "exclusive and idolatrous attachments"[6] between two persons of opposite sex against which not only Noyes but also the Shakers and many others never ceased to warn.[7]

All utopian communities were concerned with channeling the emotional energies of their members into the brotherhood rather than letting them dribble away into private and exclusive channels. They all opposed marriage outside the community since such marriages would evidently draw the member away. In some cases, endogamous marriage was indeed tolerated, but it was usually seen as a fall from full grace. In the Ebenezer community, for example, "the parties have to go through some public mortification,"[8] and in Snowhill newly married couples were degraded to the lowest rung of the social hierarchy, treated like children, and permitted to climb up to a higher and more respected social status only in a long process of re-socialization.[9] Kanter finds that, "All but one of the successful nineteenth-century groups practiced either celibacy or free

6. Charles Nordhoff, *The Communistic Societies in the United States*, New York: Schocken Books, 1965 (first published in 1875), p. 276.

7. Egon Bittner in his "Radicalism and the Organization of Radical Movements," *American Sociological Review* 28 (1963), p. 938, makes a similar point. Cf. also Vladimir C. Nahirny, "Some Observations on Ideological Groups," *American Journal of Sociology* 47 (1962), pp. 397–405.

8. Noyes, *op. cit.*, p. 140.

9. Everett Webber, *Escape to Utopia*, New York: Hastings House, 1959, pp. 288–89; and Mark Holloway, *Heavens on Earth*, New York: Library Publishers, 1951, p. 172.

love at some time in their history, as opposed to only five of the twenty-one unsuccessful communities. And of those five, although four chose free love, they practiced it in such a way that couples could form if they wished." [10] Hence, we might conclude that, in all successful utopian communities, dyadic attachments were seen as profoundly destructive. The emotional energies of the members could not be permitted to withdraw from the community.

In some communities, these anti-dyadic injunctions were justified by esoteric interpretations of biblical passages. (It is amusing to note in passing that identical biblical passages were sometimes used to justify opposed sexual practices. Thus, "In heaven they neither marry nor are given in marriage" was quoted by the Shakers in defense of celibacy and by Noyes in defense of Complex Marriage.) There is no evidence that some of the less sophisticated settlements ever consciously reflected upon the community-enhancing functions of their sexual practices. In these cases, only latent functions can be discerned. But the matter is different in such highly sophisticated colonies as Noyes' Oneida. Here we find a detailed defense of Complex Marriage not only on theological but also on sociological grounds.

As already noted, Noyes used biblical interpretations to buttress the ideological defense of Complex Marriage. He wrote, for example:

> The abolishment of exclusiveness is involved in the love-relation required between all believers by the express injunction of Christ and the apostles, and by the whole tenor of the New Testament. "The new commandment is, that we love one another," and that, not by pairs, as in the world, but *en masse*. We are required to love one another fervently. [11]

But Noyes also used sociological and social-psychological arguments:

> Love, in the exclusive form, has jealousy for its compliment; and jealousy brings on strife and division [. . .]. An association of States with custom-house lines around each, is sure to be quarrelsome. The further States in that situation are apart, and the more their interests are isolated, the better. The only way to prevent smuggling and strife in a configuration of contiguous States, is to abolish custom-house lines from the interior, and to declare free trade and free transit, collecting revenues and fostering home products by one custom-house line around the whole. This is the policy of the heavenly system—"that they *all* (not two and two) may be one." [12]

Noyes quoted with approval from an article in the transcendentalist *Dial* in which the author, Charles Lane, suggested that "the great problem of socialism now is, whether the existence of the marital family is compatible with that of the universal family, which the term 'community' signifies." "That the affections can be divided, or bent with equal ardor on two objects so opposed as universal and individual love," so Lane

10. Kanter, *op. cit.*, p. 87.
11. Noyes, *op. cit.*, p. 626.
12. *Ibid.*, pp. 634–35. Brackets are in the original.

averred, "may at least be rationally doubted [. . .]. The monasteries and convents, which have existed in all ages, have been maintained solely by the annihilation of that peculiar affection on which the separate family is based."[13]

It should be noted that, despite elaborate precautions, the Oneida colony had again and again to fight the demon of sexual separateness. "By the Community standards the most serious disadvantage of Complex Marriage," writes a modern student of Oneida, "was that couples frequently fell in love with each other. Community reports include frequent criticism of men and women who failed to suppress one of these 'exclusive' or 'special' attachments. The rule of ascending fellowship was invoked to prevent young men and women from having sexual relations, in part because they were so likely to fall in love. If it was suspected that a woman refused a man's attentions because of greater love for another, she was severely criticized for lack of appropriate 'public spirit.' "[14]

The Shakers also knew of the social-psychological implications of their communal doctrines. They stated very plainly the reasons why dyadic bonds, being inherently "selfish," militated against wider involvement:

> Carnal affections, reads an early Shaker statement, are selfish; they cleave to natural kindred. They are chiefly confined to those narrow limits which circumscribe the connective ties of flesh and blood, and seldom, if ever, extend further than to those who are excited by interest, or some other selfish motive, to indulge, flatter and exalt their selfishness [. . .] so contracted, selfish and fleeting are carnal affections.[15]

Statements such as these—and they abound in the historical record —prove that at least the more sophisticated among the utopians were quite aware of the anti-communal implications of dyadic withdrawal and "exclusive attachment." In such cases, the utopians manifestly knew why they instituted their preventive therapy. We deal here with purposive social action.

After the full institutionalization of sacerdotal celibacy in Europe, one can note the rise of forms of ritual in which the initiation of the priest into his office is symbolically depicted as his marriage to the Church. Similar symbolic transfers are common in the utopian communities. The family attachment which is denied to the members of the community is symbolically transferred in such a way that the community at large becomes an extended family. "Joining the community is like marriage"

13. *Ibid.*
14. Maren Lockwood Carden, *Oneida: Utopian Community to Modern Corporation*, Baltimore: Johns Hopkins Press, 1969, p. 58.
15. Calvin Green and Seth Wells (Eds.), *A Summary View of the Milennial Church or United Society of Believers*, Albany, N.Y.: 1848, pp. 276–77.

stated one member of Oneida.[16] The Shakers, with their strict rejection of all familistic ties, were also wont to refer to their communities as families, just as the Oneida Perfectionists. One notes a variety of ceremonial observances in the diverse utopian communities, but one can find in most of them the witting or unwitting exaltation of the community as the one true family.

Such transfers of emotion from the dyad to the community as a family writ large seem often to have been quite successful. One historian well describes this process of gradual transfer of allegiance from the family to the Family. In his account of the Rappist colony after celibacy was introduced there, he writes:

> The family became more of a house unit and an intrinsic part of the larger society rather than a separate and basically selfish organization of parents and children. Family names were unimportant anyway, for "brothers and sisters" were called by the first name [. . .]. And when parents died, the children became part of entirely different "families"; adults were moved around in like manner. Thus over a period of years the real family merged with, or was scattered throughout, the community.[17]

The abolition of family life made it possible to assure that individuals always act in their public roles; that is, that they give up their right to privacy. This proved to be an important means of social control. Robert K. Merton and Rose L. Coser have argued[18] that in modern society insulation from observability of one's role performance on the part of inferiors, peers, and superiors is one of the most important mechanisms which insure a degree of autonomy for individuals as they are variously enmeshed in group activities. "The limitations and restrictions concerning the presence of others," argues Rose Coser, "make it possible for status-occupants to present themselves in different ways with different persons."[19] This statement holds true in differentiated and segmented social structures. Here, a variety of social mechanisms insure the person a measure of privacy, a social sphere in which he is at least partly insulated from observability. But "greedy" organizations cannot allow privacy since it involves a withdrawal, be it only partial, from the group's control. Hence, such communities cannot tolerate a distinction between a private and a public sphere. For them, the public exposure of the self symbolizes in effect the complete submission of the person to the

16. William A. Hinds, *American Communities and Cooperative Colonies*, rev. ed., Chicago: Charles H. Kerr, 1902, p. 187.
17. John S. Duss, *The Harmonists*, Harrisburg: The Pennsylvania Book Service, 1943, pp. 28–29. On closely related developments in the Israeli Kibbutz, cf. Yonina Talmon, "The Family in a Revolutionary Movement—The Case of the Kibbutz in Israel," in M. F. Nimkoff (Ed.), *Comparative Family Systems*, Boston: Houghton Mifflin, 1965, pp. 259–86.
18. Robert K. Merton, *Social Theory and Social Structure*, New York: The Free Press, 1957, pp. 319 *sqq.*, Rose Laub Coser, "Insulation from Observability and Types of Social Conformity," *American Sociological Review* 26, No. 1 (February, 1961), pp. 28–39.
19. Rose Coser, *loc. cit.*, p. 28.

538   *The Sexual Requisites of Utopia*

community. The shield of privacy must be withdrawn if the member is to
be fully immersed and controlled by the collectivity.

The Shakers had watchtowers over the roofs of their buildings from
which the ministry could observe members' behavior and they had
shuttered apertures inside buildings for indoor observation. But such
means of surveillance were relatively crude since they could only help in
controlling the behavior but not the internal dispositions of the members.
Hence, the importance of the Shaker confession. Anyone seeking admission to the Shaker community was asked to give "evidence of their
sincerity [.. . .] by an honest confession of every improper transaction or
sin that lies within the reach of their memory [. . .]. It often takes years
for individuals to complete this work of thorough confession [. . .]."[20] In
fact, it appears that throughout the major part of a member's lifetime he
would periodically be urged to confess anew.

Among the Shakers, such confessions were made to elders appointed
for the purpose, though all members of the community were encouraged
to spy on each other and to report misdeeds that required the purge of
confessions.[21] Noyes' Oneida community notably improved upon this by
placing much of the burden of control of the membership not in the hands
of a hierarchical elite, but in the members themselves. What he called
"the system of mutual criticism" made each member the keeper of the
other. Here is Noyes' own account:

> This system takes the place of backbiting in ordinary society, and is regarded
> as one of the greatest means of improvement and fellowship [. . .]. Some-
> times persons are criticized by the entire family; at other times by a
> committee of six, eight, twelve, or more [. . . .]. It is an ordeal which reveals
> insincerity and selfishness; but it also often [. . .] reveals hidden virtues as
> well as secret faults. It is always acceptable to those who wish to see
> themselves as others see them [. . .]. These two agencies—daily evening
> meetings and criticisms—are found quite adequate to the maintenance of
> good order and government [. . .].[22]

Mutual criticisms, confessions, and similar forms of control helped
insure that the member could not preserve even a shred of privacy in the
face of the "greedy" community. All aspects of private life were at all
times accessible to public scrutiny. Only men and women who were
wholly public could become **perfect** members. Any attempt to withhold
information about the self **could** only be seen as involving a lack of
confidence in the community. The ideal community member had no
secrets; in fact, he had no private self.

Mutual criticism involved, of course, the whole gamut of human
failings and vices as it manifested itself in the community, but "selfish

20. Nordhoff, *op. cit.*, pp. 145–46.
21. Edward D. Andrews, *The People Called Shakers*, New York: Oxford University
Press, 1953.
22. Nordhoff, *op. cit.*, pp. 289–90.

love" and the tendency to prefer some persons over others seems to have been a major subject. Nordhoff describes one of these brainwashing sessions in which a young man was accused of being "a respecter of persons." "He showed his liking for certain individuals too plainly by calling them pet names before people." [23] The root cause of the difficulty, it finally developed in Noyes' summing up of the case, was that

> Charles, as you know, is in the situation of one who is by and by to become a father. Under these circumstances, he has fallen under the too common temptation of selfish love, and a desire to wait upon and cultivate an exclusive intimacy with the woman who was to bear a child through him. This is an insidious temptation [. . .] it must nevertheless be struggled against.

Charles, Noyes reported with satisfaction, has now agreed "to isolate himself entirely from the woman and let another man take his place at her side." Charles had further decided to sleep with the smaller children for the time being and he was hence in a fair way "to rid himself of all selfish faults." [24]

The utopian community succeeded in cutting off its members from extracommunity ties. Hence, the member came to view the community as the fount of all support and psychic sustenance. To erect walls against the intrusion of the outside world, if not always easy, proved feasible and practical among the more successful communities. But the erection of such boundaries was clearly insufficient since there was always the insidious danger of dyadic withdrawal among pairs of otherwise-devoted members. Hence, the functional necessity for institutionalized safeguards. Such safeguards involved a variety of manifestly opposed sexual practices which, however, all served the same functions: they provided the insurance that emotional energies would not be withheld from the community and could fully be harnessed for the purpose of total commitment. Control of sexual relations was supplemented by other control mechanisms, notably mutual surveillance and criticism, so that no shred of private feelings, no niche in which privacy could be cultivated, remained for the member. The good communitarian had no private self. Just because the perfect community member had sacrificed his self to the group, he was utterly at its mercy. As one can conclude from the theory of cognitive dissonance, the greater the sacrifice, the greater the pressure to uphold the value of the group in which so much has been invested. The "greedy" community had succeeded in sucking up the substance of the private self, leaving only a shell. [25]

23. *Ibid.*, p. 291.

24. *Ibid.*, pp. 292–93.

25. Certain Utopian communities that were founded later than those with which this paper is mainly concerned (the Hutterites and the Bruderhof communities in particular) permitted, and even encouraged, marriage. But it must be noted that they tended to deemphasize emotional attachments between the marital pair. In the Bruderhof community, for example, no dating or courtship is permissible. Such courtship, it is believed, "would

While sacerdotal celibacy has lasted for many centuries, few utopian communities even survived a few decades. The main reason for this differential life span seems to lie in the fact that the Catholic priesthood constituted a legitimate professional community with specialized societal functions and was a part of a wider religious organization that encompassed priests and laymen alike. The Utopian community, on the other hand, always remained a deviant community with a counterculture of societal withdrawal. It served as a meeting ground for dissatisfied members of the society at large and it may, hence, have drained away accumulating discontents into comparatively safe channels. But as society changed, so did the character of its discontents. The utopian solutions and desires of one generation no longer appealed to the next. Unlike a criminal subculture which exists in continued symbiotic relation with the official culture and whose personnel is automatically replenished in each generation by criminal deviants from society at large, the utopian counterculture arrives at so idiosyncratic a solution to the specific discontents of a period that it can no longer appeal to the dissimilar preoccupations of a later age and cannot replenish its ranks. And as to the children of the utopians, if children there were, in due time, they deserted the pathways of their fathers and escaped into the wider differentiated world. The undivided allegiance to the community, which was so effective in tying the generation of the fathers to the collective enterprise, proved dysfunctional in the long run in that it failed to provide the psychological prerequisites for the transmission of values to the next generation. By destroying the nuclear family, that indispensable link between the generations, the community destroyed the chances for its survival over time.[26]

---

lead to the explosion of what one of them called the 'always latent erotic dynamic,' " writes Benjamin Zablocki in his fine study of the Bruderhof, *The Joyful Community*, Baltimore: Penguin Books, p. 117. He also notes that the Bruderhof, like all other intentional communities, has had difficulties with the problem of sex, "but is unusual in its reluctance to admit the existence of the problem," and shows an "almost morbid avoidance of some of the more difficult aspects of life, particularly the area of sex" (p. 278).

26. Many of the themes adumbrated here are more fully developed in an honor's thesis of a student of mine, Harry F. Levine, *The Structure of Utopia: A Sociological Analysis of Five American Communistic Communities* (available at the Brandeis University Library, Waltham, Mass.). For a detailed discussion of other commitment mechanisms, see Kanter, *op. cit.*, Chap. IV.

Rosabeth Moss Kanter

Oneida,
Community of the Past

. . . The initial impetus for the building of American communes has tended to stem from one of three major themes: a desire to live according to religious and spiritual values, rejecting the sinfulness of the established order; a desire to reform society by curing its economic and political ills, rejecting the injustice and inhumanity of the establishment; or a desire to promote the psychosocial growth of the individual by putting him into closer touch with his fellows, rejecting the isolation and alienation of the surrounding society. . . .

Regardless of the rhetoric, however, the three themes have much in common. They reject the established order as sinful, unjust, or unhealthy. They stress the possibility of perfection through restructuring social institutions. They seek the recreation of a lost unity—between man and God, between man and man, or between man and himself. They stress immediacy, the opportunity to achieve such harmonies now. They frequently seek a return to the land as the pathway to perfection. And they often lead to a single development: the utopian community or commune. Despite the diversity of origins of such communities, they share many similar features in both their underlying concepts and their resulting life-styles. A prime illustration is the case of Oneida, a nineteenth-century community that is sparking much interest today. Oneida's origins were religious, but to some extent it represents a merger of all three utopian critiques.

Oneida, Community of the Past

To members of the Oneida Community, their way of life was not an experiment; rather, it was the norm, the shining example of the Kingdom of Heaven on earth. "We believed we were living under a system which the whole world would sooner or later adopt," wrote Pierrepont Noyes, son of founder John Humphrey Noyes. The elder Noyes was an activist and a realist, stressing faith in the realism of the spirit. To him, Heaven

541

was "a present, existing state, one that ought to be admitted into this world."[1]

John Noyes's vision of utopia was embodied in a community of about two hundred people, four miles from Oneida, New York, with branches in Wallingford, Connecticut, and Brooklyn, New York. The community grew out of a Bible class that Noyes, a radical graduate of Yale Theological Seminary, ran in his home in Putney, Vermont. After losing his license to preach there because of his radical teachings, he proclaimed that "Christ demanded and promised perfection here on earth," and founded the group called Perfectionists. In 1848 he moved to Oneida with a number of his followers, and the Oneida Community was officially organized around the principles of the primitive Christian church: "the believers possessed one heart and one soul and had all things in common."[2] In the words of an Oneida song:

We have built us a dome
On our beautiful plantation,
And we all have one home,
And one family relation.[3]

The pattern of community life translated these principles into practice, its most distinctive aspects being economic communism, communal living, "complex marriage" or free love, communal child-rearing, and government by mutual criticism. The community was considered one large family, sharing both the material and the spiritual life. Members had only a minimum of private property, for all recruits signed a document transferring money and major possessions to the community. The community in turn provided education and sustenance in exchange for members' labor. Even clothes were the common property of all, with the wearer merely allowed the use of them: "going-away clothes" were shared by all. No accounts were kept by members, but it was the duty of each to keep his expenses as light as possible. If women, for example, were thought to spend too much of their annual appropriation from the community for personal adornment, they might be asked to give up brooches until they had conquered the "dress spirit."[4]

Communism also informed the community work arrangements. Oneidans first supported themselves by farming, but financial difficulties indicated to members the need for industrial enterprise. Their first endeavor was canning crops for sale to grocers, then in 1852 they began the manufacture of steel traps, which became the standard brand in the

1. Pierrepont Noyes, *My Father's House* (New York, 1937), pp. 17–18; Robert Allerton Parker, *A Yankee Saint* (New York, 1935), p. 230.
2. P. Noyes, *My Father's House*, p. 4; Oneida Community, *Handbook of the Oneida Community* (Wallingford, Conn., 1867), pp. 10–11.
3. Oneida song, quoted in Mark Holloway, *Heavens on Earth* (New York, 1966), p. 179.
4. Maren Lockwood, "The Oneida Community," Ph.D. diss., Harvard University, 1962, p. 171.

United States and Canada. Other industries included a foundry and the manufacture of traveling bags, silk, and later, silverware. A carpenter's shop, joiner's shop, sawmill, tin shop, tailor shop, shoe shop, harness shop, printing press, and dental office were among the enterprises conducted for the benefit of the community. Industries were regulated by a business board, composed of heads of individual industrial departments and other interested members, which met weekly. All members were free to participate in its deliberations. Each spring there was a special session of the board to make general plans. Previous to the meeting every member was invited to hand in a note stating which industrial department he wished to work in. At this annual meeting an organization committee was appointed which selected foremen and apportioned the labor, abiding by the expressed wishes of members as far as possible.[5]

In this way, members were centrally assigned to their jobs, and jobs were rotated from year to year. In the eyes of the community, all classes of work were equally honorable. As far as possible, especially in the early years, men and women shared all kinds of work equally. As a result, women wore short skirts, pantalettes, and short hair, to make it easier to do men's work (as well as to discourage feminine vanity), and men in turn invented labor-saving devices for household chores. Two of the leading businesses were superintended by the women; women kept the community accounts; and according to the community handbook of 1867, "the sexes mingle freely in many departments of industry," side by side in the field and in the factories.[6] Sharing of work extended even to the children, who worked at least one hour and as many as three hours a day, six days a week, making chains for the trap industry. A minimum quality and quantity of work were expected before they could play.

The community worked as a group whenever the nature of the job permitted, organizing the effort into "bees." In particular, jobs that would be tedious for a few but less so when shared were handled in this way. Cleaning the buildings after the departure of visitors was one prevalent occasion for a "bee." The building of the central house, the Mansion House, was accomplished completely by members (except the plastering), and the community was continually making alterations in its buildings to accommodate new members and new needs. At the same time that participation was enhanced through "bees," nearly every member had a chance to take part in directing some aspect of community life through serving on a committee. According to one member, this "active sense of participation" led to "success and harmony."[7]

The group focus informed all aspects of life. All members of the

5. Oneida Community, *Handbook,* pp. 12–14.
6. Oneida Community, *Handbook,* p. 20.
7. Walter D. Edmonds, *The First Hundred Years, 1848–1948* (Oneida, N.Y., 1948), p. 19.

community lived in the Mansion House, slept in small rooms, with the exception of small children ate in one large dining hall at many tables, and performed most daily tasks in a public place.[8] The Mansion House had several large halls, a visitor's room, a library, two recreation rooms, a dining hall, and the printing office of the newspaper, as well as bedrooms. While older members had separate bedrooms, the younger usually shared rooms.

The whole community convened in a separate meetinghouse for daily evening meetings, consisting of prayer and discussion of community affairs. In leisure time the events most enjoyed were those that brought "their entire family together," encompassing the whole community, such as plays, operettas, concerts by the community orchestra, as well as dancing and singing. Six to seven P.M. every evening was the children's hour, when all the children congregated in one room for games, plays, and songs, and all the adults gathered to watch them. Community spirit was instilled in the children, too, for group games were especially encouraged, including card games.

Although economic communism and communal living were themselves unusual and unconventional practices for America, it was Oneida's controversial practice of complex marriage that confirmed its deviance in the eyes of outside society. The roots of the institution were in the teachings of John Humphrey Noyes, who in 1850 wrote a pamphlet called *Slavery and Marriage:* "Marriage is not an institution of the Kingdom of Heaven, and must give place to Communism . . . The abolishment of exclusiveness is involved in the love-relation required between all believers in Christ." To this end the community instituted complex marriage. Under this system every member had sexual access to every other with his or her consent. A wide selection in cohabitation was encouraged, but always under "strict regulation and governed by spiritual considerations."[9] Intercourse was supervised by Oneida's leaders and ultimately by Noyes. A man interested in a liaison had to approach a woman through a third party, generally an older woman, and his choice had the right to refuse his attentions. As there was a general feeling that the young should learn from the older, more spiritual members, who had reached a higher level of "fellowship," sexual contacts usually proceeded along these lines. Boys, for example, first had intercourse with women at menopause. To prevent breeding, a form of contraception called "male continence" was introduced by Noyes, a practice requiring a great deal of self-control on the part of the man.

While a wide range of sexual contact was encouraged, special relationships were discouraged. Couples might be broken up or one

8. Lockwood, "Oneida," p. 169.

9. John Humphrey Noyes, *History of American Socialisms* (New York, 1961), pp. 624–629. P. Noyes, *Father's House*, pp. 8–9.

member sent to a branch. Community members accepted this restriction and put it into practice. One man wrote of a sexual relationship with a woman: "Naturally our relations became more intimate, but I avoided any avowal of special love that, if reciprocated, would estrange her from the central love in the community." Though love was free and monogamous marriage unknown, outright promiscuity was also discouraged. One reporter notes that there was enforced secession of some people who were too amorously inclined. In fact, kissing and handshaking were not as prevalent as in outside society, because the community wanted these things to have meaning, and they avoided shows of affection in public because of the public's attitude toward them as "free lovers." The ceremonial leave-taking and welcome for traveling members, however, did include caresses.[10]

Although its sexual practices were attacked in the press and from the pulpit on the outside, the community denied that it practiced "free love." In the face of wild tales and gossip about its orgiastic practices, it claimed to be a private family. According to the community handbook, "free love" in the Oneida sense did not make love between all the members any less binding or responsible than in marriage.

The Perfectionists refrained from having any children from 1849 to 1869. For purposes of child-rearing, a kind of selective breeding, called "stirpiculture," was adopted in 1869. All females were encouraged to breed, and all males were allowed to have one child, but only preferred males ("stirps") could have more than one. Fifty-three women signed a statement that they considered themselves to belong first to God and second to John Humphrey Noyes, and that they would accept Noyes's choice of candidates for mating with them. A corresponding resolution was signed by thirty-eight men. In order to mate for propagation purposes, couples made application to the central committee, which passed on the fitness of the combination and, if it was disapproved, found another combination. Of fifty-one applications, forty-two were approved and nine vetoed on grounds of "unfitness." Fifty-eight stirpiculture children were born to the community, nine of them fathered by Noyes himself.[11]

Once children were born, they were raised communally. Soon after weaning, mothers sent their offspring to the Children's House, a wing of the Mansion House. This was divided into three departments: a nursery to age four, a kindergarten to age six, and the "South Room" to age twelve or fourteen. Usually after weaning, women took their turn in the children's department as assistants. Within the Children's House, as within the community as a whole, the emphasis was on group activity and

10. Allan Estlake, *The Oneida Community* (London, 1900), pp. 72, 60–63; Lockwood, "Oneida," p. 84.
11. Parker, *Yankee Saint*, pp. 257, 259–260.

love for all, rather than on selfishness or exclusive love. According to Pierrepont Noyes, who grew up there, the "physical setup of the house—the ubiquity of sitting rooms and the smallness of bedrooms —helped discourage personal isolation and exclusiveness." The heads of the children's department, not parents, raised the children, and department heads were called "papa" and "mother." In fact, the younger Noyes reports, many parent-child relationships existed between unrelated children and adults with or without children of their own. Children did visit their own parents individually once or twice a week but accepted the " 'family life' of the group as a whole . . . as the focus of their existence, and in their own immediate generation they developed a sense of solidarity . . . that they carried with them into later life." An excess of parental affection was frowned on because it was a kind of "special love" or exclusive love, just as special love between couples was discouraged by complex marriage. Children were reprimanded for any "stickiness" or special love for anyone, especially for parents, but including friends. Because of "stickiness," one boy, for example, was forbidden to see his mother for a week. Pierrepont Noyes recalled that his own weekly visits to his mother in her quarters were a privilege that could be taken away at any time.[12] The community also censured friendships that excluded others; children convicted of being partial might be temporarily separated.

Children had their own daily routine. At age twelve, for example, they worked in an industry for three hours, studied for three hours, received one hour of religious education, and had the remaining time to play. In connection with the children's hour, children held their own evening meeting, presided over by the head of the Children's House, who lectured about the dangers of Satan, the plans of God for the universe, and general moral and spiritual topics. According to Pierrepont Noyes, the children believed him unquestioningly.[13] Children were generally disciplined by nonforceful means, including verbal rather than physical punishments. One man working in the Children's House invented the Order of the O and F (obedient and faithful) for children, with badges to signify their membership in good standing. Misbehaving children were deprived of their O and F badges as a sign that they had temporarily lost some freedom of action.

For children as well as for adults, Oneida distinguished between "improvement" and "education." Improvement involved spiritual enhancement and was one of the primary goals of the community. Children, for example, were taught that reporting each other's misbehavior was a virtue, because it was desirable that "sinners" be corrected as soon as possible. This dictate was embodied in one of the Perfectionists' major

12. P. Noyes, *Father's House,* pp. 39, 66–67; Edmonds, *First Hundred Years,* p. 26.
13. P. Noyes, *Father's House,* pp. 104–106.

forms of government and social control: mutual criticism. In addition to the daily evening meetings where general or individual problems were discussed, members submitted themselves periodically for criticism by a committee of six to twelve judges; in a few cases of extreme seriousness, the entire community was present.The subject was expected to receive the criticism in silence and confess to it in writing. Judgment was made as to his good and bad points and how he might improve. Members believed the experience to be very effective. As Walter Edmonds reported:

> The Committees mixed praise with fault-finding. The essence of the system was frankness; its amelioration friendliness and affection. Yet it was always an ordeal. Without doubt the human temptation to vent personal dislikes on a victim was not resisted by everyone; but I have heard members say that the baring of secret faults by impartial criticizers called for more grace—as they used to say—than the occasional spiteful jab of an enemy. The same witnesses have testified that they were always happier and healthier after one of these spiritual baths; also that just because members had a chance to criticize one another openly, community life was singularly free from backbiting and scandal-mongering.[14]

Mutual criticism was used to ensure physical health as well as conformity to community standards. Evidently with some success, the committee exhorted those suffering from certain physical ailments to *act* like well men. Sick members might send for a criticizing committee, with the usual result that the ailing party was brought into a sweat by the ordeal, breaking the disease. As stated by one Oneidan: "If you are sick, seek for some one . . . to find out your weakest spot in character and conduct; let them put their finger on the very sore that you would best like to keep hid. Depend upon it, there is the avenue through which disease gets access to you."[15] Even for children this remedy sometimes applied. On one occasion when there was a bad epidemic of colds, the house-mother attributed them to the presence of an evil spirit, a criticism was started, and the ill children were counseled to confess Christ.

Probably the most important aim of mutual criticism was to imbue members with "public spirit" or "community spirit," and to fight egoism and selfishness. The community's ban on exclusive possessions extended beyond material goods and other persons to encompass even the self. Excessive introspection, for example, was considered a sin. There was no matter too private for mutual criticism. The Oneida handbook reported that "intercourse between the sexes" was often under discussion at meetings and the subject of criticisms. The community even published a pamphlet of criticisms of members, such as the following: "If R would turn round and instead of trying to interest others in his personal affairs, interest himself in universal truth, he would have no difficulty about

14. Edmonds, *First Hundred Years*, p. 20.
15. Parker, *Yankee Saint*, pp. 217–218.

fellowship. He would find himself in the very element of social freedom. If he would take up some study, entirely forget himself, and apply his mind to abstract truth, with perseverance, for a long season, he would be a much better judge of his own experience than he is now." In criticisms, members were often censured for their lack of "we-spirit." As one historian reported: "The odor of crushed selfishness was said to pervade the air of the communal dwelling."[16] One member gave this account of his first criticism, conducted by John Humphrey Noyes:

> Every trait of my character that I took any pride or comfort in seemed to be cruelly discounted, and after, as it were, being turned inside out and thoroughly inspected, I was, metaphorically, stood upon my head and allowed to drain till all the self-righteousness had dripped out of me . . . I felt like pouring out my soul in tears, but there was too much pride left in me yet to make an exhibition of myself. The work had only been begun. For days and weeks after I found myself recalling and reviewing them in a new light, the more I pondered, the more convinced I became of the justice of what at first my spirit had so violently rebelled against. Today I feel that I would gladly give many years of my life if I could have just one more criticism from John Humphrey Noyes.[17]

Some Oneida Perfectionists called themselves "living sacrifices to God and true communism." What the Oneidan sacrificed was not only tobacco, alcohol, and meat; nor merely individual rights over property, spouses, children, and the self; but also respectability. For Oneida's religious, economic, sexual, and familial deviance brought it into conflict with arbiters of morality in the larger society. Though the community had some good relations with immediate neighbors, often hiring them as well-paid laborers, and was well-regarded by many utopian sympathizers, free thinkers, and admirers of its industrial expertise, numerous forms of hostility were experienced. On one occasion, for example, the community boys visiting the trapshop in the village a mile away were chased, jeered, and dared to fight by the village boys. They were called "Christ boys" and "bastards" on the outside, and bastards they in fact were. Nearby Hamilton College and the clergy objected especially to Oneida. In 1873 the Association of New York Methodist Ministers denounced the ethics at Oneida as "free love and licensed indulgence" and "harlotry." Complaints about the community's "unmoralities" were registered with magistrates of two counties, and a Grand Jury investigation was prompted, although the complaint was later dropped. Even their mutual criticism was ridiculed and condemned. The New York *Times* claimed that this practice attracted members to Oneida because it embodied and legitimated scandal. Other newspapers scorned and mocked the short hair and slender figures of Oneida women. Visitors or outsiders sometimes

16. Oneida Community, *Handbook*, p. 14; Oneida Community, *Mutual Criticism* (Oneida, N.Y., 1876), p. 52; Lockwood, "Oneida," p. 78.
17. Estlake, *Oneida*, p. 67.

assailed community members with prying, obscene, and insulting questions. Even apparently innocent practices were cast in a bad light by critics; one writer, who was opposed to free love, for example, interpreted the fact that Oneida publications were mailed free in response to any request as being "malicious, shrewd proselytizing." A legal threat to take action against the community was in fact partly responsible for its eventual metamorphosis into a joint-stock company without special social and sexual practices. In 1879 the Presbyterian Church agitated for special state legislation against Oneida, and Noyes fled to Canada in response to a rumor of his intended arrest. The community had anticipated this outcome; one member said that "John Humphrey Noyes could not expect to fare better at the hands of a scurrilous public than did Christ and other reformers."[18]

The feeling of ill will was mutual. Oneida scorned the outside world as filthy and contaminating, though it did send several young men to Yale. Oneida children were horrified by the swearing and depravity of village boys. Children were forbidden to speak to outsiders, whether hired men or visitors, of which there were one hundred to one thousand at peak periods. After visitors had left, the community gathered for a ritual cleaning "bee," to efface every trace of an "unclean public" and of the "filthy invaders." Those members most exposed to contact with the outsiders underwent mutual criticism so as to be "freed from contamination by worldly influences." For members who traveled outside, there was a criticism before they left, to provide "sustaining power from the heart of the family" for the ordeal, and one on their return, "to relieve them of spiritual contamination."[19] The community thus viewed the outside world rather than itself as deviant, with the society of Perfectionists setting the example for a better, purer, and more moral life, which the rest of society would eventually adopt.

The future did not unfold in accordance with members' dreams. The Oneida Community dissolved into the Oneida joint-stock company in 1881, giving up communistic sharing, complex marriage, and much of their joint housekeeping. Today the company continues to manufacture silverware, having recently issued its first public offering of stock, and maintains a small fraction of the old community spirit. In 1962, fifty-seven people still lived in the Mansion House, and eighty-five descendents of the original Perfectionists lived in the immediate area.[20] What was once a communal utopia is now a thriving capitalistic business.

18. Parker, *Yankee Saint*, pp. 257, 268; Ellis, *First Hundred Years*, p. 50; Estlake, *Oneida*, p. 50.
19. Estlake, *Oneida*, pp. 59, 60–61.
20. Lockwood, "Oneida," pp. 51–52.

Yonina Talmon

The Family in a
Revolutionary Movement–
The Case of the Kibbutz in Israel*

Introduction

The purpose of this case study[1] is the analysis of the interrelation between changes in communal structure and modification of family organization in revolutionary and collectivist movement.[2] We will examine closely the process of institutionalization of this movement and analyze the effects of this process on the position of the family in the community and on internal family role relationships.

* This is an abridged version of a paper prepared for the International Seminar of Family Research held in Washington, August, 1962. I wish to express my sincere gratitude to M. Gluckman, D. M. Schneider, and Charlotte Green-Schwartz for their critical comments.

1. This analysis is based on a research project carried out in a representative sample of 12 of the Kibbutzin affiliated with one of the four Federations of Kibbutzim. The project has combined sociological and anthropological field methods. The data obtained from the questionnaires, from various types of interviews and from analysis of written material, were examined and carefully interpreted by direct observation. R. Bar Yoseph took an active part in the initial planning. A. Etzioni assisted me in direction of the project in its first stage. The other main research assistants were E. Ron, M. Sarell and J. Sheffer. M. Sarell and E. Cohen took over from A. Etzioni in the second stage. The main research assistants were U. Avner, B. Bonne, S. Deshen, R. Gutman-Shaku, T. Horowitz, U. Hurwitz, Z. Stup and L. Shomgar. Special thanks are due to R. Gutman-Shaku who assisted me with the collection and analysis of the material on sex-role differentiation and on aging. Z. Stup and B. Bonne assisted me with the analysis of the material on family size. U. Avner and L. Shomgar contributed much to the analysis of patterns of marriage. E. Cohen assisted me in summing up the material and made many useful suggestions.

2. For analysis of a similar process, see R. Schlesinger, *The Family in the U.S.S.R.* London: Routledge and Kegan Paul, 1949; L. A. Coser, "Some Aspects of Family Policy," *American Journal of Sociology*, Vol. 52 (1951); K. Geiger, "Changing Political Attitude in a Totalitarian Society," *World Politics*, Vol. 8 (1956) and his "Deprivation and Solidarity in the Soviet Urban Family," *American Sociological Review*, Vol. 20 (1955); N. S. Timashef, "An Attempt to Abolish the Family in Russia," in N. W. Bell and E. F. Vogel (Eds.), *Modern Introduction to the Family*. New York: Free Press of Glencoe, 1961, pp. 55–64. For material on China, see C. Yang, *The Chinese Family in the Communist Revolution*. Cambridge, Mass.: Harvard University Press, 1959; M. L. Chin, *Women in Communist China*. Cambridge, 1962 (mimeographed). Cf. also W. J. Goode, *World Revolution and Family Patterns*. New York: Free Press of Glencoe, 1963.

The main features of collective settlements or Kibbutzim are common ownership of property except for a few personal belongings, and communal organization of production and consumption. Members' needs are provided for by communal institutions on an equalitarian basis. All income goes into the common treasury; each member gets only a very small allowance for personal expenses. The community is run as a single economic unit and as one household. It is governed by a general assembly which convenes as a rule once a week. The executive agencies are a secretariat and various committees. Kibbutzim may vary in size from 40 to 50 members in newly founded settlements to more than 1000 in larger and longer established ones. The communities are usually started by a nucleus of settlers. Additional groups and individuals join the core of founders at later stages of community development. The groups of settlers are organized by youth movements and undergo a period of intensive training in longer established Kibbutzim.[3]

The process of institutionalization may be observed by an examination of the transition occurring in the collective movement as a whole, as well as by examination of the internal development in every single Kibbutz. What is the position of the family in the revolutionary stage? How does the process of differentiation and routinization affect family role relationships? We have attempted to answer these questions by comparing the patterns of family organization and role images prevalent in the Federation of the Collectives in which we conducted our study during its initial phases with the institutionalized patterns and role images most prevalent in it at present.

The Revolutionary Phase

Let us first deal with the initial phases of the movement. Structural considerations and examination of our material have led us to the hypothesis that *there is a certain fundamental incompatibility between commitment to a radical revolutionary ideology and intense collective identification on the one hand and family solidarity on the other.*[4] Kinship is based on maintenance of intergenerational ties and a certain basic continuity of transmitted tradition. A total rejection of this continuity leads to revolt against the authority of the former generation and

3. M. Spiro. *Kibbutz: Venture in Utopia*. Cambridge, Mass.: Harvard University Press, 1956; M. Holloway. *Heavens on Earth! Utopian Communities in America, 1680–1880*. London: Turnstile Press, 1951.
4. A more or less strong anti-familistic bias seems to be typical of both religious and socialist communal settlements established in America. See W. A. Hinds, *American Communal and Cooperative Colonies*. Oneida, N.Y.: Office of the American Socialist, 1878. A. E. Bestor, *Backwoods Utopias*. Philadelphia: University of Pennsylvania Press, 1959.

disrupts cross-generational kinship ties. Kinship is essentially non-selective and non-ideological. For the ascriptive "natural" kinship ties members of a revolutionary elite substitute a *Wahlverwandschaft* based on a spontaneous communion of kindred souls and on an identification with a common mission. Ideology becomes the dominant unifying factor. Relatives and friends who do not share this commitment become outsiders, almost strangers.

The urge to emigrate to the new country and establish a Kibbutz was an outcome of a kind of conversion which entailed a total change of world view and way of life. This overpowering urge did not affect either whole communities or whole families. It cut through and disrupted both kinship and local ties. The pioneering ideology appealed mainly to the young and unattached, and induced them to sever their relations with parents, to discard their former attachments and disentangle themselves from their social setting altogether. The young pioneers emigrated either on their own or with a group of comrades. The disposition to establish very cohesive communities and relegate the family to a secondary position is closely related to this radical dissociation from former ties and to familial discontinuity. The intimate person-to-person relations, the intense togetherness and the unity of purpose which permeated all contracts were more significant than kinship loyalties. External ties and conflicting loyalties were not allowed to interfere with internal cohesion.

The formation of families of procreation within the Kibbutz confronted the collectives with the problem of internal family attachments. New families are a source of centrifugal tendencies. Family ties are based on an exclusive and particularistic loyalty which sets the members of the family more or less apart from the rest of their comrades. The new elementary families may easily become competing foci of intense emotional involvement and infringe on the loyalties to the collective. Deep attachment to one's spouse and children based on purely expressive interpersonal relations may gain precedence over the more ideological and more task-oriented relations with comrades. Families are considered divisive factors also because they are intermediate units which interpose and come between the individual and the community. Inasmuch as they act as buffers and protect the individual from the direct impact of public opinion, they reduce the effectiveness of informal collective control over members.

The anti-familistic tendencies inherent in the revolutionary and collectivist ideology of the Kibbutz were enhanced by the conditions in which it developed and by the nature of the functions it performed for the society as a whole. The Kibbutzim acted as an avant-garde of the emergent society. They were therefore a unique combination of agricultural settlements, training centers and military outposts. Each new community served as a spearhead of the advancement of settlement into more outlying and more arid frontier regions and had to fight its way against great odds—eroded and barren soil, severe scarcity of water, lack of adequate training and experience, very little capital resources for basic investment and the heavy burden of self-defense in a hostile environment. Settlement entailed in most cases a long preparatory period of entrenchment, land reclamation and experimentation, during which cultivation did not yield any profit. The Kibbutzim could overcome the almost insurmountable difficulties facing them only by means of channeling most of their resources of manpower and capital into production and by restricting their input into consumption and services to the bare minimum. Centralized communal organization of the non-productive branches of their economy enabled the Kibbutzim to reduce their investment in these spheres and to utilize fully the productive capacity of their members.

The tendency to attend to the needs of its members directly on the community level rather than by means of family households was strongly reinforced by the demographic characteristics of the Kibbutz and by its function as a training center for the youth movements. The presence of a considerable number of young members without families of their own in the Kibbutz and the constant turnover of temporary trainees made development of communal service institutions imperative.

Last but not least of the factors operating in the same direction was the function of the Kibbutz as a first defense line in outlying regions and around more vulnerable types of settlements.[5] Settlement in remote frontier areas was a semi-military undertaking which required a flexible combination of activities directed towards economic development on the one hand and defense on the other. The social organization and physical layout of the Kibbutz resembled in many respects that of any army camp. Settlements composed of organizationally and ecologically independent family farms were much more difficult to tend and to defend in times of emergency. The non-familistic structure of the Kibbutz facilitated the task of merging the semi-military and economic functions.[6]

Family Functions. The inherent tension between the collective and the family and the pressure of situational exigencies led to a far-reaching limitation of the functions of the family. The Kibbutzim curtailed family

5. Material on military organization indicates clearly that there is a certain inherent incompatibility between a strong emphasis on military duties and family commitments. The tension is sometimes resolved by prohibition of marriage until completion of army service. For an interesting case in point see M. Gluckman, "The Kingdom of the Zulu," in M. Fortes and E. E. Evans-Pritchard (Eds.), *African Political Systems*. New York: Oxford University Press, 1950; and A. T. Bryant, *Olden Times in Zululand and Natal*. London: Longmans, Green, 1929.

6. In our analysis of the position of the family in the revolutionary phase we put the main emphasis on inherent ideological and structural tendencies on the one hand and on situational factors on the other. For an analysis which derives this anti-familism almost exclusively from an over-reaction against Jewish tradition, see S. Diamond, "Kibbutz and Shtetl," *Social Problems*, Vol. 5 (1957).

obligations and attachments and took over most of its functions. Husband and wife were allotted independent jobs. There was a strict ban on assigning members of the same family to the same place of work. Division of labor in the occupational sphere was based on a denial of sex-differentiation. Women participated to a considerable extent in hard productive labor as well as in defense activities. All meals were taken in the common dining hall. Communal institutions and stores supplied goods and catered services on an equalitarian basis. There was a very small personal cash allowance and standards of consumption were extremely austere and, by and large, uniform. The spouses looked after their small and simply furnished rooms but had few other household responsibilities. Interaction between the sexes in the economic sphere occurred on the level of the community as a whole and not directly between mates.

There was during this stage a far-reaching limitation of the functions of the family in the sphere of replacement as well.[7] The birth rate in the Kibbutzim was for a long time far below the level of replacement. Life in the Kibbutz leveled and standardized the fertility norms of all families within it. This seems surprising if we take into consideration the fact that the attitude toward children was very positive and that they symbolized the promise of the future. This apparent discrepancy between this child-centered position and the tendency to limit fertility drastically can be partly accounted for if we take into consideration the hazardous environmental conditions in which the Kibbutzim developed and their severe economic difficulties. Yet this is only partial explanation and there are many indications that ideological and structural pressures enhanced the tendency towards limitation of family size. During the revolutionary phase of development, the Kibbutzim emphasized recruitment by means of ideological conversion.[8] They ensured their continuity and growth by drawing reinforcements of volunteers from external sources rather than by means of natural increase. The role model of both men and women required a wholehearted devotion to work and active participation in communal activities. The emphasis on activities outside the family orbit and the masculine role prototype prevented any intense identification with the role of mother and curbed the desire for children.

A partial abdication of the parents in the sphere of socialization is another aspect of the re-structuring of family roles. The whole system

7. See Y. Talmon-Garber, "Social Structure and Family Size," *Human Relations*, Vol. 12 (1959).

8. The history of both religious and socialist communes supplies us with many analogies in this respect. Such communes are faced with a dilemma. They tend to limit the family in this respect, yet they cannot ensure their continuity without internal natural increase. See B. M. Shambaugh, *Amana—The Community of True Inspiration*. Iowa City, Iowa: State Histori-cal Society of Iowa, 1908. For an interesting discussion of the same problem in a different setting, see H. C. Lea, *Historical Sketch of Sacerdotal Celibacy in the Christian Church*. Philadelphia: Lippincott, 1867.

was organized on a basis of relative separation between family and child. The physical care and rearing of the children were basically the responsibility of the Kibbutz, not so much of their parents. In most Kibbutzim children lived apart from their parents. From birth they slept, ate and later on studied in special children's houses. Each age group led its own life and had its autonomous arrangements. Parents were not completely excluded. Children met their parents and siblings in off-hours and spent the afternoons and early evenings with them. On Saturdays and holidays they stayed with their parents most of the time. In most Kibbutzim, parents put their young children to sleep every night. There were thus frequent and intensive relations between parents and children. The main socializing agencies were, however, the peer age-group and the specialized nurses, instructors and teachers. The age-groups substituted for the sibling group. It duplicated the structure of the community and mediated between children and adults.[9]

This system of socialization can be partly accounted for by situational pressures, and it developed at first by trial and error. It enabled mothers to continue their work in communal institutions and reduced the number of workers engaged in the upbringing and education of the children. It enabled the Kibbutz to isolate the children and protect them from the ill effects of the low standard of living of their parents. Children could be accorded far better living conditions than those for adults and get specialized care. The children's houses were in more than one way an economical and convenient solution of practical problems, yet there is much more to it than just that. At the root of the matter lies the intent to transfer the main responsibility for socialization from the parents to the community. Basically, the children belonged to the community as a whole. The core of internal family activities which looms so large in other types of family has thus diminished considerably. The family almost ceased to be an autonomous unit from the point of view of division of labor.

The Sexual Ethic. Another important aspect of the process is the change of patterns in the spere of sexual relations and in internal family affairs. A number of ideological, structural and situational factors operate in this field.[10] There was, first of all, the contemptuous reaction against the set patterns of the bourgeois way of life and the attempt to do away with such restrictive conventional norms as the demands of chastity and lifelong fidelity and double standards for women and men. It was felt that sexuality should be anchored in spontaneous love. Marriage was to be a

9. Cf. M. Spiro, *Children of the Kibbutz*. Cambridge, Mass.: Harvard University Press, 1958; also Y. Talmon-Garber, "The Family and Collective Socialization in the Kibbutz," *Niv Hakvotsah*, Vol. 8 (1959) (in Hebrew).

10. For a partly analogous development, see Vera S. Dunham, "Sex—From Free Love to Puritanism" in A. Inkeles and K. Geiger (Eds.), *Soviet Society*. Boston: Houghton Mifflin, 1961, pp. 540–546.

voluntary union between free persons and was to be binding on the marital partners only as long as it continued to be based on sincere and deep attachment and as long as both partners desired to maintain it. Premarital relations were considered legitimate and were not censured. The union between a couple did not require the sanction of the marriage ceremony. A couple who maintained a stable relationship for some time and decided to establish a family applied for a room of their own and started to live together without ceremonies or celebrations. The formal wedding was usually deferred until the birth of the first child, and was performed mainly because it was the only way to legitimize children according to the law of the land. Marriage did not change the status of the wife. Wives remained members in their own right and many retained their maiden names. The right of separation and divorce was not restricted in any way.

This extremely liberal position, which put such a strong emphasis on personal autonomy and erotic gratification, was counterbalanced and checked by the deep-seated sexual modesty and reticence instilled in the members by their traditional Jewish upbringing and by the asceticism and collectivism of the Kibbutz. Members who came from comparatively small communities and traditional milieus could not eradicate the attitudes toward sex cultivated in them during childhood and adolescence. These attitudes were reinforced by the strong puritan strains in the revolutionary world view and way of life. A high evaluation of sexual gratification ran counter to the pervasive emphasis on ascetic dedication and voluntary self-abnegation. Love was problematical in this type of community also because it is anchored in the specifically personal and private sphere and, inasmuch as it leads to preoccupation with innermost emotional states, it might detract from the task-oriented concentration in collective goals.[11] Inasmuch as it evokes intense emotion, it is not very amenable to social control and tends to get out of hand.

Last but not least of all factors operating in the field was the scarcity of women. In most Kibbutzim, women were during this stage a minority—20–35 percent of the total membership. This disequilibrium between the sexes had a double effect. Inasmuch as the serious scarcity of sexual partners resulted in competition, it enhanced the tendency towards shifting relations and instability. At the same time, in an indirect way, it had the opposite effect and enhanced the deep-seated asceticism prevalent in the Kibbutz. Under such circumstances, an unequivocal emphasis on sexual gratification was bound to breed bitter frustration and destructive rivalry. Demographic disequilibrium increases the disruptive potentiality of free love and necessitates the fostering of restraint and moderation.

11. Cf. Philip E. Slater, "On Social Regression," *American Sociological Review*, Vol. 28 (1936), pp. 339–364; and W. R. Bion, "Experiences in Groups III," *Human Relations*, Vol. 2, No. 1 (1949), pp. 13–22.

In spite of the situational exigencies and the counterbalancing ideological pressures, the doctrine of free love was the dominant one and had a very strong impact on the emerging institutional patterns. Yet while maintaining their positive attitude towards erotic attraction, the Kibbutzim developed many ingenious mechanisms which toned it down and checked its disorganizing effects. Relations between the sexes were de-eroticized and neutralized by dealing with sexual problems in a straightforward, objective and "rational" manner and by minimizing the differentiation and distance between the sexes. Women adopted male style of dress and male patterns of behavior. Beauty care and personal adornment which play up and enhance femininity were completely eliminated. The Kibbutzim de-emphasized physical shame between the sexes. Larger rooms which accommodate three or more occupants were often assigned to unattached men and women, who shared their room as a matter of course. They were expected to take one another for granted and in most cases there was little erotic tension between them. Couples attempted to keep the special ties between them secret as long as they could. They tried to be as inconspicuous and as discreet as possible even when their being a "couple" was common knowledge and fully approved by public opinion. They avoided appearing together in public and when in sight of their comrades refrained from any overt signs of affection.

The emphasis on free love and the emphasis on restraint and reticence operated simultaneously and checked each other. This accounts for the fact that in spite of the complete absence of institutionalized restrictions sexual relations were, generally speaking, not taken lightly. There was hardly any promiscuous and indiscriminate mating or wild and irresponsible experimentation. A very high incidence of shifting relations, separation and divorce occurred only in a minority of Kibbutzim.

Family Role Relationships. Internal relations between members of the elementary family were patterned to a large extent on relations between co-members and emphasized equality and companionship. Execution of family tasks was based on a tenet of strict sex equality. Husbands were expected to participate in looking after the family flat and taking care of the children equally with their wives. Spouses cooperated closely and were in most respects interchangeable. Both conjugal and parents-children relationships were exceedingly non-authoritarian. Spouses had no right to impose their authority on each other, and there was hardly any differentiation between their spheres of special competence. The attitude toward children was very permissive and there were hardly any distancing mechanisms. Children were not required to approach their parents with reticence or special deference; the relationship was easygoing and uninhibited. The dominant pattern in internal family interaction was comradeship on equal terms.

The changes in family relations were mirrored to some extent in the emerging kinship terminology. The terms for husband and wife were abandoned since they were indicative of the conception of the family as a legally binding paternalistic institution. The term for establishing a family was "to enter a family room." The husband was referred to as "my young man" *(Habachur Sheli)*. By the same token the wife was called "my young woman" *(Habachura Sheli)*. Even these terms were often felt to be too familistic and members would try to circumvent and avoid them by using proper names for reference as well as for address. Children were encouraged to use their parents' proper names for both reference and address instead of "father" and "mother."[12] The terms "son" and "daughter" were extended to all children of the Kibbutz and the only distinguishing mark was the occasional use of the personal possessive pronoun when the parent was referring to his own children and the personal plural when referring to children of the Kibbutz.

The Family and the Collective. Segregation of family life was made almost impossible by the housing policy. Capital was invested mainly in expansion of productive enterprises, and in construction of communal institutions. Couples often had to wait for many months before they were allocated a room of their own. Families were requested to accommodate an additional member in their one-room apartments for some time, whenever the scarcity of housing became very acute. This was only a temporary emergency measure, yet the recurring violation of conjugal privacy expresses very clearly the precedence of collective over personal considerations. Examination of the type of houses built in the first Kibbutzim affords another indication of the same tendency. The dwelling unit consisted of one single room. A number of rooms were arranged in a row and led to one long narrow corridor or veranda. Bathrooms and sanitary facilities were built in the center of the compound and were shared by all members. The public baths and showers were important meeting places in which members exchanged information, conducted informal discussions of local problems and gossiped. Privatization of family life was made almost impossible by this type of housing policy and physical layout of the community.

Any tendency to stay away in the family rooms and to build up a segregated family life was strongly condemned. Private radios and electric kettles were banned for a long time because, among other reasons, they enhanced the attraction of the home and undermined full participation in communal affairs. There was little regard for family relationships in work allocation. Husband and wife were often assigned to jobs with different timetables and consequently did not see much of each other. There was also very little coordination of vacations and holidays.

12. On the use of personal names instead of or in conjunction with kinship terms in order to de-emphasize ascriptive kinship affiliations and in order to negate an indication of asymmetrical distribution of authority, see David M. Schneider and G. C. Homans, "Kinship Terminology and the American Kinship System," *American Anthropologist*, Vol. 57, No. 6 (December 1955), pp. 1194–1208.

Even the weekly day off of husband and wife often fell on different days. There was hardly any family entertainment or family visiting. All members of the family functioned independently and were pulled in different directions.[13] Much of life in the Kibbutz was lived in the public view. Members spent most of their free time together. They met every evening in the communal dining hall, in the reading room or the central lawn, and spent their time in committee work and heated discussions. Spontaneous community singing and folk dancing were the main recreational activities. Public opinion discouraged constant joint appearance of the couple in public. Husband and wife who stuck together and were often seen in each other's company were viewed with ridicule.

Patterns of celebrating festive occasions symbolized the overall importance of the community. There were hardly any family-centered celebrations. Weddings were as short and informal as possible and the ceremonies were performed in most cases outside the community. Wedding anniversaries and birthdays meant very little and were usually not commemorated. The Kibbutzim curtailed the functions of the family in all communal and national festivities. The family ceased to function as an independent and active unit in all ceremonies.

It should be noted that while the Kibbutzim limited the functions of the family drastically and emphasized the predominance of the Collective, they did not abolish the family altogether.[14] The anti-familistic policy was not based on a preconceived or fully worked out anti-familistic ideology. Most early formulations of ideological position did not propose to do away with the family completely. Justification for the restrictive norms was couched in terms of liberation of the family rather than of its negation and elimination. It should be stressed also that even during the earliest phases, when the anti-familistic bias was at its strongest, the family remained an identifiable unit. Families were regarded by their own members and by outsiders as distinct subgroups. There were socially regulated patterns of mating and children were recognized as offspring of particular parents. While premarital sexual relations were permitted, there was a clear-cut distinction between casual sexual experimentation, love affairs and the more durable and publicly sanctioned unions. By asking for a room of their own, the couple made public their wish to have permanent relations and eventually have children. Residence in a common bedroom-livingroom allocated by the Kibbutz conferred legitimacy

13. For a fuller analysis of the process described here, see Y. Talmon-Garber, "The Family in Collective Settlements," *Transactions of the World Congress of Sociology*, 1957; and "Family Structure and Social Change," *International Social Science Journal*, Vol. 14, No. 3 (1962), pp. 500–522.
14. See M. Spiro, "Is the Family Universal?—The Israeli Case," in N. W. Bell and E. Vogel (Eds.), *op. cit.*, pp. 55–64; also K. Gough, "The Nayar Kinship System," *Journal of the Royal Anthropological Institute*, Vol. 89, Part 1 (1959); E. R. Leach, "Polyandry, Inheritance and the Definition of Marriage," *Man*, Vol. 55, No. 199 (1955), pp. 182–185.

to the couple. While children did not actually share a common domicile with their parents, they visited their parents' room and it was their home by reference. The life of the child alternated between the two ecological centers and both nursery and his parents' room were in a real sense home to him.

The family did not relinquish its communal functions completely either. Parents contributed to the economic support of their children indirectly by working jointly rather than separately. Similarly, though educators were the designated representatives of the Kibbutz rather than of the parents, parents exercised a direct and continuous influence on the trained personnel in charge of their children. Since children's institutions were not segregated from the community either ecologically or socially, parents were able to supervise closely the way their children were raised there. They exercised a considerable direct influence on their children during the time they spent together every day.[15] While interaction of family members with one another was in many cases less frequent than interaction with outsiders, internal ties remained more continuous, more meaningful and more intense. The emotional ties that bound husband and wife and parents and children were much more intimate and more exclusive than their ties with other members of the community.

The Process of Routinization

Expansion and stabilization of the Kibbutzim reinforce the family's position and bring about a partial restoration of its lost functions. As the Kibbutzim grow and establish themselves in the area, they become less vulnerable to attacks, and defense considerations lose some of their prominence. Military training and guard duty become less time- and effort-consuming. The Kibbutzim gradually manage to consolidate their economic position as well. The dynamic drive, the ascetic dedication and perseverance inspired by the intense identification with collective values enable the settlers to overcome the enormous environmental obstacles. The Kibbutzim become ongoing economic concerns and sometimes even attain modest prosperity. The situational exigencies which put a premium on a non-familistic division of labor are less pressing

15. Cf. M. Spiro, 1958, *op. cit.*; also R. Bar Yoseph, "The Patterns of Early Socialization in the Collective Settlements in Israel," *Human Relations*, Vol. 12, No. 4 (1959), pp. 345–360; E. E. Irvine, "Observations on the Aims and Methods in Child-Rearing in Communal Settlements in Israel," *Human Relations*, Vol. 5, No. 3 (1952), pp. 247–275; Helen Faigin, "Social Behavior of Young Children in the Kibbutz," *Journal of Abnormal Social Psychology*, Vol. 56, No. 1 (1958), pp. 117–129; A. I. Rabin, "Infants and Children under Conditions of Intermittent Mothering," *American Journal of Orthopsychiatry*, Vol. 28, No. 3 (July 1958), pp. 577–586; and "Attitudes of Kibbutz Children to Parents and Family," *American Journal of Orthopsychiatry*, Vol. 29, No. 3 (January 1959), pp. 172–179.

and allow a certain amount of internal decentralization and flexibility. In some spheres, there is even a reversal of trends and practical considerations of efficiency lead to more familistic patterns.

Consolidation and economic expansion reduce the intensity of collective identification. The fusion between personal and collective aspirations occurs during a period of revolutionary ferment, in a situation of emergency. Normalization blunts the sense of utmost urgency and blurs the vision which makes such fusion possible. During the initial phases, economic activity serves as an instrument for the realization of socialist and national ideals and is therefore imbued with deep seriousness and dignity. Development of large-scale and specialized economic enterprises entails partial emancipation of the economic sphere from its subordination to the ideals of pioneering. By loosening its direct connection with the paramount values, economic activity is divested of its special aura and turns into matter-of-fact routine. Routinization of everyday activity leads to a certain dissociation between the individual and the community. Work is no longer as all-absorbing, deeply meaningful and inherently satisfying as it used to be. Purely personal aspirations and purely expressive interpersonal relations attain partial autonomy.[16]

Development and consolidation affect the position of the family in yet another way. Differentiation of functions and the concomitant crystallization of the groups which perform these functions disrupt the original homogeneity of the newly established Kibbutz. The various groups of settlers which join the core of founders of the community at different stages of its development do not assimilate fully and continue to maintain their internal solidarity. The community is gradually subdivided by distinct, overlapping and cross-cutting subgroups which mediate between the individual and the collective and partly take over control of him. The Kibbutzim become more tolerant towards internal differentiation. The family is accorded a certain amount of autonomy and assigned a place among the subgroups.

The appearance of the second generation is of crucial importance in this context because children are the main focus of semi-segregated family life in the Kibbutzim. Marriage does not entail a redefinition of roles and a new division of labor nor cause a clearly perceptible cleavage between the couple and the rest of the community. The birth of children makes manifest the partial independence of the family, and introduces a gradual shift of emphasis from disruption of inter-generation ties to continuity Children are expected to settle in the Kibbutzim founded by their parents and continue their lifework there. The family of orientation is no longer an external and alien influence. Parents and children are

16. For a fuller analysis, see Y. Talmon and E. Cohen, "Collective Settlements in the Negev," in Joseph Ben-David (Ed.), *Agricultural Planning and the Village Community in Israel.* Paris: UNESCO, 1964, pp. 58–95.

members of the same Kibbutz, who live in close proximity and share, at least to some extent, the same ideals. Identification with one's family may thus reinforce identification with the collective.

Internal processes of routinization within the Kibbutzim are intensified by external processes of routinization in the society as a whole. Acquisition of state power lessened the dependence of the social structure on voluntaristic-charismatic movements oriented to collective service. Implementation of collective goals has been increasingly relegated to bureaucratic organizations such as the army, the Settlement Agency and the Civil Service. Coupled with the functional shift came an ideological reformulation. The emphasis on long-term collective goals was superseded by concern with short-term tasks and immediate personal satisfactions. The limitation of avant-garde functions and the partial alienation from the society at large have a corrosive effect on the Kibbutzim and undermine their assurance in the final outcome of their revolutionary venture. Members are often assailed by self-doubt and insecurity. Dissociation between the Collective movement and Israeli society enhances the dissociation between individual members and their Kibbutz.

Family Functions. The shift of emphasis from discontinuity to continuity in more differentiated and less cohesive Collectives and the change of their position in the society as a whole account for the partial "emancipation" of the family. The family regains some of its lost functions in the *sphere of housekeeping.* Most families have their afternoon tea at home with their children. In some Kibbutzim, families sometimes eat their evening meal at home too. Most families do it only occasionally, as a special treat for the children, while some eat at home regularly almost every evening. Though most clothing still goes to the communal laundry, many families tend to look after their best clothes at home so that there is a little extra washing, mending and ironing now and then. The typical dwelling unit now consists of a semidetached flat containing one or two rooms, kitchenette and private sanitary facilities. While the style of the internal decoration has remained on the whole functional and uncluttered, the standard of equipment and the number of items of furniture supplied to each unit have increased considerably. The flat now requires more elaborate and more systematic care. It is in many cases an important symbol of the togetherness of the family and a physical manifestation of its separateness. Members usually tend it with care and have a strong desire to make it as neat and pleasant as possible.

The attenuation of the ascetic ideology and the change of patterns of distribution of certain items of consumption have a direct effect on the family. Many Kibbutzim have recently abolished the allocation of certain goods according to fixed and very specific standards and introduced a more flexible distributional system. Every member has a claim on an average per capita share of the allowance for clothing, for instance, and within the limits of this allowance is entitled to choose items of clothing according to his own taste and personal predilections. Freedom of choice is narrowly circumscribed within the limits of an allowance for a specified type of consumer goods, but some of the responsibility for planning in this sphere is transfered to the family.[17] Increased autonomy in the sphere of consumption has brought about the need for systematic and careful budgeting.

There is a considerable increase of the family's functions in the *sphere of reproduction*. Examination of demographic data indicates a considerable increase in the birth rate in the Kibbutzim. Economic considerations in favor of restriction of family size lose part of their weight in longer established Kibbutzim. We witness also a considerable change of the attitude towards fertility. As long as the main emphasis was on conversion and as long as reinforcements to the Kibbutzim came mainly from the youth movement and training centers, natural increase had only secondary importance. The dwindling of external recruiting sources and the difficulties experienced by the Kibbutzim in absorption of new immigrants have greatly enhanced the importance of natural increase. Emphasis has shifted from recruitment of volunteers from outside to expansion from within. The emergence of a more feminine role prototype for women and the partial emancipation of the family reinforce the tendency towards a higher birth rate. It is felt that children consolidate the position of the family in the community and contribute to a richer and more varied family life.

Parents tend to take a more active part in the *socialization of their children*. There is much closer cooperation between nurses, instructors, teachers and parents. Parents help in looking after their young children; they take turns in watching them at night and nurse them when they are ill. They help in the preparation of festivals arranged for the children and attend most of them. There is considerably more parental supervision of the children's behavior, choice of friends and reading habits. Parents try to influence their choice of future occupations and insist on their right to be consulted on this matter. Some Kibbutzim have introduced a more radical reorganization. Children in these Kibbutzim no longer sleep in the children's houses. They stay with their age-groups during the day but return home every afternoon. Duties of child care and socialization have thus partly reverted to the family.

Sex Role-Differentiation in the Occupational Sphere. The line dividing internal and external family activities has shifted considerably in all

17. See E. Rosenfeld, "Institutional Change in the Kibbutz," *Social Problems*, Vol. 5 (1957), pp. 110–136. Cf. also the research report which summarizes the results of our project in this respect; "Patterns of Allocation in the Sphere of Consumption" (in Hebrew, mimeographed, 1959).

spheres except for the occupational. There is a considerable pressure to reduce the number of hours that women work in communal enterprises but only small concessions have been made in this sphere; mothers of babies get more time off from work now and aging women start to work part-time earlier than the men. The Kibbutzim put the main emphasis on the occupational role and it has remained the major focus of activity for both men and women. Yet even here we witness considerable modifications. There is now a fairly, clear-cut sex-role differentiation in work organization. Women are mainly concentrated in occupations more closely allied to traditional houskeeping such as cooking, laundry service, nursing and teaching.[18] There are a number of intermediate spheres in which women participate alongside men, yet many occupations are completely or almost completely sex-segregated. Women participate in predominantly masculine occupations more than men do in predominantly feminine occupations. Interchangeability is thus limited and asymmetrical.

Sex differentiation in the occupational sphere was kept at a minimum as long as the women were young and had few children, and as long as all efforts were concentrated on production and the standard of living was kept very low. Communal institutions replace the mother very early but they cannot eliminate the special ties between the mother and her baby. Pregnant women are transferred to lighter tasks and nursing mothers work only part-time. As they have to nurse and feed their babies every few hours, it is more convenient for them to work in one of the communal service institutions situated near the children's houses, and they usually take a leave of absence from productive labor. The births of more children entail recurrent interruptions and discontinuity. With age, mothers usually find it increasingly difficult to return to physical labor in outlying orchards and fields. The birth of children affects work allocation in yet another way. It entails a growing need for more workers for services and child care. This process is further enhanced by the rise in the standard of living. Non-productive work now requires about 50 percent of all workers and absorbs most of the women, who usually number less than half the population of the Kibbutz. Since women cannot replace men fully in hard productive labor, it seems a waste to allow them to work in agriculture and, at the same time, to assign able-bodied men to the services. When practical considerations of utility gain precedence, considerable sex differentiation in job allocation comes to be regarded as inevitable.

The Sexual Ethic and Family Stability. So far, we have dealt with the relations between the family and other institutions. Let us now turn to

18. For a more detailed analysis of the emergence of sex-role differentiation, see Y. Talmon-Garber, "Sex-role Differentiation in an Equalitarian Society," in Lasswell, Burma and Aronson (Eds.), *Sociology and Life*. Chicago: Scott, Foresman, 1964.

internal role-relationships. There are significant changes in the norms pertaining to sexual relations and marriage. During the first phases of the development, the movement combined an extremely permissive attitude toward erotic attachment with far-reaching neutralization of relations between the sexes. The Kibbutzim do not now resort so much to de-eroticization. At the same time, their attitude towards sexual relations has become considerably less permissive. Most of the de-eroticizing mechanisms have been modified or completely discarded. The Kibbutzim now refrain from assigning members of both sexes to the same room. The emerging sex-role differentiation and the attenuation of the ascetic ideology have resulted in considerable differentiation of styles of dress and demeanor. Inconspicuous beauty care and personal adornment which discreetly underline femininity are permissible and are becoming increasingly prevalent. Couples are considerably less reticent and are not embarrassed when seen together in public.

Modifications of the doctrine of free love develop in the opposite direction. The general ideological position has remained basically liberal, yet when it comes to more specific and more practical norms, there are many reservations. Practically all feel very strongly that adolescents should not be preoccupied with sexual matters and should refrain from sexual relations altogether. After graduating from school, young members may engage in sexual relations with impunity, yet they are enjoined not to be indiscriminate and not to treat such matters in a frivolous, off-hand manner. Promiscuous experimentations are frowned upon and viewed with open disapproval. There is a considerable decrease in the age at marriage and in many cases premarital relations are just a short prelude to marriage. The time interval between commencement of sexual relations and foundation of a family is much shorter than it used to be. Normally, marriage now precedes the beginning of life together in a family apartment. Quite a number of couples postpone regular sexual relations until they marry. Most couples attach considerable importance to their marriage and want it to be a meaningful and memorable event. Wives tend now to discard their maiden names and adopt their husbands' names.

The attitude towards extra-marital relations is more critical and restrictive. While feeling that spouses should be understanding and tolerant and should not make too much fuss about a passing fancy or a temporary lapse, most members maintain that extra-marital liaisons endanger the stability and cohesion of the community and should be avoided as much as possible. They regard the right of divorce as inalienable but feel that it should be exercised only in cases of very serious and persistent estrangement. Divorce of couples who already have children is severely censured and condemned by public opinion. Officially, the Kibbutz has no right to interfere in these matters and members may do as they please, but many informal pressures are brought to bear on parents who contemplate divorce. The image of the ideal family has changed radically. Life-long companionship, mutual trust and understanding are emphasized much more than intensity of erotic attachment. Responsibility and loyalty are considered more important than spontaneity.

Both the community and the family have a vested interest in stability. Informal communication in such a closely-knit and cohesive community makes it virtually impossible to keep an extra-marital liaison secret and segregated—it soon becomes common knowledge. Since life in the Kibbutz entails close cooperation and frequent contacts between all members, the neglected spouse is exposed to recurrent encounters with the rival. Bitter jealousies which tear members apart and breed long-drawn enmities have a corrosive effect on interpersonal relations and impair the functioning of the system as a whole. A divorce is experienced by members of the family concerned as a major upheaval in their lives, since it cuts them loose from their most important source of emotional support and security. If both husband and wife stay on in the Kibbutz, they cannot possibly avoid each other. This is very irksome in cases in which the dissolution of the family left an aftermath of strong resentment. Small wonder that in most cases one spouse tends to withdraw from the Kibbutz and to leave it for good. In spite of the fact that children in the Kibbutz have a number of major socializers and a host of secondary ones, the rift between their parents and the loss of one is felt to be very harmful. It is significant that in spite of the absence of legal restrictions and economic hindrances, the rate of divorce has dropped drastically even in Kibbutzim which originally had a comparatively high rate of family dissolution. In most Kibbutzim, divorce has become a rare occurrence, and some have not had a divorce in their community for years. Families are on the whole cohesive and stable and cases of severe and protracted conflict are not common.[19]

Internal Division of Labor. Sex-role differentiation in work assignment impinges on the family. Productive labor and overall administration draw men far afield. Women's work does not take them far from their apartment or the children's houses. Since they are concentrated in occupations closely allied to housekeeping and child care, they find it easier to cope with their tasks at home. This process is accelerated when deeply-rooted sex-role images gain precedence and undermine the equalitarian ideology. The emergent division of labor is flexible and fluctuating. The husband usually helps his wife clean the flat and prepare the afternoon tea. Some husbands do it regularly, some do it now and then

19. The data on the stability of the family in the Kibbutz do not corroborate the hypothesis that limitation of the role of the father in the maintenance and placement of his children leads to instability. Cf. R. Smith, *The Negro Family in British Guiana*. New York: Humanities Press, 1956.

and some do it rarely, only in case of emergency when their wife is either very tired, ill or away. Clothes are exclusively the wife's concern. In most families the wife does most of the housekeeping and it is mainly her responsibility. Her husband is regarded as her assistant or as her temporary stand-in but not as co-worker on equal terms.[20] Budgeting of personal allowances of the whole family is almost invariably the responsibility of the wife. Officially, these allowances are personal and not transferable, but in practice this injunction is overruled and the allowances are pooled and treated as a family allowance. Since men are less concerned about scarcity of clothing and other consumer goods, a considerable part of their allowance is in fact transferred to their wives. They are usually not much interested in this small-scale budgeting and leave the planning and management of the family "finances" to their wives entirely.

Authority Pattern. The consolidation of the family unit and the emerging sex-role differentiation within it have a direct effect on the family internal authority structure. Internal discussions and disagreements are usually kept within the family, and there is a strong tendency to maintain a common front towards outsiders. We witness the emergence of a "regional" division of spheres of authority. Family authority is determined by the manner in which obligations and responsibilities are distributed between marital partners. There are also many indications that while the wife has more say in routine matters, the husband exercises more influence in matters of principle. Analysis of family decisions shows that husbands are usually more strict in their adherence to community norms and that they exert pressure on their wives in this respect. Public opinion ridicules a "weak" husband who gives way to his wife and does not prevail on her not to deviate from the accepted norms. It should be stressed that while the emergent pattern indicates a certain division of spheres of authority and favors a husband who takes a firm stand in matters of principle, it is not a clear-cut pattern, and it does not enforce an institutionalized position of pivotal authority for either spouse.

Informal Relations and Leisure-Time Activities of Husband and Wife. The tendency towards a more familistic pattern may be clearly discerned in the subtle transformation of informal relations and leisure-time activities of husband and wife. Free time spent in public has diminished considerably. There is still much organized activity on the community level and most members participate in committees, in work group discussions and in various cultural interest groups. Yet they are not as eager as they used

20. Cf. E. Bott, *Families and Social Networks.* London: Tavistock Publications, 1957, Ch. 5. The data presented here seem to indicate that Bott's hypothesis, which relates conjugal role-segregation to degree of network connectedness, needs re-examination and revision. In the Kibbutz growing differentiation between different types of social relations and loosening of social control over the family enhance sex-role differentiation rather than diminish it.

to be to participate in public discussions or attend public meetings. Spontaneous dancing and community singing sessions are rare. Husband and wife spend much of their free time together at home. They usually sit near each other during evening meals and on all public occasions. There is a far better coordination of their work schedules, vacations and holidays. Families get special consideration in this respect so that husbands and wives are able to spend their free time together. Much of the informal interchange between members occurs within the homes and entertaining and visiting are becoming joint family affairs. It is now considered impolite to invite only one of the spouses. Both husband and wife may have close friends of their own but if any of their special friends are uncongenial to the other spouse, they are gradually dropped. It is significant that increasing sex-role differentiation is accompanied by an increase in joint leisure-time activities and not by increasing segregation.

Child Care. In the sphere of child care, there is considerably more cooperation and interchangeability than in housekeeping.[21] This is clearly the effect of the system of socialization. As parents do not carry the main responsibility for either maintenance or socialization of their children, the main emphasis is put on affective ties. Parents handle their small children in an affectionate, gentle and warm way. Expressions of affection are restrained and grow less overt as the children grow up, yet the parents continue to lavish them with loving attention and do their best to be fully available to them while they are at home. The petty quarrels and persistent disagreements which often pester parent-children relationships in other types of families are quite rare here. Parents endeavor to make the few hours their children spend with them as pleasant and carefree as possible. They abstain from making too many demands on their children, and from severely penalizing misdemeanors, so as not to mar the happy hours of their daily reunion. Their main function is to minister to their children's need for security and love. Both of them interact with their children in much the same way and play a common protective role. Fathers usually take a lively interest in their children and participate actively in looking after them. Mothers have closer contacts with babies and small children but fathers come into the picture very early. Sex of the children has no marked effect either.

In spite of the considerable blurring of differences between the father role and the mother role, there are some signs of differentiation even here. The mother is as a rule more concerned with the bodily well-being of the children and takes care of them while they are at home. She usually has more contact with the children's institutions and the school and supervises the upbringing of her children there. There is not much routine disciplining in the family but, such as there is, is more often than not the

21. For the factors which enhance the tendency to de-differentiation of parental roles in the modern family, see P. E. Slater, "Parental Role-Differentiation," *American Journal of Sociology*, Vol. 67 (1961), pp. 296–308.

mother's responsibility. The source of this responsibility is primarily in her duties as housekeeper and part-time caretaker of her children. The child has to conform to certain standards of cleanliness and order. The living quarters of the family in the Kibbutz are small: in many cases one room serves all purposes. While standards of order are by no means very strict and exacting, there is a concern with the neatness of the flat. Even with a maximum of permissiveness the child has to be controlled and restricted to some extent. There are also the problems of personal cleanliness and health preservation. The father is less involved in these problems and the child may find him an ally in cases of exaggerated concern with them on the part of the mother. The father's main responsibilities are outside the home—in the yard, on the farm, in dealing with communal affairs which concern the Kibbutz as a whole. In the eyes of the growing child, the father emerges gradually as the representative of the Kibbutz and its values within the family, while the mother acts primarily as the representative of the family in the Kibbutz.[22]

Parents emphasize the unity of the family and promote closer contacts between siblings. Older children are not burdened with heavy duties and are not compelled to look after younger ones regularly, yet they are encouraged to assume some responsibility and participate at least to some extent in the care of their younger siblings. The sibling relations are not devoid of tension and rivalry. Constant sharing in the peer group often breeds a craving for a complete monopoly over the parents and persistent demands for individual attention. Yet it seems that the atmosphere at home is less competitive than in the nursery. The sibling group is as a rule smaller than the age group and, unlike it, is age-graded. Births are usually planned and an interval of at least two years is considered desirable. Thus the parents have enough time for intensive care of each child during the first years of his life, and needs and claims for attention can be graded according to age. Conflict situations are minimized by the segregation and differentiation of activities in different age groups and in different children's houses. Having siblings enhances the prestige of the older child in his age group. He will often assume a protective role towards his younger siblings and take care of them of his own accord.

We witness a "dialectical" process in the sphere of parent-children relations. The extreme limitation of the family functions in the sphere of maintenance and socialization of its children has not led to disruption of

22. Our data disprove the hypothesis that the mother figure is always the more permissive and supportive and the father more denying and demanding as far as the administering of specific disciplines and everyday relations are concerned. It reinforces the hypothesis of "positional" differentiation. The mother is the representative of the family, while the father is the representative of the community at large. For the distinction between role and position, see B. J. Berger's "Comment on Slater's Paper," *American Journal of Sociology*, Vol. 67 (1961), pp. 308–311; cf. also T. Parsons and R. Bales, *Family, Socialization and Interaction Process*. New York: The Free Press of Glencoe, 1955, Ch. 2 & 6.

family solidarity. Paradoxically, the curtailment of obligations reinforced rather than weakened parent-children relationships and enhanced the importance of the emotional ties between them. Insofar as the family has ceased to be the prime socializing agency, it avoids to some extent the inevitable ambivalence towards the agents of socialization. Parents do not have to play the two-sided role of ministering to the children's needs for care and security on the one hand, and of thwarting their wishes in various ways on the other. Since they do not carry the main responsibility for disciplining their children, they can afford to be easy and loving partners. Interaction with the parents is restricted and intermittent, yet it is continuous and consistently warm and permissive.

The role system in the children's houses is from several points of view the reverse of the role system of the family. There is a considerable turnover of child-care workers. This prevents the child from forming a strong and permanent identification with any of them. The relations in the nursery are, in addition, less affectively toned. They focus on the maintenance of a certain routine and are regulated primarily by professional criteria of competence. Diffuse general friendliness is emphasized more than love. Any attempt to monopolize the nurse must fail and the child has to learn to wait his turn and share with his peers. While the family is focused on diffuse gratification and tension release, the nursery and the school are task-oriented and emphasize performance. The child is encouraged to do things for himself and is pushed towards learning and early maturation. There is in the family a permissiveness towards slow development which is a kind of latency for the accelerated process of maturation in the nursery. Each child has an ascribed place in his family and receives his share of uncontested love and attention. The position of the child in the age group is ascribed only to a limited extent. In spite of the fact that the educators emphasize coordination of needs and cooperation, competition is not eliminated. The age group furnishes a stage for acting out dominance-submission problems. The child tests his powers in his relations with his age peers. He competes with them for his position in the group and for the approval of adults in charge of it. The family keeps the socializing situation balanced by providing the child with unconditional love and loyalty which are his right irrespective of his status in his group and which he does not have to share with his age mates.[23]

The countervailing functions of the family in the socialization process account for the overall importance of the parent-child relationship. Young children are deeply dependent, and very often over-dependent, on their parents. The children have come very often to occupy the emotional center of the parents' life. They eventually outgrow the intense involvement with their parents, and gradually become attached to their age-mates

23. Cf. R. Bar Yoseph, *op. cit.*

with whom they share uninterruptedly all their formative experiences of infancy, childhood and adolescence. Solidarity in the Kibbutz is focused primarily on horizontal ties between age equals, rather than on vertical ties between successive generations.²⁴ Adolescents gradually become firmly embedded in their group and drift away to a certain extent from their parents. The relationship with them remains straightforward, un-constrained and, in many cases, also exceedingly friendly, but it is no longer very intense and intimate. Parents resent the partial estrangement and often blame it on the usurpation of communal institutions. It is this process which is at the root of the recent reorganization of patterns of socialization.²⁵

Kinship Terms. The emerging role-relationships in the elementary family are partly mirrored in the change of terminolgy. The terms "my young man" and "my young woman" are felt to be inappropriate, especially when the couples concerned are past their prime. There are no fixed fully legitimized terms, but there is a growing tendency to refer to a husband as "my man" *(Haish Sheli)* and for the wife there are alternative terms: "my woman" *(Haisha Sheili)*, "the woman" *(Haisha)*. Sometimes members employ in a joking manner the rather poetic biblical *Raayati*. Quite often one notices a reversal to the traditional terms "husband" and "wife," which were strictly taboo in the past. These terms are employed self-consciously in a half-apologetic, half-defiant way. Almost invariably children now address and refer to their parents as father *(Aba)* and mother *(Ima)*, adding the personal possessive pronoun when using the terms for reference. Small children tend to add this personal possessive pronoun now and then also when they use the parental term for address, thus emphasizing the intimacy and exclusive-ness of the relationship. Parents often use the kinship terms "son" *(Ben)* and "daughter" *(Bat)* when addressing and referring to their children instead of their proper names.²⁶ Another significant change is the development of technonymic patterns. Children refer and address other childrens' parents by adding the name of the child to the parental term. Most adults are designated by the children as father of . . . or mother of. . . . The children use either the name of the adult's child they know best or the name of his first-born. So prevalent is this pattern that children will often refer to unmarried or childless adults as "father (or mother) of

24. For the effect of the emphasis on horizontal ties on family relationships in modern society, see E. Cummings and D. M. Schneider, "Sibling Solidarity," *American Anthropologist*, Vol. 63 (1961).

25. See Y. Talmon-Garber, "The Family and Collective Education in the Kibbutz," *Niv-Hekvutsah*, Vol. 8, No. 1, pp. 2–52 (in Hebrew). Cf. also H. Faigin, *op. cit.*; and A. I. Rabin, *op. cit.*

26. Since proper names are used for address and reference in interaction between all members of the community, the use of such personal names becomes undifferentiated and neutralized and ceases to denote special intimacy or exclusiveness.

no one." This tendency to identify a person by underlining his role as parent to a certain child is not confined only to the children; it often penetrates to adult society as well.

Wider Kinship Ties. The most important feature of the process of change from the point of view of future development is the gradual re-emergence of wider kinship ties. As long as the generational structure of the Kibbutz remained truncated, most members did not have any kin besides members of their own elementary family living in the same community. A gradual process of change sets in when the children of the founders establish families and the Kibbutz develops into a full-scale three-generational structure. The Kibbutzim have in addition accepted social responsibility for aging or sick parents[27] and transfer many of them to their children in the Kibbutz. Old parents live either in separate blocks of dwellings or in a semi-detached little flat adjoining their children's flat. Relatives who live in the same community maintain close contacts through frequent visiting and mutual help. There are many indices of the emergence of cohesive kinship groupings. Relatives very often tend to cluster and form united blocks which have a considerable influence on communal affairs.

Members tend to renew their contact with relatives who live outside the Kibbutz as well. They will stay with their relatives when they go to town and will invite them to visit. They accept personal presents from kin and reciprocate by sending farm produce from time to time. There is thus a considerable interchange between members and their relatives outside the Kibbutz. The wider kinship categories have, however, remained amorphous and fluid.[28] There is a vague sense of obligation to maintain amicable relations with all kin but actually contacts with kin outside the Kibbutz remain largely selective.[29] Congeniality of a relative is determined by many factors: political allegiance and sympathy towards the collective movement; potential of mutual help; accessibility in terms of propinquity; and, last but not least, mutual liking and compatibility on a purely personal basis.

The structure and function of the emerging kinship groupings are largely determined by patterns of mate-selection prevalent in the second generation. The most significnat factor here is the spontaneous "exogamous" tendencies manifested by members of the second generation. There is hardly any erotic attraction between them and with very few exceptions they seek their marriage partners outside their own subgroup. They tend

27. See Y. Talmon-Garber, "Aging in a Planned Society," *American Journal of Sociology*, Vol. 67, No. 3 (1961), pp. 286–295.

28. It is perhaps significant that, unlike the kin terms denoting relationships within the elementary family, wider kinship terms remain undifferentiated and classificatory.

29. On selectivity in the contacts with relatives, cf. R. Firth (Ed.), *Two Studies of Kinship in London*. London: Athlone Press, 1956; see also E. Bott, *Families and Social Network*. London: Tavistock Publications, 1957, Ch. 5.

to marry (a) members who joined their Kibbutz at later stages of its development, (b) members of other Kibbutzim, (c) members of training groups of prospective settlers organized by the youth movements and (d) outsiders who are not affiliated with the collective movement.[30]

The predilection of members of the second generation for out-group relations in the erotic sphere stems at least in part from the system of socialization. The peer group is based on diffuse and all-embracing solidarity and discourages exclusive dyadic attachments within it. The exogamous tendencies are further enhanced by the ambivalent attitude of the second generation towards local continuity.[31] Most members of the second generation have a strong loyalty to their native Kibbutz but at the same time they often feel hemmed in and isolated. The exogamous pattern expresses their craving for new experiences and their groping for new contacts.

The exogamous tendencies manifested by the second generation have far-reaching structural consequences. The prevalent patterns check the growth and consolidation of kinship blocks with the Kibbutz. Extra second-generation marriage gives rise to a less extended and less inter-connected web of intra-collective kinship affiliations than intra second-generation marriage. Normally only one of the spouses in such an out-group union is likely to have his parents and siblings living with him in the same Kibbutz. No less important is the function of out-group marriage in counteracting the tendency of the old-timers to consolidate their position as a separate and dominant group. Through their children, the established old-timers are linked to less established and more marginal members. Kinship affiliations cut across the divisions between the subgroups and link them.

Exogamous patterns of mate-selection make an important contribution on the level of the movement as well. Inter-collective unions counteract the strong separatist tendencies of the local communities and foster cooperation between them. Marriages with members of training groups strengthen the ties between the Kibbutzim and the youth movements. Such unions often create a conflict of loyalties and threaten local continuity but the gains for the movement outweigh the losses for the local community. Marriage with outsiders who do not belong and do not identify with the collective movement is more problematical and occurs less frequently. Extra-movement unions link the Kibbutzim with other sectors of the society and provide valuable connections with other elite groups, but they often lead to desertion from the Kibbutz and dissociation from the movement. It is significant that the intra-collective, inter-

30. For a fuller analysis, see Y. Talmon, "Mate Selection in Collective Settlements," *American Sociological Review* (August 1964), pp. 491–509.
31. Cf. M. Sarell, "The Second Generation in Collective Settlements," *Megamoth*, Vol. 4 (1961), pp. 123–132 (in Hebrew).

collective and intra-youth movement unions are the most prevalent. These patterns maintain a flexible balance between in-group unity and closure and inter-group connectedness. It should be noted that marriage patterns have come to serve as integrating mechanisms of major importance.

The change of the position of the family and the growing importance of the kinship groups are symbolized and made manifest by the patterns of celebrating festive occasions. Weddings have become important events both for the families concerned and the community as a whole. They are celebrated by the whole Kibbutz and are made the occasion of big, joyous parties. There is a tendency in most Kibbutzim to celebrate a number of marriages together but the couples which participate in this joint communal celebration are entitled to an additional, more exclusive party for their friends and relatives. Many families celebrate wedding anniversaries and birthdays regularly and attach considerable importance to them. Relatives gather on all important family reunions. Celebrations of communal and national festivals have become much more kinship-typed. Members of each family tend to cluster and sit near one another. Members are entitled to invite relatives who are not members of the Kibbutz to these festivals. Hundreds of such guests come to each Kibbutz from far and wide and spend their holidays with relatives there.

Supplementary Institutional Mechanics–Checks on Familism

The transformation described above indicates clearly that the Kibbutz has moved far away from the anti-familistic pole.[32] It should be stressed, however, that there are powerful internal pressures which block the trend towards familism. The tendency to revert to a familistic division of labor is held in check by two major restraining factors: (a) the collectivistic emphasis; and (b) the tendency to extension of organizational units of rationalization and specialization. The attenuation of the collectivist ideology and the shift to intergenerational continuity ease the tension between family and community but the basic rivalry does not disappear. Inasmuch as the family accepts the primacy of collective consideration, it may become a valuable ally. Inasmuch as it resents a subordinate position and disputes the authority of collective institutions, it is still a potential

32. It should be noted that the purpose of this case study is to underline the general trends. For lack of space we cannot present here our data on variation as to the extent and rate of change. Comparative data on different types of Kibbutzim and different categories of members indicate that there is considerable and patterned variation in this respect. For a comparative analysis of men versus women, first versus second generation members, leaders versus the rank and file and long established versus recently established Kibbutzin, see Y. Talmon-Garber, "Social Structure and Family Size," *ibid.*, "The Family and Collective Socialisation in the Kibbutz," *ibid.*

source of conflict and competition. The collectivistic emphasis is now much more moderate and more tolerant towards differentiation, but the tendency to limit and control the family is still operative. Furthermore, the attenuation of the collectivistic restraints is partly counterbalanced by a considerable increase in the emphasis on rationalization and specialization of the economic structure of the Kibbutz. This accelerated process of rationalization counteracts the tendency to reversal to a non-specialized and small-scale domestic pattern.

The presence of such internal restraining factors accounts for the fact that, structurally speaking, the Kibbutz has remained basically non-familistic. Both husband and wife work full time in communal institutions and most goods and services are supplied directly to members by the community. Parents make an extremely significant and indispensable contribution to the socialization of their children, but the center of gravity has remained in communal institutions. The main responsibility for preparing the children for their roles as adult members in their Kibbutz rests with the educators. Parents have only a limited influence on the process of placement of their children and on their choice of occupation.[33] The family in the Kibbutz has a strong affective orientation; it emphasizes intimacy and exclusiveness. In itself, it is hardly fit to prepare the child for life in the Kibbutz, with its emphasis on togetherness and sharing and its highly rationalized work-centered economic system.

There is also the problem of social control in adult society. The Kibbutz makes many demands on its members, but employs only a few formal means of control. Allocation of material rewards is unrelated to position of performance and there are hardly any formal sanctions in cases of faulty execution of tasks or deviance. The proper functioning of the system depends primarily on the voluntary identification of the members of the Kibbutz with collective aims and ideals. The family represents the private sphere. If it becomes an independent, largely self-sufficient and powerful unit, it is bound to undermine the primacy of collective considerations. Comprehensive ties between co-members which are based on a shared ideology and common objectives may easily be superseded by divisive and narrow loyalties based on kinship affiliation.

The Kibbutzim are very much aware of the dangers inherent in the disengagement of the family from the collective. They have tried to check this trend by reinforcing the non-familistic division of labor and have gone about it in two seemingly opposed ways. Most important is the drive to improve the efficiency of the services by means of an intensive process of rationalization, mechanization and professionalization of serv-

33. On the problems of placement, see Y. Talmon-Garber, "Occupational Placement of the Second Generation in Collective Settlements," *Megamoth*, Vol. 8 (1957), pp. 352–369 (in Hebrew).

ice branches. Until recently, collective organization of consumption lagged far behind production and did not get a fair trial in this respect. At least part of the discontent which led to the reversal of functions to the family stemmed from the fact that the service institutions were allocated very limited resources and were not effectively organized. Most service branches operated with a minimal budget and inadequate, outdated equipment. The Kibbutzim are now reorganizing and mechanizing them all. In doing so, they draw on experience accumulated in the Kibbutzim and on the advice of various outside experts. They make a persistent effort to develop scientifically tested techniques in the sphere of house-keeping and child care and to turn these occupations into semi-professions. Workers in these fields are sent for professional training in institutions outside the community. The Federations organize seminars and refresher courses in home economics, nursing and child care, in which members get some theoretical grounding and practical guidance. Training is kept up and continued by extensive reading in semi-scientific literature and by occasional lectures. These efforts have a considerable effect on service and children's institutions. A process of gradual but cumulative improvement sets in and communal institutions are able to render much more satisfactory services.

The efficiency drive leads to the formulation of precisely defined, fixed regulations and to a certain formalization of communication and control. While increasing efficiency, this process entails standardization and often leads also to rigidity and imposed uniformity. Specialized bureaucratic agencies are effective in coping with repetitive routine tasks, but are not as well fitted to solve idiosyncratic personal problems.[34] There is an inherent tendency in such agencies to treat situations and people "by the book," as if they were alike. They tend to assume sameness of needs and disregard differentiation of individual inclinations and tastes. The Kibbutzim make a special effort to avoid undue uniformization and inflexibility. They have counteracted the dysfunctions entailed in the process of bureaucratization by widening the margin of permitted varia-tion and by allowing their members more freedom of choice. Workers in charge of the communal kitchen and dining hall make special efforts to cater to different tastes by diversifying their menus and offering as many alternative courses as possible. The range of consumer choice has become much wider than it used to be and personal predilections and idiosyncrasies are not disregarded. To cite another important example, the schedule in the children's houses has become much more flexible, and parents have more free access to them. Within certain circumscribed

34. E. Litwak. "Complementary Functions of Bureaucratic and Family Organizations" (mimeographed); see also B. Moore, Jr., *Political Power and Social Theory*. Cambridge, Mass.: Harvard University Press, 1958.

limits, parents are given a free hand. Communal institutions consciously cultivate a home-like, pleasant atmosphere, and the workers in charge are enjoined to treat members in a considerate and attentive manner. Disinterest in personal problems, impatience and brusqueness are severely censured. The task of inducing a process of bureaucratization and starting a counteracting process of de-bureaucratization, simultaneously, is difficult, but not insurmountable. Kibbutzim in which this policy was implemented in a systematic and determined way have managed to formalize their institutional structure, yet avoid many of the dysfunctions entailed in such a process.

The familistic trend is very strong in most Kibbutzim and in many it seems to be gathering momentum. It is not easily curbed, yet the reorganization and the host of supplementary mechanisms evolved lately are not without avail. In some notable cases, the reorganization has brought about a partial reversal of trends. The families relinquish some of their newly acquired tasks and communal institutions are taking over again. This partial reversal of trends is particularly noticeable in the case of the relationship between the family and the communal kitchen and dining hall. In a number of Kibbutzim in our sample we were able to witness a partial comeback to the dining hall. Before the reorganization, it was very sparsely attended during the evening meal and looked almost deserted at times. The prompt service, the clean, comfortable and cheerfully decorated new hall and the good, varied food made communal dining much more attractive than it used to be and won over many of the adherents of the domestic pattern. Cooking and eating at home have not disappeared completely even after the reorganization, but most families now eat most of their meals in the communal dining hall. The familistic pattern serves as a complementary rather than a competing solution.

Reorganization and progressive professionalization check to some extent the familistic trend in the sphere of child-rearing as well. The mistrust and discontent which parents feel towards the communal children's institutions stem primarily from the tensions inherent in the collectivistic pattern itself, but the uneasiness and resentment are enhanced by faulty organization and a shortage of skilled and fully trained personnel. Collective socialization has been tried out under conditions which were far from optimal. Maintenance of educational institutions on a high level and unflagging efforts to develop and improve them bolster the confidence of parents in communal socialization and decrease the pressure for familistic innovations. Building of children's houses which are fully equipped and fully adapted to the needs of the children, careful calculation of the size of the groups and the adult-children ratio, modification of methods of recruitment and training of educators and critical appraisal and revision of educational methods increase the chances of success. Of considerable importance here are the attempts to regularize the contacts and improve communication between parents and the specialized personnel in charge of their children. Special efforts are made now to draw them into active participation in activities in the children's houses, and to enlist their cooperation in their contacts with their children at home.

The anti-familism of the revolutionary phase has thus abated, but has not disappeared altogether. It has been superseded by a moderate collectivism which regards the family as a useful though dangerous ally. The Kibbutzim still try to control and limit the family and direct it towards the attainment of collective goals. The main problem of the Kibbutzim from a dynamic point of view is how to allow the family more privacy and a certain internal autonomy without harming the cohesion of the community.

Suzanne Keller

Does the Family Have a Future?

Some thirty-five years ago, two venerable students of human behavior engaged in a six session debate on marriage and the family over the B.B.C. Their names were Bronislaw Malinowski and Robert Briffault, the one a world famous anthropologist best known for his studies of the Trobriand Islands, the other a social historian devoted to resurrecting the matriarchies of prehistory. Of the two, paradoxically, it was Briffault, the self-trained historian, who turned out to be the cultural relativist whereas Malinowski, a pioneer in crosscultural research, exhibited the very ethnocentrism his studies were designed to dispel.

Both men noted that the family was in trouble in their day. Both were distressed by this and sought to discover remedies if not solutions. Despite their common concern, however, they were soon embroiled in vivid and vociferous controversy about the nature of the crisis and its cure. *(Marriage: Past and Present,* ed. M. F. Ashley-Montagu, Boston, Porter Sargent, 1956).

Briffault concluded from his reading of the evidence that the family rests on sentiments rooted in culture and social tradition rather than in human nature. Unless one grasps these social and cultural essentials, one cannot hope to understand, much less cure, what ails it. No recourse to natural instinct or to the "dictatorship of tradition or moral coercion" could save the modern family from its destined decline.

Malinowski disagreed. The family, he admitted, might be passing through a grave crisis but the illness was not fatal. Marriage and the family, "the foundation of human society," and a key source of spiritual and material progress, were here to stay, though not without some needed improvements. Among these were the establishment of a single standard of morality, greater legal and economic equality between husband and wife, and greater freedom in parent-child relations.

The disagreement of these two men stemmed, as it so often does, not from different diagnoses but from different definitions of the phenomenon. Malinowski defined the family as a legal union of one man and one woman, together with their offspring, bound by reciprocal rights and duties, and cooperating for the sake of economic and moral survival.

Briffault defined the family much more broadly as any association involving economic production and sexual procreation. In his sense, the clan was a family.

The two agreed on only one point: parenthood and above all maternity are the pivots in the anatomy of marriage and the family. If these change so must the familial organization that contained them. Thus if one can identify such pivotal changes their difficulties are overcome while ours may be said to be just beginning.

There is good reason to suppose that such changes are now upon us. The malaise of our time reflects not simply a temporary disenchantment with an ancient institution but a profound convulsion of the social order. The family is indeed suffering a seachange.

It is curious to note how much more quickly the popular press, including the so-called women's magazines, have caught on to changing marital, sexual, and parental styles. While many of the experts are still serving up conventional and tradition-bound idols—the hard-working, responsible, breadwinner husband-father, the self-effacing, ministering, wife-mother, the grateful, respectful children—these magazines tempt the contemporary reader with less standard and more challenging fare. Whether in New York or in Athens, the newsstands flaunt their provocative titles—"Is This the Last Marrying Generation?" "Alimony for Ex-Husbands," "Why We Don't Want to Have Children," "Are Husbands Superfluous?"—in nonchalant profusion. These and other assaults on our sexual and moral codes in the shape of the new theater, the new woman, the new youth, and TV soap operas akin to a psychiatrist's case files, persuade us that something seems to be afoot in the whole sphere of marriage and family relations which many had thought immune to change. In point of fact the question is not *whether* the family is changing but how and how much; how important are these changes, how permanent, how salutary? The answers depend largely on the way we ask our questions and define our terms.

The family means many things to many people but in its essence it refers to those socially patterned ideals and practices concerned with biological and cultural survival of the species. When we speak of the family we are using a kind of shorthand, a label for a social invention not very different, in essence, from other social interventions, let us say the Corporation or the University, and no more permanent than these. This label designates a particular set of social practices concerned with procreation and child rearing; with the heterosexual partnerships that make this possible and the parent-child relations that make it enduring. As is true of all collective habits, once established, such practices are exceedingly resistant to change, in part because they evoke strong sentiments and in part because no acceptable alternatives are offered. Since most individuals are unable to step outside of their cultures, they are unable to note the arbitrary and variable nature of their conventions.

Accordingly, they ascribe to their folkways and creeds an antiquity, an inevitability, and a universality these do not possess.

The idea that the family is universal is highly misleading despite its popularity. All surviving societies have indeed found ways to stabilize the processes of reproduction and child care else they would not have survived to tell their tale. But since they differ greatly in how they arrange these matters (and since they are willing to engage in Hot and Cold Wars to defend such differences) the generalization does not help us explain the phenomenon but more nearly explains it away.

In truth there are as many forms of the family as there are forms of society, some so different from ours that we consider them unnatural and incomprehensible. There are, for example, societies in which couples do not share a household and do not have sole responsibility for their offspring; others in which our domestic unit of husband and wife is divided into two separate units, a conjugal one of biological parents and a brother-sister unit for economic sustenance. There are societies in which children virtually rear each other and societies in which the wise father does not know his own child. All of these are clearly very different from our twentieth century, industrial-urban conception of the family as a legally united couple, sharing bed and board, jointly responsible for bearing and rearing their children, and formally isolated from their next of kin in all but a sentimental sense. This product of a long and complicated evolutionary development from prehistoric times is no simple replica of the ancient productive and reproductive institutions from which it derives its name and some of its characteristic features. The contemporary family really has little in common with its historic Hebrew, Greek, and Roman ancestors.

The family of these great civilizations of the West was a household community of hundreds, and sometimes thousands, of members ("familia" is the Latin term for household). Only some of the members were related by blood and by far the larger part were servants and slaves, artisans, friends, and distant relations. In its patriarchal form (again culturally variable), this large community was formally held together by the role of eldest male who more nearly resembled the general of an army than a modern husband-father. In its prime, this household community constituted a miniature society, a decentralized version of a social organization that had grown too large and unwieldy for effective management. In this it resembles the giant bureaucracies of our own day, and their proposed decentralization into locally based, locally staffed subsystems, designed to offset the evils of remote control while nevertheless maintaining their connection with it. Far from having been universal, this ancient family type, with its gods and shrines, schools and handicrafts, was not even widely prevalent within its own social borders. Confined to the landed and propertied upper classes, it remained an unattainable ideal for the bulk of common men who made up the society.

The fallacy of universality has done students of human behavior a great disservice. By leading us to seek and hence to find a single pattern, it has blinded us to historical precedents for multiple legitimate family arrangements. As a result we have been rather impoverished in our speculations and proposals about alternative future arrangements in the family sphere.

A second common fallacy asserts that the family is *the* basic institution of society, hereby revealing a misunderstanding of how a society works. For as a social institution, the family is by definition a specialized element which provides society with certain needed services and depends on it for others. This means that you cannot tamper with a society without expecting the family to be affected in some way and vice versa. In the contemporary jargon, we are in the presence of a feedback system. Whatever social changes we anticipate, therefore the family cannot be kept immune from them.

A final fallacy concerns the presumed naturalness of the family in proof of which a motley and ill assorted grab bag of anecdotal evidence from the animal kingdom is adduced. But careful perusal of ethological accounts suggests that animals vary as greatly as we do, their mating and parental groupings including such novelties as the love death, males who bear children, total and guilt-free "promiscuity," and other "abnormal" features. The range of variation is so wide, in fact, that virtually any human arrangement can be justified by recourse to the habits of some animal species.

In sum, if we wish to understand what is happening to the family—to our family—in our own day, we must examine and observe it in the here and now. In so doing it would be well to keep in mind that the family is an abstraction at best, serving as guide and image of what a particular society considers desirable and appropriate in family relations, not what takes place in actual fact. In reality there are always a number of empirical family types at variance with this, though they usually pay lip service to the overarching cultural ideal.

Challenges to the Contemporary Industrial Family

In the United States, as in other industrial societies, the ideal family consists of a legally constituted husband-wife team, their young, dependent children, living in a household of their own, provided for by the husband's earnings as main breadwinner, and emotionally united by the wife's exclusive concentration on the home. Probably no more than one-third of all families at a particular moment in time, and chiefly in the middle and would-be middle classes, actually live up to this image. The remaining majority all lack one or more of the essential attributes—in lacking a natural parent, or in not being economically self-sufficient, or in having made other necessary modifications.

One contrasting form is the extended family in which the couple share household arrangements and expenses with parents, siblings, or other close relatives. The children are then reared by several generations and have a choice of models on which to pattern their behavior. This type, frequent in working class and immigrant milieus, may be as cohesive and effective as the ideal type but it lacks the cultural legitimacy and desirability of the latter.

A third family type, prevalent among the poor of all ethnic and racial backgrounds, is the mother-child family. Contrary to our prejudices this need not be a deviant or distorted family form for it may be the only viable and appropriate one in its particular setting. Its defects may stem more from adverse social judgments than from intrinsic failings. Deficient in cultural resources and status, it may nevertheless provide a humane and spirited setting for its members, particularly if some sense of stability and continuity has been achieved. Less fortunate are the numerous non-families, ex-families, and non-intact families such as the divorced, the widowed, the unmarriageables, and many other fragmented social forms, who have no recognized social place. None of these, however, threaten the existing order since they are seen and see themselves as involuntarily different, imperfect, or unfortunate. As such they do not challenge the ideals of family and marital relations but simply suggest how difficult it is to live up to them. When we talk of family change or decline, however, it is precisely the ideal standards which we have in mind. A challenge to them cannot be met by simple reaffirmations of old truths, disapproval, shock, or ridicule of the challengers, or feigned indifference. Such challenges must be met head on.

Today the family and its social and psychological underpinnings are being fundamentally challenged from at least three sources: (1) from accumulated failures and contradictions in marriage; (2) from pervasive occupational and educational trends including the changing relations between the sexes, the spread of birth control, and the changing nature of work; and (3) from novel developments in biology. Let me briefly examine each.

It is generally agreed that even in its ideal form, the industrial-urban family makes great, some would say excessive, demands on its members. For one thing it rests on the dyadic principle or pair relationship which, as Georg Simmel observed long ago, is inherently tragic and unstable. Whether in chess, tennis, or marriage, two are required to start and continue the game but only one can destroy it. In this instance, moreover, the two are expected to retain their separate identities as male and female and yet be one in flesh and spirit. No wonder that the image of the couple, a major source of fusion and of schism in our society, is highly contradictory according to whether we think of the sexes as locked in love or in combat. Nor do children, the symbols of their union, necessarily unify them. Their own growing pains and cultural demands force them into mutually exclusive socio-sexual identities thereby increasing the intimate polarity. In fact, children arouse parental ambivalence in a number of ways, not the least of which is that they demand all but give back all too little. And yet their upbringing and sustenance, the moral and emotional climate, as well as the accumulation of economic and educational resources needed for survival, all rest on this small, fragile, essential but very limited unit. Held together by sentimental rather than by corporate bonds, the happiness of the partners is a primary goal although no one is very sure what happiness means nor how it may be achieved and sustained.

To these potentials for stress and strain must be added the loss of many erstwhile functions to school, state, and society, and with it something of the glamour and challenge of family commitments. Few today expect the family to be employment agency, welfare state, old age insurance, or school for life. Yet once upon a time, not too long ago at that, it was all that and more. At the same time, however, with fewer resources, some new burdens have been added stemming from rising standards of child health, education, and welfare. This makes parents even more crucially responsible for the potential fate of their children over whom they have increasingly less exclusive control.

Like most social institutions in the throes of change, moreover, the modern family is also beset by numerous internal contradictions engendered by the conflict between traditional patterns of authority and a new egalitarianism between husbands and wives and parents and children. The equality of the spouses, for example, collides with the continuing greater economic responsibilities, hence authority, of the husband. The voluntary harness of love chafes under the constraint of numerous obligations and duties imposed by marriage, and dominance patterns by sex or age clash with new demands for mutuality, reciprocity, equity, and individualism. These, together with some unavoidable disillusionments and disappointments in marriage, set the stage for the influence of broader and less subjective social trends.

One such trend, demographic in nature but bound to have profound social implications, concerns the lengthened life expectancy and the shortened reproductive span for women. Earlier ages at marriage, fewer children per couple and closer spacing of children, means: the girl who marries at twenty will have all her children by age 26, have all her children in school by her early thirties, have the first child leave home for job, schooling, or marriage in her late thirties, and have all her children out of the home by her early forties. This leaves some thirty to forty years to do with as personal pleasure or social need dictates. The contrast with her grandmother is striking: later marriage, and more children spaced farther apart meant all the children in school no earlier than her middle or late thirties and the last to leave home (if he or she ever did) not before her early fifties. At which time grandmother was probably a widow and close to the end of her own lifespan. The empty nest thus not only occurs earlier today but it lasts longer, affecting not this or that unfortunate individual woman but many if not most women. Hence what may in the past have been an individual misfortune has turned into a social emergency of major proportions. More unexpected free time, more time without a socially recognized or appreciated function, more premature retirements surely put the conventional modern wife, geared to the domestic welfare of husband, home, and children at a singular disadvantage relative to the never married career woman. Destined to outlive her husband, stripped of major domestic responsibilities in her prime years, what is she to do with this windfall of extra hours and years? Surely we must expect and prepare for a major cultural shift in the education and upbringing of female children. If women cannot afford to make motherhood and domestic concerns the sole foci of their identities, they must be encouraged, early in life, to prepare themselves for some occupation or profession not as an adjunct or as a last resort in case of economic need but as an equally legitimate pursuit. The childrearing of girls must increasingly be geared to developing a feminine identity that stresses autonomy, non-dependency, and self-assertion in work and in life.

Some adjunct trends are indirectly stimulating just such a reorientation. When women are compelled, as they often are, to earn their own living or to supplement inadequate family resources necessitated by the high emphasis on personal consumption and the high cost of services increasingly deemed essential as national standards rise, conventional work-dependency patterns are shattered. For, since the male breadwinner is already fully occupied, often with two jobs, or if he cannot or will not work, his wife is forced to step in. Thus there is generated internal family pressure—arising from a concern for family welfare but ultimately not confined to it—for wives to be gainfully employed outside of the home. And fully three-fourths in the post-childbearing ages already are, albeit under far from ideal conditions. Torn between home and job, between the precepts of early childhood with its promise of permanent security at the side of a strong male and the pressures of a later reality, unaided by a society unaware or indifferent to her problems, the double duty wife must manage as best she can.

That this need not be so is demonstrated by a number of modern societies whose public policies are far better meshed with changing social realities. Surely one of our more neglected institutions—the single family household which, despite all the appliances, remains essentially backward and primitive in its conditions of work—will need some revamping and modernizing. More household appliances, more and more attractive alternatives to the individually run household, more nursery schools, and a total overhaul of work-schedules not now geared to a woman's life and interests cannot be long in coming. While these will help women in all of their multiple tasks they may also of course further challenge the presumed joys of exclusive domesticity.

All in all, it would appear that the social importance of the family relative to other significant social arenas will, as Briffault among others correctly anticipated, decline. Even today when the family still exerts a strong emotional and sentimental hold its social weight is not what it once was. All of us ideally are still born in intact families but not all of us need to establish families to survive. Marriage and children continue to be extolled as supreme social and personal goals but they are no longer —especially for men—indispensable for a meaningful existence. As individual self-sufficiency, fed by economic affluence or economic self-restraint, increases, so does one's exemption from unwanted economic as well as kinship responsibilities. Today the important frontiers seem to lie elsewhere, in science, politics, and outerspace. This must affect the attractions of family life for both men and women. For men, because they will see less and less reason to assume full economic and social respon-sibilities for four to five human beings in addition to themselves as it becomes more difficult and less necessary to do so. This, together with the continued decline of patriarchal authority and male dominance—even in the illusory forms in which they have managed to hang on—will remove some of the psychic rewards which prompted many men to marry, while the disappearance of lineage as mainstays of the social and class order, will deprive paternity of its social justification. For women, the household may soon prove too small for the scope of their ambitions and power drives. Until recently these were directed first of all to their children, secondarily to their mates. But with the decline of parental control over children a major erstwhile source of challenge and creativity is removed from the family sphere. This must weaken the mother-wife complex, historically sustained by the necessity and exaltation of motherhood and the taboo on illegitimacy.

Above all, the move towards worldwide population and birth control must affect the salience of parenthood for men and women, as a shift of cultural emphasis and individual priorities deflates maternity as woman's chief social purpose and paternity as the prod to male exertions in the world of work. Very soon, I suspect, the cultural presses of the world will slant their messages against the bearing and rearing of children. Mater-nity, far from being a duty, not even a right, will then become a rare privilege to be granted to a select and qualified few. Perhaps the day is not far off when reproduction will be confined to a fraction of the population, and what was once inescapable necessity may become voluntary, plan-ned, choice. Just as agricultural societies in which everyone had to produce food were once superseded by industrial societies in which a scant six percent now produce food for all, so one day the few may produce children for the many.

This along with changing attitudes towards sex, abortion, adoption, illegitimacy, the spread of the pill, better knowledge of human behavior, and a growing scepticism that the family is the only proper crucible for child-rearing, creates a powerful recipe for change. World-wide demands for greater and better opportunities for self-development and a growing awareness that these opportunities are inextricably enhanced or curtailed by the family as a prime determinant of life-chances, will play a major role in this change. Equal opportunity, it is now clear, cannot stop at the crib but must start there. "It is idle" commented Dr. Robert S. Morrison, a Cornell biologist, "to talk of a society of equal opportunity as long as that society abandons its newcomers solely to their families for their most impressionable years." (New York Times, October 30, 1966.) One of the great, still largely unchallenged, injustices may well be that one cannot choose one's parents.

The trends that I have sketched would affect marriage, male-female, and parent-child relations even if no other developments were on the horizon. But there are. As yet barely discernible and still far from being applicable to human beings, recent breakthroughs in biology—with their promise of a greatly extended life span, novel modes of reproduction, and dramatic possibilities for genetic intervention—cannot be ignored in a discussion devoted to the future of the family.

Revolution in Biology

If the early part of this century belonged to physics and the middle period to exploratory ventures into outer space, the next few decades belong to biology. The prolongation of life to double or triple its current span seems virtually assured, the extension of female fertility into the sixties is more than a distinct possibility, and novel ways of reproducing the human species have moved from science fiction to the laboratory. The question then arises, what will happen when biological reproduction will not only be inadvisable for the sake of collective well being but superseded by new forms and eventually by non-human forms of reproduction?

A number of already existing possibilities may give us a foretaste of what is to come. For example, the separation of conception from gestation means that motherhood can become specialized, permitting some women to conceive and rear many children and others to bear them without having to provide for them. Frozen sperm banks (of known donors) are envisioned from which prospective mothers could choose the fathers of their children on the basis of particularly admired or desired qualities, thereby advancing an age-old dream of selecting a distinguished paternity for their children based on demonstrated rather than potential male achievement. And it would grant men a sort of immortality to sire offspring long after their biological deaths as well as challenge the implicit equation now made between fathers and husbands. Finally, the as yet remote possibility to reproduce the human species without sexual intercourse, by permanently separating sex from procreation, would permit unmarried women (and men) to have children without being married, reduces a prime motive for marriage and may well dethrone— inconceivable as this may seem—the heterosexual couple. All of these pose questions of legal and social policy to plague the most subtle Solon. Who is the father of a child—the progenitor or the provider where these have become legitimately distinct roles? Who is the mother—the woman who conceives the child or the one who carries it to term? Who will decide on sex ratios once sex determination becomes routine? Along with such challenges and redefinitions of human responsibility, some see the fate of heterosexuality itself to lie in the balance. In part of course this rests on one's assumptions about the nature of sexuality and sexual identity.

Anatomy alone has never been sufficient for the classification of human beings into male and female which each society labors to develop and then calls natural. Anatomy is but one—and by no means always a reliable—identifying characteristic. Despite our beliefs, sex identification, even in the strictest physical sense, is by no means clear cut. Various endeavors to find foolproof methods of classification—for example for participation in the Olympics—have been unsuccessful, as at least nine separate and often uncorrelated components of sexual phenotype have been identified. But if we cannot count on absolute physical differentiations between the sexes, we do even less well when it comes to their social and psychological attributes. Several decades of research have shown beyond doubt that most of what we mean by the difference between the sexes is a blend of cultural myth and social necessity, which must be learned, painstakingly and imperfectly, from birth on. Once acquired, sexual identity is not fixed but needs to be reinforced and propped up in a myriad of ways of which we are quite unaware.

In the past this complicated learning process was guided by what we may call the categorical reproductive imperative which proclaimed procreation as an unquestioned social goal and which steered the procreative and sexual capacities and aspirations of men and women toward appropriate channels virtually from birth on. Many other features strengthened these tendencies—symbolism and sentiment, work patterns and friendships, all kinds of subtle and not so subtle rewards and punishments for being a "real" man, a real woman. But once the reproductive imperative is transformed into a reproductive ban what will be the rationale for the continuance of the exclusive heterosexual polarity in the future? If we keep in mind that only two out of our forty-six chromosomes are sex-carrying, perhaps these two will disappear as their utility subsides. Even without such dramatic changes, already there is speculation that heterosexuality will become but one among several forms of sexuality, these having previously been suppressed by strong social sanctions against sexual deviation as well as by their inability to reproduce themselves in standard fashion. More than three decades ago, Olaf Stapleton, one of the most imaginative science fiction writers of the century, postulated the emergence of at least six subsexes out of the familiar ancient polarity. At about the same time, Margaret Mead, in the brilliant epilogue to her book on sex and temperament (*Sex and Temperament in Three Primitive Societies,* William Morrow and Co., New York, 1935), suggested a reorganization and recategorization of human identity not along but across traditional sex lines so as to produce a better alignment between individual capacity and social necessity. In our time we have witnessed the emergence of UniSex (the term is McLuhan's) and predictions which range from the disappearance of sex to its manifold elaboration.

Some are speculating about a future in which only one of the current sexes will survive, the other having become superfluous or obsolescent. Depending on the taste, temperament—and sex—of the particular writer, women and men have alternately been so honored (or cursed). It is not always easy to tell which aspect of sex—the anatomical, psychological, or cultural—the writer has in mind but as the following comment suggests, much more than anatomy is at stake.

> Does the man and woman thing have a future? The question may not be hypothetical much longer. Within 10 years . . . we may be able to choose the sex of our offspring; and later to reproduce without mating male and female cells. This means it will someday be possible to have a world with only one sex, woman, and thereby avoid the squabbles, confusions, and headaches that have dogged this whole business of sex down the centuries. A manless world suggests several scientific scenarios. The most pessimistic would have society changing not at all, but continuing on its manly ways of eager acquisition, hot competition, and mindless aggression. In which case, half the women would become "men" and go right on getting ulcers, shouting "charge" and pinning medals on each other. (George B. Leonard, "The Man and Woman Thing," *Look* 12-25-68.)

Long before the demise of heterosexuality as a mainstay of the social order, however, we will have to come to terms with changing sexual attitudes and mores ushered in by what has been called the sexual revolution. This liberalization, this rejection of old taboos, half truths, and hypocrisies, also means a crisis of identity as men and women, programmed for more traditional roles, search for the boundaries of their sexual selves in an attempt to establish a territoriality of the soul.

Confusion is hardly, of course, a novel aspect of the human condition. Not knowing where we have come from, why we are here, nor where we are headed it could hardly be otherwise. There have always been dissatisfied men and women rejecting the roles their cultures have assigned them or the responsibilities attached to these. But these are the stuff of poetry and drama, grist for the analyst's couch or the priest's confessional, in other words private torments and agonies kept concealed from an unsympathetic world. It is only when such torments become transmuted into public grievance and so become publicly heard and acknowledged that we can be said to be undergoing profound changes akin to what we are experiencing today.

Returning now to our main question—does the family have a future—it should be apparent that I expect some basic and irreversible changes in the decades ahead and the emergence of some novel forms of human togetherness. Not that the current scene does not already offer some provocative variations on ancient themes, but most of these gain little public attention, still less approval, and so they are unable to alter professed beliefs and standards. Moreover, every culture has its own forms of self-justification and self-righteousness and in our eagerness to affirm the intrinsic superiority of our ways, we neglect to note the magnitude of variations and deviations from the ideals we espouse. What are we to make, for example, of such dubious allegiance to the monogamous ideal as serial marriages or secret adulteries? Or, less morally questionable, what of the quasi-organized part-time family arrangements necessitated by extreme occupational and geographic mobility? Consider for a moment the millions of families of salesmen, pilots, seacaptains, soldiers, sailors, and junior executives where the man of the house is not often *in* the house. These absentee husbands-fathers who magically re-enter the family circle just long enough to be appreciated, leaving their wives in charge of the homes they pay for and of the children they sired, are surely no more than part-time mates. If we know little about the adjustments they have had to make or their children's responses, this is because they clearly do not fit in with our somewhat outmoded stereotyped notions of what family relations ought to be. Or consider another home-grown example, the institution of governesses and boarding schools to rear upper class children. Where is the upper-class mother and how does she spend her time between vacations and homecoming weekends. Then there are of course many countries around the world —Israel, Sweden, the Socialist countries, some of the African societies—where all or nearly all women, most of them mothers, work outside of the home as a matter of course. And because these societies are free from guilt and ambivalence about the working mother, they have managed to incorporate these realities more gracefully into their scheme of things, developing a number of useful innovations along the way. Thus even in our own day, adaptions and modifications exist and have not destroyed all notions of family loyalty, responsibility, and commitment.

In fact, people may be more ready for change than official pronouncements and expert opinions assume. The spread of contraceptive information and the acceptance of full birth control have been remarkable. The relaxation of many erstwhile taboos has proceeded at breakneck speed and the use of public forums to discuss such vital but previously forbidden topics as abortion, homosexuality, or illegitimacy is dramatic and startling in a society rooted in Puritanism. A number of studies, moreover, show that the better educated are more open to re-examination and change in all spheres, including the family. Since these groups are on the increase, we may expect greater receptivity to such changes in the future. Even such startling proposed innovations as egg transplants, test-tube babies, and cloning are not rejected out of hand if they would help achieve the family goal most Americans prize. (See "The Second Genesis" by Albert Rosenfeld and the Louis Harris Poll, *Life,* June, 1969, pp. 31–46).

Public response to a changing moral and social climate is of course hard to predict. In particular, as regards family concerns, the reactions of women, so crucially bound up with motherhood and childrearing in their self-definitions, are of especial interest. In this connection one study of more than 15,000 women college students attending four year liberal arts colleges in the United States is relevant for its findings on how such a nationwide sample of young coeds, a group of great future significance, feels about marriage, motherhood and career. (Charles F. Westoff and Raymond H. Potvin, *College Women and Fertility Values,* Princeton University Press, 1967.) Selecting only those items on which there was wide consensus and omitting details of interest to the specialist, the general pattern of answers was unmistakeable. The large majority of these would-be wives and mothers disapproved of large families (three or more children), did not consider children to be the most important reason for marriage, favored birth control and birth planning, and thought it possible for a woman to pursue family and career simultaneously. They split evenly on the matter of whether a woman's main satisfaction should come from family rather than career, or community activities, and they were virtually united in thinking that mothers with very young children should not work. The latter strongly identifies them as Americans, I think, where nursery schools and other aids to working mothers —including moral support—are not only lacking but still largely disapproved of.

Thus if we dare to speculate further about the future of the family we will be on safe ground with the following anticipations: (1) a trend towards greater, legitimate variety in sexual and marital experience, (2) a decrease in the negative emotions—exclusiveness, possessiveness, fear and jealousy—associated with these; (3) greater room for personal choice in the kind, extent, and duration of intimate relationships, which may greatly improve their quality as people will both give and demand more of them; (4) entirely new forms of communal living arrangements in which several couples will share the tasks of child rearing and economic support as well as the pleasures of relaxation; (5) multi-stage marriages geared to the changing life cycle and the presence or absence of dependent children. Of these proposals, some, such as Margaret Mead's would have the young and the immature of any age test themselves and their capacities to relate to others in an individual form of marriage which would last only so long as it fulfilled both partners. In contrast to this, older, more experienced and more mature couples who were ready to take on the burdens of parenthood would make a deeper and longer lasting commitment. Other proposals would reverse this sequence and have couples assume parental commitments when young and, having discharged their debt to society, be then free to explore more personal, individualistic partnerships. Neither of these seems as yet to be particularly appealing to the readers who responded to Mead's proposal as set forth in Redbook Magazine. (Margaret Mead, "Marriage in Two Steps," *Redbook Magazine,* July 1966; "The Life Cycle and Its Variation: The Division of Roles," *Daedalus,* Summer, 1967; "A Continuing Dialogue on Marriage: Why Just Living Together Won't Work," *Redbook Magazine,* April 1968.)

For the immediate future, it appears that most Americans opt for and anticipate their participation in durable, intimate, heterosexual partnerships as anchors and pivots of their adult lives. They expect these to be freer and more flexible than was true in the past, however, and less bound to duty and involuntary personal restrictions. They cannot imagine and do not wish a life without them.

Speculating for the long range future, we cannot ignore the potential implications of the emerging cultural taboo on unrestricted reproduction and the shift in public concern away from the family as the central preoccupation of one's life. Hard as it may seem, perhaps some day we will cease to relate to families just as we no longer relate ourselves to clans, and instead be bound up with some new, as yet unnamed, principle of human association. If and when this happens, we may also see a world of Unisex, Multi-sex, or Nonsex. None of this can happen, however, if we refuse to shed some of our most cherished preconceptions such that monogamy is superior to other forms of marriage or that women naturally make the best mothers. Much as we may be convinced of these now, time may reveal them as yet another illusion, another example of made-to-order truths.

Ultimately all social change involves moral doubt and moral reassessment. If we refuse to consider change while there still is time, time will pass us by. Only by examining and taking stock of what is can we hope to affect what will be. This is our chance to invent and thus to humanize the future.

Name Index

Aberle, David F., 334n, 338n
Abram, A., 153n
Adam, William, 38n
Adams, Bert N., 354n
Addams, Jane, 464
Aiken, Michael, 354n
Alcott, Bronson, 213
Alcott, Louisa May, 213, 214, 215
Alexander, Franz, 118, 119, 132
Alighieri, Dante, 136
Alt, A., 32n
Andrews, Edward D., 538n
Anshen, Ruth N., 104n, 170n, 414n, 417n
Anthes, Rudolf, 31n
Arensberg, Conrad M., 376, 395-399
Ariès, Philippe, 162n, 357n
Ashley-Montagu, M. F., 64n, 579
Ashley-Montagu, W. F., 64n
Athenaeus, 35
Austen, Jane, 200-208 *passim*
Avebury, J. L., 10
Avicenna, 192

Bachofen, J. J., 61
Bacon, A. M., 446n
Bailyn, Bernard, 227n
Bailyn, Lotte, 475n, 478n, 486n
Bain, Robert K., 506n
Bales, Robert F., 14n, 15, 16n, 25n, 162n, 171n, 259, 260, 261, 263n, 266n, 281n, 297n, 302n, 305n, 330n, 461n, 569n
Banton, Michael, 44n
Barber, Elinor, 370n, 482n, 522
Baringer, Herbert R., 294n
Barker, R. G., 320n
Barnett, Clifford R., 104n
Barnett, H. G., 4
Bar Yoseph, R., 550n, 560n, 570n
Bastien, Rémy, 65n, 67, 69n, 70n, 71n
Bateson, Gregory, 372
Beach, Frank A., 304
Beaglehole, Ernest, 260n
Beaglehole, Pearl, 260n
Bee, Helen, 311
Beier, E. G., 265
Beigel, Hugo G., 144
Bell, Daniel, 401n

Bell, H. I., 39
Bell, Norman W., 170n, 263, 264, 267n, 269n, 270n, 273n, 303n, 370n, 550n, 559n
Ben-David, Joseph, 561n
Bendix, Reinhard, 402n
Bendix, Richard, 72n, 334n
Benedict, Ruth, 121n
Berger, B. J., 569n
Berger, Bennett, 402n
Berger, Peter L., 108, 157-174, 408
Bernard, J., 463n
Bernard, Jessie, 476n, 477n
Bertillon, J., 387n
Bestor, A. E., 551n
Bettelheim, Bruno, 268n
Bevan, Edwyn, 35n
Beza, Theodore, 179
Bieber, Irving, 303, 304n
Bion, W. R., 119, 556n
Birmingham, Stephen, 410
Bittner, Egon, 534n
Bittorf, Hans, 384n
Blake, Judith, 68n, 75n, 77n, 242, 276-317
Blau, Peter M., 80, 400, 401, 403n, 409
Blood, Robert O., 480n
Boccaccio, Giovanni, 143
Baker, H., 391n
Booth, Bradford, 206n
Boring, Edwin, 476n, 477
Bott, Elizabeth, 242, 267, 268, 318-333, 567n, 572n
Boulding, Kenneth, 276n
Braithwaite, Lloyd, 67n, 69n, 73n
Breasted, James Henry, 33, 34n
Briffault, Robert, 43n, 56, 58, 61, 261, 579, 580, 586
Brill, A. A., 302n
Brinton, Crane, 97n, 98
Broderick, C., 463n
Bronfenbrenner, Urie, 270n, 271, 272n, 334n, 338n, 371n, 465n
Bronson, Wanda C., 272n
Brontë, Branwell, 211, 212
Brontë, Charlotte, 205, 208-213 *passim*, 215
Brontë, Emily, 212

Subject Index

Abortion, 59, 194, 417, 418, 427, 428, 469, 591; *see also* Birth control
Achievement, as social value, 245, 246-247, 251, 449-450; *see also* Status achieved
Adolescence, 27-28, 76-77, 153-154, 245, 446-459
Adoption, 53, 58
Ambivalence, structural, 273-274, 362-373
Anomie, 157, 159, 173
Anxiety, social, 114; as a means of social control, 114, 120-122
Asymmetrical relationship, 80-81
Attitude vs. behavior: and conformity, 339-343, 365-367, 450; and consequences for authority, 364-365, 370-372; distinction made, 363-364
Attitudinal conformity, 504, 506
Authority: based on age, 430-445; and family, 14, 175-199 *passim*, 365-367, 413, 422; of father, 177-180, 271-273; male, 257-258, 321, 419; in matrilineal society, 218-219; parental, 176-183, 190-191, 198, 260, 270, 330, 362-373 *passim*, 430, 445, 453-456; of peerage, 197; of the state, 423-425; structural source of, 216-217, 367-372 *passim*; of women, 73

Bachelorhood, 134, 216-217, 398
Behavioral conformity, 504
Biological revolution, 587-589
Birth control, 57, 60, 591; *see also* Abortion, Contraception
Birth rate, 413-418; in totalitarian society, 418-419
Boston Brahmins, 237-240

Capital accumulation and marital selection, 226-240, 405
Capitalism, 491
Career women, 489
Caribbean mating system, 78-93
Celibacy, 534
Ceremonies: of exchange, 5-6, 219-222; of marriage, 191, 123-125
Child care, 464, 465-466
Child marriage, 118, 191, 192-193; *see also* Infant betrothal
China, 430-445
Chinese revolution and illegitimacy, 102-104
Church, medieval, 177
Class, social, 244-245; middle, 75, 123, 134, 148, 187, 249, 256, 260, 263, 336-353 *passim*, 362-373, 439; upper, 75, 263, 426; working, 75-76, 270, 319, 336-353 *passim*, 362-373
Class differences: in authority patterns, 352, 363-365, 426; in birth control, 417-418; in child-rearing, 334-353; in commitment to norms, 56, 73; in education, 425-426;

in marriage patterns, 75-77, 175-199; in role differentiation, 248; in social control, 155-156, 363-365; *see also* Stratification
Collectivist communities, 532-578
Commitment, 504-506
Communism, 542, 544, 548
Community: allegiance and kinship, 430-431; and dyadic withdrawal, 116-117, 122, 131; participation, 243
Complex marriage, 535-536, 542, 544-545, 546
Concubinage, 422
Conflict: of expectations, 369-370, 425, 455; between generations, 446-459; social, 269, 413, 416, 426, 443-445; of values, 251, 455-456, 457-458
Conjugal relationships, 13, 268, 318-333 *passim*, 432
Consanguinity, 47, 354-361
Consensual union, 70-77 *passim*; and social obligations, 70, 75-76; *see also* Marriage, common law
Contraception, 186, 194-195, 417; *see also* Birth control
Courtship: function of, 74-75; patterns, 75, 77; social control of, 119-126
Cousin marriage, 44, 45, 228-240, 354, 404
Cross-cousin marriage, 19-20, 222-225
Cuban revolution and illegitimacy, 104-105
Cultural transmission, 44, 45

Democratic family, 256
Descent, 20, 40-41, 55
Division of labor, 52, 134-135, 261, 269, 318, 325, 326, 329, 332
Divorce, 134, 191-192, 195, 216, 420-421, 427, 430
Dyadic de-emphasis, 533
Dyadic withdrawal, 115-116, 534; counteracted by children, 72; institutionalized, 127; in myths, 131-132; and social obligations, 116; and totalitarian society, 117, 118-119, 122, 421-422

Ebenezer community, 534
Economic role of women, 482-487
Education of women, 284-288
Elites, maintenance of, 95-96, 226-240
Emotional stability in marriage, 172-173
Endogamy, 217-218
Equality: of children, 51-52, 244; of marital partners, 198-199, 318-319, 367-368, 371, 418; and prostitution, 249-250; and social control, 449-450; of status in marriage, 75-77, 153-154; of women, 176, 180-184
Eroticism, 21-25, 28-29; repression of, within family, 27-29, 129; *see also* Love

601